Western Civilization: Ideas, Politics, and Society

McHenry County College

Volume 1

Marvin Perry | Myrna Chase | James R. Jacob |
Margaret C. Jacob| Theodore H. Von Laue

D1489645

CENGAGE
Learning·

Australia · Brazil · Japan · Korea · Mexico · Singapore · Spain · United Kingdom · United States

CENGAGE
Learning·

Western Civilization: Ideas, Politics, and
Society: McHenry County College, Volume 2

Western Civilization: Ideas, Politics, and Society, Volume I: To 1789, 10th
Edition
Marvin Perry | Myrna Chase | James R. Jacob | Margaret C. Jacob |
Theodore H. Von Laue

© 2013 Cengage Learning. All rights reserved.

Executive Editors:
Maureen Staudt
Michael Stranz

Senior Project Development Manager:
Linda deStefano

Marketing Specialist:
Courtney Sheldon

Senior Production/Manufacturing Manager:
Donna M. Brown

Production Editorial Manager:
Kim Fry

Sr. Rights Acquisition Account Manager:
Todd Osborne

For product information and technology assistance, contact us at
Cengage Learning Customer & Sales Support, 1-800-354-9706

For permission to use material from this text or product,
submit all requests online at **cengage.com/permissions**
Further permissions questions can be emailed to
permissionrequest@cengage.com

This book contains select works from existing Cengage Learning resources and
was produced by Cengage Learning Custom Solutions for collegiate use. As such,
those adopting and/or contributing to this work are responsible for editorial
content accuracy, continuity and completeness.

Compilation © 2012 Cengage Learning
ISBN-13: 978-1-285-11321-0

ISBN-10: 1-285-11321-7

Cengage Learning
5191 Natorp Boulevard
Mason, Ohio 45040
USA
Cengage Learning is a leading provider of customized learning solutions with
office locations around the globe, including Singapore, the United Kingdom,
Australia, Mexico, Brazil, and Japan. Locate your local office at:
international.cengage.com/region.

Cengage Learning products are represented in Canada by Nelson Education, Ltd.
For your lifelong learning solutions, visit **www.cengage.com/custom.**
Visit our corporate website at **www.cengage.com.**

Printed in the United States of America

Contents

Maps

Chronologies

Preface

Western civilization is a grand but tragic drama. The West has forged the instruments of reason that make possible a rational comprehension of physical nature and human culture, conceived the idea of political liberty, and recognized the intrinsic worth of the individual. But the modern West, though it has unraveled nature's mysteries, has been less successful at finding rational solutions to social ills and conflicts between nations. Science, the great achievement of the Western intellect, while improving conditions of life, has also produced weapons of mass destruction. Though the West has pioneered in the protection of human rights, it has also produced totalitarian regimes that have trampled on individual freedom and human dignity. Although the West has demonstrated a commitment to human equality, it has also practiced brutal racism.

Despite the value that Westerners have given to reason and freedom, they have shown a frightening capacity for irrational behavior and a fascination for violence and irrational ideologies, and they have willingly sacrificed liberty for security or national grandeur. The world wars and totalitarian movements of the twentieth century have demonstrated that Western civilization, despite its extraordinary achievements, is fragile and perishable. Yet the West has also shown the capacity to reassert its best values and traditions.

Western Civilization: Ideas, Politics, and Society examines the Western tradition—those unique patterns of thought and systems of values that constitute the Western heritage. While focusing on key ideas and broad themes, the text also provides a balanced treatment of economic, political, and social history for students in Western civilization courses.

The text is written with the conviction that history possesses profound meaning. Without a knowledge of history, men and women cannot fully know themselves, for all human beings have been shaped by institutions and values inherited from the past. Without an awareness of the historical evolution of reason and freedom, the dominant ideals of Western civilization,

commitment to these ideals will diminish. Without knowledge of history, the West cannot fully comprehend or adequately cope with the problems that burden its civilization and the world.

In attempting to make sense out of the past, the authors have been careful to avoid superficial generalizations that oversimplify historical events and arrange history into too neat a structure. But they do strive to interpret and to synthesize in order to provide students with a frame of reference with which to comprehend the principal events and eras in Western history.

CHANGES IN THE TENTH EDITION

For the tenth edition, every chapter has been reworked to some extent. The hundreds of carefully selected modifications and additions significantly enhance the text. Some changes deepen the book's conceptual character while others provide useful and illustrative historical detail. In several chapters the concluding essays, which strive for meaning and significance, have been enlarged and improved. We have been particularly careful to strengthen chapters dealing with intellectual history, the text's distinguishing feature. Each chapter continues to contain a profile of a significant historical figure. The most significant addition in the previous edition was the insertion in every chapter of a primary source that illuminates the narrative. These primary sources are retained in the tenth edition, and we have added questions for analysis of the documents. The Geography of Europe essay at the beginning of the book has been updated. In order to strengthen the organization of the book, we have combined two chapters of the previous edition, reducing the total number of chapters from thirty-four to thirty-three.

In Chapter 1, "The Ancient Near East," we introduced Sargon's daughter, Enheduanna, the world's oldest known poet. The sections dealing with Egypt now contain a discussion of Egyptian literature and Rameses II. In Chapter 2, "The Hebrews," we expanded the discussion of Hebrew law and strengthened the concluding section, "The Legacy of the Ancient Jews." Several short insertions strengthen and clarify the narrative in both Chapters 3 and 4—"The Greek City-State" and "Greek Thought." A section on women has been inserted in Chapter 5, "The Hellenistic Age." The most notable changes in Chapter 6, "The Roman Republic," are fuller discussions of the battle of Cannae, the Roman response to the disaster, and the military accomplishments of Julius Caesar. In Chapter 7, "The Roman Empire," we have strengthened the sections on Pax Romana and the problems of the Late Roman Empire. Chapter 8, "Early Christianity," now includes the views of Early Christian theorists towards various sexual concerns. The most noteworthy additions to Chapter 9, "The Heirs of Rome," are expanded discussions of the iconoclast struggle in Byzantium, the Islamic concept of jihad, Muslim acquisition of Greek learning, and the waning of classical culture in the West. In Chapter 10, "The High Middle Ages," more attention is given to the revival of trade and the extermination of the Cathars. Added to Chapter 11, "The Flowering of Medieval Culture," is a profile of Maimonides, medieval Judaism's most outstanding scholar. The treatment of the Black Death in Chapter 12, "The Late Middle Ages," has been expanded and upgraded.

In Chapter 13, "The Renaissance," a section has been added that explores the debt the European Renaissance owed to the Islamic civilization that developed in the Mediterranean beginning in the eighth century and that flourished in cities stretching from Baghdad and Cairo in the Near East to Cordoba in Moorish Spain. Chapter 14, "The Reformation," introduces the most recent thinking on the Reformation, and in particular the role of the major reformers, and continues its coverage into Eastern Europe. Chapter 15, "European Expansion," adds to the discussion of the preconditions within Europe for global overseas expansion in the fifteenth and sixteenth centuries. Chapter 16, "The Rise of Sovereignty," lays more emphasis on institutions of state and continues an emphasis upon the Dutch Republic, traditionally left out of most accounts of the building of the nation-state. Chapter 17, "The Scientific Revolution," supplies new perspectives on alchemy and its contribution to the formation of a new

understanding of nature. It addresses the relationship between the new science and the Industrial Revolution that began late in the eighteenth century. Chapter 18, "The Age of Enlightenment," puts more stress on the importance of the book trade for making the new ideas accessible and internationally available and highlights what is now called the Radical Enlightenment.

For this edition we have combined the chapters on the French Revolution and Napoleon into one chapter. The new Chapter 19, "The French Revolution," contains additional material on the Terror in the Vendée; providing examples of the elements of total war in the Napoleonic wars enhances the end piece, "The Meaning of the French Revolution." In Chapter 20, "The Industrial Revolution," the discussion of the major social and economic changes resulting from industrialization and urbanization has been strengthened. A generation of scholarship tracing technological and entrepreneurial change together with the resulting impact on the lives of social and national groups has been incorporated. In Chapter 22, "Revolution and Counterrevolution," we have upgraded the treatment of both the Revolution of 1830 and the revolutions of 1848. Strengthening the section "Religion in a Secular Age" is the most significant change in Chapter 23, "Thought and Culture in the Mid-Nineteenth Century." The treatment of anti-Semitism has been improved in Chapter 24, "The Surge of Nationalism." In Chapter 25, "The Industrial West," we provide expanded treatment of the complex relationship between the advance of industry and the political developments in the major European powers and the United States up to the outbreak of the first World War. In Chapter 26, "Imperialism," we have improved the discussion of the expansionist program of Western states in terms of the impact it would have on their foreign and domestic policies as well as the impact it has had on political developments in the non-Western world. Also improved is the discussion of Freud's theory of human nature in Chapter 27, "Modern Consciousness."

The principal changes in Chapter 28, "World War I," are a telling example of the enthusiasm displayed in Germany when war broke out, a deeper analysis of Germany's last offensive, and some additional material on the problems of the Provisional Government in Russia. In Chapter 29, "An Era of Totalitarianism," we have expanded the treatment of the Russian Civil War and both Stalin's and Hitler's dictatorships. In Chapter 30, "Thought and Culture in an Era of World Wars and Totalitarianism," the section on Existentialism has been restructured and abridged, and a new profile on Albert Camus has been inserted. In Chapter 31, "World War II," several topics have been expanded and deepened, particularly the collapse of France in 1940, Germany's recovery and resilience in the months following its defeat in France in 1944, the Battle of the Bulge, and the Holocaust. Two significant improvements have been inserted in the concluding section, "The Legacy of World War II": new material on the significance of the war for women and a deeper discussion of the impact of the war on Western consciousness. Chapter 32, "Europe After World War II," has been significantly restructured, and greater attention is now given to both the origins and demise of the Cold War. In Chapter 33, "The Troubled Present," the coverage of Europe contains new material on Europe's current economic problems and a new section, "New and Old Threats: Muslim Immigration and the Resurgence of Anti-Semitism." The treatments of the wars in Afghanistan and Iraq and the threat from al Qaeda have been updated. Also added to the chapter are the revolts that rocked the Arab world in 2011.

The text represents the efforts of several authors. Marvin Perry, general editor of the project, wrote Chapters 1–12, 19, 21–24, 27–31, much of the new material in Chapters 32 and 33, and the Epilogue. James R. Jacob is the author of Chapters 13 and 15. Margaret C. Jacob wrote Chapters 14 and 16–18. Myrna Chase is the author of Chapters 20, 25, and 26. The late Theodore H. Von Laue wrote the sections on Russia and the Soviet Union in Chapters 28 and 29 and was largely responsible for Chapters 32 and 33. Since Von Laue's death in 2000, Marvin Perry has reworked the sections on the Russian Revolution in Chapter 28 and the Communist regime in Chapter 29 and Myrna Chase has revised the section on tsarist Russia in Chapter 26. For several editions Marvin Perry and Angela Von Laue have reworked substantially Chapters 32 and 33. I regret that Angela Von Laue, who had added her literary and research skills to the project after her husband's death, opted for a too-early retirement. I missed working with her on the tenth edition. Over the years Marvin Perry and George Bock have edited the manuscript for continuity and clarity.

DISTINCTIVE FEATURES

The text contains several pedagogical features. Chapter outlines and introductions provide comprehensive overviews of key themes and give a sense of direction and coherence to the flow of history. Many chapters contain concluding essays that treat the larger meaning of the material. Facts have been carefully selected to illustrate key relationships and concepts and to avoid overwhelming students with unrelated and disconnected data. Appropriate quotations, many not commonly found in texts, have been integrated into the discussion. Each chapter contains notes and an annotated bibliography. Each chapter also begins with focus questions to aid students' reading of the chapter. A glossary is provided online.

Western Civilization: Ideas, Politics, and Society is available in both one- and two-volume editions, and in a third edition, *From the 1400s*. *From the 1400s* (twenty-two chapters) has been prepared for those instructors whose courses begin with the Renaissance or the Reformation.

Volume I of the two-volume edition covers the period from the first civilizations in the Near East through the Age of Enlightenment in the eighteenth century (eighteen chapters). Volume II covers the period from the growth of national states in the seventeenth century to the contemporary age (nineteen chapters). Because some instructors start the second half of their course with the period prior to the French Revolution, Volume II incorporates the last three chapters of Volume I: "The Rise of Sovereignty," "The Scientific Revolution," and "The Age of Enlightenment." Volume II also contains a comprehensive introduction that surveys the ancient world, the Middle Ages, and the opening centuries of the modern era; the introduction is designed particularly for students who did not take the first half of the course. *From the 1400s* also contains an introduction that covers the ancient world and the Middle Ages.

ANCILLARIES

We are pleased to introduce an expanded ancillary package that will help students in learning and instructors in teaching.

Instructor's Resources

PowerLecture DVD with ExamView® and JoinIn®. An all-in-one multimedia resource for class preparation, presentation, and testing. The Instructor's Resource Manual, prepared by Jennifer Deane, includes instructional objectives, chapter outlines, lecture suggestions, group learning projects, analyzing primary sources, audiovisual bibliographies, suggested readings, and Internet resources. Microsoft® PowerPoint® slides of lecture outlines, as well as images and maps from the text, can be used as offered or customized by importing personal lecture slides or other material; JoinIn PowerPoint slides with clicker content are also provided. An image library contains .jpg images from the text. The test bank, prepared by Stephen Gibson, includes key term identification, multiple-choice, essay, and map questions. ExamView, an easy-to-use assessment and tutorial system, allows instructors to create, deliver, and customize tests in minutes. Instructors can build tests with as many as 250 questions using up to twelve question types. Using the complete word-processing capabilities of ExamView, instructors can enter an unlimited number of new questions or edit existing ones.

Companion Website. This website for instructors features all of the free student assets, plus an Instructor's Resource Manual (instructional objectives, chapter outlines, lecture suggestions, group learning projects, primary source analysis, audiovisual bibliographies, suggested readings, and Internet resources) and PowerPoint presentations (lecture outlines, images and maps, and JoinIn PowerPoint slides with clicker content). In addition, access to HistoryFinder, a searchable online database with thousands of assets, allows instructors to easily create exciting presentations for their classroom by downloading art, photographs, maps, primary sources, and audio/video clips directly into a Microsoft PowerPoint slide.

WebTutor™ on Blackboard® or WebCT®. With the WebTutor text-specific, preformatted content and total flexibility, instructors can easily create and manage their own custom course website. Instructors can provide virtual office hours, post syllabi, set up threaded discussions, track student progress with the quizzing material, and much more. For students, WebTutor offers real-time access to an interactive eBook and a full array of study tools, including animations and videos that bring the book's topics to life, plus chapter outlines, summaries, learning objectives, glossary flashcards (with audio), practice quizzes, and weblinks.

CourseMate. Cengage Learning's History CourseMate brings course concepts to life with interactive learning, study tools, and exam preparation tools that support the printed textbook. Use Engagement Tracker to monitor student engagement in the course and watch student comprehension soar as your class works with the printed textbook and the textbook-specific website. An interactive eBook allows students to take notes, highlight, search, and interact with embedded media (such as quizzes, flashcards, and videos). Access to the History Resource Center, a "virtual reader," provides students with hundreds of primary sources. Learn more at www.cengage.com/coursemate.

Wadsworth Western Civilization Resource Center. Wadsworth's Western Civilization Resource Center gives your students access to a "virtual reader" with hundreds of primary sources including speeches, letters, legal documents and transcripts, poems, maps, simulations, timelines, and additional images that bring history to life, along with interactive assignable exercises. A map feature including Google Earth™ coordinates and exercises will aid in student comprehension of geography and use of maps. Students can compare the traditional textbook map with an aerial view of the location today. It's an ideal resource for study, review, and research. In addition to this map feature, the resource center also provides blank maps for student review and testing.

CourseReader: Western Civilization This application is Cengage Learning's easy, affordable way to build your own online customizable reader. Through a partnership with Gale, *CourseReader: Western Civilization* searches thousands of primary and secondary sources, readings, and audio and video clips from multiple disciplines. Select exactly and only the material you want your students to work with. Each selection can be listened to (using the "Listen" button) to accommodate varied learning styles. Additionally, an instructor can choose to add his or her own notes to readings to direct students' attention or ask them questions about a particular passage. Each primary source is accompanied by an introduction and questions to help students understand the reading. *CourseReader: Western Civilization* is the perfect complement to any class.

Student Resources

Companion Website. This website provides a variety of resources, prepared by Jeffrey Webb, to help you review for class. These study tools include glossary, crossword puzzles, short quizzes, essay questions, critical thinking questions, primary sources links, and weblinks.

WebTutor on Blackboard or *WebCT.* WebTutor offers real-time access to an interactive eBook and a full array of study tools, including animations and videos that bring the book's topics to life, plus chapter outlines, summaries, learning objectives, glossary flashcards (with audio), practice quizzes, and weblinks.

CourseMate. The more you study, the better the results. Make the most of your study time by accessing everything you need to succeed in one place. Read your textbook, take notes, review flashcards, watch videos, and take practice quizzes online with CourseMate. In addition, you can access the History Resource Center, a "virtual reader" that provides you with hundreds of primary sources.

Wadsworth Western Civilization Resource Center. Wadsworth's Western Civilization Resource Center gives you access to a "virtual reader" with hundreds of primary sources including speeches, letters, legal documents and transcripts, poems, maps, simulations, timelines, and additional images that bring history to life, along with interactive assignable exercises. A map feature including Google Earth coordinates and exercises will aid in your comprehension of geography and use of maps. You can compare the traditional textbook map with an aerial view of the location today. It's an ideal resource for study, review, and research. In addition to this map feature, the resource center also provides blank maps for student review and testing.

Rand McNally Historical Atlas of Western Civilization, 2e. This valuable resource features over forty-five maps, including maps that highlight classical Greece and Rome; maps documenting European civilization during the Renaissance; maps that follow events in Germany, Russia, and Italy as they led up to World Wars I and II; maps that show the dissolution of Communism in 1989; maps documenting language and religion in the Western world; and maps describing the unification and industrialization of Europe.

Document Exercise. Prepared by Donna Van Raaphorst, Cuyahoga Community College, *Document Exercise* is a collection of exercises based around primary sources, available in two volumes.

Music of Western Civilization. Available free to adopters, and for a small fee to students, this CD contains a broad sampling of many important musical pieces of Western civilization.

Writing for College History, 1e. Prepared by Robert M. Frakes, Clarion University, this brief handbook for survey courses in American History, Western Civilization/European History, and World Civilization guides students through the various types of writing assignments they encounter in a history class. Providing examples of student writing and candid assessments of student work, this text focuses on the rules and conventions of writing for the college history course.

The History Handbook, 1e. Prepared by Carol Berkin of Baruch College, City University of New York, and Betty Anderson of Boston University, this book teaches students both basic and history-specific study skills such as how to read primary sources, research historical topics, and correctly cite sources. Substantially less expensive than comparable skill-building texts, *The History Handbook* also offers tips for Internet research and evaluating online sources.

Doing History: Research and Writing in the Digital Age, 1e. This book was prepared by Michael J. Galgano, J. Chris Arndt, and Raymond M. Hyser of James Madison University. Whether you're starting down the path as a history major or simply looking for a straightforward and systematic guide to writing a successful paper, you'll find this text to be an indispensible handbook to historical research. This text's "soup to nuts" approach to researching and writing about history addresses every step of the process, from locating your sources and gathering information to writing clearly and making proper use of various citation styles to avoid plagiarism. You'll also learn how to make the most of every tool available to you—especially the technology that helps you conduct the process efficiently and effectively.

The Modern Researcher, 6e. Prepared by Jacques Barzun and Henry F. Graff of Columbia University, this classic introduction to the techniques of research and the art of expression is used widely in history courses but is also appropriate for writing and research methods courses in other departments. Barzun and Graff thoroughly cover every aspect of research, from the selection of a topic through the gathering, analysis, writing, revision, and publication of findings, presenting the process not as a set of rules but through actual cases that put the subtleties of research in a useful context. Part One covers the principles and methods of research; Part Two covers writing, speaking, and getting one's work published.

Acknowledgments

The authors would like to thank the following instructors for their critical reading of sections of the manuscript: Gregory Brown, University of Nevada, Las Vegas; James Carter, Saint Joseph's University; David Flaten, Tompkins Cortland Community College; Stephen Gibson, Allegany College of Maryland; Sylvia Gray, Portland Community College; Ann Kuzdale, Chicago State University; William Landon, Northern Kentucky University; Joseph McMahon, Bridgewater State College; Anne Rodrick, Wofford College; Ronald Schechter, The College of William and Mary; and Jeffrey Webb, Huntington University. Several of their suggestions were incorporated into the final version.

We are grateful to the staff of Cengage Learning who lent their considerable talents to the project. In particular, we would like to thank Associate Editor Adrienne Zicht for her conscientiousness and superb administrative skills, and Jane Lee, Senior Content Project Manager, for her careful supervision. This edition rests substantially on the editorial talents of Freda Alexander, who worked closely with us on earlier editions of the text. Over the years, both Jean Woy, Senior Consulting Editor, who has been affiliated with the text since the first edition published in 1981, and Nancy Blaine, Senior Sponsoring Editor, who has worked with us for ten years, continued to recognize and support what we are trying to do—and for this we remain grateful. Although Nancy Blaine is no longer with Cengage Learning, her replacement, Brooke Barbier, has immediately identified with the project—and for this we are also grateful. In addition, we would like to thank Cate Barr, Senior Art Director, for her creativity and artistic vision in updating the cover and interior design for this edition. Three people not part of the Cengage Learning staff made valuable contributions to the project. A special thanks to Karunakaran Gunasekaran at PreMediaGlobal, who managed the overall production with skill and dedication. Wendy Granger from the Bill Smith Group, the photo researcher, deserves praise for her fine eye and enthusiasm for the project. So, too, does Daniel Nighting, the copy editor, for his careful eye for detail.

Unfortunately, Angela Von Laue, who had assisted me since the death of her husband, Theodore Von Laue, in 2000, has taken a too-early retirement from the book. I miss her literary and research skills. I would like to express my personal gratitude to my good friend George Bock, whose creative insights in previous editions continue to contribute to the text's distinguishing character—a concern for crucial concepts and essential relationships. Our often heated but always fruitful discussions demonstrate to me the intrinsic value of the Socratic dialogue. And, as always, I am grateful to my wife, Phyllis Perry, for her encouragement and computer expertise, which have saved me much time and frustration.

Geography of Europe

The map on the following pages features the continent of Europe and parts of North Africa and the Middle East. Like most maps, it contains a selected combination of physical and political information. The physical part pertains to the natural world—the shapes of landmasses, mountains, and bodies of water—and serves as a kind of background or screen onto which the political information is projected. Categories of political information commonly featured on historical maps include the location and names of important cities and states, the changing borders of countries and empires, and the routes people traveled as they explored, migrated, traded, and fought with one another.

Europe is one of seven continents; the others are Africa, Asia, North America, South America, Australia, and Antarctica. Europe is bounded in the north by the Arctic Sea, in the west by the Atlantic Ocean, in the south by the Mediterranean Sea, and in the southeast by the Black Sea and the Caspian Sea. Off the mainland but traditionally considered a part of Europe are thousands of islands, from those of the United Kingdom, Ireland, and Iceland in the northwest, to Crete, Sicily, and Sardinia in the southeast.

Europe is quite distinctive in shape. The first thing to notice is that there is no natural border between Europe and Asia. The traditional eastern boundary is the Ural River, but looked at from a purely geographic standpoint, Europe might simply be called western Asia. The second thing to notice is how much of Europe is made up of peninsulas. In fact, Europe itself is one gigantic peninsula, with a coastline equal in distance to one and a half times around the equator (37,877 miles).

North Americans are often surprised to discover the small size of the European continent. The geographic area of France, for example, is less than that of Texas; Britain is similar in size to Alabama. The distance from London to Paris is about the same as from New York to Boston, while the distance from Berlin to Moscow is comparable to that of Chicago to Denver.

MAJOR PENINSULAS AND ISLANDS There are six major European peninsulas: the Iberian (comprising Portugal and Spain); the Apennine (Italy); the Balkan (Slovenia, Croatia, Bosnia-Herzegovina, Serbia and Montenegro, Albania, Greece, Bulgaria, and Macedonia); the Anatolian (Turkey); the Scandinavian (Norway, Sweden, and Finland); and the Jutland or Danish peninsula. The islands of Iceland, Ireland, and the United Kingdom lie to the Atlantic west, while to the east lie some of the major islands of the Mediterranean, such as Corsica, Sardinia, Sicily, Crete, and Cyprus.

SEAS, LAKES, AND RIVERS Europe's irregular coastline encloses large areas of water into bays, gulfs, and seas. Moving from west to east in the Mediterranean, we have the Tyrrhenian Sea (between Italy and the islands of Sicily, Sardinia, and Corsica), the Adriatic (between Italy and the nations of the western Balkan peninsula), the Ionian (between Italy and Greece), and the Aegean (between Greece and Turkey). The Baltic Sea is bordered on the east (moving clockwise from the north) by Finland, Russia, Estonia, Latvia, Lithuania, Poland, Germany, and Sweden. It is connected by narrow channels to the North Sea, which lies (moving clockwise from the north) between Norway, Denmark, Germany, the Netherlands, and Belgium in the east and south, to the United Kingdom in the north and west. The English Channel separates England and France; the Bay of Biscay lies between southwestern

Elevation

Meters	Feet
4,000	13,120
2,000	6,560
500	1,640
200	656
Sea level	Sea level
Below sea level	Below sea level

⊛ National capital

• Other city

Reykjavik

ICELAND

Arctic Circle

Faroe Islands
(Den.)

SWEDEN

Shetland
Islands
(U.K.)

NORWAY

Oslo

NORTHERN
IRELAND

Edinburgh

North
Sea

DENMARK

Sto

Belfast

IRELAND

Copenhagen

Baltic Sea

LIT

Dublin

UNITED
KINGDOM

NETHERLANDS

Hamburg

Kaliningra

Gdansk

Elbe R.

Cardiff

Amsterdam

London

English Channel

Berlin

GERMANY

POLA

ATLANTIC
OCEAN

Brussels

Bonn

Leipzig

Wars

BELGIUM

Frankfurt

Seine R.

Paris

Prague

Luxembourg

CZECH

LUX.

Stuttgart

REPUBLIC

CARF

Rhine R.

Loire R.

SLO

Munich

FRANCE

Zurich

LIECH.

Vienna

Bratisla

Geneva

Bern

Vaduz

AUSTRIA

Bu

Bay
of
Biscay

SWITZ.

ALPS

HUNGA

Lyons

Ljubljana

SLOVENIA

Zagreb

Turin

Milan

Po R.

CROATIA

Porto

PYRENEES

Monaco

San
Marino

SAN
MARINO

BOSNIA &
HERZEGOVINA

PORTUGAL

SPAIN

Andorra
la Vella

ANDORRA

MONACO

APENNINES

Adriatic Sea

Sarajevo

Lisbon

Madrid

Barcelona

Corsica
(Fr.)

MONT

Rome

Tagus R.

Balearic Islands
(Sp.)

Sardinia
(It.)

VATICAN
CITY

ITALY

Podgorica

ALBANIA

Naples

Tiranë

M

Gibraltar
(U.K.)

Mediterranean

Tyrrhenian
Sea

Ionian
Sea

Rabat

Algiers

Sicily
(It.)

MOROCCO

Tunis

MALTA

ALGERIA

Valletta

Sea

ATLAS MTS.

0   200   400 Km.

0   200   400 Mi.

TUNISIA

France and northern Spain. The Black Sea, on the southern border of Russia and Ukraine, is connected by two straits—the Bosphorous and the Dardanelles—to the Aegean Sea. The Caspian Sea, bordered in the north by Russia and Kazakhstan, is the world's largest saltwater lake and, at 92 feet below sea level, the lowest point in Europe.

Several of Europe's major rivers flow across the Russian plain. At 2,194 miles, the Volga is the longest river in Europe. Linked by canals and other river systems to the Arctic Ocean in the north and the Baltic Sea in the south, the Volga originates west of Moscow and empties into the Caspian Sea after flowing some 2,194 miles. At 1,777 miles, the Danube is Europe's second longest river and the principal waterway in the central part of the continent. It originates in southern Germany and flows through Austria, Slovakia, Hungary, Croatia, Serbia and Montenegro, Bulgaria, Moldova, Ukraine, and Romania, before reaching the Black Sea. The Rhine river comes next, at 766 miles, winding its way from the Swiss Alps to the Netherlands and the North Sea. Other prominent riverways in Europe include the Elbe (678 miles), which originates in the Czech Republic and passes through Germany before it, too, empties into the North Sea, and the Rhône (505 miles), which runs from Switzerland, through France, and into the Mediterranean Sea. The proximity of most areas of the European landmass to the coastline and to major river systems greatly affected the Continent's history.

LAND REGIONS Despite its relatively small size, the European continent presents a wide range of landforms, from rugged mountains to sweeping plains. These can be separated into four major regions: the Northwest Mountains, the Great European Plain, the Central Uplands, and the Alpine Mountain System. The mountains of the Northwest Region cover most of the region, running through northwestern France, Ireland, northern Great Britain, Norway, Sweden, northern Finland, and the northwest corner of Russia. The Great European Plain covers almost all of the European part of the former Soviet Union, extending from the Arctic Ocean to the Caucasus Mountains. This belt stretches westward across Poland, Germany, Belgium, the western portion of France, and southeastern England. The Central Uplands is a belt of high plateaus, hills, and low mountains. It reaches from the central plateau of Portugal, across Spain, the central highlands of France, to the hills and mountains of southern Germany, the Czech Republic, and Slovakia. The Alpine Mountain System is made up of several mountain ranges, including the Pyrenees between Spain and France, the Alps in southeastern France, northern Italy, Switzerland, and western Austria, and the Apennine range in Italy. Also included are the mountain ranges of the Balkan Peninsula, the Carpathian Mountains in Slovakia and Romania, and the Caucasus Mountains between the Black and Caspian Seas.

When studying the map of Europe, it is important to notice the proximity of Central Asia, the Middle East, and North Africa. Interaction with the peoples and cultures of these regions has had a profound impact on the course of European history.

Western Civilization
Ideas, Politics, and Society

Part One

The Ancient World: Foundation of the West

to A.D. *500*

3000
B.C.

2000
B.C.

1000
B.C.

500
B.C.

100
B.C.

A.D.
200

Politics and Society

Rise of civilization in Sumer (c. 3200)
Union of Upper and Lower Egypt (c. 2900)
Rise of Minoan civilization (c. 2600)

Rise of Mycenaean civilization (c. 2000)
Hammurabi of Babylon builds an empire
    (1792–1750)

Creation of a unified Hebrew monarchy
    under David (1000–961)
Dark Age in Greece (c. 1100–800)
Hellenic Age (c. 800–323)
Fall of Assyrian empire (612)
Persian conquest of Near East (550–525)
Formation of Roman Republic (509)

Persian Wars (499–479)
Peloponnesian War (431–404)
Conquest of Greek city-states by Philip of
    Macedon (338)
Conquests of Alexander the Great (336–323)
Hellenistic Age (323–330)
Roman conquest of Carthage and
    Hellenistic kingdoms (264–146)

Political violence and civil wars in Rome
    (88–31)
Assassination of Julius Caesar (44)
Octavian takes the title Augustus and
    becomes first Roman emperor (27)
Greco-Roman Age (30 B.C.–c. A.D. 500)
Pax Romana—the height of Roman Empire
    (27 B.C.–A.D. 180)

Military anarchy in Rome (235–285)
Goths defeat Romans at Adrianople (378)
End of Roman Empire in the West (476)

Thought and Culture

Cuneiform writing in Sumer; hieroglyphics
    in Egypt

Epic of Gilgamesh (c. 1900)
Code of Hammurabi (c. 1790)
Amenhotep IV and a movement toward
    monotheism in Egypt (c. 1369–1353)
Moses and the Exodus (1200s)

Homer's *Iliad* and *Odyssey* (700s)
Age of classical prophecy: flowering of
    Hebrew ethical thought (750–430)

Law of the Twelve Tables (c. 450)
Rise of Greek philosophy: Ionians, Pythag-
    oreans, Parmenides (500s and 400s)
Greek dramatists: Aeschylus, Sophocles,
    Euripides, Aristophanes (400s)
Greek philosophers: Socrates, Plato,
    Aristotle (400s and 300s)
Hellenistic philosophies: Epicureanism,
    Stoicism, Skepticism, Cynicism

Roman philosophers during the Republic:
    Lucretius, Cicero (1st cent. B.C.)
Rise and spread of Christianity: Jesus
    (d. A.D. 29); Paul's missionary activity
    (c. 34–64)
Gospel According to Mark (c. 66–70)
Roman historians, poets, and philosophers
    during the Pax Romana: Livy, Tacitus,
    Virgil, Horace, Ovid, Juvenal, Seneca,
    Marcus Aurelius

Church fathers: Jerome, Ambrose,
    Augustine (300s and 400s)

Chapter 1

The Ancient Near East: The First Civilizations

With the body of a lion and the face of a man, the Sphinx watches over Giza as a testament to the divine kingship of the pharaohs. (dgmata/Shutterstock.com)

Focus Questions

1. What is meant by the term *civilization*? Under what conditions did it emerge?
2. What did Mesopotamian and Egyptian civilizations have in common? How did they differ?
3. In what ways did mythopoeic thought characterize Near Eastern civilization? How does this type of thinking differ from that of science?
4. What elements of Near Eastern civilization were passed on to Western civilization?

C ivilization was not inevitable; it was an act of human creativity. The first civilizations emerged about five thousand years ago, in the Near Eastern river valleys of Sumer and Egypt. Before that time stretched the vast ages of prehistory, when our ancestors did not dwell in cities and knew nothing of writing; some 99 percent of human history took place before the creation of civilization. Today, when human beings have the capacity to destroy civilization, we might reflect on humanity's long and painful climb to a civilized state.

PREHISTORY

The period called the **Paleolithic Age,** or Old Stone Age, began with the earliest primitive toolmaking human beings who inhabited East Africa some three million years ago. It ended ten thousand years ago in parts of the Near East when people discovered how to farm. Our Paleolithic ancestors lived as hunters (no doubt also as scavengers) and food gatherers. Because they had not learned how to farm, they did not establish permanent villages. When their food supplies ran short, they abandoned their caves or tentlike structures of branches and searched for new dwelling places.

Human social development was shaped by this three-million-year experience of hunting and food gathering. For survival, groups of families formed bands consisting of around thirty people; members learned how to plan, organize, cooperate, trust, and share. The men hunted for meat, and the women cared for the young, tended the fires, and gathered fruits, nuts, berries, and grain. Hunters assisted one another in tracking and killing game, finding cooperative efforts more successful than individual forays. By sharing their kill and bringing some back to their camp for the rest of the group, they reinforced the social bond. So, too, did women who gathered food for the group. Bands that did not cooperate in the hunt, in food gathering, or in food distribution were unlikely to survive.

Hunting and food gathering also stimulated mental and physical development. Food gatherers had to know which plants were safe to eat and where to find them. Hunting required strength, speed, good eyesight and hearing, and mental

3200 B.C.*	Rise of civilization in Sumer
2900	Union of Upper and Lower Egypt
2686–2181	Old Kingdom: essential forms of Egyptian civilization take shape
2180	Downfall of Akkadian empire
1792–1750	Hammurabi of Babylon brings Akkad and Sumer under his control and fashions a code of laws
1570	Egyptians drive out Hyksos and embark on empire building
1369–1353	Reign of Amenhotep IV: a movement toward monotheism
1200	Fall of Hittite empire
612	Fall of Assyrian empire
604–562	Reign of Nebuchadnezzar: height of Chaldean empire
550–525 B.C.	Persian conquests form a world empire

*Most dates are approximations.

ability. Hunters had to study and analyze the habits of their prey, judge weather conditions, recall the location of dens and watering places, and make better tools and weapons. The physically weak and mentally deficient, unable to track animals and to cope with new problems, did not survive long. Individuals with superior intelligence and physical attributes lived longer and had more opportunities to produce offspring, passing on their characteristics and gradually improving the human species.

Although human progress was very slow during the long centuries of the Paleolithic Age, advances occurred that influenced the future enormously. Paleolithic people developed spoken language and shaped bone, wood, and stone tools that corresponded to ideas in their minds. They preserved their creations and taught other people how to use them. Succeeding generations improved on what they had learned from their ancestors. With these simple but useful tools, Paleolithic human beings dug up roots; peeled the bark off trees; trapped, killed, and skinned animals; made clothing; and fashioned fish nets. They also discovered how to control fire, which allowed them to cook their meat. By killing microbes, fire made meat safer to eat. Fire also provided warmth and protection against predators—lions and leopards, for example—that feared fire. From evidence

discovered in caves, it is certain that Paleolithic people had domesticated fire about 500,000 years ago. Some evidence points to fire use as far back as 1.5 million years.

Like toolmaking and the control of fire, language was a great human achievement. Language enabled individuals to acquire and share with one another knowledge, skills, experiences, and feelings. Thus, language was the decisive factor in the development of culture and its transmission from one generation to the next. Language helped parents teach their children rules of conduct and religious beliefs, as well as how to make tools and light fires.

Most likely, our Paleolithic ancestors developed mythic-religious ideas to explain the mysteries of nature, birth, sickness, and death. They felt that living powers operated within and beyond the world that they experienced, and they sought to establish friendly relations with these powers. To primitive peoples, the elements—sun, rain, wind, thunder, and lightning—were alive. The natural elements were spirits; they could feel and act with a purpose. To appease these forces of nature, hunters and gatherers made offerings to them. Gradually, there emerged shamans, medicine men, and witch doctors, who, through rituals, trances, and chants, seemed able to communicate with these spirits. Paleolithic people also began the practice

6

of burying their dead, sometimes with offerings, which suggests belief in life after death. Corpses were sometimes dusted with red ocher, which represented blood, a source of life. Another belief is revealed in the many small statues of women, made between forty thousand and twenty-five thousand years ago, that have been found by archaeologists in Europe and Asia. Fashioned from ivory, wood, and clay and often marked by huge breasts and distended stomachs, these fertility figurines represent a mother goddess who gave life, food, and protection.

Between thirty thousand and twelve thousand years ago, Paleolithic people sought out the dark and silent interior of caves, which they probably viewed as sanctuaries, and, with only torches for light, they painted remarkably skillful and perceptive pictures of animals on the cave walls. Even prior to civilization, human beings demonstrated artistic talent, an esthetic sense. When these prehistoric artists drew an animal with a spear in its side, they probably believed that this act would make them successful in hunting; when they drew a herd of animals, they probably hoped that this would cause game to be plentiful. This belief that something done to an image of an animal or a person will produce the same effect on the being itself is called *sympathetic magic*. Hunting societies that endured into the modern world still engage in rituals designed to protect the hunter and to ensure a kill.

Some ten thousand years ago, the New Stone Age, or **Neolithic Age**, began in the Near East. During the Neolithic Age, human beings discovered farming, domesticated animals, established villages, polished stone tools, made pottery, and wove cloth. So important were these achievements that they are referred to as the Neolithic Revolution.

Agriculture—the deliberate planting and cultivation of crops—first developed in the hilly regions of the Near East, where rainfall was plentiful and wheat and barley grew abundantly in the wild. People there also began to domesticate the sheep and wild goats that roamed the hills. In other parts of the world, farming and the domestication of animals developed independently.

Agriculture and the domestication of animals revolutionized life. Whereas Paleolithic hunters and food gatherers had been forced to use whatever nature made available to them, Neolithic farmers altered their environment to satisfy human needs. Instead of spending their time searching for grains, roots, and berries, women and children grew crops near their homes; instead of tracking animals over great distances, men could slaughter domesticated goats or sheep nearby. (Later, horses, camels, and donkeys were tamed, providing people with a means of transportation.) Since farmers had to live near their fields and could store food for the future, farming led to the rise of permanent settlements. Villages containing as many as two hundred or three hundred people had occasionally emerged in late Paleolithic times, before the discovery of agriculture. Hunter-gatherers built such villages in areas that had an abundant, stable food supply—near a river or lake well stocked with fish, or in a valley with plenty of wild wheat and barley and herds of gazelles or goats. The development of farming greatly speeded the shift to villages. It is likely that trade also impelled people to gather in village communities. Herdsmen, hunters, and food gatherers living in regions rich in salt (needed for preserving food), volcanic glass (used for mirrors, blades, and spearheads), or hematite (an iron ore that was a source of red coloring for pottery) formed trading settlements, which exchanged raw materials for food.

Villages changed the patterns of life. A food surplus freed some people to devote part of their time to sharpening their skills as basket weavers or toolmakers. The demand for raw materials and the creations of skilled artisans fostered trade, sometimes across long distances, and the formation of trading settlements. An awareness of private property emerged. Hunters had accumulated few possessions, since belongings presented a burden in moving from place to place. Villagers, however, acquired property and were determined to protect it from one another and from outsiders—nomadic herdsmen who might raid the village. Hunting bands were egalitarian; generally, no one member had more possessions or more power than another. In farming villages, a ruling elite emerged that possessed wealth and wielded power.

No doubt farming also affected our emotional development. Human beings who had evolved as hunters and foragers, enjoying considerable leisure, personal freedom, independence, and equality, were now forced to adjust to a different tempo of life—unending toil, stifling routine, and the need to obey the commands of the elites. Scholars ponder the psychological dimensions of this shift from the hunter's way of life to sedentary farming.

In recent years, archaeologists have uncovered several Neolithic villages, the oldest of which was established before 8000 B.C. Among the most famous of these sites are Çatal Hüyük in Anatolia (Turkey), Jericho in Palestine, and Jarmö in eastern Iraq. Scholars disagree on whether these communities were just highly developed villages or the first cities. The traditional view is that cities arose about 3000 B.C. in Sumer, the home of the earliest civilization. Some scholars argue that five thousand years before the Sumerian cities Jericho's two thousand inhabitants had created urban life by engaging in trade and embarking on public works. Jericho's walls were six feet six inches thick at the base and in some places twenty feet high. Their construction required cooperation and a division of labor beyond the capacity of an agricultural village. Similar communities, or primitive cities, spread throughout much of the Near East in late prehistoric times.

Neolithic people made great strides in technology. By shaping and baking clay, they made pottery containers for cooking and for storing food and water. The invention of the potter's wheel enabled them to form bowls and plates more quickly and precisely. Stone tools were sharpened by grinding them on rock. The discoveries of the wheel and the sail improved transportation and promoted trade, and the development of the plow and the ox yoke made tilling the soil easier for farmers.

The Neolithic period also marked the beginning of the use of metals. First used was copper, which was easily fashioned into tools and weapons. Copper implements lasted longer than those made of stone and flint, and they could be recast and reshaped if broken. In time, artisans discovered how to make bronze by combining copper and tin in the proper ratio. Bronze was harder than copper, a characteristic that made a sharper cutting edge possible.

During the Neolithic Age, the food supply became more reliable, village life expanded, and the population increased. Families that acquired wealth gained a higher social status and became village leaders. Religion grew more formal and structured; nature spirits evolved into deities, each with specific powers over nature or human life. Altars were erected in their honor, and ceremonies were conducted by priests, whose power and wealth increased as people gave offerings to the gods. Neolithic society was growing more organized and complex; it was on the threshold of civilization.

THE RISE TO CIVILIZATION

What we call **civilization** arose some five thousand years ago in the Near East (in Mesopotamia and Egypt) and then later in the Far East (in India and China). The first civilizations began in cities, which were larger, more populated, and more complex in their political, economic, and social structure than Neolithic villages. Because the cities depended on the inhabitants of adjacent villages for their food, farming techniques must have been developed sufficiently to produce food surpluses. Increased production provided food for urban inhabitants who engaged in nonagricultural occupations; they became merchants, craftsmen, bureaucrats, and priests.

The invention of writing enabled the first civilizations to preserve, organize, and expand knowledge and to pass it on to future generations; it also allowed government officials and priests to conduct their affairs more efficiently. Moreover, civilized societies possessed organized governments, which issued laws and defined the boundary lines of their states. On a scale much larger than Neolithic communities, the inhabitants erected buildings and monuments, engaged in trade and manufacturing, and used specialized labor for different projects. Religious life grew more organized and complex, and a powerful and wealthy priesthood emerged. These developments—cities, specialization of labor, writing, organized government, monumental architecture, and a complex religious structure—differentiate the first civilizations from prehistoric cultures.

Religion was the central force in these primary civilizations. It provided satisfying explanations for the workings of nature, helped ease the fear of death, and justified traditional rules of morality. Law was considered sacred, a commandment of the gods. Religion united people in the common enterprises needed for survival—for example, the construction and maintenance of irrigation works and the storage of food. Religion also promoted creativity in art, literature, and science. In addition, the power of rulers, regarded as gods or their agents, derived from religion.

The emergence of civilization was a great creative act and not merely the inevitable development of agricultural societies. Many communities had learned how to farm, but only a handful made the leap into civilization. How was it possible for Sumerians and Egyptians, the creators of the earliest civilizations, to make that breakthrough? This question has intrigued and baffled historians, and no single explanation is entirely convincing. Most scholars stress the relationship between civilizations and river valleys. Rivers deposited fertile silt on adjoining fields, provided water for crops, and served as avenues for trade. But environmental factors alone do not adequately explain the emergence of civilization. What cannot be omitted is the human contribution: capacity for thought and cooperative activity.

Both the Tigris and Euphrates rivers in Mesopotamia and the Nile River in Egypt deposited fertile soil when they overflowed their banks. But before these rivers could be of any value in producing crops, swamps around them had to be drained; jungles had to be cleared; and dikes, reservoirs, and canals had to be built—activities that required the cooperation of large numbers of people. Learning to work together for the good of the community was an indispensible requirement for civilization. In the process of constructing and maintaining irrigation networks, people learned to formulate and obey rules and developed administrative, engineering, and mathematical skills. The need to keep records stimulated the invention of writing. These creative responses to the challenges posed by nature spurred the early inhabitants of Sumer and Egypt to make the breakthrough to civilization, thereby altering the course of human destiny. By the time the Hebrews and the Greeks, the spiritual ancestors of Western civilization, appeared on the stage of history, civilizations had been in existence for some two thousand years.

Civilization also had its dark side. Epidemic disease thrived in urban centers, where people lived close together in unsanitary conditions, drinking contaminated water and surrounded by rotting garbage. Slavery was an essential and accepted feature of early civilizations. The authority wielded by rulers and their officials and the habits of discipline acquired by the community's members made possible the construction of irrigation works, but they were also harnessed for destructive conflicts between states. Such warfare, which involved managing large numbers of combatants, was far more lethal than the sporadic and generally disorganized acts of violence that occurred in Neolithic times. A hostile and aggressive attitude toward members of alien groups has plagued human beings since the rise of civilization. Warfare fascinated the people who created the first civilizations: scribes recounted battle after battle, warrior-kings boasted of their military conquests, and military heroes were held in the highest esteem. Cultural historian Lewis Mumford observes:

> *War was not a mere residue of more common primitive forms of aggression. . . . In all its typical aspects, its discipline, its drill, its handling of large masses of men as units, in its destructive assaults en masse, in its heroic sacrifices, its final destructions, exterminations, seizures, enslavements, war was rather the special invention of civilization: its ultimate drama.*[1]*

MESOPOTAMIAN CIVILIZATION

Mesopotamia is the Greek word for "land between the rivers." It was here, in the valleys of the Tigris and Euphrates rivers, that the first civilization began. The first to develop an urban civilization in Mesopotamia (present-day Iraq) were the Sumerians, who colonized the marshlands of the lower Euphrates, which, together with the Tigris, flows into the Persian Gulf. The Sumerians' origin is obscure, although scholars speculate that they migrated from the East, perhaps northern India.

*Numbered source notes appear at the end of each chapter, along with suggested readings.

Map 1.1 MESOPOTAMIAN AND EGYPTIAN CIVILIZATIONS The first civilizations emerged in river valleys: Mesopotamia in the valleys of the Tigris and Euphrates rivers, Egypt in the Nile Valley. (Copyright © 2013 Cengage Learning.)

They spoke a language unrelated to the tongues of their Semitic neighbors, who had migrated from Arabia into Mesopotamia and adjacent regions.

Through constant toil and imagination, the Sumerians transformed the swamps into fields of barley and groves of date palms. Around 3000 B.C., their hut settlements gradually evolved into twelve independent city-states, each consisting of a city and its surrounding countryside. Among the impressive achievements of the Sumerians were a system of symbol writing (*cuneiform*), in which pictograms and signs for numbers were engraved with a reed stylus on clay tablets to represent ideas; elaborate brick houses, palaces, and temples; bronze tools and weapons; irrigation works; trade with other peoples; an early form of money; religious and political institutions; schools; religious

and secular literature; varied art forms; codes of law; medicinal drugs; and a lunar calendar.

The history of Mesopotamia is marked by a succession of conquests. To the north of Sumer was a Semitic city* called Akkad. About 2350 B.C., the people of Akkad, led by Sargon the Great, the warrior-king, conquered the Sumerian cities. Sargon built the world's first empire, which extended from the Persian Gulf to the Mediterranean Sea. Establishing a pattern that future despotic rulers would emulate, Sargon stationed garrisons in conquered lands and appointed governors and officials to administer the territories, as well as additional bureaucrats to register and parcel

---

*Semites included Akkadians, Hebrews, Babylonians, Canaanites, Assyrians, and Aramaeans. Hebrew and Arabic are Semitic languages.

SUMERIAN ZIGGURAT. This ziggurat of the moon god, Nanna, which included an impressive temple, dominated the Sumerian city of Ur. (© Charles and Josette Lenars/Corbis.)

out the precious metals, horses, grain, and other commodities exacted from conquered peoples. He also retained a large standing army to quell revolts and to launch new imperialist ventures. The Akkadians adopted Sumerian cultural forms, including cuneiform, and spread them beyond the boundaries of Mesopotamia with their conquests. Mesopotamian religion became a blend of Sumerian and Akkadian elements. Illustrating the confluence of Akkadian and Sumerian culture was Sargon's daughter, Enheduanna, the world's oldest known poet. Serving as high priestess in the Sumerian city of Ur, Enheduanna wrote numerous poems and hymns to temple deities. In one of her hymns to the Sumerian goddess Ianna, she depicts Ianna as a fierce warrior; in a second, Ianna emerges as an overseer of home and children; and in the third surviving hymn, the poetess appeals to Ianna to help her regain her position as temple priestess after it was taken from her by a male enemy.

In succeeding centuries, the Sumerian cities were incorporated into various kingdoms and empires. The Sumerian language, which was replaced by a Semitic tongue, became an obscure language known only to priests, and the Sumerians gradually disappeared as a distinct people. But their cultural achievements endured. Akkadians, Babylonians, Elamites, and others adopted Sumerian religious, legal, literary, and art forms. The Sumerian legacy served as the basis for a Mesopotamian civilization that maintained a distinct style for three thousand years.

Religion: The Basis of Mesopotamian Civilization

Religion lay at the center of Mesopotamian life. Every human activity—political, military, social, legal, literary, artistic—was generally subordinated to an overriding religious purpose. Religion was the Mesopotamians' frame of reference for understanding nature, society, and themselves; it dominated and inspired all other cultural expressions and human activities. Wars between cities, for instance, were interpreted as conflicts between the gods of those cities, and victory ultimately depended on divine favor, not on human effort. **Myths**—narratives about the activities of the gods—explained the origins of the human species. According to the earliest Sumerian myths, the first human beings issued forth from the earth like plant life, or were shaped from clay by divine craftsmen and granted a heart by the goddess Nammu, or were formed from the blood of two gods sacrificed for that purpose.

The Mesopotamians believed that people were given life so that they could execute on earth the will of the gods in heaven. No important decisions were made by kings or priests without first consulting the gods. To discover the wishes of the gods, priests sacrificed animals and then examined their livers; or the priests might find their answers in the stars or in dreams.

The cities of Mesopotamia were sacred communities dedicated to serving divine masters, and people hoped that appeasing the gods would bring security and prosperity to their cities. The Sumerians erected ziggurats—huge multilevel mounds—on which temples were built. The ziggurat in Ur measured 205 feet by 140 feet at the base and was about 70 feet high; staircases connected its levels and led to the top platform, on which stood a majestic temple.

The ziggurat was surrounded by low walls enclosing offices and houses for the priests and shops where potters, weavers, carpenters, and tanners performed their crafts. The temple was the religious and economic heart of the city. A particular city belonged to a god, who was the real owner of the land and the real ruler of the city; often a vast complex of temples was built for the god and the god's family. In the temple, the god was offered shelter, food, clothing, and the homage of dutiful servants. Temple priests collected rents, operated businesses, and received contributions for festivals. Most inhabitants of the city worked for the temple priests as tenant farmers, agricultural laborers, or servants. Anxious to curry favor with the gods and goddesses who watched over the fields, peasants surrendered part of their crops to the temple. Priests coordinated the city's economic activity, supervising the distribution of land, overseeing the irrigation works, and storing food for emergencies. Temple scribes kept records of expenditures and receipts. By serving as stewards of the city's deities and managing their earthly estates, the priests sustained civilized life.

The gods and goddesses, invisible to human eyes but omnipresent, controlled the entire universe and everything in it. The moon, the sun, the storm, the city, the irrigation works, and the fields—each was directed by a god. Mesopotamians saw gods and demons everywhere in nature. There was a god in the fire and another in the river; evil demons stirred up sandstorms, caused disease, and endangered women in childbirth. To shield themselves from hostile forces, Mesopotamians wore charms and begged their gods for help. Each Mesopotamian offered prayers and sacrifices to a personal god or goddess, who provided protection against evil spirits.

Mesopotamians believed that they were manipulated by divine beings. When misfortune befell them, people attributed it to the gods. Even success was not due to their own efforts but to the intervention of a god who had taken a special interest in them. Compared with the gods, an individual was an insignificant and lowly creature.

Uncertainty and danger filled life in Mesopotamia. Sometimes, the unpredictable waters of the rivers broke through the dikes, flooding fields, ruining crops, and damaging cities. At other times, an insufficient overflow deprived the land of water, causing crops to fail. Great windstorms left the countryside covered with a layer of sand, and heavy thunderstorms turned fields into a sea of mud that made travel impossible. Unlike Egypt, which was protected by vast deserts, Mesopotamia had no natural barriers to invasion. Feeling themselves surrounded by unfathomable and often hostile forces, Mesopotamians lived in an atmosphere of anxiety, which permeated their civilization.

Contributing to this sense of insecurity was the belief that the gods had little love for humanity. They had created a "savage, 'man' shall be his name . . . [who] shall be charged with the service of the gods that they might be at ease."[2] Toward humans the gods behaved capriciously, maliciously, and vindictively, and it was difficult to please them.

What do the gods demand of me? Is it ever possible to please them? To these questions Mesopotamians had no reassuring answers, for the gods' behavior was a mystery to mere human beings.

> *What is good for oneself may be offense to*
> *one's god,*
> *What in one's own heart seems despicable*
> *may be proper to one's god.*
> *Who can know the will of the gods in*
> *heaven?*
> *Who can understand the plans of the*
> *underworld gods?*
> *Where have humans learned the way of a*
> *god?*
> *He who was alive yesterday is dead today.*[3]

A Mesopotamian man or woman hoped to experience the good life by being obedient to his or her older brother, father, foreman, priest, and king and to a personal deity, who could influence the decisions of the other gods. The rewards for obedience were long life, health, and worldly success. Nevertheless, the feeling persisted that happiness was either transitory or beyond reach—a pessimism that abounded in Mesopotamian literature.

A mood of uncertainty and anxiety, an awareness of the cosmos as unfathomable and mysterious, a feeling of dread about the fragility of human existence and the impermanence of human achievement—these attitudes are as old as the first civilization. The *Epic of Gilgamesh*, the finest work of Mesopotamian literature, masterfully depicts this mood of pessimism and despair. The epic deals with a profound theme: the human protest against death. The death of his close friend causes Gilgamesh to face the reality of his own death. "Despair is in my heart. What my brother is now that shall I be when I am dead. . . . I am afraid of death."[4] Gilgamesh yearns for eternal life, but he learns that when the gods created human beings, they allotted to them only death. "Where is the man who can clamber to heaven? Only the gods live forever . . . but as for us men, our days are numbered, our occupations are a breath of wind."[5]

And in contrast to the Egyptians, the Mesopotamians had little to look forward to after death.

They believed that they would either be confined to a dreary underworld whose rulers would inflict pain on them or be transformed into spirits, flying about and tormenting the living.

Government, Law, and Economy

Kingship, bestowed on a man by the gods, was the central institution in Mesopotamian society. Unlike Egyptian pharaohs, Mesopotamian kings saw themselves not as gods but rather as great men selected by the gods to represent them on earth. Gods governed through the kings, who reported to the gods about conditions in their land (which was the gods' property) and petitioned the gods for advice.

The king administered the laws, which came from the gods. Like everyone else in the land, the king had to obey divine laws. These laws provided Mesopotamians with a measure of security. The principal collection of laws in ancient Mesopotamia was the famous code of Hammurabi (c. 1792– c. 1750 B.C.), the Babylonian ruler. Unearthed by French archaeologists in 1901–1902, the code has provided invaluable insights into Mesopotamian society. The laws were inscribed on a stone slab (*stele*), near the top of which Hammurabi was depicted, standing reverently before the throne of Shamash, the sun god and patron of justice. In typical Mesopotamian fashion, Hammurabi claimed that his code rested on the authority of the gods; to violate it was to contravene the divine order.

The code reveals social status and mores in that area and time. Men were the heads of the family, although efforts were made to protect women and children from mistreatment and poverty. Thus, if a man divorced his wife because she did not bear him a son, he had to provide her with money. Punishments were generally severe— "an eye for an eye and a tooth for a tooth." The code prescribed death for housebreaking, kidnapping, aiding the escape of slaves, receiving stolen goods, and bearing false witness; however, it allowed consideration of extenuating circumstances. Being forgiven by the wronged party could also mitigate the penalty. For example, a wife who committed adultery could be spared execution if pardoned by her husband. Class distinctions were expressed in the code. Penalties varied with the status of both the wrongdoer and the victim. For instance, a person received a harsher punishment for harming a noble than for harming a commoner. Government officials engaging in extortion or bribery were punished severely. The code's many provisions relating to business transactions show the importance of trade to Mesopotamian life.

The economy of Mesopotamian cities depended heavily on foreign and domestic trade. Whereas trade in Egypt was conducted by the state bureaucracy, in Mesopotamia there was greater opportunity for private enterprise. Besides merchants, temple priests engaged in trade because they possessed surplus produce collected as rents from farmers using temple land. Early in Mesopotamian history, merchants were subservient to the king and the temple priests. Over the centuries, however, merchants began to behave as professionals—not just as agents of the palace or temple, but as private entrepreneurs.

Because of trade's importance to the life of the city, governments instituted regulations to prevent fraud. Business transactions had to be recorded in writing, and severe punishments were imposed for dishonesty. A system of weights and measures facilitated trade, and efforts were made to prevent excessive interest rates for loans.

Mesopotamians imported resources not found at home—stone, silver, and timber. In exchange, they exported textiles, fine handicrafts, and (less often because of difficulty in transporting them by donkey) agricultural products. They also imported copper from the Persian Gulf, precious metals from Afghanistan, ivory from Africa and the west coast of India, and cedar and cypress woods, oils, and essences from the Mediterranean coastal areas. Enterprising businessmen set up trading outposts in distant lands, making the Mesopotamians pioneers in international trade.

Writing, Mathematics, Astronomy, and Medicine

The Sumerians established schools, which trained the sons of the upper class in the art of cuneiform writing. Hundreds of tablets on which Sumerian students practiced their lessons have been discovered, testifying to the years of disciplined and demanding work required to master the scribal art. Virtually all scribes were men, but female scribes are at times mentioned in Mesopotamian writings. Noble women in particular were literate.

To assist their pupils, teachers prepared textbooks of word lists and mathematical problems with solutions. In translating Sumerian words into the Akkadian language, they compiled what was probably the world's first dictionary. Students who completed the course of study successfully were employed as archivists, secretaries, or accountants by the temple, the palace, the law courts, or merchants. The Sumerian system of cuneiform writing spread to other parts of the Near East.

The Mesopotamians made some impressive advances in mathematics. They devised multiplication and division tables, including even cubes and cube roots. They determined the area of right-angle triangles and rectangles, divided a circle into 360 degrees, and had some understanding of the principles that centuries later would be developed into the Pythagorean theorem and quadratic equations. But the Babylonians, who made the chief contribution in mathematics, barely advanced to the level of theorizing; they did not formulate general principles or furnish proofs for their mathematical operations.

By carefully observing and accurately recording the positions of planets and constellations of stars, Babylonian sky watchers took the first steps in developing the science of astronomy, and they devised a calendar based on the cycles of the moon. As in mathematics, however, they did not form theories to coordinate and illuminate their data. Believing that the position of the stars and planets revealed the will of the gods, astronomers did not examine the heavens to find what we call cause-and-effect connections between the phenomena. Rather, they sought to discover what the gods wanted. With this knowledge, people could organize their political, social, and moral lives in accordance with divine commands and escape the terrible consequences that they believed resulted from ignoring the gods' wishes. Thus, despite its impressive achievements, Babylonian astronomy remained essentially a mythical interpretation of the universe.

As was consistent with their religious worldview, the Mesopotamians believed that disease was caused by gods or demons. To cure a patient, priest-physicians resorted to magic; through prayers and sacrifices, they attempted to appease the gods and eject the demons from the sick body. Nevertheless, in identifying illnesses and prescribing appropriate remedies, Mesopotamians demonstrated some accurate knowledge of medicine and pharmacology.

EGYPTIAN CIVILIZATION

During the early period of Mesopotamian civilization, the people of another river valley, to the west, put themselves on the path toward civilization. The Egyptians developed their civilization in the fertile valley of the Nile. For good reason, the Greek historian Herodotus called Egypt "the gift of the Nile," for without this mighty river, which flows more than four thousand miles from central Africa northward to the Mediterranean, virtually all of Egypt would be a desert. When the Nile overflowed its banks, as it did reliably and predictably, the floodwaters deposited a layer of fertile black earth, which, when cultivated, provided abundant food to support Egyptian civilization. The Egyptians learned how to control the river—a feat that required cooperative effort and ingenuity, as well as engineering and administrative skills.

Nature favored Egypt in a number of ways. Besides water, fish and fowl, and fertile land, the Nile also provided an excellent transportation link between Upper (southern) and Lower (northern) Egypt. Natural barriers—mountains, deserts, cataracts (rapids) in the Nile, and the Mediterranean—protected Egypt from attack, allowing the inhabitants to enjoy long periods of peace and prosperity. Gold, copper, and stone abounded, along with other natural resources. In addition, the climate of Egypt is dry and salutary. To the Egyptians, nature seemed changeless and beneficent. Hence, unlike Mesopotamians, Egyptians derived a sense of security from their environment.

From the Old Kingdom to the Middle Kingdom

About 2900 B.C., a ruler of Upper Egypt, known as Narmer or Menes, conquered the Nile Delta and Lower Egypt. By 2686 B.C., centralized rule had been firmly established, and great pyramids, tombs for the pharaohs, were being constructed. The pyramids required rigorous central planning to coordinate the tens of thousands of Egyptian laborers drafted to build these immense monuments. During this Pyramid Age, or Old Kingdom (2686–2181 B.C.), royal power reached its height and the essential forms of Egyptian civilization crystallized.

The Egyptians believed the pharaoh to be both a man and a god, the earthly embodiment of the deity Horus; he was an absolute ruler of the land and held his court at the city of Memphis. The Egyptians regarded the pharaoh as a benevolent protector who controlled the floodwaters of the Nile, kept the irrigation works in order, maintained justice in the land, and expressed the will of heaven. They expected that when the pharaoh died and joined his fellow gods, he would still help his living subjects.

In time, the nobles who served as district governors gained in status and wealth and gradually came to undermine the divine king's authority. The nobles' growing power and the enormous expenditure of Egypt's human and material resources on building pyramids led to the decline of the Old Kingdom. From 2181 to 2040 B.C.— a time called the First Intermediate Period—rival families competed for the throne, thus destroying the unity of the kingdom. The civil wars and the collapse of central authority required to maintain the irrigation system cast a pall over the land, as illustrated in this ancient Egyptian poem:

> *The wrongdoer is everywhere....*
> *Plunderers are everywhere....*
> *Nile is in flood, yet none plougheth for*
> *   him....*
> *Laughter hath perished and is no longer*
> *   made.*
> *It is grief that walketh through the land,*
> *   mingled with lamentations....*
> *The storehouse is bare.*[6]

During what is called the Middle Kingdom (2040–1786 B.C.), strong kings reasserted pharaonic rule and reunited the state. The restoration of political stability reinvigorated cultural life and revived economic activity. Pharaohs extended Egyptian control south over the land of Nubia, which became a principal source of gold. A profitable trade was carried on with Palestine, Syria, and Crete.

About 1800 B.C., central authority again weakened. In the era known as the Second Intermediate Period (1786–1570 B.C.), the nobles regained some of their power, the Nubians broke away from Egyptian control, and the Hyksos (a mixture of Semites and Indo-Europeans) invaded Egypt. For centuries, desert and sea had effectively guarded Egypt from foreign invasion, but the Hyksos invaders, using horse and chariot and body armor, ended Egyptian complacency. The Hyksos succeeded in dominating Egypt for about a hundred years. Resentful of foreign rule, the Egyptians became more militant and aggressive; they learned to use the Hyksos' weapons and drove out the invaders in 1570 B.C. The period of empire building known as the New Kingdom (1570–1085 B.C.) then began.

The basic features of Egyptian civilization had been forged during the Old and Middle Kingdoms. The Egyptians looked to the past, believing that the ways of their ancestors were best. For almost three thousand years, Egyptian civilization sought to retain a harmony with the order of nature instituted at creation. Believing that the universe was changeless, the Egyptians did not value change or development—what we call progress—but venerated the institutions, traditions, and authority that embodied permanence.

Religion: The Basis of Egyptian Civilization

Religion was omnipresent in Egyptian life and accounted for the outstanding achievements of Egyptian civilization. Religious beliefs were the basis of Egyptian art, medicine, astronomy, literature, and government. The great pyramids, which took decades to finish and required the labor of thousands of people, were tombs for the pharaohs, man-gods. Magical utterances pervaded

AKHENATON. A bas-relief found in Tell el-Amarna shows Akhenaton and his family sacrificing to Aton, the sun god. (Erich Lessing/Art Resource, N.Y.)

medical practices, for disease was attributed to the gods. Astronomy evolved to determine the correct time to perform religious rites and sacrifices. The earliest examples of literature dealt wholly with religious themes. The pharaoh was a sacrosanct monarch who served as an intermediary between the gods and human beings. Justice was conceived in religious terms, something bestowed by a creator-god. Egyptians appealed to the gods to grant victory in war, provide a bountiful harvest, and protect them from illness and misfortune. The Egyptians developed an ethical code, which they believed the gods had approved. In a number of treatises compiled by high officials, now called

Books of Instruction, Egyptians were urged to tell the truth and to treat others fairly. In one *Book of Instruction* prepared at the end of the second millennium, the author, in a high ethical tone, enjoined Egyptians to express compassion for the poor, widows, and the handicapped.

Egyptian **polytheism** took many forms, including the worship of animals, for the Egyptians believed that gods manifested themselves in animal shapes. Certain gods were conceived by the Egyptians as taking various forms. Thoth, for example, was represented as the moon, a baboon, an ibis, and an ibis-headed man. The god Amon was depicted both in human form and as a ram. To the Egyptians, these different representations were not contradictory, for they did not seek logical consistency in religion. The Egyptians also believed great powers in nature—sky, sun, earth, the Nile—to be gods or the abodes of gods. Thus, the universe was alive with divinities—there were about two thousand gods in the Egyptian pantheon—and human lives were tied to the movements of the sun and the moon and to the rhythm of the seasons. In the heavens the Egyptians found answers to the great problems of human existence. In their temples, Egyptians prayed and dedicated offerings to their gods. During temple rituals, women chanted and played musical instruments.

A crucial feature of Egyptian religion was the afterlife. Through pyramid-tombs, mummification to preserve the dead, and funerary art, the Egyptians showed their yearning for eternity and their desire to overcome death. Mortuary priests recited incantations to ensure the preservation of the dead body and the continuity of existence. Inscribed on the pyramids' interior walls were so-called pyramid texts, written in *hieroglyphics*—a form of picture writing in which figures such as crocodiles, sails, eyes, and so forth represented words or sounds that would be combined to form words. The texts contained fragments from myths, historical annals, and magical lore and provided spells to assist the king in ascending to heaven.

At first, the Egyptians believed that only the pharaoh and the royal family were immortal. In time, the nobility and then the commoners claimed that they, too, could share in the blessings of the "other world." Prayers hitherto reserved for the pharaoh were, for a fee, recited by priests at the burial of commoners. Egyptians believed that

their deceased relatives would intercede with the gods in their behalf. They wrote letters to these spirits, petitioning them for help for such problems as infertility, inheritance of property, and family quarrels. Widows and widowers placed letters in the tomb of a deceased spouse in which they expressed their grief, often with great tenderness. To the Egyptians, the other world contained the same pleasures as those enjoyed on earth—friends, servants, fishing, hunting, paddling a canoe, picnicking with family members, entertainment by musicians and dancers, and good food. However, because earthly existence was not fundamentally unhappy, Egyptians did not yearn for death. Unlike early Christians, they did not reject this world or willingly endure martyrdom in order to enter a higher and better world. The following song, inscribed in a pharaoh's tomb, reveals the Egyptians' relish for life.

> *Enjoy yourself while you live,*
> *put on fine linen*
> *anoint yourself with wonderful ointments,*
> *multiply all your fine possessions on earth,*
> *follow your heart's command on earth*
> *be joyful and make merry.*[7]

Divine Kingship

"What is the king of Upper and Lower Egypt? He is a god by whose dealings one lives, the father and mother of men, alone by himself, without an equal."[8] Divine kingship was the basic institution of Egyptian civilization. Perhaps the requirements of the Egyptian environment helped forge the idea of the pharaoh as a living god because a ruler with supernatural authority, held in favor by the gods, could hold together the large kingdom and draft the mass labor required to maintain the irrigation system. Both the priesthood and a standing army answered to the pharaoh and enhanced his authority.

Through the pharaoh, the gods made known their wishes for the Egyptian people. As kingship was a divine, not a manmade, institution, it was expected to last for eternity. The Egyptians rejoiced in the rule of an all-powerful, all-knowing **god-king** who controlled the Nile, bringing fertility to the land, and could intercede in their behalf with the other deities. Even after death, when the pharaoh joined the other gods in the otherworld, he would still assist his subjects. To the Egyptians, the pharaoh was "the herdsman of everyone without evil in his heart."[9] They believed that divine kingship, which was instituted by a creator-god, was the only acceptable political arrangement, that it was in harmony with the order of the universe, and that it brought stability and authority to the nation.

The power of the pharaoh extended to all sectors of society. Peasants were drafted to serve in labor corps as miners or construction workers. Foreign trade was a state monopoly. The pharaoh authorized commercial ventures—caravan expeditions south to Nubia for ivory, gold, and ebony and sailing expeditions east to Lebanon for timber. Profits from foreign trade enriched the royal treasury. Although private ownership of land was recognized in practice, in theory, all land belonged to the pharaoh. As the supreme overlord, the pharaoh oversaw an army of government officials, who collected taxes, managed construction projects, checked the irrigation works, surveyed the land, kept records, and supervised government warehouses, where grain was stored as insurance against a bad harvest. All Egyptians were subservient to the pharaoh, and there was no conception of political liberty.

Egyptian rulers, like their Mesopotamian counterparts, believed that they had an obligation to render justice. Injustice was seen as an offense against the gods. Most pharaohs took their responsibilities seriously and tried to govern as benevolent protectors of the people as instructed by Egyptian wisdom literature.

> *Be not evil, it is good to be kindly. . . . Do right so long as thou abidest on the earth. Calm the weeper, oppress no widow, expel no man from the possessions of his father. . . . Take heed lest thou punish wrongfully. . . . Slay not a man whose good qualities thou knowest. . . . Exalt not the son of one of high degree more than him that is of lowly birth, but take to thyself a man because of his actions.*[10]

Egyptians derived a sense of security from the concept of divine kingship. It meant that earthly government and society were in harmony with the

STROLL IN THE GARDEN, EIGHTEENTH DYNASTY, c. 1350 B.C. This relief portrays members of the Egyptian royal family ("Stroll in the Garden," relief depicting Tutankhamun and his wife, Ankhesenamun, New Kingdom, c. 1330 B.C. (painted limestone), Egyptian 18th Dynasty (c. 1567–1320 B.C.)/Aegyptisches Museum, SMPK, Berlin/Ancient Art and Architecture Collection Ltd./The Bridgeman Art Library International.)

cosmos, a divine order that provided justice and security. The Egyptians believed that the institution of kingship dated from the creation of the universe, that as part of the rhythm of the universe kingship was necessary and beneficial to human beings.

The pharaoh was seen as ruling in accordance with Ma'at, which means justice, law, right, and truth. The pharaoh embodied Ma'at; his divinity assured that he would correctly determine which actions accorded with Ma'at and which did not. To oppose the pharaoh was to violate the universal and divinely ordained order of Ma'at and to bring disorder to society. Because the Egyptians regarded Ma'at, which had been established with the creation of the universe, as the right order of nature, they believed that its preservation must be the central object of human activity—the guiding norm of the state and the standard by which individuals conducted their lives. Those who did Ma'at and spoke Ma'at would be justly rewarded. Could anything be more reassuring than this belief that divine truth was represented in the person of the pharaoh, who guaranteed and defended the sacred order of the universe?

Science and Mathematics

Like the Mesopotamians, the Egyptians made practical advances in mathematics and science. They demonstrated superb engineering skills in building pyramids. For example, the pyramid of Khufu, still the largest stone building ever constructed, contains 2.3 million stone blocks, each averaging 2.5 tons. The Egyptians fashioned an effective system of mathematics, including geometry for measurements, that enabled them to solve relatively simple problems.

Controlling the floodwaters of the Nile required careful planning. Therefore, it was vital to know when the Nile would begin to overflow. Noting that the Nile flooded after the star Sirius appeared in the sky, the Egyptians developed a calendar by which they could predict the time of the flood. Eventually, they fashioned a calendar of twelve months, each having thirty days. To complete the solar year, they added a separate period of five days after the last month. The Egyptian calendar based on the sun was more accurate than the Babylonian lunar calendar.

In the area of medicine, Egyptian doctors were more capable than their Mesopotamian counterparts. They were able to identify illnesses; they recognized that uncleanliness encouraged contagion; they had some knowledge of anatomy and performed operations—circumcision and perhaps the draining of abscessed teeth. Sick people were instructed to recite an incantation designed to free their body from the demon's hold and to perform a ritual act such as being burned with hot irons. Although the progress of medicine was handicapped by the belief that supernatural forces caused illnesses, nevertheless, there is evidence that some Egyptian doctors examined the body in a scientific way. In a scroll, the Edwin Smith Surgical Papyrus (named after the nineteenth-century American Egyptologist who acquired it), the writer omitted all references to divine intervention in his advice for treating wounds and fractures. He described fractures in a matter-of-fact way and recommended healing them with splints and casts. In another papyrus document (papyrus is a writing material made from the stalks of the papyrus plant), the writer identified the various snakes, analyzed the effects of their bites, and listed treatments, including the use of specific drugs—and he did so with only minimum references to magical incantations.

Egyptian Literature

Generally only a small percentage of the population, the elite, was literate. Egyptian literature took a wide variety of forms: hymns and other religious texts; love poems; tales of adventure, romance, and fantasy; and collections of maxims prepared by elderly sages for the benefit of young rulers.

Containing hymns, litanies and other religious texts, the *Book of the Dead* was written to guide the deceased person safely between this world and the afterlife. In the Judgment Hall, before Osiris and other gods who assisted him in the judgment of souls, deceased individuals proclaimed that they did not commit any of the following sins:

> 2. *I have not robbed with violence.*
> 3. *I have not done violence [to any man].*
> 5. *I have not slain a man or a woman.*
> 11. *I have not uttered evil words.*
> 41. *I have not increased my wealth, except with such things as are [justly] mine own possessions.*[11]

The New Kingdom and the Decline of Egyptian Civilization

The New Kingdom began in 1570 B.C. with the war of liberation against the Hyksos. This war gave rise to an intense militancy, which found expression in empire building. Aggressive pharaohs conquered territory that extended as far east as

Hatchepsut

Hatchepsut, daughter of Thutmose I (1493–1482 B.C.), was an exceptional figure in Egyptian history—a female pharaoh. As the wife of her half brother, Thutmose II, she did not produce a male heir. When Thutmose II died after a three-year reign, his infant son by a secondary wife inherited the throne. But because of his tender years, Hatchepsut served as regent. By the seventh year of the regency, Hatchepsut had assumed the royal title of king of Egypt. Although females were not officially barred from becoming pharaohs, it was an unchallenged tradition that this revered position was reserved for men. To legitimize her rule, Hatchepsut had a sequence of pictures carved on the porch of her mortuary temple that told the story of her divine birth. She was conceived when the god Amon-Re, disguised as Thutmose I, visited her mother's boudoir. Amon indicated that he intended to father a female, who one day would rule Egypt. "Come to me in peace, daughter of my loins, . . . thou art the king who takes possession of the diadem [crown] on the Throne of Horus of the Living, eternally."*

Hatchepsut came to be depicted with male attire and a male body. Apparently, by casting off her female appearance, she aimed to be seen as a king, the equal of all other pharaohs, and not as a queen, who was not regarded as divine. Hatchepsut, says Egyptologist Joyce Tyldesley, "needed to make a sharp and immediately obvious distinction between her former position as queen regent and her new role as pharaoh. The change of dress was a clear sign of her altered state."†

During her twenty-year reign, from about 1479 to 1458, Hatchepsut promoted extensive building projects, including her royal tomb, and trading expeditions, particularly to the land of Punt, in present-day Eritrea and Djibouti. From Punt the Egyptians obtained myrrh and frankincense, precious resins used for making

the Euphrates River. From its subject states, Egypt acquired tribute and slaves. Conquests led to the expansion of the bureaucracy, the creation of a professional army to protect the new territorial acquisitions, and the increased power of priests, whose temples, which grew larger and more lavish, shared in the spoils. Foreign slaves acquired from imperial conquests provided much of the labor for the construction of new shrines and temples. The formation of the empire ended Egyptian isolation and accelerated commercial and cultural intercourse with other peoples. During this period, Egyptian art, for example, showed the influence of foreign forms.

A growing cosmopolitanism was paralleled by a movement toward **monotheism** during the reign of Pharaoh Amenhotep IV (c. 1369–1353 B.C.). Amenhotep sought to replace traditional polytheism with the worship of Aton, a single god of all people, a supreme force in nature represented as the sun disk. Amenhotep took the name Akhenaton ("Servant of Aton") and moved the capital from Thebes to a newly constructed holy city called Akhetaten ("Horizon of Aton," which is near present-day Tell el-Amarna). The city had palaces, administrative centers, and a temple complex honoring Aton. Akhenaton and his wife, Nefertiti, who played a prominent role in his court, dedicated themselves to Aton—the creator of the world, the maintainer of life, and the god of love, justice, and peace. Akhenaton (or Ikhnaton) also ordered his officials to remove the names and images of other gods from temples and monuments. With awe, Akhenaton celebrated Aton's power and magnificence.

> *How manifold are thy works!*
> *They are hidden from man's sight.*
> *O sole god, like whom there is no other.*
> *Thou hast made the earth according to thy*
> *   desire.*[12]

incense that was burned in temple rituals and perfumes and for the mummification of bodies. It was an arduous journey to Punt; the return of the expeditions with these treasures must have greatly increased the prestige of the female pharaoh.

After Hatchepsut's death, her monuments were mutilated and her name and image deleted in a deliberate attempt to obliterate her memory. The campaign was probably initiated by Thutmose III, but his motivation is not clear. Was he demonstrating hatred for his stepmother, who had relegated him to a subordinate role for so many years? Did he try to erase the memory of Hatchepsut in order to prevent the succession in the future of still another female pharaoh in the belief that such a situation was a grave violation of tradition and Ma'at?

_____

*Quoted in Joyce Tyldesley, *Hatchepsut: The Female Pharaoh* (New York: Penguin Books, 1998), 105.

†Ibid., 133.

Akhenaton's monotheism had little impact on the masses of Egyptians, who remained devoted to their traditional gods and ancient beliefs, and was resisted by priests, who resented his changes. The new religion could not survive the death of its founder. Akhenaton's successor, Tutankhamen (1352–1344 B.C.), abandoned the capital at Amarna and returned to Thebes. Tutankhamen was succeeded by an elderly relative, who reigned briefly. In 1340, Horemheb (1340–1315 B.C.), an army commander, seized power and had the monuments to Aton destroyed, along with records and inscriptions bearing Akhenaton's name. The great visionary was vilified as "The Blasphemer."

Historians are not certain why Akhenaton made such a radical break with tradition by propagating the worship of a single god. Was he trying to strike at the priests, whose wealth and prestige had increased considerably with Egypt's conquests? Did the break stem essentially from the vision of a great prophet? But the most significant historical questions concerning Akhenaton are these: First, was Akhenaton's religion genuine monotheism, which pushed religious thought in a new direction? And second, if this was the case, did it influence the ancient Hebrews who, according to the Old Testament, left Egypt about a century later?

These two questions have aroused controversy among historians. The principal limitation on the monotheistic character of Atonism is that there were really two gods in Akhenaton's religion—Aton and the pharaoh himself, who was still worshiped as a deity. Egyptologist John A. Wilson sheds light on this notion. Because Egyptians could not break with the central idea of their civilization, divine kingship, "one could say that it was the closest approach to monotheism possible within the thought of the day. That would still fall short of making it a belief in and worship of only one god."[13] Regarding the relationship of Atonism to a later Hebrew monotheism, Wilson says, "The mechanism of transmission from the faith of Akhenaton to the monotheism of Moses is not apparent."[14] Moreover, the Hebrews never identified God with the sun or any other object in nature.

Reigning almost 67 years from 1279 B.C. to 1213 B.C., Ramesses II is considered one of Egypt's greatest pharaohs. He campaigned to the south in Nubia, to the west in Libya, and to the east in Canaan and Syria against the Hittite empire. His inconclusive struggles with the Hittites resulted in the signing of a peace treaty, copies of which survive both in hieroglyphics and cuneiform. In order to honor Ramesses II, the Egyptian version of the treaty falsely claims that the Hittites had begged for peace. Ramesses II is most noted for the construction of numerous huge monuments, statues of himself, and temples whose walls contain extravagant glorifications of his person and achievements. Two pairs of colossal statutes of Ramesses flank the entrance to a temple at Abu Simbel in Lower Nubia.

Late in the thirteenth century B.C., Libyans, probably seeking to settle in the more fertile land of Egypt, attacked from the west, and the Peoples of the Sea, as unsettled raiders from the Aegean Sea area and Asia Minor were called, launched a series of strikes at Egypt. A weakened Egypt abandoned its empire. In the succeeding centuries, Egypt came under the rule of Libyans, Nubians,

Assyrians, Persians, and finally Greeks, to whom Egypt lost its independence in the fourth century B.C. Egyptian civilization had flourished for nearly two thousand years before it experienced an almost one-thousand-year descent into stagnation, decline, and collapse. During its long history, the Egyptians tried to preserve its ancient forms, revealed to them by their ancestors and representing for all time those unchanging values that they believed to be the way of happiness.

EMPIRE BUILDERS

The rise of an Egyptian empire during the New Kingdom was part of a wider development in Near Eastern history after 1500 B.C.—the emergence of international empires. Empire building led to the intermingling of peoples and cultural traditions and to the extension of civilization well beyond the river valleys.

One reason for the growth of empires was the migration of peoples known as Indo-Europeans. Originally from a wide area ranging from southeastern Europe to the region beyond the Caspian Sea, Indo-Europeans embarked, around 2000 B.C., on a series of migrations, which eventually brought them into Italy, Greece, Asia Minor, Mesopotamia, Persia, and India. From a core Indo-European tongue emerged the Greek, Latin, Germanic, Slavic, Persian, and Sanskrit languages.

Hittites

Several peoples established strong states in the Near East around 1500 B.C.—the Hurrians in northern Mesopotamia, the Kassites in southern Mesopotamia, and, most important, the Hittites in Asia Minor.

Penetrating Asia Minor, Indo-Europeans coalesced with native Hattic-speaking peoples to create the Hittite empire (1450–1200 B.C.). The Hittites ruled Asia Minor and northern Syria, raided Babylon, and challenged Egypt for control of Syria and Palestine.

The Hittites wanted to control the trade routes that ran along the Euphrates River into Syria. In the 1300s, the Hittite empire reached its peak and included much of Asia Minor and northern Syria. The Hittites succeeded because of their

well-trained army. Mass attacks by light, horse-drawn chariots demolished enemy lines, while foot soldiers made effective use of the battle-ax and a short curved sword.

The Hittites borrowed several features of Mesopotamian civilization, including cuneiform, legal principles, and literary and art forms. Hittite religion blended the beliefs and practices of Indo-Europeans, native inhabitants of Asia Minor, and Mesopotamians. The Hittites were probably the first people to develop a substantial iron industry. Initially, they apparently used iron just for ceremonial and ritual objects and not for tools and weapons. However, because iron ore was more readily available than copper or tin (needed for bronze), after 1200 B.C. iron weapons and tools spread throughout the Near East, although bronze implements were still used. Around 1200 B.C., the Hittite empire fell, most likely to Indo-European invaders from the north.

Small Nations

During the twelfth century B.C., a temporary lull in empire building permitted a number of small nations in Syria and Palestine to assert their sovereignty. Three of these peoples—the Phoenicians, the Aramaeans, and the Hebrews*—were originally Semitic desert nomads. The Phoenicians were descendants of the Canaanites, a Semitic people who had settled Palestine about 3000 B.C. The Canaanites who had migrated northwest into what is now Lebanon were called Phoenicians.

Settling in the coastal Mediterranean cities of Tyre, Byblos, Berytus (Beirut), and Sidon, the Phoenicians were naturally drawn to the sea. These daring explorers established towns along the coast of North Africa, on the islands of the western Mediterranean, and in Spain, and they became the greatest sea traders of the ancient world. Phoenician merchants exported lumber, glass, copper and bronze utensils, and the purple dye produced from the murex, a mollusk that was plentiful in the coastal waters. The Phoenicians (or their Canaanite forebears) devised the first alphabet—a monumental contribution to writing. Since all words could be represented by combinations of letters, it saved memorizing thousands of diagrams and aided the Phoenicians in transmitting the cul-

*The Hebrews are discussed in Chapter 2.

Map 1.2 **KINGDOMS AND PEOPLES OF THE ANCIENT WORLD** In addition to the Sumerians and Egyptians, founders of the first civilizations, other peoples contributed to the development of civilization in the Near East. The Hebrews conceived the idea of the one God, the Phoenicians invented the alphabet, and the Hittites developed a substantial iron industry. (Copyright © 2013 Cengage Learning.)

tural achievements of the Near East to the western Mediterranean. Adapted by the Greeks, who added vowels, the phonetic alphabet became a crucial component of European languages.

The Aramaeans, who settled in Syria, Palestine, and northern Mesopotamia, performed a role similar to that of the Phoenicians. As great caravan traders, they carried both goods and culture to various parts of the Near East. The Hebrews and the Persians, for example, acquired the Phoenician alphabet from the Aramaeans.

Assyria

In the ninth century B.C., empire building resumed with the Assyrians, a Semitic people from the region around the upper Tigris River. The Assyrians carefully planned their military campaigns and excelled in siege weapons—battering rams built on massive wheeled frames—which pulverized city walls that had hitherto resisted attackers. Their soldiers wore armor and wielded iron swords, and charging chariots terrorized the foe's infantry, which generally consisted of farmer-soldiers armed with little more than bows and arrows.

Although they had made forays of expansion in 1200 and 1100 B.C., the Assyrians began their march to "world" empire three centuries later. In the eighth and seventh centuries, the Assyrians became a ruthless fighting machine that stormed through Babylonia, Syria, Palestine, and Egypt. Assyrian kings believed that their gods commanded them to conquer and assisted them in their campaigns. At its height, the Assyrian empire extended from the Iranian plateau in the east to the Egyptian city of Thebes.

How did the Assyrians administer such a vast empire? An Assyrian king, who was the representative and high priest of the god Ashur, governed absolutely. Nobles appointed by the king kept order in the provinces and collected tribute, which they probably used for building palaces, temples, and canals. The Assyrians improved roads, established messenger services, and engaged in large-scale irrigation projects to facilitate effective administration of their conquered lands and promote prosperity. To keep their subjects obedient, the Assyrians resorted to terror and to deportation of troublesome subjects from their home territories. (It is also likely that masses of people were moved around for economic reasons—to replenish a diminishing labor supply.) Assyrian kings boasted of their ruthlessness toward rebellious subjects.

> 13,000 of their warriors I cut down with the sword. Their blood like the water of a stream I caused to run through the squares of their city. The corpses of their soldiers I piled in heaps. . . . [The Babylonian king's] royal bed, his royal couch, the treasure of his palaces, his property, his gods and everything from his palace without number, I carried away. His captive warriors were given to the soldiers of my land like grasshoppers. The city I destroyed, I devastated, I burned with fire.[15]

Despite an almost all-consuming concern for war, the Assyrians maintained and spread the culture of the past. They copied and edited the literary works of Babylonia, adopted the old Sumerian gods, and used Mesopotamian art forms. The Assyrian king Ashurbanipal (669–626 B.C.) maintained a great library, which contained thousands of clay tablets.

"The king knows that all lands hate us," wrote an official to King Esarhaddon (680–669 B.C.).[16] After a period of wars and revolts weakened Assyria, a coalition of Medes, or Indo-Europeans from Iran, and the Semitic Chaldeans, or Neo-Babylonians, sacked the Assyrian capital of Nineveh in 612 B.C. The conquerors looted and destroyed the city, and the surviving Assyrians fled. Assyrian power was broken.

The Neo-Babylonian Empire

The destruction of the Assyrian empire made possible the rise of a Chaldean empire, which included Babylonia, Assyria, Syria, and Palestine. Under Nebuchadnezzar, who ruled from 604 to 562 B.C., the Chaldean, or Neo-Babylonian, empire reached its height. A talented general and statesman and a brilliant administrator, Nebuchadnezzar had Babylon rebuilt. The new Babylon that arose on the shore of the Euphrates had magnificent processionways that led to palaces and temples. On his palace grounds, Nebuchadnezzar created the famous Hanging Gardens for his Median wife, according to legend. The 350-foot building was a series of vaulted terraces and was surrounded by a moat of flowing water. Trees, shrubs, and flowers decorated each terrace. In the interior, vaulted halls were stocked with vessels, fabrics, ornaments, and wines gathered from different regions of the empire. Here guests reclined on divans and were attended by slaves.

Persia: Unifier of the Near East

After Nebuchadnezzar's death, the Chaldean empire was torn by civil war and threatened by a new power—the Persians, an Indo-European people who had settled in southern Iran. (Iranians today are descendants of the ancient Persians.) Under Cyrus the Great and his son and successor, Cambyses, the Persians conquered all lands between the Nile in Egypt and the Indus River in India. This conquest took twenty-five years, from 550 to 525 B.C. The Near Eastern conception of absolute monarchy justified by religion reached its culminating expression in the person of the Persian king, who, with divine approval, ruled a vast empire, "the four quarters of the earth." Persian kings developed an effective system of administration—based in part on an Assyrian model—which gave stability and a degree of unity to their extensive territories. In so doing, they performed a creative act of statesmanship. The Persian empire was divided into twenty provinces (satrapies), each administered by a governor (satrap) responsible to the emperor. To guard against subversion, the king employed special agents—"the eyes and ears of the emperor"—who supervised

Map 1.3 THE ASSYRIAN AND PERSIAN EMPIRES In the last part of the sixth century B.C., the Persians established the greatest empire of the ancient Near East, conquering all the lands between the Nile in Egypt and the Indus River in India. (Copyright © 2013 Cengage Learning.)

the activities of the governors. Persian kings allowed the provincials a large measure of self-rule. They also respected local traditions, particularly in matters of religion, as long as subjects paid their taxes, served in the royal army, and refrained from rebellion; and they deliberately tried to win the goodwill of priests in conquered lands. But they also were brutal, impaling and mutilating opponents.

The empire was bound together by a uniform language, Aramaic (the language of the Aramaeans of Syria), which was used by government officials and merchants. Aramaic was written in letters based on the Phoenician alphabet. By making Aramaic a universal language, the Persians facilitated written and oral communication within the empire. The empire was further unified by an elaborate network of roads, an efficient postal system, a common system of weights and measures, and an empire-wide coinage, based on an invention of the Lydians from western Asia Minor.

Besides providing impressive political and administrative unity and promoting international trade, the Persians fused and perpetuated the various cultural traditions of the Near East. Persian palaces, for example, boasted the terraces of Babylon, the colonnades of Egypt, the winged bulls that decorated Assyrian palace gates, and the craftsmanship of Median goldsmiths.

The political and cultural universalism of the Persian empire had its counterpart in the emergence of an ethically oriented religion, Zoroastrianism. Named for its founder, the Persian prophet Zarathustra (Zoroaster in Greek), who probably lived in the sixth century B.C. (some scholars place him much earlier), this religion taught belief in Ahura Mazda—the Wise Lord—god of light, the embodiment of justice, wisdom, goodness, and immortality. In addition to the Wise Lord, there also existed Ahriman, the spirit of darkness, who was evil and destructive. Ahriman was in conflict with Ahura Mazda. People

PERSEPOLIS, IRAN, C. 500 B.C. The Persian ruler Darius (522–486 B.C.) constructed a thirty-acre earthen terrace almost fifty feet above the plain and built there a complex of palaces, reception halls, a treasury, and barracks for his royal guards. Persepolis became the ceremonial center of the vast Persian empire until it was destroyed by Alexander the Great's soldiers. (© George Holton/Photo Researchers, Inc.)

were free to choose whom they would follow. By choosing Ahura Mazda, they chose good over evil. To serve Ahura Mazda, one had to speak the truth and be good to others; the reward for such behavior was life eternal in paradise, the realm of light and goodness. Followers of the evil spirit could be cast into a realm of darkness and torment. In contrast to the traditional religions of the Near East, Zoroastrianism rejected magic, polytheism, and blood sacrifices and instead stressed ethics.

Persia unified the nations of the Near East into a world-state, headed by a divinely appointed king, and synthesized the region's cultural traditions. Soon it would confront the city-states of Greece, whose political system and cultural orientation differed from that of the Near East.

THE RELIGIOUS ORIENTATION OF THE NEAR EAST

Religion dominated, suffused, and inspired all features of Near Eastern society—law, kingship, art, and science. In the first civilizations, the deepest thoughts of human beings were expressed in the form of religious myths. They were the source of the vitality and creativity of Mesopotamian and Egyptian civilizations. Near Eastern art derived from religion, and science was permeated with it; literature and history dealt with the ways of the gods; and priest-kings or god-kings, their power sanctioned by divine forces, furnished the necessary authority to organize large numbers of people in cooperative ventures. Religion also encouraged and justified wars—including enslavements and massacres—which were seen as conflicts between the gods. Religious beliefs and values served as a powerful social force uniting people into a cohesive community.

A Mythmaking Worldview

A religious or **mythopoeic** (mythmaking) **view** of the world gives Near Eastern civilization its distinctive form and allows us to see it as an organic whole. Mesopotamians and Egyptians inherited from their prehistoric ancestors a great variety of communally produced imagery, rituals, and tales accounting for the origin of the world and human life. Giving free play to their imagination, they altered the old myths and elaborated new ones to resolve questions that today we try to answer with science. Mythmaking was humanity's first way of thinking; it was the earliest attempt to explain the beginnings of the universe and human history, to make nature's mysteries and life's uncertainties comprehensible. Appealing primarily to the imagination and emotions, rather than to reason, mythical thinking, as expressed in language, art, poetry, and social organization, has been a fundamental formative element of human culture.

Originating in sacred rites, ritual dances, feasts, and ceremonies, myths narrated the deeds of gods, who, in some remote past, had brought forth the world and human beings. Holding that human destiny was determined by the gods, Near Eastern people interpreted their experiences through myths. Myths also enabled Mesopotamians and Egyptians to make sense out of nature, to explain the world of phenomena. Through myths, the Near Eastern mind sought to give coherence to the universe, to make it intelligible. Mesopotamian myths, for example, attributed personal misfortune and the catastrophes that afflicted a city to supernatural forces displeased with people's behavior. These myths gave Near Eastern peoples a framework with which to pattern their experiences into a meaningful order, justify their rules of conduct, and help them to overcome the uncertainty of existence.

The civilizations of the ancient Near East were based on a way of thinking fundamentally different from the modern scientific outlook. The difference between scientific and mythical thinking is profound. The scientific mind views physical nature as an *it*—inanimate, impersonal, and governed by universal law. The mythmaking mind of the Near East saw every object in nature as a *thou*—personified, alive, with an individual will. It saw gods or demons manipulating things. The world was enchanted, imbued with mysterious spirits. The sun and stars, the rivers and mountains, the wind and lightning were either gods or the dwelling places of gods. Live agents were the forces behind natural events. An Egyptian or a Mesopotamian experienced natural phenomena—a falling rock, a thunderclap, a rampaging river—as life facing life. If a river flooded the region, destroying crops, it was because it wanted to; the river or the gods desired to punish the people. A drought was caused by the hot breath of the Bull of Heaven. Relief came when the gigantic bird Imdugud devoured the bull and released storm clouds from her wings.

The Egyptians believed that Nut, the sky goddess, gave birth to the sun, a deity who sailed west across the celestial sea before descending into his mother's womb to be reborn again in the morning. For the Egyptians, the rising and setting of the sun were not natural occurrences—a celestial body obeying an impersonal law—but a religious drama.

The scientific mind holds that natural objects obey universal rules; hence, the location of planets, the speed of objects, and the onset of a hurricane can be predicted. The mythmaking mind of the ancient Near East was not troubled by contradictions. It did not seek logical consistency and had no awareness of repetitive laws inherent in nature. Rather, it attributed all occurrences to the actions of gods, whose behavior was often erratic and unpredictable. Shamans employed magic to protect people from evil supernatural forces that surrounded them. The scientific mind appeals to reason—it analyzes nature logically and systematically and searches for general principles that govern phenomena. The mythmaking mind appeals to the imagination and feelings and proclaims a truth that is emotionally satisfying, not one that has been arrived at through intellectual analysis and synthesis. Thus, mythical explanations of nature and human experience made life seem less overwhelming and death less frightening.

Of course, Near Eastern people did engage in rational forms of thought and behavior. They certainly employed reason in building irrigation works, preparing a calendar, and performing mathematical operations. Moreover, in their daily life, men and women were often driven by purely pragmatic concerns. Fields had to be planted, goods sold, and household chores attended to. In dealing with these concerns, people did what had to be done in commonsense ways. They planned and prepared; they weighed actions as either beneficial or harmful and behaved accordingly. However, because rational or logical thought remained subordinate to a mythic-religious orientation, they did not arrive at a *consistently* and *self-consciously* rational method of inquiring into physical nature and human culture.

Thus, Near Eastern civilization reached the first level in the development of science—observing nature, recording data, and improving technology in mining, metallurgy, and architecture. But it did not advance to the level of self-conscious philosophical and scientific thought—that is, logically deduced abstractions, hypotheses, and generalizations. Mesopotamians and Egyptians did not fashion a body of philosophical and scientific ideas that were logically structured, discussed, and debated. They had no awareness of general laws that govern particular events. These later developments were the achievement of Greek philosophy. It gave a "rational interpretation to natural occurrences which had previously been explained by ancient mythologies. . . . With the study of nature set free from the control of mythological fancy, the way was opened for the development of science as an intellectual system."[17]

Near Eastern Achievements

Sumerians and Egyptians demonstrated enormous creativity and intelligence. They built irrigation works and cities, organized governments, charted the course of heavenly bodies, performed mathematical operations, constructed large-scale monuments, engaged in international trade, established bureaucracies and schools, and considerably advanced the level of technology and engineering skills. Without the Sumerian invention of writing—one of the great creative acts in history—what we mean by *civilization* could not have emerged.

Many elements of ancient Near Eastern civilization were passed on to the West. The wheeled vehicle, the plow, coinage, and the phonetic alphabet—all important to the development of civilization—derive from the Near East. In the realm of medicine, the Egyptians knew the value of certain drugs, such as castor oil; they also knew how to use splints and bandages. The innovative divisions that gave 360 degrees to a circle and 60 minutes to an hour originated in Mesopotamia. Egyptian geometry and Babylonian astronomy were utilized by the Greeks and became a part of Western knowledge. The belief that a king's power came from a heavenly source, a key idea in historic Western political thought, also derived from the Near East. In Christian art, too, one finds connections to the Mesopotamian art forms—for example, the Assyrians depicted winged angel-like beings.

Both the Hebrews and the Greeks borrowed Mesopotamian literary themes. For example, some biblical stories—the Flood, the quarrel between Cain and Abel, and the Tower of Babel—stem from Mesopotamian antecedents. A similar link exists between the Greek and the earlier Mesopotamian mythologies.

Thus, many achievements of the Egyptians and the Mesopotamians were inherited and assimilated by both the Greeks and the Hebrews, the principal founders of Western civilization. Even more important for an understanding of the essential meaning of Western civilization are the ways in which the Greeks and Hebrews rejected or transformed elements of the older Near Eastern traditions to create new points of departure for the human mind.

Mythical Thinking

The mythopoeic mind accounts for causation by personifying inanimate substances. To explain through personification is to seek the "who" behind events, to attribute these events to the will of a god (or to an object suffused with divine presence). Thus, if a river did not rise, it was because it refused to do so; either the river or the gods were angry at the people.

The following excerpts from Mesopotamian literature are examples of personification. Whereas we regard table salt as an ordinary mineral, to the Mesopotamians it was alive, a fellow being. In one passage, a person appeals to salt to end his bewitchment. In the second, an afflicted person who believes himself bewitched calls on fire to destroy his enemies.

O Salt

O Salt, created in a clean place,
For food of gods did *Enlil* [father of the Sumerian gods] destine thee.
Without thee no meal is set out in *Ekur,*
Without thee god, king, lord, and prince do not smell incense.
I am so-and-so, the son of so-and-so,
Held captive by enchantment,
Held in fever by bewitchment.

O Salt, break my enchantment! Loose my spell!
Take from me the bewitchment!—And as My Creator
I shall extol thee.

Scorching Fire

Scorching Fire, warlike son of Heaven,
Thou, the fiercest of thy brethren,
Who like Moon and Sun decidest lawsuits—
Judge thou my case, hand down the verdict.
Burn the man and woman who bewitched me;
Burn, O Fire, the man and woman who bewitched me;
Scorch, O Fire, the man and woman who bewitched me;
Burn them, O Fire;
Scorch them, O Fire;
Take hold of them, O Fire;
Consume them, O Fire;
Destroy them, O Fire.

Questions for Analysis

1. How does mythical thinking differ from scientific thinking?
2. When might the ancient Mesopotamians have turned to the gods for help?

Henri Frankfort et al., *Before Philosophy* (Baltimore: Penguin Books, 1949), 143, 147.

NOTES

1. Lewis Mumford, *Transformation of Man* (New York: Harper Torchbooks, 1972), 46–47.
2. Excerpted in James B. Pritchard, ed., *Ancient Near Eastern Texts Relating to the Old Testament*, 3rd ed., with supplement (Princeton, N.J.: Princeton University Press, 1969), 67.
3. Excerpted in James B. Pritchard, ed., *The Ancient Near East: A New Anthology of Texts and Pictures* (Princeton, N.J.: Princeton University Press, 1975), 154.

4. *The Epic of Gilgamesh*, with an introduction by N. K. Sandars (Baltimore: Penguin Books, 1960), 94.

5. Ibid., 69, 104.

6. Excerpted in Adolf Ehrman, ed., *The Ancient Egyptians* (New York: Harper Torchbooks, 1966), 94, 97, 99.

7. Quoted in Eugen Strouhal, *Life of the Ancient Egyptians* (Norman: University of Oklahoma Press, 1992), 41.

8. Quoted in Henri Frankfort, *Ancient Egyptian Religion* (New York: Harper Torchbooks, 1961), 43.

9. Quoted in John A. Wilson, "Egypt," in Henri Frankfort et al., *Before Philosophy* (Baltimore: Penguin Books, 1949), 88.

10. Excerpted in Erhman, *The Ancient Egyptians*, 76–78.

11. E. A. Wallis Budge, *The Book of the Dead* (London: Arkana, 1985), 366–371.

12. Quoted in John A. Wilson, *The Culture of Ancient Egypt* (Chicago: University of Chicago Press, Phoenix Books, 1951), 227.

13. Ibid., 225.

14. Ibid., 226.

15. Quoted in Joan Oates, *Babylon* (London: Thames and Hudson, 1979), 110–111.

16. Quoted in Georges Roux, *Ancient Iraq* (Harmondsworth, England: Penguin Books, 1966), 278.

17. S. Sambursky, *The Physical World of the Greeks* (New York: Collier Books, 1962), 18–19.

SUGGESTED READING

David, Rosalie A., *The Ancient Egyptians* (1982). Focuses on religious beliefs and practices.

Leick, Gwendolyn, *The Babylonians: An Introduction* (2003). An accessible survey.

Moscati, Sabatino, *The Face of the Ancient Orient* (1962). An illuminating survey of the various peoples of the ancient Near East.

Oates, Joan, *Babylon* (1979). A survey of the history of Babylon from its origin to Hellenistic times; includes a discussion of the legacy of Babylon.

Saggs, H. W. F., *Civilization Before Greece and Rome* (1989). Focuses on culture and society.

Sherman, David P. ed., *Ancient Egypt* (1997). Leading scholars explore ancient Egyptian culture.

Snell, Daniel C., *Life in the Ancient Near East* (1997). An excellent synthesis.

Stiebing, William H., Jr., *Ancient Near Eastern History and Culture* (2003). A sound general introduction for students.

Strouhal, Eugen, *Life of the Ancient Egyptians* (1992). Daily life of Egyptians; lavishly illustrated.

Tyldesley, Joyce, *Hatchepsut: The Female Pharaoh* (1996). A biography based largely on archeological evidence.

von Soden, Wolfram, *The Ancient Orient* (1994). A thematic treatment of ancient Mesopotamian civilization.

The Hebrews:
A New View of God
and the Individual

A sculptured relief from the triumphal Arch of Titus showing Jewish captives bearing the menorah and vessels from the holy temple burned by the Romans at the end of the Jewish revolt, first century A.D. (Vanni/Art Resource, N.Y.)

Focus Questions

1. In what ways did the Hebrew view of God mark a revolutionary break with Near Eastern thought?

2. How did Hebrew religious thought promote the ideas of moral autonomy?

3. What were the distinguishing features of Hebrew law?

4. What were the unique achievements of the Hebrew prophets?

5. Why are the Hebrews regarded as a principal source of the Western tradition?

Ancient Mesopotamia and Egypt, the birthplace of the first civilizations, are not the spiritual ancestors of the West. For the origins of the Western tradition, we must turn to the Hebrews and the Greeks. Both the Greeks and the Hebrews, of course, absorbed elements of the civilizations of Mesopotamia and Egypt, but even more significant is how they transformed this inheritance and shaped worldviews that differed markedly from the outlooks of these first civilizations. As Egyptologist John A. Wilson writes,

> The Children of Israel built a nation and a religion on the rejection of things Egyptian. Not only did they see God as one, but they ascribed to him consistency of concern for man and consistency of justice to man. . . . Like the Greeks, the Hebrews took forms from their great neighbors; like the Greeks, they used those forms for very different purposes.[1]

In this chapter, we examine one source of the Western tradition, the Hebrews, whose conception of God broke with the outlook of the Near East and whose ethical teachings helped fashion the Western idea of humanity and the dignity of the individual.

OUTLINE OF HEBREW HISTORY *

The Hebrews (Israelites or Jews) originated in Mesopotamia and migrated to Canaan, a portion of which was later called Palestine. The Hebrew patriarchs—Abraham, Isaac, and Jacob, so prominently depicted in the Old Testament—were chieftains of seminomadic clans that roamed Palestine and occasionally journeyed to Mesopotamia and Egypt. The early Hebrews absorbed some features of Mesopotamian civilization. For example, there are parallels between biblical law and the Mesopotamian legal tradition. Several biblical stories, including the Garden of Eden and the Flood, derive from Mesopotamian sources.

*Since there is a paucity of references to the early Hebrews in nonbiblical sources, scholars have to rely almost entirely on the Hebrew Bible for reconstructing much of the history of the ancient Israelites. The divergence of scholarly opinion regarding the Bible's accuracy and reliability creates additional uncertainty for the historian.

Chronology 2.1 ❖ The Hebrews

1250 B.C.*	Hebrew Exodus from Egypt
1024–1000	Reign of Saul, Israel's first king
1000–961	Creation of a united monarchy under David
961–922	Reign of Solomon: construction of the first temple
750–430	Age of classical prophecy
722	Kingdom of Israel falls to Assyrians
586	Kingdom of Judah falls to Chaldeans; the temple is destroyed
586–539	Babylonian exile
538	Cyrus of Persia allows exiles to return to Judah
515 B.C.	Second temple is dedicated

*Most dates are approximations.

The biblical account tells us that some Hebrews journeyed from Canaan to Egypt to be herdsmen and farmers, but they eventually became forced laborers for the Egyptians. Fearful of remaining permanent slaves of the pharaoh, the Hebrews yearned for an opportunity to escape. In the early thirteenth century B.C., an extraordinary leader rose among them, called Moses, who came to his people as a messenger of God. Leading the Hebrews in their Exodus from Egypt, Moses transformed them during their wanderings in the wilderness of Sinai into a nation, welded together and uplifted by a belief in Yahweh, the one God.

Arguing that there is no extrabiblical evidence for the Exodus or even for the presence of Jews in Egypt, some scholars dismiss the Exodus as fiction; although numerous Egyptian hieroglyphics detail events at the time, none of them refer specifically to Israelites in Egypt. Certainly, say these scholars, the flight of thousands of foreigners would have attracted notice. Moreover, it is highly unlikely that an escape by a large group of slaves could have succeeded when Egypt was at the peak of its power. The biblical account says that Israelites wandered in the Sinai desert for forty years, but archaeologists, who have excavated a number of sites in the Sinai mentioned in the book of Exodus, have uncovered no traces of Israelite campsites. These scholars, known as biblical minimalists, deny the Exodus from Egypt ever occurred. Other scholars reject this position, holding that there is

evidence of Asiatic slaves toiling in Egypt, some of whom might have been Hebrews. Moreover, assert these scholars, ancient Hebrew scribes would not have concocted and faithfully preserved such an inglorious history of enslavement unless the biblical account contained a core historical truth along with legend, folklore, and mythic imagery.

The Israelite Kingdom

The wandering Israelites returned to Canaan to rejoin other Hebrew tribes that had not migrated to Egypt. The colonization of Canaan, a gradual process, took many generations. Threatened by the Philistines, originally from the islands of the Aegean Sea and the coast of Asia Minor, and from whom the name Palestine derives, the twelve tribes united under the leadership of Saul, a charismatic hero, whom they acclaimed as their first king. Under Saul's successor, David, a gifted warrior and a poet, the Hebrews (or Israelites) broke the back of Philistine power and subdued neighboring peoples.

David's son Solomon erected a royal palace in Jerusalem and beside it a splendid temple honoring God. Under Solomon, Israel experienced a cultural flowering: some magnificent sections of the Old Testament took form, and music flourished. Under Solomon, ancient Israel was at the height of its power and prosperity. However, opposition

33

WALL PAINTING FROM THE SYNAGOGUE OF DURA-EUROPOS, ROMAN SYRIA, EARLY THIRD CENTURY A.D. Although a strict prohibition of the use of images inhibited representational art among the Hebrews, in Hellenistic times scenes from Hebrew history appeared on the walls and floors of Jewish synagogues. Here the prophet Samuel is depicted anointing David as king of Israel. (Art Resource, N.Y.)

to Solomon's tax policies and his favored treatment of the region of Judah in the south led to the division of the kingdom after his death in 922 B.C. The tribes loyal to Solomon's son belonged to the kingdom of Judah, whereas the other tribes organized the northern kingdom of Israel. Both second-rate powers, neither Judah nor Israel could hold on to earlier conquests.

Conquest, Captivity, and Restoration

In 722 B.C., Israel fell to the Assyrians, who deported many Hebrews to other parts of the Assyrian empire. These transported Hebrews—the so-called ten lost tribes—merged with neighboring peoples and lost their identity as the people who had made a covenant with God. By 586 B.C., the Chaldeans had conquered Judah, destroyed Solomon's temple, devastated the land, and deported several thousand Hebrews to Babylon. The prophets Isaiah, Ezekiel, and Jeremiah declared that the destruction of Judah was a punishment that the Hebrews had brought on themselves by violating God's laws. This time was the darkest moment in the history of the Hebrews. Their state was gone, neighboring peoples had overrun their land, and their holy temple was in

Map 2.1 **Hebrews and Other Peoples of the Ancient Middle East** Despite conquest and exile, the Hebrews survived as a people, retained their faith, and remained devoted to their homeland, which, they believed, God had given them. (Copyright © 2013 Cengage Learning.)

ruins. Thousands had died in battle, had been executed, or had fled to Egypt and other lands, and thousands more were in exile in Babylon. This exile is known as the Babylonian Captivity.

Still, in what is a marvel of history, the Hebrews survived as a people. Although many of the exiles in Babylon assimilated Babylonian ways, some remained faithful to their God Yahweh and the Law of Moses and longed to return to their homeland. Priests struggled to understand the misfortunes that had befallen their people and to prevent the erosion of faith in a foreign environment. They codified ancient traditions, records, and practices, particularly laws, and in the process created the Torah (see below). Thus, their faith enabled them to endure conquest and exile. When the Persians conquered Babylon, King Cyrus, in 538 B.C.,
permitted the exiles to return to Judah, now a Persian province, and to rebuild the temple. The majority of Judeans preferred to remain in prosperous and cosmopolitan Babylon. But some of them did return to Judah, and in 515 B.C. the Hebrews, now commonly called Jews, dedicated the second temple at Jerusalem.

The Hebrew Scriptures

In the following centuries, the Jews would lose their independence to Rome and become a dispersed people. But they never relinquished their commitment to God and his Law as recorded in the Hebrew Scriptures. Called *Tanak* by Jews (and Old Testament by Christians), the

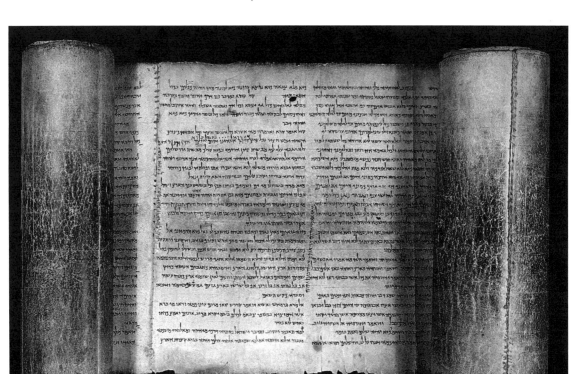

A Dead Sea Scroll, Judea, Second Century b.c. God's law, as recorded in the Holy Scriptures, still remains a unifying force among Jews. Many ancient Hebrew scrolls were found in caves near the west bank of the Dead Sea beginning in the late 1940s. The scroll depicted here contains the earliest existing copy of a complete Hebrew text of the book of the prophet Isaiah. It barely differs from more modern manuscripts. (© John Trevor, Ph.D., courtesy of the Trevor family; photo provided by the Ancient Biblical Manuscript Center, Claremont, Calif.)

Hebrew Scriptures consist of thirty-nine books* by several authors who lived in different centuries. Jews call the first five books of the Old Testament—Genesis, Exodus, Leviticus, Numbers, and Deuteronomy—the Torah (which originally meant "teaching" or "instruction"). Often, the Torah is referred to as the Pentateuch, a Greek word meaning "five books."

*In ancient times, the number of books was usually given as twenty-four. Certain books are now divided into two parts, and the twelve works by the minor prophets are now counted as individual books.

The Hebrew Scriptures represent Jewish oral and written tradition dating from about 1250 to 150 b.c. Compiled by religious devotees, not research historians, they understandably contain factual errors, imprecisions, discrepancies, legends, and folklore. However, there are also passages that offer reliable history, and historians find the Old Testament an indispensable source for studying the ancient Near East. Literary scholars study it for its poetry, legends, and themes, all of which are an integral part of the Western literary tradition. But it is as a work of religious inspiration that the Hebrew Scriptures attain their most profound importance.

The Old Testament is the record of more than a thousand years of ancient Jewish history. Containing Jewish laws, wisdom, hopes, legends, and literary expressions, it describes an ancient people's efforts to comprehend the ways of God. The Old Testament emphasizes and values the human experience; its heroes are not demigods but human beings. It depicts human strength as well as weakness. Some passages exhibit cruelty and unseemly revenge against the enemies of Israel and apostates, while others express the highest ethical values. As set forth in the Hebrew Scriptures, the Hebrew idea of God and his relationship to human beings is one of the foundations of the Western tradition.

GOD: ONE, SOVEREIGN, TRANSCENDENT, GOOD

The Hebrew view of God evolved through the history and experiences of the Hebrew people. In the days of the patriarchs, before the sojourn in Egypt, the Hebrews most likely were not monotheists. They probably devoted themselves to the god of their particular clan and expressed no hatred for the idolatrous beliefs of neighboring peoples. The chief of each clan established a special attachment to the god of his fathers, hoping that the deity would protect and assist the clan.

Some historians say that Moses' religion was not pure monotheism because it did not rule out the existence of other gods. According to this view, not until the prophets, centuries later, did the Hebrews explicitly deny that other gods existed and proclaim that Yahweh stood alone. Other scholars believe that Moses proclaimed a monotheistic idea, that this idea became the central force in the life of the Hebrews at the time of the Exodus from Egypt, and that it continues to be central today. John Bright, an American biblical scholar, suggests a judicious balance. The religion of Moses "did not deny the existence of other gods," says Bright, but it "effectively denied them status as *gods*."[2] The Hebrews could serve only Yahweh and "accorded all power and authority to Him." Consequently, Israel was

forbidden to approach [other deities] as gods. . . . The gods were thus rendered irrelevant, driven from the field. . . . To Israel only the one God was God. . . . The other gods, allowed neither part in creation, nor function in the cosmos, nor power over events. . . . were robbed of all that made them gods and rendered non-entities, in short, were "undeified." Though the full implications of monotheism were centuries in being drawn, in the functional sense Israel believed in but one God from the beginning.[3]

The Hebrew view of the one God marked a profound break with Near Eastern religious thought. The gods of other Near Eastern peoples were not truly free; their power was not without limits. Unlike Yahweh, Near Eastern gods were not eternal but were born or created; they issued from some prior realm. They also were subject to biological conditions, requiring food, drink, sleep, and sexual gratification. Sometimes they became ill or grew old or died. When they behaved wickedly, they had to answer to fate, which demanded punishment as retribution; even the gods were subject to fate's power.

The Hebrews regarded God as *fully sovereign*. He ruled all and was subject to nothing. Yahweh's existence and power did not derive from a preexisting realm, as was the case with the gods of other peoples. The Hebrews believed that no realm of being preceded God in time or surpassed him in power. They saw God as eternal and omnipotent, the source of all in the universe, and having a supreme will. He created and governed the natural world and shaped the moral laws that govern human beings. He was not subservient to fate but determined what happened.

Whereas Near Eastern divinities dwelt within nature, the Hebrew God was transcendent, above nature and not a part of it. Yahweh was not identified with any natural force and did not dwell in a particular place in heaven or on earth. Nature was God's creation but was not itself divine. Therefore, when the Hebrews confronted natural phenomena, they experienced God's magnificent handiwork, not objects with wills of their own. All natural phenomena—rivers, mountains, storms, stars—were divested of any supernatural quality. The stars and planets were creations of Yahweh, not divinities or the abodes of divinities. The Hebrews neither regarded them with awe nor worshiped them. This removal of the gods from nature is a necessary prerequisite for scientific thought.

The Hebrews demythicized nature, but concerned as they were with religion and morality, they did not create theoretical science. As testimony to God's greatness, nature inspired people to sing the praises of the Lord; it invoked worship of God, not scientific curiosity. When Hebrews gazed at the heavens, they did not seek to discover mathematical relationships but admired God's handiwork. The Hebrews did not view nature as a system governed by natural law. Rather, they saw the rising sun, spring rain, summer heat, and winter cold as God intervening in an orderly manner in his creation. The Hebrews, unlike the Greeks, were not philosophers. They were concerned with God's will, not with the human intellect; with the feelings of the heart, not the power of the mind; with righteous behavior, not abstract thought.

Unlike the Greeks, the Hebrews did not speculate about the origins of all things and the operations of nature; they knew that God had created everything. For the Hebrews, God's existence was based on religious conviction, not on rational inquiry; on revelation, not reason. It was the Greeks, not the Hebrews, who originated systematic rational thought. But Christianity, born of Judaism, retained the Hebrew view of a transcendent God and the orderliness of his creation—concepts that could accommodate Greek science.

The Hebrews also did not speculate about God's nature. They knew only that he was *good* and that he made ethical demands on his people. Unlike Near Eastern gods, Yahweh was not driven by lust or motivated by evil but was "merciful and gracious, long-suffering, and abundant in goodness and truth . . . forgiving iniquity and transgression and sin" (Psalm 145:8).[4]* In contrast to pagan gods, who were indifferent to human beings, Yahweh was attentive to human needs.

By asserting that God was *one, sovereign, transcendent*, and *good*, the Hebrews effected a

*The Bible passages in this chapter are quoted from *The Holy Scriptures* (published by the Jewish Publication Society of America).

religious revolution that separated them entirely from the worldview held by the other peoples of the ancient Near East.

THE INDIVIDUAL AND MORAL AUTONOMY

This new conception of God made possible a new awareness of the individual, who was seen as the culmination and centerpiece of God's creation. Created in the image of God, the human being is unique, qualitatively different from the rest of animate nature. Only the human being has the power of volition, the power to make choices. The Hebrews believed that God, who possessed total freedom himself, had bestowed on his people moral freedom—the capacity to choose between good and evil. Thus, in confronting God, the Hebrews developed an awareness of *self*, or *I*; the individual became conscious of his or her own person, moral autonomy, and personal worth.

Fundamental to Hebrew belief was the insistence that God did not create people to be his slaves. The Hebrews regarded God with awe and humility, with respect and fear, but they did not believe that God wanted people to grovel before him; rather, he wanted them to fulfill their moral potential by freely choosing to follow or not to follow God's Law. Thus, in creating men and women in his own image, God made them autonomous and sovereign. In God's plan for the universe, human beings were the highest creation, subordinate only to God. Of all his creations, only they had been given the freedom to choose between righteousness and wickedness, between "life and good, and death and evil" (Deuteronomy 30:15). But having the power to choose freely, men and women must bear the responsibility for their choice.

God demanded that the Hebrews have no other gods and that they make no images "nor any manner of likeness, of anything that is in heaven above, or that is in the earth beneath, . . . thou shalt not bow down unto them nor serve them" (Exodus 20:4–5). Breaking in a revolutionary way with their pagan surroundings, the Hebrews held that the one true God, both omnipotent and invisible, could not be represented in statues or other human creations. The Hebrews believed that the worship of **idols** deprived people of their freedom and dignity; people cannot be fully human if they surrender themselves to a lifeless idol. Hence, the Hebrews had to destroy images and all other forms of idolatry. A crucial element of Near Eastern religion was the use of images—art forms that depicted divinities—but the Hebrews believed that God, the Supreme Being, could not be represented by pictures or sculpture fashioned by human hands. The Hebrews rejected entirely the belief that an image possessed divine powers that could be manipulated for human advantage. Ethical considerations, not myth or magic, were central to Hebrew religious life.

By making God the center of life, Hebrews could become free moral agents; no person, no human institution, no human tradition could claim their souls. Because God alone was the supreme value in the universe, only he was worthy of worship. Thus, to give *ultimate* loyalty to a king or to a general violated God's stern warning against the worship of false gods. The first concern of the Hebrews was supposed to be righteousness, not power, fame, or riches, which were only idols and would impoverish a person spiritually and morally.

There was, however, a condition to freedom. For the Hebrews, people were not free to create their own moral precepts or their own standards of right and wrong. Freedom meant voluntary obedience to commands that originated with God. Evil and suffering were not caused by blind fate, malevolent demons, or arbitrary gods; they resulted from people's disregard of God's commandments. The dilemma is that in possessing freedom of choice, human beings also are free to disobey God, to commit a sin, which leads to suffering and death. Thus, in the Genesis story, Adam and Eve were punished for disobeying God.

For the Hebrews, to know God was not to comprehend him intellectually, define him, or prove his existence; to know God was to be righteous and loving, merciful and just. When men and women loved God, the Hebrews believed, they were uplifted and improved. Gradually, they learned to overcome the worst elements of human nature and to treat other people with respect and compassion. The Jews came to interpret the belief that man was created in God's image to mean that each human being has a divine spark in him or her, giving every person a unique dignity, which cannot be taken away.

By devotion to God, the Hebrews asserted the dignity and autonomy of human beings. Thus, the Hebrews conceived the idea of moral freedom, that each individual is responsible for his or her own actions. These concepts of human dignity and moral autonomy, which Christianity inherited, are at the core of the Western tradition.

THE COVENANT AND THE LAW

Central to Hebrew religious thought and decisive in Hebrew history was the covenant, God's special agreement with the Hebrew people.

> *And Moses went up unto God, and the Lord called unto him out of the mountain saying: "Thus shalt thou say to the house of Jacob and tell the children of Israel: Ye have seen what I did unto the Egyptians, and how I bore you on eagles' wings, and brought you unto Myself. Now therefore, if ye will hearken unto My voice indeed, and keep My covenant, then ye shall be Mine own treasure from all peoples; for all the earth is Mine; and ye shall be unto Me a kingdom of priests and a holy nation." (Exodus 19:3–6)*

By this act, the Israelites as a nation accepted God's lordship.

The Hebrews came to see themselves as a unique nation, as a "chosen people," for God had given them a special honor, a profound opportunity, and (as they could never forget) an awesome responsibility. The Hebrews did not claim that God had selected them because they were better than other peoples or because they had done anything special to deserve God's election. They believed that God, in a remarkable manner, had rescued them from bondage in Egypt and had selected them to receive the Law so that their nation would set an example of righteous behavior—"a light to the nations," said the prophet Isaiah—and ultimately lead other peoples to acknowledge God, his greatness, and his moral commands.

JUDAEA CAPTA S(ENATUS) C(ONSULTO). With a commander's baton in hand and his foot upon a helmet, a victorious centurion proclaims Rome's victory over Judea, personified weeping at the foot of the palm tree. The destruction of the city of Jerusalem under Titus was complete, but the ethics of Old Testament writing would become part of the foundation of Western civilization. (Courtesy of the American Numismatic Society.)

This divinely assigned responsibility to be the moral teachers of humanity weighed heavily on the Hebrews. They believed that God had revealed his Law—including the moral code known as the Ten Commandments—to the Hebrew people as a whole, and obedience to the Law became the overriding obligation of each Hebrew. The Law of the Torah provided Hebrews with normative guidelines for determining proper behavior. Violating the Law meant breaking the sacred covenant—an act that could lead to national disaster. As the Law originated with the one God, the necessary prerequisite for understanding and obeying it was surrendering belief in other gods forever, since they were barriers to comprehending and carrying out God's universal Law.

Justice was the central theme of Old Testament ethics. The Israelites, liberated from slavery by a righteous and compassionate God, had a moral responsibility to overcome injustice, to care for the poor, the weak, and the oppressed. Because the covenant was made with the entire Hebrew nation, society as a whole had a religious obligation to root out evil and make justice prevail. Duty to God demanded also a duty toward one's neighbor: "Thou shalt surely open thy hand unto thy poor and needy brother, in thy land" (Deuteronomy 15:11). Thus, there were laws to protect the poor, widows, orphans, resident aliens, hired laborers, and slaves. For example, in contrast to ancient Near Eastern law, which regarded slaves as property, biblical legislation emphasized the slave's humanity, although it acknowledged the slave's status as chattel. It called for the punishment of masters who used excessive force against slaves, and it required masters to allow slaves to participate in religious observances and to rest on the Sabbath.

Israelite law incorporated many elements from Near Eastern legal codes and oral traditions. But by making people more important than property, by expressing mercy toward the oppressed, and by rejecting the idea that law should treat the poor and the rich differently, Israelite law demonstrated a greater ethical awareness and a more humane spirit than other legal codes of the Near East.

And a stranger shalt thou not wrong, neither shalt thou oppress him; for ye were strangers in the land of Egypt. Ye shall not afflict any widow or fatherless child. (Exodus 22:20–21)

If thy brother, a Hebrew man, or a Hebrew woman, be sold unto thee, he shall serve thee six years; and in the seventh year thou shalt let him go free from thee. And when thou lettest him go free from thee, thou shalt not let him go empty; thou shalt furnish him liberally. . . . (Deuteronomy 15:12–14)

Thou shalt not curse the deaf, nor put a stumbling-block before the blind, but thou shalt fear thy God: I am the Lord. . . . Thou shalt love thy neighbor as thyself. (Leviticus 19:14, 18)

While biblical law valued human life and was concerned with human welfare, it also contained provisions that shock us as cruel, for example, ordering the slaughter of the enemy in war, the stoning to death of one's family members who chose to serve other gods, and the execution of homosexuals. It is unknown to what extent these prescriptions were actually carried out, and over the centuries, there arose an oral and interpretive tradition that made the written law less rigid and enabled the Hebrews to adapt to changing cultural conditions.

Hebrew law regulated all aspects of daily life, including family relationships. The father had supreme authority in the family, and this authority extended to his married sons and their wives if they remained in his household. Although polygamy was permitted, monogamy was the general rule; adultery was punishable by death.

As in other Near Eastern societies, the Jews placed women in a subordinate position. The husband was considered his wife's master, and she often addressed him as a servant or subject would speak to a superior. A husband could divorce his wife, but she could not divorce him. Only when there was no male heir could a wife inherit property from her husband or a daughter inherit from her father. Women were not regarded as competent witnesses in court and played a lesser role than men in organized worship.

On the other hand, the Jews also showed respect for women. Wise women and prophetesses such as Judith and Deborah were respected by the community and were consulted by its leaders. Prophets compared God's love for the Hebrews with a husband's love for his wife. Jewish law regarded women as persons, not as property. Even female captives taken in war were not to be abused or humiliated. The law required a husband to respect and support his wife and never to strike her. One of the Ten Commandments called for honoring both father and mother.

THE HEBREW IDEA OF HISTORY

Their idea of God made the Hebrews aware of the crucial importance of historical time. Holidays commemorating specific historical events such as the Exodus from Egypt, the receiving of the Ten Commandments on Mount Sinai, and the destruction of Solomon's temple kept the past alive and vital. Egyptians and Mesopotamians did not have a similar awareness of the uniqueness of a given event: to them, today's incident merely reproduced events experienced by their ancestors. To the Jews, the Exodus and the covenant at Mount Sinai were singular, nonrepetitive occurrences, decisive in shaping their national history. This historical uniqueness and importance of events derived from the idea of a universal God profoundly involved in human affairs—a God who cares, teaches, and punishes.

The Jews valued the future as well as the past. Regarding human history as a process leading to a goal, they envisioned a great day when God would establish on earth a glorious age of peace, prosperity, happiness, and human brotherhood. This utopian notion has become deeply embedded in Western thought.

The Hebrews saw history as the work of God; it was a divine drama filled with sacred meaning and moral significance. Historical events revealed the clash of human will with God's commands. Through history's specific events, God's presence was disclosed and his purpose made known. When the Hebrews suffered conquest and exile, they interpreted these events as divine retribution for violating the covenant and the Law, sinful acts that brought down the wrath of God upon them. For the Hebrews, history also revealed God's compassion and concern. Thus, the Lord liberated Moses and the Israelites at the Red Sea and appointed prophets to plead for the poor and the oppressed. Because historical events revealed God's attitude toward human beings, these events possessed spiritual meaning and were worth recording, evaluating, and remembering.

THE PROPHETS

Jewish history was marked by the emergence of spiritually inspired individuals called prophets who felt compelled to act as God's messengers. The prophets believed that God had commanded them to speak and had legitimated their words. The prophets cared nothing for money or possessions, feared no one, and preached without invitation. Often emerging in times of social distress and moral confusion, the prophets pleaded for a return to the covenant and the Law. Speaking in God's name, they exhorted the entire nation to make

WALL PAINTING FROM THE SYNAGOGUE IN DURA-EUROPOS, ROMAN SYRIA, EARLY THIRD CENTURY A.D. This painting shows a Hebrew prophet reading from an open scroll. (Art Resource, N.Y.)

the prophets were Amos, a shepherd from Judea in the south; his younger contemporary, Hosea, from Israel in the north; Isaiah of Jerusalem; and Jeremiah, who witnessed the siege of Jerusalem by the Chaldeans in the early sixth century B.C.

Social Justice

The flowering of the prophetic movement—the age of classical, or literary, prophecy—began in the eighth century B.C. In attacking oppression, cruelty, greed, and exploitation, the classical prophets added a new dimension to Israel's religious development. These prophets were responding to problems emanating from Israel's changed social structure. The general lack of class distinctions characterizing a tribal society had been altered by the rise of Hebrew kings, the expansion of commerce, and the growth of cities. By the eighth century, there was a significant disparity between the wealthy and the poor. Small farmers in debt to moneylenders faced the loss of their land or even bondage; the poor and their families were often dispossessed and enslaved by the greedy wealthy. To the prophets, these social evils were religious sins that would bring ruin to Israel. Amos, a mid-eighth-century prophet, felt a tremendous compulsion to speak out against these injustices. In the name of God, he denounced the pomp of the heartless rich and the hypocrisy of pious Jews who worshiped God in the prescribed manner but neglected their social obligations to their neighbors, and he demanded that the Hebrews

> *Hate the evil and love the good,*
> *And establish justice in the gate.* (Amos 5:15)

For Amos, the pursuit of justice was the most important requirement of the Law. The purpose of worship and ritual was to instill in human beings a passion for justice.

> *I hate, I despise your feasts,*
> *And I will take no delight in your solemn*
> *   assemblies.*
> *Yea, though ye offer me burnt-offerings and*
> *   your meal-offerings,*

God's religious-moral commands central to its existence. Believing that they had been dispatched by God to rescue the disobedient Hebrews from their headlong rush to destruction, the prophets reminded their brethren that because of their moral deterioration, God, who rules history, would inflict swift and terrible punishment on them. The prophets were remarkably courageous people who did not quake before the powerful. Among

Isaiah and Social Justice

The prophets' insistence that rituals were not the essence of the Law and their passion for righteousness are voiced in the Scriptures by Isaiah of Jerusalem, who lived in the mid-eighth century B.C. Scholars agree that Isaiah of Jerusalem did not write all sixty-six chapters that make up the book of Isaiah. Some material appears to have been written by his disciples and interpreters, and Chapters 40 to 55, which were composed two centuries later, are attributed to a person given the name Second Isaiah. The following verses come from Isaiah of Jerusalem.

[11]"What to me is the multitude of your
    sacrifices?
  says the LORD;
I have had enough of burnt offerings of rams
  and the fat of the fed beasts;
I do not delight in the blood of bulls, or of
  lambs, or of he-goats. . . .
[13]Bring no more vain offerings;
  incense is an abomination to me.
New moon and sabbath and the calling of
  assemblies—
  I cannot endure iniquity and solemn
  assembly.
[14]Your new moons and your appointed feasts
  my soul hates;
they have become a burden to me,
  I am weary of bearing them.
[15]When you spread forth your hands,
  I will hide my eyes from you;
even though you make many prayers,

I will not listen;
  your hands are full of blood.
[16]Wash yourselves; make yourselves clean;
  remove the evil of your doings
  from before my eyes;
cease to do evil,
[17]learn to do good;
seek justice,
  correct oppression;
defend the fatherless,
  plead for the widow.
  (Isaiah 1)

Isaiah denounces the rich and the powerful for exploiting the poor.

[13]The LORD has taken his place to contend,
  he stands to judge his people.
[14]The LORD enters into judgment
  with the elders and princes of his people:
"It is you who have devoured the vineyard,
  the spoil of the poor is in your houses.
[15]What do you mean by crushing my people,
  by grinding the face of the poor?"
  says the Lord God of hosts.
  (Isaiah 3)

Question for Analysis

1. Discuss the following statement: For Isaiah, ethical conduct was preferable to ritual acts as a way to worship God.

*I will not accept them;
Neither will I regard the peace offerings of
  your fat beasts.
Take thou away from Me the noise of thy
  songs;
And let Me not hear the melody of the
  psalteries.*

*But let justice well up as waters,
And righteousness as a mighty stream.* (Amos
  5:21–24)

Justice and righteousness are God's principal concerns and his supreme commandments, said the prophets. God's injunctions, declared Isaiah, were to

Jeremiah

In 597 B.C., the Babylonians, under King Nebuchadnezzar, captured Jerusalem, looted the temple, removed many leading citizens to Babylon, and placed Zedekiah on the throne of David as a puppet ruler. In 589 B.C., Zedekiah, ignoring the warnings of the prophet Jeremiah (born c. 645 B.C.), rebelled against Babylonian rule.

Jeremiah began prophesying when still in his teens, exhorting the Hebrews to avoid the evils of idol worship and mistreatment of their fellows. If the people did not change their ways, he warned, a "foe from the north"—clearly, he meant the Babylonians—would devastate the land and even destroy the temple. After the Babylonian conquest, Jeremiah warned Zedekiah to accept Babylonian dominion. Nebuchadnezzar,

he said, was fulfilling God's purpose. God imposed the Babylonian yoke on Judah to provide the people with an opportunity for true contrition and spiritual renewal. To oppose Babylon was to contravene God's plan and bring down his wrath on Judah. Jeremiah told King Zedekiah: "Why should you and your people die by the sword, by famine, and by pestilence, as the Lord has spoken concerning any nation that will not serve the king of Babylon?" (27:12).

Jeremiah's political advice angered royal officials and popular prophets, who urged a war of liberation. When Zedekiah rebelled, Nebuchadnezzar responded with force. The enemies of Jeremiah demanded his execution as a traitor, and he was left to die in a deep cistern. However, Zedekiah allowed the prophet to be rescued but placed him under court arrest. Shortly

> Seek justice, relieve the oppressed,
> Judge the fatherless, plead for the widow.
>   (Isaiah 1:17)

Prophets also denounced people whose principal concern was the accumulation of possessions and wealth. These objects are only transient, said Isaiah, "but the word of God will stand forever" (Isaiah 40:8).

Prophets stressed the direct spiritual-ethical encounter between the individual and God. Their concern was the inner person rather than the outer forms of religious activity. They criticized priests whose commitment to rites and rituals was not supported by a deeper spiritual insight or matched by a zeal for morality in daily life. To the prophets, an ethical sin was far worse than a ritual omission.

The prophets thus helped shape a social conscience that has become part of the Western tradition. This revolutionary social doctrine states that everyone has a God-given right to social justice and fair treatment; that each person has a religious obligation to denounce evil and oppose the mistreatment of others; and that the community has a moral responsibility to assist the unfortunate. The prophets held out the hope that life on earth could be improved, that poverty and injustice need not be accepted as part of an unalterable natural order, and that the individual was capable of elevating himself or herself morally.

Universalism

Hebrew thought displayed two tendencies: **parochialism** and universalism. Parochial-mindedness stressed the special nature, destiny, and needs of the chosen people—a nation set apart from others—for from among all the nations, God had chosen to give it his Law, the Torah. This narrow, tribal outlook was offset by **universalism,** a concern for all humanity, which found expression in the prophets who envisioned the unity of all people under God. Those prophets told of a great day when God, for whom all people were equally precious, would establish everlasting justice and peace among all nations.

afterward, the Babylonians poured through Jerusalem's breached walls; they burned the city, destroyed the temple, slaughtered nobles, and forcibly removed many people to Babylon. King Zedekiah met a dreadful end. After being forced to watch the execution of his sons, he was blinded and taken in chains to Babylon.

For Jeremiah's support, Nebuchadnezzar ordered his release from prison. Remaining in Jerusalem, the prophet sent out a message of hope to the survivors. God had punished you, he told them, because "your guilt is great, because your sins are so numerous" (30:15). But God, who loved the people of Israel "with an everlasting love" (31:3) and also recognized his abiding commitment to them, will one day "restore the fortunes of my people" (30:3). The exiles will be returned, Jerusalem rebuilt, and the temple restored, he prophesied.

> *In that day shall there be a highway out of Egypt to Assyria, and the Assyrian shall come into Egypt, and the Egyptian into Assyria; and the Egyptians shall worship with the Assyrians. In that day shall Israel be the third with Egypt and with Assyria. . . . For that the Lord of hosts hath blessed him saying: "Blessed be Egypt My people and Assyria the work of My hands, and Israel Mine inheritance."*
> (Isaiah 19:23–24)

Israel was charged with a sacred mission: to lead in the struggle against idolatry and to set an example of righteous behavior for all humanity.

The prophets were not pacifists, particularly if a war was being waged against the enemies of Yahweh. But some prophets denounced war as obscene and looked forward to its elimination. In a world where virtually everyone glorified the warrior, the prophets of universalism envisioned the day when peace would reign over the earth, when nations

> *shall beat their swords into plowshares, And their spears into pruning-hooks; Nation shall not lift up sword against nation, Neither shall they learn war any more.*
> (Isaiah 2:4)

These prophets maintained that when people glorify force, they dehumanize their opponents, brutalize themselves, and dishonor God. When violence rules, there can be no love of God and no regard for the individual.

Individualism

The prophets' universalism was accompanied by an equally profound awareness of the individual and his or her worth to God. Before Moses and the later prophets, virtually all religious tradition had been produced communally and anonymously. The prophets, however, spoke as fearless individuals who, by affixing their signatures to their thoughts, fully bore the responsibility of their religious inspiration and conviction. The prophets' emphasis on the individual's responsibility for his or her own actions is a key component of Western thought. In coming to regard God's Law as a *command to conscience, an appeal to the inner person*, the prophets heightened the awareness of the human personality. They enjoined individuals to be introspective, to examine their inner selves—their thoughts and feelings. They indicated that the individual could not know God by merely following edicts and by performing rituals; the individual must experience God. Precisely this *I-Thou* relationship could make the individual fully conscious of self and could deepen and enrich his or her personality. During the Exodus, the Hebrews were a tribal people who obeyed the Law largely out of awe and group compulsion. By the prophets' time, the Jews appeared to be autonomous individuals who heeded the Law because of a deliberate, conscious inner commitment.

The ideals proclaimed by the prophets helped sustain the Jews throughout their long and often painful historical odyssey, and they remain a vital force for Jews today. Incorporated into the teachings of Jesus, these ideals, as part of Christianity, are embedded in the Western tradition.

THE LEGACY OF THE ANCIENT JEWS

For the Jews, monotheism had initiated a process of self-discovery and self-realization unmatched by other peoples of the Near East. The great value that Westerners give to the individual and to human dignity derives in part from the ancient Hebrews, who held that man and woman were created in God's image and possessed free will and a conscience answerable to God. Inherited by Christianity, the prophets' teachings constitute the core principles of Western morality, and their command to the power structure not to abuse their authority but to pursue justice continues to inspire reformers.

Throughout the centuries, the Jewish Bible, with its view of God, human nature, divine punishment, the pursuit of righteousness, and social justice, has played a pivotal and profound role in Jewish life. Moreover, its significance has transcended the Jewish experience; it is also a cornerstone of Western civilization.

Christianity, the essential religion of Western civilization, emerged from ancient Judaism, and the links between the two, including monotheism, moral autonomy, prophetic values, and the Hebrew Scriptures as the Word of God, are numerous and strong. The historical Jesus cannot be understood without examining his Jewish background, and his followers appealed to the Hebrew Scriptures in order to demonstrate the validity of their beliefs. For these reasons, we talk of a Judeo-Christian tradition as an essential component of Western civilization.

The Hebrew vision of a future **messianic age**, a golden age of peace and social justice, is at the root of the Western idea of progress—that people can build a more just society, that there is reason to be hopeful about the future. This way of perceiving the world has greatly influenced modern reform movements. People longing to escape from oppression—African Americans in particular—have found inspiration in the Hebrews' deliverance from bondage in Egypt, the theme of Exodus.

In seeking to comprehend their relationship to God, the writers of the Hebrew scriptures produced a treasury of themes, stories, and models of literary style and craftsmanship that have been a source of inspiration for Western religious thinkers, novelists, poets, and artists to the present day. Historians and archaeologists find the Hebrew Scriptures a valuable resource in their efforts to reconstruct ancient Near Eastern history.

NOTES

1. John A. Wilson, "Egypt—the Kingdom of the 'Two Lands,'" in *The World History of the Jewish People*, vol. 1, *At the Dawn of Civilization*, ed. E. A. Speiser (New Brunswick, N.J.: Rutgers University Press, 1964), 267–268.

2. John Bright, *A History of Israel* (Philadelphia: Westminster Press, 1972), 154.

3. Ibid.

4. From *The Holy Scriptures* (Philadelphia: The Jewish Publication Society of America, 1917). The scriptural quotations are used in this chapter with the permission of The Jewish Publication Society of America.

SUGGESTED READING

Anderson, Bernhard, *Understanding the Old Testament*, 2nd ed. (1966). An excellent survey of the Old Testament in its historical setting.

Armstrong, Karen, *A History of God* (1994). Changing views of God from the ancient Hebrews until today.

Boadt, Lawrence, *Reading the Old Testament* (1984). A study of ancient Israel's religious experience by a sympathetic Catholic scholar.

Bright, John, *A History of Israel* (1972). A thoughtful, clearly written survey; one of the best of its kind.

Dever, William G., *Who Were the Israelites and Where Did They Come From?* (2003).

An archeologist explores the controversies regarding biblical accounts of the origins of the Israelites.

Finkelstein, Israel, and Neil Asher Silberman, *The Bible Unearthed: Archeology's New Vision of Ancient Israel and the Origin of Its Sacred Texts* (2001). Challenges several assumptions derived from biblical accounts.

Grant, Michael, *The History of Ancient Israel* (1984). A lucid account.

Heschel, Abraham, *The Prophets*, 2 vols. (1962). A penetrating analysis of the nature of prophetic inspiration.

Metzger, Bruce M., and Michael D. Coogan, eds., *The Oxford Companion to the Bible* (1993). A valuable reference work.

Shanks, Hershel, ed., *Ancient Israel* (1999). The revised and expanded edition contains authoritative essays on various phases of the history of ancient Israel. Highly recommended.

The Greek City-State: Democratic Politics

The Acropolis of Athens. (Robert Harding World Imagery.)

Focus Questions

1. What were the basic features and limitations of Greek democracy?

2. How did the Greek city-state differ from Near Eastern governments?

3. How did Greek political life demonstrate both the best and the worst features of freedom as well as both the capabilities and the limitations of reason?

4. Why is the Greek political experience crucial to the shaping of the Western tradition?

The Hebrew conception of ethical monotheism, with its stress on human dignity, is one principal source of the Western tradition. The second major source is ancient Greece. Both the Hebrews and the Greeks absorbed the achievements of Near Eastern civilizations, but they also developed their own distinctive viewpoints and styles of thought that set them apart from the Mesopotamians and Egyptians. The great achievements of the Hebrews lay in the sphere of religious-ethical thought; those of the Greeks lay in the development of rational thought. As Greek society evolved, says British historian James Shiel, there

> was a growing reliance on independent reason, a devotion to logical precision, progressing from myth to logos [reason]. Rationalism permeated the whole social and cultural development. . . . Architecture. . . . developed from primitive cultic considerations to sophisticated mathematical norms; sculpture escaped from temple image to a new love of naturalism and proportion; political life proceeded from tyranny to rational experiments in democracy. From practical rules of thumb, geometry moved forward in the direction of the impressive Euclidian synthesis. So too philosophy made its way from "sayings of the wise" to the Aristotelian logic, and made men rely on their own observation and reflection in facing the unexplained vastness of the cosmos.[1]

The Greeks conceived of nature as following general rules, not acting according to the whims of gods or demons. They saw human beings as having a capacity for rational thought, a need for freedom, and a worth as individuals. Although the Greeks never dispensed with the gods, they increasingly stressed the importance of human reason and human decisions. They came to assert that reason is the avenue to knowledge and that people—not the gods—are responsible for their own behavior. In this shift of attention from the gods to human beings, the Greeks broke with the mythmaking orientation of the Near East and created the rational outlook that is a distinctive feature of Western civilization.

Chronology 3.1 ❖ The Greek City-State

1700–1450 B.C.*	Height of Minoan civilization
1400–1230	Height of Mycenaean civilization
1100–800	Dark Age
750–550	Age of Colonization
c. 700	Homer
621	Draco's code of law
594	Solon is elected chief executive
546–527	Under Pisistratus, tyranny replaces oligarchy
507	Cleisthenes broadens democratic institutions
499	Ionians revolt against Persian rule
490	Athenians defeat Persians at battle of Marathon
480	Xerxes of Persia invades Greece; Greek naval victory at Salamis
479	Spartans defeat Persians at Plataea, ending Persian Wars
478–477	Formation of Delian League
431	Start of Peloponnesian War
429	Death of Pericles
413	Athenian defeat at Syracuse
404	Athens surrenders to Sparta, ending Peloponnesian War
399	Execution of Socrates
387	Plato founds a school, the Academy
359	Philip II becomes king of Macedonia
338	Battle of Chaeronea: Greek city-states fall under the dominion of Macedonia
335 B.C.	Aristotle founds a school, the Lyceum
	*Some dates are approximations.

EARLY AEGEAN CIVILIZATIONS

Until the latter part of the nineteenth century, historians placed the beginning of Greek, or Hellenic, history in the eighth century B.C. Now it is known that two related civilizations preceded Hellenic Greece: the Minoan and the Mycenaean. Although the ancient Greek poet Homer had spoken of an earlier Greek civilization in his works, historians believed that Homer's epics dealt with myths and legends, not with a historical past. In 1871,

however, a successful German businessman, Heinrich Schliemann, began a search for earliest Greece. Having been enthralled by Homer's epics as a youth, Schliemann was convinced that they referred to an actual civilization. In excavating several sites mentioned by Homer, Schliemann discovered tombs, pottery, ornaments, and the remains of palaces of what hitherto had been a lost Greek civilization. The ancient civilization was named after Mycenae, the most important city of the time. Mycenaean civilization pervaded the

Greek mainland and the islands of the Aegean Sea for much of the second millennium B.C.

In 1900, Arthur Evans, a British archaeologist, made an equally extraordinary discovery. Excavating on the island of Crete, southeast of the Greek mainland, he unearthed a civilization even older than that of the Mycenaean Greeks. The Cretans, or Minoans, were not Greeks and did not speak a Greek language, but their influence on mainland Greece was considerable and enduring. Minoan civilization lasted about 1,350 years (2600 to 1250 B.C.) and reached its height during the period from 1700 to 1450 B.C.

The centers of Minoan civilization were magnificent palace complexes whose construction was evidence of the wealth and power of Minoan kings. That the architects of these palaces and the artists who decorated the walls were sensitive to beauty is shown in the ruins uncovered at various Cretan sites. The palaces housed royal families, priests, and government officials and contained workshops that produced decorated silver vessels, daggers, and pottery for local use and for export. Numerous Cretan artifacts have been found in Egypt, Syria, Asia Minor, and Greece, attesting to a substantial export trade.

Judging by the archaeological evidence, the Minoans seemed peaceful. Minoan art did not generally depict military scenes, and Minoan palaces, unlike the Mycenaean ones, had no defensive walls or fortifications. Thus, the Minoans were vulnerable to the warlike Mycenaean Greeks, who invaded and conquered Knossos, the Minoan capital. The Minoans never recovered from this blow, and within two centuries Minoan civilization faded away.

Who were these Mycenaeans? Around 2000 B.C., Greek-speaking tribes moved southward into the Greek peninsula, where, together with the pre-Greek population, they fashioned the Mycenaean civilization. In the Peloponnesus, the Mycenaeans built palaces that were based in part on Cretan models. In these palaces, Mycenaean kings conducted affairs of state, and priests and priestesses performed religious ceremonies; potters, smiths, tailors, and chariot builders practiced their crafts in the numerous workshops, much like their Minoan counterparts. Mycenaean arts and crafts owed a considerable debt to Crete. A script that permitted record keeping probably also came from Crete. The Mycenaeans were traders, too, exchanging goods with the peoples of Egypt, Phoenicia, Sicily, southern Italy, Macedonia, and the western coast of Asia Minor.

At the apex of Mycenaean society was the king, who headed the armed forces, controlled production and trade, and was the highest judicial authority. Assisting the king were aristocrats, who were officers in the army and held key positions in the administration. The priestesses and priests were also in the upper echelons of the society; they supervised sanctuaries and other properties of the gods. Farmers, stockbreeders, and craftsmen constituted the bulk of the free population. At the bottom of the social pyramid were the slaves—mostly foreign prisoners of war.

Mycenaean civilization, which consisted of several small states, each with its own ruling dynasty, reached its height in the period from 1400 to 1230 B.C. Following that, constant warfare between the Mycenaean kingdoms (and perhaps foreign invasions) led to destruction of the palaces and the abrupt disintegration of the Mycenaean civilization about 1100 B.C. But to the later Greek civilization the Mycenaeans left a legacy of religious forms, pottery making, metallurgy, agriculture, language, a warrior culture and code of honor immortalized in the Homeric epics, and myths and legends, which offered themes for Greek drama.

THE RISE OF
HELLENIC CIVILIZATION

From 1100 to 800 B.C., the Greek world passed through the Dark Age, an era of transition between a dead Mycenaean civilization and a still unborn Hellenic civilization. The Dark Age saw the migration of Greek tribes from the barren mountainous regions of Greece to more fertile plains, and from the mainland to Aegean islands and the coast of Asia Minor. One group of invaders, the Dorians, penetrated the Peloponnesian peninsula in the south and later founded Sparta. Another group, the Ionians, settled in Attica, where Athens is located, and later crossed to Asia Minor. During this period, the Greeks experienced insecurity, warfare, poverty, and isolation. The bureaucratic system of Mycenaean government had disappeared, extensive trade had ceased, the art of writing had been forgotten, the palace workshops no longer existed, and art had reverted to primitive forms.

After 800 B.C., however, town life revived. Writing again became part of the Greek culture, this time with the more efficient Phoenician script. (Other borrowings from the Near East included artistic imagery and motifs, religious practices, craft skills, and mythological tales that were adapted and transformed by Greek poets.) The population increased dramatically, there was a spectacular rise in the use of metals, and overseas trade expanded. Gradually, Greek cities founded settlements on the islands of the Aegean, along the coast of Asia Minor and the Black Sea, and to the west in Sicily and southern Italy. These colonies, established to relieve overpopulation and land hunger, were independent, self-governing city-states, not possessions of the homeland city-states, although close ties were maintained between the two. During the two hundred years of colonization (750–550 B.C.), trade and industry expanded, the pace of urbanization quickened, and a new class emerged: the merchants, whose wealth derived from goods and money rather than from land. In time, this middle class would challenge the landholding aristocracy.

Homer, Shaper of the Greek Spirit

The poet Homer lived during the eighth century B.C., just after the Dark Age. His great narrative epics, the *Iliad* and the *Odyssey,** helped shape the Greek spirit and Greek religion. Homer was the earliest molder of the Greek outlook and character. For centuries, Greek youngsters grew up reciting the Homeric epics and admiring the Homeric heroes, who strove for honor and faced suffering and death with courage. Greek thinkers quoted Homer to illustrate moral truths.

In contrast to earlier works of mythology, Homer dealt not just with a hero's actions but also with what the hero thought and felt about his

---

*Although scholars agree that Homer composed the *Iliad,* some of them hold that the *Odyssey* was probably the work of an unknown poet who lived sometime after Homer; some say that Homer composed both epics, most likely utilizing oral poetic traditions already in circulation, in their earliest forms and that others altered them.

behavior. Homer was a poetic genius who could reveal a human being's deepest thoughts, feelings, and conflicts in a few brilliant lines. His characters, complex in their motives and expressing powerful human emotions—wrath, vengeance, guilt, remorse, compassion, and love—would intrigue and inspire Western writers down to the present.

The *Iliad* deals, in poetic form, with a small segment of the tenth and last year of the Trojan War, which had taken place centuries before Homer's time, during the Mycenaean period. At the very beginning, Homer states his theme.

> *The Wrath of Achilles is my theme, that fatal wrath which, in fulfillment of the will of Zeus, brought the Achaeans [Greeks] so much suffering and sent the gallant souls of many noblemen to Hades, leaving their bodies as carrion for the dogs and passing birds. Let us begin, goddess of song, with the angry parting that took place between Agamemnon King of Men and the great Achilles Son of Peleus.*[2]

The story goes on to reveal the cause and tragic consequences of this wrath. In depriving "the swift and excellent" Achilles of his rightful war-prize (the captive young woman Briseis), King Agamemnon has insulted Achilles' honor and has violated the solemn rule that warrior heroes treat each other with respect. His pride wounded, Achilles refuses to rejoin Agamemnon in battle against Troy and plans to affirm his honor by demonstrating that the Achaeans need his valor and military prowess. Not until many brave men have been slain, including his dearest friend Patroclus, does Achilles set aside his quarrel with Agamemnon and enter the battle.

Homer employs a *particular* event, the quarrel between an arrogant Agamemnon and a revengeful Achilles, to demonstrate a *universal* principle: that "wicked arrogance" and "ruinous wrath" will cause much suffering and death. Homer grasps that there is an internal logic to existence. For Homer, says British classicist H. D. F. Kitto, "actions must have their consequences; ill-judged actions must have uncomfortable results."[3] People, and even the gods, operate within a certain unalterable framework; their deeds are subject to the demands of fate, or necessity. With a poet's intuition, Homer sensed what would become a fundamental attitude

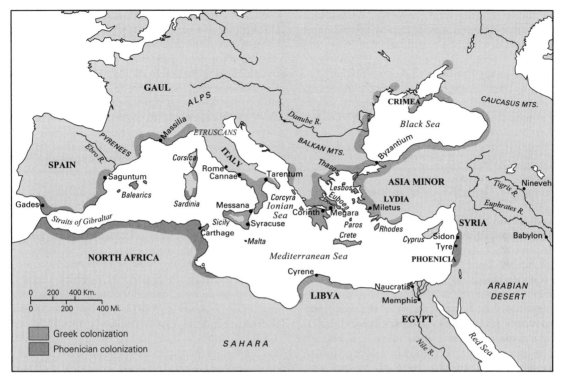

Map 3.1 **Greek Colonization of the Mediterranean Basin** From 750 to 550 B.C., the Greeks colonized the islands of the Aegean, the coasts of Asia Minor and the Black Sea, and, to the west, Sicily and southern Italy. (Copyright © 2013 Cengage Learning.)

of the Greek mind: there is a universal order to things. Later Greeks would formulate Homer's poetic insight in philosophical terms.

Although human life is governed by laws of necessity, the Homeric warrior expresses a passionate desire to assert himself, to demonstrate his worth, to gain the glory that poets would immortalize in their songs—that is, to achieve **aretē**, excellence. In the *Iliad*, Hector, prince of Troy, does battle with Achilles, even though defeat and death seem certain. He fights not because he is a fool rushing madly into a fray nor because he relishes combat, but because he is a prince bound by a code of honor and conscious of his reputation and of his responsibility to his fellow Trojans. In the code of the warrior-aristocrats, cowardice brought unbearable shame, and honor meant more than life itself. When Hector knows that he is going to be slain by Achilles, he expresses this overriding concern with

heroism and glory: "So now I meet my doom. Let me at least sell my life dearly and have a not inglorious end, after some feat of arms that shall come to the ears of generations still unborn."[4]

Heroism, the pursuit of glory and fame, and war's exhilaration are central to the *Iliad*, but Homer is also sensitive to the suffering caused by war. Battlefields littered with dead and maimed warriors fill soldiers with tears, and the grief of widows, orphans, and parents is unremitting.

Homer grasped war's tragic character: it confers honor and dignity on the victorious, but suffering, grief, enslavement, and death on the defeated. And one day, the hero, who had been lauded for his courage and prowess and had brought glory to his family and city, will also perish by the sword. This is his destiny. Homer's insights into life's tragic nature instructed the great Greek dramatists (see Chapter 4) and future Western writers.

In the warrior-aristocrat world of Homer, aretē, was principally interpreted as bravery and skill in battle. Homer's portrayal also bears the embryo of a larger conception of human excellence, one that combines thought with action. A man of true worth, says the wise Phoenix to the stubborn Achilles, is both "a speaker of words and a doer of deeds." In this passage, we find the earliest statement of the Greek educational ideal: the molding of a man who, says classicist Werner Jaeger, "united nobility of action with nobility of mind," who realized "the whole of human potentialities."[5] Thus, in Homer we find the beginnings of Greek humanism—a concern with the individual and his achievements.

To Mesopotamian and Egyptian minds, the gods were primarily responsible for the good or evil that befell human beings. In Homer's work, the gods are still very much involved in human affairs, but Homer also makes the individual a decisive actor in the drama of life. Human actions and human personality are very important. Homer's heroes demonstrate a considerable independence of will. Human beings pay respect to the gods but do not live in perpetual fear of them; they choose their own way, at times even defying the gods. As British classicist C. M. Bowra notes, "the human actors . . . pursue their own aims and deal their own blows; the gods may help or obstruct them, but success or failure remains their own. The gods have the last word, but in the interval men do their utmost and win glory for it."[6] Homer's view of the eternal order of the world and his conception of the individual striving for excellence form the foundations of the Greek outlook.

Greek Religion

During the Dark Age, Greek religion was a mixture of beliefs and cults of gods and goddesses inherited from the Mycenaean past and from an even older Indo-European past imported from Asia Minor and from the early civilizations of the Near East. The Greeks had no prophets or works of scripture like the Hebrews, but Homer's epics and Hesiod's poetry (see profile in next chapter) gave some clarity and structure to Greek religion. They were not intended to have any theological significance, but their treatment of the gods had important religious implications for the Greeks. In time, Homer's epics

formed the basis of the Olympian religion accepted throughout Greece. The principal gods were said to reside on Mount Olympus in northern Greece, and on its highest peak was the palace of Zeus, the chief deity. Although all Greeks recognized the Olympian gods, each city retained local gods and rituals that had been transmitted through generations by folk memory.

Many Greeks found an outlet for their religious feelings in the sacred ceremonies of mystic cults. Devotees of the cult of Dionysus, the god of wine and agricultural fertility, engaged in ecstatic dances and frenzied prayers for abundant harvests. Participants in the Eleusinian cult felt purified and reborn through their rituals and believed in a happy life after death. The Orphic cult, which was popular in the sixth century B.C., taught the unimportance of earthly life and the need to prepare for life after the grave. The Orphics believed that the soul, which once had enjoyed a happy existence in another world, was imprisoned in the body for an unknown fault, and that if the individual controlled his or her bodily desires, the soul would be liberated after death.

In the early stages of Greek history, most people sought to live in accordance with the wishes of the gods. Through prayer, offerings, and ritual purification, they tried to appease the gods and consulted oracles to divine the future. Although religion pervaded daily life, the Greeks had no official body of priests who ruled religious matters and could intervene in politics. Instead, religious ceremonies were conducted by citizens chosen to serve as priests. Nor was there an official creed with established doctrines. Religion was more social than spiritual; that is, it was more a way of expressing attachment to the community than finding inner peace through personal communion with a higher reality. In time, traditional religion would be challenged and undermined by a growing secular and rational spirit.

THE EVOLUTION OF THE CITY-STATE

The Break with Theocratic Politics

From 750 B.C. to the death of Alexander the Great in 323 B.C., Greek society consisted of independent city-states. The city-state based on tribal allegiances was generally the first political association during the early stages of civilization. Moreover, Greece's many mountains, bays, and islands—natural barriers to political unity—favored this type of political arrangement.

The scale of the city-state, or *polis*, was small; most city-states had fewer than 5,000 male citizens. Athens, which was a large city-state, had some 35,000 to 40,000 (some estimates are as high as 55,000) adult male citizens; the rest of its population of 350,000 consisted of women, children, resident aliens, and slaves, none of whom could participate in lawmaking. The citizens of the polis, many of whom were related by blood, knew one another well, and together they engaged in athletic contests and religious rituals. The polis gave individuals a sense of belonging, for its citizens were intimately involved in the political and cultural life of the community.

In the fifth century B.C., at its maturity, the Greeks viewed their polis as the only avenue to the good life—"the only framework within which man could realize his spiritual, moral, and intellectual capacities," in the words of Kitto.[7] The mature polis was a self-governing community that expressed the will of free citizens, not the desires of gods, hereditary kings, or priests. In the **theocracies** of the Near East, religion dominated political activity, and to abide by the mandates of the gods was the ruler's first responsibility. The Greek polis also had begun as a religious institution, in which the citizens sought to maintain an alliance with their deities. But gradually the citizens deemphasized the gods' role in political life and based government not on the magic powers of divine rulers, but on human intelligence as expressed through the community. Seers, purported to have supernatural skills, might offer advice but could not override the rulings of the Assembly. The great innovation introduced by the Greeks into politics and social theory, says classicist Mason Hammond, was "the view that law did not emanate from gods, or divine rulers, but from the human community."[8] The evolution of the Greek polis from a tribal-religious institution to a secular-rational institution was only a part of the general transition of the Greek mind from myth to reason.

The emergence of rational attitudes did not, of course, spell the end of religion, particularly for the peasants, who remained devoted to their ancient cults, gods, and shrines. Greek commanders and statesmen, at times, were not beyond consulting omens and oracles before making decisions, and considerable public revenue went to the construction of temples and the observance of religious festivals. The Greeks were careful to show respect for the gods, for many believed that these deities could aid or harm a city. Paying homage to the god of the city remained a required act of patriotism, to which Greeks unfailingly adhered.

Thus, the religious-mythical tradition never died in Greece but existed side by side with a growing **rationalism.** As Greek rationalism gained influence, traditional religious beliefs and restrictions either were made to comply more with the demands of reason or grew weaker through neglect and disuse. When Athenian **democracy** reached its height in the middle of the fifth century B.C., religion was no longer the dominant factor in politics. For many Athenians, religion had become largely ceremonial, a way of expressing loyalty to the city. They had come to rely on human reason, not divine guidance, in their political and intellectual life.

Greek political life was marred by violent party conflicts, demagoguery, intercity warfare, and the exploitation of weak states by stronger ones. Nevertheless, the Greek political achievement was extraordinary. What made Greek political life different from that of earlier Near Eastern civilizations, and also gave it enduring significance, was the Greeks' gradual realization that community problems are caused by human beings and require human solutions. Thus, the Greeks came to understand law as an achievement of the rational mind rather than as an edict imposed by the gods; law was valued because it expressed the will and needs of the community, not out of fear of the divine. The Greeks also valued free **citizenship.** An absolute king, a tyrant who ruled arbitrarily and by decree and who was above the law, was abhorrent.

The ideals of political freedom are best exemplified by Athens. Before turning to Athens, however, let us examine another Greek city, which followed a different political course.

Sparta: A Garrison State

Situated on the Peloponnesian peninsula, farther inland than most Greek cities, Sparta had been settled by Dorian Greeks. The Greek city-states dealt with overpopulation and the need for new agricultural land by founding colonies. Sparta, however, established only one colony, Tarentum, in southern Italy. Sparta's chief means of expansion was to conquer, in the eighth century B.C., its neighbors on the Peloponnesian peninsula, including Messenia. Instead of selling the Messenians abroad, the traditional Greek way of treating a defeated foe, the Spartans kept them as state serfs, or *helots*. Helots were owned by the state rather than by individual Spartans. Enraged by their enforced servitude, the Messenians, also a Greek people, desperately tried to regain their freedom. After a bloody struggle, the Spartans suppressed the uprising, but the fear of a helot revolt became indelibly stamped on Spartan consciousness.

To maintain their dominion over the Messenians, who outnumbered them ten to one, the Spartans—with extraordinary single-mindedness, discipline, and loyalty—transformed their own society into an armed camp. Agricultural labor was performed by helots; trade and crafts were left to the *perioikoi*, conquered Greeks who were free but were not citizens and had no political rights. The Spartans learned only one craft, soldiering, and were inculcated with only one conception of excellence: fighting bravely for their city.

The Spartans were trained in the arts of war and indoctrinated to serve the state. Military training for Spartan boys began at age seven; they exercised, drilled, competed, and endured physical hardships. Other Greeks admired the Spartans for their courage, obedience to law, and achievement in molding themselves according to an ideal. Spartan soldiers were better trained and disciplined and were more physically fit than other Greeks. But the Spartans were also criticized for having a limited conception of aretē.

Before Sparta converted itself into a military state, its cultural development had paralleled that of the other Greek cities. By isolating itself economically and culturally from the rest of Greece, however, Sparta became a closed provincial town and did not share in the cultural enlightenment that pervaded the Greek world. Sparta paid a heavy price for its militaristic outlook.

By 500 B.C., Sparta had emerged as the leader of the Peloponnesian League, an alliance of southern Greek city-states whose land forces were superior to those of any other combination of Greek cities. Sparta, though, was concerned with protecting its position, not with expansion. Cautious by temperament and always fearful of a helot uprising, Spartans viewed the Peloponnesian League as an instrument for defense rather than aggression.

Athens: The Rise of Democracy

The contrast between the city-states of Athens and Sparta is striking. Whereas Sparta was a land power and exclusively agricultural, Athens, located on the peninsula of Attica near the coast, possessed a great navy and was the commercial leader among the Greeks. Reluctant to send soldiers far from home, where they were needed to control the helots, Sparta's leaders pursued an isolationist foreign policy. The daring and ambitious Athenians, on the other hand, endeavored to extend their hegemony over other Greek cities. Finally, Athenians and Spartans differed in their concept of freedom. To the Spartans, freedom meant preserving the independence of their fatherland; this overriding consideration demanded order, discipline, and regimentation. The Athenians also wanted to protect their city from enemies, but, unlike the Spartans, they valued political freedom and sought the full development and enrichment of the human personality. Thus, while authoritarian Sparta became culturally sterile, Athens, with its relatively free and open society, emerged as the cultural leader of Hellenic civilization.

Greek city-states generally moved through four stages: rule by a king (monarchy), rule by landowning aristocrats (oligarchy), rule by one man who seized power (tyranny), and rule by the people (democracy). During the first stage, monarchy, the king, who derived his power from the gods, commanded the army and judged civil cases.

Oligarchy, the second stage, was instituted in Athens during the eighth century B.C. when aristocrats (*aristocracy* is a Greek word meaning "rule of the best") usurped power from hereditary kings. In the next century, aristocratic regimes experienced a social crisis. There was tension between the land-holding nobles, who dominated the government, and the newly rich and ambitious merchants, who wanted a share in governing Athens.

ZEUS, C. 460 B.C. This bronze statue was found off the Greek coast in 1926. Although his face is still stylized, his athletic body pulsates with life, capturing the essence of Zeus as the omnipotent ruler of the gods. (The Art Archive/National Archeological Museum Athens/ Gianni Dagli Orti.)

Furthermore, peasants who borrowed from the aristocracy, pledging their lands as security, lost their property and even became enslaved for non-payment of their debts. Merchants and peasants also protested that the law, which was based on oral tradition and administered exclusively by aristocrats, was unjust. The embittered and restless middle and lower classes were granted one concession. In 621 B.C., the aristocrats appointed Draco to draw up a code of law. Although Draco's code let the poor know what the law was and reduced the possibilities of aristocratic judges behaving arbitrarily, penalties were extremely severe (hence the word *draconian*), and the code provided no relief for the peasants' economic woes. As the poor began to organize and press for the cancellation of their debts and the redistribution of land, Athens was moving toward civil war.

Solon, the Reformer. In 594 B.C., Solon (c. 640–559 B.C.), a traveler and poet with a reputation for wisdom, was elected chief executive. He maintained that the wealthy landowners, through their greed, had disrupted community life and brought Athens to the brink of civil war. Solon initiated a rational approach to the problems of society by deemphasizing the gods' role in human affairs and attributing the city's ills to the specific

DETAIL OF GREEK KYLIX (CUP), C. 490–480 B.C. The frenzied dancing of the Bacchantes, worshippers of the god Dionysius, is depicted by the vase painter Macron. Maenads (mad ones) dressed in fawn skins and carrying the thrysos, a wand made of vine leaves, leap and carouse in ecstatic orgies with satyrs in worship of the god of wine and sexual liberation. (The Metropolitan Museum of Art/Art Resource, N.Y.)

behavior of individuals; he sought practical remedies for these ills; and he held that written law should be in harmony with **Dikē**, the principle of justice that underlies the human community. The concept of a just city, a unifying principle of Solon's reforms, became a formative ideal of Greek political thought. At the same time, he wanted to instill in Athenians of all classes a sense of working for the common good of the city.

Solon aimed at restoring a sick Athenian society to health by restraining the nobles and improving the lot of the poor. To achieve this goal, he canceled debts, freed Athenians enslaved for debt, and brought back to Athens those who had been sold abroad; however, he refused to confiscate and redistribute the nobles' land as the extremists demanded. He permitted all classes of free men, even the poorest, to sit in the Assembly, which elected magistrates and accepted

or rejected legislation proposed by a new Council of Four Hundred. He also opened the highest offices in the state to wealthy commoners, who had previously been excluded from these positions because they lacked noble birth. Thus, Solon undermined the traditional rights of the hereditary aristocracy and initiated the transformation of Athens from an aristocratic oligarchy into a democracy.

Solon also instituted ingenious economic reforms. Recognizing that the poor soil of Attica was not conducive to growing grain, he urged the cultivation of grapes for wine and the growing of olives, whose oil could be exported. To encourage industrial expansion, he ordered that all fathers teach their sons a trade and granted citizenship to foreign craftsmen who were willing to migrate to Athens. These measures and the fine quality of the native reddish-brown clay allowed Athens to become the leading producer and exporter of pottery. Solon's economic policies transformed Athens into a great commercial center. However, Solon's reforms did not eliminate factional disputes among the aristocratic clans or relieve much of the discontent of the poor.

Pisistratus, the Tyrant.   In 546 B.C., Pisistratus (c. 605–527 B.C.), an aristocrat, took advantage of the general instability to become a one-man ruler, driving into exile those who had opposed him. Tyranny thus replaced oligarchy. Tyranny occurred frequently in the Greek city-states. Almost always aristocrats themselves, tyrants generally posed as champions of the poor in their struggle against the aristocracy. Pisistratus sought popular support by having conduits constructed to increase the Athenian water supply; like tyrants in other city-states, he gave to peasants land confiscated from exiled aristocrats and granted state loans to small farmers.

Pisistratus' great achievement was the promotion of cultural life. He initiated grand architectural projects, encouraged sculptors and painters, arranged for public recitals of the Homeric epics, and founded festivals, which included dramatic performances. In all these ways, he made culture, formerly the province of the aristocracy, available to commoners. Pisistratus thus launched a policy that eventually led Athens to emerge as the cultural capital of the Greeks.

Cleisthenes, the Democrat.   Shortly after Pisistratus' death, a faction headed by Cleisthenes, an aristocrat sympathetic to democracy, assumed leadership. By an ingenious method of redistricting the city, Cleisthenes ended the aristocratic clans' traditional jockeying for the chief state positions, which had caused much divisiveness and bitterness in Athens. Cleisthenes replaced this practice, rooted in tradition and authority, with a new system that was rationally planned to ensure that historic allegiance to tribe or clan would be superseded by loyalty to the city as a whole.

Cleisthenes hoped to make democracy the permanent form of government for Athens. The power to govern Athens, he believed, should rest with male citizens acting as a body and not with aristocratic factions or a tyrant. To safeguard the city against tyranny, he utilized (or perhaps introduced) the practice of **ostracism.** Once a year, Athenians were given the opportunity to inscribe on a fragment of pottery (*ostracon*) the name of anyone who, they felt, endangered the state. An individual against whom six thousand votes were cast was ostracized, that is, forced to leave Athens for ten years.

Cleisthenes firmly secured democratic government in Athens. The Assembly, which Solon had opened to all male citizens, was in the process of becoming the supreme authority in the state. But the period of Athenian greatness lay in the future; the Athenians first had to fight a war of survival against the Persian empire.

ATHENIAN GREATNESS

The Persian Wars

In 499 B.C., the Ionian Greeks of Asia Minor rebelled against their Persian overlord. Sympathetic to the Ionian cause, Athens sent twenty ships to aid the revolt, an act that the Greek historian Herodotus said "was the beginning of trouble not only for Greece, but for the rest of the world as well."[9] Bent on revenge, Darius I, king of Persia, sent a small detachment to Attica. In 490 B.C., on the plains of Marathon, the citizen army of Athens defeated the Persians—for the Athenians, one of the finest moments in their history. Ten years later, Xerxes, Darius' son, organized a huge invasion force—some 250,000 men and more than 500 ships—with the aim of reducing Greece to a Persian province. Setting aside their separatist instincts, many of the city-states united to defend their independence and their liberty. Herodotus viewed the conflict as an ideological clash between Greek freedom and Asian despotism.

The Persians crossed the waters of the Hellespont (Dardanelles) and made their way into northern Greece. Herodotus describes their encounter at the mountain pass of Thermopylae with three hundred Spartans, who were true to their training and ideal of aretē and "resisted to the last with their swords if they had them, and if not, with their hands and teeth, until the Persians, coming on from the front over the ruins of the wall and closing in from behind, finally overwhelmed them."[10] Northern Greece fell to the Persians, who continued south, pillaging and burning a deserted Athens.

When it appeared that the Greeks' spirit had been broken, the Athenian statesman and general Themistocles (c. 527–460 B.C.), demonstrating in military affairs the same rationality that Cleisthenes had shown in political life, lured the Persian fleet into the narrowest entry to the Bay of Salamis. In this cramped space, the Persians were unable to deploy their more numerous ships. Excelling in ramming maneuvers and knowing what was at stake, the Athenian crews picked off the jammed Persian ships in a decisive victory. In 479 B.C., a year after the Athenian naval victory at Salamis, the Spartans defeated the Persians in the land battle of Plataea. The inventive intelligence with which the Greeks planned their military operations and a fierce desire to preserve their freedom—which, the war made them realize, was their distinguishing attribute—enabled them to defeat the greatest military power the Mediterranean world had yet seen.

The Persian Wars were decisive in the history of the West. Had the Greeks been defeated, it is very likely that their cultural and political vitality would have been aborted. The confidence and pride that came with its astonishing victory, however, propelled Athens into a golden age, which became marred by the Athenian urge for dominance in Greece.

The Persian Wars ushered in an era of Athenian imperialism, which had drastic consequences for the future. Immediately after the wars, more than 150 city-states organized a confederation, the Delian League (named after its treasury on the island of Delos), to protect themselves against a renewed confrontation with Persia. Because of its wealth, its powerful fleet, and the restless energy of its citizens, Athens assumed leadership of the Delian League. Largely thanks to the Athenian fleet, the league was able to drive both pirates and Persians from the Aegean Sea.

Although it had been conceived as a voluntary association of independent Greek states seeking protection against Persia, the league gradually came under the domination of Athens. The Athenians, seeing no contradiction between imperialism and democracy, also manipulated the league for their own economic advantage. They believed that their freedom and prosperity required subduing, exploiting, and enslaving others, and they adhered to the principle that strong states had a natural right to dominate weaker ones. They relished the empire that gave them wealth, power, and glory. Moreover, the Athenians claimed that the other city-states benefited from Athenian hegemony. Athens forbade member states to withdraw, crushed revolts, and stationed garrisons on the territory of confederate states. It used both tribute from members and the league's treasury to finance public works in Athens.

Although member states did receive protection, were not overtaxed, and enjoyed increased trade, they resented Athenian domination. As the Persian threat subsided, hatred for Athenian imperialism grew. In converting the Delian League into an instrument of Athenian imperialism, Athens may have lost an opportunity to perform a great creative act—forming a broad voluntary confederation that might have forestalled the intercity warfare that gravely weakened Hellenic civilization.

The Mature Athenian Democracy

Athenian imperialism was one consequence of the Persian Wars; another was the flowering of Athenian democracy and culture. The Athenian state was a direct democracy, in which the citizens themselves, not elected representatives, made the laws. In the Assembly, which was open to all adult male citizens and that met some forty times a year, Athenians debated and voted on key issues of state; they declared war, signed treaties, and spent public funds. All decisions were arrived at after public discussion, in which all citizens had a right to speak. It is likely that on most occasions farmers did not journey into the city to attend a meeting of the Assembly. By the middle of the fifth century B.C., the will of the people, as expressed by a majority vote in the Assembly, was supreme. Rejecting the arbitrary rule of tyrants and domination by a small circle of nobles, the Athenians conceived the idea of **isonomy**—equality of political rights for citizens of the polis, that is, the right to vote, to speak before and submit motions to the Assembly, to hold the highest public positions, and to receive equal treatment before the law.

Map 3.2 **The Aegean Basin** This map shows major battle sites. Note also the Hellespont, where Xerxes' forces crossed into Greece, and Ionia, the coast of Asia Minor, where Greek philosophy was born. (Copyright © 2013 Cengage Learning.)

The Council of Five Hundred (which had been established by Cleisthenes to replace Solon's Council of Four Hundred) managed the ports, military installations, and other state properties and prepared the agenda for the Assembly. Because its members were chosen annually by lot and could not serve more than twice in a lifetime, the Council could never supersede the Assembly. Chosen at random, its membership could not become a cabal of the most powerful and ambitious citizens. Some 350 magistrates, also chosen by lot, performed administrative tasks: collecting fines, policing the city, repairing streets, inspecting markets, and so forth. Because of the special competence that their posts required, the ten generals who led the army were, for obvious reasons, not chosen by lot but were elected annually by the Assembly.

The introduction of pay for government officials marked a great democratic advance. It meant that an average person could afford to leave his job for a year in order to serve on the Council of Five Hundred, on a commission overseeing the administration of the city, or in the law courts.

Athens has been aptly described as a government of amateurs. There were no professional civil servants, no professional soldiers and sailors, no state judges—all legal cases were decided by juries chosen by lot—and no elected lawmakers. The duties of government were performed by ordinary citizens. Such a system rested on the assumption that the average citizen was capable of participating intelligently in the affairs of state and that he would, in a spirit of civic patriotism, carry out his responsibilities to his city. In fifth-century Athens, excellence was equated with good citizenship—a concern for the good of the community that out-weighed personal aspirations. Indeed, to a surprisingly large number of Athenians, politics was an overriding concern, and they devoted considerable time and thought to civic affairs. Those who allowed private matters to take precedence over the needs of the community were denounced as useless people living purposeless lives.

Although Athens was a democracy in form, in practice aristocrats continued to dominate political life for most of the fifth century. Generals came from noble houses, as did the leading voices in the Assembly. This situation was not surprising, for aristocrats took for granted a responsibility to exercise leadership and acquired the education, particularly in public speaking and debate, needed to perform this role. The economic expansion after the Persian Wars produced a wealthy class of tradesmen, who eventually challenged aristocratic dominance in the Assembly during the last third of the fifth century B.C.

Judged by modern standards, Athenian democracy undoubtedly had its limitations and weaknesses. Modern critics point out that resident aliens were almost totally barred from citizenship and therefore from political participation. Slaves, who constituted about one-fourth of the Athenian population, enjoyed none of the freedoms that Athenians considered so precious. The Greeks regarded slavery as a necessary precondition for civilized life; for some to be free and prosperous, they believed, others had to be enslaved. The large number of slaves available for labor, they believed, permitted free citizens to devote themselves to civic affairs and to fight for the city when needed.

Slaves usually did the same work as Athenian citizens: farming, commerce, manufacturing, domestic chores. Some slaves—the three hundred Scythian archers who made up the police force and those sufficiently educated to serve the state as clerks—enjoyed a privileged position. However, slaves, including preadolescent children, who toiled in the mines suffered a grim fate. In Athens, some slaves were Greeks, but most were foreigners. Slaves were generally prisoners of war and captives of pirates. Sometimes they were foreign children sold by their parents or abandoned infants left to die, a not uncommon practice in ancient Greece and Rome. A person finding the infant might eventually sell the child into slavery.

Athenian women were another group denied legal or political rights. Most Greeks, no doubt, agreed with Aristotle, who said: "[T]he male is by nature superior, and the female inferior; and . . . the one rules and the other is ruled."[11] A girl usually was married at fourteen to a man twice her age, and the marriage was arranged by a male relative. The wedding day might be the first time that the young bride saw her future husband. Although either spouse could obtain a divorce, the children remained with the father after the marriage was dissolved. Wives did not dine with their husbands and spent much of their time in the women's quarters.

Athenian women were barred from holding public office and generally could not appear in court without a male representative. They could not act in plays, and, when attending the theater, they sat in the rear, away from the men. Greek women received no formal education, although some young women learned to read and write at home. Training in household skills was considered the only education a woman needed. Since it was believed that a woman could not act independently, she was required to have a guardian—normally her father or husband—who controlled her property and supervised her behavior. Convinced that financial dealings were too difficult for women and that they needed to be protected from strangers, men, not women, did the marketing. When a woman left the house, she was usually accompanied by a male. The Athenian wife was treated as a minor; in effect, she was her husband's ward.

Modern critics also point out the failure of Hellenic Greeks to arrive at a conception of what seventeenth- and eighteenth-century liberal thinkers were to call natural or inalienable rights and what are now generally known as human rights. The Greeks limited rights to members of a particular community; they had no awareness of the modern idea that all individuals possess as a birthright basic rights that government must respect.

Ancient critics, too, attacked Athenian democracy. Having no confidence in the ability of the common people to govern, these aristocratic critics equated democracy with mob rule. In a democracy, they said, the envious, volatile, and incompetent poor tyrannize the rich; make unwise, impetuous decisions; and are easily manipulated by clever demagogues. A political system that gives power to people of limited merit is destined to fail. The Assembly did at times make rash and foolish decisions and was swayed by the oratory of demagogues. For the most part, however, as British historian A. H. M. Jones concludes,

> *the Assembly seems to have kept its head, and very rarely to have broken its rules of procedure. . . . Moreover, the people demanded high standards of its advisors. . . . It was informed advice, and not mere eloquence, that the people expected from rising politicians, and they saw to it that they got it.*[12]

That the Athenians found democracy an indispensable form of government is proved by the paucity of revolts. In the almost two hundred years after Cleisthenes, there were only two attempts to undo the democracy, both made under the stress of the Peloponnesian War and both short-lived.

The flaws in Athenian democracy should not cause us to undervalue its extraordinary achievement. The idea that the state represents a community of free, self-governing citizens remains a crucial principle of Western civilization. Athenian democracy embodied the principle of the legal state—a government based not on force but on laws debated, devised, altered, and obeyed by free citizens.

This idea of the legal state could have arisen only in a society that was aware of and respected the rational mind. In the same way that the Greeks demythicized nature, they also removed myth from the sphere of politics. Holding that government was something that people create to satisfy human needs, the Athenians regarded their leaders neither as gods nor as priests but as men who had demonstrated a capacity for statesmanship. Athens was unique, writes Italian historian Mario Attilio Levi, for Athenians "had the audacity to maintain that human reason is itself the source of legitimacy and therefore of the right to govern and command, in a world in which the only recognized source of legitimacy was the gods."[13]

Both democratic politics and systematic political thought originated in Greece. There people first asked questions about the nature and purpose of the state, rationally analyzed political institutions, speculated about human nature and justice, and discussed the merits of various forms

ATTIC BLACK-FIGURE HYDRIA, C. 510 This hydria, or water jug, shows women drawing water from a fountainhouse. Trips to the fountainhouse provided one of the few opportunities for women to socialize outside the home. (Museum of Fine Arts, Boston/William Francis Warden Fund, 61.195.)

of government. It is to Greece that we ultimately trace the idea of democracy and all that accompanies it: citizenship, constitutions, equality before the law, government by law, reasoned debate, respect for the individual, and confidence in human intelligence.

Nevertheless, there is a fundamental difference between the Greek concept of liberty and our own. We are concerned with protecting the individual from the state, which we often see as a threat to personal freedom and a hindrance to the pursuit of our personal lives. Identifying the good of the individual with the good of the community, the Greeks were not concerned with erecting safeguards against the state; they did not view the state as an alien force to be feared or to be

Pericles on Athenian Greatness

During the Peloponnesian War, Pericles delivered a funeral oration that eloquently expressed the ideals of Athenian society. Reconstructed by Thucydides, the oration is regarded as one of the finest speeches in world history.

"Let me say that our system of government does not copy the institutions of our neighbours. It is more the case of our being a model to others, than of our imitating anyone else. Our constitution is called a democracy because power is in the hands not of a minority but of the whole people. When it is a question of settling private disputes, everyone is equal before the law; when it is a question of putting one person before another in positions of public responsibility, what counts is not membership of a particular class, but the actual ability which the man possesses. No one, so long as he has it in him to be of service to the state, is kept in political obscurity because of poverty. And, just as our political life is free and open, so is our day-to-day life in our relations with each other. We do not get into a state with our next-door neighbour if he enjoys himself in his own way, nor do we give him the kind of black looks which, though they do no real harm, still do hurt people's feelings. We are free and tolerant in our private lives; but in public affairs we keep to the law. This is because it commands our deep respect.

"We give our obedience to those whom we put in positions of authority, and we obey the laws themselves, especially those which are for the protection of the oppressed, and those unwritten laws which it is an acknowledged shame to break.

"And here is another point. When our work is over, we are in a position to enjoy all kinds of recreation for our spirits. There are various kinds of contests [in poetry, drama, music, and athletics] and sacrifices regularly throughout the year; in our own homes we find a beauty and a good taste which delight us every day and which drive away our cares. Then the greatness of our city brings it about that all the good things from all over the world flow in to us, so that to us it seems just as natural to enjoy foreign goods as our own local products. . . .

"Our love of what is beautiful does not lead to extravagance; our love of the things of the mind does not make us soft. We regard wealth as something to be properly used, rather than as something to boast about. As for poverty, no one need be ashamed to admit it: the real shame is in not taking practical measures to escape from it. Here each individual is interested not only in his own affairs but in the affairs of the state as well: even those who are mostly occupied with their own business are extremely well-informed on general politics—this is a peculiarity of ours: we do not say that a man who takes no interest in politics is a man who minds his own business; we say that he has no business here at all. We Athenians, in our own persons, take our decisions on policy or submit them to proper discussions: for we do not think that there is an incompatibility between words and deeds; the worst thing is to rush into action before the consequences have been properly debated."

Questions for Analysis

1. According to Pericles, what are the chief characteristics of a democratic society?
2. Of what was Pericles most proud regarding Athens?

Thucydides, *History of the Peloponnesian War*, trans. Rex Warner (New York: Penguin Books, 1972), 145–147.

protected against. Rather, they saw it as a moral association, a second family, which taught proper conduct and enabled them to fulfill their human potential. Given this orientation, they were not much interested in universal human rights.

Pericles: Symbol of Athenian Democracy

Pericles (c. 495–429 B.C.), a gifted statesman, orator, and military commander, was the central figure in Athenian life during the middle of the fifth century So impressive was his leadership that this period is called the Age of Pericles. During these years, Athenians achieved greatness in politics, drama, sculpture, architecture, and thought.

In the opening stage of the monumental clash with Sparta, the Peloponnesian War (431–404 B.C.), Pericles delivered an oration in honor of the Athenian war casualties (see Primary Source box). The oration, as reconstructed by Thucydides, the great Athenian historian of the fifth century B.C., contains a glowing description of the Athenian democratic ideal, which encompassed both civic and personal freedom.

Throughout the speech, Pericles contrasted the narrow Spartan concept of excellence with the Athenians' humanistic ideal of the full development of the human personality. Unlike Sparta, Athens valued both political freedom and cultural creativity; indeed, as Pericles recognized, freedom released an enormous amount of creative energy, making possible Athens's extraordinary cultural accomplishments. "Our love of what is beautiful does not lead to extravagance, our love of the things of the mind does not make us soft," continued Pericles in praise of Athenian society.[14]

THE DECLINE OF THE CITY-STATES

Although the Greeks shared a common language and culture, they remained divided politically. A determination to preserve city-state sovereignty prevented them from forming a larger political grouping, which might have contained the inter-city warfare that ultimately cost the city-state its

vitality and independence. But the creation of a Pan-Hellenic union would have required a radical transformation of the Greek character, which for hundreds of years had regarded the city-state as the only suitable political system.

The Peloponnesian War

Athenian control of the Delian League engendered fear in the Spartans and their allies in the Peloponnesian League. Sparta and the Peloponnesian states decided on war because they felt that a dynamic and imperialistic Athens threatened their independence. At stake for Athens was hegemony over the Delian League, which gave Athens political power and contributed to its economic prosperity. Neither Athens nor Sparta anticipated the catastrophic consequences that the war would have for Greek civilization.

The war began in 431 B.C. and ended in 404 B.C., with a temporary and uneasy interlude of peace from 421 to 414 B.C. Possessing superior land forces, the Peloponnesian League invaded Attica and set fire to the countryside. In 430 B.C., a plague, probably coming from Ethiopia by way of Egypt, ravaged Athens, killing about one-third of the population, including its leader, Pericles (in 429 B.C.). Because of Athenian sea power and Spartan inability to inflict a crushing defeat on Athenian ground troops, the first stage of the war ended in stalemate. In 421 B.C., the war-weary combatants concluded a peace treaty.

What led to the resumption of the war and the eventual defeat of Athens was the Athenian expedition against Sicily and its largest city, Syracuse. Athenians were intoxicated by an imperialist urge to extend the empire in the west and by prospects of riches. Swayed by speeches that stirred the emotions, the Athenian populace, believing disaster to be impossible and forsaking caution and reason, approved the Sicilian venture.

Launched with extravagant expectations, the Sicilian expedition ended in dismal failure. Athens and its allies lost fifty thousand men and two hundred ships in the venture; the expedition also cost Athens all hope of victory in the struggle with Sparta. Fearful that victory in Sicily would increase Athenian manpower and wealth, Sparta in 414 B.C. had again taken up the sword.

WRESTLERS: RELIEF FROM A STATUE BASE, ATHENIAN, LATE SIXTH CENTURY B.C. Physical fitness and athletics were highly prized by the Greeks. Poets sang the praise of Olympic champions, and sculptors captured the beauty of athletic physiques for an admiring public. (Young men wrestling, from a statue base found in the Dipylon Cemetery, Athens, c. 510 B.C. (marble) (see also 60008-9 and 60011), Greek, (6th century B.C.)/National Archaeological Museum, Athens, Greece/The Bridgeman Art Library International.)

Strengthened by financial support from Persia and by the defection of some Athenian allies, Sparta moved to end the war. Finally, with its navy decimated and its food supply dwindling, besieged Athens surrendered in 404 B.C. Sparta dissolved the Delian League, left Athens with only a handful of ships, and forced the city to pull down its long walls—ramparts designed to protect it against siege weapons. But the Spartans refused to massacre Athenian men and enslave the women and children, as some allies had urged.

The Peloponnesian War shattered the spiritual foundations of Hellenic society. During the course of the long war, men became brutalized—cities were sacked and captives murdered—selfish individualism triumphed over civic duty, moderation gave way to extremism, and politics degenerated into civil war.

The deterioration of Greek political life was exemplified by conflicts between oligarchs and democrats. Oligarchs, generally from the wealthier segments of Greek society, wanted to concentrate power in their own hands by depriving the lower classes of political rights. Democrats, generally from the poorer segment of society, sought to preserve the political rights of adult male citizens. Strife between oligarchs and democrats was quite common in the Greek city-states even before the Peloponnesian War. Both sides sought to dominate the Assembly and to manipulate

the courts; both resorted to bribery and at times even assassinated opponents. During the Peloponnesian War, in many cities, including Athens, these party conflicts erupted into savage civil war marked by fanaticism and vengeance. The moral basis of Hellenic society was wrecked. In the words of Thucydides,

> *Love of power, operating through greed and through personal ambition, was the cause of all these evils. To this must be added the violent fanaticism which came into play once the struggle had broken out. Leaders of parties in professing to serve the public interest . . . were seeking to win the prizes for themselves. In their struggle for ascendancy nothing was barred; terrible indeed were the actions to which they committed themselves, and in taking revenge they went further still. Here they were deterred neither by the claims of justice nor by the interests of the state. . . . Thus neither side had any use for conscientious motives; more interest was shown in those who could produce attractive arguments to justify some disgraceful action. As for the citizens who held moderate views, they were destroyed by both the extreme parties. . . . As the result of these revolutions, there was a general deterioration of character throughout the Greek World.*[15]

Athens shared the political problems of the Greek world during the war. Pericles had provided Athenians with effective leadership in the three decades prior to the war; when the Assembly seemed to support unwise policies, he had won it over with sound arguments. After his death in 429 B.C., the quality of leadership deteriorated. Succeeding statesmen were motivated more by personal ambition than by civic devotion; instead of soberly examining issues, they supported policies that would gain them popularity. Without Pericles' wise statesmanship, the Assembly at times acted rashly, as it did in the case of the Sicilian expedition.

Taking advantage of the decline in morale after the failure of this expedition, oligarchs gained control of Athens in 411 B.C.; a body of citizens, known as the Four Hundred, wielded power. Seeking to deprive the lower classes of political influence, the Four Hundred restricted citizenship to four thousand men. But the crews of Athenian ships, loyal to democracy, challenged the authority of the Four Hundred, who were forced to flee.

After the defeat of Athens in 404 B.C., oligarchs again gained control, this time with the support of Sparta. A ruling council of thirty men, the so-called Thirty Tyrants, held power. Led by Critias, an extreme antidemocrat, the Thirty trampled on Athenian rights, confiscating property and condemning many people to death. In the winter of 404–403 B.C., returned exiles led an uprising against the Thirty, who were unseated.

The Fourth Century

The Peloponnesian War was the great crisis of Hellenic history. The golden age of Athenian culture came to an end, and the city-states never fully recovered from their self-inflicted spiritual wounds. The civic loyalty and confidence that had marked the fifth century B.C. waned, and the fourth century was dominated by a new mentality, which the leaders of the Age of Pericles would have abhorred. A concern for private affairs superseded devotion to the general good of the polis. Increasingly, professionals, rather than ordinary citizens, administered the tasks of government, and mercenaries began to replace citizen soldiers.

The political history of the fourth century can be summed up briefly. Athens, the only state that might have united the Greek world, had lost its chance. A culturally sterile, provincial-minded, and heavy-handed Spartan government lacked the talent to govern the Greeks. In many cities, Sparta replaced democratic governments with pro-Spartan oligarchies under the supervision of a Spartan governor. But Spartan hegemony was short-lived; before long, the Greek city-states had thrown off the Spartan yoke. The quarrelsome city-states formed new systems of alliances and persisted in their ruinous conflicts. Some Greek thinkers, recognizing the futility of constant war, argued that peace should be the goal of Greek politics. However, their efforts were in vain.

In addition to wars between city-states, fourth-century Greece experienced a new outbreak of civil wars between rich and poor. Athens largely escaped these ruinous conflicts, but they engulfed many other cities. With good reason, Greek thinkers regarded social discord as the greatest of evils.

While the Greek cities battered one another in fratricidal warfare, a new power was rising in the north—Macedonia. To the Greeks, the Macedonians, a wild mountain people who spoke a Greek dialect and had acquired a sprinkling of Hellenic culture, differed little from other non-Greeks, whom they called barbarians. In 359 B.C., at the age of twenty-three, Philip II (382–336 B.C.) ascended the Macedonian throne. Having spent three years as a hostage in Thebes, Philip had learned the latest military tactics and had witnessed firsthand the weaknesses of the warring Greek states. He converted Macedonia into a first-rate military power and began a drive to become master of the Greeks.

Patient, deceitful, clever, and unscrupulous, Philip gradually extended his power over the Greek city-states. The Greeks did not correctly assess Philip's strength and were slow to organize a coalition against Macedonia, despite the efforts of Demosthenes (c. 384–322 B.C.), the Athenian orator and patriot, who urged the Greeks to unite against this threat to their freedom. In 338 B.C., at Chaeronea, Philip's forces inflicted a decisive defeat on the Greeks, and all of Greece was his. The city-states still existed, but they had

Demosthenes

Debates in the Assembly stimulated the development of oratory as an art form in Athens and other city-states. Demosthenes (384–322 B.C.), the greatest of the Greek orators, earned his reputation through disciplined effort, for he was not a naturally gifted speaker. When he first addressed the Assembly, wrote Plutarch, the second-century biographer, he was "derided for his strange and uncouth style, which was cumbered with long sentences and tortured with formal arguments to a most harsh and disagreeable excess. Besides, he had, it seems, a weakness in his voice, a perplexed and indistinct utterance and a shortness of breath, which by breaking and disjointing his sentences, much obscured the sense and meaning of what he spoke."* But the very determined Demosthenes practiced constantly until he perfected his enunciation and delivery.

Demosthenes' fame rests mainly on his Philippics—speeches delivered over a ten-year period warning Greeks of the threat posed by Philip of Macedon. He urged the city-states of Greece to unite against the common enemy and lamented the deterioration of the Greek character since the heroic struggle against Persia.

> *And we, the Greek community . . . instead of sending embassies to one another about [the danger] and expressing indignation, are in such a miserable state, so intrenched in separate towns, that to this day we can attempt nothing that interest or necessity requires; we cannot combine, or form any association for succour and alliance; we look unconcernedly on the man's growing power, . . . not caring or striving for the salvation of Greece.*†

lost their independence. The world of the small, independent, self-sufficient polis was drawing to a close, and Greek civilization was taking a different shape.

THE DILEMMA OF GREEK POLITICS

Philip's conquest of the city-states points to fundamental weaknesses of Greek politics. Despite the internal crisis and persistent warfare, the Greeks were unable to fashion any other political framework than the polis. The city-state was fast becoming an anachronism, but the Greeks were unable to see that, in a world moving toward larger states and empires, the small city-state could not compete. An unallied city-state, with its small citizen army, could not withstand the powerful military machine that Philip had created. A challenge confronted the city-states: the need to shape some form of political union, a Pan-Hellenic federation, that would end the suicidal internecine warfare, promote economic well-being, and protect the Greek world from hostile states. Because they could not respond creatively to this challenge, the city-states ultimately lost their independence to foreign conquerors.

The waning of civic responsibility among the citizens was another reason for the decline of the city-states. The vitality of the city-state depended on the willingness of its citizens to put aside private concerns for the good of the community. However, although Athens had recovered commercially from the Peloponnesian War, its citizens had suffered a permanent change in character; the abiding devotion to the polis, which had distinguished the Age of Pericles, greatly diminished during the fourth century. The factional strife, the degeneration of politics into personal ambition, the demagoguery, and the fanaticism that Thucydides had described persisted into the fourth century and were aggravated by the economic discontent of the poor. The Periclean ideal of citizenship dissipated as Athenians neglected the community to concentrate on private affairs or sought to derive personal profit

A passionate patriot, Demosthenes warned his fellow citizens that Philip, an autocratic king, wanted to conquer Athens and put an end to Athenian democracy.

There is nothing which [Philip] strives and plots against so much as our constitution, nothing in the world he is so anxious about, as its destruction. . . . First then you must assume that he is an irreconcilable enemy of our constitution and democracy; secondly, you must be convinced that all his operations and contrivances are designed for the injury of our state.[‡]

Demosthenes negotiated an alliance between Thebes and Athens, but the two were defeated by Philip at Chaeronea in 338 B.C. Demosthenes, who witnessed the battle, delivered a funeral oration for the Greek dead, but the speech is lost. After the death of Alexander the Great in 323 B.C., Demosthenes helped organize Greek resistance to Macedonian rule. The Greeks were defeated the following year, and Antipater, the Macedonian governor of Greece, ordered the execution of Demosthenes and other orators who had urged war. The aging orator and passionate patriot took poison.

Demosthenes' speeches served as a model for subsequent orators, including Cicero, Rome's greatest orator. In modern times, patriots and lovers of freedom have evoked Demosthenes' devotion to his city and its free institutions.

---

*Plutarch, *The Lives of Noble Grecians and Romans,* trans. John Dryden, rev. A. H. Clough (New York: Modern Library, n.d.), 1025.

[†]*Demosthenes' Orations,* intro. by John Warrington (London: Dent, Everyman's Library, 1954), Third Philippic, 195–196.

[‡]Ibid., Fourth Philippic, 209.

from public office. The decline in civic responsibility could be seen in the hiring of mercenaries to replace citizen soldiers and in the indifference and hesitancy with which the Athenians confronted Philip. The Greeks did not respond to the Macedonian threat as they had earlier rallied to fight off the Persian menace because the quality of citizenship had deteriorated.

Greek political life demonstrated the best and the worst features of freedom. On the one hand, as Pericles boasted, freedom encouraged active citizenship, reasoned debate, and government by law. On the other hand, as Thucydides lamented, freedom could degenerate into factionalism, demagoguery, unbridled self-interest, and civil war. Because monarchy deprives people of freedom and self-rule, the Greeks regarded monarchy as a form of government appropriate for uncivilized barbarians. Nevertheless, their political experience showed that free men in a democracy are susceptible to demagogues, will base political decisions on keyed-up emotions rather than on cool reasoning, and are capable of behaving brutally toward political opponents. Moreover, Greek democracy, which valued freedom, was unable to overcome a weakness that has afflicted despotic rulers: an incautious attitude toward power that causes the state to overreach itself. Such an attitude demonstrated a self-destructive **hubris**, excessive pride or arrogance, that Greek moralists warned against. This is how Thucydides interpreted Athens's disastrous Sicilian expedition during the Peloponnesian War. Driven by a mad passion to possess what was beyond their reach, the Athenians brought ruin to their city.

The Athenians, who saw no conflict between imperialism and democracy, considered it natural for stronger states to dominate weaker ones, an attitude that helped precipitate the destructive Peloponnesian War. A particularly egregious example of this outlook occurred during that war when Athenians decided to invade the island of Melos despite the assurances of the Melians that they represented no threat to Athens. As reported by Thucydides, the Athenian envoys told the Melians that "the strong do what they have the power to do, and the weak accept what they have to accept."[16] When the Melians resisted, the Athenians slaughtered the men, enslaved the women and children, and colonized the territory.

Greek politics also revealed both the capabilities and the limitations of reason. Originally, the polis was conceived as a divine institution in which the citizen had a religious obligation to obey the law. As the rational and secular outlook became more pervasive, the gods lost their authority. When people no longer regarded law as an expression of sacred traditions ordained by the gods but saw it as a merely human contrivance,

respect for the law diminished, weakening the foundations of the society. The results were party conflicts, politicians who scrambled for personal power, and moral uncertainty. Recognizing the danger, conservatives insisted that law must again be conceived as issuing from the gods and that the city must again treat its ancient traditions with reverence. Although the Greeks originated the lofty ideal that human beings could regulate their political life according to reason, their history, marred by intercity warfare and internal violence, demonstrates the extreme difficulties involved in creating and maintaining a rational society.

NOTES

1. James Shiel, ed., *Greek Thought and the Rise of Christianity* (New York: Barnes and Noble, 1968), 5–6.

2. Homer, *The Iliad,* trans. E. V. Rieu (Baltimore: Penguin Books, 1950), 23.

3. H. D. F. Kitto, *The Greeks* (Baltimore: Penguin Books, 1957), 60.

4. Homer, *The Iliad,* 405.

5. Werner Jaeger, *Paideia: The Ideals of Greek Culture,* trans. Gilbert Highet (New York: Oxford University Press, 1945), 1:8.

6. C. M. Bowra, *Homer* (London: Gerald Duckworth, 1972), 72.

7. Kitto, *The Greeks,* 78.

8. Mason Hammond, *The City in the Ancient World* (Cambridge, Mass.: Harvard University Press, 1972), 189.

9. Herodotus, *The Histories,* trans. Aubrey de Sélincourt (Baltimore: Penguin Books, 1954), 350.

10. Ibid., 493.

11. Aristotle, *Politics,* in *Basic Works of Aristotle,* ed. Richard McKeon (New York: Random House, 1941), 1132.

12. A. H. M. Jones, *Athenian Democracy* (Oxford: Basil Blackwell, 1969), 132–133.

13. Mario Attilio Levi, *Political Power in the Ancient World* (New York: Mentor Books, 1968), 122–123.

14. Thucydides, *History of the Peloponnesian War,* trans. Rex Warner (Baltimore: Penguin Books, 1954), 118.

15. Ibid., 210.

16. Ibid., 360.

SUGGESTED READING

Frost, Frank J., *Greek Society* (1987). Social and economic life in ancient Greece.

Hanson, Victor Davis, *A War Like No Other* (2005). A Perceptive analysis of the Peloponnesian War.

Hooper, Finley, *Greek Realities* (1978). A literate and sensitive presentation of Greek society and culture.

Kitto, H. D. F., *The Greeks* (1957). A stimulating survey of Greek life and thought.

Meier, Christian, *Athens: A Portrait of the City in Its Golden Age* (1999). Rich in details and interpretation.

———, *The Greek Discovery of Politics* (1990). Answers the question, How was it that Greek civilization, unlike all others preceding it, gave birth to democracies?

Ober, Joseph, *The Athenian Revolution* (1996). Thoughtful essays on Greek democracy and political theory.

Stockton, David, *The Classical Athenian Democracy* (1990). The evolution and nature of Greek democracy.

Go to the CourseMate website at **www.cengagebrain.com** for additional study tools and review materials—including audio and video clips—for this chapter.

Chapter 4

Greek Thought:
From Myth to Reason

Theater at Epidaurus, Greece, c. 350 B.C. (Hirmer Verlag Fotoarchiv, München.)

- **Philosophy**
- **Art**
- **Poetry and Drama**
- **History**
- **The Greek Achievement: Reason, Freedom, Humanism**

Focus Questions

1. How did the Pre-Socratic thinkers make the transition from myth to reason?

2. How did the Sophists and Socrates advance the tradition of reason and humanism?

3. Why is Plato's *Republic* considered a milestone in the emergence of political thought?

4. What do Plato and Aristotle have in common? How do they differ?

5. How did Greek drama, art, and historiography contribute to the tradition of reason and humanism?

The Greeks broke with the mythopoeic outlook of the Near East and conceived a new way of viewing nature and human society, which is the basis of the Western scientific and philosophical tradition. After an initial period of mythical thinking, by the fifth century B.C. the Greek mind had gradually applied reason to the physical world and to all human activities. This emphasis on reason marks a turning point for human civilization.

The development of rational thought in Greece was a process, a trend, not a finished achievement. The process began when some thinkers rejected mythical explanations for natural phenomena. The nonphilosophical majority never entirely eliminated the language, attitudes, and beliefs of myth from their lives and thought. For them, the world remained controlled by divine forces, which were appeased through cultic practices. Even in the mature **philosophy** of Plato and Aristotle, mythical modes of thought persisted. What is of immense historical importance, however, is not the degree to which the Greeks successfully integrated the norm of reason, but the fact that they originated this norm, defined it, and consciously applied it to their intellectual and social life.

PHILOSOPHY

The first theoretical philosophers in human history emerged in the sixth century B.C., in the Greek cities of Ionia in Asia Minor. Curious about the essential composition of nature and dissatisfied with earlier creation legends, the Ionians sought physical, rather than mythic-religious, explanations for natural occurrences. In the process, they arrived at a new concept of nature and a new method of inquiry. They maintained that nature was not manipulated by arbitrary and willful gods, nor was it governed by blind chance. The Ionians said that there is an intelligible pattern to nature; that nature contains a hidden structure—principles of order or general laws—that governs phenomena; and that these fundamental rules were ascertainable by the human mind. They implied that the origin, composition, and structure of the world can be investigated rationally and systematically. Thus, in seeking to account for rainbows, earthquakes, and eclipses, the Ionians posited entirely naturalistic explanations that relied on observation, had an awareness of cause and effect, and excluded the gods. This new outlook marks the beginning of scientific thought.

What conditions enabled the Greeks to make this breakthrough? Perhaps their familiarity with Near Eastern achievements in mathematics and science stimulated their ideas. But this influence should not be exaggerated, says Greek scholar John N. Theodorakopoulos, for Egyptians and Mesopotamians "had only mythological systems of belief and a knowledge of practical matters. They did not possess those pure and crystal-clear products of the intellect which we call science and philosophy. Nor did they have any terminology to describe them."[1] Rooted in mythological thinking, the ancient Near East experienced no eruption of theorizing about nature in pristine philosophical and scientific terms as Greece did beginning in the sixth century B.C. Perhaps the poets' conception of human behavior as subject to universal destiny was extended into the philosophers' belief that nature was governed by law. Perhaps the breakthrough was fostered by the Greeks' freedom from a priesthood and rigid religious doctrines that limit thought. Or perhaps Greek speculative thought was an offspring of the city, because if law governed human affairs, providing balance and order, should not the universe also be regulated by principles of order?

The Cosmologists: A Rational Inquiry into Nature

The first Ionian philosophers are called cosmologists because they sought to discover the underlying principles of the universe: how nature came to be the way it was. They held that some single, eternal, and imperishable substance, which underwent various modifications, gave rise to all phenomena in nature.

Ionian philosophy began with Thales (c. 624–548 B.C.) of Miletus, a city in Ionia. He was a contemporary of Solon of Athens and concerned himself with understanding the order of nature. Thales said that water was the basic element, the underlying substratum of nature, and that through some natural process—similar to the formation of ice or steam—water gave rise to everything else in the world.

Thales revolutionized thought because he omitted the gods from his account of the origins of nature and searched for a natural explanation of how all things came to be. He broke with the commonly held belief that earthquakes were caused by Poseidon, god of the sea, and offered instead a naturalistic explanation for these disturbances: that the earth floated on water and when the water experienced turbulent waves, the earth was rocked by earthquakes. Thales was the first person to predict an eclipse of the sun. To do this, he had to dismiss traditional mythical explanations and to grasp a crucial scientific principle—that heavenly objects move in regular patterns, which can be known.

Anaximander (c. 611–547 B.C.), another sixth-century Ionian, rejected Thales' theory that water was the original substance. He rejected any specific substance and suggested that an indefinite, undifferentiated substance, which he called the Boundless, was the source of all things. He believed that from this primary mass, which contained the powers of heat and cold, there gradually emerged a nucleus, the seed of the world. According to Anaximander, the cold and wet condensed to form the earth and its cloud cover, while the hot and dry formed the rings of fire that we see as the moon, the sun, and the stars. The heat from the fire in the sky dried the earth and shrank the seas. From the warm slime on earth arose life, and from the first sea creatures there evolved land animals, including human beings. Anaximander's account of the origins of the universe and nature understandably contained fantastic elements. Nevertheless, by offering a natural explanation for the origin of nature and life and by holding that nature was lawful, it surpassed the creation myths.

Like his fellow Ionians, Anaximenes, who died around 525 B.C., made the transition from myth to reason. He also maintained that a primary substance, air, underlay reality and accounted for nature's orderliness. Air that was rarefied became fire, whereas wind and clouds were formed from condensed air. If the process of condensation continued, it produced water, earth, and eventually stones. Anaximenes also rejected the old belief that a rainbow was the goddess Iris; instead, he saw it as the consequence of the sun's rays falling on dense air.

The Ionians have been called matter philosophers because they held that everything issued from a particular material substance. Other sixth-century B.C. thinkers tried a different approach. Pythagoras (c. 580–507 B.C.) and his followers, who lived in the Greek cities in southern Italy, found the nature of things not in a particular substance but in mathematical relationships. The Pythagoreans discovered that the intervals in the musical scale can be expressed mathematically. Extending this principle of structure and proportion found in sound to the universe at large, they concluded that the cosmos also contained an inherent mathematical order and harmony. Thus, the Pythagoreans shifted the emphasis from matter to form, from the world of sense perception to the logic of mathematics. The Pythagoreans were also religious mystics who believed in the immortality and transmigration of souls. Consequently, they refused to eat animal flesh, fearing that it contained former human souls.

Parmenides (c. 515–450 B.C.), a native of the Greek city of Elea in southern Italy, argued that the fundamental view of the Ionians that the universe underwent change and development over time was utterly mistaken. In developing his position, Parmenides applied to philosophical argument the **logic** used by the Pythagoreans for mathematical thinking. In putting forth the proposition that an argument must be consistent and contain no contradictions, Parmenides became the founder of formal logic.

Despite appearances, asserted Parmenides, reality—the cosmos and all that is within it—is one, eternal, and unchanging. It is made known not through the senses, which are misleading, but through the mind; not through experience, but through reason. Truth could be reached through abstract thought alone. Parmenides' concept of an unchanging reality apprehended by thought alone influenced Plato and is the foundation of **metaphysics**—the branch of philosophy that attempts to define ultimate reality, or Being.

Parmenides' thought also had religious implications. Although he did not refer to True Being as God, he did ascribe to it the attributes of oneness, transcendence, permanence, and perfection. Such a description of Being abounds with religious meaning. Particularly as developed by Plato, the quest for Being would greatly influence religious thought, including Christian theology, in the ancient world.

Democritus (c. 460–370 B.C.), from the Greek mainland, renewed the Ionians' concern with the world of matter and reaffirmed their confidence in knowledge derived from sense perception—and the senses indicated that change did occur in nature, in contrast to Parmenides' view. But Democritus also retained Parmenides' reverence for reason. His model of the universe consisted of two fundamental realities: empty space and an infinite number of atoms. Eternal, indivisible, and imperceptible, these atoms moved in the void. All things consisted of atoms, and combinations of atoms accounted for all change in nature. In a world of colliding atoms, everything behaved according to mechanical principles. (Of course, Democritus' atomic theory did not derive from any empirical evidence of atoms but was purely speculative.)

Concepts essential to scientific thought thus emerged in embryonic form with Greek philosophers: natural explanations for physical occurrences (Ionians), the mathematical order of nature (Pythagoras), logical proof (Parmenides), and the mechanical structure of the universe (Democritus). By giving to nature a rational, rather than a mythical, foundation and by holding that theories should be grounded in evidence and that one should be able to defend them logically, the early Greek philosophers pushed thought in a new direction. This new approach allowed a critical analysis of theories, whereas myths, accepted unconditionally on faith and authority, did not promote discussion and questioning. Greek thinkers established the crucial principle that a proposition is not considered true unless it can be supported by logic or empirical evidence. For the most part, the early Greek philosophers rejected the old mythical explanations of nature. Nevertheless, when they proclaimed the unity and orderliness of nature and asserted that an ultimate reality underlies the finite world, they were also expressing ideas integral to religious thought.

These early philosophers made possible theoretical thinking and the systematization of knowledge—as distinct from the mere observation and collection of data. The systematization of knowledge extended into several areas. Greek mathematicians, for example, organized

PORCH OF THE MAIDENS, ATTIC SCULPTURE FROM THE ACROPOLIS. The architect has incorporated the human form as a functional element in a rationally organized structure. The balance and harmony of the Porch of the Maidens weds humanity with art. (Vanni/Art Resource, N.Y.)

the Egyptians' practical experience with land measurements into the logical and coherent science of geometry, in which each statement followed logically from given assumptions. They established mathematics as a body of theoretical knowledge, an ordered system based on fundamental premises and necessary connections, and they developed logical procedures for arriving at mathematical proofs. Both Babylonians and Egyptians had performed fairly complex mathematical operations, but unlike the Greeks, they made no attempt to prove underlying mathematical principles—to demonstrate that certain conclusions must flow from certain hypotheses. In another area, Babylonian priests observed the heavens for religious reasons, believing that the stars revealed the wishes of the gods. The Greeks used the data collected by the Babylonians, but

not for a religious purpose; rather, they sought to discover the geometrical laws that govern the motions of heavenly bodies.

A parallel development occurred in medicine. No Near Eastern medical text explicitly attacked magical beliefs and practices. In contrast, Greek doctors, because of the philosophers' work, were able to distinguish between magic and medicine. The school of the Greek physician Hippocrates (c. 460–c. 377 B.C.), located on the island of Cos, off the Asia Minor coast, was influenced by the thought of the early Greek cosmologists. Hippocratic physicians recorded in detail their observations of ill patients, classified symptoms, and predicted the future course of the disease. They also ruled out supernatural and magical explanations and cures. The following tract from the school of Hippocrates on epilepsy, which was considered a sacred disease, illustrates the development of a scientific approach to medicine.

> *I am about to discuss the disease called "sacred." It is not, in my opinion, any more divine or sacred than any other disease, but has a natural cause, and its supposed divine origin is due to men's inexperience, and to their wonder at its peculiar character. Now . . . men continue to believe in its divine origin because they are at a loss to understand it. . . . My own view is that those who first attributed a sacred character to this malady were like the magicians, purifiers, charlatans, and quacks of our own day; men who claim great piety and superior knowledge. Being at a loss, and having no treatment which would help, they concealed and sheltered themselves behind superstition, and called this illness sacred, in order that their utter ignorance might not be manifest.*[2]

The Sophists: A Rational Investigation of Human Society

In their effort to understand the external world, the cosmologists had created the tools of reason. These early Greek thinkers were developing a new and profound awareness of the mind's capacity for theoretical thinking. And equally important, they were establishing the mind's autonomy—its ability to inquire into any subject, relying solely on its own power to think. Greek thinkers then turned away from the world of nature and attempted a rational investigation of people and society, dismissing efforts to explain the social world through inherited beliefs about the gods. The Sophists exemplified this shift in focus. They were professional teachers who wandered from city to city teaching rhetoric, grammar, poetry, gymnastics, mathematics, and music. The Sophists insisted that it was futile to speculate about the first principles of the universe, for such knowledge was beyond the grasp of the human mind. Instead, they urged that individuals improve themselves and their cities by applying reason to the tasks of citizenship and statesmanship. The Western **humanist** tradition owes much to

the Sophists who examined, at times with great insight, political and ethical concerns, cultivated the minds of their students, and invented formal secular education.

The Sophists answered a practical need in Athens, which had been transformed into a wealthy and dynamic imperial state after the Persian Wars. Because the Sophists claimed that they could teach *political* aretē—the skill to formulate the right laws and policies for cities and the art of eloquence and persuasion needed for success in public life—they were sought as tutors by politically ambitious young men, especially in Athens.

Traditionally, the Greeks had drawn a sharp distinction between Greeks, the bearers of an enlightened civilization, and uncivilized and immoderate non-Greeks, whom they called barbarians, and held that some people were slaves by nature. The dramatist Euripides expressed these sentiments: "It is natural for Hellenes to rule barbarians and not . . . for barbarians to rule Hellenes. They are a slave race, Hellenes are free."[3] Some Sophists in the fourth century B.C. arrived at a broader conception of humanity. They asserted that slavery was based on force or chance, that people were not slaves or masters by nature, and indeed that all people, Greek and non-Greek, were fundamentally alike.

The Sophists were philosophical **relativists**—that is, they held that no truth is universally valid. Protagoras, a fifth-century Sophist, said that "man is the measure of all things." By this he meant that good and evil, truth and falsehood, are matters of community and individual judgment; there are no universal standards that fit all people at all times. Human laws and ethical beliefs have evolved according to a particular community's needs; they are simply human contrivances and conventions, not objective truths or standards written into nature. While not based on moral absolutes, hopefully the city's laws derive from the judgment of wise and good men.

In applying reason critically to human affairs, the Sophists challenged the traditional religious and moral values of Athenian society. Some Sophists taught that speculation about the divine was useless. Others went further, asserting that religion was just a human invention to ensure obedience to traditions and laws. Thus, the Sophist

Critias (c. 480–403 B.C.) argued that to deter people from committing "open crimes of violence, . . . a wise and clever man invented fear (of the gods) for mortals, that there might be some means of frightening the wicked, even if they do anything or say or think it in secret. Hence he introduced the Divine (religion), saying that there is a God flourishing with immortal life, . . . who will hear everything said among mortals, and will be able to see all that is done."[4]

The Sophists also applied reason to law, with the same effect: the undermining of traditional authority. The laws of a given city, they asserted, did not derive from the gods; nor were they based on any objective, universal, and timeless standards of justice and good, for such standards did not exist. Each community determined for itself what was good or bad, just or unjust. Beginning with this premise, some Sophists simply urged that laws be changed to meet new circumstances. Some radical Sophists argued that law was merely something made by the most powerful citizens for their own benefit. (Or they said that law was a clever invention of the weak in order to check the strong, who benefited from natural advantages.) This view had dangerous implications: first, law did not need to be obeyed since it rested on no higher principle than might; and second, the strong should do what they have the power to do, and the weak must accept what they cannot resist. Both interpretations were disruptive of community life, for they stressed the selfish interests of the individual over the general welfare of the city.

Some Sophists combined this assault on law with an attack on the ancient Athenian idea of **sophrosyne**—moderation and self-discipline—because it denied human instincts. Instead of moderation, they urged that individuals should maximize pleasure and trample underfoot the traditions that restricted them from fully expressing their desires. As these radical Sophists saw it, the concept of sophrosyne was invented by the weak to enslave nobler natures.

In subjecting traditions to the critique of reason, the radical Sophists triggered an intellectual and spiritual crisis. Their doctrines encouraged loss of respect for authority, disobedience to law, neglect of civic duty, and selfish individualism. These attitudes became widespread during and after the Peloponnesian War, dangerously weakening community bonds.

Socrates: The Rational Individual

In attempting to comprehend nature, the cosmologists had discovered theoretical reason. The Sophists then applied theoretical reason to society. In the process, they created a profound problem for Athens and other city-states: the need to restore the authority of law and a respect for moral values. Conservatives argued that the only way to do so was by renewing allegiance to the sacred traditions that the Sophists had undermined.

Socrates, one of the most extraordinary figures in the history of Western civilization, took a different position. Born in Athens, probably in 469 B.C., about ten years after the Persian Wars, he was executed in 399 B.C., five years after the end of the Peloponnesian War. His life spanned the glory years of Greece, when Athenian culture and democracy were at their height, as well as the tragic years of the lengthy and shattering war with Sparta.

Both the Sophists and Socrates continued the tradition of reason initiated by the cosmologists, but unlike the cosmologists, both felt that knowledge of the individual and society was more important than knowledge of nature. For both, the old mythological traditions, which had served as a foundation for religion and morality, were no longer valid. Socrates and the Sophists endeavored to improve the individual and thought that this could be accomplished through education. Despite these similarities, Socrates' teaching marks a profound break with the Sophist movement.

Socrates attacked the Sophists' relativism, holding that people should regulate their behavior in accordance with universal values. As he saw it, the Sophists taught skills but had no insights into questions that really mattered: What is the purpose of life? What are the values by which man should live? How does man perfect his character? Here the Sophists failed, said Socrates; they taught the ambitious to succeed in politics, but persuasive oratory and clever reasoning do not instruct a man in the art of living. He felt that the Sophists had attacked the old system of beliefs but had not provided the individual with a satisfactory replacement.

Socrates' central concern was the perfection of individual human character, the achievement of moral excellence. Moral values, for Socrates, did not derive either from a transcendent God, as they did for the Hebrews, or from an inherited mythic-religious tradition. They were attained when the individual regulated his life according to objective standards arrived at through rational reflection: that is, when reason became the formative, guiding, and ruling agency of the soul. For Socrates, true education meant the shaping of character according to values discovered through the active use of reason.

Socrates wanted to subject all human beliefs and behavior to the scrutiny of reason and in this way remove ethics from the realm of authority, tradition, dogma, superstition, and myth. He believed that reason was the only proper guide to the most crucial problem of human existence: the question of good and evil. Socrates taught that rational inquiry—a questioning mind—was a priceless tool, allowing one to test opinions, weigh the merit of ideas, and alter beliefs on the basis of knowledge. To Socrates, when people engaged in critical self-examination and strove tirelessly to perfect their nature, they liberated themselves from prevailing opinions and conventions and based their conduct on convictions that they could rationally defend. Socrates believed that people with questioning minds could not be swayed by sophistic eloquence or delude themselves into thinking that they knew something when they really did not.

Socrates' fundamental premise was that wrong thinking resulted in wrongdoing and, conversely, that knowledge of what is right gave one the strength of will to do what is right. Critics, including religious thinkers, have castigated this assumption as naïve, arguing that Socrates credited others with his own extraordinary inner strength and underestimated the immense power of instinct and passions, which drive people, even those who know better, to do what is wrong.

Dialectics. In urging Athenians to think rationally about the problems of human existence, Socrates offered no systematic ethical theory, no list of ethical precepts. What he did supply was a method of inquiry called **dialectics**, or logical discussion. As Socrates used it, a dialectical exchange between individuals (or with oneself), a *dialogue*, was the essential source of knowledge. It forced people out of their apathy and smugness and

made them aware of their ignorance. It compelled them to examine their thoughts critically; confront illogical, inconsistent, dogmatic, and imprecise assertions; and express their ideas in clearly defined terms.

Dialectics affirmed that the acquisition of knowledge was a creative act. The human mind could not be coerced into knowing; it was not a passive vessel into which a teacher poured knowledge. The dialogue compelled the individual to play an active role in acquiring ideas and values by which to live. In a dialogue, individuals became thinking participants in a quest for knowledge. Through relentless cross-examination, Socrates induced his partner in discourse to explain and justify his opinions rationally, for only thus did knowledge become a part of one's being.

Dialogue implied that reason was meant to be used in relations between human beings and that they could learn from each other, help each other, teach each other, and improve each other. It implied further that the human mind could and should make rational choices. To deal rationally with oneself and with others is the distinctive mark of being human. Through the dialectical method, people could make ethical choices, impose rules on themselves, and give form to their existence.

For Socrates, the highest form of excellence was taking control of one's life and shaping it according to ethical values reached through reflection. The good life, the moral life, is attained by the exercise of reason and by the development of intelligence—this precept is the essence of Socratic teaching. Socrates made the individual the center of the universe, reason central to the individual, and moral worth the central aim of human life. In Socrates, Greek humanism found its highest expression.

Condemned to Death. Socrates devoted much of his life to what he believed was his mission: pricking the conscience of complacent Athenians and persuading them to think critically about how they lived their lives. "No greater good can happen to a man than to discuss human excellence every day,"[5] he said. Always self-controlled and never raising his voice in anger, Socrates engaged any willing Athenian in conversation about his values. Unlike the Sophists, who were paid

THE PARTHENON, ATHENS, 447–432 B.C. A masterpiece of the Doric style, the great temple dedicated to Athena Parthenos (the Maiden), the patron goddess of the city, was constructed through the efforts of Pericles. Its cult statue and the sculptural reliefs under its roofline were designed by the outstanding sculptor of the age, Phidias. In post-Hellenistic times, it served as a Christian church and then as a mosque, until it was destroyed in 1687. Between 1801 and 1812, the marble reliefs were removed by the Englishman Lord Elgin and now reside in the British Museum, in London. (Hirmer Verlag Fotoarchiv, München.)

professional teachers, Socrates never accepted a fee for his instruction. Through probing questions, he tried to stir people out of their complacency and make them realize how directionless and purposeless their lives were.

For many years, Socrates challenged Athenians without suffering harm, for Athens was generally distinguished by its freedom of speech and thought. In the uncertain times during and immediately after the Peloponnesian War, however,

PHILOSOPHER (STATUETTE), C. 280 B.C. Greek artists were the first to excel in realistic portraiture. The philosopher is neither a divinely inspired seer nor a divine king, but a person in quest of knowledge.

(Image copyright © The Metropolitan Museum of Art/Art Resource, N.Y.)

Socrates made enemies. Several of the young men close to him were antidemocrats still mistrusted by some as a threat to the recently restored democracy. When Socrates was seventy, he was accused of corrupting the youth of the city and of not believing in the city's gods but in other, new divinities. Underlying these accusations was the fear that Socrates was a troublemaker, a subversive, a Sophist who threatened the state by subjecting its ancient and sacred values to the critique of thought.

Socrates denied the charges and conducted himself with great dignity at his trial, refusing to grovel and beg forgiveness. Instead, he defined his creed:

> *If you think that a man of any worth at all ought to . . . think of anything but whether he is acting justly or unjustly, and as a good or a bad man would act, you are mistaken. . . . If you were therefore to say to me, "Socrates, . . . we will let you go, but on the condition that you give up this investigation of yours, and philosophy. If you are found following these pursuits again you shall die." I say, if you offered to let me go on these terms, I should reply: . . . As long as I have breath and strength I will not give up philosophy and exhorting you and declaring the truth to every one of you whom I meet, saying, as I am accustomed, "My good friend, you are a citizen of Athens. . . . Are you not ashamed of caring so much for making of money and for fame and prestige, when you neither think nor care about wisdom and truth and the improvement of your soul?"*[6]

Convicted by an Athenian court, Socrates was ordered to drink poison. Had he attempted to appease the jurors, he probably would have been given a light punishment, but he would not disobey the commands of his conscience and alter his principles even under threat of death. Socrates' friends wanted to arrange his escape from prison, but he refused, for this would mean violating the city's laws—an act he considered unconscionable.

Socrates did not write down his philosophy and beliefs. We are able to construct a coherent account of his life and ideals largely through the works of his most important disciple, Plato.

Plato: The Rational Society

Plato (c. 429–347 B.C.) used his master's teachings to create a comprehensive system of philosophy, which embraced both the world of nature and the social world. But Plato had a more ambitious goal than Socrates' moral reformation of the individual. He tried to arrange political life according to rational rules and held that Socrates' quest for personal morality could not succeed unless the community was also transformed on the basis of reason. In effect, Plato wanted to establish standards of thought and behavior for a city torn by moral and intellectual uncertainty. Many of the problems discussed by Western philosophers for the past two millennia were first raised by Plato. We focus on two of his principal concerns, the theory of Ideas and the theory of the just state.

Theory of Ideas.   Socrates had taught that universal standards of right and justice exist and are arrived at through thought. Building on the insights of his teacher Socrates and of Parmenides, who said that reality is known only through the mind, Plato postulated the existence of a higher world of reality, independent of the world of things that we experience every day. This higher reality, he said, is the realm of Ideas, or Forms—unchanging, eternal, absolute, and universal standards of beauty, goodness, justice, and truth. To live in accordance with these standards constitutes the good life; to know these Forms is to grasp ultimate truth.

Truth resides in this world of Forms and not in the world made known through the senses. For example, a person can never draw a perfect square, but the properties of a perfect square exist in the world of Forms. Also, a sculptor observes many bodies, and they all possess some flaw; in his mind's eye, he tries to penetrate the world of Ideas and to reproduce with art a perfect body. Again, the ordinary person only forms an opinion of what beauty is from observing beautiful things; the philosopher, aspiring to true knowledge, goes beyond what he sees and tries to grasp with his mind the Idea of beauty. Similarly, the ordinary individual has only a superficial understanding of justice or goodness; a true conception of justice or goodness is available only to the philosopher, whose mind can leap from worldly particulars to an ideal world beyond space and time.

Plato saw the world of phenomena as unstable, transitory, and imperfect, whereas his transcendent realm of Ideas was eternal and universally valid. For him, true wisdom was to be obtained through knowledge of the Ideas, not the imperfect reflections of the Ideas perceived with the senses.

A champion of reason, Plato aspired to study human life and arrange it according to universally valid standards. In contrast to Sophist relativism, he maintained that objective and eternal standards do exist. Although Plato advocated the life of reason and wanted to organize society according to rational rules, his writing also reveals a religious-mystical side. At times, Plato seems like a mystic seeking to escape from this world into a higher reality, a realm that is without earth's evil and injustice.

Because Platonism is a two-world philosophy, which believes in a higher world as the source of values and in the soul's immortality, it has had an important effect on religious thought. Christian (as well as Jewish and Muslim) thinkers could harmonize Plato's stress on a higher nonmaterial reality and an immortal soul with their faith. In subsequent chapters, we examine the influence of Platonic otherworldliness on later philosopher-mystics and Christian thinkers.

The Just State.   In adapting the rational legacy of Greek philosophy to politics, Plato constructed a comprehensive political theory. What the Greeks had achieved in practice—the movement away from mythic and theocratic politics—Plato accomplished on the level of thought: the fashioning of a rational model of the state.

Like Socrates, Plato attempted to resolve the problem caused by the radical Sophists: the undermining of traditional values. Socrates tried to dispel this spiritual crisis through a moral transformation of the individual, whereas Plato wanted the entire community to conform to rational principles. Plato said that if human beings are to live an ethical life, they must do so as citizens of a just and rational state. In an unjust state, people cannot achieve Socratic wisdom, for their souls will mirror the state's wickedness.

Plato had experienced the ruinous Peloponnesian War and the accompanying political turmoil. He saw Athens undergo one political crisis after another; most shocking of all, he had witnessed Socrates' trial and execution. Disillusioned by the corruption of Athenian morality and politics, Plato refused to participate in political life. He came to believe that under the Athenian constitution neither the morality of the individual Athenian nor the good of the state could be enhanced and that Athens required moral and political reform founded on Socrates' philosophy. Like Socrates, and in contrast to the Sophists' relativism, Plato sought permanent truth and moral certainty.

In his great dialogue, *The Republic*, Plato devised an ideal state based on standards that would rescue his native Athens from the evils that had befallen it. *The Republic* attempted to analyze society rationally and to reshape the state so that individuals could fulfill the best within themselves and attain the Socratic goal of moral excellence. For Plato, the just state could not be founded on tradition (because inherited attitudes did not derive from rational standards) or on the doctrine of might being right (a principle taught by radical Sophists and practiced by Athenian statesmen). A just state, for Plato, conformed to universally valid principles and aimed at the moral improvement of its citizens, not at increasing its power and material possessions. Such a state required leaders distinguished by their wisdom and virtue, rather than by sophistic cleverness and eloquence.

Fundamental to Plato's political theory as formulated in *The Republic* was his criticism of Athenian democracy. An aristocrat by birth and temperament, Plato believed that it was foolish to expect the common man to think intelligently about foreign policy, economics, or other vital matters of state. Yet the common man was permitted to speak in the Assembly, to vote, and to be selected, by lot, for executive office. A second weakness of democracy was that leaders were chosen and followed for nonessential reasons, such as persuasive speech, good looks, wealth, and family background.

A third danger of democracy was that it could degenerate into anarchy, said Plato. Intoxicated by liberty, the citizens of a democracy could lose all sense of balance, self-discipline, and respect for law.

> *The citizens become so sensitive that they resent the slightest application of control as intolerable tyranny, and in their resolve to have no master they end up by disregarding even the law, written or unwritten.*[7]

As liberty leads to license, Plato continued, the democratic society will deteriorate morally.

> *The parent falls into the habit of behaving like the child, and the child like the parent: the father is afraid of his sons, and they show no fear or respect for their parents, in order to assert their freedom. . . . To descend to smaller matters, the schoolmaster timidly flatters his pupils, and the pupils make light of their masters. . . . Generally speaking, the young . . . argue with . . . [their elders] and will not do as they are told; while the old, anxious not to be thought disagreeable tyrants, imitate the young and condescend to enter into their jokes and amusements.*[8]

As the democratic city falls into disorder, a fourth weakness of democracy will become evident. A demagogue—often a wealthy, handsome war hero of noble birth with an ability to stir the multitude with words—will be able to gain power by promising to plunder the rich to benefit the poor. Increasingly, the tyrant throws off all constraints and uses his authority to satisfy his desire for power and possessions. To retain his hold over the state, the tyrant

> *begins by stirring up one war after another, in order that the people may feel their need of a leader, and also be so impoverished by taxation that they will be forced to think of nothing but winning their daily bread, instead of plotting against him.*[9]

Because of these inherent weaknesses of democracy, Plato insisted that Athens could not be saved by more doses of liberty. He believed that Athens would be governed properly only when the wisest people, the philosophers, attained power.

> *Unless either philosophers become kings in their countries or those who are now called kings and rulers come to be sufficiently inspired with a genuine desire for wisdom; unless, that is to say, political power and philosophy meet together . . . there can be no rest from troubles . . . for states, nor yet, as I believe, for all mankind.*[10]

Plato rejected the fundamental principle of Athenian democracy: that the average person is capable of participating sensibly in public affairs. People would not entrust the care of a sick person to just anyone, said Plato, nor would they allow a novice to guide a ship during a storm. Yet in a democracy, amateurs were permitted to run the government and to supervise the education of the young. No wonder Athenian society was disintegrating. Plato felt that these duties should be performed only by the best people in the city, philosophers, who would approach human problems with reason and wisdom derived from knowledge of the world of unchanging and perfect Ideas. Only these possessors of truth would be competent to rule, said Plato. Whereas Socrates believed that all people could base their actions on reason and acquire virtue, Plato maintained that only a few were capable of philosophical wisdom and that these few were the state's natural rulers.

The organization of the state, as formulated in *The Republic*, corresponded to Plato's conception of the individual soul, of human nature. Plato held that the soul had three major capacities: reason (the pursuit of knowledge), spiritedness (self-assertion, courage, ambition), and desire (the "savage many-headed monster" that relishes food, sex, and possessions). In the well-governed soul, spiritedness and desire are guided by reason and knowledge—standards derived from the world of Ideas.

Plato divided people into three groups: those who demonstrated philosophical ability should be rulers; those whose natural bent revealed exceptional courage should be soldiers; and those driven by desire, the great masses, should be producers (tradespeople, artisans, or farmers). In what was a radical departure from the general attitudes of the times, Plato held that men and women should receive the same education and have equal access to all occupations and public positions, including philosopher-ruler.

Plato felt that the entire community must recognize the primacy of the intellect and sought to create a harmonious state in which each individual performed what he or she was best qualified to do and preferred to do. This would be a just state, said Plato, for it would recognize human inequalities and diversities and make the best possible use of them for the entire community. Clearly,

this conception of justice was Plato's response to the radical Sophists, who taught that justice consisted of the right of the strong to rule in their own interest or that justice was doing whatever one desired.

In *The Republic*, philosophers were selected by a rigorous system of education open to all children. Those not demonstrating sufficient intelligence or strength of character were to be weeded out to become workers or warriors, depending on their natural aptitudes. After many years of education and practical military and administrative experience, the philosophers were to be entrusted with political power. If they had been properly educated, the philosopher-rulers would not seek personal wealth or personal power; their only concerns would be pursuing justice and serving the community. To prevent the philosopher-rulers from pursuing their own interests rather than the good of the community, they would not be permitted to own property or to have families. Since the children they sired would come from a community of wives, no one would know which child was his.

The philosophers were to be absolute rulers. Although the people would lose their right to participate in political decisions, they would gain a well-governed state, whose leaders, distinguished by their wisdom, integrity, and sense of responsibility, would seek only the common good. Only thus could the individual and the community achieve well-being.

Plato repudiated the fundamental principles of a free community: the right to participate in government, equality before the law, and checks on leaders' power. Even freedom of thought was denied the great mass of people in Plato's state. Philosopher-rulers would search for truth, but the people were to be told clever stories—"noble lies," Plato called them—to keep them obedient. However, the philosopher-rulers, said Plato, would not be seekers of power or wealth. It would not be in their character as wise and virtuous people, the best products of polis education, to behave like ruthless tyrants.

The purpose of *The Republic* was to warn Athenians that without respect for law, wise leadership, and proper education for the young, their city would continue to degenerate. Plato wanted to rescue the city-state from disintegration by re-creating the community spirit that had vitalized the polis—and he wanted to re-create it not on the basis of mere tradition but on a higher level, with philosophical knowledge. The social and political institutions of Athens, Plato thought, must be reshaped according to permanent and unalterable ideals of truth and justice, and this could be done only when power and wisdom were joined. He aimed to fashion a just individual and a just state by creating conditions that permitted reason to prevail over the appetites, self-interest, and class and party loyalties.

Aristotle: A Synthesis of Greek Thought

Aristotle (384–322 B.C.) stands at the apex of Greek thought because he achieved a creative synthesis of the knowledge and theories of earlier thinkers. Aristotle studied at Plato's Academy for twenty years. Later, he became tutor to young Alexander the Great, the son of Philip of Macedon. Returning to Athens after Alexander had inherited his father's throne, Aristotle founded a school, the Lyceum.

The range of Aristotle's interests and intellect is extraordinary. He was the leading expert of his time in every field of knowledge, with the possible exception of mathematics. Even a partial listing of his works shows the universal character of his mind and his all-consuming passion to understand the worlds of nature and of humankind: *Logic, Physics, On the Heavens, On the Soul, On the Parts of Animals, Metaphysics, Nicomachean Ethics, Politics, Rhetoric,* and *Poetics.*

Aristotle undertook the monumental task of organizing and systematizing the thought of the Pre-Socratics, Socrates, and Plato. He shared with the natural philosophers a desire to understand the physical universe; he shared with Socrates and Plato the conviction that reason was a person's highest faculty and that the polis was the primary formative institution of Greek life. Out of the myriad of Aristotle's achievements, we discuss only three: his critique of Plato's theory of Ideas, his ethical thought, and his political thought.

Critique of Plato's Theory of Ideas. Like Democritus before him, Aristotle renewed confidence in **sense perception,** for which Plato had little respect; he wanted to swing the pendulum back from Plato's higher world to the material world. Possessing a scientist's curiosity to understand the facts of nature, Aristotle appreciated the world of phenomena, of concrete things. He respected knowledge obtained through the senses, as the following selection from his observations of a hen's embryo shows:

> *With the common hen after three days and three nights there is the first indication of the embryo. . . . Meanwhile the yolk comes into being . . . and, the heart appears, like a speck of blood, in the white of the egg. This point beats and moves as though endowed with life.*[11]

Aristotle retained Plato's stress on universal principles, but he wanted these principles to derive from human experience with the material world. To the practical and empirically minded Aristotle, the Platonic notion of an independent and separate world of Forms beyond space and time seemed contrary to common sense. To comprehend reality, said Aristotle, one should not escape into another world. For him, Plato's two-world philosophy suffered from too much mystery, mysticism, and poetic fancy; moreover, Plato undervalued the world of facts and objects revealed through sight, hearing, and touch, a world that was important to Aristotle. Like Plato, Aristotle desired to comprehend the essence of things and held that understanding universal principles is the ultimate aim of knowledge. But unlike Plato, he did not turn away from the world of things to obtain such knowledge.

For Aristotle, the Forms were not located in a higher world outside and beyond phenomena but existed in things themselves. He said that through human experience with such things as men, horses, and white objects, the essence of man, horse, and whiteness can be discovered through reason; the Form of Man, the Form of Horse, and the Form of Whiteness can be determined. These universals, which apply to all men, all horses, and all white things, were for both Aristotle and Plato the true objects of knowledge. For Plato, these Forms existed independently of particular objects; the Forms for men or horses or whiteness or triangles or temples existed, whether or not representations of these Ideas in the form of material objects were made known to the senses. For Aristotle, however, universal Ideas could not be determined without examination of particular things. Whereas Plato's use of reason tended to stress otherworldliness, Aristotle tried to bring philosophy back to earth.

By holding that certainty in knowledge comes from reason alone and not from the senses, Plato was predisposed toward mathematics and metaphysics—pure thought, which transcends the world of change and material objects. By stressing the importance of knowledge acquired through the rational examination of sense experience, Aristotle favored the development of empirical sciences—physics, biology, zoology, botany, and other disciplines based on the observation and investigation of nature and the recording of data. Aristotle maintained that theory must not conflict with facts and must make them more intelligible and that it was the task of science to arrange facts into a system of knowledge.

Ethical Thought. Like Socrates and Plato, Aristotle believed that a knowledge of **ethics** was possible and that it must be based on reason, for this is what distinguishes human beings from other forms of life. For him, ethical thought derived from a realistic appraisal of human nature and a commonsense attitude toward life. In *Nicomachean Ethics*, he offered this appraisal, as well as a practical guide to proper conduct. The good life, for Aristotle, was the examined life; it meant making intelligent decisions when confronted with specific problems. Individuals could achieve happiness when they exercised the distinctively human trait of reasoning, when they applied their knowledge relevantly to life, and when their behavior was governed by intelligence and not by whim, tradition, or authority.

Aristotle recognized that people are not entirely rational, that the human personality reveals a passionate element, which can never be eradicated or ignored. Aristotle held that surrendering completely to desire meant descending to the level of beasts, but that denying the passions and living as an ascetic was a foolish and unreasonable rejection of human nature. He maintained that by proper training people could learn to regulate their desires. They could achieve moral well-being, or virtue, when they avoided extremes of behavior and rationally chose the way of moderation, which

he defined as the mean between two extremes. For example, in one extreme, some people "become angry at the wrong things, more than is right, and longer, and cannot be appeased until they inflict vengeance or punishment." In the other extreme, foolish and slavish people endure every insult without defending themselves. Between these extremes is "the man who is angry at the right thing and with the right people, and, further as he ought, when he ought, and as long as he ought. . . . The good-tempered man tends to be unperturbed and not to be led by passion."[12] "Nothing in excess" is the key to Aristotle's ethics.

Aristotle believed that the contemplative life of the philosopher would yield perfect happiness. The pursuit of philosophical wisdom and beauty, he stated, offered "pleasures marvelous for their purity and their enduringness."[13] But Aristotle did not demand more from an individual than human nature would allow. He did not set impossible standards for behavior, recognizing that all persons cannot pursue the life of contemplation, for some lack sufficient leisure or intelligence. However, by applying reason to human affairs, all individuals could experience a good life.

Political Thought. Aristotle's *Politics* complements his *Ethics*. To live the good life, he said, a person must do so as a member of a political community. Only the polis would provide people with an opportunity to lead a rational and moral existence, that is, to fulfill their human potential. With this assertion, Aristotle demonstrated a typically Greek attitude. At the very moment when his pupil Alexander the Great was constructing a world-state that unified Greece and Persia, Aristotle defended the traditional system of independent city-states. Indeed, his *Politics* summed up the polis-centered orientation of Hellenic civilization.

Also in typically Greek fashion, Aristotle did not want women to participate in the political life of the city. Unlike Plato, who, in *The Republic*, gave women an equal opportunity with men to become philosopher-rulers, Aristotle, in his *Politics*, put women in an inferior category and maintained that the free male should rule over women. Though Aristotle taught that all human beings share in a rational soul, he felt that women, along with children and slaves, shared in it to a lesser degree.

Although the parts of the soul are present in all of them, they are present in different degrees. For the slave has no deliberative faculty at all; the woman has, but it is without authority, and the child has, but it is immature.... Clearly, then, moral virtue belongs to all of them; but the temperance of a man and of a woman, or the courage and justice of a man and of a woman, are not, as Socrates maintained, the same; the courage of a man is shown in commanding, of a woman in obeying.... All classes must be deemed to have their special attributes, as the poet says of women, "Silence is a woman's glory," but this is not equally the glory of man.[14]

Like Plato, Aristotle presumed that political life could be rationally understood and intelligently directed. In *Politics,* as in *Ethics,* he adopted a commonsense, practical attitude. He did not aim at utopia but wanted to find the most effective form of government for most men in normal circumstances. Exemplifying the polis outlook, Aristotle held that enhancing the good of the community is nobler and more virtuous than doing good for oneself, however worthy the act.

Aristotle emphasized the importance of the rule of law. He placed his trust in law rather than in individuals, for they are subject to unruly passions. Aristotle recognized that at times laws should be altered, but he recommended great caution; otherwise, people would lose respect for law and legal procedure.

For the law has no power to command obedience except that of habit, which can only be given by time, so that a readiness to change from old to new laws enfeebles the power of the law.[15]

Tyranny and revolution, Aristotle said, can threaten the rule of law and the well-being of the citizen. To prevent revolution, the state must maintain

the spirit of obedience to law, more especially in small matters; for transgression creeps in unperceived and at last ruins the state. [This cannot be done] unless the young are trained by habit and education in the spirit of the

constitution. [To live as one pleases] is contradictory to the true interests of the state....
Men should not think it slavery to live according to the rule of the constitution, for it is their salvation.[16]

Aristotle held "that the best political community is formed by citizens of the middle class [those with a moderate amount of property], and that those states are likely to be well-administered in which the middle class is large and stronger if possible than the other classes [the wealthy and the poor]." Both the rich, who excel in "beauty, strength, birth, [and] wealth," and the poor, who are "very weak or very much disgraced, [find it] difficult to follow rational principles. Of these two the one sort grow into violence and great criminals, the other into rogues and petty rascals." The rich are unwilling "to submit to authority . . . for when they are boys, by reason of the luxury in which they are brought up, they never learn even at school, the habit of obedience." Consequently, the wealthy "can only rule despotically." On the other hand, the poor "are too degraded to command and must be ruled like slaves."[17] Middle-class citizens are less afflicted by envy than the poor and are more likely than the rich to view their fellow citizens as equals.

ART

The classical age of Greek art spans the years from the end of the Persian Wars (479 B.C.) to the death of Alexander the Great (323 B.C.). During this period, standards were established that would dominate Western art until the emergence of modern art in the late nineteenth century.

Greek art coincided with Greek achievement in all other areas. Like Greek philosophy and politics, it too applied reason to human experience and made the transition from a mythopoeic-religious worldview to a world perceived as orderly and rational. It gradually transformed the supernatural religious themes with which it was at first preoccupied into secular human themes. Classical art was representational—that is, it strove to imitate reality, to represent the objective world realistically, as it appeared to the human eye.

Artists carefully observed nature and human beings and sought to achieve an exact knowledge of human anatomy; they tried to portray accurately the body at rest and in motion. They knew when muscles should be taut or relaxed, one hip lower than the other, the torso and neck slightly twisted—in other words, they succeeded in transforming marble or bronze into a human likeness that seemed alive. In addition to being realistic and naturalistic, Greek art was also idealistic, aspiring to a finer, more perfect representation of what was seen, depicting the essence and form of a thing more truly than it actually appeared. Thus, a Greek statue resembled no specific individual but revealed a flawless human form, without wrinkles, warts, scars, or other imperfections.

In achieving an accurate representation of objects and in holding that there were rules of beauty that the mind could discover, the Greek artist employed an approach consistent with the new scientific outlook. The Greek temple, for example, is an organized unity obeying nature's laws of equilibrium and harmony; classical sculpture captures the basic laws that govern life in motion. Such art, based on reason, which draws the mind's attention to the clear outlines of the outer world, also draws attention to the mind itself, making human beings the center of an intelligible world and the masters of their own persons.

Greek artists, just like Greek philosophers, proclaimed the importance and creative capacity of the individual. They exemplified the humanist spirit that characterized all aspects of Greek culture. Classical art placed people in their natural environment, made the human form the focal point of attention, and exalted the nobility, dignity, self-assurance, and beauty of the human being.

POETRY AND DRAMA

Through their awareness of human personality, poets and dramatists, like philosophers and artists, gave expression to the rise of the individual. One of the earliest and best of the Greek poets

was Sappho, a woman who lived around 600 B.C. on the island of Lesbos. Sappho established a school to teach music and singing to well-to-do girls and to prepare them for marriage. With great tenderness, Sappho wrote poems of friendship and love: "Some say the fairest thing on earth is a troop of horsemen, others a band of foot-soldiers, others a squadron of ships. But I say the fairest thing is the beloved."[18] And of her daughter Cleïs, she wrote:

> I have a child; so fair
> As golden flowers is she,
> My Cleïs, all my care.
> I'd not give her away
> For Lydia's * wide sway
> Nor lands men long to see.[19]

Sappho's love poetry, addressed also to women, indicates that she was bisexual. This form of sexual behavior was tolerated in ancient Greece, says classicist Lyn Hatherly Wilson, "because it was not procreative, because it did not alter a woman's virginal status, or affect her entry into marriage and male/female relations, except in ways that were considered positive."[20] Sappho was the most prominent female poet in the ancient world. She was depicted on coins and in art, and Plato praised the beauty of her lyric poetry. Sometimes, however, she was treated in an uncomplimentary way by comic playwrights who thought it inappropriate for a woman to write poetry. Her influence endured for centuries: the Roman poets Catullus, Horace, and Ovid alluded to her.

Pindar (c. 518–438 B.C.) was another Greek lyric poet. In his poem of praise for a victorious athlete, Pindar expressed the aristocratic view of excellence. Although life is essentially tragic—triumphs are short-lived, misfortunes are many, and ultimately death overtakes all—man must still demonstrate his worth by striving for excellence.

> He who wins of a sudden, some noble prize
> In the rich years of youth
> Is raised high with hope; his manhood takes
> wings;

*Ancient country in Asia Minor.

He has in his heart what is better than wealth
But brief is the season of man's delight.
Soon it falls to the ground;
Some dire decision uproots it.
—Thing of a day! such is man: a shadow in
*   a dream.*
Yet when god-given splendour visits him
A bright radiance plays over him, and how
*   sweet is life![21]*

The high point of Greek poetry is drama, an art form that originated in Greece. The Greek dramatist portrayed the sufferings, weaknesses, and triumphs of individuals. Just as a Greek sculptor shaped a clear visual image of the human form, so also a Greek dramatist brought the inner life of human beings, their fears and hopes, into sharp focus and tried to find the deeper meaning of human experience. Thus, both art and drama evidenced the growing self-awareness of the individual.

Drama originated in the religious festivals honoring Dionysus, the god of wine and agricultural fertility. A profound innovation in these sacred performances, which included choral songs and dances, occurred in the last part of the sixth century B.C. when Thespis, the first actor known to history, stepped out of the chorus and engaged it in dialogue. By separating himself from the choral group, Thespis demonstrated a new awareness of the individual.

With only one actor and a chorus, however, the possibilities for dramatic action and human conflicts were limited. Then Aeschylus introduced a second actor in his dramas, and Sophocles a third. Dialogue between individuals thus became possible. The Greek actors wore masks, and by changing them, each actor could play several roles in the same performance. This flexibility allowed the dramatists to depict the clash and interplay of human wills and passions on a greater scale. By the middle of the fifth century B.C., tragedies were performed regularly as civic festivals. The audience sat on wooden bleachers in an open-air, hillside theater (*theatron*). The acoustics of these stone theaters were so superb that a clear voice projected from the front could be heard, without amplification, in the last row. In the staging of these tragedies, the all-male chorus generally danced and sang in a circular area called the orchestra ("dancing place"), which encircled an altar. Their costumes consisted of goat skins (only later did the costumes become elaborate), larger-than-life masks, and elevated shoes.

Because of the grandeur of the dramatists' themes, the eminence of their heroes, and the loftiness of their language, Greek spectators felt intensely involved in the lives portrayed. What they were witnessing in a **tragedy** went beyond anything in their ordinary lives, and they experienced the full range of human emotions.

A development parallel to Socratic dialectics—dialogue between thinking individuals—occurred in Greek drama. Through the technique of dialogue, early dramatists first pitted human beings against the gods and destiny. Later, by placing characters in conflict with one another, dramatists arrived at the idea of individuals as active subjects responsible for their behavior and decisions, which were based on their own feelings and thoughts. Greek tragedy evolved as a continuous striving toward humanization and individualization.

Like the natural philosophers, Greek dramatists saw an inner logic in the universe and called it Fate or Destiny. When people were stubborn, narrow-minded, arrogant, and immoderate, when their "word and deed" showed no respect for justice, when they dishonored the gods, they were punished. The order in the universe required it, said Sophocles.[22]

In being free to make decisions, the dramatist says, individuals have the potential for greatness, but in choosing wrongly, unintelligently, they bring disaster on themselves and others. Also like philosophy, Greek tragedy entailed rational reflection. Tragic heroes were not passive victims of fate. They were thinking human beings who felt a need to comprehend their position, explain the reasons for their actions, and analyze their feelings. The audience was prodded to think, for a tragedy depicted a clash of viewpoints that, as in the Assembly, the audience had to analyze before choosing sides.

The essence of Greek tragedy lies in the tragic hero's struggle against cosmic forces and insurmountable obstacles, which eventually crush him. But what impressed the Greek spectators (and impresses today's readers and viewers of Greek drama) was not the vulnerability or weaknesses

Profile

Hesiod

The poet Hesiod (eighth century B.C.) lived on a farm in Boetia, in central Greece, and wrote two major poems. *Theogony* deals with the formation of the universe, and *Works and Days* depicts the life of peasants.

Theogony is replete with mythical imagery, but for several reasons scholars regard it as a precursor of Greek philosophy. First, in explaining the origins of the world through the genealogy of the gods, Hesiod produced an ordered and structured mythology that can be interpreted as nascent rational speculation. Second, the gift of law bestowed by Zeus on humanity can be viewed as an early expression of natural law—the recognition of both a physical and a moral order inherent in the universe. Crucial for philosophical thought, the concept of natural law that Hesiod expressed in mythical-religious terms was explicitly formulated in the rational categories of philosophy by Greek thinkers after Hesiod.

Whereas Homer's epics concentrate on heroes striving to win honor as defined by a chivalric aristocratic ideal, Hesiod's later poem, *Works and Days*, describes the daily ordeal of common folk struggling to feed their families. A man of the soil, Hesiod maintains that honest labor promotes the good life.

Although he was generally pessimistic, Hesiod believed that human beings could improve their lot if they embraced justice, which "is proved the best thing they have." An awareness of justice is what distinguishes human beings from other creatures.

of human beings, but their courage and determination in the face of these forces.

Aeschylus

Aeschylus (525–456 B.C.), an Athenian nobleman, had fought in the battle of Marathon. He wrote more than eighty plays, of which only seven survive. They have common themes. As an Athenian patriot, Aeschylus urged adherence to traditional religious beliefs and moral values. Like Solon, the statesman, he believed that the world was governed by divine justice, which could not be violated with impunity; when individuals evinced hubris (overweening pride or arrogance), which led them to overstep the bounds of moderation and to set themselves above the gods, they must be punished. Another principal theme was that through suffering came knowledge: the terrible consequences of sins against the divine order should remind all to think and act with moderation and caution.

Aeschylus' play *The Persians* dealt with an actual event, the defeat of the Persian emperor Xerxes by the Greeks. Xerxes' intemperate ambition to become master of Asia and Greece conflicted with the divine order of the universe. For this hubris, Xerxes and his fellow Persians must pay.

> *A single stroke has brought about the ruin of great*
> *Prosperity, the flower of Persia fallen and gone.*[23]

The suffering of Xerxes should make people aware of what they can and cannot do.

> *And heaps of corpses even in generations hence*
> *Will signify in silence to the eyes of men*
> *That mortal man should not think more than mortal thoughts.*
> *For hubris blossomed forth and grew a crop of ruin,*
> *And from it gathered in a harvest full of tears.*
> *In face of this, when Xerxes, who lacks good sense, returns*
> *Counsel him with reasoning and good advice,*
> *To cease from wounding God with overboastful rashness.*[24]

*You, Perses, should store away in your mind all
  that I tell you,
and listen to justice, and put away
  all notions of violence.
Here is the law, as Zeus established it
  for human beings;
as for fish, and wild animals, and the flying
  birds,
they feed on each other, since there is no idea of
  justice among them;
but to men he gave justice, and she in the end is
  proved the best thing
they have. If a man sees what is right and
  is willing to argue it,
Zeus of the wide brows grants him prosperity.**

Human beings are faced with the choice
between diké (straight judgment and justice),
which safeguards society, and hubris (excessive pride), which destroys it. Honoring justice
is what distinguishes a civilized society from a
state of savagery.

Throughout *Theogony* and *Works and Days*,
Hesiod used the language and imagery of
myth to express curiosity about the genesis of
the universe, concern for justice, and awareness of a universal moral order. In succeeding
centuries, Greek thinkers would discuss these
issues using the language and categories of
philosophy.

_____

*Hesiod, *Works and Days*, in *Hesiod,* trans. Richard
Lattimore (Ann Arbor: University of Michigan Press,
1973), 51.

Whereas Aeschylean drama dealt principally
with the cosmic theme of the individual in conflict
with the moral universe, later dramatists, while
continuing to use patterns fashioned by Aeschylus, gave greater attention to the psychology of
the individual.

Sophocles

Another outstanding Athenian dramatist was
Sophocles (c. 496–406 B.C.). His greatness as
a playwright lay in both the excellence of his
dramatic technique and the skill with which
he portrayed character. The people that he
created possessed violent passions and tender emotions; they were noble in their nature,
though their actions showed human frailty.
Sophocles consciously formulated a standard
of human excellence: individuals should shape
their character in the way a sculptor shapes a
form, according to laws of proportion. Sophocles felt that when these principles of harmony
were violated by immoderate behavior, a person's character would be thrown off balance
and misfortune would strike. The physical

world and human activities obey laws, said
Sophocles, and human beings cannot violate
these laws with impunity.

Whereas Aeschylus concentrated on religious
matters and Euripides (see the next section) dealt
with social issues, Sophocles wrote about the perennial problem of well-intentioned human beings struggling valiantly, but unwisely and vainly,
against the tide of fate. His characters, bent on
some action fraught with danger, resist all appeals
to caution and inescapably meet with disaster.

In *Oedipus Rex*, first performed about 429
B.C., Sophocles probes deeply into the human
psyche. Oedipus is warned not to pursue the
mystery of his birth but insists on searching for
the truth about himself: "Nothing will move me.
I will find the whole truth." (He had unsuspectingly killed his father and married his mother.*)

*Sigmund Freud's interpretation of the Oedipus story has
had a profound impact on psychoanalytic theory: "[Oedipus'] destiny moves us only because it might have been
ours. . . . It is the fate of all of us, perhaps, to direct our
first sexual impulse towards our mother and our first
hatred and . . . murderous wish against our father. Our
dreams convince us that this is so" (*The Interpretation of
Dreams*).

91

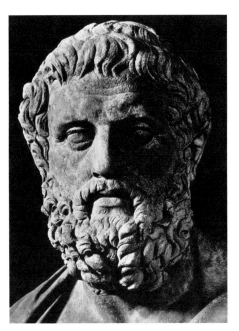

For this determination, born more of innocence than arrogance, he will suffer. Events do not turn out, as Oedipus discovers, the way a person thinks and desires that they should; the individual is impotent before a relentless fate, which governs human existence. It seems beyond imagining that Oedipus, whom all envied for his intelligence, courage, and good works, would suffer such dreadful misfortune.

But tragedy also gives Oedipus the strength to assert his moral independence. Although struck down by fate, Oedipus remains an impressive figure. The tragedy's catharsis (the purging of the audience's emotions through a work of art) comes from Oedipus' choice of his own punishment, self-inflicted blindness. Oedipus demonstrates that he still possesses the distinctly human qualities of choosing and acting, that he still remains a free man responsible for his actions. Despite his misery, Oedipus is able to confront a brutal fate with courage and to demonstrate nobility of character.

Euripides

The rational spirit of Greek philosophy permeated the tragedies of Euripides (c. 485–406 B.C.). Like the Sophists, Euripides subjected the problems of human life to critical analysis and challenged human conventions. It was this critical spirit that prompted the traditionalist Aristophanes (see the next section) to attack Euripides for introducing the art of reasoning into tragedy. The role of the gods, women's conflicts, the horrors of war, the power of passion, and the prevalence of human suffering and weakness were carefully scrutinized in Euripides' plays. Euripides blends a poet's insight with a psychologist's probing to reveal the tangled world of human passions and souls in torment. Thus, in *Medea,* he presents the deepest feelings of a Greek woman (see Primary Source box).

Euripides recognized the power of irrational, demonic forces that seethe within people—what he called "the bloody Fury raised by fiends of Hell."[25] A scorned Medea, seeking revenge against her husband by murdering their children, says:

> *I know indeed what evil I intend to do,*
> *But stronger than all my afterthoughts is my*
> *   fury,*
> *Fury that brings upon mortals the greatest*
> *   evils.*[26]

In his plays, Euripides showed that the great tragedy of human existence is that reason can offer only feeble resistance against these compelling, relentless, and consuming passions. The forces that destroy erupt from the volcanic nature of human beings.

A second distinctive feature of Euripidean tragedy is its humanitarianism. No other Greek thinker expressed such concern for a fellow human being, such compassion for human suffering. In *The Trojan Women,* Euripides depicted war as agony and not glory, and the warrior as brutish and not noble. He described the torments of women, for whom war meant the loss of homes, husbands, children, and freedom. In 416 B.C., Athens massacred the men of the small island of Melos, sold its women and children into slavery, and sacked the city, actions that

Euripides, *Medea*

The Greek dramatist Euripides applied a keen critical spirit to the great question of individual life versus the demands of society. His play Medea *focuses on a strong-willed woman whose despair at being cast off by her husband leads her to exact a terrible revenge. But in the following passage, Medea might speak for the deepest feelings of any Greek woman.*

It was everything to me to think well of one
    man,
And he, my own husband, has turned out
    wholly vile.
Of all things which are living and can form a
    judgement
We women are the most unfortunate creatures.
Firstly, with an excess of wealth it is required
For us to buy a husband and take for our bodies
A master; for not to take one is even worse.
And now the question is serious whether we
    take
A good or bad one; for there is no easy escape
For a woman, nor can she say no to her
    marriage.
She arrives among new modes of behaviour
    and manners,
And needs prophetic power, unless she has
    learnt at home,

How best to manage him who shares the bed
    with her.
And if we work out all this well and carefully,
And the husband lives with us and lightly bears
    his yoke,
Then life is enviable. If not, I'd rather die.
A man, when he's tired of the company in his
    home,
Goes out of the house and puts an end to his
    boredom
And turns to a friend or companion of his own
    age.
But we are forced to keep our eyes on one
    alone.
What they say of us is that we have a peaceful
    time
Living at home, while they do the fighting in
    war.
How wrong they are! I would very much rather
    stand
Three times in the front of battle than bear one
    child.

Question for Analysis

1. According to this passage, what were the difficulties Greek women faced?

Euripedes, *Medea*, trans. Rex Warner (London: The Bodley Head, 1944), 18.

Euripides regarded as mindless savagery. *The Trojan Women*, performed a year later, warned Athenians:

> *How are ye blind,*
> *Ye treaders down of cities, ye that cast*
> *Temples to desolation, and lay waste*
> *Tombs, the untrodden sanctuaries where lie*
> *The ancient dead; yourselves so soon to die!*[27]

By exposing war as barbaric, Euripides was expressing his hostility to the Athenian leaders who persisted in continuing the disastrous Peloponnesian War.

Aristophanes

Greek dramatists often served as political and social critics, none more so than Aristophanes (c. 448–c. 380 B.C.), the greatest of the Greek comic playwrights. He lampooned Athenian statesmen and intellectuals, censured government policies, and protested against the decay of traditional Athenian values. Behind Aristophanes' sharp wit lay a deadly seriousness, for there was much in Athens during the Peloponnesian War that angered him. As an aristocrat, he was repelled by Cleon, the common tanner who succeeded Pericles. As an admirer of the ancient values of honor, duty, and moderation, he was infuriated by corruption, which he attributed to the Sophists. As a man of common sense, he recognized that the Peloponnesian War must end. In the process of serving as a social critic, Aristophanes wrote some of the most hilarious lines in world literature.

In *Lysistrata,* an antiwar comedy, the women of Greece agree to abstain from having sexual relations with their husbands to compel the men to make peace. Lysistrata reveals the plan.

> For if we women will but sit at home,
> Powdered and trimmed, clad in our daintiest
>   lawn,*
> Employing all our charms, and all our arts
> To win men's love, and when we've won it,
>   then
> Repel them firmly, till they end the war,
> We'll soon get Peace again, be sure of that.[28]

After the plan has been implemented, many women, now sexually frustrated, seek to desert the temple where they have gathered. But the men also suffer.

> Oh me! these pangs and paroxysms of love,
> Riving my heart, keen as a torturer's wheel![29]

Through these unorthodox methods, the women achieve their goal, peace. Performed during the darkest days of the war, this play reminded its audiences to concentrate their efforts in the real world on securing peace.

In *The Clouds,* Aristophanes ridiculed the Sophist method of education both for turning the youth away from their parents' values and for engaging the youth in useless, hair-splitting logic. To Aristophanes, the worst of the Sophists was Socrates, who is depicted in *The Clouds* as a fuzzy-minded thinker with both feet planted firmly in the clouds. Socrates is made to look

ridiculous, a man who walks on air, contemplates the sun, and teaches such absurd things as "Heaven is one vast fire extinguisher" or "How many feet of its own a flea could jump." The Sophists in the play teach only how "to succeed just enough for my need and to slip through the clutches of the law." A student of these Sophists becomes "a concocter of lies . . . a supple, unprincipled, troublesome cheat."[30] To Aristophanes, Socrates was a subversive who caused Athenians to repudiate civil morality and to speculate about nonsense questions. Clearly, Aristophanes admired the Athens that had bested the Persians at the battle of Marathon and feared the rationalism that Euripides, the Sophists, and Socrates had injected into Athenian intellectual life.

HISTORY

The Mesopotamians and the Egyptians kept annals that purported to narrate the deeds of gods and their human agents, the priest-kings or god-kings. These chronicles, filled with religious sayings, royal records, and boastful accounts of military campaigns, are devoid of critical analysis and interpretation. The Hebrews valued history, but believing that God acted in human affairs, they did not remove historical events from the realm of religious-mythical thought. The Greeks initiated a different approach to the study of history. For the Greeks, history was not the record of God's wrath or benevolence—as it was for the Hebrews—but the actions solely of human beings. As the gods were eliminated from the natural philosophers' explanations for the origins of things in the natural world, mythical elements were also removed from the writing of history.

Greek historians asked themselves questions about the deeds of people, based their answers on available evidence, and wrote in prose, the language of rational thought. They not only narrated events but also examined them, says Italian historian Arnaldo Momigliano, with a "critical attitude . . . enabling [them] to distinguish between facts and fancies. To the best of my knowledge no historiography earlier than the Greek or independent of it developed these critical methods."[31]

*Fine linen dress

In the same spirit, British philosopher and historian R. G. Collingwood states:

> The Greeks quite clearly and consciously recognized both that history is, or can be, a science, and that it has to do with human actions. Greek history is not legend, it is research; it is an attempt to get answers to definite questions about matters of which one recognizes oneself as ignorant. It is not theocratic, it is humanistic; the matters inquired into are not of gods, they are of men. Moreover, it is not mythical. The events inquired into are not events in a dateless past, at the beginning of things; they are events in a dated past, a certain number of years ago. This is not to say that legend, either in the form of theocratic history or in the form of myth, was a thing foreign to the Greek mind. . . . But what is remarkable about the Greeks was not the fact that their historical thought contained a certain residue of elements which we should call non-historical, but the fact that side by side with these, it contained elements of what we call history.[32]

In several respects, however, the Greeks were unhistorical. To them, history moved in cycles; events and periods repeated themselves. Unlike the Hebrews, they had little awareness of historical uniqueness and progression. Nor was history as vital to the Greeks as it was to the Hebrews. Greek philosophers preferred fixing their minds on eternal and changeless truths rather than on the vicissitudes of history. Aristotle said that poetry (which also included drama) is "more philosophic and of greater import than history, since its statements are of the nature of universals," whereas histories deal only with particular events.[33]

Herodotus

Often called "the father of history," Herodotus (c. 484–c. 424 B.C.) wrote a history of the Persian Wars. Herodotus valued the present and recognized that it is not timeless but has been shaped by earlier happenings. To understand the conflict between Persia and Greece, the most important event during his lifetime, he first inquired into the histories of these societies. Much of his information was derived from posing questions to natives of the lands he visited. Interested in everything, Herodotus frequently interlaced his historical narrative with a marvelous assortment of stories and anecdotes.

The central theme of Herodotus' *Histories* is the contrast between Near Eastern despotism and Greek freedom and the subsequent clash of these two worldviews in the Persian Wars. Certain of their superiority, the Greeks considered the non-Hellenic world to be steeped in ignorance and darkness. Herodotus, however, was generally free of this arrogance. A fair-minded, sympathetic, and tolerant observer, he took joy in examining the wide range of human character and experience.

Though Herodotus found much to praise in the Persian empire, he was struck by a lack of freedom and by what he considered barbarity. Herodotus emphasized that the mentality of the free citizen was foreign to the East, where men were trained to obey the ruler's commands absolutely. Not the rule of law but the whim of despots prevailed in the East. When a Persian official urged some Greeks to submit to Xerxes, Herodotus wrote that the Greeks said: "You understand well enough what slavery is, but freedom you have never experienced, so you do not know if it tastes sweet or bitter. If you ever did come to experience it, you would advise us to fight for it not with spears only, but with axes too."[34] Of all the Greek city-states, Herodotus admired Athens most. Freedom had enabled Athens to achieve greatness, said Herodotus, and it was this illustrious city that had rescued the Greek world from Persia.

Another theme evident in Herodotus' work was punishment for hubris. In seeking to become king of both Asia and Europe, Xerxes had acted arrogantly; although he behaved as if he were superhuman, "he too was human, and was sure to be disappointed of his great expectations."[35] Like the Greek tragedians, Herodotus drew universal moral principles from human behavior.

In several ways, Herodotus was a historian rather than a teller of tales. First, he recognized that there is value in studying and preserving the past. Second, he asked questions about the past, instead of merely repeating ancient legends; he tried to discover what had happened, analyzed the motivations behind actions, and searched for cause-and-effect connections. Third, he demonstrated at times a cautious and critical attitude toward his sources, refusing to rely on legends based on little or no objective evidence.

> The course of my story now leads me to Cyrus: who was this man who destroyed the empire of Croesus, and how did the Persians win their predominant position in Asia? I could, if I wished, give three versions of Cyrus' history, all different from what follows; but I propose to base my account on those Persian authorities who seem to tell the simple truth about him without trying to exaggerate his exploits.[36]

Fourth, rising above inherited prejudices and a narrow parochialism, he attempted to examine disinterestedly and critically the histories of both the Greeks and the Persians. Fifth, although the gods appeared in Herodotus' narrative, they played a far less important role than they did in Greek popular mythology. Still, by retaining a belief in the significance of dreams, omens, and oracles and by allowing divine intervention, Herodotus fell short of being a thoroughgoing rationalist. Herodotus' writings contain the embryo of rational history; Thucydides brought it to maturity.

Thucydides

Thucydides (c. 460–c. 400 B.C.) also concentrated on a great political crisis confronting the Hellenic world: the Peloponnesian War. Living in Periclean Athens, whose lifeblood was politics, Thucydides regarded the motives of statesmen and the acts of government as the essence of history. He did not just catalogue facts but also sought those general concepts and principles that the facts illustrated. His history was the work of an intelligent mind trying to make sense of his times.

Thucydides applied to the sphere of political history a rationalist empiricism worthy of the Ionian natural philosophers. He strove for factual accuracy and drew conclusions based on a critical analysis of events and motives. He searched for the truth underlying historical events and attempted to present it objectively. From the Sophists, Thucydides learned that the motives and reactions of human beings follow patterns. Therefore, a proper analysis of the events of the Peloponnesian War would reveal general principles that govern human behavior and relations between states. He intended his history to be a source of enlightenment for future ages, a possession for all time, because the kinds of behavior that caused the conflict between Sparta and Athens would recur regularly throughout history, for human nature is unchanging and predictable.

> Of the events of the war I have not ventured to speak from any chance information, nor according to any notion of my own; I have described nothing but what I either saw myself, or learned from others of whom I made the most careful and particular inquiry. The task was a laborious one, because eyewitnesses of the same occurrences gave different accounts of them, as they remembered or were [partial to] one side or the other. And very likely the strictly historical character of my narrative may be disappointing to the ear. But if he who desires to have before his eyes a true picture of the events which have happened, and of the like events which may be expected to happen hereafter in the order of human things shall pronounce what I have written to be useful, then I shall be satisfied. My history is an everlasting possession, not a prize composition which is heard and forgotten.[37]

In Thucydides' history, there was no place for myths, for legends, for the fabulous—all of which were hindrances to historical truth. He recognized that a work of history was a creation of the rational mind and not an expression of the poetic imagination. The historian seeks to learn and to enlighten, not to entertain.

Rejecting the notion that the gods interfere in history, Thucydides looked for the social forces and human decisions behind events. Undoubtedly, he was influenced by Hippocratic doctors, who frowned on divine explanations for disease and distinguished between the symptoms of a disease and its causes. Whereas Herodotus occasionally lapsed into supernatural explanations, Thucydides wrote history in which the gods were absent, and he denied their intervention in human affairs. For Thucydides, history was the work of human beings, and the driving force in history was men's will to power and domination.

In addition to being a historian, Thucydides was also an astute and innovative political thinker with a specific view of government, statesmen, and international relations. He warned against the dangers of extremism unleashed by the strains of war, and he believed that when reason was forsaken, the state's plight would worsen. He had contempt for statesmen who waged war lightly, acting from impulse, reckless daring, and an insatiable appetite for territory. Consequently, he regarded the decision to attack Syracuse in Sicily, which cost so many lives, as a gross political blunder. Although Thucydides admired Athens for its democratic institutions, rule of law, sense of civic duty, and cultural achievements, he recognized an inherent danger in democracy: the emergence of demagogues, who rise to power by stirring up the populace and abuse their power when in office. He extended to international relations the Sophists' insight that people tend to act out of self-interest; national interest, he maintained, was the motivating force in relations between states. Further, he explicitly formulated the principle of balance of power as a basic formula governing international relations. What caused the Peloponnesian War, he said, was the sudden and spectacular increase of Athenian power and the Spartans' fear that this would upset the balance. Finally, Thucydides left us with an enduring insight: war unleashes terrible passions among ordinary people that culminate in slaughter and misery.

Political scientists, historians, and statesmen still turn to Thucydides for insights into the realities of power politics, the dangers of political fanaticism, the nature of imperialism, the methods of demagogues, and the effects of war on democratic politics.

THE GREEK ACHIEVEMENT: REASON, FREEDOM, HUMANISM

Like other ancient peoples, the Greeks warred, massacred, and enslaved; they could be cruel, arrogant, contentious, and superstitious; and they often violated their ideals. But their achievement was unquestionably of profound historical significance. Western thought essentially begins with the Greeks, who first defined the individual by the capacity to reason. It was the great achievement of the Greek spirit to rise above magic, miracles, mystery, authority, and custom and to discover the procedures and terminology that permit a rational understanding of nature and society. Every aspect of Greek civilization—science, philosophy, art, literature, politics, historical writing—showed a growing reliance on human reason and a diminishing dependence on the gods.

In Mesopotamia and Egypt, people had no clear conception of their individual worth and no understanding of political liberty. They were not citizens but subjects who marched to the command of a ruler whose power originated with the gods. Such royal power was not imposed on an unwilling population but was religiously accepted and obeyed.

Unlike in the Near East, monarchs were incidental to Greek political history, a development that enabled the Greeks to create both civic politics and political freedom. They saw the state as a community of free and equal citizens who made laws that served the common good. Disputes between citizens were decided by a jury of one's peers, not by the whims of a ruler or his officials. The citizens had no other masters but themselves. Denouncing arbitrary rule, they argued that power should be regulated by law and justice. The Greeks held that men are capable of governing themselves, and they regarded active participation in public affairs as a duty. For the Greeks, the state was a civilizing agent that permitted people to live the good life. Greek political thinkers arrived at a conception of the rational or legal state, in which law was an expression of reason, not of whim or divine commands; of justice, not of might; of the general good of the community, not of the self-interest of a particular class or individuals. At the beginning of the fourth century B.C., an Athenian orator eloquently captured the meaning of his city's political achievement. The Athenians, he said, "deemed that it was the way of wild beasts to be held subject to one another by force, but the duty of men to delimit justice by law, to convince by reason, and to serve these two by submitting to the sovereignty of law and the instruction of reason."[38] The ideas and terminology of this statement were totally alien to the political experience of the ancient Near East and remain an integral component of the Western democratic tradition. An offshoot of the Greek democratic experience was the emergence of political thought. Greek thinkers' discussions of justice, power, freedom, and the strengths and weaknesses of democracy are the foundation of Western political theory.

The Greeks also gave to Western civilization a conception of inner, or ethical, freedom. People were free to choose between shame and honor, cowardice and duty, moderation and excess. The heroes of Greek tragedy suffered not because they were puppets manipulated by higher powers but because they possessed the freedom of decision. The idea of ethical freedom reached its highest point with Socrates, who shifted the focus of thought from cosmology to the moral life. To shape oneself according to ideals known to the mind, to develop into an autonomous and self-directed person, became for the Greeks the highest form of freedom.

Underlying everything accomplished by the Greeks was a humanist attitude toward life. The Greeks expressed a belief in the worth, significance, and dignity of the individual. They called for the maximum cultivation of human talent, the full development of human personality, and the deliberate pursuit of excellence. In valuing human personality, the Greek humanists did

not approve of living without restraints; they aimed at creating a higher type of man. Such a man would mold himself according to worthy standards; he would make his life as harmonious and flawless as a work of art. This aspiration required effort, discipline, and intelligence. Fundamental to the Greek humanist outlook was the belief that human beings could master themselves. Although people could not alter the course of nature, for there was an order to the universe over which neither human beings nor gods had control, Greek humanists believed that people could control their own lives. Contemporary humanists continue to derive inspiration and guidelines from the literary, artistic, and philosophical creations of ancient Greece.

Despite their lauding of the human being's creative capacities, the Greeks were not naïve about human nature. Rather, intensely aware of the individual's inherent capacity for evil, Greek thinkers repeatedly warned that without the restraining forces of law, civic institutions, moral norms, and character training, society would be torn apart by the savage elements within human nature.

By discovering theoretical reason, defining political freedom, and affirming the worth and potential of human personality, the Greeks broke with the past and founded the rational and humanist tradition of the West. "Had Greek civilization never existed," wrote poet W. H. Auden, "we would never have become fully conscious, which is to say that we would never have become, for better or worse, fully human."[39]

NOTES

1. John N. Theodorakopoulos, "The Origins of Science and Philosophy," in *History of the Hellenic World: The Archaic Period* (University Park: Pennsylvania State University Press, 1975), 438.

2. Quoted in George Sarton, *A History of Science* (Cambridge, Mass.: Harvard University Press, 1952), 1:355–356.

3. Euripides, *Iphigenia at Aulis,* in *Ten Plays by Euripides,* trans. Moses Hadas and John

McClean (New York: Bantam Books, 1960), 348, lines 1400–1401.

4. Excerpted in Kathleen Freeman, *Ancilla to the Pre-Socratic Philosophers* (Cambridge, Mass.: Harvard University Press, 1957), 157–158.

5. Plato, *Apology,* trans. F. J. Church, rev. R. D. Cummings (Indianapolis: Bobbs-Merrill, 1956), sec. 28.

6. Ibid., secs. 16–17.

7. Plato, *The Republic,* trans. F. M. Cornford (New York: Oxford University Press, 1945), 289.

8. Ibid.

9. Ibid., 293.

10. Ibid., 178–179.

11. *Historia Animalium,* in *Works of Aristotle,* trans. D'Arcy Wentworth Thompson (New York: Oxford University Press, 1962), 4:561.

12. *Nicomachean Ethics,* in *Basic Works of Aristotle,* ed. Richard McKeon (New York: Random House, 1941), 996.

13. Ibid., 1104.

14. *Politics,* in *Basic Works of Aristotle,* ed. McKeon, 1144–45.

15. Ibid., 1164.

16. Ibid., 1246, 1251.

17. Ibid., 1220–21.

18. Cited in Werner Jaeger, *Paideia: The Ideals of Greek Culture,* trans. Gilbert Highet (New York: Oxford University Press, 1945), 1:135.

19. *The Oxford Book of Greek Verse in Translation,* ed. T.F. Higham and C.M. Bowra (1938), Sappho, "A Girl" (6 lines from p. 211). By Permission of Oxford University Press.

20. Lyn Hatherly Wilson, *Sappho's Sweet Bitter Songs* (London and New York: Routledge, 1966), 70.

21. Cited in H. D. F. Kitto, *The Greeks* (Baltimore: Penguin Books, 1957), 174–175.

22. See Sophocles, *Oedipus the King,* trans. Bernard M. W. Knox (New York: Washington Square Press, 1959), 61.

23. Aeschylus, *The Persians,* trans. Anthony J. Podlecki (Englewood Cliffs, N.J.: Prentice-Hall, 1970), 49, lines 250–251.

24. Ibid., 96–97, lines 818–822, 829–831.

25. *Medea,* trans. Rex Warner, in *Euripides,* vol. 3 of *The Complete Greek Tragedies,* ed. David Grene and Richard Lattimore (Chicago: University of Chicago Press, 1959–1960), 101, line 1260.

26. Ibid., 96, lines 1078–80.

27. Euripides, *The Trojan Women,* trans. Gilbert Murray (New York: Oxford University Press, 1915), 16, lines 95–97.

28. *Lysistrata,* in *Five Comedies of Aristophanes,* trans. Benjamin Bickley Rogers (Garden City, N.Y.: Doubleday Anchor Books, 1955), 292.

29. Ibid., 320.

30. *The Clouds,* in *Five Comedies of Aristophanes,* trans. Rogers, 156–157, 169–170.

31. Arnaldo Momigliano, *The Classical Foundations of Modern Historiography* (Berkeley: University of California Press, 1990), 30.

32. R. G. Collingwood, *The Idea of History* (New York: Oxford University Press, 1956), 17–18.

33. Poetics, in *Basic Works of Aristotle,* ed. McKeon, 1464.

34. Herodotus, *The Histories,* trans. Aubrey de Sélincourt (Baltimore: Penguin Books, 1954), 458.

35. Ibid., 485.

36. Ibid., 53.

37. Thucydides, *The Peloponnesian War,* trans. B. Jowett (Oxford: Clarendon Press, 1881), bk. 1, chap. 22.

38. Quoted in Jennifer Tolbert Roberts, *Athens on Trial: The Antidemocratic Tradition in Western Thought* (Princeton, N.J.: Princeton University Press, 1994), 46.

39. W. H. Auden, ed., *The Portable Greek Reader* (New York: Viking, 1952), 38.

SUGGESTED READING

Brickhouse, Thomas C. and Nicholas D. Smith, *Plato's Socrates* (1994). Informed discussions of Socrates' methodology, psychology, ethics, religion, and politics.

Brunschwig, Jacques, and Geoffrey E. R. Lloyd, eds., *Greek Thought* (2000). Essays dealing with many areas of Greek thought.

Gottlieb, Anthony, *The Dream of Reason* (2000). Superb chapters on Greek philosophy.

Guthrie, W. K. C., *The Greek Philosophers from Thales to Aristotle* (1960). A short, reliable survey of Greek philosophy.

Jaeger, Werner, *Paideia: The Ideals of Greek Culture* (1939–1944). A three-volume work on Greek culture by a distinguished classicist. The treatment of Homer, the early Greek philosophers, and the Sophists in volume 1 is masterful.

Jones, W. T., *A History of Western Philosophy*, vol. 1 (1962). Clearly written; contains useful passages from original sources.

Kitto, H. D. F., *Greek Tragedy* (1954). A valuable introduction to Greek drama.

Levi, Peter, *The Pelican History of Greek Literature* (1985). Sound insights into Greek writers.

Romm, James, *Herodotus* (1998). A study of Herodotus the historian and story teller.

The Hellenistic Age: Cultural Diffusion

Alexander the Great on Horseback. In conquering the lands from Greece to India, Alexander the Great displayed a military genius that would fascinate commanders from Caesar to Napoleon. (Alinari/Art Resource, N.Y.)

- **Alexander the Great**
- **Hellenistic Society**
- **Hellenistic Culture**
- **The Hellenistic Legacy**

Greek civilization, or Hellenism, passed through three distinct stages: the Hellenic Age, the Hellenistic Age, and the Greco-Roman Age. The **Hellenic Age** began about 800 B.C. with the early city-states, reached its height in the fifth century B.C., and endured until the death of Alexander the Great in 323 B.C. At that time, the ancient world entered the **Hellenistic Age,** which ended in 30 B.C., when Egypt, the last major Hellenistic state, fell to Rome. The **Greco-Roman Age** lasted five hundred years, encompassing the period of the Roman Empire up to the collapse of the Empire's western half in the last part of the fifth century A.D.

Although the Hellenistic Age absorbed the heritage of classical (Hellenic) Greece, its style of civilization changed. During the first phase of Hellenism, the polis was the center of political life. The polis gave Greeks an identity, and only within the polis could Greeks live a good and civilized life. With the coming of the Hellenistic Age, this situation changed. Kingdoms and empires eclipsed the city-state in power and importance. Cities retained a large measure of autonomy in domestic affairs but lost their freedom of action in foreign affairs. Dominated by monarchs, cities were no longer self-sufficient and independent communities as they had been in the Hellenic period. Monarchy—the essential form of government in the Hellenistic world—had not been admired by the Greeks of the Hellenic Age. They agreed with Aristotle that monarchy was suitable only for non-Greeks, who lacked the capacity to govern themselves.

As a result of Alexander the Great's conquests of the lands between Greece and India, tens of thousands of Greek soldiers, merchants, and administrators settled in eastern lands. Their encounters with the different peoples and cultures of the Near East widened the Greeks' horizon and weakened their ties to their native cities. Because of these changes, the individual had to define a relationship not to the narrow, parochial society of the polis, but to the larger world. The Greeks had to examine their place in a world more complex, foreign, and threatening than the polis. They had to fashion a conception of a community that would be more comprehensive than the city-state.

Hellenistic philosophers struggled with these problems of alienation and community. They

BATTLE OF ISSUS, ROMAN MOSAIC. The subject of the mosaic is believed to be Alexander's victory over the Persian king Darius III in 333 B.C. at the battle of Issus. On the right side of the mosaic, we see a realistic battle scene filled with both commotion and emotion. (Scala/Ministero per i Beni e le Attività culturali/Art Resource, N.Y.)

sought to give people the inner strength to endure in a world where the polis no longer provided security. In this new situation, philosophers no longer assumed that the good life was tied to the affairs of the city. Freedom from emotional stress—not active citizenship and social responsibility—was the avenue to the good life. This pronounced tendency of people to withdraw into themselves and seek emotional comfort helped shape a cultural environment that contributed to the spread and triumph of Christianity in the Greco-Roman Age.

In the Hellenic Age, Greek philosophers had a limited conception of humanity, dividing the world into Greeks and barbarians. In the Hellenistic Age, the intermingling of Greeks and peoples of the Near East—the fusion of different ethnic groups and cultures scattered over great distances—caused a shift in focus from the city to the **oikoumene** (the inhabited world); parochialism gave way to **cosmopolitanism** and **universalism** as people began to think of themselves as members of a world community. Philosophers came to regard the civilized world as one city, the city of humanity. This new concept was their response to the decline of the city-state and the quest for an alternative form of community.

By uniting the diverse nationalities of the Mediterranean world under one rule, Rome gave political expression to the Hellenistic philosophers' longing for a world community. But the vast and impersonal Roman Empire could not rekindle the sense of belonging, the certainty of identity, that came with being a citizen of a small polis. In time, a resurgence of the religious spirit, particularly in the form of Christianity, helped overcome the feeling of alienation by offering an image of community that stirred the heart.

ALEXANDER THE GREAT

After the assassination of Philip of Macedon in 336 B.C., his twenty-year-old son, Alexander, succeeded to the throne. Alexander inherited a proud and fiery temperament from his mother. From his tutor Aristotle, Alexander gained an appreciation for Greek culture, particularly the Homeric epics. Undoubtedly, the young Alexander was excited by these stories of legendary heroes, particularly of Achilles, and their striving for personal glory. Alexander acquired military skills and qualities of leadership from his father.

Alexander also inherited from Philip an overriding policy of state: the invasion of Persia. Such an exploit attracted the adventurous spirit of the young Alexander. A war of revenge against the Persians, who were masters of the Greek city-states of Asia Minor, also appealed to his Pan-Hellenic sentiments. Alexander was heir to the teachings of the fourth-century orator Isocrates, who urged a crusade against Persia to unite the Greeks in a common cause. Philip had intended to protect his hold on Greece by driving the Persians from Asia Minor. But Alexander, whose ambition knew no bounds, aspired to conquer the entire Persian Empire. Daring, brave, and intelligent, Alexander possessed the irrepressible energy of a romantic adventurer.

With an army of thirty-five thousand men, Alexander crossed into Asia Minor in 334 B.C. and eventually advanced all the way to India. In his military campaigns, which covered about ten thousand miles, Alexander proved himself to be a superb strategist and leader of men. Winning every battle, Alexander's army had carved an empire that stretched from Greece to India. Future conquerors, including Caesar and Napoleon, would read of Alexander's career with fascination and longing.

The world after Alexander differed sharply from that existing before he took up the sword. His conquests brought West and East closer together, marking a new epoch. Alexander himself helped implement this transformation, whether intentionally or unwittingly. He took a Persian bride, arranged for eighty of his officers and ten thousand of his soldiers to marry Asian women, and planned to incorporate thirty thousand Persian youths into his army. Alexander founded Greek-style cities in Asia, where Greek settlers mixed with the native population.

As Greeks acquired greater knowledge of the Near East, the parochialism of the polis gave way to a world outlook. As trade and travel between West and East expanded, as Greek merchants and soldiers settled in Asiatic lands, and as Greek culture spread to non-Greeks, the distinctions between barbarian and Greek lessened. Although Alexander never united all the peoples in a worldstate, his career pushed the world in a new direction, toward a fusion of disparate peoples and the intermingling of cultural traditions.

HELLENISTIC SOCIETY

Competing Dynasties

In 323 B.C., Alexander, not yet thirty-three years old, died after a sickness that followed a drinking party. He had built an empire that stretched from Greece to the Punjab of India, but he was denied the time needed to organize effective institutions to govern these vast territories. After Alexander's premature death, his generals engaged in a long and bitter struggle to see who would succeed the conqueror. Since none of the generals or their heirs had enough power to hold together Alexander's vast empire, the wars of succession ended in a stalemate. By 275 B.C., the empire was fractured into three dynasties: the Ptolemies in Egypt, the Seleucids in western Asia, and the Antigonids in Macedonia. Macedonia—Alexander's native country—continued to dominate the Greek cities, which periodically tried to break its hold. Later, the kingdom of Pergamum, in western Asia Minor, emerged as the fourth Hellenistic monarchy. These Hellenistic kings were not native rulers enjoying local support (except in Macedonia) but were foreign conquerors. Consequently, they had to depend on mercenary armies and loyal administrators.

In the third century B.C., Ptolemaic Egypt was the foremost power in the Hellenistic world. The Seleucid Empire, which stretched from the Mediterranean to the frontiers of India and encompassed many different peoples, attempted to extend its power in the west but was resisted by the Ptolemies. Finally, the Seleucid ruler Antiochus III

(223–187 B.C.) defeated the Ptolemaic forces and established Seleucid control over Phoenicia and Palestine. Taking advantage of Egypt's defeat, Macedonia seized several of Egypt's territories.

Rome, a new power, became increasingly drawn into the affairs of the quarrelsome Hellenistic kingdoms. By the middle of the second century B.C., it had imposed its will on them. From that time on, the political fortunes of the western and eastern Mediterranean were inextricably linked.

Hellenistic society was characterized by a growing cosmopolitanism—a mingling of peoples, an interchange of cultures, and a broad outlook. Greek traditions spread to the Near East, while Mesopotamian, Egyptian, Hebrew, and Persian traditions—particularly religious beliefs—moved westward. A growing cosmopolitanism replaced the parochialism of the city-state. Although the rulers of the Hellenistic kingdoms were Macedonians and their high officials and generals were Greeks, the style of government was modeled after that of the ancient Middle Eastern kingdoms. In the Hellenic Age, the law had expressed the will of the community, but in this new age of monarchy, the kings laid down the law. To promote loyalty, the Macedonian rulers encouraged the Near Eastern cultic practice of worshiping the king as a god or as a representative of the gods. In Egypt, for example, the priests conferred on the Macedonian king the same divine powers and titles traditionally held by Egyptian pharaohs. In accordance with ancient tradition, statues of the divine king were installed in Egyptian temples, suffusing political power with supernatural authority, in marked contrast to the democratic spirit of the Greek Assembly.

Following Alexander's lead, the Seleucids founded cities in the east patterned after the city-states of Greece. The cities, which were often founded to protect trade routes and as fortresses against hostile tribes, adopted the political institutions of Hellenic Greece, including a popular assembly and a council. Hellenistic kings generally did not intervene in the cities' local affairs. Thousands of Greeks settled in these cities, which were Greek in architecture and contained Greek schools, temples, theaters where performances of classical plays were staged, and gymnasia. Gymnasia were essentially places to exercise, train in sports, and converse, but some had libraries and halls where public lectures and competitions of orators and poets were held. Hellenistic kings brought books, paintings, and statues from Greece to their cities. Hellenistic cities, inhabited by tens of thousands of people from many lands and dominated by a Hellenized upper class, served as centers and agents of Hellenism, which non-Greeks adopted. The ruling class in each Hellenistic city was united by a common Hellenism, which overcame national, linguistic, and racial distinctions. *Koine* (or shared language), a form of spoken Greek spread by soldiers, administrators, merchants, teachers, and others, became a common tongue throughout much of the Mediterranean world. Greek was the language both of government and culture.

Hellenistic cities engaged in economic activity on a much greater scale than the classical Greek city-states. Increased trade integrated the Near East and Greece into a market economy, and business methods became more developed and refined. The middle and upper classes enjoyed homes, furniture, and jewelry more elegant than those of Periclean Athenians, and some people amassed great fortunes. In contrast to the ideal of citizenship, which distinguished the fifth-century polis, many Greeks who settled in Egypt, Syria, and other eastern lands ran roughshod over civil law and moral values and engaged in competitive struggles for wealth and power.

The greatest city of the time and the one most representative of the Hellenistic Age was Alexandria, in Egypt, founded by Alexander. Strategically located at one of the mouths of the Nile, it became a hub of commerce and culture. The most populous city of the Mediterranean world, Alexandria had about 300,000 inhabitants fifty years after its founding. At the beginning of the Christian era, it contained perhaps a million people: Macedonians, Greeks, Romans, Jews, Syrians, Ethiopians, and Arabs.

Alexandria was an unrivaled commercial center; goods from the Mediterranean world, eastern Africa, Arabia, and India circulated in its marketplaces. Two handsome boulevards, squares, fountains, and great temples added to the city's beauty. Its library, created by the first two Ptolemies, had about half a million books. The library was part of a larger complex, the museum, which contained an astronomical observatory

Map 5.1 **THE DIVISION OF ALEXANDER'S EMPIRE AND THE SPREAD OF HELLENISM** None of Alexander's generals could hold together the vast empire, which fractured into competing dynasties. (Copyright © 2013 Cengage Learning.)

and botanical and zoological gardens. Some of the greatest poets, philosophers, physicians, and scientists of the Mediterranean world utilized these facilities. Athens and other classical Greek cities seemed like provincial towns compared to Alexandria.

Aside from the proliferation of Greek urban institutions and ideas, Hellenistic cosmopolitanism expressed itself in an increased movement of peoples, the adoption of common currency standards, and an expansion of trade. International trade was made easier by improvements in navigation techniques, better port facilities, the extension of the monetary economy at the expense of barter, and the rapid development of banking. The makeup of Hellenistic armies also reflected the cosmopolitanism of the age. Serving the Hellenistic kings were men from lands stretching from India to the little-known areas north of the

Danube. In Egyptian and Syrian cities, a native elite emerged who spoke Greek, wore Greek-style clothes, and adopted Greek customs.

Cultural exchange permeated all phases of cultural life. Sculpture showed the influence of many lands. Historians wrote world histories, not just local ones. Greek astronomers worked with data collected over the centuries by the Babylonians. Like other Near Eastern people, the Jews—both those in Judea and the **Diaspora** (Jews who lived outside Palestine)—came under the influence of Hellenism. Some Jewish scholars, admiring Greek learning, expressed Jewish religious ideas in philosophical terms; God was identified with reason, and Moses' Law with the rational order of the universe. They wanted to show that Mosaic Law, revealed by God, was compatible with the truth discovered by natural reason. The Hebrew Scriptures were translated

NIKE, THE GODDESS OF VICTORY, ON A GOLD EARRING, HELLENISTIC PERIOD. The calm, timeless, idealized forms of classical period sculpture gave way to a new style—the Hellenistic, marked by more dynamic, emotion-laden realism. This new aesthetic form reflected the cosmopolitan character of the Greek culture that emerged from Alexander's conquests. (Museum of Fine Arts, Boston/Henry Lillie Pierce Fund, 98.788.)

centers it was often only a thin veneer. Many non-Greeks learned Greek and received a Greek education, which was a necessity for advancement in the state bureaucracy, and some assumed Greek names. But for most, Hellenization did not go much deeper. The countryside lacked even the veneer of Greek culture. Retaining traditional attitudes, the countryside in the East resisted Greek ways. In the villages, local and traditional law, local languages, and family customs remained unchanged; religion, the most important ingredient of the civilizations of the Near East, also kept its traditional character, even if ancestral gods were given Greek names.

To be sure, Hellenistic society was male dominated, but the status of women did show some improvement over the classical period. Some royal mothers and daughters exercised political power, even if behind the scenes, and royal women had access to great wealth as indicated by their cash contributions to cities. Some non-royal ladies held important priestly offices, and far more than in the classical era, women contributed to high culture as poets, harpists, artists, and architects. Two of the new schools of philosophy, Epicureanism and Cynicism, welcomed female participation.

HELLENISTIC CULTURE

Literature, History, and Art

The Hellenistic Age saw a great outpouring of literary works. Callimachus (c. 305–240 B.C.), an Alexandrian scholar-poet, felt that no one could duplicate the great epics of Homer or the plays of the fifth-century B.C. dramatists. He urged poets to write short, finely crafted poems instead of composing on a grand scale. A student of his, Apollonius of Rhodes, took issue with him and wrote the *Argonautica*. This Homeric-style epic tells the story of Jason's search for the Golden Fleece.

The poet Theocritus (c. 315–250 B.C.), who lived on the island of Sicily, wrote pastorals that showed great sensitivity to natural beauty. He responded with uncommon feeling to the sky and wind, to the hills, trees, and flowers, and to the wildlife of the countryside.

into Greek—the *Septuagint*—for use by Greek-speaking Jews living in Alexandria and other areas outside of Judea. Greek words entered the Hebrew language, and newly constructed synagogues employed Hellenistic architectural styles.

Greeks increasingly demonstrated a fascination with Near Eastern religious cults. Philosophers helped break down the barriers between peoples by asserting that all inhabit a single fatherland. As the philosopher Crates said, "My fatherland has no single tower, no single roof. The whole earth is my citadel, a home ready for us all to live in."[1]

The spread of Greek civilization from the Aegean to the Indus River gave the Hellenistic world a cultural common denominator, but **Hellenization** did not transform the East and make it one with the West. Hellenization was limited almost entirely to the cities, and in many urban

DRUNKEN OLD WOMAN. Hellenistic genre sculpture depicted people in everyday situations as individuals, rather than as types. This sculpture of a drunken old woman is a marble copy of a third- or second-century B.C. Hellenistic work. (© imagebroker.net/SuperStock.)

The Athenian playwright Menander (c. 342–291 B.C.) depicted Athenian life at the end of the fourth century. Menander's plays, unlike Aristophanes' lampoons of inept politicians, dealt little with politics. Apparently, Menander reflected the attitude of his fellow Athenians, who, bored with public affairs, had accepted their loss of freedom to Macedonia and were preoccupied with their private lives. Menander dealt sympathetically with human weakness and wrote about stock characters: the clever slave, the young playboy, bragging soldiers, compassionate prostitutes, the elderly seducer, the heroine in trouble. Menander also expressed a warm concern for people, urging them to recognize the humanity of their fellows—whether Greeks, barbarians, or slaves—and to treat one another with kindness and respect.

The leading historian of the Hellenistic Age was Polybius (c. 200–118 B.C.), a Greek, whose history of the rise of Rome is one of the great works of historical literature (see Primary Source box). Reflecting the universal tendencies of the Hellenistic Age, Polybius endeavored to explain how Rome had progressed from a city-state to a world conqueror.

Hellenistic art, like Hellenistic philosophy, expressed a heightened awareness of the individual. Whereas Hellenic sculpture aimed to depict ideal beauty—the perfect body and face—Hellenistic sculpture, moving from idealism to realism, captured individual character and expression, often of ordinary people—an old fisherman, a crippled man, a drunken lady, a dwarf. Scenes of daily life were realistically portrayed. Wealthy merchants commissioned artists to embellish their private homes. Monarchs, eager to glorify their reigns, sought the services of eminent artists to produce royal portraits, victory monuments, paintings of great battles, temples, and tombs. Continuing a practice initiated during the Hellenic Age, Hellenistic cities commissioned artists. What was new, however, was the proliferation of portrait statues honoring prominent civic leaders, orators, poets, philosophers, and playwrights.

Science

During the Hellenistic Age, Greek scientific achievement reached its height. When Alexander invaded Asia Minor, the former student of Aristotle brought along surveyors, engineers, scientists, and historians, who continued with him into Asia. The vast amount of data in botany, zoology, geography, and astronomy collected by Alexander's staff stimulated an outburst of activity. To integrate so much information, scientists had to specialize in the various disciplines. Hellenistic scientists preserved and expanded the tradition of science developed in the Hellenic Age. They attempted a rational analysis of nature; they engaged in research, organized knowledge in logical fashion, devised procedures for mathematical proof, separated medicine from magic, grasped the theory of experiment, and applied scientific principles to mechanical devices. Hellenistic science, says historian Benjamin Farrington, stood "on the threshold of the modern world. When modern science began in the sixteenth century, it took up where the Greeks left off."[2]

Although Alexandria was the principal center of scientific research, Athens still retained some of its former luster in this area. After Aristotle died in 322 B.C., he was succeeded as head of the Lyceum by Theophrastus and then by Strato. Both wrote treatises on many subjects—logic, ethics, politics, physics, and botany. Theophrastus systematized knowledge of botany in a manner similar to Aristotle's treatment of animals. Strato is most famous for his study of physics. It is likely that Strato, in his investigation of physical problems, did not rely on logic alone but performed a series of experiments to test his investigations.

Because of its library, the finest in the ancient world, and its state-supported museum, Alexandria attracted leading scholars and superseded Athens in scientific investigation. The museum was really a research institute—the first institution in history specifically established for the purpose of scientific research—in which some of the best minds of the day studied and worked.

Alexandrian doctors advanced medical skills. They improved surgical instruments and techniques and, by dissecting bodies, added to anatomical knowledge. Through their research, they discovered organs of the body not known until then, made the distinction between arteries and veins, divided nerves into those comprising the motor and the sensory system, and identified the brain as the source of intelligence. Their investigations advanced knowledge of anatomy and physiology to a level that was not significantly improved until the sixteenth century A.D.

Knowledge in the fields of astronomy and mathematics also increased. Eighteen centuries before Copernicus, Alexandrian astronomer Aristarchus (310–230 B.C.) said that the sun was the center of the universe, that the planets revolved around it, and that the stars were situated at great distances from the earth. But these revolutionary ideas were not accepted, and the belief in an earth-centered universe persisted. In geometry, Euclid, an Alexandrian mathematician who lived around 300 B.C., creatively synthesized earlier developments. Euclid's hundreds of geometric proofs, derived from reasoning alone—his conclu-

sions flowed logically and flawlessly from given assumptions—are a profound witness to the power of the rational mind.

Alexander's expeditions had opened the eyes of Mediterranean peoples to the breadth of the earth and had stimulated explorations and geographic research. Eratosthenes (c. 275–194 B.C.), an Alexandrian geographer, sought a scientific understanding of this enlarged world. He divided the planet into climatic zones, declared that the oceans are joined, and with extraordinary ingenuity and accuracy measured the earth's circumference.

Archimedes of Syracuse (c. 287–212 B.C.), who studied at Alexandria, was a mathematician, a physicist, and an ingenious inventor. His mechanical inventions, including war engines, dazzled his contemporaries. However, Archimedes dismissed his practical inventions, preferring to be remembered as a theoretician. In one treatise, he established the general principles of hydrostatics, a branch of physics that deals with the pressure and equilibrium of liquids at rest.

Philosophy

Hellenistic thinkers preserved the rational tradition of Greek philosophy. Like their Hellenic predecessors, they regarded the cosmos as governed by universal principles intelligible to the rational mind. For the philosophers of both ages, a crucial problem was the achievement of the good life. Also, both Hellenic and Hellenistic thinkers sought rules for human conduct that accorded with rational standards; both believed that individuals attain happiness through their own efforts, unaided by the gods. In the tradition of Socrates, Hellenistic thinkers taught a morality of self-mastery. But although they retained the inheritance of the classical age, they also transformed it, for they had to adapt thought to the requirements of a cosmopolitan society.

In the Hellenic Age, the starting point of philosophy was the citizen's relationship to the city; in the Hellenistic Age, the point of departure was the solitary individual's relationship to humanity and the individual's personal destiny in a larger and more complex world. Philosophy tried to deal with the feeling of alienation—of not

Polybius

Rome's expansion from a city-state to a world empire that embraced many different nationalities and the extension of citizenship to non-Romans exemplified the universalism and cosmopolitanism of the Hellenistic Age. So too did Polybius' *Histories,* which sought to account for Rome's unprecedented accomplishment.

In 168 B.C. at the battle of Pynda, the Romans defeated Macedonia, which ruled Greece, ending its independence. After the battle, Polybius, along with a thousand other Greeks who had shown sympathy for Macedonia, was deported to Rome to be questioned. Protected by an influential Roman family, no harm came to him.

In the tradition of Thucydides, Polybius believed that a historian had a duty to teach moral lessons and to enlighten by pointing to general principles governing the course of historical events. Like Thucydides, he believed that there are lessons to be learned from a study of history and that his work would instruct current and future officials regarding the proper course of action under given circumstances. But whereas Thucydides wrote about the Peloponnesian War, which involved the Greek city-states, Polybius, reflecting the spirit of the Hellenistic Age, took the entire Mediterranean world as his subject. His aim was to recount how "the Romans succeeded in less than fifty-three years in bringing under their rule the whole inhabited world, an achievement which is without parallel in human history."* No question was of greater importance, he said, than to understand how Rome acquired this supremacy. Polybius stated explicitly that, unlike his predecessors who wrote specialized narrow studies dealing with aspects of Greek or Persian history, he was attempting a unique project—a systematic world history that "examine[s] the general and comprehensive

belonging—resulting from the weakening of the individual's attachment to the polis and to arrive at a conception of community that corresponded to the social realities of a world grown larger. Unlike Plato and Aristotle, Hellenistic philosophers were moralists, not great speculators and theorists. The Hellenistic schools of philosophy, in contrast to their predecessors, were far less concerned with the scientific understanding of nature. Also in contrast to earlier Greek thinkers, they were less concerned with political organization. Philosophy was now chiefly preoccupied with providing the individual with practical guidelines for living; it tried to alleviate spiritual uneasiness and loss of security. It aspired to make people ethically independent so that they could achieve happiness in a hostile and competitive world. As the philosopher Epicurus said: "Empty are the words of that philosopher who offers no therapy for human suffering. For just as there is no use in medical expertise if it does not give therapy for bodily disease, so too there is no use in philosophy if it does not expel the suffering of the soul."[3] To "expel the suffering of the

soul"—to conquer fear and anxiety and to achieve happiness—said Hellenistic philosophers, people must not allow themselves to be troubled by cares and concerns that are ultimately trivial.

In striving for tranquility of mind and relief from conflict, Hellenistic thinkers reflected the general anxiety that pervaded their society. They retained respect for reason and aspired to the rational life, but by stressing peace of mind and the effort to overcome anxiety, they were performing a quasi-religious function. Philosophy was trying to provide comfort for the individual suffering from feelings of loneliness and insignificance. This attempt indicated that Greek civilization was undergoing a spiritual transformation. (We examine the full meaning of this transformation in Chapters 7 and 8.) The gravitation toward religion in an effort to relieve despair gathered momentum in the centuries that followed. Thus, Hellenistic philosophies helped prepare people to accept Christianity, which promised personal salvation. Ultimately, the Christian answer to the problems of alienation and the need for community would scheme of events."† Such a study, he held, was an avenue to a wisdom closed to historians who write monographs on parochial, insignificant, and obscure topics.

Among the reasons Polybius gave for Rome's success was its political system, which balanced aristocratic and democratic elements: the Senate, representing the aristocracy, wielded great power, but the Assembly, representing the commoners, also played an important role in political life. Polybius held that such a political balance promoted loyalty and effective government. Polybius was greatly impressed with the Roman army. The discipline and dedication of citizen soldiers, he said, help explain Rome's success in creating a world empire.

---

*Polybius, *The Rise of the Roman Empire,* trans. Ian Scott-Kilvert (New York: Penguin Classics, 1979), 41.

†Ibid., 44.

---

predominate over the Greco-Roman attempt at resolution.

The Hellenistic world gave rise to four principal schools of philosophy: Epicureanism, Stoicism, Skepticism, and Cynicism.

Epicureanism.   In the tradition of Plato and Aristotle, Epicurus (342–270 B.C.) founded a school in Athens at the end of the fourth century B.C. He broke with the attitude of the Hellenic Age in significant ways. Unlike classical Greek philosophers, Epicurus, reflecting the Greeks' changing relationship to the city, taught the value of passivity and withdrawal from civic life. To him, citizenship was not a prerequisite for individual happiness. Wise persons, said Epicurus, would refrain from engaging in public affairs, for politics is marred by clashing factions and treachery that deprive individuals of their self-sufficiency, their freedom to choose and to act. Nor would wise individuals pursue wealth, power, or fame, as the pursuit would only provoke anxiety. For the same reason, wise persons would not surrender to

hate or love, desires that distress the soul. A wise person would also try to live justly, for one who behaves unjustly is burdened with troubles. Nor could there be happiness when one worried about dying or pleasing the gods.

To Epicurus, dread that the gods punished people in this life and could inflict suffering after death was the principal cause of anxiety. To remove this source of human anguish, he favored a theory of nature that had no place for supernatural intervention in nature or in people's lives. Therefore, he adopted the physics of Democritus, which taught that all things consist of atoms in motion. In a universe of colliding atoms, there could be no higher intelligence ordering things; there was no room for divine activity. Epicurus taught that the gods probably did exist but that they could not influence human affairs; hence, it was pointless to worry about them. Individuals should order their lives without considering the gods. Epicurus embraced atomism, not as a disinterested scientist aspiring to truth, but as a moral philosopher seeking to liberate emotional life from fear of the gods.

People could achieve happiness, said Epicurus, when their bodies were "free from pain" and their minds "released from worry and fear." Although Epicurus wanted to increase pleasure for the individual, he rejected unbridled hedonism. Because he believed that happiness must be pursued rationally, he thought that the merely sensuous pleasures with unpleasant aftereffects (such as overeating and excessive drinking) should be avoided. In general, Epicurus espoused the traditional Greek view of moderation and prudence. Most important for achieving the good life, said Epicurus, was the company of friends.

By opening his philosophy to men and women, slave and free, Greek and barbarian, and by separating ethics from politics, Epicurus fashioned a philosophy adapted to the post-Alexandrian world of kingdoms and universal culture.

Stoicism.   Around the time of the founding of Epicurus' school, Zeno (335–263 B.C.) also opened a school in Athens. Zeno's teachings, called Stoicism, became the most important philosophy in the Hellenistic world. Epicurus backed away from civic participation and political life as snares that deprived the individual of self-sufficiency. Stoics, however, developed a new formula for the individual's membership in a political community. By teaching that the world constituted a single

111

Epicureanism: Living Well

Epicureanism was named for its founder, Epicurus, who established a school at Athens in 307 or 306 B.C. To achieve peace of mind, taught Epicurus, one should refrain from worrying about death or pleasing the gods, avoid intense involvements in public affairs, cultivate friendships, and pursue pleasure prudently. The following excerpts from Epicurus' works reveal his prescription for living well in a world grown more complex.

. . . We must grasp this point, that the principal disturbance in the minds of men arises because they think that these celestial bodies are blessed and immortal, and yet we have wills and actions and motives inconsistent with these attributes; and because they are always expecting or imagining some everlasting misery (inflicted on them by the gods), such as is depicted in legends, or even fear the loss of feeling in death . . . and, again, because they are brought to this pass not by reasoned opinion, but rather by some irrational presentiment . . . and, by learning the true causes of celestial phenomena and all other occurrences that come to pass from time to time, we shall free ourselves from all which produces the utmost fear in other men.

It is vain to ask of the gods what a man is capable of supplying for himself.

But the many at one moment shun death as the greatest of evils, at another yearn for it as a respite from the evils of life. But the wise man neither seeks to escape life nor fears the cessation of life, for neither does life offend him nor does the absence of life seem to be any evil.

A man cannot dispel his fear about the most important matters if he does not know what is the nature of the universe but suspects the truth of some mythical story. So that without natural science it is not possible to attain our pleasures unalloyed.

When, therefore, we maintain that pleasure is the end, we do not mean the pleasures-of-profligates and those that consist in sensuality, as is supposed by some who are either ignorant or disagree with us or do not understand, but freedom from pain in the body and from trouble in the mind.

Of all the things which wisdom acquires to produce the blessedness of the complete life, far the greatest is the possession of friendship.

We must release ourselves from the prison of affairs and politics.

A free life cannot acquire many possessions, because this is not easy to do without servility to mobs or monarchs. . . .

The noble soul occupies itself with wisdom and friendship. . . .

Questions for Analysis

1. What did Epicurus believe were the chief causes of emotional distress among human beings?
2. What advice did he offer for achieving inner peace and happiness?

Epicurus: The Extant Remains translated by Cyril Bailey (1926), 440 words from pp. 53, 85, 89, 101, 115, 117, 119. By permission of Oxford University Press.

society, Stoicism gave theoretical expression to the world-mindedness of the age. By arriving at the concept of a world-state, the city of humanity, Stoicism offered an answer to the problem of community and alienation posed by the decline of the city-state. By stressing gaining control over one's inner life in dealing with life's misfortunes, Stoicism offered an avenue to individual happiness in a world fraught with uncertainty.

At the core of Stoicism was the belief that the universe contained a principle of order, variously called Divine Reason (*Logos*), the Divine Fire, or God—more the fundamental force of the universe than a living being. This ruling principle underlay reality and permeated all things; it ordered the cosmos according to law. The Stoics reasoned that, being part of the universe, people too shared in the **Logos** that operated throughout

16,400	Thule / Arctic Circle
	Ierne
	Britannia / ATLANTIC OCEAN
34,900	Tanais / Jaxartes
	Ister / Oxus
29,900	
25,200	TAURUS MTS / IMAUS MTS / Rhodian Parallel
23,800	Rhodes / Ganges
	Alexandria / Indus
16,800	Syene
11,800	Meroë / Tropic
8,400	Nile / ATLANTIC
	OCEAN
stades 0	Equator

RECONSTRUCTION OF THE MAP OF THE WORLD BY ERATOSTHENES (C. 275–194 B.C.). Geographical knowledge expanded enormously among the Hellenistic Greeks. The first systematic scientific books on geography were credited to Eratosthenes, head of the Alexandrian library, the greatest scientific and humanistic research center in the Hellenistic world. Eratosthenes estimated the circumference of the earth with remarkable accuracy for his time. His map illustrates the limits of the world known to the Greeks. (From John Onians, *Art and Thought in the Hellenistic Age* [Thames and Hudson, 1979]. Reprinted by permission of Thames and Hudson Ltd.)

the cosmos. Inherent in every human soul and discovered through reason, the Logos enabled people to act virtuously and intelligently and to comprehend the principles of order that governed nature. This **natural law** provides human beings with an awareness of what is and is not correct behavior, especially when dealing with other human beings. Living in accordance with natural law is the avenue to both virtue and happiness. Natural law alone commands our ultimate obedience.

Since reason was common to all, human beings were essentially brothers and fundamentally equal. Reason gave individuals dignity and enabled them to recognize and respect the dignity of others. To the Stoics, all people, Greek and barbarian, free and slave, rich and poor, were fellow human beings, and one law, the law of nature, applied to all of them. What people had in common as fellow human beings far outweighed differences based on culture. All rational human beings were fellow

citizens of a cosmopolis, a world community. Thus, the Stoics, like the Hebrews, arrived at the idea of a common humanity subject to the same moral obligations.

Pericles had spoken of the Athenians' obligation to abide by the laws and traditions of their city; Stoics, viewing people as citizens of the world, emphasized the individual's duty to understand and obey the natural law that governed the cosmos and applied to all. Socrates had taught a morality of self-mastery—reason exercising control over feelings; the Stoics spread Socrates' philosophy beyond Athens, beyond Greece, and enlarged it, offering it as a way of life for all. Like Socrates, the Stoics believed that a person's distinctive quality was the ability to reason and that happiness came from the disciplining of emotions by the rational part of the soul. Also like Socrates, the Stoics maintained that individuals should progress morally, thus perfecting their character.

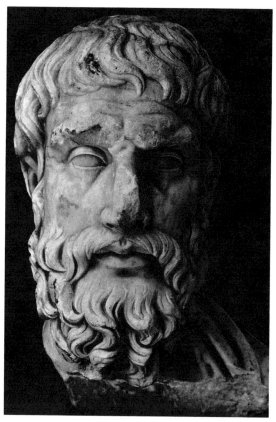

MARBLE PORTRAIT OF EPICURUS. The direct gaze and inner calm of the philosopher suggest the essence of his teachings. Epicurus believed that happiness came from a rationally ordered life. He urged his followers to disengage from the uncertainties and stress of politics, business, family, and religion.
(The Metropolitan Museum of Art/Art Resource, N.Y.)

In the Stoic view, wise persons ordered their lives according to the natural law—the Logos, or law of reason—that underlay the cosmos. To live in agreement with nature—that is, to follow the dictates of reason—was the aim of moral activity. This harmony with the Logos would give these individuals the inner strength to resist the torments inflicted by others, by fate, and by their own passionate natures. Self-mastery and inner peace, or happiness, would follow. Such individuals would remain undisturbed by life's misfortunes, for their

souls would be their own. Even slaves were not denied this inner freedom; although their bodies were subjected to the power of their masters, their minds still remained independent and free.

Stoicism had an enduring influence on the Western mind. To some Roman political and legal thinkers, the Empire fulfilled the Stoic ideal of a world community, in which people of different nationalities held citizenship and were governed by a worldwide law that accorded with the law of reason, or natural law—a moral order operating throughout the universe. Stoic beliefs—that by nature we are all members of one family, that each person is significant, that distinctions of rank and race are of no account, and that human law should not conflict with natural law—were incorporated into Roman jurisprudence, Christian thought, and modern liberalism. There is continuity between the Stoic idea of natural law and the principle of inalienable rights, rights to which all are entitled by nature, stated in the American Declaration of Independence. In the modern age, the principle of natural law provided theoretical justification for human rights that are the birthright of each individual.

Skepticism. The Epicureans tried to withdraw from the evils of this world and to attain personal happiness by reducing physical pain and mental anguish. The Stoics sought happiness by actively entering into harmony with universal reason, that is, with nature. Both philosophies sought peace of mind, but the Stoics did not disengage themselves from political life and often exerted influence over Hellenistic rulers. Skepticism, another school of philosophy, attacked the Epicurean and Stoic belief that there is a definite avenue to happiness. Skeptics held that one could achieve spiritual comfort by recognizing that none of the beliefs by which people lived were true or could bring happiness. For the Skeptic, nothing can be known with certainty. Therefore, suspending judgment—that is, recognizing the existence of alternative viewpoints and disdaining a commitment to dogmatic beliefs—calms the mind and brings contentment.

Some Skeptics taught indifference to all theory and urged conformity to accepted views whether or not they were true. This attitude would avoid arguments and explanations. Gods might not exist, said the Skeptics, but to refuse to worship them or to deny their existence would only cause trouble; therefore, individuals should follow the crowd. The life of the mind—metaphysical speculation inquiring into the origin of things, and clever reasoning—did not bring truth or happiness, so why should one bother with it? Suspending judgment, recognizing the inability to understand, not committing oneself to a system of belief—by these means one could achieve peace of mind. Instead of embracing doctrines, said the Greek writer Lucian, individuals should go their way "with ever a smile and never a passion."[4] This was the position of those Skeptics who were suspicious of ideas, particularly all encompassing rational systems, and hostile to intellectuals.

The more sophisticated Skeptics did not run away from ideas but pointed out their limitations; they did not avoid theories but refuted them. In doing so, they did not reject reason. Rather, they focused on a problem of reason: whether indeed it could arrive at truth. Thus, Carneades of Cyrene (213–129 B.C.) insisted that all ideas, even mathematical principles, must be regarded as hypotheses and assumptions, not as absolutes. Just because the universe showed signs of order, Carneades argued, one could not assume that it had been created by God. Since there was never any certainty, only probability, morality should derive from practical experience rather than from dogma.

Cynicism. The Cynics were not theoretical philosophers but supreme individualists who rebelled against established values and conventions—against every barrier of society that restrained individuals from following their own natures. Cynics regarded laws and public opinion, private property and employment, and wives and children as hindrances to the free life. Extreme individualists, the Cynics had no loyalty to family, city, or kingdom and ridiculed religion, philosophy, and literature. They renounced possessions and showed no respect for authority. When Diogenes, a fourth-century B.C. Cynic, met Alexander the Great, he is supposed to have asked only that the great conqueror get out of his light.

Cynics put their philosophy into practice. They cultivated indifference and apathy and scorned wealth, fame, and noble birth. To harden themselves against life's misfortunes, they engaged in strenuous exercise, endured cold and hunger, and lived ascetically. Not tied down by property or employment,

Cynics wandered shoeless from place to place, wearing dirty and ragged clothes and carrying staffs. To show their disdain for society's customs, Cynics grew long scraggly beards, used foul language, and cultivated bad manners. Diogenes supposedly said: "Look at me, . . . I am without a home, without a city, without property, without a slave; I sleep on the ground; I have neither wife nor children, no miserable governor's mansion, but only earth, and sky, and one rough cloak. Yet what do I lack? Am I not free from pain and fear, am I not free?"[5]

In their attack on inherited conventions, Cynics strove for self-sufficiency and spiritual security. Theirs was the most radical philosophical quest for meaning and peace of soul during the Hellenistic Age.

THE HELLENISTIC LEGACY

The Hellenistic Age encompassed the period from the death of Alexander to the formation of the Roman Empire. During these three centuries, Greek civilization spread eastward as far as India and westward to Rome. As Greeks settled in the Near East and intermingled with Egyptians, Syrians, Persians, and others, the parochialism of the Greek polis gave way to a new cosmopolitanism, an interest in the culture of other ethnic groups, and to universalism, an awareness that people were members of a world community that transcended citizenship in one's native city. Both philosophy and the arts reflected these new concerns.

Rome, conqueror of the Mediterranean world and transmitter of Hellenism, inherited the universalist tendencies of the Hellenistic Age and embodied them in its law, institutions, and art. So too did Christianity, which welcomed converts from every ethnic background and held that God loved all people and that Christ died for all humanity. The Stoic idea of natural law that applies to all human beings and its corollary that human beings are fundamentally equal were crucial to the formulation of the modern idea that the individual is endowed with **natural rights** that no government can violate. A parallel can be drawn between the Hellenistic Age, in which Greek civilization spread to the Near East, and our own age, in which the ideas, institutions, and technology of Western civilization have been exported throughout the globe.

NOTES

1. Quoted in John Ferguson, *The Heritage of Hellenism* (New York: Science History Publications, 1973), 30.

2. Benjamin Farrington, *Greek Science* (Baltimore: Penguin Books, 1961), 301.

3. Quoted in Anthony Gottlieb, *The Dream of Reason* (New York: W. W. Norton, 2000), 283–284.

4. Quoted in J. H. Randall Jr., *Hellenistic Ways of Deliverance and the Making of the Christian Synthesis* (New York: Columbia University Press, 1970), 74.

5. Epictetus, *The Discourses as Reported by Arrian, the Manual and Fragments,* trans. W. A. Oldfather (Cambridge, Mass.: Harvard University Press, 1966), 2:147.

SUGGESTED READING

Bonnard, André, *Greek Civilization,* vol. 3 (1961). Self-contained chapters on various phases of late classical and Hellenistic periods.

Cartledge, Paul, *Alexander the Great* (2004). A recent biography.

Chamoux, François, *Hellenistic Civilization* (2003). Strong on the ways Greek ideas and cultural forms were received in different lands.

Ferguson, John, *The Heritage of Hellenism* (1973). A good introduction to Hellenistic culture.

Gergel, Tania, ed., Alexander *the Great: The Brief Life and Towering Exploits of History's Greatest Conqueror As Told by His Original Biographers* (2004). A convenient anthology of original sources.

Grant, Michael, *From Alexander to Cleopatra* (1982). A fine survey of all phases of Hellenistic society and culture.

Koester, Helmut, *Introduction to the New Testament,* vol. 1, *History, Culture, and Religion of the Hellenistic Age* (1982). An intelligent guide.

Tripolitis, Antonia, *Religions of the Hellenistic Age* (2002). An excellent survey.

Wallbank, F. W., *The Hellenistic World* (1982). A survey of the Hellenistic world that makes judicious use of quotations from original sources.

The Roman Republic: City-State to World Empire

A Roman Warship with Legionnaires on a Relief from the Temple of Fortuna Primigenia, First Century B.C. Roman soldiers fought on sea as well as on land, conquering nations throughout the Mediterranean area during the eras of the Republic and the Empire. (Scala/Art Resource, N.Y.)

Focus Questions

1. What was the significance of the conflict between plebeians and patricians?
2. What factors enabled the city-state of Rome to conquer Italy and the Mediterranean world?
3. What was the significance of Roman expansion?
4. What were the reasons for the collapse of the Roman Republic?

Rome's great achievement was to transcend the narrow political orientation of the city-state and to create a world-state that unified the different nations of the Mediterranean world. Regarding the polis as the only means to the good life, the Greeks had not desired a larger political unit and had almost totally excluded foreigners from citizenship. Although Hellenistic philosophers had conceived the possibility of a world community, Hellenistic politics could not shape one. Rome overcame the limitations of the city-state mentality and developed an empire-wide system of law and citizenship. The Hebrews were distinguished by their prophets and the Greeks by their philosophers. The Romans produced no Amos or Isaiah, and no Plato or Aristotle; their genius found expression in law and government and in the transmission of the Greek cultural achievement.

Historians divide Roman history into two broad periods: the period of the **Republic** began in 509 B.C. with the overthrow of the Etruscan monarchy; the period of the **Empire** began in 27 B.C., when Octavian (Augustus) became in effect the first Roman emperor, ending almost five hundred years of republican self-government. By conquering the Mediterranean world and extending Roman law and, in some instances, citizenship to different nationalities, the Roman Republic transcended the parochialism typical of the city-state. The Republic initiated the trend toward political and legal universalism, which reached fruition in the second period of Roman history, the Empire.

EVOLUTION OF THE ROMAN CONSTITUTION

By the eighth century B.C., peasant communities existed on some of Rome's seven hills near the Tiber River in central Italy. To the north stood Etruscan cities and to the south Greek cities. The more advanced civilizations of both Etruscans and Greeks were gradually absorbed by the Romans.

The origin of the Etruscans remains a mystery, although some scholars believe that they came from Asia Minor and settled in north-central Italy. From them, Romans acquired architectural styles and skills in road construction, sanitation,

Chronology 6.1 ❖ The Roman Republic

509 B.C.	Expulsion of the Etruscan monarch
450	Law of Twelve Tables
287	End of the Struggle of the Orders
264–241	First Punic War: Rome acquires provinces
218–201	Second Punic War: Hannibal is defeated
149–146	Third Punic War: destruction of Carthage
133–122	Land reforms by the Gracchi brothers; they are murdered by the Senate
88–83	Conflict between Sulla and the forces of Marius; Sulla emerges as dictator
79	After restoring rule by Senate, Sulla retires
73–71	Slave revolt is led by Spartacus
58–51	Caesar campaigns in Gaul
49–44	Caesar is dictator of Rome
31 B.C.	Antony and Cleopatra are defeated at Actium by Octavian

hydraulic engineering (including underground conduits), metallurgy, ceramics, and portrait sculpture. Symbols of authority and rule—purple robes, ivory-veneer chariots, thrones for state officials, and a bundle of rods and an ax held by attendants—were also borrowed from the Etruscans. Etruscan words and names entered into the Latin language, and Roman religion absorbed Etruscan gods.

The Etruscans had expanded their territory in Italy during the seventh and sixth centuries B.C., and they controlled the monarchy in Rome. However, defeated by Celts, Greeks, and finally Romans, the Etruscans had ceased to exercise any political power in Italy by the third century B.C.

Rome became a republic at the end of the sixth century B.C.—the traditional date is 509 B.C.—when the landowning aristocrats, or **patricians**, overthrew the Etruscan king. In the opening phase of republican history, religion governed the people, dictated the law, and legitimized the rule of the patricians—aristocrats by birth who regarded themselves as the preservers of sacred traditions. Gradually, the Romans loosened the ties between religion and politics and hammered out a constitutional system that paralleled the Greek achievement of rationalizing and secularizing politics and law. In time, the Romans, like the Greeks, came to view law as an expression of the public will and not as the creation of god-kings, priest-kings, or a priestly caste.

The impetus for the growth of the Roman constitution came from a conflict—known as the Struggle of the Orders—between the patricians and the commoners, or **plebeians.** At the beginning of the fifth century B.C., the patrician-dominated government consisted of two annually elected executives called consuls, the Centuriate Assembly, and the Senate. Patricians owned most of the land and controlled the army. The two consuls, who came from the nobility, commanded the army, served as judges, and initiated legislation. To prevent either consul from becoming an autocrat, decisions had to be approved by both of them. In times of crisis, the consuls were authorized by the Senate to nominate a dictator; he would possess absolute powers during the emergency, but these powers would expire after six months. The consuls were aided by other annually elected magistrates and administrators. The Centuriate Assembly was a popular assembly but, because of voting procedures, was controlled by the nobility. The Assembly elected consuls and other magistrates and made the laws, which also needed Senate approval. The Senate advised the Assembly but did not itself enact laws; it controlled public finances and foreign policy. Senators either were appointed for life terms by the consuls or were former magistrates. The Senate was the principal organ of patrician power.

The tension between patricians and commoners stemmed from plebeian grievances, which included enslavement for debt, discrimination in the courts, prevention of intermarriage with patricians, lack of political representation, and the absence of a written code of laws. Resenting their inferior status and eager for economic relief, the plebeians organized and waged a struggle for political, legal, and social equality. They had one decisive weapon: their threat to secede from Rome, that is, not to pay taxes, work, or serve in the army. Realizing that Rome, which was constantly involved in warfare on the Italian peninsula, could not endure without plebeian help, the pragmatic patricians begrudgingly made concessions. Thus, the plebeians slowly gained legal equality.

Early in the fifth century, the plebeians won the right to form their own assembly (the Plebeian Assembly, which was later enlarged and called the Tribal Assembly). This Assembly could elect tribunes, officials who were empowered to protect plebeian rights. As a result of plebeian pressure, in about 450 B.C., the first Roman code of laws was written. Called the Twelve Tables, the code gave plebeians some degree of protection against unfair and oppressive patrician officials, who could interpret customary law in an arbitrary way. Other concessions gained later by the plebeians included the right to intermarry with patricians; access to the highest political, judicial, and religious offices in the state; and the elimination of slavery as payment for debt. In 287 B.C., a date generally recognized as the termination of the plebeian-patrician struggle, laws passed by the Tribal Assembly no longer required Senate approval. Now the plebeians had full civil equality and legal protection, and their assembly had full power to enact legislation.

Despite these reforms, Rome was still ruled by an upper class. The oligarchy that now held power consisted of patricians and influential plebeians who had joined forces with the old nobility. Marriages between patricians and politically powerful plebeians strengthened this alliance. Generally only wealthy plebeians became tribunes, and they tended to side with the old nobility rather than defend the interests of poor plebeians. By using bribes, the ruling oligarchy of patricians and wealthy plebeians maintained control over the Assembly, and the Senate remained a bastion of aristocratic power.

A patron–client relationship extending back to the days of the monarchy reinforced upper-class rule. In early Rome, a plebeian seeking protection for himself and his family in the courts looked to a patrician for assistance. In return, the plebeian gave his patrician patron both military and political support. Enduring over the centuries, the patron–client relationship assured powerful nobles of their commoner clients' support in the Assembly, and it provided clients with food, money, and protection.

Thus, from beginning to end, an upper class—sometimes expanded to allow entry of new talent and wealth—governed the Roman Republic. This aristocracy's view of liberty always remained elitist: freedom for Rome's best men to achieve virtue (*virtus*), dignity (*dignitas*), and fame (*fama*) by competing with one another for political power and privilege. Cicero (see below), himself a member of the ruling elite, aptly summed up its outlook: "the safety of the State depends upon the wisdom of its best men, especially since Nature has provided not only that those men who are superior in virtue and in spirit should rule the weaker, but also that the weaker should be willing to obey the stronger."[1] Like others of the upper class, Cicero held that "the perversity and rashness of popular assemblies" precluded them from governing effectively.[2] In the Greek cities, tyrants had succeeded in breaking aristocratic dominance, thereby clearing a pathway for democratic government. But in the Roman Republic, the nobility maintained its tight grip on the reins of power until the civil wars of the first century B.C.

Deeming themselves Rome's finest citizens, the ruling oligarchy led Rome during its period of expansion and demonstrated a sense of responsibility and a talent for statesmanship. In noble families, parents and elders prepared the young for public service. They recounted the glorious deeds of ancestors who had served Rome, and they reminded youngsters of their responsibility to bring additional honors to the family by winning distinction as a commander, orator, or jurist.

STATUE PORTRAIT, FIRST CENTURY A.D. The Romans valued family, city, and tradition. Here a noble proudly exhibits the busts of his ancestors. (Scala/Art Resource, N.Y.)

In this way, a son would prove his worth as a man and as a Roman.

During their two-hundred-year class struggle, the Romans forged a constitutional system based on civic needs rather than on religious mystery. The essential duty of government ceased to be the regular performance of religious rituals and became the maintenance of order at home and the preservation of Roman might and dignity in international relations. Although the Romans retained the ceremonies and practices of their ancestral religion—correct observance was a way of showing respect for tradition—public interest, not religious tradition, determined the content of law and was the standard by which all the important acts of the city were judged. When Romans chose a course of action in public life, they rarely took into consideration the fear of displeasing the gods. By the late Republic, Romans did not seem concerned about divine intervention in their daily lives; the prospect of divine punishment seemed quite remote. In the opening stage of republican history, law was priestly and sacred, spoken only by priests and known only to men of religious families. Gradually, as law was written, debated, and altered, it became disentangled from religion. Another step in this process of secularization and rationalization occurred when the study and interpretation of law passed from the hands of priests to a class of professional jurists, who analyzed, classified, systematized, and sought commonsense solutions to legal problems.

The Roman constitution was not a product of abstract thought, nor was it the gift of a great lawmaker such as the Athenian Solon. Rather, like the unwritten British constitution, the Roman constitution evolved gradually and empirically in response to specific needs. The Romans, unlike the Greeks, were distinguished by practicality and common sense, not by a love of abstract thought. In their pragmatic and empirical fashion, they gradually developed the procedures of public politics and the legal state.

Undoubtedly, the commoners' struggle for rights and power did arouse hatred on both sides. But in contrast to the domestic strife in Greek cities, Rome's class conflict did not end in civil war. This peaceful solution testifies to the political good sense of the Romans. Fear of foreign powers and the tradition of civic patriotism prevented the patrician–plebeian conflict from turning into a fight to the death. At the time of the class struggle, Rome was also engaged in the extension of its power over the Italian peninsula. Without civic harmony and stability, Rome could not have achieved expansion.

ROMAN EXPANSION TO 146 B.C.

By 146 B.C., Rome was the dominant state in the Mediterranean world. Roman expansion occurred in three main stages: the uniting of the Italian peninsula, which gave Rome the forces that transformed it from a city-state into a great power; the collision with Carthage, from which Rome emerged as ruler of the western Mediterranean; and the subjugation of the Hellenistic states, which brought Romans in close contact with Greek civilization. As Rome expanded territorially, its leaders enlarged their vision. Instead of restricting citizenship to people having ethnic kinship, Rome assimilated other peoples into its political community. Just as Roman law had grown to cope with the earlier grievances of the plebeians, so too it adjusted to the new situations resulting from the creation of a multinational empire. The city of Rome was evolving into the city of humanity—the cosmopolis envisioned by the Stoics.

The Uniting of Italy

During the first stage of expansion, Rome extended its hegemony over Italy, subduing in the process neighboring Latin kinsmen, semicivilized Italian tribes, the once-dominant Etruscans, and Greek city-states in southern Italy. At the beginning, Roman warfare was principally motivated by the hunger for more farmland. As Rome expanded and its territory and responsibilities increased, it was often drawn into conflict to protect its widened boundaries and its allies. Also fueling Roman expansion was an aristocratic ethos, which placed the highest value on glory and reputation. Demonstrating prowess in war, aristocrats believed, was the finest way to win the esteem of fellow Romans, bring honor to their families, and enhance their own political careers.

Rome's conquest of Italy stemmed in part from superior military organization, grueling training, and iron discipline. From the Greeks they acquired the most advanced methods of siegecraft. Also copying the Greeks, the Romans organized their soldiers into battle formations; in contrast, their opponents often fought as disorganized hordes, which were prone to panic and flight. Fighting as part of a unit strengthened the courage and confidence of the Roman soldier, for he knew that his comrades would stand with him. Roman soldiers who deserted their posts or fled from battle were punished and disgraced, an ordeal more terrible than facing up to the enemy. The promise of glory and rewards also impelled the Roman soldier to distinguish himself in battle.

Ultimately, Rome's success was due to the character of its people and the quality of its statesmanship. The Roman farmer-soldier was dedicated, rugged, persevering, and self-reliant. He could march thirty miles a day laden with arms, armor, and equipment weighing sixty pounds. In the face of danger, he remained resolute and tenacious, obedient to the poet Virgil's maxim: "Yield you not to ill fortune, but go against it with more daring." Romans willingly made sacrifices so that Rome might endure. In conquering Italy, they were united by a moral and religious devotion to their city strong enough to overcome social conflict, factional disputes, and personal ambition.

Despite its army's might, Rome could not have mastered Italy without the cooperation of other Italian peoples. Like other ancient peoples, Rome plundered, enslaved, and brutalized, at times with great ferocity. But it also endeavored, through generous treatment, to gain the loyalty of those it had conquered. Some defeated Italian communities retained a measure of self-government but turned the conduct of foreign affairs over to Rome and contributed contingents to the army when Rome went to war. Other conquered people received partial or full citizenship. In extending its dominion over Italy, Rome displayed a remarkable talent for converting former enemies into allies and eventually into Roman citizens. No Greek city had ever envisaged integrating nonnatives into its political community.

Polybius: The Roman Army

The discipline and dedication of the citizen soldiers help explain Rome's success in conquering a world empire. In the following account, Polybius (see Profile in Chapter 5) tells how the commanders enforced obedience and fostered heroism.

A court-martial composed of the tribunes immediately sits to try him [a soldier], and if he is found guilty, he is punished by beating (*fustuarium*). This is carried out as follows. The tribune takes a cudgel and lightly touches the condemned man with it, whereupon all the soldiers fall upon him with clubs and stones, and usually kill him in the camp itself. But even those who contrive to escape are no better off. How indeed could they be? They are not allowed to return to their homes, and none of their family would dare to receive such a man into the house. Those who have once fallen into this misfortune are completely and finally ruined. The *optio* [lieutenant] and the *decurio* [sergeant] of the squadron are liable to the same punishment if they fail to pass on the proper orders at the proper moment to the patrols and the *decurio* of the next squadron. The consequence of the extreme severity of this penalty and of the absolute impossibility of avoiding it is that the night watches of the Roman army are faultlessly kept. . . .

The Romans also have an excellent method of encouraging young soldiers to face danger. Whenever any have especially distinguished themselves in a battle, the general assembles the troops and calls forward those he considers to have shown exceptional courage. He praises them first for their gallantry in action and for anything in their previous conduct which is particularly worthy of mention, and then he distributes gifts such as the following: to a man who has wounded one of the enemy, a spear; to one who has killed and stripped an enemy, a cup if he is in the infantry, or horse-trappings if in the cavalry—originally the gift was simply a lance. These presentations are not made to men who have wounded or stripped an enemy in the course of a pitched battle, or at the storming of a city, but to those who during a skirmish or some similar situation in which there is no necessity to engage in single combat, have voluntarily and deliberately exposed themselves to danger.

At the storming of a city the first man to scale the wall is awarded a crown of gold. In the same way those who have shielded and saved one of their fellow-citizens or of the allies are honoured with gifts. . . . The men who receive these trophies not only enjoy great prestige in the army and soon afterwards in their homes, but they are also singled out for precedence in religious processions when they return. On these occasions nobody is allowed to wear decorations save those who have been honoured for their bravery by the consuls, and it is the custom to hang up the trophies they have won in the most conspicuous places in their houses, and to regard them as proofs and visible symbols of their valour. So when we consider this people's almost obsessive concern with military rewards and punishments, and the immense importance which they attach to both, it is not surprising that they emerge with brilliant success from every war in which they engage.

Question for Analysis

1. How did the Romans ensure good discipline and promote bravery among their soldiers?

Polybius, *The Rise of the Roman Empire*, trans. Ian Scott-Kilvert (New York: Penguin Books, 1984), 332–334.

The Italian Confederation formed by Rome was a unique and creative organization that conferred on Italians a measure of security and order previously unknown. Rome prevented internecine wars within the peninsula, suppressed internal revolutions within city-states, and protected the Italians from barbarians (Gallic invaders from the north). In the wars of conquest outside Italy, a share of the glory and plunder fell to all Italians, another benefit of the confederation.

By 264 B.C., Rome had achieved two striking successes. First, it had secured social cohesion by redressing the grievances of the plebeians. Second, it had increased its military might by conquering Italy, thus obtaining the human resources with which it would conquer the Mediterranean world.

Conquest of the Mediterranean World

When Rome finished unifying Italy, there were five great powers in the Mediterranean area: the Seleucid monarchy in the Near East, the Ptolemaic monarchy in Egypt, the kingdom of Macedonia, Carthage in the western Mediterranean, and the Roman-dominated Italian Confederation. One hundred twenty years later, by 146 B.C., Rome had subjected the other states to its dominion—"an event for which the past affords no precedent," said the contemporary Greek historian Polybius.

Roman expansion beyond Italy did not proceed according to predetermined design. Indeed, some Roman leaders considered involvement in foreign adventures a threat to both Rome's security and its traditional way of life. But it is difficult for a great power not to get drawn into conflicts as its interests grow, and, without planning it, Rome acquired an overseas empire.

Shortly after asserting supremacy in Italy, Rome engaged Carthage, the other great power in the western Mediterranean, in a prolonged conflict. Founded about 800 B.C. by Phoenicians, the North African city of Carthage had become a prosperous commercial center. Its wealth was derived from a virtual monopoly of trade in the western Mediterranean and along the western coasts of Africa and Europe. The Carthaginians (*Poeni* in Latin) had acquired an empire comprising North Africa and coastal regions of southern Spain, Sardinia, Corsica, and western Sicily.

War between the two great powers began because Rome feared Carthage's designs on the northern Sicilian city of Messana. Rome was apprehensive about the southern Italian city-states that were its allies, fearing that Carthage would use Messana either to attack them or to interfere with their trade. Rome decided that the security of its allies required intervention in Sicily.

The two powers had stumbled into a collision, the First Punic War (264–241 B.C.), that neither had deliberately sought. Although Rome suffered severe losses—including the annihilation of an army that had invaded North Africa and the destruction of hundreds of ships in battle and storms—the Romans never considered anything but a victor's peace. Drawing manpower from loyal allies throughout Italy, Rome finally prevailed over Carthage, which had to surrender Sicily to Rome. Three years later, Rome seized the islands of Corsica and Sardinia from a weakened Carthage. With the acquisition of these territories beyond Italy, which were made into provinces, Rome had the beginnings of an empire.

Carthaginian expansion in Spain in order to recoup wealth—Spain was rich in metals—and to obtain manpower for the depleted Carthaginian forces precipitated the Second Punic War (218–201 B.C.). Coming from Spain, the Carthaginian army was commanded by Hannibal (247–183 B.C.), whose military genius astounded the ancients. Hannibal led a seasoned army, complete with war elephants for charging enemy lines, through passes in the Alps so steep and icy that men and animals sometimes lost their footing and fell to their deaths. Some twenty-six thousand men survived the crossing into Italy; fifteen thousand more were recruited from Gallic tribesmen of the Po valley. At the battle of Cannae (216 B.C.), 50,000 Carthaginian mercenaries, principally Libyans, Numidians, Gauls, and Spaniards, faced some 60,000 Roman citizen-soldiers. In a brilliant encircling maneuver, the Carthaginian forces completely destroyed the largest army Rome had ever put into the field. The butchering by hand of the trapped Roman soldiers lasted for hours.

Romans were in a state of shock. Mixed with grief for the dead was the fear that Hannibal would crown his victory with an attack on Rome itself. To prevent panic, the Senate ordered women and children indoors, limited mourning to thirty days, and prepared to raise a new army. Adding to Rome's distress was the defection of many southern Italian allies to Hannibal.

These were the Republic's worst days. Nevertheless, says the Roman historian Livy, the Romans did not breathe a word of peace. Hannibal could not follow up his victory at Cannae with a finishing blow, for Rome wisely would

CAST MADE FROM TRAJAN'S COLUMN. Emperor Trajan (A.D. 98–117) constructed a column to commemorate his campaigns. One of the reliefs depicts a Roman fleet landing at the port of Acona. During the First Punic War, Rome had become a naval power able to counter Carthage's fleet. (© DeA Picture Library/Art Resource, N.Y.)

not allow its army to be lured into another major engagement. Nor did Hannibal possess the manpower to capture the city itself, with its formidable fortifications. In addition, most of Rome's Italian allies remained loyal, although many south Italian cities went over to Hannibal. Rome quickly raised and equipped new legions, even enlisting seventeen-year olds and promising freedom to slaves and amnesty to criminals who volunteered to serve. To finance the army, taxes were doubled and women surrendered their jewelry to the state. Most important, the Roman fleet prevented supplies from reaching the Carthaginians.

When Rome invaded North Africa, threatening Carthage, Hannibal was forced to withdraw his troops from Italy in order to defend his homeland. Hannibal, who had won every battle in Italy, was defeated by Scipio Africanus at the battle of Zama in North Africa in 202 B.C., ending the Second Punic War. Carthage was compelled to surrender Spain and to give up its elephants and its navy. Sheer determination, its vast reserves of manpower, and the state's willingness to garner its wealth to strengthen its legions explain Rome's victory.

The Second Punic War left Rome as the sole great power in the western Mediterranean; it also hastened Rome's entry into the politics of the Hellenistic world. In the year after Cannae, during Rome's darkest ordeal, Philip V of Macedonia formed an alliance with Hannibal. Fearing that the Macedonian ruler might have intentions of invading Italy, Rome initiated the First Macedonian War and won it in 205 B.C. To end Macedonian influence in Greece, which Rome increasingly viewed as a Roman protectorate, the Romans fought two other wars with Macedonia. Finally, in 148 B.C., Rome created the province of Macedonia.

Intervention in Greece led to Roman involvement in the Hellenistic kingdoms of the Near East and Asia Minor—Seleucia, Egypt, and Pergamum. The Hellenistic states became client kingdoms of Rome and consequently lost their freedom of action in foreign affairs.

Roman imperialism is a classic example of a great power being snared into overseas adventures. To achieve security, Rome protected its allies, prevented endemic warfare, and thwarted any would-be conquerors of Italy. In the course of these actions came considerable spoils of war, but Rome's principal motives for expansion were strategic and political, not economic.

In 146 B.C., the same year that Rome's hegemony over the Hellenistic world was assured, Rome concluded an unnecessary Third Punic War with Carthage. Although Carthage was by then a second-rate power and no longer a threat to Rome's security, Rome had launched this war of annihilation against Carthage in 149 B.C. The Romans were driven by old hatreds and the traumatic memory of Hannibal's near conquest. Rome sold Carthaginian survivors into slavery, obliterated the city, and turned the territory into the Roman province of Africa. Rome's savage and irrational behavior toward a helpless Carthage was an early sign of the deterioration of senatorial leadership; there would be others.

Rome had not yet reached the limits of its expansion, but there was no doubt that by 146 B.C. the Mediterranean world had been subjected to its will. No power could stand up to Rome.

Consequences of Expansion

As a result of Rome's eastern conquests, thousands of Greeks came to Rome; many were educated persons who had been enslaved because of the conquests. This influx accelerated the process of Hellenization—the adoption of Greek culture—which had begun earlier with Rome's contact with the Greek cities of southern Italy.

A crucial consequence of expansion was Roman contact with the legal experience of other peoples, including the Greeks. Roman jurists, demonstrating the Roman virtues of pragmatism and common sense, selectively incorporated into Roman law elements of the legal codes and traditions of these nations. Thus, Roman jurists empirically fashioned the *jus gentium*, the law of nations, or peoples, which gradually was applied throughout the Empire (see "Law," in Chapter 7).

Rome's conquests also contributed to the rise of a business class, whose wealth was derived from trade, army supply contracts, construction, and tax collecting in the provinces. Rome had no professional civil service, and the collection of public revenues was open to bidding—the highest bidder receiving a contract to collect customs duties, rents on public lands, and tribute in the provinces. The collector's profit came from milking as much tax money as he could from the provincials. These financiers belonged to a group called the Equites, which also included prosperous landowners. Generally, the interests of the Equites paralleled those of the ruling oligarchy. At times, however, they did support generals—notably Julius Caesar—who challenged senatorial rule.

The immense wealth brought to Rome from ransacked eastern cities and overworked Spanish silver mines gave the upper classes a taste for luxury. The rich built elaborate homes, which they decorated with fine furniture and works of art and staffed with servants, cooks, and tutors. They delighted in sumptuous banquets, which contained all types of delicacies. Wealthy matrons wore fancy gowns and elaborate hairstyles. These excesses prompted Roman moralists to castigate the people for violating traditional values. Moralists lamented that the new prosperity produced a deterioration in the Roman character.

Roman conquerors had transported to Italy hundreds of thousands of war captives, including Greeks, from all over the Empire. The enslavement and deportations would continue in the first century B.C. (Julius Caesar, for example, enslaved some one million Gauls.) It is estimated that between 80 and 8 B.C. more than two million enslaved aliens were transported to Italy. By the middle of that century, slaves constituted about one-third of Italy's population, compared with about 10 percent before the Second Punic War. The wars of conquest (and piracy) had made the slave trade a vast and lucrative commercial venture. Like the Greeks, Romans considered slavery indispensable for the preservation of civilized life. Roman jurists and intellectuals regarded the division of humanity into masters and slaves as a rule of nature and viewed the slave as an animate tool, an object that produced and served; like other forms of property, slaves could be sold or rented out by their masters. The more fortunate or more capable slaves worked as domestic servants, artisans, bookkeepers, scribes, and administrators; the luckless and more numerous, branded and chained, toiled from dawn to dusk on the growing number of plantations or died early laboring in mines under inhuman conditions. So brutal was their existence that they begged for death, reported a Roman observer. Except for the very poor, every free Roman owned at least one slave. Roman masters often treated their slaves brutally: torture was common, and masters sexually exploited both male and female slaves for their own pleasure or compelled them to work as prostitutes. But strong personal bonds between master and slave also existed—for example, there are accounts of slaves enduring torture and death to protect their masters from enemies.

Although slave uprisings were not common, their ferocity terrified the Romans. In 135 B.C., slaves in Sicily revolted and captured some key towns, defeating Roman forces before being subdued. In 73 B.C., gladiators led by Spartacus broke out of their barracks and were joined by tens of thousands of runaways. Spartacus aimed to escape from Italy to Gaul and Thrace, the homelands of many slaves. The slave army, which grew to some 150,000, defeated Roman armies and devastated southern Italy before the superior might of Rome prevailed. Some 6,000 of the defeated slaves were tortured and crucified on the road from Capua to Rome.

Republican Rome treated the people in overseas lands differently from its Italian allies. Italians were drafted into the Roman army, but provincials as a rule served only in emergencies, for Rome was not certain of their loyalty or of their readiness to meet Roman standards of discipline. Whereas Rome had been somewhat generous in extending citizenship to Italians, provincials were granted citizenship only in exceptional cases. All but some favored communities were required to pay taxes to Rome. Roman governors, lesser officials, and businessmen found the provinces a source of quick wealth; they were generally unrestrained by the Senate, which was responsible for administering the overseas territories. Exploitation, corruption, looting, and extortion soon ran rampant. "No administration in history has ever devoted itself so whole-heartedly to fleecing its subjects for the private benefit of its ruling class as Rome of the last age of the Republic," concludes E. Badian.[3] The Roman nobility proved unfit to manage a world empire.

Despite numerous examples of misrule in the provinces, Roman administration had many positive features. Rome generally allowed its subjects a large measure of self-government and did not interfere with religion and local customs. Usually, the Roman taxes worked out to be no higher, and in some instances lower, than those under previous regimes. Most important, Rome reduced the endemic warfare that had plagued these regions.

Essentially, Rome used its power for constructive ends: to establish order; to build roads, aqueducts, and public buildings; and to promote Hellenism. When Rome destroyed, it rebuilt creatively; when it conquered, it spread civilization and maintained peace. But no doubt its hundreds of thousands of prisoners of war, uprooted, enslaved, and degraded, did not view Roman conquest as beneficial; nor did the butchered Spanish tribesmen or the massacred Carthaginians.

Caspian Sea

Volga R.

Don R.

Dnieper R.

CRIMEA

Black Sea

ARMENIA

Tigris R. PARTHIA

Euphrates R.

Seleucia

Damascus

SYRIA

Antioch

CAPPADOCIA

JUDEA

Jerusalem

PONTUS

PHRYGIA

CILICIA

Cyprus

ARABIAN DESERT

Red Sea

EGYPT

Nile R.

Alexandria

Pergamum

ASIA

Rhodes

THRACE

MOESIA

Athens

Crete

Mediterranean Sea

MACEDON

Actium

DACIA

Danube R.

PANNONIA

VINONICUM

DALMATIA

Brundisium

Adriatic Sea

Cannae

Tarentum

LIBYA

SAHARA

Messana

Sicily

Elbe R.

GERMANY

RAETIA

NORICUM

CISALPINE GAUL

Po R.

ETRUSCANS

Tiber R.

Rome

Corsica

Sardinia

Carthage

NUMIDIA

NORTH AFRICA

Rhine R.

North Sea

Rhône R.

GAUL

NARBONENSIS

Balearics

MAURETANIA

BRITAIN

Ebro R.

NEARER SPAIN

FARTHER SPAIN

ATLANTIC OCEAN

0   200   400 Km.

0   200   400 Mi.

Roman territories c. 140 B.C.

Roman territories added by 44 B.C.

Major battle

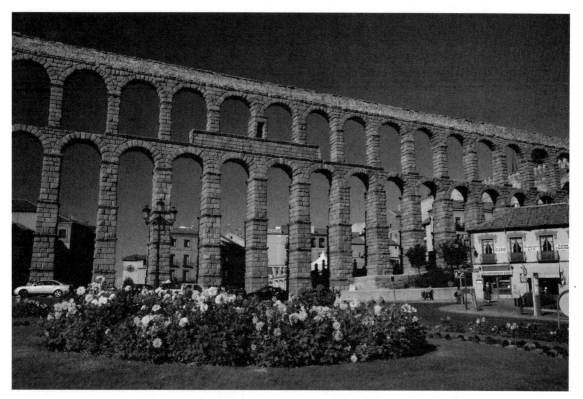

RUINS IN SPAIN. This Roman aqueduct in Spain stands as an impressive reminder of the ancient Romans' engineering skills. (© Alan Copson/JAI/Corbis.)

To these hapless victims, Rome appeared as an evil oppressor, not as the creator of a cosmopolis that brought order and security.

CULTURE IN THE REPUBLIC

One of the chief consequences of expansion was increased contact with Greek culture. During the third century B.C., Greek civilization started to exercise an increasing and fruitful influence on the Roman mind. Greek teachers, both slave and free,

◀ *Map 6.1* ROMAN CONQUESTS DURING THE REPUBLIC The conquest of Italy gave Rome the manpower to expand throughout the Mediterranean world. In the Second Punic War, Rome defeated its greatest rival, Carthage. (Copyright © 2013 Cengage Learning.)

came to Rome and introduced Romans to Hellenic cultural achievements. As they conquered the eastern Mediterranean, Roman generals began to ship libraries and works of art from Greek cities to Rome. Roman sculpture and painting imitated Greek prototypes. In time, Romans acquired from Greece knowledge of scientific thought, philosophy, medicine, and geography. Roman writers and orators used Greek history, poetry, drama, and oratory as models. The Elder Pliny (A.D. 23–79), who wrote on many topics but is most famous for *Natural History*, refers to Homer's poetry as "the most valuable work of the human mind."[4] Cicero, Rome's greatest orator, tells us that ambitious young men eager to learn the art of oratory but unaware of the existence of any "course of training or any rules of art . . . attain[ed] what skill they could by means of their natural ability. . . . But later, having heard the Greek orators, gained acquaintance with their literature and called in

Greek teachers, our people were fired with a really incredible enthusiasm for eloquence."[5]

Adopting the humanist outlook of the Greeks, the Romans came to value human intelligence and eloquent and graceful prose and poetry. Wealthy Romans retained Greek tutors, poets, and philosophers in their households and sent their sons to Athens to study. By the late Republic, educated Romans could speak and read Greek. Thus, Rome creatively assimilated the Greek achievement and transmitted it to others, thereby extending the orbit of Hellenism. To be sure, some conservative Romans were hostile to the Greek influence, which they felt threatened traditional Roman values that had accounted for Roman greatness. Cato the Elder (234–149 B.C.) and other Roman moralists denounced Socrates for undermining respect for Athenian law and warned that Greek philosophy might lure Roman youth into similar subversive behavior. Moreover, said these moralists, Greek philosophy, with its endless discussions of abstract themes, contrasted with the virtue most cherished by Romans—*gravitas*, or seriousness, which enabled Romans to conduct public affairs effectively. Philosophy seemed designed for a life of leisure and inaction, whereas a virtuous Roman was actively involved in practical civic matters. But the tide of Hellenism could not be stemmed.

Plautus (c. 254–184 B.C.), Rome's greatest playwright, adopted features of fourth- and third-century Greek comedy. His plays had Greek characters and took place in Greek settings; the actors wore the Greek style of dress. His characters resembled those found in Menander's comedies: a cunning slave, a lovesick youth, a foolish old man, a braggart soldier. The plots often consisted of a struggle between two antagonists over a woman or money, or both. The plays usually had the ending desired by the audience: the "good guy" won, and the "bad guy" received a fitting punishment. The pains of love were a common theme.

> *Not the throes of all mankind*
> *Equal my distracted mind.*
> *I strain and I toss*
> *On a passionate cross;*
> *Love's goad makes me reel,*
> *I whirl on Love's wheel,*
> *In a swoon of despair*

> *Hurried here, hurried there—*
> *Torn asunder, I am blind*
> *With a cloud upon my mind.*[6]

Terence (c. 185–159 B.C.), another playwright, was originally from North Africa and was brought to Rome as a slave. His owner, a Roman senator, provided the talented youth with an education and freed him. Terence demonstrated humaneness, a quality that can be seen in his attitude toward child rearing.

> *I give—I overlook; I do not judge it necessary*
> *to exert my authority in everything. . . . I think*
> *it better to restrain children through a sense*
> *of shame and liberal treatment than through*
> *fear. . . . This is the duty of a parent to ac-*
> *custom a son to do what is right rather of his*
> *own choice, than through fear of another.*[7]

Catullus (c. 84–c. 54 B.C.) is generally regarded as one of the greatest lyric poets in world literature. He was a native of northern Italy whose father had provided him with a gentleman's education. In his early twenties, Catullus came to Rome and fell in love with Clodia; she was the wife of the governor of Cisalpine Gaul, who was away at the time. For the older Clodia, Catullus was a refreshing diversion from her many other lovers. Tormented by Clodia's numerous affairs, Catullus struggled to break away from passion's grip.

> *I look no more for her to be my lover*
> *As I love her. That thing could never be.*
> *Nor pray I for her purity—that's over.*
> *Only this much I pray, that I be free.*
> *Free from insane desire myself, and guarded*
> *In peace at last. O heaven, grant that yet*
> *The faith by which I've lived may be*
> *   rewarded.*
> *Let me forget.*[8]

Lucretius (c. 96–c. 55 B.C.), the leading Roman Epicurean philosopher, was influenced by the civil war fostered by two generals, Marius and Sulla, which is discussed later in this chapter. Distraught by the seemingly endless strife, Lucretius yearned for philosophical tranquility. Like Epicurus, he believed that religion prompted people to perform evil deeds and caused them to experience terrible anxiety about death and eternal punishment. In his work *On the Nature of Things*, Lucretius expressed his appreciation of Epicurus. Like his mentor, Lucretius denounced superstition and religion for fostering psychological distress and advanced a materialistic conception of nature, one that left no room for the activity of gods—mechanical laws, not the gods, governed all physical happenings. To dispel the fear of punishment after death, Lucretius marshaled arguments to prove that the soul perishes with the body. He proposed that the simple life, devoid of political involvement and excessive passion, was the highest good and the path that would lead from emotional turmoil to peace of mind. Epicurus' hostility to traditional religion, disparagement of politics and public service, and rejection of the goals of power and glory ran counter to the accepted Roman ideal of virtue. On the other hand, his glorification of the quiet life amid a community of friends and his advice on how to deal with life's misfortunes with serenity had great appeal to first-century Romans like Lucretius, who were disgusted with civil strife.

Rome's finest orator, as well as a leading statesman, Cicero (106–43 B.C.) was an unsurpassed Latin stylist and a student of Greek philosophy. His letters, more than eight hundred of which have survived, provide modern historians with valuable insights into the politics of the late Republic. His Senate speeches have been models of refined rhetoric for all students of the Latin language. Cicero's discussion of such topics as republicanism, citizenship, friendship, virtue, duty, and justice had an enduring influence on Western moral and political thought. Dedicated to republicanism and public-spiritedness, Cicero sought to prevent one-man rule and in his writings exhorted fellow Romans to serve their city.

Cicero was drawn to Stoicism, the most influential philosophy in Rome. Stoicism's stress on virtuous conduct and performance of duty coincided with Roman ideals, and its doctrine of a natural law that applies to all nations, regardless of ethnicity or culture, harmonized with the requirements of a world empire. Cicero admired the Stoic goal of the self-sufficient sage who sought to accord his life with standards of virtue inherent in nature. Natural law commands people to do what is right and deters them from doing what is

wrong, and our gift of reason enables us to abide by its commands. Thus, knowledge and virtue are closely linked. Cicero adopted the Stoic belief that the law of the state should conform with the rational and moral norms embodied in natural law, for adherence to such rationally formulated law creates a moral bond among citizens.

He also shared the Stoic view that because natural law applies to all, we are all citizens of a single commonwealth and belong to a society of humanity. As he expressed it,

> there is no difference in kind between man and man; for Reason, which alone raises us above the level of the beasts and enables us to draw inferences, to prove and disprove, to discuss and solve problems, and to come to conclusions, is certainly common to us all, and though varying in what it learns, at least in the capacity to learn it is invariable. . . . In fact, there is no human being of any race who, if he finds a guide, cannot attain virtue.[9]

In the eighteenth century, the Founding Fathers of the United States praised Cicero's natural law philosophy, which coincided with their belief in inalienable rights; his condemnation of tyranny; and his advocacy of liberty, republicanism, and constitutional government.

COLLAPSE OF THE REPUBLIC

In 146 B.C., Roman might spanned the Mediterranean world. After that year, the principal concerns of the Republic were no longer foreign invasions but adjusting city-state institutions to the demands of empire and overcoming critical social and political problems at home. The Republic was unequal to either challenge. Instead of developing a professional civil service to administer the conquered lands, Roman leaders attempted to govern an empire with city-state institutions that had evolved for a different purpose. The established Roman administration proved unable to govern the Mediterranean world. In addition, Rome's ruling elites showed little concern for the welfare of their subjects, and provincial rule worsened as governors, tax collectors, and soldiers shamelessly exploited the provincials.

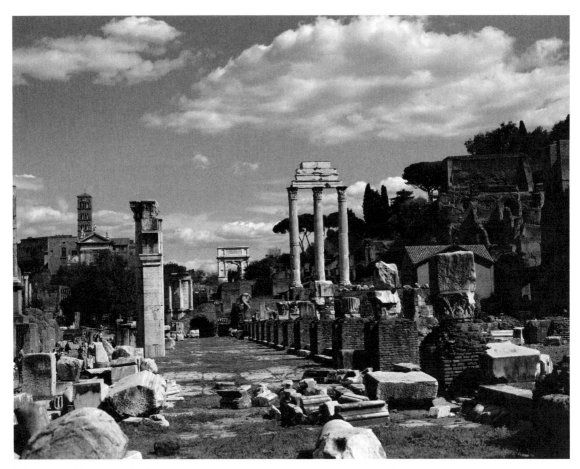

FORUM IN ROME. The forum, a large rectangular space that served as a marketplace, was the center of a Roman city. In Rome itself, the forum evolved into a political center surrounded by large public buildings. (Hiroshi Higuchi/Getty Images.)

During Rome's march to empire, all its classes had demonstrated a magnificent civic spirit in fighting foreign wars. With Carthage and Macedonia no longer threatening Rome, this cooperation deteriorated, as Cato the Elder had forewarned: "What was to become of Rome, when she should no longer have any state to fear?"[10] Internal dissension tore Rome apart as the drive for domination formerly directed against foreign enemies turned inward against fellow Romans. Civil war replaced foreign war.

The Romans had prevailed over their opponents partly because of their traditional virtues: resoluteness, simplicity of manners, and willingness to sacrifice personal interests for the good of Rome. But the riches flowing into Rome from the plundered provinces caused these virtues to decay, and rivalry for status and a frenzied pursuit of wealth overrode civic patriotism. This "perverted greed" and "lack of principle," said the poet Horace (65–8 B.C.), had caused "impious slaughter, . . . intestine [domestic] fury, . . . and lawless licence."[11] And the masses, landless and afflicted with poverty and idleness, withdrew their allegiance from the state.

In this time of agony, both great and self-seeking individuals emerged. Some struggled to restore the social harmony and political unity that had prevailed in the period of expansion. Others, political adventurers, attacked the authority of the Senate to gain personal power. The Senate, which had previously exercised leadership creatively and responsibly, degenerated into a self-serving oligarchy that resisted reform and fought to preserve its power and privilege.

Neither the Senate nor its opponents could rejuvenate the Republic. Eventually it collapsed, a victim of class tensions, poor leadership, power-hungry demagogues, and civil war. Underlying all these conditions were the breakdown of social harmony and the deterioration of civic patriotism. The Republic had conquered an empire only to see the character of its citizens decay. In a high moral tone, the historian Sallust (c. 86–34 B.C.) condemned the breakdown of republican values.

> *Growing love of money, and the lust for power which followed it, engendered every kind of evil. Avarice destroyed honor, integrity, and every other virtue, and instead taught men to be proud and cruel, to neglect religion, and to hold nothing too sacred to sell. Ambition tempted many to be false.... At first these vices grew slowly and some times met with punishments; later on, when the disease had spread like a plague, Rome changed: her government, once so just and admirable, became harsh and unendurable.*[12]

Crisis in Agriculture

The downhill slide of the Republic began with an agricultural crisis. During the long war with Hannibal in Italy, each side had tried to deprive the other of food supplies; in the process, they ruined farm land, destroyed farmhouses and farm equipment, and slaughtered animals. With many Roman soldier-farmers serving in the army for long stretches of time, fields lay neglected. Returning veterans with small holdings lacked the wealth to restore their land. They were forced to sell their farms to wealthy landowners at low prices.

Another factor that helped to squeeze out the owners of small farms was the importation of hundreds of thousands of slaves to work on large plantations called **latifundia**. This massive use

of slaves was unprecedented in Roman history. Farmers who had formerly increased their meager incomes by working for wages on neighboring large estates were no longer needed. Sinking ever deeper into poverty and debt, farmers gave up their lands and went to Rome, seeking work. The dispossessed peasantry found little to do in Rome, where there was not enough industry to provide them with employment and where much of the work was done by slaves. Congregated in rundown, crime-ridden slums and chronically unemployed, the urban poor faced a daily struggle for survival. The once sturdy and independent Roman farmer, who had done all that his country had asked of him, was becoming part of a vast urban underclass—destitute, embittered, and alienated. The uprooting of a formerly self-reliant peasantry was Hannibal's posthumous revenge on Rome; severing the civic bond, it would prove even more deadly than Cannae.

The Gracchan Revolution

In 133 B.C., Tiberius Gracchus (163–133 B.C.), who came from one of Rome's most honored families, was elected tribune. Distressed by the injustice done to the peasantry and recognizing that the Roman army depended on the loyalty of small landowners, Tiberius made himself the spokesman for land reform. He proposed a simple and moderate solution for the problem of the landless peasants: implementing an old law barring any Roman from using more than 312 acres of the state-owned land obtained in the process of uniting Italy. For many years, the upper class had ignored this law, occupying vast tracts of public land. By reenacting the law, Tiberius hoped to free land for distribution to landless citizens.

Rome's leading families viewed Tiberius as a revolutionary threatening their property and political authority. They thought him a dangerous democrat who would undermine the Senate, the seat of aristocratic power, in favor of the Assembly, which represented the commoners. When Tiberius sought reelection as a tribune, a violation of constitutional tradition, the senators were convinced that he was a rabble-rouser who aimed to destroy the republican constitution and become a one-man ruler. To preserve the status quo, with

Cleopatra

Cleopatra (69–30 B.C.), the Greek queen of Egypt, belonged to the Ptolemaic family, the Macedonian Greeks who ruled Egypt during the Hellenistic Age. Cleopatra spoke Greek, received a Greek education, and viewed herself as Greek, but in contrast to her Ptolemaic predecessors, she also learned to speak the Egyptian tongue. Aspiring to revive Ptolemaic power, which had once extended into Palestine and Lebanon, she had the political good sense to realize that this could not be accomplished by antagonizing Rome, which dominated the Mediterranean world.

Cleopatra became Julius Caesar's mistress when the Roman leader stopped at Alexandria. In 47 B.C., she bore a son, declaring that Caesar was the father, and in the next year she followed Caesar to Rome. Three years after Caesar's assassination, she became Mark Antony's lover and bore him twins. She worked closely with Antony, who competed with Octavian for control of the Roman world. At the naval battle of Actium in 31 B.C., Antony and Cleopatra escaped to Egypt, where Octavian pursued them. When Antony's forces either surrendered to Octavian without a fight or fled, Cleopatra barricaded herself inside her mausoleum. Thinking that she had killed herself, Antony plunged a sword into his body. A messenger told the dying Antony that Cleopatra was still alive and wished to see him. Slaves carried him to her. Because the mausoleum's doors were sealed, he had to be hoisted with great difficulty to an opening in the wall by Cleopatra and her female servants.

wealth and power concentrated in the hands of a few hundred families, senatorial extremists killed Tiberius and some three hundred of his followers, dumping their bodies into the Tiber.

The cause of land reform was next taken up by Gaius Gracchus (153–121 B.C.), a younger brother of Tiberius. An emotional and gifted speaker, Gaius won the support of the city poor and was elected tribune in 123 B.C. A more astute politician than his brother, Gaius increased his following by favoring the Equites, the new class of plebeian businessmen, and by promising full citizenship to all Italians. He aided the poor by reintroducing his brother's plan for land distribution and by enabling them to buy grain from the state at less than half the market price. But like his brother, Gaius aroused the anger of the senatorial class, which ordered his murder. After his death, three thousand of his followers were executed without trial.

By killing the Gracchi, the Senate had substituted violence for reason and made murder a means of coping with troublesome opposition. Soon the club and the dagger became common weapons in Roman politics, hurling Rome into an era of political violence that ended with the destruction of the Republic. Though the Senate considered itself the guardian of republican liberty, in reality it was expressing the determination of a few hundred families to retain their control over the state. This is a classic example of a once-creative minority clinging tenaciously to power long after it has ceased to govern effectively or to inspire allegiance. The Senate, which had led Rome to world dominance, became a self-seeking, unimaginative, entrenched oligarchy that was dragging the Republic and the Mediterranean world into disaster.

Rome in the first century B.C. was very different from the Rome that had defeated Hannibal. Entranced by luxuries flowing into Rome from its eastern conquests and determined to retain oligarchic rule, the senatorial families neglected their responsibility to the state. Many upper-class Romans, burning to achieve the dignity and glory that would mark them as great men, tried to climb onto the crowded stage of Roman politics, but the best roles were already reserved for members of the senatorial families. With so few opportunities, aspirants to political power stopped at nothing.

Roman politics in the century after the Gracchi was bedeviled by intrigues, rivalries, personal

Plutarch, the ancient biographer, described the scene:

Those that were present say that nothing was ever more sad than this spectacle, to see Antony, covered all over with blood and just expiring, thus drawn up, still holding up his hands to her, and lifting up his body with the little force he had left. . . . When she had got him up, she laid him on the bed, tearing all her clothes, which she spread upon him; and beating her breast with her hands, lacerating herself, and disfiguring her own face with the blood from his wounds, she called him her lord, her husband, her emperor.*

Antony died shortly afterward. Captured by the Romans, Cleopatra feared that Octavian would parade her in a victory celebration at Rome. To avoid such a humiliation, the proud Cleopatra poisoned herself, ending the Ptolemaic dynasty in Egypt. In a last letter, she requested to be buried beside Antony.

Cleopatra's life and death have intrigued historians; writers, including Shakespeare; and Hollywood producers. Her true character remains elusive. She had sufficient allure to attract both Caesar and Antony and sufficient ruthlessness to murder her younger brother, and co-ruler, in order to make her son co-ruler. No doubt her determination and ambition made her an equal partner with Antony in their political quest.

---

*Plutarch, *The Lives of Noble Grecians and Romans*, trans. John Dryden, rev. A. H. Clough (New York: The Modern Library, n.d.), 1148.

ambition, and violence. Political adventurers exploited the issue of cheap grain and free land in order to benefit their careers. Whereas the Gracchi were sincere reformers, these later champions of social reform were unscrupulous demagogues who cleverly charmed and manipulated the city poor with bread and circuses: low-cost food and free admission to games. These demagogues aspired to the tribunate of the plebes, an office possessing powers formidable enough to challenge the Senate and not too difficult to obtain since ten tribunes were elected each year. By riding a wave of popular enthusiasm, these political adventurers hoped to sweep aside the Senate and concentrate power in their own hands. The poor, denied land and employment, demoralized, alienated, and lulled into political ignorance by decades of idleness, food handouts, and free entertainment, were ready to back whoever made the most glittering promises. The Senate behaved like a decadent oligarchy, and the Tribal Assembly, which had become the voice of the urban mob, demonstrated a weakness for demagogues, an openness to bribery, and an abundance of deceit and incompetence. The Roman Republic had passed the peak of its greatness.

Rival Generals

Marius (157–86 B.C.), who became consul in 107 B.C., adopted a military policy that eventually contributed to the wrecking of the Republic. Until about 100 B.C., soldiers served essentially at their own expense, paying for their arms, armor, and food. This meant that only men of some substance could serve. Short of troops for a campaign in Numidia in North Africa, Marius disposed of the traditional property requirement for entrance into the army and filled his legions with volunteers from the urban poor, a dangerous precedent. These new soldiers, disillusioned with Rome, served only because Marius held out the promise of pay, loot, and land grants after discharge. In effect, they were Marius's clients. Their loyalty was not to Rome but to Marius, and they remained loyal to their commander only as long as he fulfilled his promises.

Marius set an example that other ambitious commanders followed. They saw that a general could use his army to advance his political career, that by retaining the confidence of his soldiers he could cow the Senate and dictate Roman policy. The army, no longer an instrument of government, became a private possession of generals. Seeing its authority undermined by generals appointed by the Assembly, the Senate was forced to seek army commanders who would champion the cause of senatorial rule. In time, Rome would be engulfed in civil wars as rival generals used their troops to strengthen their political affiliations and to further their own ambitions.

Meanwhile, the Senate continued to deal ineffectively with Rome's problems. When Rome's Italian allies—who had provided the manpower needed to conquer the Empire—pressed for citizenship, the Senate refused to make concessions. The Senate's shortsightedness plunged Italy into a savage war known as the Social War. As it ravaged the peninsula, the Romans reversed their policy and conferred citizenship on the Italians. The unnecessary and ruinous rebellion petered out.

While Rome was fighting its Italian allies, Mithridates, king of Pontus in northern Asia Minor, invaded the wealthy Roman province of Asia. In 88 B.C., he incited the local population to massacre eighty thousand Italian residents of the province, a devastating blow to Rome's economy and prestige. Mithridates and his forces crossed into Greece and occupied Athens and other cities. Faced with this crisis, the Senate entrusted command to Sulla (138–78 B.C.), who had distinguished himself in the Social War. But supporters of Marius, through intrigue and violence, had the order rescinded and the command given to Marius.

Sulla refused to accept his loss of command, which deprived him of honor and opportunity for riches; with his loyal troops, he proceeded to the capital. This was a fateful moment in Roman history: the first march on Rome by a Roman legion, the first prolonged civil war, and the first time a commander and his troops defied the government. The competition for honor, the overriding concern of Roman aristocrats, had taken Rome down a perilous path. Sulla won the first round. But when Sulla left Rome to fight Mithridates in Greece, Marius and his troops retook the city and, in a frenzy, lashed out at Sulla's supporters. The killing lasted for five days and nights.

Marius died shortly afterward. Sulla, on his return, quickly subdued Marius's supporters and became dictator of Rome. He instituted a terror that far surpassed Marius's violence. Without legal sanction and with cold-blooded cruelty, Sulla marked his opponents for death; the state seized their property and declared their children and grandchildren ineligible for public office.

Sulla resolved to use his absolute power to revive the Senate's rule and make it permanent. He believed that only rule by an aristocratic oligarchy could protect Rome from future military adventurers and assure domestic peace. Therefore, he restored the Senate's right to veto acts of the Assembly, limited the power of the tribunes and the Assembly, and, to prevent any march on Rome, reduced the military authority of provincial governors. To make the Senate less oligarchic, he increased its membership to six hundred. Having put through these reforms, Sulla retired.

Julius Caesar

The Senate failed to wield its restored authority effectively. The Republic was still menaced by military commanders who used their troops for their own political advantage, and underlying problems remained unsolved. In 60 B.C., a triumvirate, a ruling group of three—consisting of Julius Caesar (c. 100–44 B.C.), a politician; Pompey, a general; and Crassus, a wealthy banker—conspired to take over Rome. The ablest of the three was Caesar. Descended from an ancient noble family, Caesar had first gained public recognition for his demonstration of conspicuous bravery in Rome's assault on the rebellious Greek city of Mytilene. Upon returning to Rome, he distinguished himself as an orator—his star was rising.

Recognizing the importance of a military command as a prerequisite for political prominence, Caesar gained command of the legions in Gaul in 59 B.C. The following year he began the conquest of the part of Gaul not under Roman control, bringing the future France into the orbit of Greco-Roman civilization. The campaign was brilliantly described in his *Commentaries*, although, to be sure, the work was a deliberate attempt to apprise the Roman public of his military prowess. The successful Gallic campaigns and the invasion of Britain revealed Caesar's exceptional talent for generalship: he acted decisively, moved troops rapidly, and had excellent rapport with his men. By plundering Gaul, he also acquired a fortune

BUST OF CAESAR. Julius Caesar tried to rescue a dying Roman world by imposing strong rule. He paved the way for the transition from republican to imperial rule. (Scala/Art Resource, N.Y.)

that could be used to further his political career. Indeed, Caesar's victories alarmed the Senate, which feared that the popular general would use his devoted troops and soaring reputation to seize control of the state.

Meanwhile, the triumvirate had fallen apart. In 53 B.C., Crassus had perished with his army in a disastrous campaign against the Parthians in the East. The bonds between Pompey and Caesar were weak, consisting essentially of Pompey's

marriage to Caesar's daughter Julia. After her death in 54 B.C., Pompey and Caesar grew apart. Pompey, who was jealous of Caesar's success and eager to expand his own power, drew closer to the Senate. Supported by Pompey, the Senate ordered Caesar to relinquish his command. Caesar realized that without his troops he would be defenseless; he decided instead to march on Rome. After Caesar crossed the Rubicon River into Italy in 49 B.C., civil war again ravaged the Republic. Pompey proved no match for so talented a general; the Senate acknowledged Caesar's victory and appointed him to be dictator, a legal office, for ten years.

Caesar realized that republican institutions no longer operated effectively and that only strong and enlightened leadership could permanently end the civil warfare destroying Rome. His reforms were designed to create order out of chaos. Caesar responded to the grievances of the provincial subjects by lowering taxes, making the governors responsible to him, restraining Roman businessmen from ruthlessly draining the provinces' wealth, and generously extending citizenship. To gain greater support for Rome, he also granted citizenship to more Italians. To aid the poor in Rome, he began a public works program, which provided employment and beautified the city. He also relocated more than a hundred thousand veterans and members of Rome's lower class to the provinces, where he gave them land. To improve administration, he reorganized town governments in Italy, reformed the courts, and planned to codify the law. He attempted to conciliate the senatorial class by treating former enemies with moderation and generosity.

In February 44 B.C., Rome's ruling class—jealous of Caesar's success and power and afraid of his ambition—became thoroughly alarmed when his temporary dictatorship was converted into a lifelong office. The aristocracy saw this event as the end of senatorial government and their rule, which they equated with liberty, and as the beginning of a Hellenistic type of monarchy. On March 15 of that year, a group of aristocrats, regarding themselves as defenders of centuries-old republican traditions and institutions, assassinated Caesar. The group included the general and orator Marcus Junius Brutus. Cicero expressed the feeling that motivated the conspirators.

Our tyrant deserves his death, [for his] was the blackest crime of all. [Caesar was] a man who was ambitious to be king of the Roman people and master of the whole world. . . . The man who maintains that such an ambition is morally right is a madman, for he justifies the destruction of law and liberty.[13]

The Republic's Last Years

The assassination of Julius Caesar did not restore republican liberty but plunged Rome into renewed civil war. Thousands more died in battle or were killed in the proscriptions—lists of Roman citizens declared by their political enemies to be outlaws. Those proscribed had their property confiscated and could be executed. Two of Caesar's trusted lieutenants, Mark Antony and Lepidus, joined with Octavian, Caesar's adopted son, and defeated the armies of Brutus and Cassius, two conspirators in the plot against Caesar. After Lepidus was forced into political obscurity, Antony and Octavian fought each other, with control of Rome as the prize. In 31 B.C., at the naval battle of Actium in western Greece, Octavian crushed the forces of Antony and his wife, Egypt's Queen Cleopatra (who had earlier borne Julius Caesar's son). Octavian emerged as master of Rome and four years later became, in effect, the first Roman emperor. The Roman Republic, whose death throes had lasted for decades and kept the Mediterranean world in turmoil, had finally perished.

The Roman Republic, which had amassed power to a degree hitherto unknown in the ancient world, was wrecked not by foreign invasion but by internal weaknesses: the personal ambitions of power seekers; the degeneration of senatorial leadership and the transformation of political rivalry into violence and terror, in which opponents were condemned to death and their property confiscated; the formation of private armies, in which soldiers gave their loyalty to their commander rather than to Rome; the transformation of a self-reliant peasantry into an impoverished and demoralized city rabble; and the deterioration of the ancient virtues that had been the source of the state's vitality. Before 146 B.C., the threat posed by foreign enemies, particularly Carthage, had forced Romans to work together for the benefit of the state, and the equilibrium achieved during the patrician–plebeian struggle was maintained. This social cohesion broke down when foreign danger diminished. In the ensuing century of turmoil, the apparatus of city-state government failed to function effectively.

Thus, the high point of Roman rule was not achieved under the Republic. The city-state constitution of the Republic was too limited to govern an immense empire. Rome first had to surpass the narrow framework of city-state government before it could unite the Mediterranean world in peace and law. The genius of Augustus (Octavian), the first emperor, made this development possible.

NOTES

1. Cicero, *De Republica*, trans. Clinton Walker Keyes (Cambridge, Mass.: Harvard University Press, Loeb Classical Library, 1994), 79.

2. Ibid., 81.

3. E. Badian, *Roman Imperialism in the Late Republic* (Ithaca, N.Y.: Cornell University Press, 1971), 87.

4. Quoted in Alan Wardman, *Rome's Debt to Greece* (New York: St. Martin's Press, 1976), 62.

5. Cicero, *De Oratore,* trans. E. W. Sutton (Cambridge, Mass.: Harvard University Press, Loeb Classical Library, 1967), 14.

6. Quoted in J. Wright Duff, *A Literary History of Rome* (New York: Barnes and Noble, 1960), 136–137.

7. Terence, *The Brothers,* trans. H. T. Riley (London: Henry G. Bohn, 1853), 202–203.

8. Catullus, quoted in E. A. Havelock, *The Lyric Genius of Catullus* (New York: Russell and Russell, 1929), 63.

9. Cicero, *De Legibus,* trans. C. W. Keyes (Cambridge, Mass.: Harvard University Press, Loeb Classical Library, 1928), 329–330.

10. Quoted in Eli Sagan, *The Honey and the Hemlock* (New York: Basic Books, 1991), 25.

11. Horace, *The Odes and Epodes,* trans. C. E. Bennett (Cambridge, Mass.: Harvard University Press, 1988), ode 24, pp. 255–256.

12. Sallust, *The Conspiracy of Catiline,* trans. S. A. Handford (Baltimore: Penguin Books, 1963), 181–182.

13. Cicero, *De Officiis,* trans. Walter Miller (Cambridge, Mass.: Harvard University Press, Loeb Classical Library, 1913), 357.

SUGGESTED READING

Boren, H. C., *Roman Society* (1977). A social, economic, and cultural history of the Republic and the Empire, written with the student in mind.

Christ, Karl, *The Romans* (1984). A good survey.

Crawford, M., *The Roman Republic* (1982). A reliable survey, with many quotations from original sources.

Dupont, Florence, *Daily Life in Ancient Rome* (1989). Everyday private and public lives of Roman citizens.

Errington, R. M., *The Dawn of Empire: Rome's Rise to World Power* (1972). A study of Rome, the reluctant imperialist.

Grant, Michael, *History of Rome* (1978). A synthesis of Roman history by a leading classical scholar; valuable in regard to both the Republic and the Empire.

Holland, Tom, *Rubicon: The Last Years of the Roman Republic* (2003). Well-written and intelligent.

McGeouch, Kevin M., *The Romans* (2004). A comprehensive analysis of Roman society and culture in the Republic and the Empire.

Ogilvie, R. M., *Roman Literature and Society* (1980). An introductory survey of Latin literature.

Wood, Neal, *Cicero's Social and Political Thought* (1988). An important work for understanding ancient thought and Cicero's impact on later Western political philosophy.

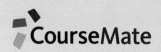

CourseMate

Go to the CourseMate website at **www.cengagebrain.com** for additional study tools and review materials—including audio and video clips—for this chapter.

Chapter 7

The Roman Empire: A World-State

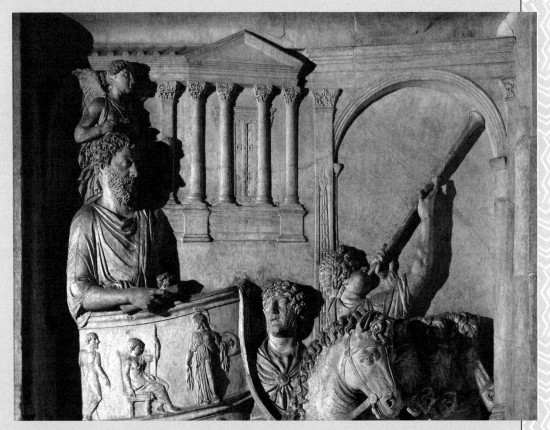

Marcus Aurelius, Roman Emperor (161–180) In this relief, Marcus rides through the Roman Forum in ceremonial triumph after defending the Empire against barbarian incursions.

(Alfredo Dagli Orti/© The Art Archive/Corbis.)

Focus Questions

1. What is the historical significance of Augustus?
2. Why is the Pax Romana regarded as one of the finest periods in world history? What continuity is there between the Pax Romana and the Hellenistic Age?
3. How did Roman law evolve? How did it incorporate Stoic principles?
4. Why is the third century regarded as an age of crisis?
5. What are the reasons for the decline of the Roman Empire?
6. What is Rome's legacy to Western civilization?

Rome's republican institutions, designed for a city-state, proved incapable of coping with the problems created by the conquest of a world empire. Invincible against foreign enemies, the Republic collapsed from within. But after Octavian's brilliant statesmanship brought order out of chaos, Rome entered its golden age under the rule of emperors. For more than two hundred years, from 27 B.C. to A.D. 180, the Mediterranean world enjoyed unparalleled peace and stability. The Roman world-state, erected on a Hellenic cultural foundation and cemented with empirewide civil service, laws, and citizenship, gave practical expression to Stoic cosmopolitanism and universalism. Yet even this impressive monument had structural defects, and in the third century A.D. the Empire was wracked by crises from which it never fully recovered. In the fifth century, Germanic tribesmen overran the western half of the Empire, which had by then become a shadow of its former self.

During its time of trouble, Rome also experienced an intellectual crisis. Forsaking the rational and secular values of classical humanism, many Romans sought spiritual comfort in Near Eastern religions. One of these religions, Christianity, won out over its competitors and was made the official religion of the Empire. With the triumph of Christianity in the Late Roman Empire, Western civilization took a new direction. Christianity would become the principal shaper of the European civilization that emerged from the ruins of Rome.

AUGUSTUS AND THE FOUNDATIONS OF THE ROMAN EMPIRE

After Octavian's forces defeated those of Antony and Cleopatra at the battle of Actium in 31 B.C., no opponents could stand up to him. The century of civil war, political murder, corruption, and mismanagement had exhausted the Mediterranean world, which longed for order. Like Caesar before him, Octavian recognized that only a strong monarchy could rescue Rome from civil war and anarchy. But learning from Caesar's assassination, he also knew that republican ideals were far from dead. To exercise autocratic power openly, like a Hellenistic monarch, would have aroused the hostility of the

141

Chronology 7.1 ❖ The Roman Empire

27 B.C.	Senate grants Octavian the title Augustus, and he becomes, in effect, the first Roman emperor; start of the principate and the Pax Romana
A.D. 14	Death of Augustus; Tiberius gains the throne
66–70	Jewish revolt: Romans capture Jerusalem and destroy the second temple
79	Eruption of Mount Vesuvius and destruction of Pompeii and Herculaneum
132–135	Hadrian crushes another Hebrew revolt
180	Marcus Aurelius dies: end of the Pax Romana
212	Roman citizenship is granted to virtually all free inhabitants of Roman provinces
235–285	Military anarchy; Germanic incursions
285–305	Diocletian tries to deal with the crisis by creating a regimented state
378	Battle of Adrianople: Visigoths defeat the Roman legions
406	Imperial borders collapse, and Germanic tribes move into the Empire
410	Rome is plundered by Visigoths
455	Rome is sacked by Vandals
476	End of the Roman Empire in the West

Roman ruling class, whose assistance and goodwill Octavian desired.

Octavian demonstrated his political genius by reconciling his military monarchy with republican institutions: he held absolute power without abruptly breaking with a republican past. Magistrates were still elected, and assemblies still met; the Senate administered certain provinces, retained its treasury, and was invited to advise Octavian. With some truth, Octavian could claim that he ruled in partnership with the Senate. By maintaining the facade of the Republic, Octavian camouflaged his absolute power and contained senatorial opposition, which already had been weakened by the deaths of leading nobles in battle or in the purges that Octavian had instituted against his enemies. Moreover, Octavian's control over the armed forces made resistance futile, and the terrible violence that followed Caesar's assassination made senators amenable to change.

In 27 B.C., Octavian shrewdly offered to surrender his power, knowing that the Senate, purged of opposition, would demand that he continue to lead the state. By this act, Octavian could claim to be a legitimate constitutional ruler leading a government of law, not one of lawless despotism so hateful to the Roman mentality. In keeping with his policy of maintaining the appearance of traditional republican government, Octavian refused to be called king or even, like Caesar, dictator; instead, he cleverly disguised his autocratic rule by taking the inoffensive title *princeps* (first citizen). The Senate also honored Octavian by conferring on him the semireligious and revered name of *Augustus*. (The rule of Augustus and his successors is referred to as the *principate*.)

The reign of Augustus signified the end of the Roman Republic and the beginning of the Roman Empire—the termination of senatorial rule and aristocratic politics and the emergence of one-man rule. The old Roman aristocracy, decimated by war and the proscriptions employed by Antony, Lepidus, and Octavian, had to adjust to a political situation in which they no longer predominated. As the historian Tacitus recognized, Augustus accomplished a profound revolution in Roman political life: "The country had been transformed, and there was nothing left of the fine old Roman character. Political equality was a thing of the past; all eyes watched for imperial commands."[1] Under Augustus, who ruled

THE PANTHEON, C. A.D. 125. The Pantheon, the most complete surviving building of Roman antiquity, was built by Emperor Hadrian in the second century A.D. In the temple, Greek forms of ornamentation are combined with Roman building techniques. The vast hemispherical dome was constructed by pouring concrete into great wooden forms; then the interior was faced with marble. In contrast to a Greek temple, where the exterior is paramount, the Roman temple emphasizes interior space. (Alinari/Art Resource, N.Y.)

from 27 B.C. to A.D. 14, the power of the ruler was disguised; in ensuing generations, however, emperors would wield absolute power openly. As Rome became more autocratic and centralized, it took on the appearance of an oriental monarchy.

Augustus introduced the practice of emperor worship. In the eastern provinces, where Middle Eastern and Hellenistic monarchs had been traditionally regarded as divine, the person of Augustus was worshiped as a god. In Italy, where the deification of leaders was alien to the republican spirit, divine honors were granted to Augustus's genius, or spirit of leadership; once deceased, Augustus and his successors were deified. The imperial cult, with its ceremonies, processions, temples, and statues, strengthened the bonds of loyalty that

Caspian Sea

Volga R.

Don R.

Dnieper R.

Black Sea

CRIMEA

Constantinople
(Byzantium)

THRACE

ARMENIA

Tigris R.   PARTHIA

Euphrates R.

Babylon

ARABIAN DESERT

Red Sea

Jerusalem

JUDEA

SYRIA

CAPPADOCIA

PONTUS

PHRYGIA

PISIDIA

CILICIA

ASIA

Pergamum

Cyprus

Rhodes

Nile R.

EGYPT

Alexandria

LIBYA

Crete

Mediterranean Sea

Athens

ACHAEA
(GREECE)

Actium

DACIA

MOESIA

MACEDON

PANNONIA

VINDONNA

DALMATIA

Adriatic Sea

Pompeii

Sicily

NORICUM

RAETIA

Aquileia

CISALPINE
GAUL

Po R.

Tiber R.

Rome

Danube R.

Elbe R.

GERMANY

Rhine R.

BELGIUM

Seine R.

GAUL

NARBONENSIS

Rhône R.

Corsica

Sardinia

Balearics

Carthage

NUMIDIA

NORTH AFRICA

SAHARA

MAURETANIA

Ebro R.

NEARER SPAIN

FARTHER SPAIN

BRITAIN

North Sea

ATLANTIC
OCEAN

400 Mi.

400 Km.

200

200

0

0

Roman Empire under Augustus

Territory added by Hadrian's reign

Line dividing eastern and western
parts of the Roman Empire

Major battle

tied subjects to the emperor. By the third century, Italians and other peoples in the western territories generally viewed the living emperor as a god-king.

Despite his introduction of autocratic rule, Augustus was by no means a self-seeking tyrant, but a creative statesman. Heir to the Roman tradition of civic duty, he regarded his power as a public trust delegated to him by the Roman people. He was faithful to the classical ideal, which required that the state should promote the good life by protecting civilization from barbarism and ignorance; he sought to rescue a dying Roman world by restoring political order and reviving the moral values and civic spirit that had contributed to Rome's greatness.

To prevent a renewal of civil war and to safeguard the borders of the Empire, Augustus reformed the army. As commander in chief, he could guard against the reemergence of ambitious generals like those whose rivalries and private armies had wrecked the Republic. Augustus maintained the loyalty of his soldiers by ensuring that veterans, on discharge, would receive substantial bonuses and land in Italy or in the provinces. By organizing a professional standing army made up mostly of volunteers who generally served for twenty-five years, Augustus was assured a well-trained and loyal force capable of maintaining internal order, extending Roman territory, and securing the frontier.

For the city of Rome, Augustus had aqueducts and water mains built, which brought water to most Roman homes, and he beautified the city by restoring ancient monuments and temples and building new ones. He created a fire brigade, which reduced the danger of great conflagrations in crowded tenement districts, and he organized a police force to contain violence. He improved the distribution of free grain to the impoverished urban masses and financed the popular gladiatorial combats out of his own funds.

◀ *Map 7.1* THE ROMAN EMPIRE UNDER AUGUSTUS AND HADRIAN During the Pax Romana, the Roman Empire expanded beyond the Rhine and Danube Rivers, the imperial boundary during the reign of Augustus. (Copyright © 2013 Cengage Learning.)

In Italy, Augustus had roads repaired, and he fostered public works. He arranged for Italians to play a more important role in the administration of the Empire. For the Italians' security, his army suppressed brigandage, which had proliferated in the countryside during the preceding century of agony, and he guarded the northern borders from barbarian incursions.

By ending the civil wars and their accompanying devastation and by ruling out forced requisition of supplies and extortion of money, Augustus earned the gratitude of the provincials. Also contributing to his empirewide popularity were his efforts to correct tax abuse and to end corruption through improving the quality of governors and enabling aggrieved provincials to bring charges against Roman officials. An imperial bureaucracy, which enabled talented and dedicated men to serve the state, gradually evolved. In addition, Augustus continued the sensible practice of not interfering with the traditional customs and religions of the provinces. During his forty-year reign—the longevity itself was a stabilizing factor—Rome overcame the chaos of the years of revolution. The praise bestowed on him by grateful provincials was not undeserved. One decree from the province of Asia called Augustus

> the savior of all mankind in common whose provident care has not only fulfilled but even surpassed the hopes of all: for both land and sea are at peace, the cities are teeming with the blessings of concord, plenty, and respect for law, and the culmination and harvest of all good things bring fair hopes for the future and contentment with the present.[2]

THE PAX ROMANA

The brilliant statesmanship of Augustus inaugurated Rome's greatest age. For the next two hundred years, the Mediterranean world enjoyed the blessings of the **Pax Romana**, the Roman peace. The ancient world had never experienced such a long period of peace, order, efficient administration, and prosperity. Although both proficient and inept rulers succeeded Augustus, the essential features of the Pax Romana persisted.

Profile

Epictetus

Born a slave, Epictetus (c. A.D. 55–135) belonged to an official (himself a former slave) who served the emperors Nero and Domitian. Even before he was given his freedom, Epictetus received a good education from his master. In A.D. 89, Domitian, fearful that philosophers would cast doubt on the emperor's divinity, banished all philosophers from Rome and Italy. Epictetus moved to Epirus in Greece, where he attracted students. One student recorded and organized Epictetus's thoughts into eight books, four of which were lost. Epictetus presented his views in the form of maxims: admonitions from a teacher to his students to pursue the moral life. His ideas greatly influenced Marcus Aurelius, the Roman emperor and Stoic philosopher.

Like other Stoic philosophers, Epictetus was concerned with attaining peace of mind—an inner contentment that produces happiness. For Epictetus, happiness did not depend on material possessions, status, reputation, or the affection others have for us. By pursuing these externals, he said, we become subject to the people who are needed to procure them for us: "If you are absorbed in externals, you must necessarily be tossed up and down, according to the inclination of your master. Who is your master? Whosoever controls those things which you seek."*

Epictetus maintained that to achieve happiness we must reduce desires, shun things that are beyond our power to control, and deliberately strive for inner dignity and moral integrity. Human beings, said Epictetus, can shield themselves from life's uncertainties and misfortunes, even slavery, by taking control of the part of themselves that belongs to no one else: their minds. Epictetus defined man as a rational

The Successors of Augustus

The first four emperors who succeeded Augustus were related either to him or to his third wife, Livia. They constituted the Julio-Claudian dynasty, which ruled from A.D. 14 to 68. Although their reigns were marked by conspiracies, summary executions, and assassinations, the great achievements of Augustus were preserved and strengthened. The Senate did not seek to restore republicanism and continued to assist the princeps; the imperial bureaucracy grew larger and more professional; the army, with some exceptions, remained a loyal and disciplined force.

The Julio-Claudian dynasty came to an end in A.D. 68, when the emperor Nero committed suicide. Nero had grown increasingly tyrannical and had lost the confidence of the people, the senatorial class, and the generals, who rose in revolt. In the year following his death, anarchy reigned as military leaders competed for the throne. After a bloody civil war, the execution of two emperors, and the suicide of another, Vespasian gained the principate. Vespasian's reign (A.D. 69–79) marked the beginning of the Flavian dynasty. By rotating commanding officers and stationing native troops far from their homelands, Vespasian improved discipline and discouraged mutiny. By having the great Colosseum of Rome constructed for gladiatorial contests, he earned the gratitude of the city's inhabitants. Vespasian also had nationalist uprisings put down in Gaul and Judea.

In Judea, Roman rule clashed with Jewish religious-national sentiments. Recognizing the tenaciousness with which Jews clung to their faith, the Roman leaders deliberately refrained from interfering with Hebraic religious beliefs and practices. Numerous privileges, such as exemption from emperor worship because it conflicted with the requirements of strict monotheism, were extended to Jews not only in Judea but throughout the Empire. Sometimes, however, the Romans engaged in activities that outraged the Jews. For example, Pontius Pilate, the Roman procurator in being. It is reason that distinguishes man from wild beasts and cattle. He wrote:

> *Take care, then to do nothing like a wild beast; otherwise you have destroyed the man; you have not fulfilled what your nature promises. Take care too, to do nothing like cattle; for thus likewise the man is destroyed. In what do we act like cattle? When we act gluttonously, lewdly, rashly, sordidly, inconsiderately, into what are we sunk? Into cattle. What have we destroyed? The rational being. When we behave contentiously, injuriously, passionately, and violently, into what we have sunk? Into wild beasts. . . . By all these means the nature of man is destroyed.*[†]

---

*Epictetus, *Discourses*, based on translation of Thomas Wentworth Higginson (Roslyn, N.Y.: Walter J. Black, Classics Club, 1944), bk. 2, chap. 2, p. 92.

†Ibid., bk. 2, chap. 9, pp. 106–107.

Judea from A.D. 26 to 36, at one point ordered a Roman army unit into Jerusalem with banners bearing the image of the emperor. The entire Jewish nation was aroused. To the Jews, this display of a pagan idol in their holy city was an abomination. Realizing that the Jews would die rather than permit this act of sacrilege, Pilate ordered the banners removed. Another explosive situation emerged when the emperor Caligula (A.D. 37–41) ordered that a golden statue of himself be placed in Jerusalem's temple. Again, the order was rescinded when the Jews demonstrated their readiness to resist.

Relations between the Jews of Judea and the Roman authorities deteriorated progressively in succeeding decades. Militant Jews, who rejected Roman rule as a threat to the purity of Jewish life, urged their people to take up arms. Feeling a religious obligation to reestablish an independent kingdom in their ancient homeland and unable to reconcile themselves to Roman rule, the Jews launched a full-scale war of liberation in A.D. 66. In A.D. 70, after a five-month siege had inflicted terrible punishment on the Jews, Roman armies captured Jerusalem and destroyed the temple, the central site and focus of Jewish religious life. After the conquest of Jerusalem, some fortresses, including Masada on the western side of the Dead Sea, continued to resist. The defenders of Masada withstood a Roman siege until A.D. 73; refusing to become Roman captives, they took their own lives.

Vespasian was succeeded by his sons Titus (A.D. 79–81) and Domitian (A.D. 81–96). The reign of Titus was made memorable by the eruption of Mount Vesuvius, which devastated the towns of Pompeii and Herculaneum. After Titus's brief time as emperor, his younger brother Domitian became ruler. Upon crushing a revolt led by the Roman commander in Upper Germany, a frightened Domitian executed many leading Romans. These actions led to his assassination in A.D. 96, ending the Flavian dynasty. The Flavians, however, succeeded in consolidating and extending the borders of the Empire.

The Senate selected one of its own, Nerva, to succeed the murdered Domitian. Nerva's reign (A.D. 96–98) was brief and uneventful. But he introduced a wise practice that would endure until A.D. 180: he adopted as his son and designated as his heir a man with proven ability, Trajan, the governor of Upper Germany. This adoptive system assured a succession of competent rulers.

During his rule (A.D. 98–117), Trajan eased the burden of taxation in the provinces, provided for the needs of poor children, and had public works built. With his enlarged army, he conquered Dacia (parts of Romania and Hungary), where he seized vast quantities of gold and silver. He made the territory into a Roman province, adding to the large frontier Rome had to protect. The settlement of the region by many of Trajan's veterans led to its Romanization.

Trajan's successor, Hadrian (A.D. 117–138), abandoned what remained of Trajan's eastern conquests. He strengthened border defenses in Britain and fought the second Hebrew revolt in Judea (A.D. 132–135). After initial successes, including the capture of Jerusalem, the Jews were again defeated by superior Roman might. The majority of Palestinian Jews were killed, sold as slaves, or forced to seek refuge in other lands. The Romans renamed the province Syria Palestina; they forbade Jews to enter Jerusalem, except once a year, and encouraged non-Jews to settle the land. Although the Jews continued to maintain a presence in Palestine, they had become a dispossessed and dispersed people.

After Hadrian came another ruler who had a long reign, Antoninus Pius (A.D. 138–161). He introduced humane and just reforms. He set limits on the right of masters to torture their slaves to obtain evidence, and he established the principle that an accused person be considered innocent until proven guilty. During the reign of Antoninus, the Empire remained peaceful and prosperous.

Marcus Aurelius (A.D. 161–180), the next emperor, was also a philosopher whose *Meditations* eloquently expressed Stoic thought. Frequent strife marked his reign. Roman forces had to fight the eastern kingdom of Parthia. The Roman legions were victorious in this campaign but brought back from the East an epidemic that decimated the population of the Empire. Marcus Aurelius also had to deal with Germanic incursions into Italy and the Balkan Peninsula—incursions far more serious than any faced by previous emperors.

From the accession of Nerva in A.D. 96 to the death of Marcus Aurelius in A.D. 180, the Roman Empire was ruled by "the Five Good Emperors." During this period, the Empire was at the height of its power and prosperity, and nearly all its peoples benefited. The four emperors preceding Marcus Aurelius had no living sons, so they had resorted to the adoptive system in selecting successors, which served Rome effectively. But Marcus Aurelius chose his own son, Commodus, to succeed him. With the accession of Commodus—a misfit and a megalomaniac—in A.D. 180, the Pax Romana came to an end.

"The Time of Happiness"

The Romans called the Pax Romana "the Time of Happiness." They saw it as the fulfillment of Rome's mission: the creation of a world-state that provided peace, security, ordered civilization, and the rule of law. Roman legions defended the Rhine–Danube river frontiers from incursions by Germanic tribesmen, held the Parthians at bay in the east, and subdued the few uprisings that occurred. Nerva's adoptive system of selecting emperors provided Rome with internal stability and a succession of emperors with exceptional ability. These Roman emperors did not use military force needlessly but fought for sensible political goals; generals did not wage war recklessly but tried to limit casualties, avoid risks, and deter conflicts by a show of force.

Constructive Rule.   Roman rule was constructive. The Romans built roads—some fifty-three thousand miles of roads, from Scotland to the Euphrates—improved harbors, cleared forests, drained swamps, irrigated deserts, and cultivated undeveloped lands. The aqueducts they constructed brought fresh water for drinking and bathing to large numbers of people, and the effective sewage systems enhanced the quality of life. Goods were transported over roads made safe by Roman soldiers and across a Mediterranean Sea swept clear of pirates. A wide variety of goods circulated throughout the Empire. A stable currency, generally not subject to depreciation, contributed to the economic well-being of the Mediterranean world.

Scores of new cities sprang up, and old ones grew larger and wealthier. Although these municipalities had lost their power to wage war and had to bow to the will of the emperors, they retained considerable freedom of action in local matters. Imperial troops guarded against civil wars within the cities and prevented warfare between cities—two traditional weaknesses of city life in the ancient world. Some two thousand municipalities served as centers of Greco-Roman civilization, which spread to the farthest reaches of the Mediterranean, continuing a process initiated during the Hellenistic Age. Regions of North Africa, Gaul, Britain, and South Germany, hitherto untouched by Hellenism, were brought into the orbit of Greco-Roman civilization. Barriers between Italians and provincials broke down as Spaniards, Gauls, Africans, and other provincials rose to high positions in the army and in the imperial administration and even became emperors. Citizenship, generously granted, was finally extended to virtually all free people by an edict of A.D. 212.

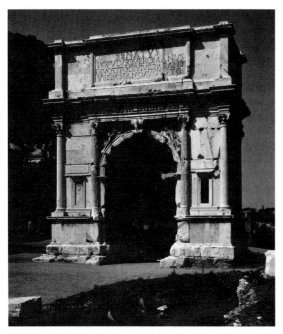

ARCH OF TITUS, C. A.D. 81, CONCRETE FACED WITH MARBLE, ROME. The arch stands at the crest of the Sacred Way to commemorate Titus' successful capture of Jerusalem in A.D. 70. It was dedicated in A.D. 81 by his brother, the Emperor Domitian.
(Scala/Art Resource, N.Y.)

BASALT BUST OF LIVIA. Octavian's third wife, Livia (58 B.C.–A.D. 29), was admired for her wisdom and dignity, and the emperor valued her counsel.
(Alinari/Art Resource, N.Y.)

Improved Conditions for Both Slaves and Women. Conditions improved for those at the bottom of society, the slaves. At the time of Augustus, slaves may have accounted for a quarter of the population of Italy. But their numbers declined as Rome engaged in fewer wars of conquest. The freeing of slaves also became more common during the Empire. Urban slaves, who were often skilled artisans, could be induced to work more effectively if there was the hope of **manumission**. Often, nobles liberated and set up in business skilled and enterprising slaves in return for a share of the profits. Freed slaves became citizens, with most of the rights and privileges of other citizens; their children suffered no legal disabilities. (The poet Terence, the Stoic philosopher Epictetus, and the father of the poet Horace were all freed slaves.)

During the Republic, slaves had been terribly abused; they were often mutilated, thrown to wild beasts, crucified, or burned alive. Several emperors issued decrees protecting slaves from cruel masters. Claudius forbade masters to kill sick slaves; Vespasian forbade masters to sell slaves into prostitution. Domitian prohibited the castration of slaves, and Hadrian barred the execution of slaves without a judicial sentence.

The status of women had been gradually improving during the Republic. In the early days of the Republic, a woman lived under the absolute authority first of her father and then of her husband. By the time of the Empire, a woman could own property and, if divorced, keep her dowry. A father could no longer force his daughter to marry against her will, although upper-class marriages were usually based on political and social considerations. Women could make business arrangements and draw up wills without the consent of their husbands. Roman women, unlike their Greek counterparts, were not secluded in their homes but could come and go as they pleased. Upper-class women of Rome had far greater opportunities for education than did those of Greece, and some formed groups that read and discussed poetry.

Supervising the household remained the principal responsibility of Roman women. The Romans regarded marriage as a sacred civic duty. Seeking to restore traditional values, Augustus issued decrees encouraging Romans to marry. Romans greatly admired the woman who loved only one man and had only one husband, but in reality promiscuity, adultery, divorce, and remarriage were quite common. A wife could obtain a divorce just as easily as her husband, but as a rule children remained with their father. Despite the frequency of divorce, there is evidence that husbands and wives held genuine affection for each other.

The history of the Empire, indeed Roman history in general, was filled with talented and influential women. Cornelia, the mother of Tiberius and Gaius Gracchus, influenced Roman politics through her sons. The historian Sallust said that Sempronia, the wife of a consul and the mother of Brutus, one of the assassins of Julius Caesar, was "well-educated in Greek and Latin literature.... She could write poetry, crack a joke, and converse at will.... She was in fact a woman of ready wit and considerable charm."[3] Livia, the dynamic wife of Augustus, was often consulted on important government matters, and during the third century there were times when women controlled the throne.

An Orderly World Community.

From Britain to the Arabian Desert, from the Danube River to the sands of the Sahara, some fifty to seventy million people with differing native languages, customs, and histories were united by Roman rule into a world community. Unlike officials of the Republic, when corruption and exploitation in the provinces were notorious, officials of the Empire felt a strong sense of responsibility to preserve the Roman peace, institute Roman justice, and spread Roman civilization.

In creating a stable and orderly political community with an expansive conception of citizenship, Rome resolved the problems posed by the limitations of the Greek city-state: civil war, intercity warfare, and a parochial attitude that divided people into Greek and non-Greek. Rome also brought to fruition an ideal of the Greek city-state—the protection and promotion of civilized life. By constructing a world community that broke down barriers between nations, by preserving and spreading Greco-Roman civilization, and by developing a rational system of law that applied to all humanity, Rome completed the trend toward universalism and cosmopolitanism that had emerged in the Hellenistic Age. The Roman world-state was the classical mind's response to the problem of community posed by the decline of the city-state in the era of Alexander the Great. Aelius Aristides, a second-century rhetorician, although Greek, proudly considered himself a Roman and glowingly extolled the Roman achievement.

> *Neither sea nor any intervening distance on land excludes one from citizenship. No distinction is made between Asia and Europe in this respect. Everything lies open to everybody; and no one fit for office or a position of trust is an alien.... You have made the word "Roman" apply not to a city but to a universal people.... You no longer classify peoples as Greek or barbarian.... You have redivided mankind into Romans and non-Romans.... Under this classification there are many in each city who are no less fellow citizens of yours than those of their own stock, though some of them have never seen this city.*[4]

medicine, and geography. Roman writers used Greek models; sharing in the humanist outlook of the Greeks, they valued human achievement and expressed themselves in a graceful and eloquent style. The diffusion of Hellenism throughout the Mediterranean world produced a cultural unity among elites that underlay the Pax Romana. Roman cultural life reached its high point during the reign of Augustus, when Rome experienced the golden age of Latin literature.

Literature and History. At the request of Augustus, who wanted a literary **epic** to glorify the Empire and his role in founding it, Virgil (70–19 B.C.) wrote the *Aeneid*, a masterpiece in world literature. The *Aeneid* is a long poem that recounts the tale of Aeneas and the founding of Rome. The first six books, which describe the wanderings of Aeneas, a survivor of Troy, show the influence of Homer's *Odyssey*; the last six, dealing with the wars in Italy, show the *Iliad*'s imprint. Whereas Homer's epics focused on the deeds and misdeeds of heroic warriors, the *Aeneid* is a literary epic of national glory. The most profound ideas and feelings expressed in the *Aeneid* are Roman virtues—patriotism, devotion to the family, duty to the state, and a strong sense of religion. Intensely patriotic, Virgil ascribed to Rome a divine mission to bring peace and civilized life to the world, and he praised Augustus as a divinely appointed ruler who had fulfilled Rome's mission. The Greeks might be better sculptors, orators, and thinkers, said Virgil, but only the Romans knew how to govern an empire.

BAS-RELIEF FROM CONSTANTINE'S ARCH. Emperor Marcus Aurelius dispenses aid to needy citizens.
(Alinari/Art Resource, N.Y.)

Roman Culture and Law During the Pax Romana

During the late Roman Republic, Rome had creatively assimilated the Greek achievement (see Chapter 6) and transmitted it to others who had little or no contact with Hellenism. Rome had acquired Greek scientific thought, philosophy,

> *For other peoples will, I do not doubt,*
> *still cast their bronze to breathe with softer*
> *   features,*
> *or draw out of the marble living lines, plead*
> *   causes better,*
> *trace the ways of heaven with wands and tell*
> *   the rising*
> *constellations; but yours will be the rulership*
> *   of nations,*
> *remember, Roman, these will be your arts:*
> *to teach the ways of peace to those you*
> *   conquer, to spare*
> *defeated peoples, to tame the proud.*[5]

Aelius Aristides: The Blessings of the Pax Romana

In the following reading, Aelius Aristides (A.D. 117–187), a Greek intellectual, glowingly praises the Pax Romana in an oration that was probably delivered in Rome. In the tradition of Roman orators, Aristides used hyperbole and exaggeration. Nevertheless, the oration does capture the universalism and cosmopolitanism that characterized the Roman Empire.

"But the most marvelous and admirable achievement of all, and the one deserving our fullest gratitude, is this. . . . You alone of the imperial powers of history rule over men who are free. You have not assigned this or that region to [unscrupulous governors]. . . . Just as citizens in an individual city might designate magistrates, so you, whose city is the whole world, appoint governors to protect and provide for the governed, as if they were elective, not to lord it over their charges. As a result, so far from disputing the office as if it were their own, governors make way for their successors readily when their term is up, and may not even await their coming. Appeals to a higher jurisdiction are as easy as appeals from parish to county. . . .

"But the most notable and praiseworthy feature of all, a thing unparalleled, is your magnanimous conception of citizenship. All of your subjects (and this implies the whole world) you have divided into two parts: the better endowed and more virile, wherever they may be, you have granted citizenship and even kinship; the rest you govern as obedient subjects. Neither the seas nor expanse of land bars citizenship; Asia and Europe are not differentiated. Careers are open to talent. . . . Rich and poor find contentment and profit in your system; there is no other way of life. Your polity is a single and all-embracing harmony. . . .

. . . "[You] established cities in diverse parts. The cities you filled with colonists; you introduced arts and crafts and established an orderly culture. . . . Your military organization makes all others childish. Your soldiers and officers you train to prevail not only over the enemy but over themselves. The soldier lives under discipline daily, and none ever deserts the post assigned him.

"You alone are, so to speak, natural rulers. Your predecessors were masters and slaves in turn; as rulers they were counterfeits, and reversed their positions like players in a ball game. . . . You have measured out the world, bridged rivers, cut roads through mountains, filled the wastes with posting stations, introduced orderly and refined modes of life. . . .

"Be all gods and their offspring invoked to grant that this empire and this city flourish forever and never cease until stones float upon the sea and trees forbear to sprout in the springtide. May the great Ruler and his sons be preserved to administer all things well."

Question for Analysis

1. What did Aristides find so admirable in Rome's imperial system?

Moses Hadas, ed., *A History of Rome: From Its Origins to 529 A.D. as Told by the Roman Historians* (Garden City, N.Y.: Doubleday Anchor Books, 1956), 143–145.

In his *History of Rome,* the historian Livy (59 B.C.–A.D. 17) also glorified Roman virtues, customs, and deeds. He praised Augustus for attempting to revive traditional Roman morality, to which Livy felt a strong attachment. Modern historians criticize Livy for failing to utilize important sources of information in this work, for relying on biased authorities, and for allowing fierce patriotism to warp his judgment. Although Livy was a lesser historian than Thucydides or Polybius, his work was still a major achievement, particularly in its depiction of the Roman character, which helped make Rome great.

An outstanding poet, Horace (65–8 B.C.) was the son of a freed slave. He broadened his education by studying literature and philosophy in Athens, and Greek ideals are reflected in his writings. Horace enjoyed the luxury of country estates, banquets, fine clothes, and courtesans, along with the simple pleasures of mountain streams and clear skies. His poetry touched on many themes—the joy of good wine, the value of moderation, and the beauty of friendship. Desiring to blend reason and emotion, Horace urged men to seek pleasurable experiences but to avoid extremes and to keep desire under rational control. He also reminded Romans of the terrible civil wars that had ruined the Republic.

> *What plain is not enriched with Latin blood, to bear witness with its graves to our unholy strife. . . . What pool or stream has failed to taste the dismal war! What sea has Italian slaughter not discolored! What coast knows not our blood![6]*

Unlike Virgil, Livy, or Horace, Ovid (43 B.C.–A.D. 17) did not experience the civil wars during his adult years. Consequently, he was less inclined to praise the Augustan peace. His poetry showed a preference for romance and humor, and he is best remembered for his advice to lovers contained in his most famous work, *The Art of Love.* Written when Ovid was fifty years old, the work deals with the art of seduction. Book I tells how to attract a woman who is the object of a man's desire; Book II explains how a man can keep a woman's love; Book III advises women about men. To the man who wants to win a woman, Ovid gave this counsel:

> *First of all, be quite sure that there isn't a woman who cannot be won, and make up your mind that you will win her. Only you must prepare the ground.*
>
> *You must play the lover for all you're worth. Tell her how you are pining for her.*
>
> *Never cease to sing the praises of her face, her hair, her taper fingers, and her dainty foot.*
>
> *Tears too are a mighty useful resource in the matter of love. They would melt a diamond. Make a point, therefore, of letting your mistress see your face all wet with tears.*
>
> *Women are things of many moods. You must adapt your treatment to the special case.[7]*

The writers who lived after the Augustan age were of a lesser quality than their predecessors, although the historian Tacitus (A.D. 55–c. 118) was an exception. Sympathetic to republican institutions, Tacitus denounced Roman emperors and the imperial system in his *Histories* and *Annals.* In *Germania,* he turned his sights on the habits of the Germanic peoples. He described the Germans as undisciplined but heroic, with a strong love of freedom.

The satirist Juvenal (A.D. c. 55–138) attacked the evils of Roman society, such as the misconduct of emperors, the haughtiness of the wealthy, the barbaric tastes of commoners, and the failures of parents. He also described the noise, congestion, and poverty of the capital, as well as its criminal element.

> *But these aren't your only terrors. For you can never restrain*
> *The criminal element. Lock up your house, put bolt and chain*
> *On your shop, but when all's quiet, someone will rob you or he'll*
> *Be a cutthroat perhaps and do you in quickly with cold steel.[8]*

In addition, Juvenal expressed venomous views toward women. He describes the humiliations husbands must face—infidelity, poisonings, public harlotry, and being ignored, intimidated, and dominated. All of this, says Juvenal, is a consequence of a wife's failure to live up to the obligations of the married state—being silent, loyal, obedient, respectful of her husband, and caring for the children.

Philosophy. Stoicism was the principal philosophy of the Pax Romana, and its leading exponents were Seneca, Epictetus (A.D. c. 60–c. 117), and the emperor Marcus Aurelius. Perpetuating the rational tradition of Greek philosophy, Roman Stoics saw the universe as governed by reason, and they esteemed the human intellect. Like Socrates, they sought the highest good in this world, not in an afterlife, and envisioned no power above human reason. Moral values were obtained from reason alone. The individual was self-sufficient and depended entirely on rational faculties for knowing and doing good. Stoics valued self-sufficient persons who attained virtue and wisdom by exercising rational control over their lives. Roman thinkers also embraced the Stoic doctrine that all people, because of their capacity to reason, belong to a common humanity.

Lucius Annaeus Seneca (4 B.C.–A.D. 65), a student of rhetoric and philosophy, served the emperor Nero. After Nero accused him of participating in a conspiracy against the throne, Seneca was forced to commit suicide. Seneca's Stoic humanitarianism was expressed in his denunciation of the gladiatorial combats and in his concern for slaves. He urged Romans "to consider, that he whom you call your slave, is sprung from the same origin, enjoys the same climate, breathes the same air, and is subject to the same condition of life and death as yourself."[9]

The emperor Marcus Aurelius, the last of the great Stoics, also had to deal with serious problems confronting the Empire. While commanding troops engaged in fighting plundering tribesmen in the Balkans, he wrote in Greek the *Meditations*, a classic work of Stoic thought. In Stoicism,

he sought the strength to overcome the burdens of ruling an empire, the fear of death, and the injustices and misdeeds committed by his fellows.

> *Hour by hour resolve firmly, like a Roman and a man, to do what comes to hand with correct and natural dignity, and with humanity, independence, and justice. Allow your mind freedom from all other considerations. This you can do, if you will approach each action as though it were your last, dismissing the wayward thought, the emotional recoil from the commands of reason, the desire to create an impression, the admiration of self, the discontent with your lot. See how little a man needs to master, for his days to flow on in quietness and piety: he has but to observe these few counsels, and the gods will ask nothing more.[10]*

Science. The two most prominent scientists during the Greco-Roman age were Ptolemy, the mathematician, geographer, and astronomer, who worked at Alexandria in the second century A.D., and Galen (A.D. c. 130–c. 201), who investigated medicine and anatomy. Ptolemy's thirteen-volume work, *Mathematical Composition*—more commonly known as the *Almagest*, a Greek-Arabic term meaning "the greatest"—summed up antiquity's knowledge of astronomy and became the authoritative text during the Middle Ages. In the Ptolemaic system, a motionless, round earth stood in the center of the universe, and the moon, sun, and planets moved about the earth in circles, or in combinations of circles. The Ptolemaic system was built on a faulty premise, as modern astronomy eventually showed. However, it did work—that is, it did provide a model of the universe that adequately accounted for most observed phenomena. The Ptolemaic system would not be challenged until the middle of the sixteenth century.

As Ptolemy's system dominated astronomy, so the theories of Galen dominated medicine down to modern times. By dissecting both dead and living animals, Galen attempted a rational investigation of the body's working parts. Although his work contains many errors, he made essential contributions to the knowledge of anatomy. Thanks to Arab physicians who preserved his writings during the Middle Ages, Galen's influence continued in the West into early modern times.

Art, Architecture, and Engineering. Romans borrowed art forms from other peoples, particularly the Greeks, but they borrowed creatively, transforming and enhancing their inheritance. Roman portraiture continued trends initiated during the Hellenistic Age. Imitating Hellenistic models, Roman sculptors realistically carved every detail of a subject's face: unruly hair, prominent nose, lines and wrinkles, a jaw that showed weakness or strength. Sculpture also gave expression to the imperial ideal. Statues of emperors conveyed nobility and authority; reliefs commemorating victories glorified Roman might and grandeur.

The Romans most creatively transformed the Greek inheritance in architecture. The Greek temple was intended to be viewed from the outside; the focus was exclusively on the superbly balanced exterior. By using arches, vaults, and domes, the Romans built structures with large, magnificent interiors. The vast interior, massive walls, and overarching dome of the famous Pantheon, a temple built in the early second century, during the reign of Hadrian, symbolizes the power and majesty of the Roman world-state.

The Romans excelled at engineering. They built amphitheaters, public baths, and aqueducts that carried water to Roman cities—some still survive. Roman engineers with an eye for natural barriers and drainage problems carefully selected routes and designed great embanked roads, the finest in the ancient world.

Law. Expressing the Roman yearning for order and justice, law was Rome's great legacy to Western civilization. Roman law passed through two essential stages: the formation of civil law (*jus civile*) and the formation of the law of nations (*jus gentium*). The basic features of the civil law evolved during the two-hundred-year Struggle of the Orders, at the same time that Rome was extending its dominion over Italy. The Twelve Tables, drawn up in the early days of the patrician–plebeian struggle (described at the beginning of Chapter 6), established for the Roman state written rules of criminal and civil law that applied to all citizens. Over the centuries, the civil law was expanded by statutes enacted by the assemblies, by the legal decisions of jurisdictional magistrates, by the rulings of emperors, and by the commentaries of professional jurists, who, aided by familiarity with Greek logic, engaged in systematic legal analysis.

During the period of the Republic's expansion outside Italy, contact with the Greeks and other peoples led to the development of the second branch of Roman law, jus gentium, which combined Roman civil law with principles selectively drawn from the legal tradition of Greeks and other peoples. Roman jurists identified the jus gentium with the natural law (*jus naturale*) of the Stoics. The jurists said that a law should accord with rational principles inherent in nature: uniform and universally valid standards that can be discerned by rational people. Serving to bind different peoples together, the law of nations harmonized with the requirements of a world empire and with Stoic ideals, as Cicero pointed out.

> *True law is right reason in agreement with nature; it is of universal application, unchanging and ever lasting. . . . And there will not be different laws at Rome and at Athens or different laws now and in the future, but one eternal and unchangeable law will be valid for all nations and all times.*[11]

The law of nations came to be applied throughout the Empire, although it never entirely supplanted local law. In the eyes of the law, a citizen was not a Syrian or a Briton or a Spaniard but a Roman. In effect, through jus gentium, an international law, Rome transformed what was a theoretical principle for the Stoics into a political reality.

After the fall of the western Roman Empire, Roman law fell into disuse in Europe. Gradually reintroduced in the twelfth century, it came to

THE COLOSSEUM, ROME, A.D. 70–80. The joint work of the emperor Vespasian and his sons Titus and Domitian, this huge amphitheater was the largest in the ancient world. It was the site of innumerable spectacles, sham sea battles, gladiatorial games, wild beast hunts, and the deaths of Christian martyrs.
(Scala/Art Resource, N.Y.)

form the basis of the common law in all Western European lands except Britain and its dependencies. Some provisions of Roman law are readily recognizable in modern legal systems, as the following excerpts illustrate:

> *Justice is a constant, unfailing disposition to give everyone his legal due.*
> *No one suffers a penalty for what he thinks.*
> *In the case of major offenses it makes a difference whether something is committed purposefully or accidentally.*

> *The guilt or punishment of a father can impose no stigma upon the son, for every individual is subjected to treatment in accordance with his own action, and no one is made the inheritor of the guilt of another.*
> *In inflicting penalties, the age . . . of the guilty party must be taken into account.*[12]

Entertainment. Despite its many achievements, Roman civilization presents a paradox. On the one hand, Roman culture and law evidence high standards of civilization. On the other hand, the Romans institutionalized barbaric practices: battles to the death between armed gladiators and the tormenting and slaughtering of wild beasts.

The major forms of entertainment in both the Republic and the Empire were chariot races, wild animal shows, and gladiatorial combat. Chariot races were gala events in which the most skillful riders and the finest and best-trained stallions raced in an atmosphere of extreme excitement. The charioteers, many of them slaves hoping that victory would bring them freedom, became popular heroes. The rich staked fortunes on the races, and the poor bet their last coins.

The Romans craved brutal spectacles. One form of entertainment pitted wild beasts against each other or against men armed with spears. Another consisted of battles, sometimes to the death, between highly trained gladiators. The gladiators, mainly prisoners of war and condemned criminals, learned their craft at schools run by professional trainers. Some gladiators entered the arena armed with a sword, others with a trident and a net. The spectators were transformed into a frenzied mob that lusted for blood. If they were displeased with a losing gladiator's performance, they would call for his immediate execution.

Over the centuries, these spectacles grew more bizarre and brutal. Hundreds of tigers were set against elephants and bulls; wild bulls tore apart men dressed in animal skins; women battled in the arena; dwarfs fought each other. One day in the Colosseum, which could seat fifty thousand people, three thousand men fought one another; on the day the Colosseum opened in A.D. 80, nine thousand beasts were slaughtered. In fact, much of the African trade was devoted to supplying animals for the contests.

Few Romans questioned these barbarities, which became a routine part of daily life. Occasionally, however, thoughtful Romans had strong doubts. After watching a public spectacle, the Stoic philosopher Seneca wrote in disgust: "There is nothing more harmful to one's character than attendance at some spectacle, because vices more easily creep into your soul while you are being entertained. When I return from some spectacle, I am greedier, more aggressive and . . . more cruel and inhuman."[13]

SIGNS OF TROUBLE

The Pax Romana was one of the finest periods in ancient history. But even during the Time of Happiness, signs of trouble appeared that would grow to crisis proportions in the third century.

Internal Unrest

The Empire's internal stability was always subject to question. Were the economic foundations of the Empire strong and elastic enough to endure hard blows? Could the Roman Empire retain the loyalty of so many diverse nationalities, each with its own religious and cultural traditions? Were the mass of people committed to the values of Greco-Roman civilization, or would they withdraw their allegiance and revert to their native traditions if imperial authority weakened?

Most people in the Mediterranean world welcomed Roman rule and could not conceive of a world without the Empire that brought them peace and security. Nevertheless, during the Pax Romana, dissident elements did surface, particularly in Gaul, Egypt, and Judea. Separatist movements in Gaul were crushed by Roman forces. To provide free bread for Rome's poor, Roman emperors exploited the Egyptian peasantry. Weighed down by forced labor, heavy taxes, requisitions, and confiscations, Egyptian peasants frequently sought to escape from farm work. And the Romans suppressed two uprisings by the Jews of Judea.

The unrest in Egypt, Gaul, and Judea demonstrated that not all people at all times welcomed the grand majesty of the Roman peace and that localist and separatist tendencies persisted in a universal empire. In the centuries that followed, as Rome staggered under the weight of economic, political, and military difficulties, these native loyalties reasserted themselves. Increasingly, the masses, and even the Romanized elite of the cities, withdrew their support from the Roman world-state.

Social and Economic Weaknesses

A healthy world-state required empirewide trade to serve as an economic base for political unity, expanding agricultural production to feed the cities, and growing internal mass markets to stimulate industrial production. But the economy of the Empire during the Pax Romana had serious defects. The means of communication and transportation were slow, which hindered long-distance commerce. Roman roads, built for military rather than commercial purposes, were often too narrow for large carts and in places were too steep for any vehicles. Consequently, transporting goods by land, even short distances, necessitated huge price increases that hampered trade. Many nobles, considering it unworthy for a gentleman to engage in business, chose to squander their wealth rather than invest it in commercial or industrial enterprises. Lacking the stimulus of capital investment, the economy could not expand.

Limited employment opportunities resulted from the Greco-Roman civilization's failure to improve its technology substantially and from reliance on slave labor. Also, because manual labor was considered degrading, fit only for a slave, there was little incentive for innovation that might have triggered economic growth and expanded employment opportunities. Because of these factors, millions of people simply did not engage in productive labor. Moreover, scarce employment left the masses with little purchasing power; this too adversely affected business and industry. Many unemployed inhabitants of Italian towns lived on free or cheap grain provided by the state. To feed this unemployed underclass, the government kept the price of grain artificially low. This practice discouraged farmers from planting more crops and expanding grain production and forced many of them to seek other livelihoods. As more farmers left the countryside, the towns became increasingly swollen with an impoverished proletariat. Rural areas eventually faced a serious shortage of laborers due to this population migration.

Ultimately, only a small portion of the urban population—landlords whose estates were outside the city, merchants, and administrators—reaped the benefits of the Roman peace. They basked in luxury, leisure, and culture. The urban poor, on the other hand, derived few of the economic gains and shared little in the political and cultural life of the city. The privileged classes bought off the urban poor with bread and circuses, but occasionally mass discontent expressed itself in mob violence. Outside the cities, the peasantry—still the great bulk of the population—was exploited to provide cheap food for the city dwellers.

Such a parasitical, exploitative, and elitist social system might function in periods of peace and tranquility, but could it survive crises? Would the impoverished people of town and country—the overwhelming majority of the population—remain loyal to a state whose benefits barely extended to them and whose sophisticated culture, which they hardly comprehended, virtually excluded them?

Cultural Stagnation and Transformation

Perhaps the most dangerous sign for the future was the spiritual paralysis that crept over the ordered world of the Pax Romana. A weary and sterile Hellenism underlay the Roman peace. The ancient world was undergoing a transformation of values that foreshadowed the end of Greco-Roman civilization.

During the second century A.D., Greco-Roman civilization lost its creative energies, and the values of classical humanism were challenged by mythic-religious movements. No longer regarding reason as a satisfying guide to life, the educated elite subordinated the intellect to feelings and an unregulated imagination. No longer finding the affairs of this world to have purpose, people placed their hope in life after death. The Roman world was undergoing a religious revolution and seeking a new vision of the divine.

The application of reason to nature and society, as we have seen, was the great achievement of the Greek mind. Yet despite its many triumphs, Greek rationalism never entirely subdued the mythic-religious mentality, which draws its strength from human emotion. The masses of peasants and slaves remained attracted to religious forms. **Ritual**, mystery, magic, and ecstasy never lost their hold on the ancient world—nor, indeed, have they on our own scientific and technological society. During the Hellenistic Age, the tide of rationalism gradually receded, and the nonrational, an ever-present undercurrent, showed renewed vigor. This resurgence of the mythical mentality could be seen in the popularity of the occult, magic, alchemy, and astrology. Feeling themselves controlled by heavenly powers, burdened by danger and emotional stress, and fearing fate as fixed in the stars, people turned for deliverance to magicians, astrologers, and exorcists.

They also became devotees of the many Near Eastern religious cults that promised personal salvation. More and more people felt that the good life could not be achieved by individuals through their own efforts; they needed outside help. Philosophers eventually sought escape from this world through union with a divine presence greater than human power. Increasingly, the masses, and then even the educated elite, came to believe that the good life could be found not on earth but only in a world beyond the grave. Seeing themselves as isolated souls wandering aimlessly in a social desert, people sought refuge in religion. Reason had been found wanting; the time for faith and salvation was at hand.

The Roman Empire had imposed peace and stability, but it could not alleviate the feelings of loneliness, anxiety, impotence, alienation, and boredom that had been gaining ground in the Mediterranean world since the fourth century B.C. A spiritual malaise descended on the Greco-Roman world. Among the upper classes, the philosophical and scientific spirit withered; rational and secular values were in retreat. Deprived of the excitement of politics and bored by idleness and pleasure, the best minds, says historian Michael Rostovtzeff,

> *lost faith in the power of reason. . . . Creative genius dwindled; science repeated its previous results. The textbook took the place of research; no new artistic discoveries were made, but echoes of the past were heard. . . . [Writers] amuse[d] the mind but [were] incapable of elevating and inspiring it.*[14]

Asia Minor. The various mystery cults possessed many common features. Converts underwent initiation rites and were bound by oath to secrecy. The initiates, in a state of rapture, attempted to unite with the deity after first purifying themselves through baptism (sometimes with the blood of a bull), fasting, having their heads shaved, or drinking from a sacred vessel. Communion was achieved by donning the god's robe, eating a sacred meal, or visiting the god's sanctuary. This sacramental drama propelled initiates through an intense mystical experience of exaltation and rebirth. Cultists were certain that their particular savior-god would protect them from misfortune and ensure their soul's immortality.

Of special significance was the cult of Mithras, which had certain parallels with early Christianity and was its principal competitor. Originating in Persia, Mithraism spread westward into the Roman Empire. Because it stressed respect for the masculine virtues of bravery and camaraderie, it became particularly popular with the army. The god Mithras, whose birth date was celebrated on December 25, had as his mission the rescuing of humanity from evil. He was said to demand high standards of morality, to judge souls after death, and to grant eternal life to his faithful followers.

The popularity of magic and mystery demonstrates that many people in Roman society either did not comprehend or had lost faith in the rational and secular values of classical humanism. Religion proved more comforting to the spirit. People felt that the gods could provide what reason, natural law, and civic affairs could not: a sure way of overcoming life's misfortunes and discouragements, a guarantee of immortality, a sense of belonging to a community of brethren who cared, an exciting outlet for bottled-up emotions, and a sedative for anxiety at a time when dissatisfaction with the human condition showed itself in all phases of society and life.

The Spread of Mystery Religions

The proliferation of Eastern mystery religions was a clear expression of this transformation of classical values. During the Hellenistic era, slaves, merchants, and soldiers brought many religious cults westward from Persia, Babylon, Syria, Egypt, and

The Spiritualization of Philosophy

The religious orientation also found expression in philosophy, which demonstrated attitudes markedly at odds with classical humanism. These attitudes, commonly associated with religion, included indifference to the world, withdrawal, and pessimism

HADRIAN'S WALL. Between A.D. 122 and 127, the Romans constructed an elaborate defensive system in Britain consisting of a wall of solid masonry and a series of forts. Built on high ground, Hadrian's Wall extended from the estuary of the Solway to that of the Tyne, a distance of seventy-three miles. (© Patrick Ward/Corbis.)

about the earthly state. From trying to understand nature and individuals' relationships to one another, the philosophers more and more aspired to a communion with a higher reality. Like the mystery religions, philosophy reached for something beyond this world in order to comfort the individual. In Neo-Platonism, which replaced Stoicism as the dominant school of philosophy in the late Roman Empire, religious yearnings were transformed into a religious system that transcended reason.

Plotinus (A.D. c. 205–c. 270), the most influential spokesman of Neo-Platonism, went far beyond Marcus Aurelius's natural religion; in aspiring to the ecstatic union of the soul with God, he subordinated philosophy to mysticism and the occult. Plato's philosophy, we have seen, contained both a major and a minor key. The major key stressed a rational interpretation of the human community and called for reforming the polis on the basis of knowledge, whereas the minor key urged the soul to rise to a higher world of reality. Plotinus was intrigued by Plato's otherworldliness.

What Plotinus desired was union with the One, or the Good, sometimes called God—the source of all existence. Plotinus felt that the intellect could neither describe nor understand the One, which transcended all knowing, and that joining with the One required a mystical leap, a purification of the soul that dispensed with logic, evidence, and proof. This vision, which induced the soul to return to its true home, was for Plotinus something greater and more compelling than reason.

For Plotinus, philosophy became a religious experience, a contemplation of the eternal. His successors held that through acts of magic the soul can unite with the One. Compared with this union with the divine One, of what value was knowledge of the sensible world or a concern for human affairs? For Plotinus, the principal goal of life was not comprehension of the natural world or fulfillment of human potential or betterment of the human community but attaining spiritual truth—knowledge of the One—through a transrational experience. Neo-Platonism, concludes historian of philosophy W. T. Stace, "is founded upon . . . the despair of reason." It seeks to reach the Absolute not through reason but through "spiritual intoxication." This marks a radical transformation of philosophical thinking.

> For philosophy is founded upon reason. It is the effort to comprehend, to understand, to grasp the reality of things intellectually. Therefore it cannot admit anything higher than reason. To exalt intuition, ecstasy, or rapture, above thought—this is the death of philosophy. . . . In Neo-Platonism, therefore, ancient philosophy commits suicide. This is the end. The place of philosophy is taken henceforth by religion.[15]

By the time of the late Roman Empire, mystery religions intoxicated the masses, and mystical philosophy beguiled the educated elite. Classical civilization was being transformed. Philosophy had become subordinate to religious belief; secular values seemed inferior to religious experience. The earthly city had raised its eyes toward heaven. The culture of the Roman world was moving in a direction in which the quest for the divine was to predominate over all human enterprises.

THE DECLINE OF ROME

Third-Century Crisis

At the death of Marcus Aurelius in A.D. 180, the Empire was politically stable, economically prosperous, and militarily secure. In the third century, the ordered civilization of the Pax Romana ended. Several elements caused this disruption. The Roman Empire was plunged into military anarchy, raided by Germanic tribes, and burdened by economic dislocations. During these critical times, effective leadership was lacking, for the adoptive system abandoned by Marcus Aurelius was not restored.

The degeneration of the army was a prime reason for the third-century crisis. During the great peace, the army had remained an excellent fighting force, renowned for its discipline, organization, and loyalty. In the third century A.D., however, there was a marked deterioration in the quality of Roman soldiers. Lacking loyalty to Rome and greedy for spoils, soldiers used their weapons to prey on civilians and to make and unmake emperors. Fearful of being killed by their unruly troops who wanted spoils or of being murdered by a suspicious emperor, generals were driven to seize the throne. Once in power, they had to buy the loyalty of their soldiers and guard against assassination by other generals. From A.D. 235 to 285, military mutiny and civil war raged as legion fought legion. During this period, there were twenty-six soldier-emperors, twenty-five of whom died violently. The once stalwart army neglected its duty of defending the borders against barbarian incursions and disrupted the internal life of the Empire.

Perhaps the degeneration of the army can be explained by the liberal granting of citizenship. In A.D. 212, citizenship was extended to virtually all freeborn inhabitants of the Empire. Previously, many army recruits had been drawn from among provincials, who were attracted by the promise of citizenship and its advantages. These recruits generally were men of a high caliber who were interested in bettering themselves and their families' lot. With citizenship no longer an inducement for enlistment, says Edward T. Salmon,

> recruits were now only too likely to be drawn from the lowest and most primitive elements . . . men of the rough and reckless type, who were joining the army chiefly in order to get weapons in their hands with which they would be able to extort for themselves an even greater share of the Empire's collective wealth . . . men who knew little and cared less about Rome's mission and who, when not preying upon the civilians, had not the slightest compunction about preying upon one another.[16]

During the third century, Rome also had to deal with a revived Persian Empire that forced the Romans to shift large contingents of legions eastward. Taking advantage of the weakened borders and military anarchy, Germanic tribesmen crossed the Rhine–Danube frontier to loot and destroy. The Goths raided coastal cities of Asia Minor and Greece and even burned much of Athens. In the Western Empire, other Germanic tribes penetrated Gaul, Spain, and Italy and engaged the Romans in a full-scale battle near Milan. At the same time that the European defense lines were being breached, a reborn Persian Empire, led by the Sassanid dynasty, attacked and for a while conquered Roman lands in the east. Some sections of the Empire, notably in Gaul, attempted to break away; these moves reflected an assertion of local patriotism over Roman universalism. The "city of mankind" was crumbling.

These eruptions had severe economic repercussions. Cities were pillaged and destroyed, farmland ruined, and trade disrupted. To obtain funds and supplies for the military, emperors confiscated goods, exacted forced labor, and devalued the currency by reducing the gold and silver content of coins and adding base metals: zinc, tin, and lead. Cheap money caused a ruinous inflation, leading many people to turn to barter as a medium of exchange. These measures led many citizens to withdraw their loyalty from Rome.

Repeated invasions, civil war, pillage by Germanic tribes and by Roman soldiers, soaring prices, a debased coinage, declining agricultural production, disrupted transportation, and the excessive demands of the state caused economic havoc and famine in the cities. Compounding the problem was a great plague that spread across North Africa and the Balkans in midcentury. Driven to desperation by famine and plague, by invading barbarians and plundering Roman soldiers, and by the extortions and requisitions of government officials, many people fled the cities. The urban centers of the ancient world, creators and disseminators of high civilization, were caught in a rhythm of breakdown. As cities decayed, the center of life gravitated back to the countryside. Large, fortified estates, or villas, owned by the emperor or wealthy aristocrats, provided refuge for the uprooted and destitute of town and country. In the countryside, people had no deep commitment to classical civilization, which had made little headway against native languages, religions, and manners.

During the third century A.D., the spiritual crisis intensified as the rational foundations of Greco-Roman civilization eroded further. People turned increasingly to the mystery cults, which offered relief from earthly misery, a sense of belonging, and a promise of immortality. In philosophy, creative energies were directed not toward a greater understanding of nature or society but toward a knowledge of the divine, which, taught the philosophers, was the path to happiness. Hellenism was breaking down.

Diocletian and Constantine: The Regimented State

The emperors Diocletian (A.D. 285–305) and Constantine (A.D. 306–337) tried to contain the awesome forces of disintegration. At a time when agricultural production was steadily declining, they had to feed the city poor and an expanded army of more than 500,000, strung out over the Empire. They also had to prevent renewed outbreaks of military anarchy, drive the Germans back across the Danube frontier, and secure the eastern region against renewed aggression from Persia. Their solution was to weaken municipal institutions, tighten the reins of central government, and extort more taxes and requisitions from the citizens. In the process, they transformed Rome into a bureaucratic, regimented, and militarized state, which some historians refer to as "a vast prison."

Ruling like a Near Eastern despot, Diocletian completed a trend that had been developing for generations. He imitated the pomp of the East, wore magnificent robes and jewels, and demanded that subjects prostrate themselves in his presence. Cities lost their traditional right of local self-government—a loss that also culminated an earlier trend. To increase the size of the army, Diocletian drafted prisoners of war and hired German mercenaries. He also established, on vacant or deserted Roman lands, colonies of Germans from which soldiers could be recruited. To ensure continuous production of food and goods, as well as the collection of taxes, the state forced unskilled workers and artisans to hold their jobs for life and to pass them on to their children. For the same reasons, peasants were turned into virtual serfs, bound to the land that they cultivated. An army of government agents was formed to hunt down peasants who fled the land to escape crushing taxes and poverty.

Also frozen into their positions were city officials, or *curiales*. They often found it necessary to furnish from their own pockets the difference between the state's tax demands and the amount that they could collect from an already overtaxed population. This system of a hereditary class of tax collectors and of crippling taxes to pay for a vastly expanded bureaucracy and military establishment enfeebled urban trade and industry. Such conditions killed the civic spirit of townspeople, who desperately sought escape. By overburdening urban dwellers with taxes and regulations, Diocletian and Constantine helped shatter the vitality of city life, on which Roman prosperity and civilization depended. During the Pax Romana, municipal authorities had enjoyed considerable autonomy; now the state bureaucracy extended its often onerous and rapacious power everywhere.

Rome was governed by a despotism characteristic of the Near East—a highly centralized monarchy regimenting the lives of its subjects. Whereas Augustus had upheld the classical ideal that the commonwealth was a means of fostering the good life for the individual, Diocletian adopted the Eastern attitude that the individual lives for the state. The absolutism inherent in the concept of the principate had eclipsed the republican elements that had endured in the Augustan political settlement.

To guard against military insurrection, Diocletian appointed a loyal general as emperor to govern the western provinces of the Empire while he ruled the eastern regions; although both emperors bore the title Augustus, Diocletian remained superior. (Each emperor then chose an heir-designate, who received his own territory to govern. For a time, the Empire was a tetrarchy—a government by four.) By building an imperial capital, Constantinople, at the Bosporus, a strait where Asia meets Europe, Constantine furthered this trend of dividing the Empire into eastern and western halves.

Tribal Migrations and Invasions

Nearly two centuries after Diocletian's reign, the Roman historian Zosimus described the emperor's accomplishment.

> *By the foresight of Diocletian the frontiers were everywhere studded with cities and forts and towers, and the whole army stationed along them. It was thus impossible for the barbarians to break through, since at every point they encountered an opposing force strong enough to repel them.*[17]

By imposing some order on what had been approaching chaos, Diocletian and Constantine prevented the Empire from collapsing. Rome was given a reprieve. A long period of peace might have brought economic recovery, but misfortune continued to burden Rome, and the process of breakdown and disintegration resumed.

In the last part of the fourth century, the problem of guarding the frontier grew more acute. The Huns, a nomadic people from central Asia, swept across the plains of Russia. With their formidable cavalry—the Huns were expert riders and archers—they subdued the Ostrogoths, a Germanic tribe that had established itself in Ukraine, and forced the Germanic Visigoths, who had migrated along the Danube in what is now Romania, to seek refuge within the eastern Roman Empire. Enraged by their mistreatment at the hands of Roman officials, the Visigoths took up arms. In 378, Goths and Romans fought each other in a historic battle at Adrianople. The Visigoths' cavalry cut to pieces the Roman forces, largely tribal mercenaries, and killed and captured perhaps as many as two-thirds of the Roman army. Emperor Valens perished in what was Rome's worst defeat since Cannae in the war with Hannibal. The Visigoths were on Roman territory to stay. The battle of Adrianople signified that Rome could no longer defend its borders. Since it was the Visigoth cavalry that prevailed over a Roman army composed mainly of foot soldiers, the battle also signified that cavalry had begun to supersede infantry as a principal instrument of warfare.

Map 7.2 INCURSIONS AND MIGRATIONS, C. A.D. 300–500 In the fifth century, Germanic tribes, seeking land and desperate to escape the Huns, overran the weakened Roman borders. (Copyright © 2013 Cengage Learning.)

Other Germanic tribes increased their pressure on the Empire's borders. Attracted by the warmer climate, riches, and advanced civilization of the Roman Empire, they were also looking for new lands to farm and were frightened by the advent of the Huns. The borders finally collapsed at the very end of 406 as Vandals, Alans, Suebi, and other tribes joined the Goths in devastating and overrunning the Empire's western provinces. In 408–409, the Visigoths, led by Alaric, besieged Rome itself, extorting huge sums in return for permitting food to enter the city. Then, in 410, they rampaged through the city, which for eight hundred years had remained free of foreign attack,

slaughtering, destroying, and plundering. Saint Jerome lamented: "Who could believe that Rome, built upon the conquest of the whole world, would fall to the ground? that the mother herself would become the tomb of her peoples?"[18]

Economic conditions continued to deteriorate. Cities in Britain, Gaul, Germany, and Spain lay abandoned. Other metropolises saw their populations dwindle and production stagnate. The great network of Roman roads was not maintained, and trade in the West almost disappeared or passed into the hands of Greeks, Syrians, and Jews from the East. Everywhere famine, the extortion of taxes by government officials, the proliferation of marauding outlaws (many of them driven from their homes by the excessive financial demands of the state bureaucracy), and murderous warfare added to the misery of the Roman populace and the decomposition and fragmentation of the Empire.

In 451, Attila (c. 406–453), who had united Mongol tribes, led his Huns into Gaul, where he suffered his only defeat at the hands of a coalition of Germans and the remnants of the Roman army. He died two years later, having come within a hairsbreadth of turning Europe into a province of a Mongolian empire. But Rome's misfortunes persisted. In 455, Rome was again pillaged, this time by the Vandals. Additional regions fell under the control of Germanic chieftains. Germanic soldiers in the pay of Rome gained control of the government and dictated the choice of emperor. In 476, Germanic officers overthrew the Roman emperor Romulus and placed a fellow German, Odoacer, on the throne. This act is traditionally regarded as the end of the Roman Empire in the West. By the end of the fifth century, the western empire had fragmented into separate Germanic kingdoms.

Reasons for Rome's Decline

What were the underlying causes of the decline and fall of the Roman Empire in the West? Surely, no other question has intrigued the historical imagination more than this one. Implicit in the answers suggested by historians and philosophers is a concern for their own civilization. Will it suffer the same fate as Rome?

To analyze so monumental a development as the fall of Rome, some preliminary observations are necessary. First, the fall of Rome was a process lasting hundreds of years; it was not a single event that occurred in A.D. 476. Second, only the western half of the Empire fell. The eastern half—wealthier, more populous, less afflicted with civil wars, and less exposed to barbarian invasions—survived as the Byzantine Empire until the middle of the fifteenth century. Third, no single explanation suffices to account for Rome's decline; multiple forces—internal problems and external threats—operated concurrently to bring about the fall.

The Role of the Germanic Tribes. Was Rome's fall suicide or murder? Did the Germans walk over a corpse, or did they contribute substantially to Rome's decline and fall? Undoubtedly, an empire enfeebled by internal rot succumbed to the Germanic migrations. Perhaps a stronger Rome might have secured its borders, as it had done during the Pax Romana. But the Germanic attacks occurred mainly in the west, and the western Empire, poorer and less populated than the eastern portion, reeled under these increasingly numerous and more severe barbarian onslaughts. The pressures exerted by the Germans along an immense frontier also aggravated Rome's internal problems. The barbarian attacks left border regions depopulated and impoverished, as expenditures for the military drained the western Empire's resources. The Empire imposed high taxes and labor services on its citizens in order to strengthen the armed forces, causing the overburdened middle and lower classes to hate the imperial government that took so much from them.

Moreover, as more and more territory fell to the barbarian invaders, the Roman state was deprived of badly needed tax revenues. Containing the threat from a revived Persian Empire made it more difficult for Rome to deal with the Germanic invaders: it necessitated stationing a large force on the eastern frontier that could have been deployed in the west, and it imposed a heavy financial burden on the Empire, preventing it from funding larger armies against the barbarians.

Spiritual Considerations. The classical mentality, once brimming with confidence about the potentialities of the individual and the power of the intellect, suffered a failure of nerve. The urban upper class, on whom the responsibility for preserving cosmopolitan Greco-Roman culture traditionally rested, became dissolute and apathetic and no longer took an interest in public life. The aristocrats secluded themselves behind the walls of their fortified country estates; many did not lift a finger to help the Empire. The townspeople demonstrated their disenchantment by avoiding public service and by rarely organizing resistance forces against the barbarian invaders. Hounded by the state and persecuted by the army, many farmers viewed the Germans as liberators. The great bulk of the Roman citizenry, disillusioned and indifferent, simply gave up, despite the fact that they overwhelmingly outnumbered the Germanic invaders.

Political and Military Considerations. The Roman government itself contributed to this spiritual malaise through its increasingly autocratic tendencies, which culminated in the regimented rule of Diocletian and Constantine. The insatiable demands and regulations of the state in the late Roman Empire sapped the initiative and civic spirit of its citizens. The ruined middle and lower classes withdrew their loyalty. For many, the state had become the enemy, and its administration was hated and feared more than the barbarians. Salvianus of Marseilles (c. A.D. 400–470), a monk from Gaul, described the disaffection toward Rome that led many to welcome the barbarians as liberators.

> *Meanwhile the poor are being robbed, widows groan, orphans are trodden down, so that many, even persons of good birth, who have enjoyed a liberal education, seek refuge with the enemy to escape death under the trials of general persecution. They seek among the barbarians the Roman mercy, since they cannot endure the barbarous mercilessness they find among the Romans. . . . So you find men passing over everywhere, now to the Goths . . . , or whatever other barbarians have established their power anywhere. . . . Hence the name of Roman citizen, once . . . much valued . . . , is now voluntarily repudiated and shunned, and is thought not merely valueless, but even almost abhorrent.*[19]

Related to the political decline was the government's inability to retain the allegiance of its armies and to control ambitious military commanders, who used their troops to seize the throne and its immense power. The internal security and stability of the Empire was thus constantly imperiled by army leaders more concerned with grandiose personal dreams than with defending the Empire's borders. These civil wars imposed terrible financial burdens on the Empire and gravely weakened the frontier defenses—compounding the problem of forces spread thinly over thousands of miles and presenting an invitation to the Germans to increase their pressure.

During the Pax Romana, superior training and organization, rigorous discipline, a professional system of command, and a network of walls and forts enabled the Roman legions to protect the frontiers against incursions. The Roman soldier, for whom discipline was a deeply ingrained tradition, knew that his comrades would not desert the field, no matter how hard the fighting—an attitude that usually meant certain victory against untrained barbarian hordes. However, in the Late Roman Empire, the quality of Roman soldiers deteriorated, and the legions failed to defend the borders, even though the Germanic invaders were fewer numerically. During the third century, the army consisted predominantly of the provincial peasantry. These nonurban, non-Italian, semicivilized soldiers, often the dregs of society, were not committed to Greco-Roman civilization. They had little comprehension of Rome's mission and at times used their power to attack the cities and towns and to prey on hapless citizens. The emperors also recruited large numbers of Germans into the army—barbarians had been used as auxiliary troops since Julius Caesar—to fill depleted ranks. Ultimately, the army consisted predominantly of barbarians, as both legionnaires and officers. Although these Germans made brave soldiers, they too had little loyalty to Greco-Roman civilization and to the Roman state. This deterioration of the Roman army occurred in part because many young citizens evaded conscription. No longer imbued with patriotism, they considered military service a servitude to be shunned.

The deterioration of the Roman army is seen also on the level of tactics. Roman soldiers continued to fight in organized units, but the training and discipline required for fighting in close-order formations had lapsed. Barbarian units serving with the Roman army under their own commanders did not easily submit to traditional discipline. Thus, Rome lost the tactical superiority that it had once enjoyed over the barbarians.

Economic Considerations. Contributing to the decline of the Roman Empire in the west were population decline, the lack of technological advance, the heavy burden of taxation, and economic decentralization, which abetted political decentralization.

During the late Roman Empire, the population shrank. The epidemic during the reign of Marcus Aurelius, which might have been the bubonic plague, lasted fifteen years. A second plague struck the Empire during the reign of Commodus, Marcus Aurelius's son. Other plagues in the middle of the third century and constant warfare further reduced the population. The birth rate did not rise to compensate for these losses. Worsening economic conditions and lack of hope in the future apparently discouraged people from increasing the size of their families.

The decline in population adversely affected the Empire in at least three important ways. First, at the same time that the population was declining, the costs of running the Empire were spiraling, a situation that created a terrible burden for taxpayers. Second, fewer workers were available for agriculture, the most important economic activity of the Empire. Third, population decline reduced the manpower available for the army, forcing emperors to permit the establishment of Germanic colonies within the Empire's borders to serve as feeders for the army. This situation led to the barbarization of the army.

The Roman peace brought stability, but it failed to discover new and better ways of producing goods and agricultural products. To be sure, some advances in technology did take place during the Hellenistic Age and the Pax Romana: rotary mills for grain, screw presses, and improvements in glass-blowing and field-drainage methods. But the high intellectual culture of Greece and Rome rested on a meager economic and technological foundation. The widespread use of slave labor probably precluded a breakthrough in technology, for slaves had little incentive to invent more efficient ways of producing. The upper classes, identifying manual labor with slavery, would not condescend to engage in the mechanical arts. This failure to improve the level of technology limited employment opportunities for the masses. Because the masses could not increase their purchasing power, business and industry were without a mass internal market that might have acted as a continual stimulus for the accumulation of capital and for economic expansion.

Instead of expanding industry and trade, towns maintained their wealth by exploiting the countryside. The Roman cities, centers of civilized life and opulence, lacked industries. They spent but did not produce. Provided with food and entertainment—"bread and circuses"—the unproductive city dwellers, driven out of the labor force by slavery and economic stagnation, were a heavy burden for the state. The towns were dominated by landlords whose estates lay beyond the city and whose income derived from grain, oil, and wine. Manufacturing was rudimentary, confined essentially to textiles, pottery, furniture, and glassware. The methods of production rarely improved; the market was limited; the cost of transportation, particularly by land, was high; and agricultural productivity was low—the labor of perhaps nineteen peasants was required to support one townsman. Such a fundamentally unhealthy economy could not weather the dislocations caused by uninterrupted warfare and the demands of the military and a mushrooming bureaucracy.

With the barbarians pressing on the borders, the increased military expenditures overstrained the Empire's resources. To pay for the food, uniforms, arms, and armor of the soldiers, taxes were raised, growing too heavy for peasants and townspeople, particularly since the large landowners did not pay their fair share. The state also requisitioned wood and grain and demanded that citizens maintain roads and bridges. The government often resorted to force to collect taxes and exact services. Crushed by these demands, many peasants simply abandoned their farms and sought the protection of large landowners or turned to banditry.

Making the situation worse was the administrative separation of the Empire into eastern and western parts, undertaken by Diocletian and Constantine. As a result, western emperors could no longer rely on financial aid from the wealthier east to pay for the defense of the borders. Slow communications and costly transport continued to hamper the empirewide trade, which was required to sustain political unity. Meanwhile, industries gravitated outward, to search for new markets in the frontier army camps and for new sources of slaves in border regions. This dispersion further weakened the bonds of economic unity. Gradually, trade became less international and more local, and provincial regions grew more self-sufficient. The strife of the third century intensified the drift toward economic self-sufficiency in the provinces, a condition that promoted localism and separatism.

Contributing to the economic decentralization was the growth of industries on latifundia, the large, fortified estates owned by wealthy aristocrats. Producing exclusively for the local market, these estates contributed to the impoverishment of urban centers by reducing the number of customers available to buy goods made in the cities. As life grew more desperate, urban craftsmen and small farmers, made destitute by the state, sought the protection of these large landlords, whose estates grew in size and importance. The growth of latifundia was accompanied by the decline of cities and the transformation of independent peasants into virtual serfs.

These great estates were also new centers of political power, which the imperial government could not curb. A new society was taking shape in the late Roman Empire. The center of gravity shifted from the city to the landed estate, from the imperial bureaucrat to the local aristocrat. These developments epitomized the decay of ancient civilization and presaged a new era, the Middle Ages.

THE ROMAN LEGACY

Rome left the West a rich heritage, which endured for centuries. The idea of a world empire united by a common law and effective government never died. In the centuries following the collapse of Rome, people continued to be attracted to the idea of a unified and peaceful world-state. By preserving and adding to the philosophy, literature, science, and arts of ancient Greece, Rome strengthened the basic foundations of the Western cultural tradition. Latin, the language of Rome, lived on long after Rome perished. The Western church fathers wrote in Latin, and during the Middle Ages, Latin was the language of learning, literature, and law. From Latin came Italian, French, Spanish, Portuguese, and Romanian. Roman law, the quintessential expression of Roman genius, influenced church law and formed the basis of the legal codes of most European states. Finally, Christianity, the core religion of the West, was born within the Roman Empire and was greatly influenced by Roman law (the church's **canon law** owed much to Roman jurisprudence) and organization (the pope, head of the church and ruling from Rome, was the counterpart of the Roman emperor, and bishoprics were established in regions that coincided with the Empire's administrative structure). The ideal of a single Christian society embracing many different nationalities, so dear to medieval thinkers, was superimposed on the model of the Roman Empire.

NOTES

1. Tacitus, *The Annals of Imperial Rome,* trans. Michael Grant (Baltimore: Penguin Books, 1959), 31.

2. Cited in David Magie, *Roman Rule in Asia Minor* (Princeton, N.J.: Princeton University Press, 1950), 490.

3. Sallust, *The Conspiracy of Cataline,* trans. S. A. Handford (Baltimore: Penguin Books, 1963), 193.

4. Excerpted in Naphtali Lewis and Meyer Reinhold, eds., *Roman Civilization, Sourcebook II: The Empire* (New York: Harper and Row, 1966), 136.

5. *From The Aeneid of Virgil,* trans. Allen Mandelbaum, copyright © 1971 by Allen Mandelbaum. Used by permission of Bantam Books, division of Random House, Inc.

6. *The Odes and Epodes of Horace,* trans. C. E. Bennett (Cambridge, Mass.: Harvard University Press, Loeb Classical Library, 1914), 109.

7. *The Art of Love and Other Love Books of Ovid* (New York: Grosset and Dunlap, The Universal Library, 1959), 117–118, 130–132, 135.

8. *The Satires of Juvenal,* trans. Hubert Creekmore (New York: Mentor Books, 1963), 58–61.

9. Adapted from Seneca, *The Epistles,* trans. Thomas Morell (London: W. Woodfall, 1786), vol. 1, epistle 47.

10. Marcus Aurelius, *Meditations,* trans. Maxwell Staniforth (Baltimore: Penguin Classics, 1964), bk. 2.

11. Cicero, *De Republica,* trans. Clinton Walker Keyes (Cambridge, Mass.: Harvard University Press, Loeb Classical Library, 1994), 211.

12. Excerpted in Lewis and Reinhold, eds., *Roman Civilization, Sourcebook II: The Empire,* 535, 539, 540, 547, 548.

13. Seneca, *The Epistles,* vol. 1, epistle 7.

14. Michael Rostovtzeff, *Rome* (New York: Oxford University Press, 1960), 322.

15. W. T. Stace, *A Critical History of Greek Philosophy* (London: Macmillan, 1924), 377.

16. Excerpted in Mortimer Chambers, ed., *The Fall of Rome* (New York: Holt, Rinehart and Winston, 1963), 45–46.

17. Quoted in Stephen Williams, *Diocletian and the Roman Recovery* (New York: Methuen, 1985), 101.

18. Excerpted in James Harvey Robinson, ed., *Readings in European History* (Boston: Ginn, 1904), 45.

19. Salvian, *On the Government of God,* trans. Eva M. Sanford (New York: Octagon, 1966), 141–142.

SUGGESTED READING

Boardman, John, et al., eds., *The Oxford History of the Classical World* (1986). Essays on all facets of Roman culture.

Christ, Karl, *The Romans* (1984). Good chapters on social and cultural life in the Empire.

Clarke, M. L., *The Roman Mind* (1968). Studies in the history of thought from Cicero to Marcus Aurelius.

Ferrill, Arther, *The Fall of the Roman Empire: The Military Explanation* (1986). Examines the deterioraton of the Roman Army.

Galinsky, Karl, *Augustan Culture* (1996). Weaves together the history and culture of the period.

Goldsworthy, Adrian, *How Rome Fell* (2009). An important recent study of Rome's decline, paying special attention to Rome's frequent internal wars starting in the third century.

Grant, Michael, *The Fall of the Roman Empire* (1990). A clearly written synthesis.

Heather, Peter, *The Fall of the Roman Empire: A New History of Rome and the Barbarians* (2006). A readable, thoughtful analysis.

Jenkyns, Richard, ed., *The Legacy of Rome: A New Appraisal* (1992). Essays on Rome's influence upon later centuries.

Southern, Pat, *Augustus* (1998). A helpful biography.

White, Lynn, ed., *The Transformation of the Roman World* (1973). A useful collection of essays on the transformation of the ancient world and the emergence of the Middle Ages.

Early Christianity: A World Religion

Christ Gives the Law to Saints Peter and Paul, fifth century, Santa Costanza, Rome. This mosaic portrays a haloed, beardless Christ bestowing the law in the manner of an emperor delivering an edict. (Vanni/Art Resource, N.Y.)

Focus Questions

1. How did Saint Paul transform a Jewish sect into a world religion?

2. What factors contributed to the triumph of Christianity in the Roman Empire?

3. How was early Christianity influenced by Judaism, Greek philosophy, and Hellenistic mystery religions?

4. What factors contributed to Christian anti-Judaism? What is the historical significance of the negative image of Jews and Judaism taught by early Christians?

5. What are the core features of Saint Augustine's theology?

6. What do the worldviews of Christianity and Greco-Roman humanism have in common? Why are they essentially different?

As confidence in human reason and hope for happiness in this world waned in the last centuries of the Roman Empire, a new outlook began to take hold. Evident in philosophy and in the popularity of Eastern religions, this viewpoint stressed escape from an oppressive world and communion with a higher reality. Christianity evolved and expanded within this setting of declining classicism and heightening otherworldliness. As one response to a declining Hellenism, Christianity offered a spiritually disillusioned Greco-Roman world a reason for living: the hope of personal immortality. The triumph of Christianity marked a break with classical antiquity and a new stage in the evolution of the West, for there was a fundamental difference between the classical and the Christian concepts of God, the individual, and the purpose of life.

THE ORIGINS OF CHRISTIANITY

A Palestinian Jew named Jesus was executed by the Roman authorities during the reign of Tiberius (A.D. 14–37), who succeeded Augustus. At the time, few people paid much attention to what proved to be one of the most pivotal events in world history. In the quest for the historical Jesus, scholars have stressed the importance of both his Jewishness and the religious ferment that prevailed in Palestine in the first century B.C. Jesus' ethical teachings are rooted in the moral outlook of the Old Testament prophets. Jesus, who prayed as a Jew, taught as a Jew to fellow Jews, and valued Jewish law and prophetic teachings, could only conceive of himself as a Jew. Hans Küng, the prominent Swiss student of religion, elaborates on this point.

> Jesus was a Jew, a member of a small, poor, politically powerless nation living at the periphery of the Roman Empire. He was active among Jews and for Jews. His mother Mary, his father Joseph, his family, his followers were Jews. His name was Jewish (Hebrew Yeshu'a). . . . His Bible, his worship, his prayers were Jewish. In the situation at that time he could not have thought of any proclamation among the gentiles. His message was for the Jewish people, but for this people

171

Chronology 8.1 ❖ Early Christianity

c. A.D. 29	Crucifixion of Jesus
c. 34–64	Missionary activity of Saint Paul
c. 66–70	The Gospel According to Mark is written
250–260	A decade of brutal persecution of Christians by the Romans
313	Constantine grants toleration of Christianity
c. 320	First convent is founded
325	Council of Nicaea rules that God and Christ are of the same substance, coequal and coeternal
391–392	Theodosius I prohibits public acts of pagan worship and the public profession of pagan religion; during his reign, Christianity becomes the state religion
430	Death of Saint Augustine
451	Council of Chalcedon rules that Christ is truly God and truly man
529	Saint Benedict founds monastery at Monte Cassino

in its entirety without any exception. From this basic fact it follows irrevocably that without Judaism there would be no Christianity. The Bible of the early Christians was the "Old Testament." The New Testament Scriptures became part of the Bible only by being appended to the Old. The gospel of Jesus Christ everywhere quite consciously presupposes the Torah and the Prophets.[1]

Judaism in the First Century B.C.

In the first century B.C., four principal social-religious parties, or sects, existed among the Palestinian Jews: Sadducees, Pharisees, Essenes, and Zealots. Composed of the upper stratum of Jewish society—influential landed gentry and hereditary priests, who controlled the temple in Jerusalem—the religiously conservative Sadducees insisted on a strict interpretation of **Mosaic Law** (Torah) and the perpetuation of temple ceremonies. Claiming to be the descendants of Sadok, the high priest of Solomon, Sadducees believed that they were maintaining the ancient Hebrew teachings concerning the Torah, which they interpreted literally. Rejecting the concepts of the resurrection of the dead and of an afterlife,

they held that God meted out rewards and punishments on earth. Challenging the aristocratic Sadducees, the Pharisees adopted a more liberal attitude toward Mosaic Law. They allowed discussion on varying interpretations of the Law and granted authority to oral tradition—an "oral Torah," which was communicated from one generation to another—as well as to written Scripture. Unlike the Sadducees, the Pharisees believed in life after death. The concept of personal immortality is barely mentioned in the Hebrew Scriptures. A later addition to Hebrew religious thought, probably acquired from Persia, the idea had gained wide acceptance by the first century A.D. The Pharisees had the support of most of the Jewish people. All later forms of Judaism developed from the Pharisees.

Besides the afterlife, another widely recognized idea in the first century B.C. was the belief in a **Messiah**, a redeemer chosen by God to liberate Israel from foreign rule. In the days of the Messiah, it was predicted, Israel would be free, the exiles would return, and the Jews would be blessed with peace, unity, and prosperity. The Messiah, in contrast to wicked Roman rulers, would govern justly and righteously.

The third religious party, the Essenes, established a semimonastic community near the Dead

172

SARCOPHAGUS OF BAEBIA HERTOFILA, LATE THIRD CENTURY, MUSEO DELLE TERME, ROME. Symbolizing the Christian Eucharist, Jesus distributes the bread and the wine of the Last Supper to his disciples. (Scala/Art Resource N.Y.)

Sea. Like the Sadducees, they considered themselves to be the true descendants of Sadok, but they rejected the temple priests as corrupt. Only those priests affiliated with their sect were deemed pure. In 1947, leather scrolls in hermetically sealed cylinders were found near the Essene community of Qumran, about fourteen miles from Jerusalem, close to the Dead Sea. Dated from between c. 200 B.C. and A.D. 66–70, the *Wady Qumran Manuscripts*, commonly called the Dead Sea Scrolls, contain the oldest extant Hebrew manuscripts and also documents that are unique to the sect of the Essenes, founded by a man they refer to as "the Teacher of Righteousness." The Essenes believed in the physical resurrection of the body, like the Pharisees, but gave this doctrine a more compelling meaning by tying it to the immediate coming of God's kingdom. Certain that the Messiah was about to come, the Essenes saw themselves as the first generation of God's people.

By adding to our knowledge of Palestinian Judaism in the first century, the scrolls shed light on the period in which Christianity arose and the New Testament was written. Because of the similarity between many of the teachings of Jesus,

particularly in the Sermon on the Mount, and the teachings of the Essenes' Teacher of Righteousness, some modern scholars have suggested that Jesus may have been a member of the Essene community. These scholars argue that the teachings of Jesus concerning the imminent coming of the kingdom of God parallel the messianic expectations of the Essenes.

The fourth sect, the Zealots, demanded that the Jews neither pay taxes to Rome nor acknowledge the authority of the Roman emperor. Devoted patriots, the Zealots engaged in acts of resistance to Rome, which culminated in the great revolt of A.D. 66–70, discussed in Chapter 7.

Jesus (c. 4 B.C.–c. A.D. 29) practiced his ministry within this context of Jewish religious-national expectations and longings. The hopes of Jesus' early followers encompassed a lower-class dissatisfaction with the aristocratic Sadducees; a Pharisee emphasis on prophetic ideals and the afterlife; an Essene preoccupation with the end-of-days, the nearness of God, and the need for repentance; and a conquered people's yearning for a Messiah who would liberate their land from Roman rule and establish God's reign.

Jesus: The Inner Person

Historians are able to speak with greater certainty about social-religious developments in Judea at the time of Jesus than they can about Jesus himself. In reconstructing what Jesus did and believed, the historian labors under a handicap, for the sources are few. Jesus himself wrote nothing, and nothing was written about him during his lifetime. In the generations following his death, both Roman and Jewish historians paid him scant attention. Consequently, virtually everything known about Jesus derives from the Bible's New Testament, which was written decades after Jesus' death by devotees seeking to convey a religious truth and to propagate a faith.

Modern historians in quest of the historical Jesus have rigorously and critically analyzed the New Testament; their analyses have provided some insights into Jesus and his beliefs. Nevertheless, much about Jesus remains obscure. Very little is known about his childhood. Like other Jewish youths, he was taught Hebrew religious-ethical thought and the many rules that governed daily life. At about the age of thirty, no doubt influenced by John the Baptist, who likely was once part of the Essene community, Jesus began to preach the coming of the reign of God and the need for people to repent—undergo moral transformation—so that they could enter God's kingdom. "Now after John was arrested, Jesus came into Galilee, preaching the gospel of God, and saying, 'The time is fulfilled, and the kingdom of God is at hand; repent, and believe in the gospel [good news]'" (Mark 1:14–15).[2]* This apocalyptic vision that the existing world was coming to an end and would be replaced by God's perfect kingdom had been preached by John the Baptist and other religious thinkers before him.

For Jesus, the coming of the kingdom was imminent; the process leading to the establishment of God's kingdom on earth had already begun. A new order would soon be established in which God would govern his people righteously and mercifully. Hence, the present moment became critical for him—a time for spiritual preparedness and repentance—because an individual's thoughts, goals, and actions would determine whether he or she would gain entrance into the kingdom. People had to radically change their lives. They had to eliminate base, lustful, hostile, and selfish feelings; stop pursuing wealth and power; purify their hearts; and show their love for God and their fellow human beings.

Most likely Jesus' early followers perceived him as a prophet. Like the Hebrew prophets, Jesus saw ethics as the core of Mosaic Law: "So whatever you wish that men would do to you, do so to them; for this is the law and the prophets" (Matthew 7:12). Like the prophets, he denounced injustice and oppression, urged mercy and compassion, and expressed a special concern for the poor and downtrodden.

Jesus did not intend to lead his fellow Jews, who called him rabbi, away from their ancestral religion: "'Think not that I have come to abolish the law and the prophets; I have come not to abolish them but to fulfil them'" (Matthew 5:17). Although Jesus did not negate the Law, some of his interpretations offended Jewish leaders.

While not seeking to break with his past or to reject Jewish law, Jesus was distressed by the Judaism of his day. Following the prophets, the rabbis taught the Golden Rule, as well as God's love and mercy for his children, but it seemed to Jesus that these ethical considerations were being undermined by an exaggerated rabbinical concern with ritual, restrictions, and the fine points of the Law. Jesus believed that the center of Judaism had shifted from prophetic values to obedience to rules and prohibitions regulating the smallest details of daily life. (To Jewish leaders, of course, these detailed regulations governing eating, washing, Sabbath observance, family relations, and so forth were God's commands intended to sanctify all human activities.) To Jesus, such a rigid view of the Law distorted the meaning of prophetic teachings. Rules dealt only with an individual's visible behavior; they did not engage the person's inner being and lead to a moral transformation based on love, compassion, and selflessness. Observing the Lord's command to rest on the Sabbath—for example, by not eating an egg laid on Saturday or by not lifting a chair on that day—did not purify a person's heart.

For Jesus, the best way to realize the true meaning of Jewish law was through moral purity, which finds expression in a love for one's fellows. The inner person concerned Jesus, and it was an inner change that he sought: "For

---

*The biblical quotations in this chapter are taken from the Revised Standard Version of the Holy Bible.

from within, out of the heart of man, come evil thoughts, fornication, theft, murder, adultery, coveting, wickedness, deceit, licentiousness, envy, slander, pride, foolishness. All these evil things come from within, and they defile a man" (Mark 7:21–23). To Jesus, the spirit of Mosaic Law was more important than the letter of the Law; for him, right living and a pure loving heart were Judaism's true essence. With the fervor of a prophet, he urged a moral transformation of human character through a direct encounter between the individual and God. By preaching active love for others and genuine compassion for sufferers and by stressing a personal and intimate connection between the individual and God, Jesus associated himself more with the Hebrew prophetic tradition than with the Hebrew rituals, rules, and prohibitions that served to perpetuate a national and cultural tradition of a distinct people.

It was inevitable that Jewish scribes and priests, guardians of the faith, would regard Jesus, who had become a popular preacher, as a threat to ancient traditions. To Jewish leaders, he was a troublemaker and a subversive. They accused him of associating with social outcasts, sinners, and imperial tax collectors; undermining respect for the Sabbath by violating God's strict command prohibiting any form of labor on this holy day; proclaiming spiritual truth in his own name and on his own authority; and claiming that he, above all other men, had a special and intimate relationship with God and that by associating with him a sinner would be forgiven. Stated succinctly, Jewish leaders believed that Jesus was setting the authority of his person over Mosaic Law—an unpardonable blasphemy in their eyes. They saw Jesus as a false prophet who was leading the people astray.

The Romans, who ruled Palestine, had little interest in Jewish intrareligious disputes. They feared Jesus as a political agitator, as a charismatic leader who could ignite Jewish messianic expectations into a revolt against Rome. After Jewish leaders turned Jesus over to the Roman authorities, the Roman procurator, Pontius Pilate, sentenced him to death by crucifixion, a customary punishment for someone guilty of high treason. Jesus' execution was consistent with Roman policy in Judea, for the Romans routinely arrested

and executed Jews suspected of inciting unrest against Roman rule. Inscribed on the cross on which he was crucified were the words "King of the Jews," a seemingly clear indication of why Pilate ordered his death. Although it is questionable if Jesus ever intended to challenge Roman authority, Pilate was taking no chances. He wanted to eliminate this popular leader before he might ignite a popular uprising.

Some Jews, believing that Jesus was an inspired prophet or even the long-awaited Messiah, had become his followers; the chief of these were the Twelve Disciples. At the time of Jesus' death, Christianity was not a separate religion but a small Hebrew sect with dim prospects for survival. What established the Christian movement and gave it strength was the belief of Jesus' followers that he was raised from the dead on the third day after he was buried. The doctrine of the resurrection enabled people to regard Jesus as more than a superb ethical soul, more than a righteous rabbi, more than a prophet, more than the Messiah; it made possible belief in Jesus as a divine **savior-god** who had come to earth to show people the way to heaven. For early Christians, Jesus' death and belief in his resurrection took on greater importance than his life. For these believers, Jesus the savior-god became the center of their emerging church.

There is no evidence that Jesus, who never preached to Gentiles, intended to establish a new church; this was accomplished by his followers. In the years immediately following the crucifixion, the religion of Jesus was confined almost exclusively to Jews, who could more appropriately be called Jewish-Christians. The word *Christian* came from a name given Jesus: *Christ* (the Lord's Anointed, the Messiah). Missionaries of this dissenting Christian movement within Judaism were called Apostles—those sent out to preach the gospel about Christ. They addressed themselves to Jews and to converts to Judaism who, because they did not adhere fully to Mosaic Law, were not wholly accepted by the Jewish community.

Before this new Jewish messianic movement could realize the universal implications of Jesus' teachings and become a world religion, as distinct from a reformist Jewish sect, it had to separate itself both ideologically and socially from the corporate body of Judaism. Instrumental in this

Map 8.1 THE JOURNEYS OF SAINT PAUL Paul, a Greek-speaking citizen of Rome and thus free to travel throughout the Empire, won converts to the new religion. (Copyright © 2013 Cengage Learning.)

development was the work of a Hellenized Jew named Saul, known to the world as Saint Paul.

Saint Paul: From a Jewish Sect to a World Religion

Saint Paul (A.D. c. 5–c. 67) came from the Greek city of Tarsus in southeastern Asia Minor. Originally called Saul, he belonged to the Diaspora, or the "Dispersion"—the millions of Jews living outside Palestine. Though the Jews of the Diaspora retained their ancient faith, they were also influenced by Greek culture. An example is the Alexandrian Jew Philo (c. 20 B.C.–c. A.D. 50), who tried to demonstrate that Hebrew Scriptures could be explained and justified in terms of Greek philosophy.

Non-Jews, or *Gentiles* (from Latin *gens*, or "nation"), who came into contact with Jews of

the Diaspora were often favorably impressed by Hebrew monotheism, ethics, and family life. Some Gentiles embraced Hebrew monotheism but refused to adhere to provisions of the Law requiring circumcision and dietary regulations. Among these Gentiles and non-Palestinian Jews who were greatly influenced by the Greco-Roman milieu, Jesus' Apostles would find receptive listeners.

Reared in Tarsus, a stronghold of Greek culture, Saul knew Greek well, but it is unlikely, despite a respectable writing style, that he had great knowledge of Greek literature, philosophy, and science. Trained in the outlook of the Pharisees, the young Saul went to Jerusalem to study with Rabban Gamaliel, an outstanding Pharisee teacher. In Jerusalem, Saul persecuted Jesus' followers in the time after his crucifixion, but then Saul underwent a spiritual transformation and became a follower of Jesus. Serving as a zealous missionary of Jewish

SAINT PAUL MOSAIC FROM THE BAPTISTRY OF THE ARIANS, RAVENNA, ITALY. Inspired by Jesus' life and death, Paul taught that Jesus was a resurrected redeemer who held the promise of salvation for both Jews and Gentiles. (Scala/Art Resource N.Y.)

Christianity in the Diaspora, Saul, now called by his Roman name, Paul, preached to his fellow Jews in synagogues throughout the Roman Empire and wrote letters of advice back to the congregations he had started. Not having much success with his fellow Jews and recognizing that the Christian message applied to non-Jews as well, Paul urged spreading it to the Gentiles. His knowledge of Greek was of inestimable value in his missionary work with both Diaspora Jews and Gentiles.

Although he was neither the first nor the only missionary to the Gentiles, Paul was without doubt the most important. In the process of his missionary activity—and he traveled extensively throughout the Roman Empire—he formulated doctrines that represented a fundamental break with Judaism and became the heart of this new religion. Paul taught that all people, both Jews and Gentiles, were sinners as a consequence of Adam's original defiance of God; that Jesus had come to earth to save all people from sin and death; that by suffering and dying on the cross he had atoned for the sins of all and made it possible for people to have eternal life in heaven; and that by believing in Jesus people could gain this salvation. Alone, one was helpless, possessed by sin, unable to overcome one's wicked nature. Jesus was the only hope, said Paul. "Wretched man that I am! Who will deliver me from this body of death? Thanks be to God through Jesus Christ our Lord!" (Romans 7:24–25).

Christ: A Savior-God. To the first members of the Christian movement, Jesus was both a prophet who proclaimed the power and purpose of God and the Messiah whose coming heralded a new age. To Paul, Jesus was a resurrected redeemer who offered salvation to all peoples. Paul taught that the crucified Messiah had suffered and died for the sins of human beings; that through Jesus God had shown his love of humanity and revealed himself to all people, both Jews and Gentiles; and that this revelation supplanted the earlier one to the Jewish people.

Increasingly Jesus' followers came to view the sacrificed Messiah as a savior-god, indeed, as God incarnate. The idea of a slain savior-god was well known in the mystery religions of the eastern Mediterranean. Like these religions, Christianity initiated converts into the mysteries of the faith, featured a sacramental meal, and in time developed a priesthood. But the similarities between

Christianity and the mystery cults should not be overstressed since the differences are more profound.

Unlike the cultic gods, Jesus had actually lived in history. Hence, people could identify with him, which enormously increased the appeal of this new religion. Moreover, the deities of the mystery religions were killed against their will by evil powers. In Jesus, it was said, God had become a man and suffered pain and death out of compassion for human beings, to show a floundering humanity the way that would lead from sin to eternal life. This suffering Savior evoked from distressed human beings deep feelings of love and loyalty. Adherents of the mystery cults were not required to undergo a profound moral transformation. Christian converts, however, felt a compelling obligation to make their behavior, in the words of Paul, "worthy of the God who calls you" (Thessalonians 2:12) and to obey Jesus' command: "Be perfect as your heavenly Father is perfect" (Matthew 5:48). Finally, Christians, with their Jewish heritage, would tolerate no other divinity but God. Pagans, on the other hand, often belonged to more than one cult, or at least recognized the divinity of gods in other cults.

The Break with Judaism.   In attempting to reach the Gentiles, Paul had to disentangle Christianity from a Jewish sociocultural context. Thus, he held that neither Gentile nor Jewish followers of Jesus were bound by the hundreds of rituals and rules that constitute Mosaic Law.* Paul saw no distinctive difference between Jew and Gentile; in his view, the ministry of Jesus was intended for all. As a consequence of Jesus' coming, Paul maintained, Mosaic regulations hindered missionary activity among the Gentiles. For Paul, not the Law of Moses but love of and faith in Christ was

the new avenue to God and salvation. The followers of Jesus fulfilled Hebrew history; they were the new Israel.

To Paul, the new Christian community was the true fulfillment of Judaism: it was the means to moral transformation and eternal life. The Jews regarded their faith as a national religion, bound inseparably with the history of their people. Paul saw the new Christian community not as a nation but as an oikoumene, a world community. Jesus fulfilled not only the messianic aspirations of the Jews but also the spiritual needs and expectations of all peoples. To this extent, Christianity shared in the universalism of the Hellenistic Age.

In preaching the doctrine of a risen Savior and insisting that Mosaic Law had been superseded, Paul (whatever his intentions) was breaking with his Jewish roots and transforming a Jewish sect into a new religion. Separating Christianity from Judaism enormously increased its appeal for non-Jews, who were attracted to Hebrew ethical monotheism but repelled by practices such as circumcision, dietary regulations, and other strict requirements of Mosaic Law. Paul built on Jesus' appeal for individual spiritual renewal and his empathy for all humanity (both also concerns of the ancient Hebrew prophets) to create a religion intended not for a people with its own particular history, culture, and land, but for all humankind.

THE SPREAD AND TRIUMPH OF CHRISTIANITY

By establishing Christianity's independence from Judaism and its practices, Paul made the new religion attractive to the Greco-Roman world. Originating in the first century, Christianity took firm root in the second, grew extensively in the third, and became the official religion of the Roman Empire at the end of the fourth century.

The Appeal of Christianity

The triumph of Christianity was related to a corresponding decline in the vitality of Hellenism and a shift in cultural emphasis—a movement from reason to emotion and revelation. Offering

---

*Paul's understanding of Mosaic Law is a matter of controversy. Some scholars argue that he regarded the Law as obsolete and broke with his ancestral faith. Other scholars, arguing that Paul did not forsake the Law, point to a famous passage: "Do we then nullify the law by this faith? Not at all! Rather we uphold the law" (Romans 3:31). Paul, who continually described himself as a Pharisee, lived an observant life and celebrated Jewish festivals. For these scholars, Paul never stopped revering the Torah but taught that Jesus, the Messiah, fulfilled the Torah's higher purpose—the biblical prophecy of the Messiah's coming.

comforting solutions to the existential problems of life and death, religion demonstrated a greater capacity than reason to stir human hearts. Hellenism had invented the tools of rational thought, but the power of mythical thought was never entirely subdued. By the Late Roman Empire, science and philosophy were unable to compete with mysticism, myth, and the divine.

This deterioration of the classical outlook was demonstrated by the growing popularity of Eastern religions and the spiritualization of philosophy. Mystery cults, which promised personal salvation, were spreading and gaining followers. Astrology and magic, which offered supernatural explanations for the operations of nature, were also popular. Stoicism and Epicureanism were performing a religious function by trying to help individuals overcome emotional stress, while Neo-Platonists yearned for a mystical union with the One. This recoil from rational and worldly values helped prepare the way for Christianity. In a culturally stagnating and spiritually troubled Greco-Roman world, Christianity gave new meaning to life and offered new hope to disillusioned men and women.

During the Hellenistic Age, the individual had struggled with the problems of alienation and lack of community. With the decline of the independent city-state, the individual searched for a new frame of reference, a new form of attachment. The Roman Empire represented one possible allegiance. But for many people, it was not a satisfying relationship; the individual found it difficult to be devoted to a political organization so vast, remote, and impersonal. The Christian message of a divine Savior and a concerned Father, as well as of brotherly love, inspired men and women who were dissatisfied with the world of the here and now— who felt no attachment to city or empire, derived no inspiration from philosophy, and suffered from a profound sense of loneliness. Christianity offered the individual what the city and the Roman world-state could not: an intensely personal relationship with God, an intimate connection with a higher world, and membership in a community of the faithful who cared for one another.

Stressing the intellect and self-reliance, Greco-Roman thought did not provide for the emotional needs of many people. Christianity addressed itself to this deficiency in the Greco-Roman outlook. Particularly those who were poor, oppressed, or enslaved were attracted to the personality, life, death, and resurrection of Jesus, his love for all, and his concern for suffering humanity. They found spiritual sustenance in a religion that offered a hand in love and taught that a person need not be well-born, rich, educated, or talented to be worthy, that God draws no distinction between the lowly poor and enslaved and the mightiest aristocrats. To people burdened with misfortune and terrified by death, Christianity held the promise of eternal life, a kingdom of heaven where they would be comforted by God the Father. Thus, Christianity gave to the common person what the aristocratic values of Greco-Roman civilization generally did not: hope, a sense of dignity, and inner strength. By and large, classical philosophy offered little compassion for the sufferer, but the cardinal principle of Christianity was that Jesus had endured earthly torments because of his love for all human beings and that even the lowliest could be redeemed.

Christianity succeeded not only through the appeal of its message but also through the power of its organization. To retain the devotion of the faithful, win new converts, protect itself from opponents, and administer its services, Christianity developed an organized body of followers. This body became the Christian church, which grew into a strong organization uniting the faithful. To city dwellers—lonely, alienated, disillusioned with public affairs; stranded mortals groping for a sense of community—the church that called its members "brother" and "sister" filled an elemental need of human beings to belong. Another attraction for Christian converts was the absence of painful or expensive initiation rites, such as those required for entrance into Mithraism, a leading rival (see "The Spread of Mystery Religions" in Chapter 7). Unlike Mithraism, the church also welcomed women converts, who were often the first to join and who brought their menfolk after them. Among the reasons that the church drew women was its command to husbands to treat their wives kindly, remain faithful, and provide for the children. Moreover, in the eyes of God, women were spiritually equal with men. The church also won new converts and retained the loyalty of its members by furnishing social services for the poor and infirm; welcoming slaves, criminals, sinners, and other outcasts; and offering community and comfort during difficult times.

Blandina

During the reign of the emperor Marcus Aurelius, a number of Christians in Lyons, Gaul, including Blandina, a frail young slave, were imprisoned and accused of engaging in cannibalism and incest. The Roman authorities tortured Blandina, hoping that she would implicate the Christian community in these abhorrent crimes. Despite the torments inflicted on her, Blandina would not speak falsely against her fellow Christians. The historian Eusebius described her terrible ordeal:

> Blandina was filled with such power that those who took it in turns to subject her to every kind of torture from morning to night were exhausted by their efforts and confessed themselves beaten—they could think of nothing else to do to her. They were amazed that she was still breathing, for her whole body was mangled and her wounds gaped; they declared that torment of any one kind was enough to part soul and body, let alone a succession of torments of such extreme severity. But the blessed woman, wrestling magnificently, grew in strength as she proclaimed her faith, and found refreshment, rest, and insensibility to her sufferings in uttering the words: "I am a Christian: we do nothing to be ashamed of."

For several days Blandina had to watch other Christians being whipped, roasted, and set upon by wild beasts in the amphitheater. Finally, after surviving

---

The ability of an evolving Christianity to assimilate elements from Greek philosophy and even from the mystery religions also contributed in no small measure to its growth. By becoming infused with Greek philosophy, Christianity could present itself in terms intelligible to those versed in Greek learning and thus attract educated people. Philosophers who converted to Christianity proved to be able defenders of their newly adopted faith. Because some Christian doctrines (the risen savior-god, the virgin and her child, life after death, communion with the divine), practices (purification through baptism), and holy days (December 25 was the birth date of the god Mithras) either paralleled or were adopted from the mystery religions, it became relatively easy to win converts from these rivals.

Christianity and Rome

At first, the Roman government, which was generally tolerant of religions, did not interfere much with the Christian movement. In fact, Christianity benefited in many ways from its association with the Roman Empire. Christian missionaries, among them some of the Twelve Disciples, who were the original followers of Christ, traveled throughout the Empire over roads and across seas made safe by Roman arms. The common Greek dialect, Koine, spoken in most parts of the Empire, facilitated the missionaries' task. Had the Mediterranean world been fractured into separate and competing states, the spread of Christianity might well have faced an insurmountable obstacle. The universalism of the Roman Empire, which made citizenship available to peoples of many nationalities, prepared the way for the universalism of Christianity, which welcomed membership from all nations. Early Christians grafted onto Rome's imperial mission a spiritual, evangelical cause: "Go ye therefore and teach all nations" (Matthew 28:19).

As the number of Christians increased, Roman officials began to fear the Christians as subversives, preaching allegiance to God and not to Rome, and as a self-absorbed sect that did not want to fit into the Empire. To many Romans, Christians were disloyal citizens, strange people who would not accept the state gods, would not engage in sacrifices to Roman divinities, scorned gladiatorial contests, stayed away from public baths, glorified nonviolence, refused to honor deceased emperors as gods, and worshiped a crucified criminal as Lord. Romans *similar torments, she was "dropped into a basket and thrown to a bull. Time after time the animal tossed her, but she was indifferent now to all that happened to her, because of her hope and sure hold on all that her faith meant, and of her communing with Christ. Then she, too, was sacrificed, while the heathen themselves admitted that never yet had they known a woman suffer so much or so long."**

---

*Eusebius, *The History of the Church from Christ to Constantine,* trans. G. A. Williamson (New York: New York University Press, 1966), 196, 202.

ultimately found in Christians a scapegoat for the ills burdening the Empire, such as famines, plagues, and military reverses. Were not these afflictions divine punishment for Christians' refusal to honor ancestral gods and traditions? In an effort to stamp out Christianity, emperors occasionally resorted to persecution. Christians were imprisoned, beaten, starved, beheaded, burned alive, torn apart by wild beasts in the arena for the amusement of the Romans, and crucified. The authorities freed accused Christians who agreed to renounce their faith. But many Christians embraced the opportunity for martyrdom; they believed they were reenacting the passion of Jesus, who had sacrificed himself for humanity.

However, the early persecutions, beginning with those incited under Emperor Nero in A.D. 64, were local, did not cause much loss of life, and were too sporadic to impede the growth of Christianity. The persecutions in the mid-third century and during Diocletian's rule caused the brutal deaths of many Christians but did not last long enough to seriously threaten the new religion. Actually, they strengthened the determination of most of the faithful and won new converts, who were awed by the extraordinary courage of the martyrs willingly dying for their faith.

Unable to crush Christianity by persecution, Roman emperors decided to gain the support of the growing number of Christians within the Empire. In A.D. 313, Constantine, probably genuinely attracted to Christianity, issued the Edict of Milan, granting toleration to Christians. By allowing the free flow of Christian teachings and instituting legislation favorable to the church, Constantine and his successors accelerated the growth of Christianity and the Christianization of the Empire. By A.D. 392, Theodosius I had made Christianity the state religion of the Empire and declared the worship of pagan gods illegal. With Christianity in power, persecution did not end, but its target shifted to pagans, Jews, and Christians with unorthodox views. The polytheistic religions of the Roman world did not claim to possess an exhaustive truth—they did not assert that a particular god or a particular form of worship should prevail over all others and that wrongful religious expressions should be rooted out. People were relatively free to select their own credo and engage in their own acts of worship. Christianity, in contrast, possessing an exclusive attitude toward truth, felt compelled to cleanse society of false gods and beliefs. Such an outlook often led Christians to view nonbelievers as enemies of God deserving of punishment. Thus, mobs, often driven by fanatic clergy, hurled non-Christian writings into bonfires, destroyed pagan altars and sacred images, and squelched pagan rites and festivals. Emperors, often pushed by the clergy, passed decrees calling for fining, imprisoning, torturing, and executing adherents of pagan cults.

Christianity and Greek Philosophy

Christianity synthesized both the Hebrew and the Greco-Roman traditions. Having emerged from Judaism, Christianity assimilated Hebrew monotheism and prophetic morality and retained the Old Testament as the Word of God. Without this Hebraic foundation, Christianity cannot be understood. As the new religion evolved, it also assimilated elements of Greek philosophy. The ability to combine a historic Judaic monotheism, which had many admirers in the Gentile world, with Greek rational philosophy was a crucial reason for Christianity's triumph in the Roman Empire. But there was a struggle between conservatives, who wanted no dealings with pagan philosophy, and those

Map 8.2 THE SPREAD OF CHRISTIANITY Aided by dedicated missionaries, Christianity expanded throughout the Mediterranean world and later into Germanic lands. (Copyright © 2013 Cengage Learning.)

believers who recognized the value of Greek thought to Christianity.

To conservative church fathers—early Christian writers whose works are accepted as authoritative by the church—classical philosophy erred completely because it did not derive from divine revelation. As the final statement of God's truth, Christianity superseded both pagan philosophy and pagan religions. According to the church fathers, the simple peasant who accepted Christ possessed more knowledge than the most learned philosopher who did not. These conservatives feared that studying classical authors would contaminate Christian morality (did not Plato propose a community of

wives, and did not the dramatists treat violent passions?) and promote heresy (was not classical literature replete with references to pagan gods?). For these church fathers, there could be no compromise between Greek philosophy and Christian revelation. For them, faith was more reliable than all the demonstrations of human reason. "What indeed has Athens to do with Jerusalem?" asked Tertullian (A.D. 150–225). "With our faith, we desire no further belief. For this is our faith that there is nothing which we ought to believe besides."[3]

Some church fathers, including several who had a Greek education, resisted this anti-intellectualism. Defending the value of studying classical literature, they maintained that such literature, if properly taught, could aid in the moral development of children because it presented many examples of virtuous deeds. Some church fathers claimed that Greek philosophy contained a dim glimmer of God's truth, a pre-Christian insight into divine wisdom. Christ had corrected and fulfilled an insight reached by the philosophical mind. Knowledge of Greek philosophy, they also contended, helped Christians explain their beliefs logically and argue intelligently with pagan critics of Christian teachings. Thus, Clement of Alexandria (c. A.D. 150–220) brought reason to the support of faith in his attempt to make Christianity more intellectually respectable in his world.

> *Rather, philosophy is a clear image of truth, a divine gift to the Greeks. Before the advent of the Lord, philosophy helped the Greeks to attain righteousness, and is now conducive to piety, it supplies a preparatory teaching for those who will later embrace the faith. God is the cause of all good things: some given primarily in the form of the Old and the New Testament; others are the consequence of philosophy. Perchance too philosophy was given to the Greeks primarily till the Lord should call the Greeks to serve him. Thus philosophy acted as a schoolmaster to the Greeks, preparing them for Christ, as the laws of the Jews prepared them for Christ.*[4]

Utilizing the language and categories of Greek philosophy, Christian intellectuals transformed Christianity from a simple ethical creed into a theoretical system, a theology. Greek philosophy enabled Christians to explain rationally God's existence and revelation in order to show that Christian teachings did not violate the laws of logic. Christ was depicted as the divine or incarnate Logos (reason) in human form. Educated believers could argue that the fundamental principles that Greek philosophers maintained operated in the universe were established by God the Father. The Stoic teaching that all people are fundamentally equal because they share in universal reason could be formulated in Christian terms: all are united in Christ. Christians could interpret the church to be the true fulfillment of the Stoic idea of a polity embracing the entire world. Stoic ethics, which stressed moderation, self-control, and brotherhood,

could be assimilated by Christian revelation. Particularly in Platonism, which drew a distinction between a world perceived by the senses and a higher order—a transcendent world that should be the central concern of human existence—Christian thinkers found a congenial vehicle for expressing Christian beliefs. The perfect and universal Forms, or Ideas, which Plato maintained were the true goal of knowledge and the source of ethical standards, were held by Christians to exist in God's mind.

That Greek philosophy had a strong hold on church doctrine was immensely important, for it meant that rational thought, the priceless achievement of the Greek mind, was not lost. But Greek philosophy had to sacrifice its ability to think freely to the needs of Christian revelation: reason had to serve faith. And in any conflict between reason and faith, faith would prevail. Although Christianity made use of Greek philosophy, Christian truth ultimately rested on faith, not reason. As Tertullian stated, it is precisely because faith in a crucified Lord contradicted all human logic that he would believe: "And the Son of God died; it is by all means to be believed, because it is absurd. And He was buried, and rose again; the fact is certain because it is impossible."[5]

THE GROWTH OF CHRISTIAN ORGANIZATION, DOCTRINE, AND ATTITUDES

Early in its history, the church gradually developed along hierarchical lines. Those members of the Christian community who had the authority to preside over the celebration of the Mass—breaking bread and offering wine as Christ had done in the Last Supper—were called either priests or bishops. Gradually, the designation *bishop* was reserved for the one clergyman in the community with the authority to resolve disputes over doctrines and practices. Regarded as the successors to Jesus' Twelve Disciples, bishops supervised religious activities within their regions. The most influential bishops ministered to the leading cities of the Empire: Rome, Alexandria, Antioch, and Milan. In creating a diocese that was supervised by a bishop and had its center in a leading city, the church adapted Roman administrative techniques.

The Primacy of the Bishop of Rome

The bishop of Rome, later called the *pope* ("father"), claimed primacy over the other bishops, maintaining that the Apostle Peter founded the Roman see (official seat of authority) and that both Peter and Paul were martyred in Rome. Moreover, as the traditional capital of the Empire, Rome seemed the logical choice to serve as the center of the church.

In developing the case for their supremacy over the church organization, bishops of Rome increasingly referred to the famous New Testament passage in which Jesus says to his disciple Simon (also called Peter): "'And I tell you, you are Peter, and on this rock I will build my church'" (Matthew 16:18). Because *Peter* in Greek means "rock" (*petra*), it was argued that Christ had chosen Peter to succeed him as ruler of the universal church. It was commonly accepted that Saint Peter had established a church in Rome and was martyred there, so it was argued further that the Roman bishop inherited the power that Christ had passed on to Peter. Thus, the argument continued, the bishop of Rome held a unique office: of all the bishops, only he had inherited the powers originally granted by Christ to Peter. Because the Apostles had been subordinate to Peter, so too must the bishops defer to Peter's successor.

The Rise of Monasticism

Some devout Christians committed to living a perfect Christian life were distressed by the wickedness of the world about them, including the moral laxity of those clergy who chased after wealth and pomp. Seeking to escape from the agonies and corruptions of this world, some ardent Christians withdrew to deserts and mountains in search of solitude and spiritual renewal. In their zeal to emulate Jesus' self-denial, they sometimes practiced extreme forms of asceticism: self-flogging, wearing spiked corsets, eating only herbs, or living for years atop a column high above the ground.

Gradually, colonies of these hermits sprang up, particularly in Egypt and Syria; in time, the leaders of these monastic communities drew up written rules for prayer and work. Saint Basil (c. 329–c. 379), a Greek who was bishop of Caesarea in Cappadocia (eastern Asia Minor), established the rules that became the standard for monasteries in the East. Basil required monks to refrain from bodily abuses and to engage in manual labor. Through farming, weaving, and construction, monks could make a monastery self-supporting and have the means to assist the needy. Aware of the lure of materialism and selfishness, Basil forbade his monks to own personal property other than clothing and insisted that they spend much of their time in silence.

The monastic ideal spread from east to west. The principal figure in the shaping of **monasticism** in the West was Saint Benedict (c. 480–c. 543), who founded a monastery at Monte Cassino, Italy, in 529. The Rule of Saint Benedict (see Primary Source box) required the monks to live in poverty and to study, labor, and obey the abbot, the head of the monastery. They had to pray often, work hard, talk little, and surrender private property. In imposing discipline and regulations, Benedict eliminated the excessive and eccentric individualism of the early monks. Benedict demonstrated the same genius for administration that the Romans had shown in organizing and governing their empire. Benedict's rule became the standard for monasteries throughout Western Europe.

Scriptural Tradition and Doctrinal Disputes

The earliest surviving Christian writings are Paul's Epistles, written some twenty-five to thirty years after the death of Jesus. Jesus' sayings were preserved by word of mouth. Sometime around A.D. 66–70, about forty years after the crucifixion, Saint Mark formulated the Christian message from this oral tradition and perhaps from some material that had been put in writing earlier. Later, Saint Matthew and Saint Luke, relying heavily on Mark's account, wrote somewhat longer Gospels. The Gospels of Mark, Matthew, and Luke are called *synoptic* because their approach to Jesus is very similar. The remaining Gospel, written by Saint John around A.D. 110, varies significantly from the synoptic Gospels. The Gospel of John uses the Stoic concept of Logos to present Jesus as the divine being. John identifies Jesus with the eternal word, or Logos, which became the incarnate Son of God: "In the beginning was the Word and the Word was with God, and the Word was God. . . . And the Word became Flesh and dwelt among us"

(John 1:1, 14). The synoptic Gospels; the Gospel According to Saint John; Acts of the Apostles; the twenty-one Epistles, including those written by Saint Paul; and Revelation constitute the twenty-seven books of the Christian New Testament. Christians also accepted the Old Testament of the Hebrews as God's Word. The New Testament was written not by historians with the critical spirit of a Thucydides or a Polybius but by men moved by the fervor of faith. Under these circumstances, it is understandable that it contains discrepancies, some nonhistorical legends, and polemics.

The early Christians had a Bible and a clergy to teach it. But the Holy Writ could be interpreted differently by equally sincere believers, and controversies over doctrine threatened the loose unity of the early church. The most important controversy concerned how people viewed the relationship between God and Christ. Arius (250–336), a Greek priest in Alexandria, led one faction; he denied the complete divinity of Christ, one of the basic tenets of the church. To Arius, Christ was more than man but less than God; the Father and the Son did not possess the same nature, or essence. Arius said that there was no permanent union between God and Christ; the Father alone is eternal and truly God.

The Council of Nicaea (325), the first assembly, or ecumenical council, of bishops from all parts of the Roman world, was called to settle the controversy. The council condemned Arius and ruled that God and Christ were of the same substance, coequal and coeternal. The position adopted at Nicaea became the basis of the Nicene Creed, which remains the official doctrine of the church. Although Arianism, the name given the heresy of Arius, won converts for a time, it eventually died out, helped along by persecution. This meant that the Catholic church alone would shape the distinctive character of the new civilization that emerged in the Middle Ages.

Christianity and Society

Although salvation was their ultimate aim, Christians still had to dwell within the world and deal with its imperfections. In the process, Christian thinkers challenged some of the mores of Greco-Roman society and formulated attitudes that would endure for centuries.

Influenced by passages in the New Testament that condemned acts of revenge and the shedding of blood, and concerned only with the heavenly kingdom, some early Christians refused military service. Others, however, held that in a sinful world, defense of the state was necessary, and without concealment or apology they served in the army. With the barbarians menacing the borders, Christian officials could not advocate nonviolence. Christian theorists began to argue that under certain circumstances—to punish injustice or to restore peace—war was just. But even such wars must not entail unnecessary violence.

Christians denounced the gladiatorial combats and contests between men and beasts as bloodlust and murder, and regarded attendance at these spectacles as tantamount to participating in murder. Nevertheless, these spectacles persisted even after the majority of the population had converted to Christianity. When the games finally ended, it was probably due more to the growing poverty of the western Empire than to the Christian conscience.

Numerous women joined the Christian movement and a number suffered martyrdom, but positions of authority were reserved for men, including ordination as priests. The early Christian view of women was rooted in the patriarchal tradition of Jewish society. Paul subjected the wife to her husband's authority. "Wives, be subject to your husbands, as to the Lord. For the husband is the head of the wife as Christ is the head of the church" (Ephesians 5:22–23). Paul wanted women to remain quiet at church meetings. "If there is anything they desire to know, let them ask their husbands at home. For it is shameful for a woman to speak in church" (1 Corinthians 14:35). But Paul also held that all are baptized in Christ: "There is neither Jew nor Greek, there is neither slave nor free, there is neither male nor female; for you are all one in Christ Jesus" (Galatians 3:28). Consequently, both sexes were subject to divine law, and both possessed moral autonomy. The early church held to strict standards on sexual matters. It condemned adultery and esteemed virginity pledged for spiritual reasons.

Christians waged no war against slavery, which was widely practiced and universally accepted in the ancient world. Paul commanded slaves to obey their masters, and many Christians, including leaders of local churches, were slave owners. Although

Saint Benedict of Nursia: The Christian Way of Life

In the following selection from his monastic book of rules, Saint Benedict of Nursia advises his monks on the attitudes and conduct necessary to live a virtuous Christian life.

What Are the Instruments of Good Works?

In the first place, to love the Lord God with the whole heart, whole soul, whole strength, then his neighbor as himself.

Then not to kill, not to commit adultery, not to steal, not to covet, not to bear false witness, to honor all men, and what anyone would not have done to him, let him not do to another. To deny himself, that he may follow Christ, to chasten the body, to renounce luxuries, to love fasting. To relieve the poor, to clothe the naked, to visit the sick, to bury the dead, to help in tribulation, to console the afflicted.

To make himself a stranger to the affairs of the world, to prefer nothing before the love of Christ, not to give way to anger, not to bear any grudge, not to harbour deceit in the heart, not to forsake charity. Not to swear, lest haply he perjure himself, to utter truth from his heart and his mouth. Not to return evil for evil, not to do injuries, but rather to bear them patiently, to love his enemies, not to curse against those that curse him, but rather to bless them, to endure persecution for righteousness' sake. Not to be proud, not given to wine, not gluttonous, not addicted to sleep, not slothful, not given to murmur, not a slanderer. To commit his hope to God; when he sees anything good in himself to attribute it to God, and not to himself, but let him always know that which is evil is his own doing; and impute it to himself. To fear the day of judgment, to dread hell, to desire eternal life with all spiritual longing, to have the expectation of death every day before his eyes. To watch over his actions at all times, to know certainly that in all places the eye of God is upon him; those evil thoughts which come into his heart to dash to pieces on Christ, and to make them known to his spiritual senior. To keep his lips from evil and wicked discourse, not to be fond of much talking, not to speak vain words or such as provoke laughter, not to love much or violent laughter. To give willing attention to the sacred readings, to pray frequently every day, to confess his past sins to God, in prayer, with tears and groanings; from thence forward to reform as to those sins.

Not to fulfill the desires of the flesh, to hate his own will, in all things to obey the commands of the abbot, even though he himself (which God forbid) should do otherwise, remembering our Lord's commands: "What they say, do; but what they do, do ye not." Not to desire to be called a saint before he is one, but first to be one that he may be truly called one; every day to fulfill the commands of God in his deeds, to love chastity, to hate no one, not to have jealousy or envy, not to love contention, to avoid self-conceit; to reverence seniors, to love juniors, to pray for enemies in the love of Christ, to be reconciled with his adversary, before the going down of the sun, and never to despair of the mercy of God. . . .

Question for Analysis

1. According to Saint Benedict, how should a Christian lead a virtuous life?

Oliver J. Thatcher, ed., *Library of Original Sources* (Milwaukee: University Research Extension, 1907), 4:133–134.

Christians did not try to alter the legal status of slaves, they did teach that slaves, too, were children of God; they sought their conversion; they urged owners not to treat slaves harshly; and they considered it a virtue for owners to free slaves. In the modern world, the Christian teaching that all persons are spiritually equal before God would arouse some Christians to fight for the abolition of slavery.

Christian theorists condemned sex outside of marriage, adultery, prostitution, homosexuality, and abortion, and insisted that the sex drive should be confined to reproduction, as Clement of Alexandria wrote: "Yet marriage in itself merits esteem and the highest approval, for the Lord wished men to 'be fruitful and multiply.' He did not tell them, however, to act like libertines, nor did He intend them to surrender themselves to pleasure as though born only to indulge in sexual relations. . . . To indulge in intercourse without intending children is to outrage nature."[6]

Christianity and the Jews

Increasingly, Christians identified opponents—Jews, pagans, and heretics—with Satan, the fallen angel, and viewed conflicts in a moral context: a struggle between God's faithful and Satan's servants. Over the centuries, the view that they were participants in a cosmic struggle between good and evil led Christians to demonize adversaries, a practice that exacerbated hatred and justified mistreatment and even massacre. Christian attitudes and behavior toward Jews poignantly illustrate this point.

Numerous links connect early Christianity and Judaism. Jesus himself and his earliest followers, including the Twelve Disciples, were Jews who were faithful to Jewish law. Jesus attended synagogue and frequently quoted the Hebrew Scriptures, which to him and his disciples was the authoritative word of God, to support a particular viewpoint. Jesus' message was first spread in synagogues throughout the Roman Empire. Early Christianity's affirmation of the preciousness of the human being, created in God's image; its belief that God rules history; its awareness of human sinfulness; its call for repentance; and its appeal to God for forgiveness are rooted in Judaism. The Christian reference to God as a "merciful Father" derives from Jewish prayer. Also rooted in Judaism are the moral norms

proclaimed by Jesus in the Sermon on the Mount and on other occasions. For example, "Thou shalt love thy neighbor as thyself" was the motto of the Jewish sage Hillel, a contemporary of Jesus, who founded a school. The great value that the Torah gives to charity was inherited by Christianity. Jesus' use of parables to convey his teachings, the concept of the Messiah, respect for the Sabbath, and congregational worship also stem from Judaism. Moreover, Christians viewed the Hebrew Scriptures as God's Word. In addition, a deep understanding of the New Testament requires knowledge of the Old Testament, for its thought and language permeate the Christian Gospels.

However, over the years, particularly after more and more non-Jews became followers of Christ, Christians forgot or devalued the Jewish roots of their faith, and some thinkers began to show hostility toward Judaism and Jews that had tragic consequences in later centuries. Several factors fueled this anti-Judaism: resentment against Jews for their refusal to embrace Jesus; the polemics of the Jewish establishment against followers of Jesus; the role in Jesus' death ascribed to Jews by the New Testament; resentment against those Christians who Judaized, that is, continued to observe Jewish festivals and the Jewish Sabbath, regard the synagogue as holy, and practice circumcision; and anger that Judaism remained a vital religion, for this undermined the conviction that Christianity was the fulfillment of Judaism and the one true faith.

What made Christian anti-Judaism particularly ominous was the effort of some theologians to **demonize** the Jewish people. The myth emerged that the Jews, murderers of the incarnate God who embodied all that was good, were a cursed people, children of the Devil, whose suffering was intended by God. Thus, Origen (c. 185–c. 251) maintained that "the blood of Jesus [falls] not only upon those who lived then but also upon all generations of the Jewish people following afterwards until the end of the world."[7] In the late fourth century, John Chrysostom described Jews as "inveterate murderers, destroyers, men possessed by the Devil. . . . [T]hey murder their offspring and immolate them to the devil." The synagogue, he said, was "the domicile of the devil as is also the soul of the Jews." Their rites are "criminal and impure," and their religion is "a disease." For the "odious assassination of Christ," there is "no expiation possible, . . . no pardon." Jews will live "under the yoke of servitude without end."[8] Since the Devil was very real to early and medieval Christians, the Jew became identified with evil. Christians developed a mindset, concludes the Reverend Robert A. Everett, that was "unable to see anything positive in Judaism. . . . Judaism and the Jewish people came to have no real value for Christians except as a negative contrast to Christianity."[9] Because of this "teaching of contempt" and the "diabolization of the Jew," the Christian ethic of love did not extend to Jews.

> *Once it is established that God has cursed the Jews, how can one argue that Christians should love them? If Jews have been fated by God to have . . . a long history of suffering, who are Christians to alter their history by doing anything to relieve Jewish suffering? The theology of victimization thus precludes Christian love as a basis of relating to Jews.*[10]

The diabolization of the Jew, which bore no relationship to the actual behavior of Jews or to their highly ethical religion, and the "theology of victimization," which held that the Jews were collectively and eternally cursed for denying Christ, became powerful myths, which, over the centuries, poisoned Christians' hearts and minds against Jews, spurring innumerable humiliations, persecutions, and massacres by Christians who believed that their actions were pleasing to God. Alongside this hatred of Jews and antipathy to their suffering, there also evolved the belief that the Jews, faithless and perfidious though they were, should be permitted to survive, for their dispersal among the nations was evidence of divine punishment and the truth of Christianity. Moreover, one day the Jews would see the light and convert to the true faith.

SAINT AUGUSTINE: THE CHRISTIAN WORLDVIEW

During the early history of Christianity, learned fathers of the church explained and defended church teachings. Most of the leading early fathers wrote in Greek, but in the middle of the fourth century, three great Latin writers—Saint Jerome, Saint Ambrose, and Saint Augustine—profoundly influenced the course of Christianity in the West.

As a youth, Saint Jerome (c. 340–420) studied Latin literature in Rome. Throughout his life, he remained an admirer of Cicero, Virgil, Lucretius, and other great Latin writers, and he defended the study of classical literature by Christians. Criticized for attacking the luxurious living and laxness of the clergy, he left Rome and established a monastery near Bethlehem, where he devoted himself to prayer and study. His greatest achievement was the translation of the Old and New Testaments from Hebrew and Greek into Latin. Jerome's text, the common, or Vulgate, version of the Bible, became the official edition of the Bible for the Western church.

Saint Ambrose (340–397), bishop of Milan, Italy, urged clerics not to pursue wealth but to practice humility and avoid favoring the rich over the poor. Ambrose sought to defend the autonomy of the church against the power of the state. Emperors are not the judges of bishops, he wrote. His dictum that "the Emperor is within the church, not above it" became a cardinal principle of the medieval church.

The most important Christian theoretician in the Late Roman Empire was Saint Augustine (354–430), bishop of Hippo, in North Africa. Born in the North African province of Numidia, Augustine attended school at Carthage, where he studied the Latin classics. Struggling to find meaning in a world that abounded with evil, Augustine turned to Manichaeism, an Eastern religious philosophy whose central doctrine was the struggle of the universal forces of light and good against those of darkness and evil. But Augustine still felt spiritually restless. In Milan, inspired by the sermons of Ambrose, he abandoned Manichaeism and devoted his life to following Christ's teachings. After serving as a priest, he was appointed bishop of Hippo in 395. At the turn of the fifth century, when the Greco-Roman worldview was disintegrating and the Roman world-state was collapsing, Augustine wrote his greatest and most influential work, *The City of God*. He became the chief architect of the Christian outlook that succeeded a dying classicism.

In 410, when Augustine was in his fifties, Visigoths sacked Rome—a disaster for which the classical consciousness was unprepared. Throughout the Empire, people panicked. Non-Christians blamed the tragedy on Christianity, saying that the

CHRIST ENTHRONED. This detail from the funerary sarcophagus of Junius Bassus, dating from A.D. 359, shows Christ sitting on a throne. (Hirmer Verlag Fotoarchiv, München.)

Christians had predicted the end of the world and by refusing to offer sacrifices to ancient gods had turned those deities against Rome. Even Christians expressed anxiety. Why were the righteous also suffering? Where was the kingdom of God on earth that had been prophesied in the Scriptures?

Augustine's *City of God* was a response to the crisis of the Roman Empire, just as Plato's *Republic* had been a reaction to the crisis of the Athenian polis. Whereas Plato expressed hope that a state founded on rational principles could remedy the abuses of Athenian society, Augustine maintained that the worldly city could never be the central concern of a Christian. The ideal state, he wrote, could not be realized on earth; it existed only in heaven. The misfortunes of Rome, therefore, should not distress a Christian unduly, for

Christianity belonged to the realm of the spirit and could not be identified with any state. The collapse of Rome did not diminish the greatness of Christianity because the true Christian was a citizen of a heavenly city that could not be pillaged by ungodly barbarians but would endure forever. Compared with God's heavenly city, Rome and its decline were unimportant. What really mattered in history, Augustine said, was not the coming to be or the passing away of cities and empires, but the individual's spiritual destiny, his or her entrance into heaven or hell.

Yet Augustine remained a man of this world. Although the earthly city was the very opposite of the heavenly city, he insisted that people must still deal with this earthly abode. Christians could not reject their city entirely but must bend it to fit a Christian pattern. The city that someday would rise from the ruins of Rome must be based on Christian principles. Warfare, economic activity, education, and the rearing of children should all be conducted in a Christian spirit. The church could not neglect the state but must guide it to protect human beings from their own sinful natures. The state must employ repression and punishment to restrain people, who were inherently sinful, from destroying one another. But the earthly city would never know tranquility, said Augustine, for it would always be inhabited predominantly by wretched sinners. People should be under no illusion that it could be transformed into the City of God. Because human beings are infected with sin, everywhere in human society we see

> *love for all those things that prove so vain and . . . breed so many heartaches, troubles, griefs, and fears; such insane joys in discord, strife, and war; such wrath and plots of enemies . . . such fraud and theft and robbery; such perfidy . . . homicide and murder, cruelty and savagery, lawlessness and lust; all the shameless passions of the impure—fornication and adultery . . . and countless other uncleannesses too nasty to be mentioned; the sins against religion—sacrilege and heresy . . . the iniquities against our neighbors—calumnies and cheating, lies and false witness, violence to persons and property . . . and the innumerable other miseries and maladies that fill the world, yet escape attention.*[11]

Augustine did not hold that Christ, by his sacrificial death, had opened the door to heaven for all. Most of humanity remained condemned to eternal punishment; only a handful were blessed with the gift of faith and the promise of heaven. Whereas the vast majority of people, said Augustine, were citizens of a doomed earthly city, the small number endowed with God's grace constituted the City of God. These people lived on earth as visitors only, for they awaited deliverance to the Kingdom of Christ, where together with the good angels and God they would know perfect happiness. But the permanent inhabitants of the earthly city were destined for eternal punishment in hell. A perpetual conflict existed between the two cities and between their inhabitants; one city

stood for sin and corruption, the other for God's truth and perfection. For Augustine, the highest good was not of this world but consisted of eternal life with God.

Augustine's distinction between this higher world of perfection and a lower world of corruption remained influential throughout the Middle Ages. But the church, rejecting Augustine's doctrine that only a limited number of people are predestined for heaven, emphasized that Christ had made possible the salvation of all who would embrace the precepts and injunctions of the church. Leading Protestant reformers of the sixteenth century, however, accepted Augustine's position.

Augustine repudiated the distinguishing feature of classical humanism: the autonomy of reason. For him, ultimate wisdom could not be achieved through rational thought alone. Reason had to be guided by faith. Without faith, there could be no true knowledge, no understanding. Philosophy had no validity if it did not first accept as absolutely true the existence of God and the authority of his revelation. Valid ethical standards could not be formulated by reason alone but were revealed to people by the living God. Christian truth did not rest on theoretical excellence or logical consistency; it was true because its source was God.

Augustine's belief contrasts with that of Socrates, who insisted that through rational reflection each individual could arrive at standards of good and evil. For the humanist Socrates, ultimate values were something that the individual could grasp through thought alone and could defend rationally. For Augustine, reason alone could not serve as a proper guide to life. He maintained that individuals, without divine guidance, lacked the capacity to comprehend ultimate truth or to regenerate themselves morally. Without God, they could not attain wisdom or liberate themselves from a wicked and sinful human nature: "the happiness of man can come not from himself but only from God, and . . . to live according to oneself is sin."[12]

Thus, in contrast to the classical view that asserted the primacy of reason, Augustine argued for the primacy of faith. He denied the classical view that reason *alone* could attain wisdom or could instruct people how to live. The wisdom that Augustine sought was Christian wisdom, God's revelation to humanity. The starting point for this wisdom, he said, was belief in God and

THE LADDER OF DIVINE ASCENT, TWELFTH-CENTURY ICON, ST. CATHERINE'S MONASTERY, MOUNT SINAI. Monks climbing a ladder to heaven, while demons are trying to prevent them from leaving earth. (Erich Lessing/Art Resource, N.Y.)

the Scriptures. For Augustine, secular knowledge for its own sake had little value; the true significance of knowledge lay in its role as a tool for comprehending God's will. Let us utilize truths useful to the faith that pagan philosophers might have chanced upon, he said. Augustine adapted the classical intellectual tradition to the requirements of Christian revelation.

With Augustine, the human-centered outlook of classical humanism, which for centuries had been undergoing transformation, gave way to a God-centered worldview. The fulfillment of God's will, not the full development of human talent, became the chief concern of life. The *City of God* encompassed several themes that would concern Christian thinkers for centuries: the meaning of

history and the place of the individual, the state, and the church in God's plan.

Augustinian Christianity is a living philosophy because it still has something vital to say about the human condition. To those who believe that people have the intelligence and goodwill to transform their earthly city into a rational and just community that promotes human betterment, Augustine offers a reminder of human sinfulness, weakness, and failure. Nor will new and ingenious political and social arrangements alter a defective human nature. He cautions the optimist that progress is not certain; that people, weak and ever prone to wickedness, are their own worst enemies; that success is illusory; and that misery is the essential human reality.

CHRISTIANITY AND CLASSICAL HUMANISM: ALTERNATIVE WORLDVIEWS

Christianity and classical humanism are the two principal components of the Western tradition. The value that modern Western civilization places on the individual derives ultimately from classical humanism and the Judeo-Christian tradition. Classical humanists believed that human worth came from the capacity of individuals to reason and to shape their character and life according to rational standards. Christianity also places great stress on the individual. In the Christian view, God cares for each person; he wants people to behave righteously and to enter heaven; Christ died for all because he loves humanity. Christianity espouses active love and genuine concern for fellow human beings. Without God, people are as Augustine described them: "foul, crooked, sordid, . . . vicious." With God, the human personality can undergo a moral transformation and become loving, good, and free. The idea of a Christian conscience, prompted by God and transcending all other loyalties, reinforces respect for all human beings regardless of cultural and national differences. Also promoting respect for each person is the presupposition of natural equality stemming from the Christian belief that each individual, regardless of birth, wealth, or talent, is precious to God.

There are striking parallels between Christian and Stoic ethics. Both Christians and Stoics believed that there is an essential "brotherhood of man," that all human beings are related and possess a fundamental dignity. Both urged suppressing wild passions, expressing concern for others, living simply, and heeding the inner voice of conscience that commands human beings to do what is right.

But Christianity and classical humanism also represent two essentially different worldviews. The triumph of the Christian outlook signified a break with the essential meaning of classical humanism; it pointed to the end of the world of antiquity and the beginning of an age of faith, the Middle Ages. With the victory of Christianity, the ultimate goal of life shifted. Life's purpose was no longer to achieve excellence in this world through the full and creative development of human capacities, but to attain salvation in a heavenly city. A person's worldly accomplishments amounted to very little if he or she did not accept God and his revelation. The Christian ideal of the isolated and contemplative monk, who rejected the world in order to serve God, was alien to the spirit of classical humanism, which valued active citizenship and active participation in worldly activities. Equally foreign to the Greco-Roman mind was another idea introduced by Christianity: the need to escape from a sinful human nature, a consequence of Adam and Eve's defiance of God. This view of a corrupt human nature and an unclean human body, particularly in Augustine's formulation, became deeply embedded in the European mind during the Christian centuries—the Middle Ages.

In the classical view, history had no ultimate end, no ultimate meaning; periods of happiness and misery repeated themselves endlessly. In the Christian view, history is filled with spiritual meaning. It is the profound drama of individuals struggling to overcome their original sin in order to gain eternal happiness in heaven. History began with Adam and Eve's fall and would end when Christ returns to earth, evil is eradicated, and God's will prevails. For the Christian, Christ on the cross was both the central event and a turning point in world history.

Classicism held that there was no authority higher than reason, that individuals had within themselves, through unaided reason, the ability to understand the world and life. Christianity teaches that, without God as the starting point, knowledge is formless, purposeless, and prone to error. Classicism, unlike Judaism or Christianity, possessed no truths or moral precepts revealed by a divine power. Rather, classicism held that ethical standards were expressions of universal reason, laws of nature, which the human mind could discover. Through reason, individuals could discern the norms by which they should regulate their lives. Reason would enable them to govern desires and will; it would show where their behavior was wrong and teach them how to correct it. Because individuals sought what was best for themselves, they would obey the voice of reason. Christianity, on the other hand, maintains that ethical standards emanate from the personal will of God. Without submission to God's commands, people remain wicked forever; the human will, essentially sinful, cannot be transformed by the promptings of reason. Only when individuals turn to God for forgiveness and guidance can they find the inner strength to overcome their sinful nature. People cannot perfect themselves through scientific knowledge; it is spiritual insight and belief in God that they require and that must serve as the first principle of their lives. For classicism, the ultimate good was sought through independent thought and action; for Christianity, the ultimate good comes through knowing, obeying, and loving God.

Although some Christian thinkers dismissed Greek philosophy as erroneous and useless, others respected the Greek intellectual tradition and rejected attempts to eradicate it. Rather, they sought to fit it into a Christian framework—that is, rational inquiry must be guided by and never conflict with Christian teachings. By holding that the mind is limited in its capacity to think for itself and must be guided by faith and clerical authority, Christianity contributed to the waning of the classical tradition in the Late Roman Empire. For centuries, articles of faith would predominate over empirical observation and logic. Nevertheless, by preserving the Greek philosophical tradition—even if it remained subordinate to the Christian outlook—Christian thinkers performed a task of immense historical significance.

Christianity inherited the Hebrew view of the overriding importance of God for humanity: God, who is both lawgiver and judge, makes life intelligible and purposeful. For the Christian, God is a

PORTRAIT OF CHRIST. Painted on a ceiling in the Catacomb of Domitilla around the second century A.D., this is among the oldest surviving portraits of Jesus. (Scala/Art Resource, N.Y.)

living being, loving and compassionate, in whose company one seeks to spend eternity; one knows God essentially through faith and feeling. Although the Greek philosophers had a conception of God, it was not comparable to the God of the Hebrews and Christians. For the Greeks, God was a logical abstraction, a principle of order, the prime mover, the first cause, the mind of the universe, pure thought, the supreme good, the highest truth; God was a concept, impersonal, unfeeling, and uninvolved with human concerns. The Greeks approached God through the intellect, not the heart; they neither loved nor worshiped God. In addition, because religion was at the periphery, not the center, of classical humanism, the idea of God did not carry the same significance as it did for Christianity.

Christianity maintained that there was a prescribed way to worship the one true God, that belief in other gods was an abomination, and that nonbelievers (or infidels) and heretics were wicked sinners hated by God. Over the centuries, this outlook sanctioned fanaticism, persecution, and holy war, with accompanying massacres—a terrible legacy that constitutes the dark side of monotheism. Unlike the monotheistic faiths—Judaism, Christianity, and Islam—Greek and Roman polytheism had no concepts of **martyrdom** for the true faith and holy war against the infidel and consistently tolerated many different religious beliefs and practices as long as they did not threaten the state.

In the classical world, the political community was the avenue to justice, happiness, and self-realization. In Christianity, the good life was identified not with worldly achievement but with life eternal, and the ideal commonwealth could only be one that was founded and ruled by Christ. It was entrance into God's kingdom that each person must make the central aim of life. Christian thinkers viewed the state as an inferior community to their own—the church of Christ, which had ties to the spiritual realm, the highest good. Therefore, they held that secular power should submit to ecclesiastical authority. For the next thousand years, this distinction between heaven and earth, this otherworldly, theocentric outlook, would define the Western mentality.

In the Late Roman Empire, when classical values were in decay, Christianity was a dynamic and creative movement. Possessing both institutional and spiritual strength, Christianity survived the fall of Rome. Because it retained elements of Greco-Roman civilization and taught a high morality, Christianity served as a civilizing agent in the centuries that followed Rome's collapse. Indeed, Christianity was the essential shaper of the European civilization that emerged in the Middle Ages.

Notes

1. Hans Küng, "Christianity and Judaism," in *Jesus' Jewishness,* ed. James H. Charlesworth (New York: Crossroad, 1991), 259.

2. The biblical quotations, used with permission, are from the Holy Bible, Revised Standard Version (New York: Thomas Nelson & Sons, 1952). The Revised Standard Version is the text used for biblical quotations throughout, except where noted otherwise.

3. Tertullian, "On Prescription Against Heretics," chap. 7, in *The Ante-Nicene Fathers,* ed. Alexander Roberts and James Donaldson (New York: Charles Scribner's Sons, 1918), 3:246.

4. Clement of Alexandria, *Stromata (Miscellanies),* trans. William Wilson, in *Ante-Nicene Christian Library,* vol. 4, *The Writings of Clement of Alexandria,* ed. Alexander Roberts and James Donaldson (Edinburgh: T & T Clark, 1867–1872), 303–304.

5. Tertullian, "On the Flesh of Christ," in *The Ante-Nicene Fathers,* ed. Roberts and Donaldson, 525.

6. From Clement of Alexandria, *Christ the Educator,* trans. Simon P. Woo, C. P. (New York: Fathers of the Church, 1954), 175.

7. *Origenis, Commentariorum in Evangelium Secundum Matthaeum, in Patrologiae Cursus Completus,* Series Graeca Prior, ed. J. P. Migne (Paris: Parisiorum, 1862), vol. 13 (trans. J. Castora), cols. 1494–1495, pars. 775–776.

8. Quoted in Edward H. Flannery, *The Anguish of the Jews* (London: Macmillan, 1965), 48.

9. Randolph Braham, ed., *The Origins of the Holocaust: Christian Anti-Semitism* (Boulder, Colo: Social Science Monographs and Institute for Holocaust Studies of the City University of New York, 1986), 36.

10. Ibid., 37.

11. Saint Augustine, *The City of God,* trans. Gerald G. Walsh et al., abridged (Garden City, N.Y.: Doubleday Image Books, 1958), 519.

12. Ibid., 300.

Suggested Reading

Armstrong, Karen, *A History of God* (1994). Good material on early Christianity.

Benko, Stephen, *Pagan Rome and the Early Christians* (1984). How Romans and Greeks viewed early Christianity.

Bettenson, Henry, and Chris Maunder, eds., *Documents of the Christian Church* (1999). A new edition of this invaluable reference work.

Chadwick, Henry, *The Early Church* (1967). A survey of early Christianity in its social and ideological context.

Charlesworth, James, ed., *Jesus' Jewishness* (1991). Essays by prominent scholars exploring the Jewish context of early Christianity.

Ferguson, Everett, ed., *Encyclopedia of Early Christianity* (1990). Entries on all aspects of early Christianity.

———, *Backgrounds of Early Christianity* (1993). A clear and thorough examination of the milieu in which Christianity was born.

Le Beau, Bryan F., Leonard Greenspoon, and Dennis Hamm, S. J., eds., *The Historical Jesus Through Catholic and Jewish Eyes* (2000). A collection of perceptive essays on Jesus' Jewish background.

Perkins, Pheme, *Reading the New Testament* (1978). Introduces the beginning student to the New Testament.

Perry, Marvin, and Frederick M. Schweitzer, eds., *Jewish-Christian Encounters Over the Centuries* (1994). Useful essays on Jesus, Paul, the Dead Sea Scrolls, and early Christian anti-Judaism.

Walsh, Michael, *The Triumph of the Meek: Why Early Christianity Succeeded* (1986). An informed and clearly written account of a major scholarly concern.

Wills, Garry, *What Jesus Meant* (2006). A fresh and intriguing reading of the gospels by an eminent Catholic intellectual.

———, *What Paul Meant* (2006). An interpretation of Paul's writings that sheds light on Jesus and his followers.

Part Two

The Middle Ages: The Christian Centuries,

500 to 1400

Politics and Society	Thought and Culture
Germanic kingdoms established on former Roman lands (5th and 6th centuries)	Boethius, *Consolation of Philosophy* (523)
Saint Benedict founds monastery at Monte Cassino (529)	Law code of Justinian (529)
Pope Gregory I sends missionaries to convert Anglo-Saxons (596)	Byzantine church Hagia Sophia (532–537)
	Cassiodorus establishes a monastic library at Vivarium (540)
Spread of Islam (622–732)	The Koran
Charles Martel defeats Muslims at Tours (732)	Bede, *Ecclesiastical History of the English People* (c. 700)
	Muslim Golden Age (700s and 800s)
Charlemagne crowned emperor of Romans	Carolingian Renaissance (768–814)
Alfred the Great, ruler of Saxon kingdom of Wessex (871–899)	Alfred the Great promotes learning in England (871–899)
Muslim, Magyar, and Viking invasions of Latin Christendom (9th and early 10th centuries)	
Growth of feudalism (800–1100)	
German king Otto I becomes first Holy Roman Emperor (962)	
Split between the Byzantine and Roman churches (1054)	Romanesque style in architecture (1000s and 1100s)
Norman conquest of England (1066)	
Start of First Crusade (1096)	
Philip Augustus expands central authority in France (1180–1223)	Flowering of medieval culture (12th and 13th centuries): universities, Gothic architecture, scholastic philosophy, revival of Roman law
Development of common law and jury system in England (1100s)	
Pontificate of Innocent III: height of papal power (1198–1216)	
Magna Carta (1215)	Aquinas, *Summa Theologica* (1267–1273)
Destruction of Baghdad by Mongols (1258)	
Hundred Years' War (1337–1453)	Dante, *Divine Comedy* (c. 1307–1321)
Black Death (1347–1351)	Chaucer, *Canterbury Tales* (c. 1388–1400)
Great Schism of papacy (1378–1417)	

The Heirs of Rome: Byzantium, Islam, and Latin Christendom

Coronation of Charlemagne. (Scala/Art Resource, N.Y.)

- **Byzantine Civilization: The Medieval Christian East**
- **Islamic Civilization: Its Development and Dissemination**
- **Latin Christendom: The Rise of Europe**
- **The Church: Shaper of Medieval Civilization**
- **The Kingdom of the Franks**
- **Medieval Society**

Focus Questions

1. How did Latin Christendom blend Christian, Greco-Roman, and Germanic traditions?
2. In what ways were Greco-Roman ideas and institutions alien to Germanic traditions?
3. What was Byzantium's long-term influence on world history?
4. What does Islam have in common with Christianity? How do they differ?
5. What was the significance of medieval Muslim intellectual life?
6. What conditions led to the rise of feudalism and manorialism?

The triumph of Christianity, the decay of the Roman Empire, and the establishment of Germanic kingdoms on once-Roman lands constituted a new phase in Western history: the end of the ancient world and the beginning of the Middle Ages, a period that spanned a thousand years. In the ancient world, the locus of Greco-Roman civilization had been the Mediterranean Sea; the heartland of Western medieval civilization gradually shifted to the north, to regions of Europe that Greco-Roman civilization had barely penetrated. **Latin Christendom** (Western and Central Europe) was only one of three new civilizations based on religion that emerged after the decline of the Roman Empire; Byzantium and Islam were the other two. Both of these Eastern civilizations influenced the emerging Europe in important ways.

BYZANTINE CIVILIZATION: THE MEDIEVAL CHRISTIAN EAST

Although the Roman Empire in the West fell to the Germanic tribes, the eastern provinces of the Empire survived. They did so because they were richer, more urbanized, and more populous and because the main thrust of the Germanic and Hunnish invaders had been directed at the western regions. In the eastern parts, Byzantine civilization took shape. Its religion was Christian, its culture Greek, and its machinery of administration Roman. The capital, Constantinople, was built on the site of the ancient Greek city of Byzantium, on a peninsula in the Straits of Bosporus—the dividing line between Asia and Europe. Constantinople was a fortress city perfectly situated to resist attacks from land and sea.

During the Early Middle Ages (500–1050), Byzantine civilization was economically and culturally far more advanced than the Latin West. At a time when few westerners (Latin Christians) could read or write, Byzantine scholars studied the literature, philosophy, science, and law of ancient Greece and Rome. Whereas trade and urban life had greatly declined in the West, Constantinople was a magnificent Byzantine city of schools, libraries, open squares, and bustling markets.

199

Chronology 9.1 ❖ The Rise of Europe

496	Clovis adopts Roman Christianity
523	Boethius writes *Consolation of Philosophy*
540	Cassiodorus establishes a monastic library at Vivarium
596	Pope Gregory I sends missionaries to convert the Anglo-Saxons
717	Charles Martel becomes mayor of the palace under a weak Merovingian king
732	Charles Martel defeats the Muslims at Tours
751	Pepin the Short, with papal support, deposes the Merovingian ruler and becomes king of the Franks
755	Pepin donates to the papacy lands taken from the Lombards
768	Charlemagne becomes king of the Franks
774	Charlemagne defeats the Lombards
782	Alcuin of York heads Charlemagne's palace school
c. 799	Charlemagne subdues the Saxons
800	Charlemagne is crowned emperor of the Romans by Pope Leo III
814	Charlemagne dies and is succeeded by his son, Louis the Pious
840	Death of Louis the Pious: the empire is divided among his sons
c. 840s	Height of Viking attacks
c. 890	Magyars invade central Europe

Over the centuries, many differences developed between the Eastern church and the Roman church. The pope in Rome resisted domination by the Byzantine emperor, and the Byzantines denied the pope's claim to authority over all Christians. The two churches quarreled over ceremonies, holy days, and the display of holy images or icons. Fearing that some of his subjects were actually worshipping these images, in 726, Emperor Leo III ordered the destruction of all images of Christ, the Virgin, and the saints and persecuted monks who continued to venerate them. This decree greatly angered many Christians and the pope, who excommunicated Leo III. After a storm of protest convulsed the empire, the Empress Irene in 787 and the Empress Theodora in 843 restored the images. The iconoclastic struggle contributed to the rift between Byzantium and the papacy. The final break came in 1054 when the Christian church split into the Roman Catholic church in the West and the Eastern (Greek) Orthodox church in the East.

Political and cultural differences widened the rift between Latin Christendom and Byzantium. Latin Christians refused to recognize that the Byzantine emperors were, as they claimed, successors to the Roman emperors. In the Byzantine Empire, Greek was the language of religion and intellectual life; in the West, it was Latin.

Imperial Growth and Decline

Byzantine emperors were absolute rulers who held that God had chosen them to rule and to institute divine will on earth. As successors to the Roman emperors, they claimed to rule all the lands once part of the Roman Empire. The first great Byzantine ruler was Justinian, who reigned nearly forty years, from 527 to 565. Justinian often relied on the advice of his wife, Theodora. Theodora's background was unusual for an empress; she was not from the nobility but was the daughter of a bear trainer in the circus and had been an actress,

Map 9.1 THE BYZANTINE EMPIRE In the centuries after Justinian regained lands in the western Mediterranean that had been lost to Germanic invaders, the Byzantines faced attacks from Avars, Bulgars, Lombards, Persians, Arabs, Latin Christians, Seljuk Turks, and the Ottoman Turks, who captured Constantinople in 1453. (Copyright © 2013 Cengage Learning.)

a profession most people considered degrading. In a number of crises, the strong-willed and astute Theodora gave Justinian the courage to act decisively.

Justinian's most lasting achievement was the appointment of a commission of scholars to collect and codify Rome's ancient laws and the commentaries of learned jurists. The result was the *Corpus Juris Civilis,* which became the official body of law of the Byzantine Empire. In the twelfth century, it was gradually reintroduced into Western Europe, where it became the basis of civil law in many European lands.

Justinian sought to regain the lands in the western Mediterranean that had been conquered by Germanic invaders. During his reign, Byzantine forces retook North Africa from the Vandals, part of southern Spain from the Visigoths, and Italy from the Ostrogoths, establishing a western capital at Ravenna.

Besides draining the treasury, the long and costly wars led to the neglect of defenses in the Balkan Peninsula and the Near East. The Balkans were invaded by Slavic tribes from the Black Sea region and by Avars and Bulgars, originally from Central Asia; Syria was ravaged by the Persians.

RAVENNA MOSAICS. Theodora, Emperor Justinian's wife, was a strong-willed woman who exercised considerable authority and often advised her husband on matters of state. (North Wind Picture Archives/AP Images.)

Nor were the conquered territories in the west secure. The Germanic Lombards, who had moved into northern Italy in the late sixth century, conquered much Byzantine territory that had been recently recovered from the Ostrogoths. By 629, the Visigoths had driven the Byzantines from Spain.

In the early seventh century, the Byzantines faced a renewed threat from the Persians, who seized the Byzantine provinces of Syria, Palestine, and Egypt. In an all-out effort, however, Emperor Heraclius (610–641) regained the provinces and in 627 crushed the Persians near the ruins of the ancient city of Nineveh. But the exhausted Byzantine Empire had become vulnerable to the Muslim Arabs, who had moved swiftly out of the Arabian Desert seeking to propagate Islam, their new faith (discussed later in this chapter).

By 642, the Arabs had stripped the Byzantine Empire of Syria, Palestine, and Egypt, and by the beginning of the eighth century, they had taken North Africa. Near the end of the seventh century and again in 717, the Muslims besieged Constantinople. But the Byzantine fleet was armed with a new weapon, "Greek fire"—a fiery explosive liquid shot from tubes—which set enemy ships aflame and made blazing pools on the water's surface. Thus, the light Byzantine ships were able to repulse the better-built Arabian ships.

The Arabs' failure to take Constantinople was crucial not only for the Byzantine Empire but also for the history of Christianity. Had this Christian

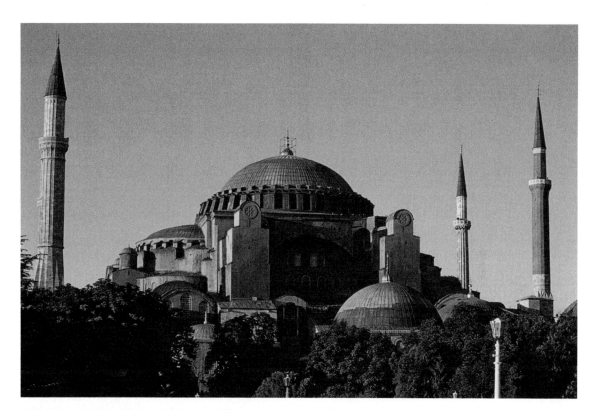

CHURCH OF THE HOLY WISDOM (HAGIA SOPHIA), CONSTANTINOPLE, 532–537. The largest church ever built in the Byzantine world, Hagia Sophia was constructed by Emperor Justinian. The interior of its immense dome was decorated with golden mosaics simulating the light of heaven. After the Turkish conquest of Constantinople in 1453, the mosaics were painted white, the church was converted into a mosque, and minarets (towers from which the faithful were summoned for prayer five times a day) were constructed. (© Peter M. Wilson/Corbis.)

fortress fallen in the eighth century, the Arabs would have been able to overrun the Balkan Peninsula and sail up the Danube River into the European heartland. After this defeat, however, Islamic armies largely concentrated their conquests outside Europe.

But soon new enemies threatened. By 1071, the Normans from France had driven the Byzantines from Italy. In the same year, the Seljuk Turks, a people from Central Asia who had adopted Islam, defeated the Byzantines in Asia Minor and subjugated most of the peninsula, the heart of the Byzantine Empire. Internal dissension, however, led to the breakup of the Seljuk Empire.

Seeking to exploit Seljuk weakness and to regain lost territories, the Byzantines appealed to Latin Christians for help. Although European Christians had little love for the Byzantines, they did want to free Christian holy places from the Muslims. For this purpose, they undertook a series of Crusades, beginning in the late eleventh century (see Chapter 10). In 1204, during the Fourth Crusade, Latin Christian knights—greedy for riches—and Venetian merchants—eager to gain control of the rich Byzantine trade—decided to take Constantinople rather than fight the Muslims.

The Latin Christians looted the city, destroying sacred books, vandalizing churches, and carrying huge amounts of gold, jewels, Christian relics, and works of art back to Western Europe. They also set up kingdoms on Byzantine lands and tried to force Latin forms of Christianity on the Byzantine Greeks. Not until 1261 were the westerners driven from Constantinople. The Byzantine Empire regained its independence, but its power was disastrously weakened. Crushing taxes, decreasing agricultural production, declining trade, and civil war continued to sap the tottering empire.

The deathblow to the empire was dealt by another group of Turks from central Asia. The Ottoman Turks had accepted Islam and had begun to build an empire. They drove the Byzantines from Asia Minor and conquered much of the Balkans. By the beginning of the fifteenth century, the Byzantine Empire consisted of only two small territories in Greece and the city of Constantinople. In 1453, the Ottoman Turks broke through Constantinople's great walls and plundered the city. After more than ten centuries, the Byzantine Empire came to an end.

The Bequest of Byzantium

During its thousand years, Byzantium made a significant impact on world history. First, it prevented the Muslim Arabs from advancing into Eastern Europe. Had the Arabs broken through Byzantine defenses, much of Europe might have been converted to the new faith of Islam. A far-reaching accomplishment was the codification of the laws of ancient Rome under Justinian. This monumental achievement preserved Roman law's principles of reason and justice. Today's legal codes in much of Europe and Latin America trace their roots to the Roman law recorded by Justinian's lawyers. The Byzantines also preserved the philosophy, science, mathematics, and literature of ancient Greece.

Contacts with Byzantine civilization stimulated learning in both the Islamic world to the east and Latin Christendom to the west. Speros Vryonis, a student of Byzantine civilization, states: "The Byzantines carried the torch of civilization unextinguished at a time when the barbarous Germanic and Slav tribes had reduced much of Europe to near chaos: and they maintained this high degree of civilization until Western Europe gradually emerged and began to take form."[1] Byzantium exerted an important religious, cultural, and linguistic influence on Latin Romanians, eastern Slavs (Russians and Ukrainians), and southern Slavs (Serbs and Bulgars). From Byzantium, the Slavs acquired legal principles, art forms, and an alphabet (the Cyrillic, based on the Greek) for writing their languages. (On the other hand, the western Slavs—Poles, Czechs, and Slovaks—came under the influence of Latin Christianity and Latin culture.)

ISLAMIC CIVILIZATION: ITS DEVELOPMENT AND DISSEMINATION

The Prophet: The Founding of a New Religion

The second Eastern civilization to arise after Rome's fall was based on the vital new religion of Islam, which emerged in the seventh century among the Arabs of Arabia. Its founder was Muhammad (c. 570–632), a prosperous merchant in Mecca, a trading city near the Red Sea. At times the introspective Muhammad withdrew from worldly affairs and devoted himself to meditation. He began to experience visions, which he interpreted as messages from God. When Muhammad was about forty, he believed that he was visited in his sleep by the angel Gabriel, who ordered him to "recite in the name of the Lord!" Transformed by this experience, Muhammad came to believe that he had been chosen as a prophet, the carrier of God's revelation.

Although most desert Arabs worshiped tribal gods, many Arabs, including Muhammad, in the towns and trading centers were familiar with Judaism and Christianity, and some had accepted the idea of one God. Rejecting the many deities of the tribal religions, Muhammad offered the Arabs a new monotheistic faith, Islam, which means "surrender to Allah (God)."

Islamic standards of morality and rules governing daily life are set by the Koran, the holy book that Muslims believe contains the words of

Allah as revealed to Muhammad. For Muslims, the Koran is both God's final word and infallible. Muslims see their religion as the completion and perfection of Judaism and Christianity; they believe both of those monotheistic predecessors were superseded by Allah's revelation to Muhammad. Muslims regard the ancient Hebrew prophets as sent from God and value their messages about compassion and the oneness of humanity. They also regard Jesus as a great prophet but do not consider him divine and view the Trinity as a form of polytheism. They see Muhammad as the last and greatest of the prophets and believe that he was entirely human, not divine. Muslims worship only Allah, the creator and ruler of heaven and earth, a single, all-powerful God who is merciful, compassionate, and just. According to the Koran, on the Day of Judgment, unbelievers and the wicked "shall dwell amidst scorching winds and seething water: in the shade of pitch-black smoke . . . sinners that deny the truth . . . shall eat . . . [bitter] fruit . . . [and] drink boiling water."[2] Faithful Muslims who have lived virtuously are promised paradise, which they believe to be a garden where they will experience bodily pleasures and spiritual delights.

An essential feature of Islam is the obligation of the faithful to obey the Five Pillars of the faith: (1) A Muslim must accept and repeat the statement of faith: "There is no God but Allah, and Muhammad is his Prophet." (2) At least five times a day, a believer must face the holy city of Mecca and pray. (3) Muslims have a religious duty to be generous to the poor. (4) During the holy month of Ramadan, believers should not eat or drink between sunrise and sunset. (5) Muslims are expected to make at least one pilgrimage to the holy city of Mecca.

Muhammad's religion began to win followers, but the ruling elite of Mecca would not accept this new faith. To escape persecution, Muhammad and his small band of followers left Mecca in 622 for Medina, a town about two hundred miles away. Their flight, known as the *Hegira,* or "emigration," is one of the most important events in Muslim history and is commemorated by yearly pilgrimages. The date of the Hegira became year one of the Muslim calendar.

In Medina, Muhammad gained converts and won respect as a judge, rendering decisions on

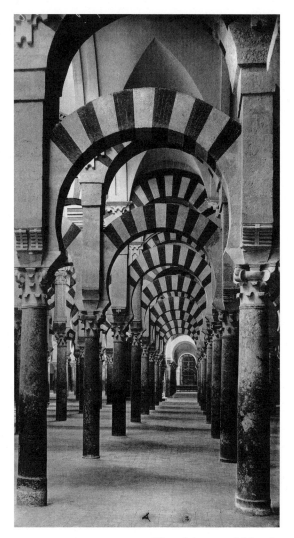

MOSQUE OF CÓRDOBA. The richness of Islamic culture and architecture is evident in Spain, where Muslim rule lingered until the conquest of Granada in 1492. The arch of alternating stone would find its way into Christian churches, most memorably at Vezelay in southern France. (Roger Viollet/Getty Images.)

such matters as family relations, property inheritance, and criminal behavior. Preaching a holy war against unbelievers, Muhammad urged followers to raid the trading caravans from Mecca and to subdue unfriendly Bedouin tribes. He tried to convert the Jews of Medina, but they would not accept him as a prophet and mocked his unfamiliarity with the Hebrew Scriptures and the learned writings of the rabbis. To a large extent, political considerations determined Muhammad's attitude toward Jews, who sided with his Meccan enemies. He expelled several thousand Jews from Medina, seized Jewish property, beheaded some six hundred Jewish men, and enslaved women and children. Later, he permitted the Arabian Jews the free exercise of their religion and guaranteed the security of their property. In 630, Mecca surrendered to a Muslim army virtually without a fight. Muhammad demonstrated leniency and forgiveness toward his former enemies and persecutors, a wise decision that helped gain him the support of the Meccans. Soon Bedouin tribes all over Arabia embraced Islam and recognized the authority of the Prophet Muhammad.

In a little more than two decades, Muhammad united the often feuding Arabian tribes into a powerful force dedicated to Allah and the spreading of the Islamic faith. After Muhammad's death in 632, his friend and father-in-law, Abu Bakr, became his successor, or caliph. Regarded as the defender of the faith, whose power derived from Allah, the caliph governed in accordance with Muslim law as defined in the Koran. Islam gave the many Arab tribes the unity, discipline, and organization to succeed in their wars of conquest. Under the first four caliphs, who ruled from 632 to 661, the Arabs, with breathtaking speed, overran Persia's empire, seized large parts of the Byzantine Empire, and invaded Europe.

Muhammad had conveyed to his followers their religious obligation to perform jihad, literally striving in the path of God. *Jihad* is a complex term whose two essential meanings are an internal striving by the individual for moral self-improvement and a collective military struggle to defend Islam against its enemies and to extend Muslim power over other lands so that all people will be subject to God's laws as revealed to Muhammad. Historically the doctrine of jihad held that the Islamic community (*umma*), the recipient of Allah's revelation was commanded to make Allah's directives supreme over the whole world. Either by conversion or conquest, infidels were destined to submit to Islamic jurisdiction.

Muslim warriors believed that they were engaged in a holy war to spread Islam to nonbelievers and that those who died in the jihad were assured a place in paradise. A desire to escape from the barren Arabian Desert and to exploit the rich Byzantine and Persian lands was another compelling reason for expansion. In the east, Islam's territory eventually extended into India and to the borders of China; in the west, it encompassed North Africa and most of Spain. The Muslims' northward push lost momentum and was halted in 717 by the Byzantines at Constantinople and in 732 by the Franks at the battle of Tours, in central France.

The Muslim State and Society

After the death of Muhammad, Muslims sought authoritative guidance on religious, social, and moral questions that the Koran did not specifically address. The most important source for such guidance was the *Hadith*—a collection of sayings, stories, and actions of the Prophet on a wide range of topics. The Koran coupled with the Hadith provided directions for a complete way of life for Muslims.

The Islamic state was a theocracy: government and religion were inseparable; there could be no distinction between secular and spiritual authority. Muslims viewed God as the source of all law and political authority and the caliph as his earthly deputy. Divine law regulated all aspects of human relations. The ruler who did not enforce Koranic law failed in his duties. Thus, Islam was more than a religion; it was also a system of government, society, law, and thought that bound its adherents into an all-encompassing community. Muslim jurists called for the creation of a single society governed by Islamic law. And this world-state had a religious obligation to subdue the non-Muslim world. This goal, to be achieved by jihad, endured in the Muslim mind over the centuries and is a principal aim of Muslim extremists today. The separation of church and state, which became firmly rooted in the West in modern times, still remains an alien concept in much of the Muslim world.

Over the centuries, many Christians and Jews living in Muslim lands, for a variety of reasons, some of them economic and social, converted to the new faith. Those who retained their ancestral faith had to accept a subordinate status—they could not bear arms, were assessed a special tax, at times were barred from testifying in court against a Muslim, and were required to wear a distinguishing mark on their clothing, a sign of their humiliation. Nevertheless, as "people of the book," Jews and Christians were protected communities, and despite instances of loss of property and life, including massacres, the two groups generally went about their business and practiced their religions relatively free of persecution. Generally Jews were physically safer in Muslim than in Christian lands.

Muslims perceived themselves as members of a single community of the faithful, but the emergence of sects ruptured the unity of Islam. The principal division—one that still incites bitter animosity—was between the Sunnis and the Shiites. The Sunnis, who were in the majority, followed traditional teachings and established practices as defined by the consensus of the Muslim community. The Shiites (*Shia* means "Party") maintained that not the existing caliphs but the descendants of Muhammad, starting with Ali, cousin and son-in-law of Muhammad and the fourth caliph, were the rightful rulers of the Islamic community.

Ali had been murdered in 661; his older son, in 669. The massacre in 680 of Ali's younger son, Husayn, and some of Husayn's followers and relatives gave rise to passionate devotion to the house of Ali, which is still expressed in processions, poetry, and self-mortification. To Shiites, the anniversary of Husayn's death remains the most important religious holiday in the Muslim calendar. Suffering and martyrdom are central to Shia.

Shiites viewed Ali and his descendants as *imams*, holy men, innocent of all sin, the most excellent of beings, selected by God to inherit Muhammad's spiritual and political powers. The imams linked the new generation with Muhammad's original inspiration. Shiites believed that without the imams' guidance, the true meaning of Islam could not be grasped.

The Muslim Golden Age

The Arabs who first burst into the Byzantine and Persian empires had no tradition of science or philosophy. But they were quick to absorb the learning of Byzantines and Persians who had preserved and studied ancient Greek works. In the eighth and ninth centuries, under the Abbasid caliphs based in Baghdad, Muslim civilization entered its golden age. Islamic civilization creatively integrated Arabic, Byzantine, Persian, and Indian cultural traditions. During the Early Middle Ages, when learning was at a low point in Western Europe, the Muslims forged a high civilization.

Muslim science, philosophy, and mathematics, based largely on the achievements of the ancient Greeks, made brilliant contributions to the sum of knowledge at a time when Latin Christendom had lost much of Greco-Roman thought and culture. The Muslims had acquired Greek learning from the older Persian and Byzantine civilizations, which had kept alive the Greek inheritance. By translating Greek works into Arabic and commenting on them, Muslim scholars performed the great historical task of preserving the philosophical and scientific heritage of ancient Greece. Muslim scholars, often affiliated with impressive universities, also creatively interpreted these Greek works and in some areas, particularly mathematics, pushed the frontiers of knowledge beyond what the Greeks had achieved. This intellectual heritage was passed on to Christian Europe, a transmission of immense historical significance, as the historian W. Montgomery Watt explains:

> *When one becomes aware of the full extent of Arab experimenting, Arab thinking and Arab writing, one sees that without the Arabs European science and philosophy would not have developed when they did. The Arabs were no mere transmitters of Greek thought, but genuine bearers, who both kept alive the disciplines they had been taught and extended their range. When about 1100, Europeans became seriously interested in . . . science and philosophy . . . [they] had to learn all they could from the Arabs before they themselves could make further advances.*[3]

There are numerous examples of Muslim brilliance in mathematics, medicine, science, and philosophy. From India, the Muslims acquired the concept of zero and "Arabic" numerals, passing these ideas on to the West. Euclid's *Elements*, the creative synthesis of Greek geometry, was translated into Arabic and studied by Muslim scholars who produced numerous commentaries on the work. Muslim mathematicians also did original work in algebra and trigonometry. Also translated into Arabic was another important Greek writing, Ptolemy's *Almagest,* which synthesized astronomical knowledge. Muslim astronomers corrected some of Ptolemy's calculations, pointed out theoretical inconsistencies, and explored problems he had not considered. In physics, the Muslim Arabs' most significant contribution was in the field of optics. Rejecting Euclid's and Ptolemy's explanation that the eye emits visual rays, they recognized that vision is a consequence of rays of light. Building on the medical knowledge of the Greeks, Muslim physicians became the best-trained and most skillful doctors of the time. Surgeons performed amputations, removed cancerous tissue, devised new medicines, and used anesthetics when performing operations. The best Muslim hospitals had separate wards for fevers, surgical cases, eye diseases, and dysentery. Well ahead of their time were those Muslim doctors who recommended humane treatment for the mentally ill. The Persian al-Razi, or Rhazes, who headed the hospital in Baghdad in the ninth century, wrote a medical encyclopedia in which he discussed measles, kidney stones, poisons, skin diseases, and ways of maintaining one's health. The works of Rhazes, translated into Latin, were widely consulted in Latin Christendom.

Muslim thinkers employed the categories of Greek philosophy to explain Islamic doctrine. Al-Farabi (c. 870–950), who wrote commentaries on Aristotle, offered proofs for God's existence based on Aristotelian logic that were later studied by medieval Christian philosophers. The most eminent Muslim thinker, Ibn-Sina, known to the West as Avicenna (980–1037), was a poet, doctor, scientist, and philosopher who wrote on every field of knowledge. His philosophical works, which relied heavily on Aristotle, had an important influence on medieval Christian thinkers. Another giant of Muslim learning was Ibn-Rushd, whom Westerners call Averroës (1126–1198). Averroës insisted that the Koran did not oppose the study of philosophy and held that the ancient Greeks—even though they were not Muslims—had discovered truth. His commentaries on Aristotle were studied in Western universities, where they sparked an important controversy (see page 265).

Mongol Invasions and Ottoman Dominance

The Arab empire, stretching from Spain to India, was unified by a common language (Arabic), a common faith, and a common culture. By the eleventh century, however, the Arabs began losing their dominance in the Islamic world. The Seljuk Turks, who had taken Asia Minor from the Byzantines, also conquered the Arabic lands of Syria, Palestine, and much of Persia. Although the Abbasid caliphs remained the religious and cultural leaders of Islam, political power was exercised by Seljuk sultans. In the eleventh and twelfth centuries, the Muslims lost Sicily and most of Spain to Christian knights, and European Crusaders carved out kingdoms in the Near East.

In the thirteenth century came a new wave of invaders, the Mongols from central Asia. Led by Genghis Khan, Mongolian archers, mounted on fast-moving ponies, poured across Asia into Muslim lands. By 1227, when Genghis Khan died, the eastern part of the Muslim world had fallen to the Mongols. After the death of Genghis Khan, some Mongol forces swept across Russia and threatened Central Europe; others continued to advance on Muslim lands in the Near East. Storming Baghdad in 1258, the Mongols burned, plundered, and killed with savage fury; among the fifty thousand people slaughtered was the last Abbasid caliph. The Mongols devastated the palaces, libraries, and schools that had made Baghdad the cultural capital of the Islamic world. A year later, they marched into Syria, again killing and looting. Their brutal advance westward was finally stopped in 1260 in Palestine by Egyptian forces.

By the beginning of the fourteenth century, the Mongols, who had by this time converted to Islam, remained in Persia and were unable to advance westward. In the late fourteenth century, however, the Mongols, under Tamerlane, again menaced the Near East. Another bloody conqueror, Tamerlane cowed opposition with huge pyramids built from the skulls of thousands of slaughtered victims. After Tamerlane's death in 1404, his empire disintegrated, and its collapse left the way open for the Ottoman Turks.

The Ottoman Empire reached its height in the sixteenth century with the conquest of Egypt, North Africa, Syria, and the Arabian coast. The

The Art of the Ancient World and the Middle Ages

1. Praxiteles. *Hermes with Young Dionysus*, c. 350 B.C. (Archaeological Museum, Olympia, Archaia, Greece/The Bridgeman Art Library.)

The art of the classical period (c. fifth century B.C.) was important not only to the ancient Greeks but also to the Romans and to later generations, from the Renaissance to the postmodern period of the late twentieth century. Through the ages, classical art has been kept alive—adopted, adapted, altered, and appreciated—by artists and craftspeople. Why has the classical style remained at the forefront of artistic endeavor?

The classical period has given us the first works of the Western world to represent the human form with accuracy. The body itself was the sculptors' subject. Their aim was to shape their marble so as to make a general and schematic figure lifelike. Classical sculpture has been a powerful learning device for aspiring artisans from Michelangelo to nineteenth-century artists such as Auguste Rodin. Ancient sculptures—and plaster casts made from them—have been used as teaching tools by educators since the Renaissance. Learning to draw from casts of ancient works was the traditional first step in an artist's education; even many abstract artists of the twentieth century had a solid grounding in works of the classical period.

2. Venus de Milo. Greek statue from the first century B.C., probably an imitation of a fourth-century work. (Vanni/Art Resource, N.Y.)

3. Lysippos. Roman copy of *Apoxyomenos (Scrapers)*, original c. 325–300 B.C. (Apoxyomenos (marble), Roman, (1st century AD)/Vatican Museums and Galleries, Vatican City, Italy/Bildarchiv Steffens Ralph Rainer Steffens/The Bridgeman Art Library International.)

The balanced, rhythmical composition of classical sculpture and architecture is another element that has influenced later artists. Earlier works—from the Greek Archaic period (sixth century B.C.) as well as from ancient Egypt and Mesopotamia—are solid, blocklike, and devoid of any sense of movement. Classical sculptors, by contrast, were able to bring the stone alive with innovative poses, luxuriant drapery, and a careful balancing between relaxation and tension.

The works of Praxiteles embody the ideal of classical sculpture and offer visual proof that the Greeks' search for beauty and truth extended beyond their literature and philosophy. Praxiteles (fl. 375–330 B.C.) is renowned for the quality of his marble sculpture, such as *Hermes with Young Dionysus* (Figure 1), considered one of his finest works. Little is known of Praxiteles himself, but much has been written about his art.

The Hermes statue has many of the attributes that distinguish the best classical sculpture. The stance is relaxed: an S-curve takes the weight off one leg and shifts it to the opposite hip. This *contrapposto*, or counterbalanced, pose draws attention to every part of the god's body. The turned and slightly tilted head is a departure from the fully frontal works of earlier periods. The drapery is a careful, three-dimensional rendering of drapery in vase painting from the same period. It is realistic and so fluid that viewers might forget they are looking at marble.

A roughly contemporary work, the *Venus de Milo* (Figure 2) by an unidentified artist, embodies many of the same principles as the Hermes figure. Venus puts her weight on one leg, tensing some muscles and relaxing others. Drapery loosely covers her waist and has the look of soft cotton.

A contemporary of Praxiteles, Lysippos (fl. fourth century B.C.), is credited with changing the "canon of proportions" established by his predecessor Polyclitus. The canon of proportions rules that earlier sculptors followed in carving their masterpieces, assured a certain uniformity in the rendering of the human form. Heads were always a certain proportion of the whole, eyes were placed at a certain level within the face, and so on. But the work of Lysippos is notably different.

One of Lysippos' best-known works, the *Apoxyomenos (Scraper)* (Figure 3), shows a youthful athlete cleaning himself with a *strigyl* (scraper) after exercising. What distinguishes this work from the works of other artists are the proportions. Lysippos' youth has a smaller head and a more slender body. Although he stands with his weight on one foot, his hips are not as sharply angled as the hips of other classical figures, in which the S-curve is more clearly pronounced. Even the face of the athlete foretells a new era in art. Unlike the serene, perfect faces of other classical figures, the Apoxyomenos' expression seems thoughtful and dreamy, not remote and dispassionate.

Distinguished by its portrayal of emotion and drama, *The Laocoön Group* (Figure 4) is one of the most famous works of Western art. Dated to the second century B.C., the work depicts the death of Laocoön, a priest of the god Apollo, and his twin sons, killed by sea serpents because they tried to prevent the entry into Troy of the huge wooden horse in which Greek warriors were concealed. The sculptors, Agesander, Atheodorou, and Polydoros of Rhodes, convey the violence and intensity of events through the exaggeration of facial features, musculature, and pose.

This work from the Hellenistic period differs from its classical predecessors in its emotionality and exaggeration of the human form. Laocoön's face shows anguish over the loss of his sons, and his muscles bulge as he strains to

4. Hellenistic Sculpture. *The Laocoön Group*, second century B.C. (Scala/Art Resource, N.Y.)

wrest himself from the serpent's grasp. Laocoön's children are depicted as smaller than their father yet as fully mature men.

Many historians have described the art of Rome as unoriginal and deriving from classical Greek works. The Romans did make multiple copies of many Greek prototypes, but they also excelled in areas of the decorative arts in which we have no evidence of Greek virtuosity. The Romans developed distinctive styles in wall painting (fresco), mosaic, and minor metal arts; their contributions to architecture are also noteworthy.

Frescoes are made by painting directly on wet or damp plaster. Some fresco painters limit their work to small scenes; others cover entire walls with landscapes, people, and architectural elements. Roman fresco painters were adept at reproducing the look of marble and other materials. The *trompe l'oeil* (literally "fool the eye") style of Roman fresco painters demonstrates their skill at reproducing the world around them.

5. Detail of a Pompeian Wall Fresco, Lady Playing the Cithera, first century B.C. (© The Art Gallery Collection/Alamy.)

As can be seen in Figure 5, Roman painters were able to convincingly present three-dimensional objects on a two-dimensional surface. This first-century B.C. fresco, *Lady Playing the Cithera* (a harplike musical instrument), from a villa at Boscoreale, near Pompeii, is an excellent example of the fresco painter's art. Though painted on a flat surface, the chair is set at an angle and projects outward toward the viewer. The chair's three-dimensionality is further emphasized by the placement of the young attendant, who stands behind it, holding on to its back.

Roman sculptors tended to follow closely the classical Greek and Hellenistic traditions. Some art historians assert that originality in Roman sculpture is evident only in lifelike portrait busts of the emperors, often planted firmly on the necks of copies of Greek or Hellenistic gods and heroes. To an extent, this is the case with the life-size *Augustus of the Prima Porta* (Figure 6), a work probably completed during the reign of Augustus (27 B.C.–A.D. 14) or shortly after his death and deification. Many elements of this work are direct borrowings from classical and Hellenistic prototypes. It is

the head, however, that sets this work apart from its forebears. The face of Augustus is a lifelike representation of the emperor, if we assume that the great number of coins bearing Augustus's image offer an accurate likeness. Unlike Greek sculpture, which idealized the human form, this Roman work presents an image that would be recognized by all who viewed it.

Roman works such as the Augustus statue also served as illustrations of contemporary events. Carvings on the breastplate in *Augustus of the Prima Porta* portray the Romans' victory over the Parthians. Pictorial narratives of other Roman achievements were sculpted on freestanding columns and triumphal arches, as well as on the walls of buildings. In this way, Roman rulers were able to transmit news and information throughout their vast empire to people who could not read or who did not speak Latin.

The art and architecture of the Byzantine era and the Middle Ages show a transformation in subject matter. Christianity, with its theme of resurrection and salvation, dominated the period. Both Latin and Greek churches used art to spread Christian teachings and to buttress their authority. Because few people could read or write, both churches relied on sculpture, painting, and drawing to convey the essence of Christianity.

Figure 7, the mosaic *The Court of Justinian*, from the Church of San Vitale in the Italian city of Ravenna, shows the emperor Justinian and his attendants and dates to c. A.D. 547. The emperor stands in the center of the scene and is flanked by officials and local clergy. The contrast between this work and the Boscoreale fresco (Figure 5) is noteworthy. Here, the emphasis is on two-dimensionality and the vertical. All of the figures face front; there is little attempt to show depth or three-dimensionality, except for the somewhat unsuccessful overlapping of figures. These Byzantine figures, with small heads, tiny feet, and disproportionate arms, are elongated and slender, unlike the figures of the Roman painting or the Greek sculptures shown earlier.

As political and spiritual ruler of the Byzantine Empire, Justinian is flanked by twelve companions, drawing a parallel between him and Jesus Christ. His golden halo brings to mind the one usually shown around Christ's head; the attributes of Christianity, including a cross, a censer (incense burner), and a shield bearing a symbolic version of Jesus' name, remind viewers of Justinian's dual roles.

Easily recognized symbols and images such as the halo became part of a common language for transmitting the message of Christ and the church. This is exemplified by the *Enthroned Madonna and Child*, from the Byzantine school (Figure 8) in the thirteenth century, in which the Madonna is shown in what now seems to be a conventional pose—seated on an elaborate chair or throne, facing front, holding the child on her left knee, and supporting him with her left hand. The Madonna is heavily robed, but the artist was able to depict the clothes with the fluidity of the painter responsible for the Boscoreale fresco (Figure 5).

The *Enthroned Madonna and Child*'s origins are Eastern—the Byzantine school having developed in Byzantium, the capital of the eastern Roman Empire. Byzantium (renamed Constantinople in A.D. 330) had a certain sphere of influence in the West, attested to by the Ravenna mosaic (Figure 7), and, as a result, a fusion of Eastern and Western styles is evident in works such as the *Enthroned Madonna*. What is typically Byzantine about this work is the richness of color and the use of gold—in the background and in the Madonna's robes. The faces of the figures owe more to Western art, however. Soft modeling and careful shading make them look almost as if they were superimposed by another artist at another time.

The Last Supper of the thirteenth-century Magdalen Master (Figure 9) preserves the austere and otherworldly emphasis of the Eastern style exhibited by such works as the Ravenna Mosaic. It captures a pivotal moment, when Christ announces to his disciples that he will be betrayed by one of them, and instructs them to commemorate him by consuming bread and wine as his body and blood. (Compare with da Vinci's *Last Supper*, Figure 5 in the art essay "The Renaissance.") This event becomes

6. *Augustus of the Prima Porta.* (Scala/Art Resource, N.Y.)

the basis for the Christian sacrament of the Eucharist.

The painting is two-dimensional. There is no depth, no background, and no foreground. The table does not recede into the picture. The objects on its surface seem stacked vertically one on top of another. The tablecloth lacks texture. The figures seated at the table are immobile, rigid, lifeless, expressionless, severe, and monotonously spaced. There is a prevailing impersonality in the composition.

The painting perfectly exemplifies the characteristic style of Eastern and medieval art, which

7. Mosaic. *The Court of Justinian, c.* A.D. 547. (Scala/Art Resource, N.Y.)

is nonperspectival, usually two-dimensional, and profoundly impersonal.

At this point, Western art begins to undergo another transformation. Styles and subject matter change, paralleling developments in politics and society. Artists working at the end of the Middle Ages and on the verge of the Renaissance include the brothers Jan and Hubert van Eyck. Figure 10 shows *The Last Judgement* (c. 1420–1425), one panel of a diptych (a two-paneled work) painted by one or both of them (the other panel portrays the Crucifixion). *The Last Judgement* illustrates some of the stylistic elements that distinguish these artists. The image is divided in two horizontally. In the upper half, which represents heaven, the mood is one of calm and

order; below, on earth and in hell, pandemonium reigns. This suggestion of the promise of heaven and the threat of hell was intended to motivate people to heed Christian teachings and clerical authority.

The van Eycks portrayed this idea with a clarity and realistic feeling unseen in other works. Their virtuosity is paralleled by the work of a slightly earlier Italian artist, Giotto di Bondone (1267–1337), whose style also marked a definite break with his peers, and whose work stands on the cusp between the Renaissance and what preceded it.

Giotto's *Kiss of Judas*, in the Scrovengi Chapel in Padua, dates from 1305 (Figure 11). A work of the Late Middle Ages, or Gothic period, it represents a major shift in artistic direction; its lifelike depiction of the human figures seen in the foreground anticipates later perspectival painting. To understand this change in representational art in the fourteenth century, it is necessary to remember what was happening in Italy at the time. Although the art was meant to reflect the kingdom of heaven, actual events in the kingdom on earth played a great role.

As noted earlier, Byzantium and Byzantine art influenced Italian art and society in the medieval period. Images, symbols, and techniques that flourished in Eastern workshops took root in Italy, culminating in what art historians call a neo-Byzantine style in the early thirteenth century, soon after the Crusaders conquered Constantinople in 1204. Italian artists adopted the Byzantine style, which had its roots in classical Greek prototypes. The combination of Byzantine, Greek, and native Italian styles produced the new way of seeing epitomized by Giotto.

8. Byzantine School. *Enthroned Madonna and Child*, thirteenth century. (Virgin and Child (tempera on panel), Byzantine, (14th century)/Church of Sveti Kliment, Ohrid, Macedonia/Giraudon/The Bridgeman Art Library International.)

9. Studio of Magdalen Master. *The Last Supper*, late thirteenth century. (Reunion des Musées Nationaux, Art Resource, N.Y.)

11. Giotto di Bondone. *Kiss of Judas*, c. 1305, Scrovengi Chapel, Padua, Italy. (Alinari/Art Resource, N.Y.)

10. Hubert or Jan van Eyck. *The Last Judgement*, c. 1420–1425. (© The Metropolitan Museum of Art/Art Resource, N.Y.)

Map 9.2 THE EXPANSION OF ISLAM, 622–732 From 632 to 661, the Arabs, with breathtaking speed, overran the Persian Empire, seized some of Byzantium's provinces, and invaded southern Europe. Their northward momentum was halted in 717 by the Byzantines at Constantinople and in 732 by the Franks at the battle of Tours in central France. (Copyright © 2013 Cengage Learning.)

Turkish conquest of much of Hungary in the 1520s and the siege of Vienna (1529) spread panic in Europe. The Ottomans developed an effective system of administration but could not restore the cultural brilliance, the thriving trade, or the prosperity that the Muslim world had known under the Abbasid caliphs of Baghdad. The vitality that had kept the Muslim world more advanced than Western Europe for most of the Middle Ages dissipated.

LATIN CHRISTENDOM: THE RISE OF EUROPE

The centuries of cultural greatness of the Islamic and the Byzantine civilizations enriched the Western world. They did not, however, produce the major breakthroughs in science, technology, philosophy, economics, and political thought that gave rise to the modern world. That process was the singular achievement of Europe. During the Middle Ages, a common European civilization—Latin Christendom—evolved. It integrated Christian, Greco-Roman, and Germanic elements. Christianity was at the center of medieval civilization, Rome was the spiritual capital and Latin the language of intellectual life, and Germanic customs pervaded social and legal relationships.

During the Early Middle Ages (500–1050), Latin Christendom was culturally far behind the two Eastern civilizations and did not catch up until the twelfth century. In succeeding centuries, however, it produced the movements that ushered in the modern age: the Renaissance, the

Reformation, the Scientific Revolution, the Age of Enlightenment, the French Revolution, and the Industrial Revolution.

Political and Economic Transformation

From the sixth to the eighth century, Europeans struggled to overcome the disorder created by the breakup of the Roman Empire and the deterioration of Greco-Roman civilization. In the process, a new civilization, with its own distinctive style, took root. It grew out of the intermingling of Greco-Roman civilization, the Christian outlook, and Germanic traditions, although centuries would pass before it would come to fruition.

In the fifth century and after, Germanic invaders founded kingdoms in North Africa, Italy, Spain, Gaul, and Britain—lands formerly belonging to the Roman Empire. Even before the invasions, these Germanic tribes had acquired some knowledge of Roman culture and were attracted to it. Therefore, the new rulers sought not to destroy Roman civilization but to share in its advantages. For example, Theodoric the Great (474–526), the Ostrogoth ruler of Italy, retained the Roman Senate, civil service, and schools; and rich aristocratic Roman families continued to hold high government offices. The Burgundians in Gaul and the Visigoths in Spain maintained Roman law for their conquered subjects; and the Frankish ruler Clovis (c. 466–511) wore Roman imperial colors and took Roman titles. All the Germanic kingdoms tried to maintain Roman systems of taxation; furthermore, Latin remained the official language of administration.

However, torn by warfare, internal rebellion, and assassination, the Germanic kingdoms provided a poor political base on which to revive a decadent and dying classical civilization. Most of the kingdoms survived for only a short time and had no enduring impact. An exception to this trend occurred in Gaul and south-central Germany, where the most successful of the Germanic kingdoms was established by the Franks—the founders of the new Europe.

The Roman world was probably too far gone to be rescued, but even if it had not been, the Germans were culturally unprepared to play the role of restorer. By the end of the seventh century, the old Roman lands in Western Europe showed a marked decline in central government, town life, commerce, and learning. Though vigorous and brave, the Germanic invaders were essentially a rural and warrior people, tribal in organization and outlook. Their native culture, without cities or written literature, was primitive compared with the literary, philosophical, scientific, and artistic achievements of the Greco-Roman world. The Germans were not equipped to reform the decaying Roman system of administration and taxation or to cope with the economic problems that had burdened the Empire. Nor could they maintain roads and irrigation systems, preserve skills in the arts of stoneworking and glassmaking, or breathe new life into the dying humanist culture.

Roman ideas of citizenship and the legal state were totally alien to Germanic tradition. The Germans gave loyalty to their kin and to a tribal chief, not to an impersonal state that governed citizens of many nationalities. The king viewed the land he controlled as a private possession that could be divided among his sons after his death—a custom that produced numerous and devastating civil wars and partitions. Unlike the Romans, the Germanic invaders had no trained civil servants to administer the state and no organized system of taxation to provide a secure financial base for government.

The Germans also found Roman law strange, although the Germanic kingdoms did make attempts to retain Roman law codes. Roman law incorporated elements of Greek philosophy and was written, whereas Germanic law at the time of the invasions consisted of unwritten tribal customs. Roman law applied to all people throughout the Empire, regardless of nationality; a German could be judged only by the law of his own tribe. Roman judges investigated evidence and demanded proof; Germanic courts, in the absence of clear evidence, relied on trial by ordeal. In a typical ordeal, a bound defendant was thrown into a river. Sinking meant innocence; floating was interpreted as divine proof of guilt, because the pure water had "rejected" the evildoer. Although primitive by Roman standards, Germanic law did help lessen blood feuds between families. Before long, the Germanic kingdoms began to put customary tribal law, which had absorbed and continued to absorb elements from Roman law, into writing. Replacing Roman law and spreading throughout

Europe, Germanic law became an essential element of medieval society.

The distinguishing feature of classical civilization, its vital urban institutions, had deteriorated in the Late Roman Empire. The shift from an urban to a rural economy accelerated under the kingdoms created by Germanic chieftains. Although the Germanic kings retained Roman cities as capitals, they did not halt the process of decay that had overtaken urban centers. These rulers settled their people in the countryside, not in towns; they did not significantly utilize cities as instruments of local government; and they failed to maintain Roman roads. Although towns did not vanish altogether, they continued to lose control over the surrounding countryside and to decline in wealth and importance. They were the episcopal seats (sees) of bishops, rather than centers of commerce and intellectual life. Italy remained an exception to this general trend. There, Roman urban institutions persisted, even during the crudest period of the Early Middle Ages. Italian cities kept some metal currency in circulation and traded with one another and with Byzantium.

Shrinking commerce during the Early Middle Ages was part of the process of decline begun in the Late Roman Empire. Although commerce never wholly disappeared, it was predominantly localized. Furthermore, it was controlled by colonies of Jews, Syrians, and Greeks—a sign of the economic inertia of Latin Christians. From the last decade of the fifth century to the middle of the seventh century, Byzantine merchants established themselves in the western lands and exchanged papyrus, spices, and textiles for European slaves. Then, in the second half of the seventh century, this trade dropped off greatly; as Muslim power expanded to control the Mediterranean, Byzantine merchants had to turn eastward for markets. Thus, the bonds between East and West weakened, and Europe shifted its axis northward, away from the Mediterranean. Few goods exchanged hands, and few coins circulated; people produced for themselves what they needed.

The Waning of Classical Culture

Greco-Roman humanism, in retreat since the Late Roman Empire, continued its decline in the centuries immediately following Rome's demise. The old Roman upper classes abandoned their heritage and absorbed the ways of their Germanic conquerors, the Roman schools closed, and Roman law faded into disuse. Aside from clerics, few people could read and write Latin, and even learned clerics were rare. Europeans' knowledge of the Greek language was almost totally lost, and the Latin rhetorical style deteriorated. Many literary works of classical antiquity were either lost or unread. Raids by Germanic tribes and later by Muslims, Magyars, and Vikings (see below) devastated libraries. Many works by great authors were lost forever. For example, only seven of the one hundred dramas written by Sophocles have survived. Gone were attempts to understand the natural world through reason; magic and the occult prevailed among both pagans and Christians. The literature of the seventh century, concerned principally with the lives of saints, was devoid of the humanist themes that had motivated Greek and Roman poets and dramatists. European culture was much poorer than the high civilizations of Byzantium, Islam, and ancient Rome.

During this period of cultural poverty, the few persons who were learned generally did not engage in original thought but salvaged and transmitted remnants of classical civilization. Given the context of the times, this was a considerable achievement. These individuals retained respect for the inheritance of Greece and Rome while remaining devoted to Christianity. In a rudimentary way, they were struggling to create a Christian culture that combined the intellectual tradition of Greece and Rome with the religious teachings of the Christian church.

An important figure in the intellectual life of this transitional period was Boethius (480–c. 525), a descendant of a noble family. Boethius had received a classical education at the Platonic Academy at Athens before Emperor Justinian closed it in 529. He was the last Latin-speaking scholar of the Roman world to have mastered the Greek language and to have intimate knowledge of Greek philosophy. Later, Boethius served the Ostrogoth Theodoric I, who ruled Italy. Recognizing that Greco-Roman civilization was dying, Boethius tried to rescue the intellectual heritage of antiquity. He translated into Latin some of Aristotle's treatises on logic and wrote commentaries on

Aristotle, Cicero, and Porphyry (a Neo-Platonist philosopher). He also wrote treatises on theology and textbooks on arithmetic, astronomy, and music. A sudden turn of fortune deprived him of power, prestige, and possessions and confronted him with imminent death when Theodoric ordered him executed in 524 or 525 for allegedly participating in a plot against the throne.

While in prison awaiting execution, Boethius wrote *The Consolation of Philosophy,* which is regarded as one of the masterpieces of world literature. In it, Boethius pondered life's meaning: "Think you that there is any certainty in the affairs of mankind when you know that often one swift hour can utterly destroy a man?"[4] Alone in his dungeon, he turned for guidance and consolation to the philosophical training of his youth. He derived comfort from Lady Philosophy, who reassured him, in the tradition of Socrates and the Stoics, that "if then you are master of yourself, you will be in possession of that which you will never wish to lose, and which Fortune will never be able to take from you."[5] No tyrant can "ever disturb the peculiar restfulness which is the property of a mind that hangs together upon the firm basis of its reason."[6] In the life and thought of Boethius, the classical tradition lived on. He was a bridge between a classical civilization too weakened to be revived and a Christian civilization still in its embryonic stage.

Until the twelfth century, virtually all that Latin Christendom knew of Aristotle came from Boethius's translations and commentaries. Similarly, his work in mathematics, which contains fragments from Euclid, was the principal source for the study of that discipline in the Early Middle Ages. In his theological writings, he strove to demonstrate that reason did not conflict with orthodoxy—an early attempt to attain a rational comprehension of belief, or, as he expressed it, to join faith to reason. Boethius's effort to examine Christian doctrines rationally, a principal feature of medieval philosophy, would grow to maturity in the twelfth and thirteenth centuries. Writing in the sixth century, Boethius was a forerunner of this movement.

Cassiodorus (c. 490–575), a contemporary of Boethius, was born in southern Italy of a good family; he served three Ostrogoth kings. Although Cassiodorus wrote the twelve-volume *History of the Goths* and some theological treatises, his prime legacies were the establishment of a monastic library containing Greek and Latin manuscripts and his advocacy of higher education to improve the quality of the clergy. In his educational writings, he justified the importance of studying secular literature as an aid to understanding sacred writings. Even though his works were not original, they did rescue some ideas of the ancients from oblivion; these ideas would bear fruit again in later centuries. Cassiodorus's plans for founding a university in Rome modeled after the one in Alexandria did not materialize; in fact, six hundred years would elapse before universities would arise in Latin Christendom. Leaving political office, Cassiodorus retired to a monastery, where he helped initiate the monastic practice of copying ancient texts. Without this tradition, many key Christian and Greco-Roman works would undoubtedly have perished.

In Spain, Isidore of Seville (c. 576–636) compiled an encyclopedia, *Etymologiae,* covering a diversity of topics, from arithmetic and God to furniture. Isidore derived his information from many secular and religious sources. Quite understandably, his work contained many errors, particularly in its references to nature. For centuries, though, the *Etymologiae* served as a standard reference work and was found in every monastic library of note.

The translations and compilations made by Boethius, Cassiodorus, and Isidore, the books collected and copied by monks and nuns, and the schools established in monasteries (particularly those in Ireland, England, and Italy) kept intellectual life from dying out completely in the Early Middle Ages. Amid the deterioration of political authority, the stagnation of economic life, and the decline in learning, a new civilization was emerging. Germanic and Roman peoples intermarried, and Roman, Germanic, and Christian traditions intermingled. But it was the church more than anything else that gave form and direction to the emerging civilization.

THE CHURCH: SHAPER OF MEDIEVAL CIVILIZATION

The Church as Unifier

Christianity was the integrating principle and the church was the dominant institution of the Middle Ages. During the Late Roman Empire, as the Roman state and its institutions decayed, the church gained power and importance; its organization grew stronger, and its membership increased. Unlike the Roman state, the church was a healthy and vital institution. The elite of the Roman Empire had severed their commitment to the values of classical civilization, whereas church leaders were intensely devoted to their faith.

During the invasions of the fifth and sixth centuries, the church, retaining an effective administrative system, assumed many political functions formerly performed by the Roman state and continued to convert the Germanic tribes. By teaching a higher morality, the church tamed the warrior habits of the Germanic peoples. By preserving some of the high culture of Greece and Rome, it opened Germans' minds to new ideas. A unifying and civilizing agent, the church provided people with an intelligible and purposeful conception of life and death. In a dying world, the church was the only institution capable of reconstructing civilized life.

Thus, the Christian outlook, rather than the traditions of the Germanic tribes, was the foundation of medieval civilization. During the course of the Middle Ages, people came to see themselves as participants in a great drama of salvation. There was only one truth: God's revelation to humanity. There was only one avenue to heaven, and it passed through the church. God had established the church to administer the rites through which his love was bestowed on people. The church had the awesome responsibility of caring for human souls. Without the church, it was believed, people would remain doomed sinners. To the medieval mind, society without the church was inconceivable. Membership in a universal church replaced citizenship in a universal empire. Across Europe, from Italy to Ireland, a new society centered on Christianity was forming.

Monks and the Papacy

Monks helped construct the foundations of medieval civilization. During the seventh century, intellectual life on the European continent continued its steady decline. In the monasteries of Ireland and England, however, a tradition of learning persisted. Early in the fifth century, Saint Patrick began the conversion of the Irish to Christianity. In Ireland, Latin became firmly entrenched as the language of both the church and scholars at a time when it was in danger of disappearing in many parts of Europe. Irish monks preserved and cultivated Latin and even kept some knowledge of Greek alive. Irish scholars engaged in biblical analysis, and, besides copying manuscripts, they decorated them, with an exquisite eye for detail. In England, the Anglo-Saxons, both women and men, who converted to Christianity mainly in the seventh century, also established monasteries that kept learning alive. Double monasteries existed, in which monks and nuns obeyed a common rule and one superior, sometimes an abbess. The Venerable Bede (673–735) wrote commentaries on Scripture and translated the fourth Gospel (Saint John's) into Anglo-Saxon. Bede is best known for his *Ecclesiastical History of the English People,* one of the finest medieval historical works.

In the sixth and seventh centuries, Irish and Anglo-Saxon monks and nuns built monasteries in continental Europe and converted people in the surrounding areas. They became the chief agents in Christianizing people in northern Europe. Thus, monks and nuns made possible a unitary European civilization based on a Christian foundation. By copying and preserving ancient texts, they also kept alive elements of ancient civilization.

During the Early Middle Ages, when cities were in decay, monasteries, whose libraries contained theological works and ancient Latin classics, were the main cultural centers; they would remain so until the rebirth of towns in the High Middle Ages. Monks instructed peasants in superior methods of farming and were partly responsible for the reclamation of lands that had been neglected or devastated during the great invasions and for the clearing of new lands. Monasteries also offered succor to the sick and the destitute and served as places of refuge for travelers. To the medieval mind, the monks' and nuns' selfless devotion to God, adoption of apostolic poverty, and dedication to prayer and contemplation represented the highest expression of the Christian way of life; it was the finest and most certain path to salvation. It was not uncommon for both men and women, with old age or even death approaching, to take the vows so that they might die as monks or nuns. Regarding the monks as soldiers in the

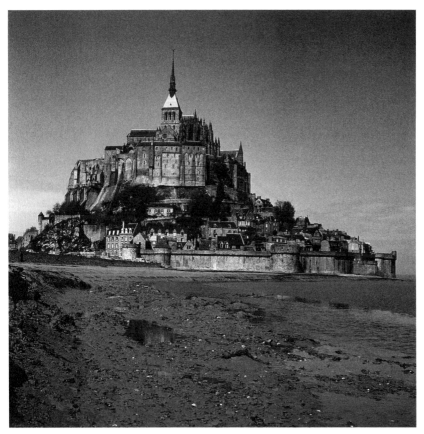

MONASTERY OF MONT ST. MICHEL. The monastic institutions throughout Western Europe stood firm amid the intellectual and cultural confusion of the Early Middle Ages. By copying ancient manuscripts and studying Latin, monks preserved elements of classical civilizations. (© Paul Almasy/Corbis.)

war against paganism, unorthodoxy, and heresy, the popes protected monasteries and encouraged their spread.

The Early Middle Ages was a formative period for the **papacy**, as well as for society in general. The status of the papacy was closely tied to events in Italy. In the late sixth century, the papacy was compelled to protect Rome and the surrounding territory from the Lombards, the last Germanic people to settle in once-Roman lands. At this critical stage, Gregory I, the Great (590–604), became pope. A descendant of a prominent Roman family and a monk, Gregory turned out to be one of the ablest medieval popes. He used Roman methods of administration effectively to organize and administer papal property in Italy, Sicily, Sardinia, Gaul, and other regions. The papacy owned huge estates worked by serfs. It also owned timberlands and mines, which provided the income for maintaining the clergy, churches, monasteries, hospitals, and orphanages in Rome and other places. Because of Gregory's efforts, the papacy became the leading financial institution of the day.

Gregory tried to strengthen the pope's authority within the church, insisting that all bishops and the Byzantine church in Constantinople were subject to papal authority. Establishing monasteries, he tightened the bonds between the monks and the papacy, and it was he who

THE CONSOLATION OF PHILOSOPHY. Fortune turns her wheel as Philosophy consoles the imprisoned Boethius, who faces death. (Bridgeman-Giraudon/Art Resource, N.Y.)

dispatched Benedictine monks to England to win over the Anglo-Saxons. The newly established Anglo-Saxon church looked to Rome for leadership. Gregory realized that to lead Christendom effectively the papacy must exercise authority over churches outside Italy—a policy adopted by popes who succeeded him.

He was also an intellectual who wrote commentaries on the books of the Bible and authored many works dealing with Christian themes: the duties of bishops, the lives of saints and monks, miracles, and purgatory. Because of his many writings, Gregory is regarded as a father of the Latin church. An astute diplomat, he knew that

the papacy required the political and military support of a powerful kingdom to protect it from its enemies, especially the Lombards. Accordingly, he set his sights on an alliance with the Franks. Finally materializing 150 years later, this alliance between the papacy and Frankish kings helped shape medieval history.

THE KINGDOM OF THE FRANKS

From their homeland in the Rhine River valley, the Frankish tribes had expanded into Roman territory during the fourth and fifth centuries.

Map 9.3 THE CAROLINGIAN WORLD Resting more on the personal qualities of Charlemagne than on any firm economic or political foundation, the Carolingian empire did not survive the emperor's death in 814. (Copyright © 2013 Cengage Learning.)

The ruler Clovis united the various Frankish tribes and conquered most of Gaul. In 496, he converted to Roman Christianity. Clovis's conversion to Catholicism was an event of great significance. A number of other Germanic kings had adopted the Arian form of Christianity, which the church had declared heretical. By embracing Roman Christianity, the Franks became a potential ally of the papacy.

Clovis's successors could not maintain control over their lands, and power passed to the mayor of the palace, the king's chief officer. Serving as mayor of the palace from 717 to 741, Charles Martel subjected all Frankish lands to his rule. In addition, at the battle of Tours in 732, he defeated the Muslims. Although the Muslims continued to occupy the Iberian Peninsula, they would advance no farther north into Europe.

Charles Martel was succeeded by his son, Pepin the Short, who in 751 deposed the king. With the approval of the papacy and his nobles, Pepin was crowned king by Boniface, a prominent bishop. Two years later, Pope Stephen II anointed Pepin again as king of the Franks and appealed to him to protect the papacy from the Lombards. Pepin crossed into Italy, defeated the Lombards, and turned over captured lands to the papacy. This famous Donation of Pepin made the pope ruler of the territory between Rome and Ravenna, which became known as the Papal States.

The Era of Charlemagne

The alliance between the Franks and the papacy was continued by Pepin's successor, Charlemagne (Charles the Great), who ruled from 768 to 814. Charlemagne continued the Carolingian policy of expanding the Frankish kingdom. He destroyed the Lombard kingdom, added Bavaria to his kingdom, and, after long, terrible wars, compelled the Saxons to submit to his rule and convert to Christianity—thousands were beheaded when they were slow to choose between baptism or execution. He also conquered a region in northern Spain, the Spanish March, which served as a buffer between the Christian Franks and the Muslims in Spain.

Immense difficulties arose in governing the expanded territories. Size seemed an insuperable obstacle to effective government, particularly since Charlemagne's administrative structure, lacking trained personnel, was primitive by Islamic, Byzantine, or Roman standards. The empire was divided into about 250 counties administered by counts—nobles personally loyal to the ruler. Men from powerful families, the counts served as generals, judges, and administrators, implementing the king's decisions. To supervise the counts, Charlemagne created *missi dominici* (royal messengers)—generally two laymen and a bishop or abbot—who made annual journeys to the different counties. The purpose of the missi dominici was to prevent counts and their subordinates from abusing their power and undermining Charlemagne's authority.

On Christmas Day in Rome in the year 800, Pope Leo III crowned Charlemagne emperor of the Romans. The initiative for the coronation probably came from the papacy, not from Charlemagne. The meaning of this event has aroused conflicting opinions among historians, but certain conclusions seem justified. The title signified that the tradition of a world empire still survived despite the demise of the western Roman Empire three hundred years earlier. But because it was the pope who crowned Charlemagne, this meant that the emperor had a spiritual responsibility to spread and defend the faith. Thus, Roman universalism was fused with Christian universalism.

The Frankish Empire, of course, was only a dim shadow of the Roman Empire. The Franks had no Roman law or Roman legions; there were no cities that were centers of economic and cultural activity; and officials were not trained civil servants with a world outlook, but uneducated war chieftains with a tribal viewpoint. Yet Charlemagne's empire did embody the concept of a universal Christian empire, an ideal that would endure throughout the Middle Ages.

The crowning of a Germanic ruler as emperor of the Romans by the head of the church represented the merging of Germanic, Roman, and Christian traditions, which is the essential characteristic of medieval civilization. This blending of traditions was also evident on a cultural plane, for Charlemagne, a Germanic warrior-king, showed respect for classical learning and Christianity, both non-Germanic traditions.

Carolingian Renaissance

Charlemagne felt that it was his religious duty to raise the educational level of the clergy so that they understood and could properly teach the faith. To do so required overcoming the illiteracy or semiliteracy of clergymen and preparing sacred Scriptures that were uniform, complete, and free of errors. Charlemagne also fostered education to train administrators who would be capable of overseeing his empire and the royal estates; such men had to be literate. He himself learned Latin and spoke it fluently.

To achieve his purpose, Charlemagne gathered some of the finest scholars in Europe. Alcuin of York, England (735–804), was given charge of the palace school attended by Charlemagne and

Saint Boniface

Of the many English monks and nuns who converted inhabitants of the Netherlands and Germany, none was more important than Saint Boniface (c. 680–754). In 716, Boniface, then a monk called Wynfrid who had earned a reputation as a Latin scholar, left England for Frisia in order to restore the churches that had been destroyed when the Frisians revolted against Frankish rule and Christian proselytizing. Consecrated bishop in 722, he extended his missionary activity into Bavaria and Thuringia. Working closely with the papacy, he founded monasteries, including the famous Abbey of Fulda; converted pagans; and imposed Christian standards of behavior on both clergy and laypeople. For example, he prohibited idol worship and the selling of slaves to heathens for sacrifices. In a letter to Pope Zacharias, he expressed his displeasure with deacons who "have four or five concubines in their beds, still read the Gospel and are not ashamed or afraid to call themselves deacons—nay rather, entering upon the priesthood, they continue in the same vices, add sin to sin, declare that they also have a right . . . to celebrate mass."* He also denounced "any layman, be he emperor, king, official, or count [who] may capture a monastery from the power of a bishop, an abbot, or an abbess and begin to hold property bought by the blood of Christ—the ancient fathers called such a man a robber, sacrilegious, a murderer of the poor, a devil's wolf entering the sheepfold of Christ, to be condemned with the ultimate anathema before the judgment of Christ."†

Boniface maintained a correspondence with his cousin Lioba, an English-born nun, who became abbess of the convent Boniface founded at Tauberbischofsheim, near the Main River. Shortly before his death, Boniface visited with Lioba at her convent. He urged her not to "forsake the land of your pilgrimage. . . . Hold

his sons and daughters, high lords, and youths training to serve the emperor. Throughout France, Alcuin expanded schools and libraries, promoted the copying of ancient manuscripts, and imposed basic literary standards on the clergy.

The focus of the Carolingian Renaissance was predominantly Christian: an effort to train clergymen and improve their understanding of the Bible and the writings of the church fathers. This process raised the level of literacy and improved the Latin style. Most important, monastic copyists continued to preserve ancient texts, which otherwise might never have survived; the oldest surviving manuscripts of many ancient Greek and Roman works are Carolingian copies.

Compared with the Greco-Roman past, with the cultural explosion of the twelfth and thirteenth centuries, or with the great Italian Renaissance of the fifteenth century, the Carolingian Renaissance seems slight indeed. Although it did rediscover and revive ancient Roman works and adopt Roman architecture and artistic forms, it did not recapture the worldly spirit of Greece and Rome. Carolingian scholars did not engage in independent philosophical speculation or search for new knowledge, nor did they achieve that synthesis of faith and reason that would be constructed by the great theologians of the twelfth and thirteenth centuries. The Carolingian Renaissance did, however, reverse the process of cultural decay, which had characterized much of the Early Middle Ages. Learning would never again fall to the low level it had reached during the centuries following the decline of Rome.

During the era of Charlemagne, a distinct European civilization took root. It blended the Roman heritage of a world empire, the intellectual achievement of the Greco-Roman mind, Christian otherworldliness, and the customs of the Germanic peoples. This nascent civilization of Latin Christendom differed from Byzantine and Islamic civilizations, and Latin Christians were growing conscious of the difference. But the new medieval civilization was still centuries away from its high point, which would be reached in the twelfth and thirteenth centuries.

Charlemagne's empire also engendered the ideal of a unified Latin Christendom: a single bravely to your course, carry on the good work day by day, and heed not the body's weakness. Time is not long, suffering is not hard, if your eyes are set upon eternity."‡

When Boniface died, Archbishop Cuthbert of Canterbury praised him for bringing "savage peoples from their long and devious wanderings in the wide abyss of eternal perdition into the glorious pathways of the heavenly fatherland by the inspiration of his holy words and by the example of his pious and gentle life."§ When Lioba died in 780, she was buried at Fulda to be joined with Boniface.

*The Letters of Saint Boniface, trans. Ephraim Emerton (New York: Columbia University Press, 1940), 80.

†Ibid., 140.

‡Quoted in Eleanor Duckett, The Wandering Saints of the Early Middle Ages (New York: Norton, 1959), 227.

§The Letters of Saint Boniface, 184.

Christian community under one government. This new collectivity would supersede the separate Germanic tribal units. Over the centuries, the pursuit of this ideal of a Christian world-state, Christendom, would inspire many people, both clergy and laity.

The Breakup of Charlemagne's Empire

After Charlemagne's death in 814, his son, Louis the Pious, inherited the throne. Louis aimed to preserve the empire, but the task was virtually impossible. The empire's strength rested more on the personal qualities of Charlemagne than on any firm economic or political foundation. In particular, it never developed an empirewide system of taxation, such as the one that had supported the Roman Empire for centuries. Moreover, the empire was simply too large and consisted of too many diverse peoples to be governed effectively. Besides Frankish nobles, who sought to increase their own power at the emperor's expense, Louis had to deal with his own rebellious sons. After

Louis died in 840, the empire was divided among the three surviving sons.

The Treaty of Verdun in 843 gave Louis the German the eastern part of the empire, which marked the beginning of Germany; to Charles the Bald went the western part, which was the start of France; and Lothair received the Middle Kingdom, which extended from Rome to the North Sea. The Middle Kingdom would become a source of conflict between France and Germany into the twentieth century. As central authority waned, large landowners increasingly exercised authority in their own regions. Simultaneous invasions from all directions furthered this movement toward localism and decentralization.

In the ninth and tenth centuries, Latin Christendom was attacked on all sides. From bases in North Africa, Spain, and Sicily, Muslims ravaged regions of southern Europe, even as far as the suburbs of Rome. They deported shiploads of Christians to North Africa to be sold in slave markets. The Magyars, originally from western Asia and linguistically related to Finns and Turks, crossed the Carpathian Mountains in the ninth century and established themselves on the plains of the Danube; their horsemen launched lightning raids into northern Italy, western Germany, and parts of France. Defeated in Germany in 933 and again in 955, the Magyars withdrew to what is now Hungary; they ceased their raids and adopted Christianity.

Still another group of invaders, the Northmen, or Vikings, sailed from Scandinavia in their long, open, wooden ships to raid the coasts and river valleys of Western Europe. Superb seamen, the Vikings crossed the North Atlantic and settled in Iceland and Greenland; from there, they almost certainly traveled to and landed on the coast of North America. In addition to their conquests and explorations, the Vikings also produced rich poetry, excelled at crafts, and contributed greatly to the revival of trade in the High Middle Ages.

In pursuit of slaves, jewels, and precious metals hoarded in monasteries, the Viking invaders plundered, destroyed, raped, and murdered. Villages were devastated, monasteries were looted and their libraries set ablaze, ports were ruined, and the population was decimated. Trade was at a standstill, coins no longer circulated, and farms were turned into wastelands. The European economy, already gravely weak, collapsed; the political authority of kings disappeared; and cultural life and learning withered.

These terrible attacks heightened political insecurity and accelerated anew the process of decentralization that had begun with the decline of Rome. During these chaotic times, counts came to regard as their own the land that they administered and defended for their king. At a time when monarchs could no longer guarantee the safety of their subjects, the inhabitants of a district looked on the count or local lord, frequently a former Carolingian official, as their ruler, for his men and fortresses protected them. In their regions, nobles exercised public power formerly held by kings, an arrangement later designated as *feudalism.*

Wherever great lords failed to protect their territories from neighboring counts or from invaders, political power was further fragmented. In other areas, local nobles chipped away at a count's authority in his county. In his region, the local lord, aided by warrior-knights, exercised virtually supreme authority; people turned to him for protection and for the administration of justice. Europe had entered an age of feudalism, in which the essential unit of government was not a kingdom but a local region, and political power lay in the hands of local lords.

MEDIEVAL SOCIETY

Arising during a period of collapsing central authority, invasion, scanty public revenues, and declining commerce and town life, feudalism attempted to provide some order and security. Feudalism was not a planned system devised logically from general principles but rather an improvised response to the challenge posed by ineffectual central authority. Feudal practices differed from locality to locality and in some regions barely took root. Although it was only a stopgap means of government, feudalism did bring some order, justice, and law during an era of breakdown, localism, and transition. It would remain the predominant political arrangement until kings reasserted their authority in the High and Late Middle Ages.

Feudalism made an enduring impact on Western civilization. It contributed to Western notions about honor, the deportment of gentlemen, and romantic love (see Chapter 11). Most important, feudal traditions laid the groundwork for the principle of limiting a king's power and for the practice of parliamentary government (see Chapters 10 and 12).

Feudalism was built on an economic foundation known as *manorialism.* Although pockets of free peasantry remained, a village community, or manor, consisting of serfs bound to the land became the essential agricultural arrangement for much of the Middle Ages. The manorial village was the means of organizing an agricultural society with limited markets and money. Neither lords nor priests performed economically productive work. Their ways of life were made possible by the toil of serfs.

Manorialism and feudalism presupposed a stable social order: clergy who prayed, lords who warred, and serfs who toiled. People believed that society functioned smoothly when individuals accepted their status and performed their proper role. In the words of an eleventh-century cleric,

> *Mankind, since the beginning of time has been divided in three, those who pray, those who cultivate, those who fight, and each of the three is comforted on either side by the two others. He who, forsaking the world, gives himself to a life of prayer owes it to the warriors that he is able to carry out his holy task in safety, while he owes his bodily nourishment to the farmers. Similarly, the farmers ascend to God through the prayers of the ecclesiastics and are defended by the weapons of the warriors. So also, the warriors are fed by the produce of the fields and benefit from the income therefrom, while the holy prayers of the pious whom they protect will expiate the crimes which they commit in battle.*[7]

A person's rights, duties, and relationship to law depended on his or her ranking in the social order. To change position was to upset the organic unity of society. And no one, serfs included, should be deprived of the traditional rights associated with his or her rank. This arrangement was justified by the clergy.

> *God himself has willed that among men, some must be lords and some serfs, in such a fashion that the lords venerate and love God, and that the serfs love and venerate their lord following the word of the Apostle; serfs obey your temporal lords with fear and trembling; lords treat your serfs according to justice and equity.*[8]

Bishop Adalbero of Laon: *The Tripartite Society*

Medieval thinkers came to see their society divided into three different but complementary groups: clergy, lords, and serfs. Each group had its own responsibilities—priests guided the souls of the faithful; lords protected society from its enemies; and the serfs' toil provided sustenance for everyone. Written in about 1020, the following statement by Bishop Adalbero of Laon, France, illustrates the tripartite nature of medieval society.

The community of the faithful is a single body, but the condition of society is threefold in order. For human law distinguishes two classes. Nobles and serfs, indeed, are not governed by the same ordinance. . . . The former are the warriors and the protectors of the churches. They are the defenders of the people, of both great and small, in short, of everyone, and at the same time they ensure their own safety. The other class is that of the serfs. This luckless breed possesses nothing except at the cost of its own labour. Who could, reckoning with an abacus, add up the sum of the cares with which the peasants are occupied, of their journeys on foot, of their hard labours? The serfs provide money, clothes, and food, for the rest; no free man could exist without serfs. Is there a task to be done? Does anyone want to put himself out? We see kings and prelates make themselves the serfs of their serfs; [but in truth] the master, who claims to feed his serf, is fed by him. And the serf never sees an end to his tears and his sighs. God's house, which we think of as one, is thus divided into three; some pray, others fight, and yet others work. The three groups, which coexist, cannot bear to be separated; the services rendered by one are a precondition for the labours of the two others; each in his turn takes it upon himself to relieve the whole. Thus the threefold assembly is none the less united, and it is thus that law has been able to triumph, and that the world has been able to enjoy peace.

Question for Analysis

1. According to Bishop Adalbero, what was the virtue of the triparite society?

Jacques Le Goff, *Medieval Civilization*, trans. Julia Barrow (Oxford: Blackwell, 1990), 255.

Vassalage

Feudal relationships enabled lords to increase their military strength. The need for military support was the principal reason for the condition of vassalage. A vassal was a knight who in a solemn ceremony pledged loyalty to a lord. This feature of feudalism derived from an ancient Germanic ceremony during which warriors swore personal allegiance to the head of the war-band. Among other things, the vassal gave military service to his lord and received in return a *fief*, which was usually land sufficient to support his needs. This fief was inhabited by peasants, and the crops that they raised provided the vassal with his means of support.

Besides rendering military assistance and supplying knights, the vassal owed several other obligations to his lord in return for the fief and the lord's protection. These duties included sitting in the lord's court and judging cases, such as the breach of feudal agreements between the lord and his other vassals; providing lodgings when the lord traveled through the vassal's territory; offering a gift when the lord's son was knighted or when his eldest daughter married; and raising a ransom should the lord be captured by an enemy.

Both lord and vassal felt honor-bound to abide by the oath of loyalty. It became an accepted custom for a vassal to renounce his loyalty to his lord if the latter failed to protect him from enemies, mistreated him, or increased the vassal's obligations as fixed by the feudal contract. Similarly, if a vassal did not live up to his obligations, the lord would summon him to his court, where the vassal would be tried

CHESS PIECES. These grim and foreboding chessmen depict the medieval nobility's concern with combat. (© The Trustees of the British Museum/Art Resource, N.Y.)

for treachery. If found guilty, he could lose his fief and perhaps his life. Sometimes disputes between vassals and lords erupted into warfare. Because a vassal often held land from more than one lord and sometimes was himself a lord to vassals, situations frequently became awkward, complex, and confusing. On occasion, a vassal had to decide to which lord he owed *liege homage* (prime loyalty).

As feudalism evolved, the king came to be regarded as the chief lord, who had granted fiefs to the great lords, who in turn had divided them into smaller units and regranted them to vassals. Thus, all members of the ruling class, from the lowliest knights to the king, occupied a place in the feudal hierarchy. In theory, the king was the highest political authority and the source of land tenure, but in actual fact he was often less powerful than other nobles of the realm.

Feudalism would decline when kings converted their theoretical powers into actual powers. The decline of feudalism was a gradual process; conflict between the crown and the aristocracy would persist, with varying degrees of intensity, for several centuries, but the future belonged to the centralized state being shaped by kings, not to feudal fragmentation.

Feudal Law

Feudal law, which incorporated many features of traditional Germanic law, differed markedly from Roman law. Roman law was universal, having been enacted by a central government for a world empire. It was also rational, for it sought to be in accord with natural law that applied to all; and it was systematic, for it offered a framework of standards that applied to individual cases. Feudal law, in contrast, was local, covering only a small region. Moreover, it was personal. In the Roman view, the individual as a citizen owed obligations to the state, whereas under feudalism, a vassal owed loyalty and service to a lord according to the terms of a personal agreement made between them.

In the feudal view, lords and kings did not make law; rather, they were guided by tradition and precedent. They discovered and confirmed law by examining ancient customs. Therefore, feudal patterns of landownership, military service, and wardship came to be regarded as an expression of ancient, unchanging, and inviolable custom. Consequently, if the vassal believed that his lord had violated the feudal agreement, that is, had broken faith with him and had transgressed tradition, the vassal would demand restoration of customary rights before an audience of his fellow vassals. Often lords battled one another, believing that they were defending their rights. Similarly, lords claimed the right to resist kings who did not honor their feudal agreements.

Feudal Warriors

Feudal lords viewed manual labor and commerce as degrading for men of their rank. They considered only one vocation worthy: that of warrior. Through combat, the lord demonstrated his valor, earned his reputation, measured his individual worth, derived excitement, added to his wealth, and defended his rights. Warfare was his whole purpose in life. During the twelfth century, to relieve the boredom of peacetime, nobles staged gala tournaments in which knights, fighting singly or in teams, engaged each other in battle to prove their skill and courage. The victors in these pageants gained prestige in the eyes of fellow nobles and admiring ladies and received prizes—falcons, crowns, and substantial amounts of money. The feudal glorification of combat became deeply ingrained in Western society and endured into the twentieth century. Over the centuries, a code of behavior, called *chivalry*, evolved for the feudal nobility. A true knight was expected to fight bravely, demonstrate loyalty to his lord, and treat other knights with respect and courtesy.

In time, the church interjected a religious element into the warrior culture of the feudal knight. It sought to use the fighting spirit of the feudal class for Christian ends: knights could assist the clergy in enforcing God's will. Thus, to the Germanic tradition of loyalty and courage was added a Christian component. As a Christian gentleman, a knight was expected to honor the laws of the church and to wield his sword in the service of God. He was supposed to protect women, children, and the weak and to defend the church against heretics and infidels. The very ceremony of knighthood was placed within a Christian framework. A priest blessed the future knight's arms and prayed that the knight would always "defend the Just and Right."

Regarding the private warfare of lords as lawless violence that menaced social life, the church, in the eleventh century, imposed strictures called the Peace of God and the Truce of God. These restrictions limited feudal warfare to certain days of the week and certain times of the year. Thus, the church tried to regulate warfare according to moral principles. Although only partially effective, these religious restraints did offer Christian society some respite from plundering and incessant warfare.

Noblewomen

Feudal society was very much a man's world. In theory, women were deemed to be physically, morally, and intellectually inferior to men; in practice, they were subjected to male authority. Fathers arranged the marriages of their daughters. Girls from aristocratic families were generally married at age sixteen or younger to a man often twice as old. The wife of a lord was at the mercy of her husband; if she angered him, she might expect a beating. A French law code of the thirteenth century stated: "In a number of cases men may be excused for the injuries they inflict on their wives, nor should the law intervene. Provided he neither kills nor maims her, it is legal for a man to beat his wife when she wrongs him."[9] Although the church taught that both men and women were precious to God and spiritual equals, church tradition also regarded women as agents of the Devil—evil temptresses who, like the biblical Eve, used their

NOBLEWOMEN. **At times, medieval ladies joined their husband's hunting party.** (akg-images)

sexuality to lure men into sin—and church law also permitted wife beating.

In Mary, the mother of Jesus, however, Christians had an alternative image of women to the image suggested by Eve, one that placed women in a position of honor. Devotion to the Virgin Mary reached its high point in the twelfth and thirteenth centuries with the growing belief in the Immaculate Conception (the idea, which later became a doctrine, that Mary was conceived free of original sin and remained free of sin throughout her life).* Moreover, medieval Christians believed that Mary, by dedicating her entire life to Jesus in his work of redemption, cooperated with him

in his ministry and could intercede with him in behalf of individual Christians. The numerous artistic depictions of Mary as the Mother of God and the Queen of Heaven, as well as the multitude of churches named after the Virgin, are evidence of the popular piety that the cult of Mary generated throughout the Middle Ages.

Aristocratic girls who did not marry often entered a convent. (Peasant daughters, because they were needed on the farm—they probably worked as hard and as well as men—rarely became nuns. Moreover, their parents could not afford the dowry, payable in land, cash, or goods, required by the convent for admission.) The nunneries provided an outlet for the talents of unmarried noblewomen. Abbesses demonstrated organizational skills in supervising the convent's affairs. Some nuns acquired an education and, like their male counterparts, copied manuscripts and thus preserved knowledge and ideas of the past. The nun Hroswitha (c. 935–c. 1001) of Gandersheim, in Saxony, Germany, produced poetry, history, and plays. Inspired by the Roman poet Terence, she wrote six dramas—the first since Roman times—along with a history of Germanic rulers and one of her own convent.

As the lady of the castle, the lord's wife performed important duties. She assigned tasks to the servants; made medicines; preserved food; taught young girls how to sew, spin, and weave (she was responsible for providing the lord and his companions with most of the clothes they required); and, despite her subordinate position, took charge of the castle when her husband was away. If the lord was taken prisoner in war, she raised the ransom to pay for his release. Sometimes she put on armor and went to war. For amusement, noblewomen enjoyed chess and other board games, played musical instruments, or embroidered tapestries to cover castle walls. A lady might also join her husband on the hunt, a favorite recreation of the medieval nobility.

Agrarian Life

The origins of manorialism can be traced in part to the Late Roman Empire, when peasants depended on the owners of large estates for protection and security. This dependence increased during the

---

*The Immaculate Conception did not become Roman Catholic dogma until 1854, when Pope Pius IX promulgated the bull *Ineffabilis Deus*.

Early Middle Ages, especially during the invasions of Northmen, Magyars, and Muslims in the ninth and tenth centuries. Peasants continued to sacrifice their freedom in exchange for protection, or, in some cases, they were too weak to resist the encroachments of local magnates. Like feudalism, manorialism was not an orderly system but consisted of improvised relationships and practices that varied from region to region.

A lord controlled at least one manorial village; great lords might control hundreds. A small manor included a dozen families; a large one, as many as fifty or sixty. The manorial village was never completely self-sufficient because salt, millstones, and metalware were generally obtained from outside sources; it did, however, constitute a balanced economic setting. Peasants grew grain and raised cattle, sheep, goats, and hogs; blacksmiths, carpenters, and stonemasons built and repaired dwellings and implements; the village priest cared for the souls of the inhabitants; and the lord defended the manor and administered the customary law.

The serf and his family lived in a dismal, one-room cottage that they shared with chickens and pigs. In the center burned a small fire, the smoke escaping through a hole in the roof. In cold weather when the fire was strong, the room filled with smoke. When it rained, water came through the thatched roof and turned the earthen floor into mud. The odor from animal excrement was ever present.

Poor roads, few bridges, and dense forests made travel difficult; thieves and warring knights made it unsafe. Peasants generally lived, worked, and died on the lord's estate and were buried in the village churchyard. Few had any contact with the world beyond the village of their birth. When a manor was attacked by another lord, the peasants found protection inside the walls of their lord's house. In many places, by the twelfth century, this building had become a well-fortified stone castle.

In return for protection and the right to cultivate fields and to pass these holdings on to their children, serfs owed obligations to their lord, and their personal freedom was restricted in a variety of ways. Bound to the land, they could not leave the manor without the lord's consent. Before serfs could marry, they had to obtain the lord's permission and pay a fee. The lord could select a wife for his serf and force him to marry her. Sometimes a serf, objecting to the lord's choice, preferred to pay a fine: "Thomas of Oldbury came on summons and was commanded to take Agatha of Halesowen to wife; he said he would rather be fined."[10] These rules also applied to serfs' children, who inherited their parents' obligations. In addition to working their allotted land, the serfs had to tend the fields reserved for the lord. Other services exacted by the lord included digging ditches, gathering firewood, building fences, repairing roads and bridges, and sewing clothes. Probably somewhat more than half of a serf's workweek was devoted to these labor obligations. Serfs also paid a variety of dues to the lord, most notably for using the lord's mill, bake-oven, and winepress.

Serfs did derive some benefits from manorial relationships. They received protection from roving brigands and warring nobles, and they possessed customary rights, which the lord generally respected, to cottages and farmland. But in a world periodically threatened with famine and epidemics, serfs faced an unrelenting struggle to survive, a struggle made all the more difficult by the contempt lords had for them. Medieval literature often depicted peasants as repulsive creatures—ugly, dirty, cowardly, and uncouth.

If a lord demanded more services or dues than were customary, or if he interfered with their right to cottages or strips of farmland, the peasants might demonstrate their discontent by refusing to work for the lord. Up to the fourteenth century, however, open rebellion was rare because lords possessed considerable military and legal power. The manorial system promoted attitudes of dependency and servility among the serfs; their hopes for a better life were directed toward heaven.

Medieval agriculture suffered from several deficiencies. Among them was the short supply of fertilizer; farmers depended solely on animal manure. Inadequate wooden plows and primitive methods of harnessing draft animals resulted in low yields. Yet as the Middle Ages progressed, important improvements in agriculture (discussed in Chapter 10) took place and had wide ramifications for medieval economic and social life. In the High Middle Ages, the revival of an urban economy and the reemergence of central authority would undermine manorial (and feudal) relationships.

❖   ❖   ❖

NOTES

1. Speros Vryonis Jr., *Byzantium and Europe* (New York: Harcourt, Brace and World, 1967), 193.

2. *The Koran,* trans. N. J. Dawood (Baltimore: Penguin Books, 1961), 108–109.

3. W. Montgomery Watt, *The Influence of Islam on Medieval Europe* (Edinburgh: Edinburgh University Press, 1972), 43.

4. Boethius, *The Consolation of Philosophy,* trans. W. V. Cooper (New York: Modern Library, 1943), 26.

5. Ibid., 29.

6. Ibid., 34.

7. Quoted in Jean-Pierre Poly and Eric Bournazel, *The Feudal Transformation 900–1200,* trans. Caroline Higgitt (New York: Holmes and Meier, 1991), 149.

8. Quoted in V. H. H. Green, *Medieval Civilization in Western Europe* (New York: St. Martin's Press, 1971), 35.

9. Cited in Frances Gies and Joseph Gies, *Women in the Middle Ages* (New York: Thomas Y. Crowell, 1978), 46.

10. Quoted in G. G. Coulton, *Medieval Village, Manor, and Monastery* (New York: Harper Torchbooks, 1960), 82.

SUGGESTED READING

Angold, Michael, *Byzantium: The Bridge from Antiquity to the Middle Ages* (2001). An excellent introduction.

Collins, Roger, *Early Medieval Europe 300–1000* (1999). A clearly and expertly written text.

Fossier, Robert, ed., The *Cambridge Illustrated History of The Middle Ages, Vol. 1, 350–950* (2000). Excellent essays on major themes.

Gies, Frances, and Joseph Gies, *Life in a Medieval Castle* (1974). The castle as the center of medieval life; passages from journals, songs, and account books.

Holmes, George, ed., *The Oxford History of Medieval Europe* (1988). Essays by several scholars; good opening essay on transformation of the Roman world.

Lewis, A. R., *Emerging Medieval Europe* (1967). Good discussions of both economic and social changes.

Lewis, Bernard, ed. and trans., *Islam from the Prophet Muhammad to the Capture of Constantinople,* 2 vols. (1979). A valuable collection of original sources.

Lucas, Angela M., *Women in the Middle Ages* (1983). Women and religion, marriage, and letters.

Rowling, Marjorie, *Life in Medieval Times* (1973). All phases of medieval daily life.

Tierney, Brian, *Western Europe in the Middle Ages* (1970). An outstanding text.

Zacour, Norman, *An Introduction to Medieval Institutions* (1969). Comprehensive essays on all phases of medieval society.

The High Middle Ages: Vitality and Renewal

Miniature painting of Flemish citizens receiving a city charter, Chronique de Hainout, fifteenth century. (Bibliotheque Royal de Belgique.)

- **Economic Expansion**
- **The Rise of States**
- **The Growth of Papal Power**
- **Christians and Jews**

Focus Questions

1. What were the signs of vitality and recovery in European economic, political, and religious life during the High Middle Ages?
2. What factors contributed to the rise of towns? What was the significance of the medieval town?
3. Why was there a conflict between church and state during the Middle Ages?
4. What prompted lords and commoners to heed the papacy's call for a crusade?
5. What conditions led to the rise of states? What were the essential differences characterizing the development of medieval England, France, and Germany?
6. What factors led to the rise of anti-Semitism during the Middle Ages? How does anti-Semitism demonstrate the power of mythical thinking?

*B*y the end of the eleventh century, Europe showed many signs of recovery and vitality. The invasions of Magyars and Vikings had ended, and powerful lords and kings imposed greater order on their territories. Improvements in technology and the clearing of new lands increased agricultural production. More food, the fortunate absence of plagues, and the limited nature of feudal warfare contributed to a population increase. The revival of long-distance trade and the emergence of towns were other visible signs of economic expansion. Offensives against the Muslims—in Spain, in Sicily, and (at the end of the century) in the Holy Land—demonstrated Europe's growing might and self-confidence. So too did the German conquest and colonization of lands on the northeastern frontier of Latin Christendom.

Reform movements strengthened the bonds between the church and the people and increased the power of the papacy. During the High Middle Ages (1050–1300), the pope, as Christ's deputy, sought to direct, if not rule, all Christendom. European economic and religious vitality was paralleled by a cultural flowering in philosophy, literature, and the visual arts. The civilization of Latin Christendom had entered its golden age.

ECONOMIC EXPANSION

A period of economic expansion, the High Middle Ages witnessed an agricultural revolution, a commercial revolution, the rebirth of towns, and the rise of an enterprising and dynamic middle class.

Agricultural Revolution

During the Middle Ages, important advances were made in agriculture. Many of these innovations occurred in the Early Middle Ages but were adopted only gradually and were not used everywhere. In time, however, they markedly increased production. By the end of the thirteenth century, medieval agriculture had reached a technical level far superior to that of the ancient world.

One innovation was a heavy plow that cut deeply into the soil. This new plow enabled farmers to work more quickly and effectively. As a

Chronology 10.1 ❖ The High Middle Ages

910	Founding of the Abbey of Cluny
962	Otto I crowned emperor of the Romans, beginning the Holy Roman Empire
987	Hugh Capet becomes king of France
1054	Split between the Byzantine and the Roman churches
1061–1091	Norman conquest of Sicily
1066	Norman conquest of England
1075	Start of the Investiture Controversy
1096	First Crusade begins
c. 1100	Revival of the study of Roman law at Bologna
1163	Start of the construction of the Cathedral of Notre Dame
1198–1216	Pontificate of Innocent III: height of the church's power
1267–1273	Saint Thomas Aquinas writes *Summa Theologica*
c. 1321	Dante completes *Divine Comedy*

result, they could cultivate more land, including the heavy, moist soils of northern Europe, which had offered too much resistance to the light plow. Another important advance in agricultural technology was the invention of the collar harness. The old yoke harness worked well with oxen but tended to choke horses, which, because they move faster and have greater stamina than oxen, are more valuable for agricultural work. The introduction of the horseshoe to protect the soft hooves of horses added to their ability to work on difficult terrain. The widening use of the water mill by the tenth century and the introduction of windmills in the twelfth century replaced ancient, less effective hand-worked mills for grinding grain.

The gradual emergence of the three-field system of managing agricultural land, particularly in northern Europe, increased production. In the old, widely used two-field system, half the land was planted in autumn with winter wheat, while the other half was left fallow to restore its fertility. In the new three-field system, one-third of the land was planted in autumn with winter wheat, a second third was planted the following spring with oats and vegetables, and the last third remained fallow. The advantages of the three-field system were that two-thirds of the land were farmed and only one-third was left unused and that the diversification of crops made more vegetable protein available.

Greater agricultural production reduced the number of deaths caused by starvation and dietary disease and thus contributed to a population increase. Grain surpluses also meant that draft animals and livestock could survive the winter. The growing numbers of animals provided a steady source of fresh meat and milk and increased the quantity of manure for fertilizer.

Soon the farmland of a manorial village could not support the growing village population. Consequently, peasants had to look beyond their immediate surroundings and colonize trackless wasteland. Lords vigorously promoted this conversion of uncultivated soil into agricultural land because it increased their incomes. Monastic communities also actively engaged in this enterprise. Almost everywhere peasants were draining swamps, clearing forests, and establishing new villages. Their endeavors during the eleventh and twelfth centuries

A Painting from an Anglo-Saxon Calendar, Eleventh Century. The heavy, iron-pointed, wheeled plough was of immense importance in extending farming to the heavier wet soils of northern Europe's lowlands. It made possible the growing agricultural exploitation of lands recovered from floodplains, forests, and marshes. (HIP/Art Resource, N.Y.)

brought vast areas of Europe under cultivation for the first time. New agricultural land was also acquired through expansion, the most notable example being the organized settlement of lands toward the east by German colonists.

The colonization and cultivation of virgin lands contributed to the decline of serfdom. Lords owned vast tracts of forests and swamps that would substantially increase their incomes if cleared, drained, and farmed. But serfs were often unwilling to move from their customary homes and fields to do the hard labor needed to cultivate these new lands. To lure serfs away from their villages, lords promised them freedom from most or all personal services. In many cases, the settlers fulfilled their obligations to the lord by paying rent rather than by performing services or providing foodstuffs, thus making the transition from serfs to freemen. In time, they came to regard the land as their own. As a result of these changing economic conditions, the percentage of French peasants who were serfs fell from 90 percent in 1050 to about 10 percent in 1350.

The improvement in agricultural technology and the colonization of new lands altered the conditions of life in Europe. Surplus food and the increase in population freed people to work at nonfarming occupations, making possible the expansion of trade and the revival of town life.

The Revival of Trade

Expanding agricultural production, the end of Viking attacks, greater political stability, the growth of a considerable money supply, and an increasing population produced a revival of commerce. During the Early Middle Ages, Italians and Jews kept alive a small amount of long-distance trade between Catholic Europe and the Byzantine and Islamic worlds. In the eleventh century, sea forces of Italian trading cities cleared the Mediterranean of Muslim fleets, which had blocked trade. As in Roman times, goods could circulate once again from one end of the sea to the other. The expanding population of northern Europe provided a market for Eastern silks, sugar, spices, and dyes, and Italian merchants were quick to exploit this demand.

By the start of the eleventh century, the European economy showed unmistakable signs of recovery from the disorders of the previous century. During the next two centuries, local, regional, and long-distance trade gained such momentum that some historians describe the period as a commercial revolution that surpassed the commercial activity of the Roman Empire during the Pax Romana. A class of traders emerged, many of them former serfs who had started trading by taking to the road as humble peddlers. Gradually they acquired business contacts in other lands, know-how, and ambition.

Crucial to the growth of trade were international fairs, where merchants and craftspeople set up stalls and booths to display their wares: swords, leather saddles, tools, rugs, shoes, silks, spices, furs, fine furniture, and other goods. Each fair lasted about three to six weeks; then the merchants would move on to another site. The Champagne region in northeastern France was the great center for fairs because the count of Champagne provided protection for merchants from thieves both en route to and at the fair, judges to guarantee the enforcement of contracts, and the necessary equipment, including covered stalls and accurate scales.

The principal arteries of trade flowed between the eastern Mediterranean and the Italian cities; between Scandinavia and the Atlantic coast; between northern France, Flanders, and England; and from the Baltic Sea in the north to the Black Sea and Constantinople via Russian rivers. The fine woolen cloth manufactured in Flanders provided the main stimulus for commerce along the Atlantic coast, and Flemish merchants prospered. In exchange for Flemish cloth, Scandinavians traded hunting hawks and fur; the English traded raw wools; and the Germans traded iron and timber. A wine trade also flourished between French vineyards and English wine merchants. Progress in navigation, including the use of the compass borrowed from the Arabs, and improvements in sails greatly aided long-distance commerce.

Because of their strategic position, Italian towns acted as intermediaries between the trade centers of the eastern Mediterranean and those of Latin Christendom. In Egyptian and North African ports, Italian merchants established enclaves where they set up permanent residence and conducted business. Luxury goods from as far away as India and China were transported to Italy by Italian ships and then taken overland to parts of Germany and France. In addition, the Italians extended their trade and increased their profits by sailing westward into the Atlantic Ocean and then north to the markets of Spain, the Netherlands, and England. On return voyages, they brought back wool and unfinished cloth, which in turn stimulated the Italian textile industry. Because individual merchants often lacked sufficient capital for these large-scale enterprises, groups of merchants formed partnerships. By enabling merchants to pool their capital, reduce their risks, and expand their knowledge of profit-making opportunities, these arrangements furthered commerce.

Increased economic activity led to other advances in business techniques. The development of banking and credit instruments made it unnecessary for merchants to carry large amounts of cash. The international fairs not only were centers of international trade but also served as capital markets for international credit transactions. The arrangements made by fair-going merchants to settle their debts were the origin of the bill of exchange, which allowed one currency to be converted into another. The invention of double-entry bookkeeping gave merchants an overview of their financial situation: the value of their goods and their ready cash. Without such knowledge, no large-scale commercial activity could be conducted on a continuous basis. Another improvement in business techniques was the formation of commercial law, which defined the rules of conduct for debts and contracts. Finally, a system of insurance emerged to provide protection for merchants whose goods were in transit. For a fee, a syndicate of brokers—the risk was too great for a single broker—would compensate the merchant whose cargo was lost at sea due to storms or piracy.

The Rebirth of Towns

In the eleventh century, towns emerged anew throughout Europe, and in the next century, they became active centers of commercial and intellectual life. Towns were a revolutionary force—socially, economically, and culturally. Because they provided new opportunities, other than food production, for commoners, towns contributed to the decline of manorialism. A new class of merchants and craftspeople came into being. This new class—the middle class—comprised those who, unlike the lords and serfs, were not affiliated with the land. The townsperson was a new type of person, with a value system different from that of the lord, the serf, or the cleric.

LOCAL MARKET IN FLORENCE. The birth of towns in the eleventh and twelfth centuries was a revolutionary development. Towns gave rise to a middle class that moved away from the outlook of traditional medieval society—clergy, lords, and peasants. This picture depicts the commercial vitality of a market in Florence. (Reunion des Musees Nationaux/Art Resource, N.Y.)

What spurred town growth was the increased food supply resulting from advances in agricultural technology. Surplus farm production meant that the countryside could support an urban population of artisans and professionals. Expanding trade also fostered urbanization. Towns emerged in places that were natural for trade: seacoasts, riverbanks, crossroads, and market sites. They also sprang up outside fortified castles and monasteries and on surviving Roman sites. The colonies of merchants who gathered at these locations were joined by peasants skilled in crafts or willing to work as laborers. From a medieval record comes this description of a town taking shape:

After this castle was built, certain traders began to flock to the place in front of the gate to the bridge of the castle, that is merchants, tavernkeepers, then other outsiders drifted in for the sake of food and shelter of those who might have business transactions with the count, who often came there. Houses and inns were erected for their accommodation, since there was not room for them within the chateau. These habitations increased so rapidly that soon a large ville came into being.[1]

Medieval towns were protected from outside attack by thick, high walls, towers, and drawbridges. Most towns had a small population. The larger ones—Florence, Ghent, and Paris—had between fifty thousand and a hundred thousand inhabitants by the start of the fourteenth century; Venice and Milan had somewhat more than a hundred thousand. Covering only small areas, these walled towns were crowded with people. Booths and wares of merchants and artisans lined the narrow and crooked streets, which were strewn with refuse—animal blood and bones dumped by butchers, rotten fish discarded by fishmongers, and human waste thrown from windows. Such unsanitary conditions were a breeding ground for contagious disease.

During the day, the streets were jammed with merchants hawking their goods, women carrying baskets, men carting produce and merchandise, beggars pleading, children playing, and thieves lurking. A festive occasion, such as a procession honoring a patron saint, sometimes brought traffic to a standstill. A hanging—in Paris decomposing corpses on gallows were a permanent fixture—a beheading, or the burning of a heretic was looked upon as another festive occasion and always attracted a huge crowd. At night, the streets were deserted; few people ventured forth because the few elderly watchmen were no match for the numerous thieves. Even greater danger came from fires, which raged through overcrowded streets lined with wooden houses. Quarrels between individuals or groups were often settled violently.

Merchants and craftspeople organized guilds to protect themselves from outside competition. The merchant guild in a town prevented outsiders from doing much business. Craftsmen new to a town had to be admitted to the guild of their trade before opening a shop. Competition between members of the same guild was discouraged. To prevent any one member from making significantly more money than another, a guild required its members to work the same number of hours, pay employees the same wages, produce goods of equal quality, and charge customers a just price. These rules were strictly enforced. Guilds also performed social and religious functions. Guild members attended meetings in the guildhall, celebrated holidays together, and marched in processions. The guilds cared for members who were ill or needy and extended help to widows and children of deceased members.

Women took an active part in the economic life of towns, working with men, usually their husbands, in the various crafts—as cobblers, tailors, hatters, bakers, goldsmiths, and so forth. Women brewed beer; made and sold charcoal; sold vegetables, fish, and poultry; and ran inns. In many towns, the wives and widows of master craftsmen were admitted to guilds. These guildswomen had many of the privileges of a master, including the right to train apprentices.

Because many towns were situated on land belonging to lords or on the sites of old Roman towns ruled by bishops, these communities at first came under feudal authority. In some instances, lords encouraged the founding of towns, for urban industry and commerce brought wealth to the region. However, tensions soon developed between merchants, who sought freedom from feudal restrictions that interfered with their pursuit of financial gain, and lords and bishops, who wanted to preserve their authority over the towns. Townspeople, or burghers (a *burg* is a fortified town), refused to be treated as serfs bound to a lord and liable for personal services and customary dues. The burghers wanted to travel, trade, marry, and dispose of their property as they pleased; they wanted to make their own laws and levy their own taxes. Sometimes by fighting, but more often by payments of money, townspeople obtained charters from the lords giving them the right to set up their own councils. These assemblies passed laws, collected taxes, and formed courts, which enforced the laws. Towns became more or less self-governing municipalities, the first since Greco-Roman days.

The leading citizens of the towns, the patricians, were members of the merchant guilds who engaged in commerce, industry, and banking. Some patricians in the prosperous Italian towns enjoyed great wealth, owned considerable real estate, and conducted business transactions involving large sums. These people generally dominated town politics; often they obtained country estates and intermarried with the feudal aristocracy. Successful doctors and lawyers also belonged to the urban elite. Below them on the social scale were master craftsmen in the more lucrative crafts (goldsmiths, for example) and large retailers. Then came small retailers, masters in the less profitable crafts, and journeymen training to be masters. At the bottom were the laboring poor—the bulk of the population—who had no special skills and were subject to unemployment.

In virtually every medieval city, the church was the largest property owner. Because the church frowned on the pursuit of wealth, many businessmen had guilt pangs, particularly in old age, about the way they had earned their livelihood. Compounding their guilt and fear of hellfire was an awareness of having violated the church's strict prohibitions against practicing usury. To allay these concerns about the destiny of their souls, businesspeople often bequeathed money and property to the church. These bequests helped to finance hospitals and schools, which were the church's responsibility.

In a number of ways, towns loosened the hold of lords on serfs. "City air makes a man free," went a medieval proverb. Seeking freedom and fortune, serfs fled to the new towns, where, according to custom, lords could no longer reclaim them after a year and a day. Enterprising serfs earned money by selling food to townspeople. When the serfs acquired a sufficient sum of money, they bought their freedom from lords, who needed cash to pay for goods bought from merchants. Lords increasingly began to accept fixed cash payments from serfs in place of labor services or foodstuffs. As serfs met their obligations to lords with money, they gradually became rent-paying tenants and, in time, were no longer bound to the lord's land. The manorial system of personal relations and mutual obligations was disintegrating.

The activities of townspeople made them a new breed; they engaged in business and had money and freedom. Their world was the market rather than the church, the castle, or the manor. Townspeople were freeing themselves from the prejudices both of feudal aristocrats, who considered trade and manual work degrading, and of the clergy, who cursed the pursuit of riches as sordid and shameful and an obstacle to salvation. They revived the Greco-Roman ideal of active citizens devoted to their city. Processions, celebrations, and feasts commemorating holy days or memorable events in the town's history strengthened civic bonds. An emerging secular civic life, combined with the new value given to business and the need for some secular education in order to handle business transactions, produced a spiritual counterforce to Christian otherworldliness that would gain momentum in succeeding centuries. The townspeople were critical, dynamic, and progressive—a force for change.

THE RISE OF STATES

The revival of trade and the burgeoning of towns signaled a growing vitality in Latin Christendom. Another sign of strength was the greater order and security provided by the emergence of states.

While feudalism fostered a Europe that was split into many local regions, each ruled by a lord, the church envisioned a vast Christian commonwealth, **Respublica Christiana,** governed by an emperor who was guided by the pope. During the High Middle Ages, the ideal of a universal Christian community seemed close to fruition. Never again would Europe possess such spiritual unity.

But other forces were propelling Europe in a different direction. Aided by educated and trained officials who enforced royal law, tried people in royal courts, and collected royal taxes—all of which served to reduce the power of local lords— kings expanded their territory and slowly fashioned strong central governments. Gradually, subjects began to transfer their prime loyalty from the church and the lords to the person of the king. These developments laid the foundations of European states. Not all regions followed the same pattern. Whereas England and France achieved a large measure of unity during the Middle Ages, the areas that later became Germany and Italy remained divided, with numerous independent territories.

England

After the Roman legions abandoned England in the fifth century, the Germanic Angles and Saxons invaded the island and established several small kingdoms. In the ninth century, the Danes— one group of the Northmen who raided Western Europe—conquered most of Anglo-Saxon England. But the Saxon kingdom of Wessex, ruled by Alfred the Great (871–899), survived. To resist the Danes, Alfred strengthened his army and built a fleet. To stem the decline of learning that accompanied the Danish invasions, Alfred, like Charlemagne, founded a palace school, bringing to it scholars from other areas. Alfred himself studied Latin and translated a work of Pope Gregory I into Anglo-Saxon. He also had other works translated into Anglo-Saxon, including Boethius's *Consolation of Philosophy.* Alfred's descendants gradually regained land from the Danes and reestablished Anglo-Saxon control over the island.

In 1066, the Normans—those Northmen who had first raided and then settled in France— defeated the Anglo-Saxons in the battle of Hastings and became masters of England. Normans replaced the Anglo-Saxon aristocracy and ecclesiastical hierarchy. Determined to establish effective control over his new kingdom, William the Conqueror (1027–1087), duke of Normandy (in western France), kept one-sixth of conquered England for himself. In accordance with feudal practice, he distributed the rest among his Norman nobles, who swore an oath of loyalty to him and provided him with military assistance. But William made certain that no feudal baron had enough land or soldiers to threaten his power. The Norman conquest strengthened the king's position as never before.

To tighten royal control, William retained some Anglo-Saxon administrative practices. The land remained divided into *shires* (counties) administered by *sheriffs* (royal agents). This structure gave the king control over local government. To determine how much money he could demand, William ordered a vast census taken of people and property in every village. Census data, compiled in the *Domesday Book,* indicated the number of tenants, cattle, sheep, and pigs and the quantities of farm equipment throughout the realm. Thus, better than any other monarch of his day, William knew what the assets of his kingdom were. Because William conquered England in one stroke, his successors did not have to travel the long, painful road to national unity that French monarchs had to take.

Crucial to shaping national unity was the development of common law. When Henry I became king in 1100, England had conflicting baronial claims and legal traditions, which were a barrier to unity. These legal traditions included Anglo-Saxon law, feudal law introduced by the Normans from France, church law, and the commercial law emerging among the town businesspeople. During the reigns of Henry I (1100–1135) and Henry II (1154–1189), royal judges traveled to different parts of the kingdom. Throughout England, important cases began to be tried in the king's court rather than in local courts, thereby increasing royal power. The decisions of royal judges were recorded and used as guides for future cases. In this way, a law common to the whole land gradually came to prevail over the customary law of a specific locality. Because common law applied to all England, it served as a force for unity. It also provided a fairer system of justice. Common law remains the foundation of the English legal system and the legal systems of lands settled by English people, including the United States.

Henry II made an early form of trial by jury a regular procedure for many cases heard in the king's court, laying the foundations of the modern judicial system. Twelve men familiar with the facts of the case appeared before the king's justices and were asked under oath if the plaintiff's statement was true. The justices based their decisions on the answers. Henry II also ordered representatives of a given locality to report under oath to visiting royal judges any local persons who were suspected of murder or robbery. This indictment jury was the ancestor of the modern grand jury.

The growth of an efficient financial administration paralleled the development of a strong judicial system. The Exchequer, the royal accounting office, was formed during the early years of Henry I's reign. Its officials saw to the collection of all revenues owed the king. Like the judges, these officials formed a class of professional administrators who were personally loyal to the king.

King John (1199–1216) inadvertently precipitated a situation that led to another step in the political development of England. Fighting a costly and losing war with the king of France, John had coerced his vassals into giving him more and more revenue; he had also punished some vassals without a proper trial. In 1215, the angry barons rebelled and compelled John to fix his seal to a document called Magna Carta, or Great Charter. Magna Carta is celebrated as the root of the uniquely English respect for basic rights and liberties. Although essentially a feudal document directed against a king who had violated feudal barons' rights, Magna Carta stated certain principles that eventually could be interpreted more widely.

Over the centuries, these principles were expanded to protect the liberties of the English against governmental oppression. Magna Carta stated that no unusual feudal dues "shall be imposed in our kingdom except by the common consent of our kingdom." In time, this right came to mean that the king could not levy taxes without the consent of Parliament, the governmental body that represents the English people. Magna Carta also provided that "no freeman shall be taken or imprisoned . . . save by the lawful judgment of his peers or by the law of the land." The barons who drew up the document had intended

WOMEN WORKERS. At times noble ladies fought side by side with men when their castle was attacked. Here women hurl rocks and shoot arrows at the attackers. (Bibliotheque Royale de Belgique.)

it to mean that they must be tried by fellow barons. As time passed, these words were regarded as a guarantee of trial by jury for all men, a prohibition against arbitrary arrest, and a command to dispense justice fully, freely, and equally. Implied in Magna Carta is the idea that the king cannot rule as he pleases but must govern according to the law: not even the king can violate the law of the nation. Centuries afterward, when the English sought to limit the king's power, they would interpret Magna Carta in this way.

Anglo-Saxon England retained the Germanic tradition that the king should consider the advice of the leading men in the land. William the Conqueror continued this practice by seeking the opinions of leading nobles and bishops. In the thirteenth century, it became accepted custom that the king should not decide major issues without consulting these advisers, who assembled together as the Great Council. Lesser nobility and townspeople also began to be summoned to meet with the king. These two groups were eventually called the House of Lords

(bishops and nobles) and the House of Commons (knights and burghers). Thus did the English Parliament evolve, and by the mid-fourteenth century, it was a permanent institution of government.

Frequently in need of money but unable to levy new taxes without the approval of Parliament, the king had to turn to that body for help. Parliament used this control over money matters to enhance its power. The tradition grew that the power to govern rested not with the king alone but with the king and Parliament together.

During the Middle Ages, England became a centralized and unified state. But the king did not have unlimited power; he was not above the law. The rights of the people were protected by certain principles implicit in the common law and Magna Carta and by the power of Parliament.

France

In the 150 years after Charlemagne's death, the western part of his empire, which was destined to become France, faced terrible ordeals. Charlemagne's heirs fought one another for the crown; the Vikings raided everywhere their ships would carry them; Muslims from Spain plundered the southern coast; and strong lords usurped power for themselves. With the Carolingian family unable to maintain the throne, the great lords bestowed the title of king on one of their own. In 987, they chose Hugh Capet (987–996), the count of Paris. Because many great lords held territories far larger than those of Hugh, the French king did not seem a threat to noble power. But Hugh strengthened the French monarchy by having the lords also elect his son as his co-ruler. This practice continued until it became understood that the crown would remain with the Capetian family.

With the accession of Louis VI (1108–1137), a two-hundred-year period of steadily increasing royal power began. Louis started this trend by successfully subduing the barons in his own duchy. A decisive figure in the expansion of French royal sway was Philip Augustus (1180–1223). Philip struck successfully at King John of England (of Magna Carta fame), who held more territory as feudal lord in France than Philip did. When William, duke of Normandy, conquered England in 1066, he became ruler of England and Normandy;

Map 10.1 THE KINGDOM OF FRANCE, **1180–1314** Through wars, alliances, and marriages, French kings expanded their territory. (Copyright © 2013 Cengage Learning.)

William's great-grandson Henry II acquired much of southern France through his marriage to Eleanor of Aquitaine (c. 1122–1204) in 1152. Thus, as a result of the Norman Conquest and intermarriage, the destinies of France and England were closely intertwined until the end of the Middle Ages. By stripping King John of most of his French territory (Normandy, Anjou, and much of Aquitaine),

Philip trebled the size of his kingdom and became stronger than any French lord.

Louis IX (1226–1270)—pious, compassionate, and conscientious and a genuine lover of peace—was perhaps the best-loved French monarch of the Middle Ages. Departing from feudal precedent, Louis issued ordinances for the entire realm without seeking the consent of his vassals.

One ordinance prohibited private warfare among the nobility. Another promoted the nationwide circulation of coins produced by royal mints. These ordinances furthered royal power and promoted order.

Under Louis IX and his successors, the power of the French monarch continued to grow. Kings added to their lands by warfare and marriage; they devised new ways of raising money, including taxing the clergy. A particularly effective way of increasing the monarch's power was by extending royal justice. In the thirteenth century, the king's court, the *parlement,* became the highest court in France. Quarrels between the king and his vassals were resolved in the parlement, and many cases previously tried in lords' courts were transferred to the king's court. Moreover, because the decision of feudal courts could be appealed to the parlement, lords no longer had the last say on legal questions.

At the beginning of the fourteenth century, Philip IV (the Fair) engaged in a struggle with the papacy (see page 279). Seeking to demonstrate that he had the support of his subjects, Philip summoned representatives of the church (First Estate), the nobility (Second Estate), and the townspeople (Third Estate) to meet in a national assembly known as the Estates General. This assembly would be called again to vote funds for the crown. Unlike the English Parliament, the Estates General never became an important body in French political life, and it never succeeded in controlling the monarch. Whereas the basis for limited monarchy had been established in England, no comparable checks on the king's power developed in France. By the end of the Middle Ages, French kings had succeeded in creating a unified state, but regional and local loyalties remained strong and persisted for centuries.

Germany

After the destruction of Charlemagne's empire, its German territories were broken into large duchies. Following traditional Germanic practice, the ruling dukes elected one of their own as king. The German king, however, had little authority outside his own duchy. Some German kings tried not to antagonize the dukes, but Otto the Great (936–973) was determined to control them. He entered into an alliance with German bishops and archbishops, who could provide him with fighting

THIRTEENTH-CENTURY POLITICS. The representative assembly, antecedent of the modern parliament, was an original achievement of the Middle Ages. Here the king of Aragon presides over the *cortes,* an assembly representing clergy, nobles, and townspeople. (MAS Barcelona/Institut Amattler d'Art Hispanic.)

men and trained administrators—a policy continued by his successors.

In 951, Otto marched into northern Italy in an attempt to assert his influence. Ten years later, he returned to protect the pope from his Italian enemies. In 962, emulating the coronation of Charlemagne, the pope crowned Otto "Emperor of the Romans" (later the title would be changed to "Holy Roman Emperor").

The revival of the empire meant that the history of medieval Germany was closely tied to that of Italy and the papacy. Otto and his successors wanted to dominate both Italy, which had been part of Charlemagne's empire, and the pope—an ambition that embroiled the Holy Roman Emperor in a life-and-death struggle with the papacy. The papacy allied itself with the German dukes and the Italian cities, enemies of the emperor. German intervention in papal politics and Italian lands was the principal reason that German territories did not achieve unity in the Middle Ages.

The Emergence of Representative Institutions

One great contribution of the Middle Ages to the modern world was the representative institution. Representative assemblies, or parliaments, had their beginnings at the end of the twelfth century in the Spanish kingdom of León. In the thirteenth century, they developed in other Spanish kingdoms—Castile, Aragon, Catalonia, and Valencia—as well as in Portugal, England, and the Holy Roman Empire. In the fourteenth century, parliaments formed in France and the Netherlands.

Kings generally came to accept the principles that parliamentary consent was required for levying taxes and that the king should consult parliament about important laws and obtain its approval. By and large, the parliaments had grown out of royal dependence on the nobility for military support. Because of this dependence, monarchs considered it wise to listen to the opinions of the lords. Consequently, it became customary for the king to summon councils to discuss matters of war and peace and other vital questions. Since the high clergy constituted an important group in the realm, they too were consulted. As towns gained in wealth and significance, townspeople were also asked to royal councils. Leading nobles came to represent the nobility as an order of society; members of the upper clergy—archbishops, bishops, and abbots—represented the entire clergy; and deputies from the towns represented the townspeople. An important tradition had been established: the duty of the monarch to seek advice and consent on issues of concern to his subjects. Perhaps the practice of representative government was influenced by those church lawyers who held that the pope should seek the guidance of the Christian community as expressed in church councils—meetings of representatives of the clergy.

To be sure, in succeeding centuries, parliaments would be either ignored or dominated by kings. Nevertheless, the principle of constitutional government—government by consent—was woven into the fabric of Western society. The representative parliament is unique to Western civilization; it has no parallel in the political systems of the non-European world. Originating in the Middle Ages, the representative assembly is a distinct achievement and contribution of Western civilization.

THE GROWTH OF PAPAL POWER

In the High Middle Ages, a growing spiritual vitality accompanied economic recovery and increasing political stability. It was marked by several developments. The common people were showing greater devotion to the church. Within the church, reform movements were attacking clerical abuses, and the papacy was becoming more powerful. A holy war against the Muslims was drawing the Christian community closer together. During this period, the church tried with great determination to make society follow divine standards: it tried to shape institutions and cultural expressions according to a comprehensive Christian outlook.

The Sacraments

As the sole interpreters of God's revelation and the sole ministers of his sacraments—sacred rites—the clergy imposed and supervised the moral outlook of Christendom. Divine grace was channeled through seven sacraments, which could be administered only by the clergy, the indispensable intermediary between individuals and God. On persons who resisted its authority, the church could impose the penalty of excommunication—expulsion from the church and denial of the sacraments, without which there could be no salvation.

The seven sacraments involved the church in the lives of individuals from birth to death. Baptism cleansed individuals—usually infants—of the stain of original sin. Confirmation granted additional **grace** to previously baptized young adults. Matrimony made marriage a holy union. Extreme unction, administered to the dying, was intended to remove the remains of sin. The sacrament of the Eucharist, derived from Gospel accounts of Christ's Last Supper, took place within a liturgical service, the Mass. In a solemn ceremony, bread and wine were miraculously transformed into the substance of the body and blood of Christ, which the priest administered, allowing believers to partake of Christ's saving grace. The sacrament of penance required sinners to show sorrow for their sins, to confess them to a priest, and to perform an act of contrition: prayer, fasting, almsgiving, or a pilgrimage to a holy shrine. Through the priest, the sinner could receive absolution and be rescued from spending eternity in hell. This sacrament enabled the church to enforce its moral standards throughout Latin Christendom. The final sacrament, ordination, consecrated men to serve as clergy.

Gregorian Reform

By the tenth century, the church was Western Europe's leading landowner, owning perhaps a third of the land in Italy and vast properties in other lands. However, the papacy was in no position to exercise commanding leadership over Latin Christendom. The office of pope had fallen under the domination of aristocratic families; they conspired and on occasion murdered in order to place one of their own on the wealthy and powerful throne of Saint Peter. As the papacy became a prize for Rome's leading families, it was not at all unusual for popes themselves to be involved in conspiracies and assassinations. Also weakening the authority of the papacy were local lords, who dominated churches and monasteries by appointing bishops and abbots and by collecting the income from church taxes. These bishops and abbots, appointed by lords for political reasons, lacked the spiritual devotion to maintain high standards of discipline among the priests and monks.

What raised the power of the papacy to unprecedented heights was the emergence of a reform movement, particularly in French and German monasteries. High-minded monks called for a reawakening of spiritual fervor and the elimination of moral laxity among the clergy. They particularly denounced the concern for worldly goods, the taking of mistresses, and the diminishing commitment to the Benedictine rule. Of the many monasteries that took part in this reform movement, the Benedictine monks of Cluny, in Burgundy, France, were the most influential.

In the middle of the eleventh century, popes came under the influence of the monastic reformers.

In 1059, a special synod, convened by the reform-minded Pope Nicholas II, moved to end the interference of Roman nobles and German Holy Roman Emperors in choosing the pope. Henceforth, a select group of clergymen in Rome, called *cardinals,* would be responsible for picking a new pontiff.

The reform movement found its most zealous exponent in the person of Hildebrand, who became Pope Gregory VII in 1073. Gregory insisted that human society was part of a divinely ordered universe, governed by God's universal law, and as the supreme spiritual leader of Christendom, the pope was charged with the mission of establishing a Christian society on earth. As successor to Saint Peter, the pope had the final word on matters of faith and doctrine. All bishops came under his authority; so too did kings, whose powers should be used for Christian ends. Disobeying the pope, God's viceroy on earth, constituted disobedience to God himself. The pope was responsible for instructing rulers in the proper use of their God-given powers, and kings had the solemn duty to obey these instructions. If the king failed in his Christian duty, the pope could deny him his right to rule. Responsible for implementing God's law, the pope could never take a subordinate position to kings.

Like no other pope before him, Gregory VII made a determined effort to assert the preeminence of the papacy over both the church hierarchy and secular rulers. This determination led to a bitter struggle between the papacy and the German monarch and future Holy Roman Emperor Henry IV. The dispute was a dramatic confrontation between two competing versions of the relationship between secular and spiritual authority.

Through his reforms, Gregory VII intended to improve the moral quality of the clergy and to liberate the church from all control by secular authorities. He forbade priests who had wives or concubines to celebrate Mass, deposed clergy who had bought their offices, excommunicated bishops and abbots who had received their estates from a lay lord, and expelled from the church lay lords who invested bishops with their office. The appointment of bishops, Pope Gregory insisted, should be controlled entirely by the church.

This last point touched off the conflict, called the Investiture Controversy, between King Henry and Pope Gregory. Bishops served a dual function. On the one hand, they belonged to the spiritual community of the church; on the other hand, as members of the nobility and holders of estates, they were also integrated into the feudal order. Traditionally, emperors had both granted bishops their feudal authority and invested them with their spiritual authority. In maintaining that no lay rulers could confer ecclesiastical offices on their appointees, Pope Gregory threatened Henry's authority.

In earlier times, seeking allies in the conflict with feudal nobility, German kings had made vassals of the upper clergy. In return for a fief, bishops had agreed to provide troops for a monarch in his struggle against the lords. But if kings had no control over the appointment of bishops—in accordance with Pope Gregory's view—they would lose the allegiance, military support, and financial assistance of their most important allies. To German monarchs, bishops were officers of the state who served the throne. Moreover, if they agreed to Gregory's demands, German kings would lose their freedom of action and be dominated by the Roman pontiff. Henry IV regarded Gregory VII as a fanatic who trampled on custom, meddled in German state affairs, and challenged legitimate rulers established by God, thereby threatening to subordinate kingship to the papacy.

With the approval of the German bishops, Henry called for Pope Gregory to descend from the throne of Saint Peter. Gregory in turn excommunicated Henry and deposed him as king. German lands were soon embroiled in a civil war as German lords used the quarrel to strike at Henry's power. Finally, Henry's troops crossed the Alps, successfully attacked Rome, and installed a new pope, who crowned Henry emperor of the Romans. Gregory died in exile in 1085.

In 1122, the papacy and Emperor Henry V reached a compromise. Bishops were to be elected exclusively by the church and invested with the staff and the ring—symbols of spiritual power—by the archbishop, not the king. This change signified that a bishop owed his role as spiritual leader to the church only. But the king would grant the bishop the scepter, to indicate that the bishop was also the recipient of a fief and the king's vassal, owing feudal obligations to the crown. This compromise, called the Concordat of Worms, recognized the dual function of the bishop as a spiritual leader in the church and a feudal landowner.

Similar settlements had been reached with the kings of France and England several years earlier.

The conflict between the papacy and the German rulers continued after the Concordat of Worms—a contest for supremacy between the heir of Saint Peter and the heir of Charlemagne. German monarchs wanted to control the papacy and the prosperous northern Italian cities. When Frederick I (1152–1190), known as Frederick Barbarossa (Red Beard), tried to assert authority over these cities, they resisted. In 1176, the armies of an alliance of Italian cities, supported by the pope, trounced Frederick's forces at the battle of Legnano. The Italian infantry showed that it could defeat knights on horseback, and Frederick was compelled to recognize the independence of the Italian cities. His numerous expeditions to Italy weakened his authority. German princes strengthened themselves at the expense of the monarchy, thereby continuing to preclude German unity.

The Crusades

Like the movement for spiritual renewal associated with the Cluniac reformers, the Crusades—wars to regain the Holy Land from the Muslims—were an outpouring of Christian zeal and an attempt by the papacy to assert its preeminence. Along with the renewal of commerce and the growth of towns, the Crusades were a sign of vitality and self-confidence in Western Europe. The victims of earlier Muslim attacks, Latin Christians now took the offensive. Furthermore, the Crusades were part of a general movement of European expansion during the High Middle Ages. Latin Christians were venturing forth as pioneers to open new lands to cultivation and as conquerors to expand the borders of Christendom.

By the middle of the eleventh century, forces from the cities of Genoa and Pisa had driven the Muslims from Sardinia. By 1091, Normans had taken Sicily from the Muslims and southern Italy from Byzantium. With the support of the papacy, Christian knights engaged in the long struggle to drive the Muslims from Spain; by 1248, after more than two centuries of conflict, only the small southern kingdom of Granada remained in Muslim hands. Germans conquered and colonized lands south of the Baltic coast inhabited by

DEPICTION OF THE SIEGE OF TYRE IN 1124. The fall of the city gave Christians control of the Syrian coast. (Tyre being blockaded by the Venetian fleet and besieged by Crusader knighthood, from the Estoire d'Outremer (vellum and gold leaf), William of Tyre (c.1130–85)/Bibliotheque Nationale, Paris, France/The Bridgeman Art Library International.)

non-Christian Slavs, Balts, and Prussians. German settlers brought with them Christianity and German language and culture. They cleared vast tracts of virgin land for farming and established towns, bishoprics, and monasteries in a region where urban life had been virtually unknown.

In the eleventh century, the Seljuk Turks, who had earlier embraced Islam, conquered vast regions of the Near East, including Anatolia, a province of the Byzantine Empire. With the death of the Turkish sultan in 1092, the Seljuk Empire broke up, which reduced the pressure on Byzantium. Seeking to strengthen his army in preparation for the reconquest of Anatolia, Byzantine emperor Alexius appealed to Western rulers for mercenaries.

Pope Urban II, at the Council of Clermont (in France) in 1095, exaggerated the danger confronting Eastern Christianity. He called for a holy crusade against the heathen Turks, whom he accused of defiling and destroying Christian churches. Several months later, he expanded his objectives

to include the conquest of Jerusalem. A Christian army, mobilized by the papacy to defend the faith and to regain the Holy Land from nonbelievers, accorded with the papal concept of a just war; it would channel the endemic violence of Europe's warrior class in a Christian direction. A crusade against the Muslims also held the promise of bringing the Eastern church, which had formally broken with Rome in 1054, under papal leadership. In organizing a crusade for Christian ends, Urban II, like Gregory VII in his struggle with Henry IV, sought to demonstrate the supremacy of the pope.

What motivated the knights and others who responded to Urban's appeal? To some younger sons with no hope of inheriting land at home, a crusade offered an opportunity to gain land by conquest. No doubt the Crusaders regarded themselves as armed pilgrims dedicated to rescuing holy places from the hated Muslims. Through the years, Christian pilgrims had made the journey to Jerusalem to do penance for crimes against the church and to demonstrate their piety. These pilgrims and other devout Christians found it deplorable that Christian holy places were controlled by heathen Muslims. Moreover, Urban declared that participation in a crusade was itself an act of penance, an acceptable way of demonstrating sorrow for sin. In their eagerness to recruit warriors, popular preachers went even further: they promised cancellation of penalties for sin. To a knight, a crusade was no doubt a great adventure that promised land, glory, and plunder, but it was also an opportunity to remit sins by engaging in a holy war. The enthusiasm with which knights became Christian warriors demonstrated the extent to which the warrior mentality of the nobles had become permeated by Christian principles.

Stirred by popular preachers, the common people also became gripped by the crusading spirit. The most remarkable of the evangelists was Peter the Hermit, who rode his donkey through the French countryside arousing the religious

Map 10.2 **THE HOLY ROMAN EMPIRE, c. 1200** ▶
Unable to overcome the German princes, Holy Roman Emperors, unlike French and English rulers, could not build a unified state during the Middle Ages. Germany did not achieve unity until the late nineteenth century. (Copyright © 2013 Cengage Learning.)

CAPTURE OF JERUSALEM. Gripped by religious frenzy, the Crusaders, "dripping with blood," massacred the Muslim and Jewish inhabitants of Jerusalem. (Snark/Art Resource, N.Y.)

zeal of plain folk. Swayed by the old man's eloquence, thousands of poor people abandoned their villages and joined Peter's march to Jerusalem. As this army of the poor crossed Germany, the credulous peasants expected to find Jerusalem just beyond the horizon; some thought that Peter was leading them straight to heaven. While Peter's army made its way to Constantinople, another army of commoners recruited in Germany sought to do God's work by massacring the Jews of the Rhineland, despite the efforts of bishops to protect them. Unlike Peter's army, these commoners never reached Constantinople; after plundering Hungary, they were slaughtered by Hungarians (Magyars). Camped in the suburbs of Constantinople, Peter's restless recruits crossed from Byzantine-controlled land into Turkish territory, where they too were massacred. Faith alone could not win Jerusalem.

Departing later than the commoners, an army of knights assembled at Constantinople in the spring of 1097. After enduring the long march through Anatolia, the Christian army arrived at Antioch in Syria, which it captured after a long siege. In June 1099, three years after Urban's appeal, the soldiers of the First Crusade (1096–1099) stood outside the walls of Jerusalem. Using siege weapons, they broke into the city and slaughtered Muslims and Jews. An eyewitness recorded the scene.

> *It was impossible to look upon the vast numbers of the slain without horror; everywhere lay fragments of human bodies, and the very ground was covered with the blood of the slain. It was not alone the spectacle of headless bodies and mutilated limbs strewn in all directions that roused horror in all who looked upon them. Still more dreadful was it to gaze upon the victors themselves, dripping with blood from head to foot, an ominous sight which brought terror to all who met them. . . .*

> *When at last the city had been set in order in this way, arms were laid aside. Then, clad in fresh garments, with clean hands and bare feet, in humility and contrition, [the victors] began to make the rounds of the venerable places which the Saviour had deigned to sanctify and make glorious with His bodily presence. With tearful sighs and heartfelt emotion they pressed kisses upon these revered spots.[2]*

Weakened by local rivalries and religious quarrels, the Muslim world failed to unite against the Christian invaders, who, besides capturing Jerusalem, carved out four small states in Syria and Palestine. How long could these Christian states, islands in a Muslim sea, endure against a Muslim counteroffensive?

Never resigned to the establishment of Christian states in their midst, Muslim leaders called for a jihad, or holy war. In 1144, one of the Crusader states, the County of Edessa, in Syria, fell to the resurgent forces of Islam. Alarmed by the loss of

Map 10.3 THE ROUTES OF THE CRUSADES ▶
In 1291, almost two hundred years after Pope Urban II's appeal for a crusade, the last Christian stronghold in the Near East had fallen.

245

Saladin

Salah al-Din Yusuf (1137–1193), known to the Western world as Saladin, recaptured Jerusalem from the Franks in 1187. Born into a prominent Kurdish family, Saladin served the emir of Syria, whose troops invaded Egypt in 1167. Rising quickly, Saladin was appointed vizier of Egypt and then confirmed as sultan of Egypt and Syria. After extending his authority over Muslim-controlled territories of Egypt, Syria, and Palestine, Saladin, deeply committed to jihad, turned against the Franks. In particular, he vowed to liberate Islamic holy places in Jerusalem from Christian control.

In 1187, Saladin lured the Franks into an engagement at Hittin, near Tiberias, in northern Palestine. Marching all day, the exhausted and thirst-crazed Franks suffered terrible losses when, in desperation, they threw themselves at the prepared Muslim lines, which blocked the Franks from reaching Lake Tiberias and its life-giving water. After the victory at Hittin, Saladin's forces took several Christian strongholds, most of which surrendered without a fight. Then Saladin turned on Jerusalem.

Living up to his reputation as a man of honor and magnanimity, Saladin made the Christian inhabitants of Jerusalem a generous proposal. If the Franks surrendered, Christians would be free to leave the city with their property, and Christian pilgrims would not be harmed. But the Frankish lords would not surrender without a fight the city where Jesus had been crucified. On September 20, 1187, Saladin's soldiers besieged Jerusalem and began battering its walls. A Muslim historian

Edessa, Pope Eugenius II called for the Second Crusade (1147–1149), which was a complete failure.

After 1174, Saladin, a brilliant commander, became the most powerful leader in the Muslim Near East. In 1187, he invaded Palestine, annihilated a Christian army near Nazareth, and recaptured Jerusalem. In contrast to Christian knights of the First Crusade, who filled Jerusalem with blood and corpses, Saladin permitted no slaughter. The capture of Jerusalem led to the Third Crusade (1189–1192), in which some of Europe's most prominent rulers participated—Richard I, the Lion-Hearted, of England; Philip Augustus of France; and Frederick Barbarossa of Germany. The Crusaders captured Acre and Jaffa, but Jerusalem remained in Muslim hands.

Pope Innocent III, who called the Fourth Crusade (1202–1204), was enraged by the actions of the Crusaders. They had first attacked the Christian port of Zara, which was controlled by the king of Hungary, and then looted and defiled churches and massacred Byzantines in Constantinople. This shameful behavior, along with the belief that the papacy was exploiting the crusading ideal to extend its own power, weakened both the crusading zeal of Christendom and the moral authority of the papacy. It also left a legacy of bitterness and distrust that still taints relations between the Eastern Orthodoxy and other Christians.

Other Crusades followed, including even the Children's Crusade in 1212. Stirred by Stephen of Cloyes, a young shepherd boy who claimed that Christ had communicated with him, thousands of French peasant children, accompanied by priests, marched to Marseilles, where they expected the Mediterranean Sea to part, permitting them to continue their march to the Holy Land. When the miracle did not occur, the children boarded seven ships offered to them by William the Pig and Hugo the Iron, two seemingly pious townsmen. Two of the ships were lost in a terrible storm, and the other five were captured by Muslim pirates, with whom William and Hugo had worked out a deal. The children were sold into slavery in North Africa, and as far as is known, none ever returned (one priest eventually did).

Despite other crusades, the position of the Christian states in the Near East continued to deteriorate. In 1291, almost two centuries after Pope noted: "Then began the fiercest struggle imaginable; each side looked on the fight as an absolute religious obligation. There was no need for a superior authority to drive them on."* On October 2, the Muslims rushed through the breached walls and captured the city. In stark contrast to the Christian conquest of Jerusalem in 1099, Saladin permitted no massacre and no plundering. The Franks could escape enslavement by paying a moderate ransom, and in an extraordinary display of tolerance, Saladin guarded Christian holy places from Muslims seeking revenge for earlier Frankish brutalities.

---

*Excerpted in Francesco Gabriel, ed., *Arab Historians of the Crusades* (Berkeley: University of California Press, 1969), 130.

Urban's appeal, the last Christian strongholds in the Near East fell.

The Crusades had some immediate effects on Latin Christendom. They may have contributed to the decline of feudalism and the strengthening of monarchy because many lords were killed in battle or squandered their wealth financing expeditions to the Holy Land. The Crusades did foster trade between Latin Christendom and the East, but the revival of trade had already begun and would have proceeded without the Crusades. The Crusades sparked an interest in geography and travel; introduced Westerners to new foods, clothing, and architecture; and became a theme in literature. Nevertheless, they did not significantly influence European intellectual progress. The Crusaders had no contact with Muslim centers of learning in the Near East; it was through Spain and Sicily that Muslim learning penetrated Latin Christendom and helped stimulate the cultural awakening of the twelfth and thirteenth centuries. Over the centuries, some have praised the Crusades for inspiring idealism and heroism. Others, however, have castigated the movement for corrupting the Christian spirit and unleashing religious intolerance and fanaticism—including the massacre of Jews in the Rhineland and of Muslims and Jews in Jerusalem—which would lead to strife in future centuries. The Crusades remain a crucial component of the ideology of contemporary Islamic extremists.

Dissenters and Reformers

Freedom of religion is a modern concept; it was totally alien to the medieval outlook. Regarding itself as the possessor and guardian of divine, and therefore ultimate, truth, the church felt a profound obligation to purge Christendom of **heresy**—beliefs that challenged Christian orthodoxy. To the church, heretics had committed treason against God and were carriers of a deadly infection. Heresy was the work of Satan; lured by false ideas, people might abandon the true faith and deny themselves salvation. The church could never create a Christian world community if heretics rebelled against clerical authority and created divisions among the faithful. In the eyes of the church, heretics not only obstructed individual salvation but also undermined the foundations of society. The church believed that it had a sacred duty to eradicate this moral defect.

To compel obedience, the church used its power of excommunication. An excommunicated person could not receive the sacraments or attend church services—fearful punishments in an age of faith. In dealing with a recalcitrant ruler, the church could declare an interdict on his territory, which in effect denied the ruler's subjects the sacraments (although exceptions could be made). The church hoped that the pressure exerted by an aroused populace would compel the offending ruler to mend his ways.

The church also conducted heresy trials. Before the thirteenth century, local bishops were responsible for locating heretics and putting them on trial. Gregory IX (1227–1241) started to use Franciscans and Dominicans (see page 249) as official investigators, in effect creating a permanent tribunal, the Inquisition, directly under the pope's authority. An inquisitor and his staff established themselves in a region suspected of heresy. After taking testimony, often in secret, the inquisitors summoned suspects to answer accusations made against them. The accused were not told the names of their accusers, nor could they have legal defense or examine evidence of witnesses. They were tortured (torture had been sanctioned by Roman law), and those who persisted in their beliefs might be turned over to the civil authorities to be burned at the stake.

Religious dissent in the Middle Ages was often reformist in character. Inspired by the Gospels, reformers criticized the church for its wealth and involvement in worldly affairs. They called for a return to the simpler, purer life of Jesus and the Apostles. Reform movements drew support from the new class of town dwellers; the church often rebuked the way of life in towns and only slowly adjusted to the townspeople's spiritual needs.

The Waldensians.   In their zeal to emulate the moral purity and material poverty of the first followers of Jesus, reform-minded dissenters attacked ecclesiastical authority. The Waldensians, followers of Peter Waldo, a rich merchant of Lyons, were a case in point. Peter was greatly moved by a passage in Matthew: "If thou wilt be perfect go sell what thou hast and give to the poor and thou shalt have treasure in heaven" (19:22). In the 1170s, Peter distributed his property to the poor and attracted both male and female supporters. Like their leader, they committed themselves to poverty and to preaching the Gospel in the vernacular, or native tongue, rather than in the church's Latin, which many Christians did not understand. The Waldensians considered themselves true Christians, faithful to the spirit of the apostolic church. Repelled by Waldensian attacks against the immorality of the clergy and by the fact that these laypeople were preaching the Gospel without the permission of ecclesiastical authorities, the church condemned the movement as heretical. Despite persecution, however, the Waldensians continued to survive as a group in northern Italy.

The Cathari.   Catharism was the most radical heresy to confront the medieval church. This belief represented a curious mixture of Gnosticism and Manichaeism—Eastern religious movements that had competed with Christianity in the days of the Roman Empire—and of doctrines condemned as heretical by the early church. Carried to Italy and southern France by Bulgarian missionaries, Catharism gained followers in regions where opposition to the worldliness and wealth of the clergy was already strong.

Cathari tenets differed considerably from those of the church. The Cathari believed in an eternal conflict between the forces of the god of good and those of the god of evil. Because the evil god, whom they identified with the God of the Old Testament, created the world, this earthly home was evil. The soul, spiritual in nature, was good but was trapped in wicked flesh. Because sexual activity was responsible for imprisoning the spirit in the flesh, the Cathari urged abstinence to avoid the birth of still another wicked human being. They also abstained from eggs, cheese, milk, and meat because these foods were the products of sexual activity. (This rigorous asceticism was demanded only of a select few, the *perfecti* [perfect ones]; simple believers could marry, and their diets were not restricted.) The Cathari taught that, since the flesh is evil, Christ would not have taken a human form; hence, he could not have suffered on the cross or have been resurrected. Nor could God have issued forth from the evil flesh of the Virgin. According to Catharism, Jesus was not God but an angel. In order to enslave people, the evil god created the church, which demonstrated its wickedness by pursuing power and wealth. They saw themselves as the true church, the successors of Jesus' apostles. Repudiating the existing church, the Cathari organized their own ecclesiastical hierarchy. People were impressed with the ascetic and moral lifestyle of the perfecti.

The center for the Catharist heresy was southern France, where a strong tradition of protest existed against the moral laxity and materialism of the clergy. When the Cathari did not submit to peaceful persuasion, Innocent III called on kings and lords to exterminate Catharism with the sword before the infection spread throughout Christendom. Lasting from 1208 to 1229, the war against the Cathari was marked by brutality and fanaticism. An army of crusading knights led by a papal legate assembled in northern France; it headed south, massacring heretics in the belief they were doing the work of God. Soon command of the crusading army passed to Simon de Montfort, a minor baron with great ambition. De Montfort slaughtered suspected heretics throughout the county of Toulouse, and for a short time he held the title of count of Toulouse. The crusading knights had effectively broken the power of the nobles who had protected the heretics. Innocent III sent legates to the region to arrest and try the Cathari. Under his successor, Dominican and Franciscan inquisitors completed the task of exterminating them virtually to the last person, a horrendous slaughter that some refer to as medieval genocide.

The Franciscans and the Dominicans.

Driven by a zeal for reform, devout laypeople condemned the clergy for moral abuses. Sometimes their piety and resentment exploded into heresy; at other times, it was channeled into movements that served the church. Such was the case with the two great orders of friars, the Franciscans and the Dominicans.

Like Peter Waldo, Saint Francis of Assisi (c. 1181–1226) came from a wealthy merchant family. After undergoing an intense religious experience, Francis abandoned his possessions and devoted his life to imitating Christ. Dressed as a beggar, he wandered into villages and towns preaching, healing, and befriending. Unlike the monks who withdrew into walled fortresses, Francis proclaimed Christ's message to the poor of the towns. Like Peter Waldo, he preached a religion of personal feeling; like Jesus, he stretched out a hand of love to the poor, to the helpless, to the sick, and even to lepers, whom everyone feared to approach. The saintly Francis soon attracted disciples, called Little Brothers, who followed in the footsteps of their leader.

To suspicious churchmen, the Little Brothers seemed to be another heretical movement protesting against a wealthy and worldly church. However, Francis respected the authority of the priesthood and the validity of the sacraments. Recognizing that such a popular movement could be useful to the church, Innocent III allowed Francis to continue his mission. Innocent hoped that the Franciscans would help keep within the church those members of the laity who had deep religious feelings but were dissatisfied with the leadership of the traditional hierarchy.

As the Franciscans grew in popularity, the papacy exercised greater control over their activities; in time, the order was transformed from a spontaneous movement of inspired laymen into an organized agent of papal policy. The Franciscans served the church as teachers and missionaries in Eastern Europe, North Africa, the Near East, and China. The papacy set aside Francis's prohibition against

the Brothers owning churches, houses, and lands corporately. His desire to keep the movement a lay order was abandoned when the papacy granted the Brothers the right to hear confession. Francis's opposition to formal learning as irrelevant to preaching Gospel love was rejected when the movement began to urge university education for its members. Those who protested against these changes as a repudiation of Francis's spirit were persecuted, and a few were even burned at the stake as heretics.

The Dominican order was founded by Saint Dominic (c. 1170–1221), a Spanish nobleman who had preached against the Cathari in southern France. Believing that those well versed in Christian teaching could best combat heresy, Dominic, unlike Francis, insisted that his followers engage in study. In time, the Dominicans became some of the leading theologians in the universities. Like the Franciscans, they went out into the world to preach the Gospel and to proselytize. Dominican friars became the chief operators of the Inquisition. For their zeal in fighting heresy, they were known as "hounds of the Lord."

Innocent III: The Apex of Papal Power

During the pontificate of Innocent III (1198–1216), papal theocracy reached its zenith. More than any earlier pope, Innocent made the papacy the center of European political life. In the tradition of Gregory VII, he forcefully asserted the theory of papal monarchy. As head of the church, Vicar of Christ, and successor of Saint Peter, Innocent claimed the authority to intervene in the internal affairs of secular rulers when they threatened the good order of Christendom. According to Innocent, the pope, "lower than God but higher than man . . . judges all and is judged by no one."[3]

Innocent applied these principles of papal supremacy in his dealings with the princes of Europe. When King Philip Augustus of France repudiated Ingeborg of Denmark the day after their wedding and later divorced her to marry someone else, Innocent placed an interdict on France to compel Philip to take Ingeborg back. For two decades, Innocent III championed Ingeborg's cause until she finally became the French queen. When King John of England rejected the papal candidate for

Pope Innocent III: "Royal Power Derives Its Dignity from the Pontifical Authority"

In the tradition of Gregory VII, Innocent III (1198–1216), the most powerful of medieval popes, asserted the claim for papal supremacy.

The Creator of the universe set up two great luminaries in the firmament of heaven; the greater light to rule the day, the lesser light to rule the night. In the same way for the firmament of the universal Church, which is spoken of as heaven, he appointed two great dignities; the greater to bear rule over souls (these being, as it were, days), the lesser to bear rule over bodies (those being, as it were, nights). These dignities are the pontifical authority and the royal power. Furthermore, the moon derives her light from the sun, and is in truth inferior to the sun in both size and quality, in position as well as effect. In the same way the royal power derives its dignity from the pontifical authority; and the more closely it cleaves to the sphere of that authority the less is the light with which it is adorned; the further it is removed, the more it increases in splendour.

Question for Analysis

1. Why were papal claims likely to stir a conflict with royal rulers?

Henry Bettenson and Chris Maunder, *Documents of the Christian Church* (New York: Oxford University Press, 1999), 123.

archbishop of Canterbury, Stephen Langton, Innocent first laid an interdict on the country. Then he excommunicated John, who expressed his defiance by confiscating church property and by forcing many bishops into exile. However, when Innocent urged Philip Augustus of France to invade England, John backed down. He accepted Innocent's nominee for archbishop, returned the property to the church, welcomed the exiles back, and, as a sign of complete capitulation, turned his kingdom over to Innocent to receive it back as a fief. Thus, as vassals of the papacy, John and his successors were obligated to do homage to the pope and to pay him a feudal tribute. Innocent also laid interdicts on the Spanish kingdoms of Castile and León and on Norway and strove to make the Holy Roman Emperor subservient to the papacy.

Innocent called the Fourth Crusade against the Muslims and a crusade against the heretical Cathari. The culminating expression of Innocent's supremacy was the Fourth Lateran Council, summoned in 1215. Comprising some twelve hundred clergy and representatives of secular rulers, the council issued several far-reaching decrees. It maintained that the Eastern Orthodox church was subordinate to the Roman Catholic church, prohibited the state from taxing the clergy, and declared laws detrimental to the church null and void. The council made bishops responsible for ferreting out heretics in their dioceses and ordered secular authorities to punish convicted heretics. Insisting on high standards of behavior for the clergy, it also required each Catholic to confess his or her sins to a priest at least once a year and to perform the prescribed penance. Through this directive, the church tightened its control over the conscience of Europe. The council also decreed that in the sacrament of the Eucharist the body and blood of Christ are actually present in the bread and wine used in the sacrament. This meant that the priest at the altar was God's agent in the performance of a wondrous miracle.

CHRISTIANS AND JEWS

In their relations with heretics, pagans, and Muslims, medieval Christians demonstrated a narrow and hostile attitude that ran counter to the Gospel message that all human beings were children of God and that Christ had suffered for all humanity.

Muslims were seen, in the words of Pope Urban II, as a "vile breed," "infidels," and "enemies of God." While the clergy denounced war among Christians, they considered it a duty to wage holy war against non-Christians. And knights regarded fighting the Muslims in Spain and the Holy Land as a heartfelt expression of their Christian ideals.

Medieval Christians also showed hatred for Jews—a visibly alien group in a society dominated by the Christian worldview. The First Crusade was a turning point for medieval Jews. Until then, there were few instances of organized violence against Jewish communities. If we are warring against God's enemies, reasoned zealous Crusaders, why not annihilate the Lord's enemies living in our midst? In 1096, bands of Crusaders, proclaiming that they were seeking vengeance against "Christ-killers," slaughtered Jews in French and German towns. The Crusaders were often aided by townspeople driven by hateful images of Jews and eager to seize Jewish property. The efforts of bishops to protect the Jews proved largely unsuccessful. In the German city of Mainz, more than a thousand Jews lost their lives. Some, in an act of martyrdom, chose to kill themselves and their children rather than submit to forced baptism or face a crueler death at the hands of the Crusaders. One contemporary wrote:

> I know not whether by a judgment of the Lord, or by some error of mind, they rose in a spirit of cruelty against the Jewish people scattered throughout these cities and slaughtered them without mercy, . . . asserting it to be their duty against the enemies of the Christian faith. . . . The Jews of [Mainz], knowing of the slaughter of their brethren, . . . fled in hope of safety to Bishop Rothard. . . . He placed the Jews in the very spacious hall of his own house, [but the Crusaders] attacked the Jews in the hall with arrows and lances. Breaking the bolts and doors, they killed the Jews, about seven hundred in number, who in vain resisted the force and attack of so many thousands. They killed the women, also, and with their swords pierced tender children of whatever age and sex.[4]

This venomous hatred of Jews unleashed by the First Crusade triggered numerous other massacres during the Middle Ages, at times fomented by clergy.

Viewing the Jews as possessions to be exploited, kings and lords taxed and fined them relentlessly and periodically expelled Jews from their territories in order to confiscate their property. In 1290, Jews were expelled from England, and in 1306, from France. Between 1290 and 1293, expulsions, massacres, and forced conversions led to the virtual disappearance of a centuries-old Jewish community life in southern Italy. In Germany, savage riots periodically led to the torture and murder of Jews. In 1348–1349, when the Black Death (see page 275) raged across Europe, Jews were accused of spreading the plague by poisoning well water; thousands of them were burned alive in Basel, Freiburg, Strasbourg, Mainz, and other towns.

Several factors contributed to anti-Jewish feelings during the Middle Ages. To medieval Christians, the Jews' refusal to embrace Christianity was an act of wickedness, particularly since the church taught that the coming of Christ had been prophesied by the Old Testament. Related to this prejudice was the portrayal of the crucifixion in the Gospels. In the minds of medieval Christians, the crime of deicide—the killing of God—eternally stained the Jews as a people; medieval Christians saw Jews as dangerous, criminal people rejected by God and deserving of ceaseless punishment. Christian theologians taught that they were to remain forever in subjection to Christians. It was just such a view that led town magistrates and princes periodically to confiscate Jewish property, at times after burning the helpless Jews alive in a public spectacle. The flames of hatred were fanned by the absurd allegation that Jews, made bloodthirsty by the spilling of Christ's blood, tortured and murdered Christians, particularly children, to obtain blood for ritual purposes. Although some popes condemned the charges as groundless, this blood libel was widely believed by the credulous masses and incited numerous riots, which led to the torture, burning alive, and expulsion of countless Jews and the pillaging of their property.

The role of Jews as moneylenders also provoked animosity toward them. Jews were increasingly excluded from international trade and most professions and were barred from the guilds and

ANTI-SEMITISM. Holding the Jews responsible for the Black Death, Christians committed mass murder. In Basel, several hundred Jews were herded into a wooden house and burned to death. Some six thousand Jews were burned alive in Mainz. Flames consumed another two thousand in a huge pyre outside Strasbourg, and their property was distributed to the local townspeople. In this picture depicting the slaughter of the Jews of Strasbourg, the townspeople evidently enjoy the spectacle. (Bibliothèque Royale de Belgique.)

in some areas from landholding as well. Hence, virtually the only means of livelihood open to them was moneylending—in reality an important activity in an expanding economy. This activity, which was in theory forbidden to Christians, aroused the hatred of the individual peasants, clergy, lords, and kings who did the borrowing.

The policy of the church toward the Jews was that they should not be harmed, and several medieval popes sought to protect Jewish life and property from wanton violence. But the church also wanted Jews to live in humiliation, a fitting punishment for their act of deicide and continued refusal to embrace Christianity. Thus, the Fourth Lateran Council barred Jews from public office, ordered them to remain off the streets during Christian festivals, and required them to wear a distinguishing badge on their clothing, a symbol of their

degradation. Christian art, literature, and religious instruction depicted the Jews in a derogatory manner, often identifying them with the Devil, who was very real and very terrifying to medieval Christians. Such people deserved no mercy, reasoned medieval Christians. Indeed, nothing was too bad for them. Because Jews were seen as evil allies of Satan engaged in a diabolical plot against God and Christendom, Jew-hatred was regarded as an expression of Christian virtue, a message routinely spread by preachers. Deeply etched into the minds and hearts of Christians, the distorted image of the Jew as a contemptible creature persisted in the European mentality into the twentieth century.

Despite their precarious position, medieval Jews maintained their faith, expanded their tradition of biblical and legal scholarship, and developed a flourishing Hebrew literature. The work of Jewish translators, doctors, and philosophers contributed substantially to the flowering of medieval culture in the High Middle Ages. The foremost Jewish scholar of the Middle Ages was Moses ben Maimon (1135–1204), also called by the Greek name Maimonides (see profile in Chapter 11.) In both Muslim and Christian lands Maimonides achieved fame during his lifetime as a philosopher, theologian, mathematician, and physician.

NOTES

1. Quoted in J. W. Thompson, *Social and Economic History of the Middle Ages* (New York: Frederick Ungar, 1959), 2:772.
2. William of Tyre, *A History of Deeds Done Beyond the Sea*, trans. Emily Atwater Babcock and A. C. Krey (New York: Columbia University Press, 1943), 372, 373.
3. Excerpted in Brian Tierney, ed., *The Crisis of Church and State, 1050–1300* (Englewood Cliffs, N.J.: Prentice-Hall, 1964), 132.
4. Excerpted in A. C. Krey, ed., *The First Crusade: The Accounts of Eye-Witnesses and Participants* (Princeton, N.J.: Princeton University Press, 1921), 54–55.

SUGGESTED READING

Chazan, Robert, *Medieval Stereotypes and Modern Antisemitism* (1997). The deterioration of the image of the Jew in the High Middle Ages.

Duby, Georges, ed., *A History of Private Life*, vol. 2, *Revelations of the Medieval World* (1988). Among the topics discussed are sex, child-rearing, old age, and aristocratic households.

Fossier, Robert, ed., *The Cambridge Illustrated History of The Middle Ages*, vol. 2, *950–1250* (1997). Valuable essays.

Gimpel, Jean, *The Medieval Machine* (1977). Technological advances in the Middle Ages.

Lopez, R. S., *The Commercial Revolution of the Middle Ages, 950–1350* (1976). How an undeveloped society succeeded in developing itself.

Madden, Thomas E., ed., *Crusades* (2004). Essays by specialists on medieval crusading movements.

McCall, Andrew, *The Medieval Underworld* (2004). Accounts of witches, heretics, homosexuals, thieves and others considered on the margins of society.

Pernoud, Regine, ed., *The Crusades* (1964). A compilation of original sources.

Pounds, N. J. G., *An Economic History of Medieval Europe* (1974). A lucid survey.

Spufford, Peter, Power and Profit: *The Merchant in Medieval Europe* (2002). A detailed study replete with interesting accounts.

The Flowering
of Medieval Culture:
The Christian Synthesis

School of Bologna manuscript illumination. (Bildarchiv Preussischer Kulturbesitz/Art Resource, N.Y.)

Focus Questions

1. What conditions contributed to the revival of learning during the High Middle Ages?
2. What were scholastic philosophers trying to accomplish?
3. How does the medieval view of the universe differ from the modern view?
4. How did religion pervade much of medieval philosophy, science, literature, art, and architecture?

Europe in the High Middle Ages showed considerable vitality. The population grew, long-distance trade revived, new towns emerged, states started to take shape, and papal power increased. The culminating expression of this recovery and resurgence was the cultural flowering in philosophy, the visual arts, and literature. Creative intellects achieved on a cultural level what the papacy accomplished on an institutional level: the integration of life around a Christian viewpoint. The High Middle Ages saw the restoration of some of the learning of the ancient world, the rise of universities, the emergence of an original form of architecture (the Gothic), and the erection of an imposing system of thought, called **scholasticism**. Medieval theologian-philosophers fashioned Christian teachings into an all-embracing philosophy, which represented the spiritual character of medieval civilization. They perfected what Christian thinkers in the Roman Empire had initiated and what the learned men of the Early Middle Ages were groping for: a synthesis of Greek philosophy and Christian **revelation**.

THE REVIVAL OF LEARNING

In the late eleventh century, Latin Christendom began to experience a cultural revival; all areas of life showed vitality and creativeness. In the twelfth and thirteenth centuries, a rich civilization with a distinctive style united the educated elite in the lands from England to Sicily. Gothic cathedrals, an enduring testament to the creativeness of the religious impulse, were erected throughout Europe. Universities sprang up in several cities. Roman authors were again read, and their style was imitated. The quality of written Latin—the language of the church, learning, and education—improved, and secular and religious poetry, both in Latin and in the vernacular, abounded. Roman law emerged anew in Italy, spread to northern Europe, and regained its importance (lost since Roman times) as worthy of study. Some key works of ancient Greece were translated into Latin and studied in universities. Employing the rational tradition of Greece, men of genius harmonized Christian doctrines and Greek philosophy. During this period, the status and influence of learned men grew considerably.

Map 11.1 MEDIEVAL CENTERS OF LEARNING Medieval universities established in the West a tradition of learning that has never died. There is direct continuity between the universities of our own day and the medieval centers of learning.

(Copyright © 2013 Cengage Learning.)

Several conditions contributed to this cultural explosion, known as the Twelfth-Century Awakening. As attacks of Vikings, Muslims, and Magyars ended and kings and great lords imposed more order and stability, people found greater opportunities for travel and communication. The revival of trade and the growth of towns created a need for literacy and provided the wealth required to support learning. Increasing contact with Islamic and Byzantine cultures in Spain

256

and Sicily led to the translation into Latin of ancient Greek works preserved by these Eastern civilizations. By preserving Greek philosophy and science—and by commenting creatively on these classical works—Islamic civilization acted as a bridge between antiquity and the cultural revival of the High Middle Ages. The Twelfth-Century Awakening was also kindled by the legacy of the Carolingian Renaissance, whose cultural lights had dimmed but never wholly vanished in the period of disorder after the dissolution of Charlemagne's empire.

In the Early Middle Ages, the principal educational centers were the monastic schools. During the twelfth century, cathedral schools in towns gained importance. Paid a stipend by a local church, their teachers taught grammar, rhetoric, and logic. But the chief expression of expanding intellectual life was the university, a distinct creation of the Middle Ages.

The origins of the medieval university are obscure and varied. The first universities were not planned but grew spontaneously. They developed as students eager for knowledge and skills needed for high positions in government gathered around prominent teachers. The renewed importance of Roman law for business and politics, for example, drew students to Bologna to study with acknowledged masters.

The university was really a guild or corporation of masters or students who joined together to defend their interests against church or town authorities or the townspeople. A university might emerge when students united because of common needs, such as protection against townspeople who overcharged them for rooms and necessities. Organized into a body, students could also make demands on their instructors. At Bologna, professors faced fines for being absent or for giving lectures that drew fewer than five students; they were required to leave behind a deposit as security to ensure their return if they took a journey. A corporation of students formed the University at Bologna. The University of Paris, which evolved from the Cathedral School of Notre Dame, was the creation of a corporation of masters.

University students attended lectures, prepared for examinations, and earned degrees. They studied grammar, rhetoric, logic, arithmetic, geometry, astronomy, music, medicine, and, when ready, church law and theology, which was considered queen of the sciences. The curriculum relied heavily on Latin translations of ancient texts, chiefly the works of Aristotle. In mathematics and astronomy, students read Latin translations of Euclid and Ptolemy, while students of medicine studied the works of two great medical men of the ancient world, Hippocrates and Galen.

But sometimes students followed other pursuits. Instead of studying, they turned to drinking, gambling, and fighting. At Oxford University, it was reported that students "went through the streets with swords and bows and arrows and assaulted all who passed by."[1] Fathers complained that their sons preferred "play to work and strumming a guitar while the others are at their studies."[2] Students often faced financial problems, and they knew whom to ask for help: "Well-beloved father, to ease my debts . . . at the tavern, at the baker's, with the doctor . . . and to pay . . . the laundress and the barber, I send you word of greetings and of money."[3]

Universities performed a crucial function in the Middle Ages. Students learned the habit of reasoned argument. Universities trained professional secretaries and lawyers, who administered the affairs of church and state and of the growing cities; these institutions of learning also produced theologians and philosophers, who shaped the climate of public opinion. Since the curriculum and the texts studied were essentially the same in all lands, the learning disseminated by universities tightened the cultural bonds that united Christian Europe. Medieval universities established in the West a tradition of learning that has never died; there is direct continuity between the universities of our own day and the medieval ones.

THE MEDIEVAL WORLDVIEW

A distinctive worldview, based essentially on Christianity, evolved during the Middle Ages. This outlook differed from both the Greco-Roman and the modern scientific and secular views of the world. In the Christian view, not the individual but the Creator determined what constituted the good life. Thus, reason that was not illuminated by revelation was either wrong or inadequate, for God had revealed the proper rules for the regulation of individual and social life. Ultimately, the good life was not of this world but came from a union with God in a higher world. This Christian belief as formulated by the church made life and death purposeful and intelligible; it dominated the thought of the Middle Ages.

The Universe: Higher and Lower Worlds

Medieval thinkers sharply differentiated between spirit and matter, between a realm of grace and an earthly realm, between a higher world of perfection and a lower world of imperfection. Moral values derived from the higher world, which was also the final destination for the faithful. Two sets of laws operated in the medieval universe, one for the heavens and one for the earth. The cosmos was a giant ladder, with God at the summit; earth, composed of base matter, stood at the bottom, just above hell, where, farthest from God, dwelled Satan, his evil spirits, and the souls of the damned.

From Aristotle and Ptolemy, medieval thinkers inherited the theory of an earth-centered universe—the *geocentric theory*—which they imbued with Christian symbolism. The geocentric theory held that revolving around the motionless earth at uniform speeds were seven transparent spheres, in which were embedded each of the seven "planets"—the moon, Mercury, Venus, the sun, Mars, Jupiter, and Saturn. A sphere of fixed stars (that is, the stars, like chandeliers in a ceiling, stayed in a constant relationship to one another) enclosed this planetary system. Above the firmament of the stars were the three heavenly spheres. The outermost, the Empyrean Heaven, was the abode of God and the Elect. Through the sphere below—the Prime Mover—God transmitted motion to the planetary spheres. Underneath this was the lowermost sphere, the Crystalline Heaven, composed of a clear transparent substance.

An earth-centered universe accorded with the Christian idea that God created the universe for men and women and that salvation was the

GOD AS ARCHITECT OF THE UNIVERSE, FRENCH OLD TESTAMENT MINIATURE PAINTING, THIRTEENTH CENTURY. To the medieval Christian, God was the creator of the world. The universe had a known hierarchical order—a "great chain of being"—extending from God downward to the lowest form of being. (Osterreichische Nationalbibliothek, Vienna: Cod. 2554, fol. lv.)

primary aim of life. Because God had created people in his image, they deserved this central position. Although they might be at the bottom of the cosmic ladder, only they, of all living things, had the capacity to ascend to heaven, the realm of perfection.

Also acceptable to the Christian mentality was the sharp distinction drawn by Aristotle between the world above the moon and the one below it. Aristotle held that terrestrial bodies were made of four elements: earth, water, air, fire. Celestial bodies, which occupied the region encompassing the moon and the area above, were composed of a fifth element, the ether—too clear, too pure, and too perfect to be found on earth. The planets and stars existed in a world apart; they were made of the divine ether and followed celestial laws, which did not apply to earthly objects. Whereas earthly bodies underwent change—ice converting to water, a burning log converting to ashes—heavenly objects were incorruptible, immune to all change. Unlike earthly objects, they were indestructible.

Heavenly bodies also followed different laws of motion than earthly objects. Aristotle said that it was natural for celestial bodies to move eternally in uniform circles, such motion being considered a sign of perfection. According to Aristotle, it was also natural for heavy bodies (stone) to fall downward and for light objects (fire, smoke) to move upward toward the celestial world; the falling stone and the rising smoke were finding their natural place in the universe. This view of the universe would be shattered by the Scientific Revolution of the sixteenth and seventeenth centuries.

The Individual: Sinful but Redeemable

At the center of medieval belief was the idea of a perfect God, who had conceived and created the universe, and wretched and sinful human beings. God had given Adam and Eve freedom to choose; rebellious and presumptuous, they had used their freedom to disobey God. In doing so, they made evil an intrinsic part of the human personality. But God, who had not stopped loving human beings, showed them the way out of sin. God became man and died so that human beings might be saved. Men and women were weak, egocentric, and sinful. With God's grace, they could overcome their sinful nature and gain salvation; without grace, they were utterly helpless.

The medieval individual's understanding of self stemmed from a comprehension of the universe as a **hierarchy** instituted by and culminating in God. On earth, the basest objects were lifeless stones devoid of souls; higher than stones were plants, endowed with a primitive type of soul, which allowed for reproduction and growth. Still higher were animals, which had the capacity for motion and sensation. The highest of the animals were human beings; unlike other animals, they could grasp some part of universal truth. Far superior to them were the angels, for they apprehended God's truth without difficulty. At the summit of this graduated universe was God, who was pure

Being, without limitation, and the source of all existence. God's revelation reached down to humanity through the hierarchical order. From God, revelation passed to the angels, who were also arranged hierarchically. From the angels, the truth reached men and women, grasped first by prophets and apostles and then by the multitudes. Thus, all things in the universe, from angels, men, and women to the lowest earthly objects, occupied a place peculiar to their nature and were linked by God in a great, unbroken chain.

Medieval individuals derived a sense of security from this hierarchical universe, in which the human position was clearly defined. Although they were sinners who dwelt on a corruptible earth, at the bottom of the cosmic hierarchy, they *could* ascend to the higher world of perfection above the moon. As children of God, they enjoyed the unique distinction that each human soul was precious; all Christians commanded respect, unless they were heretics. (A heretic forfeited dignity and could be justly executed.)

Medieval thinkers also arranged knowledge in a hierarchical order: knowledge of the spiritual surpassed all worldly knowledge, that is, all the sciences. Therefore, the true Christian understood that the pursuit of worldly knowledge could not proceed properly unless guided by divine revelation. To know what God wanted of the individual was the summit of self-knowledge and permitted entry into heaven. Thus, God was both the source and the end of knowledge. The human capacity to think and to act freely constituted the image of God within each individual; it ennobled man and woman and offered them the promise of associating with God in heaven.

True, human nobility derived from intelligence and free will. But if individuals disobeyed God, they brought misery on themselves. To challenge the divine will with human will constituted the sin of pride, contempt for God, and a violation of the divine order. Such sinful behavior invited self-destruction.

In the medieval view, neither nature nor the human being could be understood apart from God and his revelation. All reality emanated from God and was purposefully arranged in a spiritual hierarchy. Three great expressions of this view of life were scholastic philosophy, *The Divine Comedy* of Dante, and the Gothic cathedral.

PHILOSOPHY-THEOLOGY

Medieval philosophy, or scholasticism, applied reason to revelation. It explained and clarified Christian teachings by means of concepts and principles of logic derived from Greek philosophy. Scholastics tried to show that the teachings of faith, though not derived from reason, were not contrary to reason, that logic could confirm church dogma. They tried to prove through reason what they already held to be true through faith. For example, the existence of God and the immortality of the soul, which every Christian accepted as articles of faith, could also, they thought, be demonstrated by reason. In struggling to harmonize faith with reason, medieval thinkers constructed an extraordinary synthesis of Christian revelation and Greek thought.

The scholastic masters used reason not to challenge but to serve faith: to elucidate, clarify, and buttress it. They did not break with the central concern of Christianity, that of earning God's grace and achieving salvation. Although this goal could be realized solely through faith, scholastic thinkers insisted that a science of nature did not obstruct the pursuit of grace and that philosophy could assist the devout in the contemplation of God. They did not reject those Christian beliefs that were beyond the grasp of human reason and therefore could not be deduced by rational argument. Instead, they held that such truths rested entirely on revelation and were to be accepted on faith. To medieval thinkers, reason did not have an independent existence but ultimately had to acknowledge a suprarational, superhuman standard of truth; Greek philosophy had to be interpreted to accord with Christian revelation. They wanted rational thought to be directed by faith for Christian ends and guided by scriptural and ecclesiastical authority. Ultimately, faith had the final word.

Not all Christian thinkers welcomed the use of reason. Regarding Greek philosophy as an enemy of faith (would not reason lead people to question belief in miracles?), a fabricator of heresies (would not reason encourage disbelief in essential church teachings?), and an obstacle to achieving communion of the soul with God (would not a deviation from church teachings, under the influence of pagan philosophy, deprive people of salvation?), conservative theologians opposed the use of reason to elucidate Christian revelation. For if reason could demonstrate the proof of Christian teachings, as its advocates insisted, it could also be used, warned conservatives, to challenge and reject those teachings. In a sense, the conservatives were right. By revitalizing Greek thought, medieval philosophy nurtured a powerful force that eventually would shatter the medieval concepts of nature and society and weaken Christianity. Modern Western thought was created by thinkers who refused to subordinate reason to religious authority. Reason proved to be a double-edged sword: it both ennobled and undermined the medieval worldview.

Saint Anselm and Abelard

An early scholastic, Saint Anselm (1033–1109) was abbot of the Benedictine monastery of Bec in Normandy. He used rational argument to serve the interests of faith. Like Augustine before him and other thinkers who followed him, Anselm said that faith was a precondition for understanding. Without belief, there could be no proper knowledge. He developed philosophical proof for the existence of God. Anselm argued as follows: We can conceive of no being greater than God. But if God were to exist only in thought and not in actuality, his greatness would be limited; he would be less than perfect. Hence, he exists. Anselm's motive and method reveal something about the essence of medieval philosophy. He does not begin as a modern might: "If it can be proven that God exists, I will adopt the creed of Christianity; if not, I will either deny God's existence (atheism) or reserve judgment (agnosticism)." Rather, Anselm accepts God's existence as an established fact because he believes what Holy Scripture says and what the church teaches. He then proceeds to employ logical argument to demonstrate that God can be known not only through faith but also through reason. He would never use reason to subvert what he knows to be true by faith. In general, this attitude would characterize later medieval thinkers, who also applied reason to faith.

As a young teacher of theology at the Cathedral School of Notre Dame, Peter Abelard (1079–1142) acquired a reputation for brilliance and combativeness. His tragic affair with Héloise, whom he tutored and seduced, has become one of the great

Peter Abelard: The Synthesis of Reason and Faith

Dialectics, a method of logical analysis, as applied to the Bible and the writings of early Christian thinkers, was brilliantly taught by Peter Abelard in the cathedral school at Paris. In his book Sic et Non *(Yes and No), Abelard listed some 150 questions on which the early church authorities had taken differing positions over the centuries. He suggested that these issues could be resolved by the careful application of the dialectical method to the language of the texts.*

Although he never intended to challenge the Christian faith, Abelard raised, with his critical scrutiny, fears that the dialectical approach would undermine faith and foster heresy, and he was forced to quit his teaching post. Nevertheless, the new scholastic rationalistic approach swept the schools of Europe. In the following reading, Abelard describes the critical use of rational methods in textual analysis.

We must be careful not to be led astray by attributing views to the [Church] Fathers which they did not hold. This may happen if a wrong author's name is given to a book or if a text is corrupt. For many works are falsely attributed to one of the Fathers to give them authority, and some passages, even in the Bible, are corrupt through the errors of copyists. . . . We must be equally careful to make sure that an opinion quoted from a Father was not withdrawn or corrected by him in the light of later and better knowledge. . . . Again the passage in question may not give the Father's own opinion, but that of some other writer whom he is quoting. . . .

We must also make a thorough inquiry when different decisions are given on the same matter under canon [church] law. We must discover the underlying purpose of the opinion, whether it is meant to grant an indulgence or exhort to some perfection. In this way we may clear up the apparent contradiction. . . . If the opinion is a definitive judgment, we must determine whether it is of general application or directed to a particular case. . . . The when and why of the order must also be considered because what is allowed at one time is often forbidden at another, and what is often laid down as the strict letter of the law may be sometimes moderated by a dispensation. . . .

Furthermore we customarily talk of things as they appear to our bodily senses and not as they are in actual fact. So judging by what we see we say it is a starry sky or it is not, and that the sun is hot or has no heat at all, when these things though variable in appearance are ever constant. Can we be surprised, then, that some matters have been stated by the Fathers as opinions rather than the truth? Then again many controversies would be quickly settled if we could be on our guard against a particular word used in different senses by different authors. . . .

A careful reader will employ all these ways of reconciling contradictions in the writings of the Fathers. But if the contradictions are so glaring that they cannot be reconciled, then the rival authorities must be compared and the view that has the heaviest backing be adopted. . . .

By collecting contrasting divergent opinions I hope to provoke young readers to push themselves to the limit in the search for truth, so that their wits may be sharpened by their investigation. It is by doubting that we come to investigate, and by investigating that we recognize the truth.

Questions for Analysis

1. Describe the methods of literary analysis promoted by Peter Abelard.
2. Why did Abelard's new method of textual analysis create so much controversy?

Excerpted in David Ayerst and A. S. S. Fisher, eds., *Records of Christianity*, vol. 2, *Christendom* (Oxford: Blackwell, 1977), 196–197.

Maimonides

Moses ben Maimon, also called by the Greek name Maimonides (1135–1204), was recognized as the foremost Jewish sage of his day. His works were also read and respected by Muslim and Christian thinkers, including Thomas Aquinas and Albert the Great. Born in Córdoba, Spain, then under Muslim rule, his family was forced to flee the country when the Almohads, a fanatical fundamentalist group from North Africa, conquered Córdoba and demanded that Jews and Christians convert or face death. Maimonides' family went into exile, moving about Spain and then emigrating to Morocco and later to a suburb of Cairo. When his brother David, a merchant, perished at sea with the family's fortune, Maimonides, who had read widely in Arabic translations of Greek and Muslim medical works, became a physician. Gaining a reputation, he served as court physician to Saladin and the Egyptian royal family.

During his lifetime, Maimonides achieved fame as a philosopher, theologian, mathematician, and physician. Maimonides was intimately familiar with the works of Arab philosophers and Arabic translations of ancient Greek philosophy, particularly Aristotle. Like Christian scholastics and Muslim philosophers, Maimonides tried to harmonize faith with reason, to reconcile the Hebrew Scriptures and the Talmud (Jewish biblical commentary) with the teachings of Aristotle.

romances in Western literature. Héloise had a child and entered a nunnery; Abelard was castrated on orders of Canon Fulbert, Héloise's guardian, and sought temporary refuge in a monastery. After resuming his career as a teacher in Paris, Abelard again had to seek refuge, this time for writing an essay on the **Trinity** that church officials found offensive. After further difficulties and flights, he again returned to Paris to teach dialectics. Not long afterward, his most determined opponent, Bernard of Clairvaux, accused Abelard of using the method of dialectical argument to attack faith. To Bernard, a monk and a **mystic,** subjecting revealed truth to critical analysis was fraught with danger.

> *The deepest matters become the subject of un-dignified wrangling. . . . Virtues and vices are discussed with no trace of moral feelings, the sacraments of the Church with no evidence of faith, the mystery of the Holy Trinity with no spirit of humility or sobriety: all is presented in a distorted form, introduced in a way different from the one we learned and are used to.*[4]

Hearkening to Bernard's powerful voice, the church condemned Abelard and confined him to a monastery for the rest of his days.

Abelard believed that it was important to apply reason to faith and that careful and constant questioning led to wisdom. Since all knowledge derives from God, said Abelard, it is good to pursue learning. In *Sic et Non* (Yes and No), he took 150 theological issues and, by presenting passages from the Bible and the church fathers, showed that there were conflicting opinions. He suggested that the divergent opinions of authorities could be reconciled through proper use of dialectics (see Primary Source box). But like Anselm before him, Abelard did not intend to refute traditional church doctrines. Reason would buttress, not weaken, the authority of faith. After his condemnation in 1141, Abelard wrote:

> *I will never be a philosopher, if this is to speak against St. Paul, I would not be an Aristotle if this were to separate me from Christ. . . . I have set my building on the cornerstone on which Christ has built his Church. . . . I rest upon the rock that cannot be moved.*[5]

The Recovery of Aristotle

During the Early Middle Ages, scholars in the Muslim world translated the works of Aristotle into Arabic and wrote commentaries on them.

Reflecting the value that Jews gave to education, Maimonides insisted that every Jewish man, whether he be rich or poor, old or young, healthy or unhealthy, and even if burdened with family responsibilities, was obliged to study daily the Hebrew Scriptures. Drawing on the deeply ingrained Jewish tradition calling for care for the poor, Maimonides listed eight degrees of almsgiving. The highest was to help a needy person become self-supporting. Just below was giving charity in such a way that both the donor and the recipient are unknown to each other.

In his numerous medical writings, Maimonides displayed a scientific bent in treating the sick, and to preserve health he urged drinking clean water, breathing fresh air, and eating healthy foods.

The preservation of ancient Greek thought was a major contribution of Islamic civilization. During the High Middle Ages, these works were translated into Latin by learned Europeans.

The introduction into Latin Christendom of the major works of Aristotle created a dilemma for religious authorities. Aristotle's comprehensive philosophy of nature and man, a product of human reason alone, conflicted in many instances with essential Christian doctrine. For Aristotle, God was an impersonal principle that accounted for order and motion in the universe, the unmoved mover. For Christianity, not only was God responsible for order in the physical universe, but he was also a personal being—a loving Father concerned about the deeds of his children. Whereas Christianity taught that God created the universe at a specific point in time, Aristotle held that the universe was eternal. Nor did Aristotle believe in the personal immortality of the soul, another cardinal principle of Christianity. For Aristotle, it was impossible for the soul to exist independently of the body.

Some church officials feared that the dissemination of Aristotle's natural philosophy would endanger faith. Would the teachings of Christ and the church fathers have to answer to pagan philosophy? Would Athens prevail over Jerusalem?

At various times in the first half of the thirteenth century, the teaching of Aristotle's scientific works was forbidden at the University of Paris. However, because the ban did not apply throughout Christendom and was not consistently enforced in Paris, Aristotle's philosophy continued to be studied.

Thomas Aquinas: The Synthesis of Faith and Reason

Rejecting the position of conservatives, who insisted that philosophy would contaminate faith, Saint Thomas Aquinas (c. 1225–1274) upheld the value of human reason and natural knowledge. He set about reconciling Aristotelianism with Christianity. Aquinas taught at Paris and at various institutions in Italy. His greatest work, *Summa Theologica,* is a systematic exposition of Christian thought and the crowning expression of the medieval attempt to integrate Aristotle with Christianity. As a devout Catholic and member of the Dominican order, he of course accepted the truth of revelation. He never used reason to undermine faith.

Aquinas divided revealed truth into two categories: beliefs whose truth can be demonstrated by reason and beliefs that reason cannot prove to be either true or false. For example, he believed that philosophical speculation could prove the existence of God and the immortality of the human soul but could not prove or disprove the doctrines of the Trinity, the **Incarnation,** and the **Redemption** because those articles of faith wholly surpassed the capacity of human reason. This fact, however, did not detract from their certainty. Doctrines of faith did not require rational proof to be valid. They were true because they originated with God, whose authority is unshakable.

Can the teachings of faith conflict with the evidence of reason? For Aquinas, the answer was emphatically no. He said that revelation could not be the enemy of reason because revelation did not contradict reason and reason did not corrupt the purity of faith. Revelation supplemented and perfected reason. If there appeared to be a conflict between philosophy and faith, it was certain that reason had erred somewhere, for the doctrines of faith were infallible. Since *both* faith and reason came from God, they were not in competition with each other but, properly understood, supported each other and formed an organic unity. Consequently, reason should not be feared, for it was another avenue to God. Because there was an inherent agreement between true faith and correct reason—they both ultimately stemmed from God—contradictions between the two were only a misleading appearance. Although philosophy had not yet been able to resolve the dilemma, for God no such contradictions existed. In heaven, human beings would attain complete knowledge, as well as complete happiness. While on earth, however, they must allow faith to guide reason; they must not permit reason to oppose or undermine faith.

Because reason was no enemy of faith, applying it to revelation need not be feared. As human reasoning became more proficient, said Aquinas, it also became more Christian, and apparent incompatibilities between faith and reason disappeared. Recognizing that both faith and reason point to the same truth, the wise person accepts the guidance of religion in all questions that relate directly to knowledge needed for salvation. There also existed a wide range of knowledge that God had not revealed and that was not required for salvation. Into this category fell much knowledge about the natural world of things and creatures, which human beings had perfect liberty to explore.

Thus, in exalting God, Aquinas also paid homage to human intelligence, proclaimed the value of rational activity, and asserted the importance of physical reality revealed through human senses. Consequently, he valued the natural philosophy of Aristotle. Correctly used, Aristotelian thought would assist faith. Aquinas's great effort was to synthesize Aristotelianism with the divine revelation of Christianity. That the two could be harmonized he had no doubt. He made use of Aristotelian categories in his five proofs of God's existence. In his first proof, for example, Aquinas argued that a thing cannot move itself. Whatever is moved must be moved by something else, and that by something else again. "Therefore, it is necessary to arrive at a first mover, moved by no other; and this everyone understands to be God."[6]

Aquinas upheld the value of reason. To love the intellect was to honor God and not to diminish the truth of faith. He had confidence in the power of the rational mind to comprehend most of the truths of revelation, and he insisted

NOTRE-DAME DE CHARTRES, BEGUN C. 1194, CHARTRES, FRANCE. Because the two spires topping the west façade towers were constructed nearly four centuries apart, they provide an interesting contrast between early and late Gothic architecture. The simple north spire was built between 1160 and 1170; the south spire, constructed in the early sixteenth century, is a good example of the flamboyant Gothic style.
(Nat Farbman/Time and Life Pictures/Getty Images.)

that in nontheological questions about specific things in nature—those questions not affecting salvation—people should trust only to reason and experience.

Aquinas gave new importance to the empirical world and to scientific speculation and human knowledge. The traditional medieval view, based largely on Saint Augustine, drew a sharp distinction between the higher world of grace and the lower world of nature, between the world of spirit and the world of sense experience. Knowledge derived from the natural world was often seen as an obstacle to true knowledge. Aquinas altered this tradition by affirming the importance of knowledge of the social order and the physical world. He gave human reason and worldly knowledge a new dignity. Thus, the City of Man was not merely a sinful place from which people tried to escape in order to enter God's city; it was worthy of investigation and understanding. But Aquinas remained a medieval thinker, for he always maintained that secular knowledge should be supervised and corrected by revealed truth, and he never questioned the truth of the medieval Christian view of the world and the individual. As historian Steven Ozment explains,

> Aquinas brought reason and revelation together, but strictly as un-equals. . . . In this union, reason, philosophy, nature, secular man and the state ultimately had value only in subservience to the higher goals of revelation, theology, grace, religious man, and the church. . . . Thomist theology was the most sophisticated statement of the medieval belief in the secondary significance of the lay and secular world, a congenial ideology for a church besieged by independent and aggressive secular political powers.[7]

Strict Aristotelianism: The Challenge to Orthodoxy

Some teachers in the Faculty of Arts at Paris, relying heavily on the commentaries of Averroës, the great Muslim thinker (see page 208), found Aquinas's approach of Christianizing or explaining away Aristotle unacceptable. Unlike Aquinas, they did not seek to reconcile Aristotle's philosophy with Christian dogma. They held that certain Aristotelian propositions contradicting faith were philosophically true, or at least could not be proven false. These teachers maintained that it was impossible to refute these propositions by natural reason alone—that is, without recourse to faith. For example, by reason alone Aristotle had demonstrated that the world was eternal and that the processes of nature were unalterable. The first doctrine conflicted with the Christian belief that God created the universe at a point in time; the second conflicted with the belief that God could work miracles.

But these teachers did not take the next step and argue that Aristotle was correct and faith wrong. They maintained only that Aristotle's arguments could not be refuted by natural reason and that philosophers—as philosophers, not as Christians—should base their judgments on rational arguments only, not on miracles and revelation. These strict Aristotelians did not deny the truths of faith, but they did assert that natural reason could construct conclusive proofs for propositions that the church had explicitly stated to be false.

In 1277, the bishop of Paris condemned 219 propositions, many of them taught by these expositors of Aristotle at the University of Paris. Included in the condemnation were some propositions held by the great Aquinas. This move attempted to prevent Aristotle's philosophical naturalism from undermining Christian beliefs. Consequently, the condemnation was a triumph for conservative theologians, who had grown increasingly worried about the inroads made by Aristotelianism. To them, even the Christian Aristotelianism of Aquinas was suspect, for it could lead people astray, endangering their salvation.

Condemnations generally hinder the pursuit of knowledge, but, ironically, the condemnation of 1277 may have had the opposite effect. It led some thinkers to examine critically and reject elements of Aristotle's natural philosophy. This development may have served as a prelude to modern science, which, born in the sixteenth and seventeenth centuries, grew out of a rejection of Aristotelian physics.

SCIENCE

During the Early Middle Ages, few scientific works from the ancient world were available to Western Europeans. Scientific thought was at its lowest ebb since its origination more than a thousand years earlier in Greece. By contrast, both Islamic and Byzantine civilizations preserved and, in some instances, added to the legacy of Greek science. In the High Middle Ages, however, many ancient texts were translated from Greek and Arabic into Latin and entered Latin Christendom for the first time. The principal centers of translation were Spain, where Christian and Muslim civilizations intersected, and Sicily, which had been controlled by Byzantium up to the last part of the ninth century and then by Islam until Christian Normans completed the conquest of the island by 1091. Often learned Jews, who knew both Arabic and Latin, served as translators. These translations of ancient Greek scientific works and of Arabic commentaries stimulated interest in nature.

In the thirteenth and fourteenth centuries, a genuine scientific movement did occur. Impressed with the naturalistic and empirical approach of Aristotle, some medieval scholars spent time examining physical nature. Among them was the Dominican Albert the Great (Albertus Magnus). Born in Germany, Albert (c. 1206–1280) studied at Padua and taught at the University of Paris, where Thomas Aquinas was his student. To Albert, philosophy meant more than employing Greek reason to contemplate divine wisdom; it also meant making sense of nature. Albert devoted himself to mastering, editing, and commenting on the vast body of Aristotle's works.

While retaining the Christian stress on God, revelation, the supernatural, and the afterlife, Albert (unlike many earlier Christian thinkers) considered nature a valid field for investigation. In his writings on geology, chemistry, botany, and zoology, Albert, like Aristotle, displayed respect for the concrete details of nature, utilizing them as empirical evidence.

> I have examined the anatomy of different species of bees. In the rear, i.e. behind the waist, I discovered a transparent, shining bladder. If you test this with your tongue, you find that it has a slight taste of honey. In the body there is only an insignificant spiral-shaped intestine and nerve fibers which are connected with the sting. All this is surrounded with a sticky fluid.[8]

Showing a modern-day approach, Albert approved of inquiry into the material world, stressed the value of knowledge derived from experience with nature, sought rational explanations for natural occurrences, and held that theological debates should not stop scientific investigations. He pointed to a new direction in medieval thought.

Robert Grosseteste (c. 1175–1253), chancellor of Oxford University, was also a scholar of the scientific movement. He declared that the roundness of the earth could be demonstrated by reason. In addition, he insisted that mathematics was necessary in order to understand the physical world, and he carried out experiments on the refraction of light.

Another Englishman, the monk and philosopher Roger Bacon (c. 1214–1294), foreshadowed the modern attitude of using science to gain mastery over nature. He recognized the practical advantages that might come and predicted these great changes.

> Machines for navigation can be made without rowers so that the largest ships on rivers or seas will be moved by a single man in charge with greater velocity than if they were full of men. Also oars can be made so that without animals they will move with unbelievable rapidity. . . . Also flying machines can be constructed so that a man sits in the midst of the machine revolving some engine by which artificial wings are made to beat the air like a flying bird. Also a machine small in size can be made for walking in the sea and rivers, even to the bottom without danger.[9]

Bacon valued the study of mathematics and read Arabic works on the reflection and refraction of light. Among his achievements were experiments in optics and the observation that light travels much faster than sound. His description of the anatomy of the vertebrate eye and optic nerves was the finest of that era, and he recommended dissecting the eyes of pigs and cows to obtain greater knowledge of the subject.

The study of the ancient texts of Hippocrates and Galen and their Islamic commentators, particularly Avicenna's Canon of Medicine, which synthesized Greek and Arabic medicine, elevated medicine to a formal discipline. Although these texts contained numerous errors and contradictions, they had to be mastered, if only to be challenged, before modern medicine could emerge. In addition, medieval doctors dissected animals and, in the late fourteenth century, human bodies. From practical experience, medieval doctors, monks, and laypeople added to the list of plants and herbs that would ease pain and heal.

Medieval scholars did not make the breakthrough to modern science. They kept the belief that the earth was at the center of the universe and that different sets of laws operated on earth and in the heavens. Although some medieval thinkers explicitly urged seeking natural explanations to account for physical occurrences, medieval science was never wholly removed from a theological setting. Modern science self-consciously seeks the advancement of specifically scientific knowledge, but in the Middle Ages many questions involving nature were raised merely to clarify a religious problem.

Medieval scholars and philosophers, however, did advance knowledge about optics, the tides, and mechanics. They saw the importance of mathematics for interpreting nature, and they performed some experiments. By translating and commenting on ancient Greek and Arabic works, medieval scholars provided future ages with ideas to reflect on and to reject and surpass, a necessary precondition for the emergence of modern science.

Medieval thinkers also developed an anti-Aristotelian physics, which some historians of science believe influenced Galileo, the creator of modern mechanics, more than two centuries later. To explain why heavy objects do not always fall downward—why an arrow released by a bow moves in a straight line before it falls—Aristotle said that when the arrow leaves the bow, it separates the air, which then moves behind the arrow and pushes it along. Aristotle, of course, had no comprehension of the law of inertia, which, as formulated by Isaac Newton in the seventeenth century, states that a body in motion will continue in a straight line unless interfered with. Unable to imagine that being in motion is as natural a condition as being at rest, Aristotle concluded that an outside force must maintain continual contact with the moving object. Hence, the flying arrow requires the "air-engine" to keep it in motion.

In the fourteenth century, Jean Buridan, a professor at the University of Paris, rejected Aristotle's theory. Buridan argued that the bowstring transmits to the arrow a force called impetus, which keeps the arrow in motion. Whereas Aristotle attributed the arrow's motion to the air, which was external to the arrow, Buridan found the motive force to be an agent imparted to the arrow by the bowstring. Though still far from the modern theory of inertia, Buridan's impetus theory was an advance over Aristotle's air-engine. In the impetus theory, a moving body requires a cause to keep it in motion. In the theory of inertia, as noted above, once a body is in motion, no force is required to keep it moving in a straight line.

Late medieval physics went beyond Aristotle in other ways as well, particularly in the importance given to expressing motion mathematically. The extent to which late medieval thinkers influenced the thinkers of the Scientific Revolution is a matter of debate. Some historians view modern science as a child of the Middle Ages. Other historians believe that the achievements of medieval science were slim and that modern science owes very little to the Middle Ages.

THE RECOVERY OF ROMAN LAW

During the Early Middle Ages, Western European law essentially consisted of Germanic customs, some of which had been written down. Although some elements of Roman law endured as custom, the formal study of Roman law disappeared. The late eleventh and the twelfth centuries saw the revival of Roman law, particularly in Bologna, Italy. Irnerius lectured on the *Corpus Juris Civilis,* Roman laws and judicial commentaries codified by Byzantine jurists in the sixth century by order of the emperor Justinian. He made Bologna the leading center for the study of Roman law. Irnerius and his students applied to the study of law the methods of organization and logical analysis that scholastic theologians used in studying philosophical texts.

Unlike traditional Germanic law, which was essentially tribal law, Roman law assumed the existence of universal principles, which could be grasped by the human intellect and expressed in the law of the state. Roman jurists had systematically and rationally structured the legal experience of the Roman people. The example of Roman law stimulated medieval jurists to organize their own legal tradition. Intellectuals increasingly came to insist on both a rational analysis of evidence and judicial decisions based on rational procedures. Law codes compiled in parts of France and Germany and in the kingdom of Castile were influenced by the recovery of Roman law.

Roman law also influenced church law, which was derived from the Bible, the church fathers, church councils, and the decisions of popes. In the last part of the eleventh century, church scholars began to codify church (or canon) law and were helped by the Roman legal tradition.

LITERATURE

Medieval literature was written both in Latin and in the vernacular—the normal spoken language, as distinct from the language of learning. Much of medieval Latin literature consisted of religious hymns and dramas depicting the life of Christ and saints.

Medieval university students, like their modern counterparts, lampooned their elders and social conventions, engaged in drinking bouts, and rebelled against the rigors of study. They put their feelings into poetry written in Latin. For them, youth and study did not mix.

> Let's away with study,
>   Folly's sweet.
> Treasure all the pleasure of our youth:
>   Time enough for age
> To think of Truth.
> So short a day,
> And life so quickly hasting
> And is study wasting
>   Youth that would be gay![10]

And, of course, their thoughts turned to romance.

> All I care for is to play,
>   Gaze upon my treasure,
> Now and then to touch her hand,
>   Kiss in modest measure;
> But the fifth act of love's game,
>   Dream not of that pleasure![11]

Poor or errant students who had given up their studies roamed the roads as free spirits. These vagabonds sometimes composed poetry that ridiculed clerics and sang the praises of wine, gambling, and women.

> Down the highway-broad I walk,
> Like a youth in mind,
> Implicate myself in vice,
> Virtue stays behind,
> Avid for the world's delight
> More than for salvation,
> Dead in soul, I care but for
> Body's exultation.[12]

Vernacular literature emerged in the High Middle Ages. The French chansons de geste—epic poems of heroic deeds that had first been told orally—were written in the vernacular of northern France. The poems dealt with Charlemagne's battles against the Muslims, with rebellious nobles, and with feudal warfare. The finest of these epic poems, The Song of Roland, expressed the feudal ethic: loyalty to one's lord and devotion to Christianity were the highest virtues and treachery an unpardonable crime.

The Nibelungenlied, the best expression of the heroic epic in Germany, is often called "the Iliad of the Germans." Like its French counterpart, it dealt with heroic feats.

> In stories of our fathers, high marvels we are
>   told
> Of champions well-approved in perils
>   manifold.
> Of feasts and merry meetings, of weeping and
>   of wail,
> And deeds of gallant daring I'll tell you in my
>   tale.[13]

The roman—a blending of old legends, chivalric ideals, and Christian concepts—combined love with adventure, war, and the miraculous. Among the romans were the tales of King Arthur and his Round Table. Circulating by word of mouth for centuries, these tales spread from the British Isles to France and Germany.

Another form of medieval poetry, which flourished particularly in Provence, in southern France, dealt with the romantic glorification of women. Sung by troubadours, many of them nobles, the

MILLEFLEURS TAPESTRY: TWO MUSICIANS, SCHOOL OF THE LOIRE, FRANCE, C. 1500. The courtly love tradition, in which women were worshipped and untouchable, inspired poetry. Troubadours sang this poetry, which expressed a changing attitude toward women. By inviting poets to their courts and writing poetry themselves, noblewomen actively influenced the rituals and literature of courtly love. (© The Collection of the Frick Art and Historical Center, Pittsburgh, Pennsylvania.)

courtly love poetry expressed a changing attitude toward women. Although medieval men generally regarded women as inferior and subordinate, courtly love poetry ascribed to noble ladies superior qualities of virtue. To the nobleman, the lady became a goddess worthy of devotion, loyalty, and worship. He would honor her and serve her as he did his lord; for her love, he would undergo any sacrifice. Troubadours sang love songs that praised ladies for their beauty and charm and expressed both the joys and the pains of love.

> *I sing of her, yet her beauty*
> *is greater than I can tell,*
> *with her fresh color, lively eyes,*
> *and white skin, untanned*
> *and untainted by rouge.*

> *She is so pure and noble*
> *that no one can speak ill of her.*
> *But above all, one must praise,*
> *it seems to me, her truthfulness,*
> *her manners and her gracious speech*
> *for she never would betray a friend.*[14]

Noblewomen actively influenced the rituals and literature of courtly love. They often invited poets to their courts and wrote poetry themselves. Sometimes a lady troubadour expressed disdain for her husband and desire for the knight whom she truly loved.

> *I should like to hold my knight*
> *Naked in my arms at eve,*
> *That he might be in ecstasy*
> *As I cushioned his head against my breast,*
> *For I am happier far with him*
> *Than Floris with Blancheflor;*
> *I grant him my heart, my love,*
> *My mind, my eyes, my life.*

> *Fair friend, charming and good,*
> *When shall I hold you in my power?*
> *And lie beside you for an hour*
> *And amorous kisses give to you;*
> *Know that I would give almost anything*
> *To have you in my husband's place,*
> *But only if you swear*
> *To do everything I desire.*[15]

Ladies demanded that knights treat them with gentleness and consideration and that knights dress neatly, bathe often, play instruments, and compose (or at least recite) poetry. To prove worthy of his lady's love, a knight had to demonstrate patience, charm, bravery, and loyalty. It was believed that a knight would ennoble his character by devoting himself to a lady.

Courtly love involved not a husband–wife relationship but a noble's admiration and yearning for another woman of his class. Among nobles, marriages were arranged for political and economic reasons. The rituals of courtly love, it has been suggested, provided an outlet for erotic feelings condemned by the church. They also enhanced the skills and refined the tastes of the noble. The rough warrior acquired wit, manners, charm, and a facility with words. He was becoming a courtier and a gentleman.

THE VISITATION, WEST PORTAL, REIMS CATHEDRAL, C. 1225–1245. The reflection of Roman art exhibited by these statues of the expectant mothers (Mary and Elizabeth) of Jesus and John the Baptist suggests that the sculptor was well versed in the classical tradition. The carving of the draperies and the poses of the figures reveal classical traits, but instead of being idealizations, the figures display human warmth. (Scala/Art Resource/N.Y.)

The greatest literary figure of the Middle Ages was Dante Alighieri (1265–1321) of Florence. Dante appreciated the Roman classics and wrote not just in Latin, the traditional language of intellectual life, but also in Italian, his native tongue. In this respect, he anticipated the Renaissance. In the tradition of the troubadours, Dante wrote poems to his beloved Beatrice.

In *The Divine Comedy,* Dante synthesized the various elements of the medieval outlook and summed up, with immense feeling, the medieval understanding of the purpose of life. Written while Dante was in exile, *The Divine Comedy* describes the poet's journey through hell, purgatory, and paradise. Dante arranges hell into nine concentric circles; in each region, sinners are punished in proportion to their earthly sins. The poet experiences all of hell's torments—burning sand, violent storms, darkness, and fearful monsters that whip, claw, bite, and tear sinners apart. The ninth circle, the lowest, is reserved for Lucifer and traitors. Lucifer has three faces, each a different color, and two bat-like wings. In each mouth, he gnaws on the greatest traitors in history: Judas Iscariot, who betrayed Jesus, and Brutus and Cassius, who assassinated Caesar. Those condemned to hell are told: "All hope abandon, ye who enter in."

In purgatory, Dante meets sinners who, although they undergo punishment, will eventually enter paradise. He and Beatrice ascend to the highest heaven, a realm of light that radiates truth, goodness, and gentleness. In paradise, the poet meets the great saints and the Virgin Mary. He glimpses the Vision of God. In this mystical experience, the aim of life is realized.

ARCHITECTURE

Two styles of architecture evolved during the Middle Ages: Romanesque and Gothic. The **Romanesque** style dominated the eleventh century and the greater part of the twelfth. In imitation of ancient Roman structures, Romanesque buildings used massive walls to support stone barrel-and-groin vaults with rounded arches. Thick walls were needed to hold up the great weight of the roofs. Because the walls had few spaces for windows, little light entered the interior of Romanesque buildings.

The development of the pointed arch permitted supports that lessened the bearing pressure of the roof on the walls. This new style, called **Gothic,** allowed buildings to have lofty, vaulted ceilings and huge windows, which permitted sunlight to flood the interior. Whereas Romanesque buildings produced an impression of massive solidity, Gothic buildings created an illusion of lightness and upward motion. The Gothic cathedral gave visual expression to the medieval conception of a hierarchical universe. As the historian Joan Gadol puts it, "Inside and out, the Gothic cathedral is one great movement upward through a mounting series of grades, one ascent through horizontal levels marked by arches, galleries, niches, and towers. . . . [T]he material ascends to the spiritual, the natural is assumed into the supernatural—all in a graduated rise."[16] This illusion of upward reach to the heavens is created by the tall and narrow proportions of the interior spaces, the springing pointed arches, and the marching patterns of closely spaced columns and colonnettes.

The magnificently designed stained-glass windows and complex sculptural decoration of Gothic cathedrals depicted scenes from the Bible and the lives of saints, as well as scenes from daily life, for the worshipers, many of whom were illiterate. The reduction of wall space, which allowed these massive glass illustrations, was made possible by the flying buttresses on the buildings' exteriors. These great arcs of masonry carry the weight and thrust of the stone vaults out to the exterior walls. The light cage of buttresses surrounding the cathedral makes the exterior silhouette appear as airy and diffuse as the interior spaces. The architects and builders thought only of honoring God, not themselves; their identity remains a mystery.

Gothic cathedrals took many decades to complete and required donations from the devout. Only in an age of intense religious faith could such energy have been spent to glorify God. These vast building projects, many of them in northern France, were made possible by economic prosperity. Funds were raised from a variety of sources. Cathedrals owned income-producing properties, such as farmland, mills, and forests, and received donations from pilgrims visiting the relics of famous saints. Clerics also collected tolls and taxes on goods shipped to fairs through their region.

The Gothic style was to remain vigorous until the fifteenth century, spreading from France to England, Germany, Spain, and beyond. Revived from time to time thereafter, it has proved to be one of the most enduring styles in Western art and architecture.

Not too long ago, some intellectuals viewed the Middle Ages as a period of ignorance and superstition, an era of cultural sterility that stood between the high civilizations of ancient Greece and Rome and the modern West. This view of the Middle Ages as a dark age has been abandoned, and quite properly so, for the High Middle Ages saw the crystallization of a rich and creative civilization. To be sure, its religious orientation sets it apart both from classical civilization and from our own modern secular and scientific civilization. But the *Summa Theologica* of Aquinas, *The Divine Comedy* of Dante, and the Gothic cathedral all attest to the creativeness and genius of the medieval religious spirit.

❖   ❖   ❖

NOTES

1. Quoted in G. G. Coulton, *Life in the Middle Ages* (New York: Macmillan, 1928), 1:74.

2. Quoted in Charles Homer Haskins, *The Rise of Universities* (Ithaca, N.Y.: Cornell University Press, 1957), 79.

3. Quoted in Coulton, *Life in the Middle Ages*, 3:113.

4. Quoted in Anders Piltz, *The World of Medieval Learning* (Oxford: Blackwell, 1981), 83.

5. Quoted in David Knowles, *The Evolution of Medieval Thought* (New York: Vintage Books, 1964), 123.

6. *Summa Theologica*, excerpted in *Introduction to Saint Thomas Aquinas,* ed. Anton C. Pegis (New York: Modern Library, 1948), 25.

7. Steven Ozment, *The Age of Reform* (New Haven, Conn.: Yale University Press, 1980), 20.

8. Quoted in Piltz, *The World of Medieval Learning,* 176.

9. Quoted in A. C. Crombie, *Medieval and Early Modern Science* (Garden City, N.Y.: Doubleday Anchor Books, 1959), 1:55–56.

10. Quoted in Marcia L. Colish, *Medieval Foundations of the Western Intellectual Tradition, 400–1400* (New Haven, Conn.: Yale University Press, 1997), 202.

11. Excerpted in David C. Riede and J. Wayne Baker, eds., *The Western Intellectual Tradition* (Dubuque, Ia.: Kendall/Hunt, 1980), 1:62.

12. Excerpted in E. H. Zeydel, ed., *Vagabond Verse: Secular Latin Poems in the Middle Ages* (Detroit: Wayne State University Press, 1966), 61.

13. *The Fall of the Nibelungers,* trans. William Nanson Lettsom (London: Williams and Norgate, 1890), 1.

14. Excerpted in Anthony Bonner, ed., *Songs of the Troubadours* (New York: Schocken Books, 1972), 42–43.

15. Quoted in Frances Gies and Joseph Gies, *Women in the Middle Ages* (New York: T. Y. Crowell, 1978), 45.

16. Joan Gadol, *Leon Battista Alberti, Universal Man of the Early Renaissance* (Chicago: University of Chicago Press, 1969), 149–150.

SUGGESTED READING

Bonner, Anthony, ed., *Songs of the Troubadours* (1972). Collection of troubadour poetry.

Colish, Marcia L., *Medieval Foundations of the Western Intellectual Tradition, 400–1400* (1997). A lucid account; highly recommended.

Cook, William R. and Ronald B. Herzman, *The Medieval World View: An Introduction* (1983). A lucid summary of the medieval outlook; excellent for students.

Copleston, F. C., *A History of Medieval Philosophy* (1974). A lucid, comprehensive survey of medieval philosophy.

Gilson, Etienne, *Reason and Revelation in the Middle Ages* (1966). A superb brief exposition of the medieval philosophical tradition.

Gimpel, Jean, *The Cathedral Builders* (1984). The financial, political, and spiritual forces behind the building of cathedrals.

Harren, Michael, *Medieval Thought: The Western Intellectual Tradition from Antiquity to the Thirteenth Century* (1992). An up-to-date introduction to the major themes of medieval thought.

Pieper, Josef, *Scholasticism* (1964). Written with intelligence and grace.

Piltz, Anders, *The World of Medieval Learning* (1981). A valuable survey of medieval learning intended for non-specialists.

Wieruszowski, Helene, *The Medieval University* (1966). A good survey, followed by documents.

The Late Middle Ages: Crisis and Dissolution

The Jacquerie Enraged French peasants attack the castle of a lord.

(© Mary Evans Picture Library/The Image Works.)

- **An Age of Adversity**
- **The Decline of the Papacy**
- **The Breakup of the Thomistic Synthesis**
- **The Middle Ages and the Modern World: Continuity and Discontinuity**

Focus Questions

1. Why is the fourteenth century described as an age of adversity?
2. What led to the decline of the medieval papacy? What is the historical significance of this development?
3. What is the significance of thinkers who challenged the Thomistic synthesis?
4. What is the legacy of the Middle Ages to the modern world?
5. How does the characteristic outlook of the Middle Ages differ from that of the modern age?

By the start of the fourteenth century, Latin Christendom had experienced more than 250 years of growth. On an economic level, agricultural production had expanded, commerce and town life had revived, and the population had increased. On a political level, kings had become more powerful, bringing greater order and security to large areas. On a religious level, the papacy had demonstrated its strength as the spiritual leader of Christendom, and the clergy had been reformed. On a cultural level, a unified worldview, blending faith and reason, had been forged.

During the Late Middle Ages, roughly the fourteenth and early fifteenth centuries, medieval civilization was in decline. The fourteenth century, an age of adversity, was marked by crop failures, famine, population decline, plagues, stagnating production, unemployment, inflation, devastating warfare, and abandoned villages. Violent rebellions by the poor of the towns and countryside were ruthlessly suppressed by the upper classes. The century witnessed flights into mysticism, outbreaks of mass hysteria, and massacres of Jews; it was an age of pessimism and general insecurity. The papacy declined in power, heresy proliferated, and the synthesis of faith and reason, erected by Christian thinkers during the High Middle Ages, began to disintegrate. These developments were signs that the stable and coherent civilization of the thirteenth century was drawing to a close.

But all was not decline and gloom. On the positive side, representative institutions developed, and thinkers showed a greater interest in the world of nature. And in Italy, the dynamic forces of urbanism and secularism were producing a period of cultural and humanistic flowering known as the Renaissance.

AN AGE OF ADVERSITY

Economic Problems, the Black Death, and Social Tension

In the Late Middle Ages, Latin Christendom was afflicted with severe economic problems. The earlier increases in agricultural production did not continue. Limited use of fertilizers and limited knowledge of conservation exhausted the topsoil.

Chronology 12.1 ❖ The Late Middle Ages

1303	The French attack papal summer palace at Anagni
1309–1377	Babylonian Captivity: the popes, all French, reside at Avignon and are influenced by the French monarchy
1323–1328	Peasants' Revolt in Flanders
1328	End of France's Capetian dynasty; Edward III of England tries to gain the French throne
1337–1453	Hundred Years' War between England and France
1346	Battle of Crécy: the English defeat the French
1347–1351	Black Death reaches Italian ports and ravages Europe
1356	Battle of Poitiers: the English defeat the French
1358	Jacquerie, the French peasants' revolt
1377	Pope Gregory XI returns papacy to Rome
1378	Florentine laborers revolt
1378–1417	Great Schism: Christendom has two and then three popes
1381	English peasants revolt
1382	Weavers revolt in Ghent
1415	Battle of Agincourt: Henry V of England defeats the French; Jan Hus, a Bohemian religious reformer, is burned at the stake
1429	Joan of Arc liberates Orléans
1431	Joan of Arc is condemned as a witch
1453	The English are driven from France, except Calais: end of the Hundred Years' War
1460	Pope Pius II condemns the Conciliar Movement as heretical

As more grazing land was converted to the cultivation of cereals, animal husbandry decreased, causing a serious shortage of manure needed for arable land. Intermittent bouts of prolonged heavy rains and frost also hampered agriculture. From 1301 to 1314, there was a general shortage of food, and from 1315 to 1317, famine struck Europe. People subsisted by scavenging. On roads and in villages, people died of starvation, and the dead remained unattended. Throughout the century, starvation and malnutrition were widespread. In Bruges, for example, two thousand of the town's thirty-five thousand inhabitants died of starvation.

Other economic problems abounded. A shortage of silver, caused by technical problems in sinking deeper shafts in mines, led to the debasement of coins and spiraling inflation, which hurt the feudal nobility in particular. Prices for manufactured luxury goods, which the nobility craved, rose rapidly. At the same time, the dues that the nobility collected from peasants diminished. To replace their revenues, lords and knights turned to plunder and warfare.

Compounding the economic crisis was the Black Death, or bubonic plague, a bacillus carried by fleas on black rats. The disease probably first struck Mongolia in 1331–1332, and from there it crossed into Russia. Carried back from Black Sea ports, the plague reached Sicily in 1347 and then spread swiftly throughout much of Europe

John Wycliff: Concerning the Pope's Power

John Wycliffe (c. 1320–1384), a respected English theologian challenged the church's core doctrine that salvation was attainable only by adhering to its sacraments as administered by the clergy. Anticipating the Protestant Reformation of the sixteenth century, Wycliffe maintained that inspiration from Scripture, not obedience to the church, was the path to salvation. He specifically rejected the church doctrine that the clergy were indispensable intermediaries between human beings and God. In calling for a return to the spiritual purity of the early Christians, he attacked the luxurious life style of bishops and the pope. The following text, originally written in Middle English, was rendered into Modern English by Alfred J. Andrea.

Christ was a very poor man from His birth to His death and forswore worldly riches and begging . . . but Antichrist, in contrast to this, from the time that he is made pope to the time of his death, covets worldly wealth and tries in many shrewd ways to gain riches. Christ was a most meek man and urged that we learn from Him, but people say that the pope is the proudest man on earth, and he makes lords kiss his feet, whereas Christ washed His apostles' feet. Christ was a most unpretentious man in life, deeds, and words. People say that this pope is not like Christ in this way, for whereas Christ went on foot to cities and little towns alike, they say this pope desires to live in a castle in a grand manner. Whereas Christ came to John the Baptist to be baptized by him, the pope summons people to come to him wherever he might be, yea, as though Christ Himself, and not the pope, had summoned them to Him. Christ embraced young and poor in token of his humility; people say that the pope desires to embrace worldly prestige and not good people for the sake of God, lest he dishonor himself. Christ was busy preaching the Gospel, and not for worldly prestige or for profit;

through human contact. Some historians contend that the Black Death may have consisted of two diseases, the bubonic plague and anthrax, which was transmitted by eating meat from diseased cattle. The first crisis lasted until 1351, and other serious outbreaks occurred in later decades. The crowded cities and towns, where sewage made rats more fecund, had the highest mortality rate—as much as sixty percent. Perhaps twenty million people—about one-quarter to one-third of the European population—perished in the worst disaster in recorded history caused by natural forces. Contemporaries viewed the disaster as divine punishment for humanity's sins.

Overwhelmed by terror, people abandoned their sick children, spouses, and parents. Panic-stricken people drifted into debauchery, lawlessness, and frenzied forms of religious life. Confidence in the church declined as many priests fled, depriving the sick of spiritual comfort and the dying of last rites. Organized bands of flagellants marched from region to region beating themselves and one another with sticks and whips in a desperate effort to appease God, who, they believed, had cursed them with the plague. Expressing the pervasive gloom and pessimism of these times, art concentrated on morbid scenes of decaying flesh, open graves laden with worm-eaten corpses—even the Madonna was represented as a corpse being eaten by snakes and frogs—dances of death, and the torments of hell. Sometimes this hysteria was directed against Jews, who were accused of causing the plague by poisoning wells. Terrible massacres of Jews, often by mass burnings, occurred despite the pleas of the people say that the pope allows this, but he would gladly make laws to which he gives more prestige and sanction than Christ's law. Christ so loved His flock that He laid down his life for them and suffered sharp pain and death in order to bring them to bliss. People say that the pope so loves the prestige of this world that he grants people absolution that guarantees a straight path to Heaven so that they might perform acts that redound to his honor. And so this foolishiness could be the cause of the death, in body and soul, of many thousands of people. And how does he follow Christ in this way? Christ was so patient and suffered wrongs so well that He prayed for His enemies and taught His apostles not to take vengeance. People say that the pope of Rome wishes to be avenged in every way, by killing and by damning and by other painful means that he devises. Christ taught people to live well by the example of His own life and by His words, for He did what He taught and taught in a manner that was consonant with His actions. People say that the pope

acts contrary to this. His life is not an example of how other people should live, for no one should live like him, inasmuch as he acts in a manner that accords to his high state. In every deed and word, Christ sought the glory of God and suffered many assaults on His manhood for this goal; people say that the pope, to the contrary, seeks his own glory in every way, yea, even if it means the loss of the worship of God. And so he manufactures many groundless gabblings.

If these and similar accusations are true of the pope of Rome, he is the very Antichrist and not Christ's vicar on earth.

Questions for Analysis

1. Why was John Wycliffe critical of the church?
2. Why did the church regard his teachings as a serious threat to its mission?

Source: From Alfred Andrea, *The Medieval Record*, 1E. © 1997 Wadsworth, a part of Cengage Learning, Inc. Reproduced by permission. www.cengage.com/permissions.

papacy. Whole Jewish communities in Germany and Switzerland were exterminated. Invited by Duke Casimir II, who hoped they would stimulate economic activity, many Jews fled to Poland.

The millions of deaths caused production of food and goods to plummet. However, depopulation was a boon for surviving artisans, who found opportunities and higher wages in depopulated towns desperate for skilled workers. A diminishing labor pool also benefited peasants, who were able to attain lighter burdens from strapped lords, and free peasants who toiled as laborers demanded higher wages. The combination of lower agricultural prices and increasing wages hurt aristocratic landowners. As their agricultural income lessened, nobles tried to make peasants bear the brunt of the crisis. A law decreed in England in

1349 required peasants to work for lords at fixed wages. Similar regulations of wages in German, Spanish, and Portuguese principalities aggravated tensions between peasants and nobles.

Economic and social tensions, some of them antedating the Black Death, escalated into rebellions. Each rebellion had its own specific causes, but a general pattern characterized the uprisings in the countryside. When kings and lords, breaking with customary social relationships, imposed new and onerous regulations, the peasants rose in defense of their traditional rights. No doubt their revolt was also fueled by an instinctive hatred for the haughty lords, who, for centuries, had treated peasants with contempt. In 1323, the lords' attempt to reimpose old manorial obligations infuriated the free peasants of Flanders,

THE GREAT PLAGUE. The Black Death, or bubonic plague, devastated Europe, carrying off entire villages. A new piety swept through European art in the plague's aftermath. The elegant French courtly love style was replaced by morbid scenes of decaying flesh and suffering saints. (Snark/Art Resource, N.Y.)

whose condition had improved in earlier decades. The Peasants' Revolt lasted five bloody years. In 1358, French peasants took up arms in protest against the plundering of the countryside by soldiers. Perhaps twenty thousand peasants died in the uprising known as the Jacquerie. In 1381, English peasants revolted, angered over legislation that tied them to the land and imposed new taxes. John Ball, who claimed to be a priest, expressed egalitarian sentiments.

> My good friends, things cannot go on well in England, nor ever will until everything shall be in common; when there shall neither be vassal nor lord, and all distinctions leveled; when the lords shall be no more masters than ourselves. But ill have they used us! and for what reason do they thus hold us in bondage? Are we not all descended from the same parents, Adam and Eve? and what can they show, or what reasons give, why they should be more the masters than ourselves? except, perhaps, in making us labor and work, for

them to spend. . . . They have handsome manors, when we must brave the wind and rain in our labors in the field; but it is from our labor they have wherewith to support their pomp.[1]

Like the revolts in Flanders and France, the uprising in England failed. To the landed aristocracy, the peasants were sinners attacking a social system ordained by God. Possessing superior might, the nobility suppressed the peasants, sometimes with savage cruelty.

Social unrest afflicted the towns as well as the countryside. The wage earners of Florence (1378), the weavers of Ghent (1382), and the poor of Paris (1382) rose up against the ruling oligarchy. These revolts were generally initiated not by the poorest and most downtrodden but by those who had made some gains and were eager for more. The rebellions of the urban poor were crushed just like the peasant uprisings.

The Hundred Years' War

Compounding the adversity was the series of conflicts known as the Hundred Years' War (1337–1453). Because English kings ruled parts of France, conflicts between the two monarchies were common. In the opening phase of the war, the English inflicted terrible defeats on French knights at the battles of Crécy (1346) and Poitiers (1356). Using longbows, which allowed them to shoot arrows rapidly, English archers cut down wave after wave of charging French cavalry. The war continued on and off throughout the fourteenth century. During periods of truce, gangs of unemployed soldiers roamed the French countryside killing and stealing, actions that precipitated the Jacquerie.

After the battle of Agincourt (1415), won by the English under Henry V, the English controlled most of northern France. It appeared that England would shortly conquer France and join the two lands under one crown. At this crucial moment in French history, a young, illiterate peasant girl, Joan of Arc (1412–1431), helped rescue France. Believing that God commanded her to drive the English out of France, Joan rallied the demoralized French troops, leading them in battle. In 1429, she liberated the besieged city of Orléans. Later she was captured and imprisoned by the English, and in 1431 she was condemned as a heretic and a witch by a hand-picked church court and was burned at the stake. Inspired by Joan's death, the French drove the English from all French territory except the port of Calais.

During the Hundred Years' War, French kings introduced new taxes, which added substantially to their incomes. These monies furnished them with the means to organize a professional army of well-paid, loyal troops. By evoking a sense of pride and oneness in the French people, the war also contributed to a growing, but still incomplete, national unity. The English, too, emerged from the war with a greater sense of solidarity, and Parliament, because it had to finance the war, gained in stature. However, the war had horrendous consequences for the French peasants. Thousands of farmers were killed, and valuable farmland was destroyed by English armies and marauding bands of mercenaries. In a portentous development, the later stages of the Hundred Years' War saw the use of gunpowder and heavy artillery.

THE DECLINE OF THE PAPACY

The principal sign of breakdown in the Late Middle Ages was the waning authority and prestige of the papacy. In the High Middle Ages, the papacy had been the dominant institution in Christendom, but in the Late Middle Ages, its power disintegrated. The medieval ideal of a unified Christian commonwealth guided by the papacy was shattered. Papal authority declined in the face of the growing power of kings, who championed the parochial interests of states. The papacy's prestige and its capacity to lead diminished as it became more embroiled in European politics. Many pious Christians felt that the pope behaved more like a secular ruler than like an Apostle of Christ. Political theorists and church reformers further undermined papal authority.

Conflict with France

Pope Boniface VIII (1294–1303) vigorously upheld papal claims to supremacy over secular rulers. In the famous bull *Unam Sanctam* (1302), he declared:

> *If the earthly power errs, it shall be judged by the spiritual power . . . but [the pope] can be judged only by God not by man. . . . Whoever therefore resists this power so ordained by God resists the ordinance of God. . . . Therefore, we declare, state, define, and pronounce that it is altogether necessary to salvation for every human creature to be subject to the Roman Pontiff.*[2]

But in trying to enforce this idea of papal supremacy on proud and increasingly powerful kings, Boniface suffered defeat and humiliation.

Philip IV of France (1285–1314) taxed the church in his land to raise revenue for war. In doing so, he disregarded the church prohibition against the taxing of its property without papal permission. In 1296, in the bull *Clericis Laicos,* Pope Boniface VIII decreed that kings and lords who imposed taxes on the clergy and the clergy who paid them would be excommunicated. Far from bowing to the pope's threat, Philip acted forcefully to assert authority over the church in his kingdom. Boniface backed down from his position, declaring that the French king could tax the clergy in times of national emergency. Thus, the matter was resolved to the advantage of the state.

A second dispute had more disastrous consequences for Boniface. Philip tried and imprisoned a French bishop despite Boniface's warning that this was an illegal act and a violation of church law and tradition, which held that the church, not the state, must judge the clergy. Philip summoned the first meeting of the Estates General to gain the backing of the nation. Shortly afterward, Boniface threatened to excommunicate Philip. The outraged monarch raided the papal summer palace at Anagni in September 1303 and captured the pope. Although Boniface was released, this shocking event proved too much for him, and a month later he died.

Boniface's two successors, Benedict XI (1303–1304) and Clement V (1305–1314), tried to conciliate Philip. In particular, Clement decided to remain at Avignon, a town on the southeastern French frontier, where he had set up a temporary residence.

From 1309 to 1377, a period known as the Babylonian Captivity, the popes were all French and resided in Avignon, not Rome. During this time, the papacy, removed from Rome and

A DEAD MAN BEFORE HIS JUDGE: A MINIATURE PAINTING FROM THE ROMAN BOOK OF HOURS, FRANCE, C. 1420. God the Father, bearing the orb and sword of universal sovereignty, hears the final prayer of a dying man and sends an angel to liberate the man's soul from the clutches of a demon. A preoccupation with death and demons was characteristic of late medieval Christian art. (© Art Media/HIP/The Image Works.)

deprived of revenues from the Papal States in Italy, was often forced to pursue policies favorable to France. The growing antipapalism among the laity further damaged the papal image. Laypeople were repelled by the luxurious style of living at Avignon and by the appointment of high churchmen to lands where they did not know the language and showed little concern for the local population. Criticism of the papacy increased.

The conflict between Boniface and Philip provoked a battle of words between proponents of papal supremacy and defenders of royal rights. The most important critique of clerical intrusion into worldly affairs was *The Defender of the Peace* (1324) by Marsiglio of Padua (c. 1290–c. 1343). Marsiglio held that the state ran according to principles that had nothing to do with religious commands originating in a higher realm. Religion dealt with a supernatural world and with principles of faith that could not be proved by reason, wrote Marsiglio. Politics, in contrast, dealt with a natural world and with the affairs of the human community. Political thinkers should not try to make the earthly realm conform to articles of faith. According to Marsiglio, the state was self-sufficient; it needed no instruction from a higher authority. Thus, Marsiglio denied the essential premises of medieval papal political theory: that kings received their power from God; that the pope, as God's vicar, was empowered to guide kings; that the state, as part of a divinely ordered world, must conform to and fulfill supranatural ends; and that the clergy were above the laws of the state. Marsiglio viewed the church as a spiritual institution with no temporal power. "Christ himself," said Marsiglio, "refuse[d] rulership in this world . . . and taught that all men, both priests and non-priests, should be subject . . . to the coercive judgment of the rulers of this world."[3] Marsiglio even went so far as to suggest that the church should be subordinate to the state; his concept of an autonomous state that did not answer to clerical authority anticipates modern political thought.

The Great Schism and the Conciliar Movement

The Avignon popes were often competent men who, despite the hard times that had overtaken the papacy, tried to bolster papal power. They tightened their hold over church administration by reserving for themselves certain appointments and collections of fees formerly handled by local bishops. Through a deliberate effort at financial centralization, including the imposition of new taxes and the more efficient collection of old ones, the Avignon popes substantially increased papal income.

Although Pope Gregory XI returned the papacy to Rome in 1377, the papacy was to suffer

PORTRAIT OF JOAN OF ARC: WITCH OR SAINT? Claiming that heavenly voices had called upon her to lead the armies of France to victory over the English, a young peasant girl, Joan of Arc, persuaded the French crown prince to give her command of the army. Victorious in battle, she fulfilled all that was required of her, including the crowning of the new King at Rheims. Captured soon after, she was tried as a witch by an English-dominated court and executed in Rouen in 1431. She has been a heroine and inspiration to many modern artists, poets, and dramatists. (The Art Archive/Archives Nationales Paris/Marc Charmet.)

another humiliation: the Great Schism. Elected pope in 1378, Urban VI immediately displayed tactlessness, if not mental imbalance, by abusing and even imprisoning cardinals. Fleeing from Rome, the cardinals declared that the election of Urban had been invalid and elected Clement VII as the new pope. Refusing to step down, Urban excommunicated Clement, who responded in kind. To the utter confusion and anguish of Christians throughout Europe, there were now two popes: Urban ruling from Rome and Clement from Avignon.

Prominent churchmen urged the convening of a general council to end the disgraceful schism, which obstructed the papacy from performing its sacred duties. Held in 1409 and attended by hundreds of churchmen, the Council of Pisa deposed both Urban and Clement and elected a new pope. Since neither deposed pope recognized the council's decision, Christendom then had three popes. A new council was called at Constance in 1414. In the struggle that ensued, each of the three popes either abdicated or was deposed in favor of an appointment by the council. In 1417, the Great Schism ended.

During the first half of the fifteenth century, church councils met at Pisa (1409), Constance (1414–1418), and Basel (1431–1449) in order to end the schism, combat heresy, and reform the church. The Conciliar Movement attempted to transform the papal monarchy into a constitutional system in which the pope's power would be regulated by a general council. Supporters of the movement held that the papacy could not reform the church as effectively as a general council representing the clergy. But the Conciliar Movement ended in failure. As the Holy Roman Emperor and then the French monarch withdrew their support from the councils, the papacy regained its authority over the higher clergy. In 1460, Pope Pius II condemned the Conciliar Movement as heretical.

Deeply embroiled in European power politics and the worldly life of Renaissance Italy, the papacy often neglected its spiritual and moral responsibilities. Many devout Christians longed for religious renewal and a return to simple piety; the papacy did not hear this cry for reform. The papacy's failure to provide creative leadership for reform made possible the Protestant Reformation of the sixteenth century. By splitting Christendom into Catholic and Protestant, the Reformation destroyed forever the vision of a Christian world commonwealth guided by God's vicar, the pope.

Fourteenth-Century Heresies

Another threat to papal power and to the medieval ideal of a universal Christian community guided by the church came from radical reformers who questioned the function and authority of the entire church hierarchy. These heretics in the Late Middle Ages were forerunners of the Protestant Reformation. The two principal dissenters were the Englishman John Wycliffe (c. 1320–1384) and the Czech Jan Hus (c. 1369–1415).

By stressing a personal relationship between the individual and God and by claiming that the Bible itself, rather than church teachings, is the ultimate Christian authority, Wycliffe, a respected English theologian teaching at the University of Oxford, challenged the fundamental position of the medieval church: that the avenue to salvation passed through the church alone. He argued that Scripture, which was the final authority, needed no further development by church authorities and that the sacraments are not necessary for salvation. He denounced the wealth of the higher clergy and sought a return to the spiritual purity and material poverty of the early church. To Wycliffe, the wealthy, elaborately organized hierarchy of the church was unnecessary and wrong. The splendidly dressed and propertied bishops bore no resemblance to the simple people who first followed Christ. Indeed, these worldly bishops, headed by a princely and tyrannical pope, were really anti-Christians, the "fiends of Hell." Wycliffe wanted the state to confiscate church property and the clergy to embrace poverty. By denying that priests changed the bread and wine of Communion into the substance of the body and blood of Christ, Wycliffe rejected the special powers of the clergy.

In Bohemia, Wycliffe's ideas were enthusiastically received by Czech reformers led by Jan Hus. Like Wycliffe, Hus advocated vernacular translations of the Bible, which would be accessible to common people, and he upbraided the upper clergy for their luxury and immorality.

Both movements were declared heretical. The church deprived the Lollards—an order of poor priests that spread Wycliffe's teachings—of their priestly functions. In the early fifteenth century, some of Wycliffe's followers were burned at the stake, as was Jan Hus. Nevertheless, the church could not crush the dissenters' followers or eradicate their teachings. To some extent, the doctrines of the Reformation would parallel the teachings of Wycliffe.

THE BREAKUP OF THE THOMISTIC SYNTHESIS

In the Late Middle Ages, the papacy lost power as kings, political theorists, and religious dissenters challenged papal claims to supreme leadership. The great theological synthesis constructed by the scholastic theologians of the twelfth and thirteenth centuries was also breaking down. The process of fragmentation evident in the history of the church took place in philosophy as well.

Saint Thomas Aquinas's system culminated the scholastic attempt to show the basic agreement of philosophy and religion. In the fourteenth century, a number of thinkers cast doubt on the possibility of synthesizing Aristotelianism and Christianity, that is, reason and faith. Consequently, philosophy grew more analytical and critical. Denying that reason could demonstrate the truth of Christian doctrines with certainty, philosophers tried to separate reason from faith. Whereas Aquinas had said that reason proved or clarified much of revelation, fourteenth-century thinkers asserted that the basic propositions of Christianity were not open to rational proof. Whereas Aquinas had held that faith supplemented and perfected reason, some philosophers were now proclaiming that reason often contradicted faith.

Duns Scotus (1265–1308), a Scottish Franciscan, held that human reason cannot prove that God is omnipotent, that he forgives sins, that he rewards the righteous and punishes the wicked, or that the soul is immortal. These Christian doctrines, which scholastic philosophers believed could be proven by reason, were for Scotus the province of revelation and faith, not reason.

To be sure, this new outlook did not urge abandoning faith in favor of reason. Faith had to prevail in any conflict with reason because faith rested on God, the highest authority in the universe. But the relationship between reason and revelation was altered. Articles of faith, it was now held, had nothing to do with reason; they were to be believed, not proved. Reason was not an aid to theology but a separate sphere of activity. This new attitude snapped the link between reason and faith that Aquinas had so skillfully forged. The scholastic synthesis was disintegrating.

The chief proponent of the new outlook was William of Ockham (c. 1285–1349). In contrast to Aquinas, Ockham insisted that natural reason could not prove God's existence, the soul's immortality, or any other essential Christian doctrine. Reason could say only that God probably exists and that he probably endowed humankind with an immortal soul. But it could not prove these propositions with certainty. The tenets of faith were beyond the reach of reason, said Ockham; there was no rational foundation to Christianity. For Ockham, reason and faith did not necessarily complement each other as they did for Aquinas; it was neither possible nor helpful to join reason to faith. Ockham, however, sought not to undermine faith—only to disengage it from reason.

In the process of proclaiming the authority of theology, Ockham furthered the use of reason to comprehend nature. His approach, separating natural knowledge from religious dogma, made it easier to explore the natural world empirically without fitting it into a religious framework. Thus, Ockham is a forerunner of the modern mentality, which is characterized by a separation of reason from religion and an interest in the empirical investigation of nature.

THE MIDDLE AGES AND THE MODERN WORLD: CONTINUITY AND DISCONTINUITY

Medieval civilization began to decline in the fourteenth century, but no "dark age" comparable to the three centuries following Rome's fall descended on Europe; its economic and political institutions and technological skills had grown too strong. Instead, the waning of the Middle Ages opened up possibilities for another stage in Western civilization: the modern age.

The modern world is linked to the Middle Ages in innumerable ways. European cities, the middle class, the state system, English common law, universities—all had their origins in the Middle Ages. During medieval times, important advances were made in business practices, including partnerships, systematic bookkeeping, and the bill of exchange, which paved the way for modern banking. By translating and commenting on the writings of Greek and Arabic thinkers, medieval scholars preserved a priceless intellectual heritage without which the modern mind could never have evolved. In addition, numerous strands connect the thought of the scholastics and that of early modern philosophers.

Feudal traditions lasted long after the Middle Ages. Up to the French Revolution, for instance, French aristocrats enjoyed special privileges and exercised power over local government. In England, the aristocracy controlled local government until the Industrial Revolution transformed English society in the nineteenth century. Retaining the medieval ideal of the noble warrior, aristocrats continued to dominate the officer corps of European armies through the nineteenth century and even into the twentieth. Aristocratic notions of duty, honor, loyalty, and courtly love have endured into our own day.

During the Middle Ages, Europeans began to take the lead over the Muslims, the Byzantines, the Chinese, and all other peoples in the use of technology. Medieval technology and inventiveness stemmed in part from Christianity, which taught that God had created the world specifically for human beings to subdue and exploit. Consequently, medieval people tried to employ animal power and labor-saving machinery to relieve human drudgery. Moreover, Christianity taught that God was above nature, not within it, so the Christians faced no spiritual obstacle to exploiting nature—unlike, for instance, the Hindus. In contrast to classical humanism, the Christian outlook did not consider manual work degrading; even monks combined it with study.

The Christian stress on the sacred worth of the individual (each person had an immortal soul that was God's concern), on human equality (differences in rank and birth were of no account to God on **Judgment Day**), and on the higher law of God (divine precepts had a greater pull on conscience than did the state's laws) has never ceased to influence Western civilization. Even though in modern times the various Christian churches have not often taken the lead in political and social reform, the ideals identified with the Judeo-Christian tradition have become part of the Western heritage. As such, they have inspired social reformers who may no longer identify with their ancestral religion.

In structuring canon (church) law into a coherent and rational system, church jurists provided a model for legal systems in emerging European states. Moreover, specific elements of canon law have become an integral part of modern Western law. Medieval jurists, for example, argued for the replacement of trials by ordeals of fire or water, which were central to ancient Germanic folk law, with rational trial procedures and insisted that marriages based on fraud or duress could be invalidated.

Believing that God's law was superior to state or national decrees, medieval philosophers provided a theoretical basis for opposing tyrannical kings who violated Christian principles. The idea that both the ruler and the ruled are bound by a higher law would, in a secularized form, become a principal element of modern liberal thought.

Feudalism also contributed to the history of liberty. According to feudal custom, the king, as a member of the feudal community, was duty-bound to honor agreements made with his vassals. Lords possessed personal rights, which the king was obliged to respect. Resentful of a king who ran roughshod over customary feudal rights, lords also negotiated contracts with the crown, such as Magna Carta (1215), to define and guard their customary liberties. To protect themselves from the arbitrary behavior of a king, feudal lords initiated what came to be called *government by consent* and the *rule of law*.

During the Middle Ages, then, there gradually emerged the idea that law was not imposed on inferiors by an absolute monarch but required the collaboration of the king and his subjects; that the king, too, was bound by the law; and that lords had the right to resist a monarch who violated agreements. A related phenomenon was the rise of representative institutions, with which the king was expected to consult on the realm's affairs. The most notable of such institutions was the British Parliament; though subordinate to the king, it became a permanent part of the state. Later, in the seventeenth century, Parliament would successfully challenge royal authority. Thus, continuity exists between the feudal tradition of a king bound by law and the modern practice of limiting the authority of the head of state.

Although the elements of continuity are clear, the characteristic outlook of the Middle Ages is as different from that of the modern age as it was from the outlook of the Greco-Roman past. Religion—often expressing a disdain of earthly pursuits and a preoccupation with the world to come—was the integrating feature of the Middle Ages, whereas science and secularism—a preoccupation with worldly life—determine the modern outlook. The period from the Italian Renaissance of the fifteenth century through the eighteenth-century Age of Enlightenment saw a gradual breaking away from the medieval worldview—a rejection of the medieval conception of nature, the individual, and the purpose of life. The transition from medieval to modern was neither sudden nor complete, for there are no sharp demarcation lines separating historical periods. Although many distinctively medieval ways endured in the sixteenth, seventeenth, and even eighteenth centuries, these centuries saw as well the rise of new intellectual, political, and economic forms, which marked the emergence of **modernity**.

Medieval thought began with the existence of God and the truth of his revelation as interpreted by the church, which set the standards and defined the purposes for human endeavor. The medieval mind rejected the fundamental principle of Greek philosophy: the autonomy of reason. Without the guidance of revealed truth, reason was seen as feeble. Philosophical inquiry was permissible only if the mind arrived at clerically approved conclusions.

Scholastics engaged in genuine philosophical speculation and demonstrated impressive signs of logical thinking, but they did not allow philosophy to challenge the basic premises of their faith. For them, the dissemination of views that contradicted church doctrine had to be prohibited lest they corrupt the mind of the faithful. Unlike either ancient or modern thinkers, medieval scholars ultimately believed that reason alone could not provide a unified view of nature or society. A rational soul had to be guided by a divine light. For all medieval philosophers, the natural order depended on a supernatural order for its origin and purpose. To understand the natural world properly, it was necessary to know its relationship to the higher world. The discoveries of reason had to accord with Scripture as interpreted by the church. In medieval thought, says the historian-philosopher Ernst Cassirer,

WISDOM URGES MEDIEVAL SCHOLARS FORWARD. During the Middle Ages, Europeans made considerable advances in technology. The astrolabe, suadrant, sundials, and mechanical clocks shown here exemplify medieval technical skills. (Bibliothèque Royale de Belgique.)

neither science nor morality, neither law nor state, can be erected on its own foundations. Supernatural assistance is always needed to bring them to true perfection. . . . Reason is and remains the servant of revelation; within the sphere of natural intellectual and psychological forces, reason leads toward, and prepares the ground for, revelation.[4]

In the modern view, both nature and the human intellect are self-sufficient. Nature is a mathematical system that operates without miracles or any other form of divine intervention. To comprehend nature and society, the mind needs no divine assistance; it accepts no authority above reason. The modern mentality finds it unacceptable to reject the conclusions of science on the basis of clerical authority and revelation or to ground politics, law, or economics on religious dogma. It refuses to settle public issues by appeals to religious belief, which is now seen as a strictly private concern.

The medieval philosopher understood both nature and society to be a hierarchical order. The heavens were qualitatively superior in purpose and substance to the earthly realm. God was the source of moral values, and the church was responsible for teaching and upholding these ethical norms. Kings acquired their right to rule from God. The entire social structure constituted a hierarchy: the clergy, the highest order, guided society according to Christian standards; lords defended Christian society from its enemies; and serfs, lowest in the social order, toiled for the good of all. In the hierarchy of knowledge, a lower form of knowledge derived from the senses, and the highest type of knowledge, theology, dealt with God's revelation. To the medieval mind, this hierarchical ordering of nature, society, and knowledge had a divine sanction.

Rejecting the medieval division of the universe into higher and lower realms and superior and inferior substances, the modern view postulated the uniformity of nature and of nature's

Profile

Joan of Arc

A crucial phase in the Hundred Years' War occurred in 1415 when England inflicted an overwhelming defeat on the French at Agincourt. The victorious English imposed on the French the Treaty of Troyes (1420). Its terms stipulated that the daughter of Charles VI, the French monarch, would marry the English ruler, Henry V, and that their future son would reign over the dual monarchy of England and France. This provision deprived Charles VI's only living son, the dauphin Charles, from succeeding to the throne. From Bourges in central France, the dauphin continued the struggle against the English invaders and their Burgundian allies. In 1428, the English besieged Orléans in preparation for an attack on Bourges. The dauphin's position seemed hopeless.

At this critical moment, Joan of Arc appeared on the scene. Born to a peasant family in northern France, Joan very early demonstrated extreme piety. At age thirteen, she experienced revelations—voices from angels and saints who guided her behavior. When she was about sixteen, her voices instructed her to raise the siege of Orléans and have Charles anointed king of France at Rheims. Joan the maid, as she was called, attracted followers who believed that Joan was sent by God to rescue Orléans from the English.

Demonstrating great resolve, Joan, dressed in men's clothing and accompanied by believers in her mission, made the arduous journey to the dauphin's castle. Charles reluctantly granted an audience to Joan, whom some of his counselors considered mad. After listening to Joan detail her divine mission, Charles had her examined by his clerks and sages, who reported that the uneducated, but devout, peasant girl was neither a heretic nor a sorceress. With the military position worsening, the desperate dauphin provided Joan with an army—perhaps this religiously inspired maid had indeed been sent by God. Wearing a full set of armor and wielding a lance, Joan demonstrated remarkable leadership and courage, which inspired her troops. She also showed a facility for military planning. To the inhabitants of Orléans, it seemed that God had provided them with a deliverer. When she entered the city, crowds pressed to touch her. Aided by the citizens of Orléans, Joan's army attacked the English fortifications. Hit by

laws: the cosmos knows no privilege of rank; heavenly bodies follow the same laws of nature as earthly objects. Space is geometric and homogeneous, not hierarchical, heterogeneous, and qualitative. The universe was no longer conceived as finite and closed but as infinite, and the operations of nature were explained mathematically. The modern thinker studies mathematical law and chemical composition, not grades of perfection. Spiritual meaning is not sought in an examination of the material world. Roger Bacon, for example, described seven coverings of the eye and then concluded that God had fashioned the eye in this manner in order to express the seven gifts of the Spirit. This way of thinking is alien to the modern outlook. So too is the medieval belief that natural disasters, such as plagues and famines, are God's punishments for people's sins.

The outlook of the modern West also broke with the rigid division of medieval society into three orders: clergy, nobles, and commoners. The intellectual justification for this arrangement, as expressed by the English prelate John of Salisbury (c. 1115–1180), has been rejected by modern westerners: "For inferiors owe it to their superiors to provide them with service, just as the superiors in their turn owe it to their inferiors to provide them with all things needful for their protection and succor."[5] To be sure, Christian theorists also maintained that as God's children, all human beings are in principle equal in God's eyes. Opposing the feudal principle that an individual's obligations and rights are a function of his or her rank in society, the modern view stressed equality of opportunity and equal treatment under the law. It rejected the idea that society should be guided an arrow above the breast, Joan had the wound dressed and immediately returned to the fray. In a decisive encounter, the maid grabbed her standard from a squire and led a successful assault on an English fortress. Soon after, the English abandoned the siege: the maid's forces had liberated the city. Several months later, Joan achieved her greatest victory, an open-field battle at Patay, which caught the English by surprise. Following the battle, the dauphin was crowned Charles VII at Rheims.

Meanwhile, in the ongoing conflict with the English and Burgundians, Joan could not escape a Burgundian siege and was taken prisoner. Charles VII made no effort to ransom Joan; he simply abandoned her. Purchasing the now-famous prisoner from the Burgundians, the English organized a show trial in Rouen, conducted by learned but hostile French clerics, to prove that the despised Joan was a heretic and a witch. The proceedings took about five months. During that time, Joan wore leg irons; at night in her dungeon, her jailers chained the leg irons to the foot of the bed. During the interrogation, Joan displayed remarkable self-control, dignity, cleverness, and even eloquence and humor, which often exasperated the inquisitors. The inquisitors asked Joan if she would defer to the church when told that her voices were illusions; Joan replied that her voices had not commanded her to disregard the church but she served the Lord first, a rebellious act that amounted to heresy.

When the judges accused her of lying and threatened to inflict torture unless she altered her statements, Joan replied: "Truly, though you were to have my limbs torn off and send the soul out of my body, I should not say otherwise; and if I did tell you otherwise, I should always thereafter say that you had made me speak so by force."*

After the judges ruled that she had been doing the work of the Devil, Joan was declared a heretic and condemned to burn at the stake. The sentence was carried out on May 30, 1431, and her ashes were thrown into the Seine. In 1456, the church nullified the condemnation, and in 1920 Joan was declared a saint.

---

*Quoted in Régine Pernoud, *Joan of Arc: By Herself and Her Witnesses*, trans. Edward Hyans (Lanham, Md.: Scarborough House, 1994), 206.

by clergy who were deemed to possess a special wisdom, by nobles who were entitled to special privileges, and by monarchs who were thought to receive their power from God.

The modern West also rejected the personal and customary character of feudal law. As the modern state developed, law assumed an impersonal and objective character. For example, if the lord demanded more than the customary forty days of military service, the vassal might refuse to comply because he would see the lord's request as an unpardonable violation of custom and agreement, as well as an infringement on his liberties. In the modern state, with a constitution and a representative assembly, if a new law increasing the length of military service is passed, it merely replaces the old law. People do not refuse to obey it because the government has broken faith or violated custom.

In the modern world, the individual's relationship to the universe has been radically transformed. Medieval people lived in a geocentric universe that was finite in space and time. The universe was small, enclosed by a sphere of stars, beyond which were the heavens. The universe, it was believed, was some four thousand years old, and, in the not-too-distant future, Christ would return and human history would end. People in the Middle Ages knew why they were on earth and what was expected of them; they never doubted that heaven would be their reward for living a Christian life. Preparation for heaven was the ultimate aim of life. J. H. Randall Jr., a historian of ideas, eloquently sums up the medieval view of a purposeful universe in which the human being's position was clearly defined.

> *The world was governed throughout by the omnipotent will and omniscient mind of God, whose sole interests were centered in man, his trial, his fall, his suffering and his glory. Worm of the dust as he was, man was yet the central object in the whole universe. . . . And when his destiny was completed, the heavens would be rolled up as a scroll and he would dwell with the Lord forever. Only those who rejected God's freely offered grace and with hardened hearts refused repentance would be cut off from this eternal life.*[6]

This comforting medieval vision is alien to the modern outlook. Today, in a universe some thirteen to fourteen billion years old, in which the earth is a tiny speck floating in an endless cosmic ocean, where life evolved over tens of millions of years, many westerners no longer believe that human beings are special children of God; that heaven is their ultimate goal; that under their feet is hell, where grotesque demons torment sinners; or that God is an active agent in human history. To many intellectuals, the universe seems unresponsive to the religious supplications of people, and life's purpose is sought within the limits of earthly existence. Science and secularism have driven Christianity and faith from their central position to the periphery of human concerns.

In the nineteenth and twentieth centuries, Christian thinkers lamented the waning of faith. Distressed by all-consuming secularism, crude materialism, and vicious class and national antagonisms, these thinkers attributed the ills of the modern West to a diminishing commitment to Christianity and called for spiritual renewal. Some of them, looking back nostalgically to the Middle Ages, when life had an overriding religious purpose and few doubted the truth of Christian teachings, contended that the modern West would benefit from a reaffirmation of those Christian concerns and values that had energized medieval society.

The modern outlook developed gradually in the period from the Renaissance to the eighteenth-century Age of Enlightenment. Mathematics rendered the universe comprehensible. Economic and political thought broke free of the religious frame of reference. Science became the great hope of the future. The thinkers of the Enlightenment wanted to liberate humanity from superstition, ignorance, and traditions that could not pass the test of reason. They saw themselves as emancipating culture from theological dogma and clerical authority. Rejecting the Christian idea of a person's inherent sinfulness, they held that the individual was basically good and that evil resulted from faulty institutions, poor education, and bad leadership. Thus, the concept of a rational and free society in which individuals could realize their potential slowly emerged.

❖ ❖ ❖

Notes

1. Jean Froissart, *Chronicles of England, France, Spain* (London: Henry G. Bohn, 1849), 653.

2. Excerpted in Brian Tierney, ed., *The Crisis of Church and State, 1050–1300* (Englewood Cliffs, N.J.: Prentice-Hall, 1964), 189.

3. Marsilius of Padua, *Marsilius of Padua: The Defender of the Peace,* trans. Alan Gewirth (New York: Columbia University Press, 1956), 2:119.

4. Ernst Cassirer, *The Philosophy of the Enlightenment* (Boston: Beacon Press, 1955), 40.

5. John of Salisbury, *Policraticus,* trans. John Dickinson (New York: Russell and Russell, 1963), 243–244.

6. J. H. Randall Jr., *The Making of the Modern Mind* (Boston: Houghton Mifflin, 1940), 34.

Suggested Reading

Bowsky, W. M., ed., *The Black Death* (1971). Readings on the impact of the plague.

Goodich, Michael, ed., *Other Middle Ages: Witnesses at the Margin of Medieval Society* (1998). Selections dealing with disenfranchised members of medieval society in the High and Late Middle Ages.

Cantor, Norma F., *In the Wake of the Plague: The Black Death and the World It Made* (2001). A readable and current synthesis of latest scholarship.

Holmes, George, *Europe: Hierarchy and Revolt, 1320–1450* (1975). A good survey of the period.

Lerner, Robert E., *The Age of Adversity* (1968). A short, readable survey of the fourteenth century.

Nirenberg, David, *Communities of Violence: Persecution of Minorities in the Middle Ages* (1996). Focuses on medieval beliefs that triggered violent attacks on minorities.

Ozment, Steven E., *The Age of Reform, 1250–1550* (1980). An intellectual and religious history of late medieval and Reformation Europe.

Pegg, Mark Gregory, *A Most Holy War: The Albigensian Crusade and the Battle for Christendom* (2008). A gripping narrative of medieval mass murder.

Russell, Burton Jeffrey, *Witchcraft in the Middle Ages* (1972). Describes the development of a phenomenon that is deeply rooted in the nonrational.

Spinka, M., *John Hus and the Czech Reform* (1941). A reliable work on Hus and the Hussite wars.

 CourseMate

Go to the CourseMate website at **www.cengagebrain.com** for additional study tools and review materials—including audio and video clips—for this chapter.

Part Three

Early Modern Europe: From Renaissance to Enlightenment

1350–1789

1300

1400

1500

1600

1700

Politics and Society

Hundred Years' War (1337–1453)

War of Roses in England (1455–1485)
Rule of Ferdinand and Isabella in Spain
(1469–1516)
Charles VIII of France (1483–1498)
Henry VII; beginning of Tudor dynasty in
England (1485–1509)
French invasion of Italy (1494)
Columbus reaches America (1492)

Henry VIII of England (1509–1547)
Francis I of France (1515–1547)
Charles V, Holy Roman emperor (1519–
1556)
Henry VIII of England breaks with Rome
(1529–1536)
Council of Trent (1545–1563)
Treaty of Augsburg in Germany (1555)
Philip II of Spain (1556–1598)
Elizabeth I of England (1558–1603)
Religious wars in France (1562–1598)
Revolt of the Netherlands from Spain
(1566–1609)
Defeat of Spanish Armada (1588)

Thirty Years' War (1618–1648)
English revolutions (1640–1660, 1688–1689)
Louis XIV of France (1643–1715)
Peter the Great of Russia (1682–1725)

War of Spanish Succession (1702–1714)
War of Austrian Succession (1740–1748)
Frederick the Great of Prussia (1740–1786)
Maria Theresa of Austria (1740–1780)
Seven Years' War (1756–1763)
Catherine the Great of Russia (1762–1796)
American Declaration of Independence (1776)
American Revolution (1776–1783)
Beginning of French Revolution (1789)

Thought and Culture

Italian Renaissance begins (c. 1350)

Early Renaissance artists: Brunelleschi,
Masaccio, van Eyck
Printing with movable type (c. 1445)
Humanists: Valla, Pico della Mirandola
Late Renaissance artists: Botticelli,
Leonardo da Vinci, Michelangelo,
Raphael, Bellini, Giorgione, Titian
Renaissance spreads to northern Europe
(late 15th–early 16th centuries)

Humanists: Castiglione, Erasmus,
Montaigne, Rabelais, More, Machiavelli,
Cervantes, Shakespeare
Luther writes Ninety-Five Theses (1517)
Calvin, *The Institutes of the Christian Religion*
(1536)
Copernicus, *On the Revolution of the
Heavenly Spheres* (1543)

Scientists: Kepler, Galileo, Newton
Philosophers: Bacon, Descartes, Spinoza,
Hobbes, Bayle, Locke

Enlightenment thinkers: Voltaire,
Montesquieu, Rousseau, Diderot, Hume,
Adam Smith, Thomas Jefferson, Kant

Chapter 13

The Renaissance: Transition to the Modern Age

The School of Athens, *by Raphael (1483–1520). The ancient Greek philosophers, with Plato and Aristotle at the center, are depicted here, assembled in classical grandeur. Painted to decorate the Vatican, the papal palace in Rome, the picture exudes the Renaissance reverence for classical antiquity and reflects the widely held view that ancient philosophy represented a foreshadowing of Christianity and was essentially in harmony with it.* (Alinari/Art Resource, N.Y.)

Focus Questions

1. What conditions gave rise to the Italian Renaissance?
2. What is the historical significance of Renaissance humanism?
3. How did Machiavelli's political thought mark a break with the medieval outlook?
4. What were the effects of the printing press on European civilization?

From the Italian Renaissance of the fifteenth century through the Age of Enlightenment of the eighteenth century, the outlook and institutions of the Middle Ages disintegrated and distinctly modern forms emerged. The radical change in European civilization could be seen on every level of society. On the economic level, commerce and industry expanded greatly, and capitalism in some countries largely replaced medieval forms of economic organization. On the political level, central government grew stronger at the expense of feudalism. On the religious level, the rise of Protestantism fragmented the unity of Christendom. On the social level, middle-class townspeople, increasing in number and wealth, were playing a more important role in economic and cultural life. On the cultural level, the clergy lost its monopoly on learning, and the otherworldly orientation of the Middle Ages gave way to a secular outlook in literature and the arts. Theology, the queen of knowledge in the Middle Ages, surrendered her crown to science. Reason, which in the Middle Ages had been subordinate to revelation, asserted its independence.

Many of these tendencies manifested themselves dramatically during the Renaissance. The word *renaissance* means "rebirth," and it is used to refer to the attempt by artists and thinkers to recover and apply the ancient learning and standards of Greece and Rome. In historical terms, the Renaissance is both a cultural movement and a period. As a movement, it was born in the city-states of northern Italy and spread to the rest of Europe. As a period, it ran from 1350 to 1600. Until the late fifteenth century, the Renaissance was restricted to Italy. What happened there in the fourteenth and fifteenth centuries sharply contrasts with civilization in the rest of Europe, which, until the end of the fifteenth century, still belonged to the Late Middle Ages.

The nineteenth-century historian Jacob Burckhardt in his classic study *The Civilization of the Renaissance in Italy* (1860) held that the Renaissance was the point of departure for the modern world. During the Renaissance, said Burckhardt, individuals showed increasing concern with worldly life and self-consciously aspired to shape their destinies—attitudes that are the key to modernity.

Burckhardt's thesis has been challenged, particularly by medievalists, who view the Renaissance

Chronology 13.1 ❖ The Renaissance

1200–1300	Bologna, Padua, and Ravenna become centers of legal studies
1300–1450	Republicanism reigns in northern Italian city-states
1304–1374	Petrarch, "father of humanism"
1378	Ciompi revolt in Florence
c. 1407–1457	Lorenzo Valla, author of *Declamation Concerning the False Decretals of Constantine*
c. 1445	Johann Gutenberg invents movable metal type
1454	Peace of Lodi is signed
1494	Charles VIII of France invades northern Italy; Pope Julius II commissions frescoes by Michelangelo for the Vatican's Sistine Chapel
1513	Machiavelli writes *The Prince*
1528	*The Book of the Courtier*, by Baldesar Castiglione, is published
1535	Sir Thomas More, English humanist and author of *Utopia*, is executed for treason

as an extension of the Middle Ages, not as a sudden break with the past. These critics argue that Burckhardt neglected important links between medieval and Renaissance culture. One distinguishing feature of the Renaissance, the revival of classical learning, had already emerged in the High Middle Ages to such an extent that historians speak of "the renaissance of the twelfth century" and the "Twelfth-Century Awakening." The Renaissance owes much to the legal and scholastic studies that flourished in the Italian universities of Padua and Bologna before 1300. Town life and trade, hallmarks of Renaissance society, were also a heritage from the Middle Ages.

To be sure, the Renaissance was not a complete and sudden break with the Middle Ages. Many medieval ways and attitudes persisted. Nevertheless, Burckhardt's thesis that the Renaissance represents the birth of modernity has much to recommend it. Renaissance writers and artists themselves were aware of their age's novelty. They looked back on the medieval centuries as "the Dark Ages" that followed the grandeur of ancient Greece and Rome, and they believed that they were experiencing a rebirth of cultural greatness. Renaissance artists and writers were fascinated by the cultural forms of Greece and Rome; they sought to imitate **classical** style and to capture the secular spirit of antiquity. In the process, they broke with medieval artistic and literary forms. They valued the full development of human talent and expressed fresh excitement about the possibilities of life in this world. This outlook represented a new trend in European civilization.

The Renaissance, then, was an age of transition that saw the rejection of certain elements of the medieval outlook, the revival of classical cultural forms, and the emergence of distinctly **modern** attitudes. As mentioned earlier, this rebirth began in Italy during the fourteenth century. It gradually spread north and west to Germany, France, England, and Spain during the late fifteenth and sixteenth centuries.

ITALY: THE BIRTHPLACE OF THE RENAISSANCE

The city-states of northern Italy that spawned the Renaissance were developed urban centers where the elite had the wealth, freedom, and inclination to cultivate the arts and to enjoy the fruits of worldly life. In Italy, moreover, reminders of ancient Rome's grandeur were visible everywhere. Roman roads, monuments, and manuscripts intensified Italians' links to their Roman past.

The Political Evolution of the City-States

During the Middle Ages, the feudal states of northern Italy had been absorbed into the Holy Roman Empire. They continued to owe nominal allegiance to the German emperor during the early Renaissance. But protracted wars with the papacy had sapped the empire's vitality. Its consequent weakness allowed the states of northern Italy to develop as autonomous political entities. The weakening of the papacy in the fourteenth century also promoted this development.

In their size and their varied types of governments, the city-states in northern Italy resembled those of ancient Greece. Among the more important were Rome, Milan, Florence, Venice, Mantua, Ferrara, Padua, Bologna, and Genoa. They differed markedly from most of Europe in two fundamental respects.

First, by the late eleventh and twelfth centuries, these city-states were flourishing commercial and banking centers and monopolized trade in Mediterranean areas, including trade between the East and the West. Merchant fleets, especially those of Venice and Genoa, carried goods from ports in the eastern Mediterranean westward into the Atlantic and from there north to the Baltic Sea. In contrast to the rest of Europe, the wealth of these cities lay not in land but in commerce and industry. When popes, monarchs, and feudal magnates of Europe needed money, they borrowed it from Italian, especially Florentine, merchant-bankers.

Second, the predominance of business and commerce within these city-states meant that the feudal nobility, which held the land beyond the city walls, played a much lesser role in government than they did elsewhere in Europe. By the end of the twelfth century, the city-states no longer were dominated by the feudal nobility, or landed aristocracy. The aristocracy and the rich merchants had to share power, and when their alliances broke down, as they often did, the two groups struggled for power based on their opposing interests and outlooks. The interests of the smaller merchants and the artisans in the towns also had to be catered to. When they were not, those groups rioted and rebelled, as they did, for instance, in 1378, during the revolt of the *Ciompi* (wool-workers) in Florence.

Politically, the city-states in northern Italy were inherently unstable. The instability had two sources: internal conflicts between merchants and nobles and external rivalries among the city-states themselves. The city-states managed to keep both the papacy and the Holy Roman Empire at bay, sometimes by playing one giant against the other. But the price of this continued independence was that the city-states, without any externally imposed power structure, had to seek their own solutions to their instability. Out of this situation came experiments in the form and technique of government. The origins of modern political thought and practice can be discerned in this experimentation, which is an important link between the Renaissance and the modern age.

The political experimentation in the northern Italian city-states can usefully, if only roughly, be divided into two periods: the first (1300–1450) marked by the defense of **republicanism**; the second (1450–1550), by the triumph of **despotism**. By the end of the twelfth century, the city-states had adopted a fairly uniform pattern of republican self-government built around the office of a chief magistrate. Elected by the citizens on the basis of a broad franchise, the chief magistrate ruled with the advice of two councils—a large public one and a small secret one. His powers were tightly circumscribed by the **constitution**; with his term of office restricted ordinarily to six months, he could be removed from government or punished at the end of his tenure.

The city-states not only developed republican institutions but also devised important theories to defend and justify their liberty and self-government in the face of their external enemies, the papacy and the empire. With the emperor, they argued that their customary feudal subjection to imperial authority must be radically adjusted to fit the changed reality that they were in fact self-governing. With the papacy, they contended that Christ had denied all political jurisdiction to the clergy, including the pope, and that this fact undercut the papal claim to political control in Italy and elsewhere.

However, given the city-states' internal instability and rivalry, their republicanism proved precarious. During the fourteenth and early fifteenth centuries, the republican institutions in one city after another toppled in favor of despotic rule.

Three conditions were responsible for this development. First, class war between rich merchants and nobles caused one group or the other, or both, to seek a resolution of the crisis by turning to one-person rule. Second, the economic disasters, famine, and disease of the period from 1350 to 1450 encouraged the drift toward despotism. Northern Italy was particularly hard hit by the bubonic plague. The citizenry lost faith in the ability of short-term republican governments to cope with such emergencies and put its trust in long-term, one-man rule. Third, and perhaps most important, the city-states, in wars with their rivals, had come to rely on mercenary troops. The leaders of those troops, the notorious *condottieri*—unschooled in and owing no loyalty to the republican tradition—simply seized power during emergencies.

Some city-states held out for a long time against the trend toward despotism. Among those that did, Florence was by far the most successful. In the process, the Florentines developed new arguments and theories for the maintenance of republicanism and liberty (discussed later in this chapter). But by the middle of the fifteenth century, even Florentine republicanism was giving way before the intrigues of a rich banking family, the Medicis. They had installed themselves in power in the 1430s, with the return of Cosimo de' Medici from exile. Cosimo's grandson, Lorenzo the Magnificent, completed the destruction of the republican constitution in 1480, when he managed to set up a government staffed by his own supporters.

The one city-state where republicanism survived until the advent of Napoleon was Venice. Protected from the rest of Italy by lagoons, Venice during the Middle Ages controlled a far-flung and exceptionally lucrative seagoing trade and a maritime empire stretching along the Adriatic and the

PORTRAIT OF A MAN, CALLED *THE SOLDIER*, 1475, BY ANTONELLO DA MESSINA (D. 1479). This soldier could have been either a mercenary, hired to fight for pay, or a citizen-soldier who ideally would have fought not just for money but out of loyalty to his city-state, and who, as such, was thought to be the embodiment of civic virtue—honest, strong, and brave. (The Art Archive/Musee du Louvre, Paris/Alfredo Dagli Orti.)

eastern Mediterranean seas. Venetian maritime commercial successes were matched by political ones at home. For centuries, Venice managed to govern itself without a major upheaval; its republican constitution made this stability possible. Its chief executive offices, the Council of Ten, were elective, but after 1297 both these offices and the electorate were narrowly restricted by law to old patrician families. Venice was an aristocratic **republic**. The government proved remarkably effective because the ruling elite was able to instill in its young a sense of public duty that was passed on from one generation, and one century, to the next. Because Venetian government was at once stable and republican, it served as a model to republican theorists in seventeenth- and eighteenth-century Europe.

◀ *Map 13.1* ITALIAN CITY-STATES, C. 1494
During the Renaissance, Italy was divided between large kingdoms in the south, dominated by the Spanish monarchy, and smaller city-states in the north, each with its own government and army and often hostile to one another. The French king Charles VIII took advantage of these divisions by invading and occupying much of northern Italy beginning in 1494. (Copyright © 2013 Cengage Learning.)

Aside from Venice, the city-states in northern Italy were not only internally unstable but also constantly warring with one another. By the middle of the fifteenth century, however, five major powers had emerged from the fighting: the kingdom of Naples and Sicily in the south; the Papal States, a papacy-controlled territory running across the center of the Italian peninsula; and the city-states of Florence, Venice, and Milan in the north. In 1454, these five powers, largely through the efforts of Cosimo de' Medici, concluded the Peace of Lodi. For the next forty years, they were relatively peaceful, until the French king Charles VIII invaded northern Italy in 1494.

The Peace of Lodi endured so long thanks to diplomacy. The essential techniques of modern diplomacy were worked out and applied in the second half of the fifteenth century in Italy. The practices of establishing embassies with ambassadors, sending and analyzing intelligence reports, consulting and negotiating during emergencies, and forming alliances all developed during this period. Some historians also see this time in Italian history as the seedbed for the notion of balance of power, which eventually became fundamental to the diplomacy of all Europe. Later, in the early modern period, European governments formed alliances so that no single state or group of allied states could dominate the Continent. Some elements of this balance of power were anticipated in the struggles among the Italian city-states.

Renaissance Society

The new way of life in the city-states paralleled developments in relations among them. Prosperous merchants played a leading role in the political and cultural life of the city. With the growth of commerce and industry, the feudal values of birth, military prowess, and a fixed hierarchy of lords and vassals decayed in favor of ambition and individual achievement, whether at court, in the counting-house, or inside the artist's studio. The old feudal chivalric code was not destroyed but transformed to serve different purposes.

The new urban, commercial **oligarchies** could not justify their power in the old way, through heredity. Moreover, they had to function within the inherently unstable political climate of the city-states. Faced with this dual problem, the oligarchs fell back on the feudal idea of honor and developed elaborate codes. These codes differed in significant ways from their medieval antecedents. First came a depreciation (though never a complete elimination) of birth as a basis of merit and a corresponding emphasis on effort, talent, and (in the case of the artist) creative genius. Second, honor was no longer defined in narrow, largely military terms; it was expanded to include both the civic and courtly virtues of the worthy citizen and courtier and the artistic achievement of the painter, sculptor, architect, and poet.

The new code, however, did remain elitist and even aristocratic. Indeed, the new oligarchs of the Renaissance, because of their newness and insecurity, were all the more anxious to adopt the aristocratic outlook of the old nobility. The *nouveaux riches* (newly rich) aped the feudal aristocracy in dress and manners, even as they accommodated the code of knightly chivalry to the demands of a new urban and commercial culture. Renaissance society was a highly unstable compound of old and new.

Marriage and Family Life. City life profoundly altered family structures, marriage patterns, and relations between the sexes. Elsewhere in Europe, most people still lived on the land and tended to marry early in order to produce large families to work the fields. But in cities, early marriage could be a liability for a man who was attempting to make his fortune. The results were that older men married young brides and that wives usually outlived their husbands. Because a widow inherited her husband's property, she was not pressed to remarry and was likely to bring up her children in a single-parent household. According to the historian David Herlihy, the fact that so many women were responsible for nurturing their children may have encouraged the development of the Renaissance ideal of a gentleman, which emphasized civility, courtliness, and an appreciation of art, literature, and the feminine graces.

The large number of single, relatively prosperous, and leisured adults probably explains why Renaissance cities were reputed for sodomy, prostitution, and triangles involving an older husband, a young wife, and a young lover. Such sexual behavior was encouraged by the relative anonymity of the large cities and by the constant influx of young men of talent from the country districts.

Whatever the effect on their sons, upper-class women enjoyed greater freedom in greater numbers than they had since the fall of Rome. If they were married, they had the income to pursue pleasure in the form of clothes, conversation, and romance. If a well-to-do husband died while his wife was still young, she had no financial reasons to remarry and was free, to a degree previously unknown, to go her own way.

Patronage of the Arts. Members of the urban upper class became patrons of the arts, providing funds to support promising artists and writers. Urban patricians, whose wealth was based on commerce and banking, not land, had become dominant in both republican Florence and despotic Milan. Unable to claim power by birth or to rely on traditional loyalties, they looked to culture to provide the trappings and justification of power.

For the newly rich, art could serve a political function. In its sheer magnificence, art could manifest power. Art, like literature, could also serve as a focus of civic pride and patriotism. Just as insecure rulers contended on the battlefield, they competed for art and artists to bolster their egos. Art became a desirable political investment, especially when, in the fifteenth century, economic investments were not offering as much return as they had a century or two before. The popes invested in art as well. Having lost the battle for temporal dominion in Europe, the papacy concentrated on increasing its direct dominion in Italy by consolidating and expanding the Papal States. As an adjunct to this policy, the popes heaped wealth on artists to enhance papal prestige. Indeed, the popes became the most lavish patrons of all, as the works of Michelangelo, Botticelli, and Raphael testify.

The result of this new patronage by popes and patricians was an explosion of creativity. The amount, and especially the nature, of this patronage also helped shape both art and the artist. For the first time since antiquity, portraiture became a separate genre and was developed much further than ever before. Patrician rivalry and insecurity of status, fed by the Renaissance ethic of achievement and reward, produced a scramble for honor and reputation. This fostered the desire to be memorialized in a painting, if not in a sculpture. A painter like Titian was in great demand.

Secularism. Renaissance society was marked by a growing **secular** outlook. Intrigued by the active life of the city and eager to enjoy the worldly pleasures that their money could obtain, wealthy merchants and bankers moved away from the medieval preoccupation with salvation. Although they were neither nonbelievers nor atheists, for them religion increasingly had to compete with worldly concerns. Consequently, members of the urban upper class paid religion less heed or at least did not allow it to interfere with their quest for a full life. The challenge and pleasure of living well in this world seemed more exciting than the promise of heaven. This outlook found expression in Renaissance art and literature.

Individualism. Individualism was another hallmark of Renaissance society. Urban life released people of wealth and talent from the old constraints of manor and church. The urban elite sought to assert their own personalities, discover and express their individual feelings, and demonstrate their unique talents. They strove to win fame and glory and to fulfill their ambitions. This Renaissance ideal was explicitly elitist. It applied only to the few, entirely disregarding the masses, and it valued what was distinctive and superior in an individual, not what was common to all. Concerned with the distinctions of the few, it did not consider the needs or rights of the many. Individualism became deeply embedded in the Western soul and was expressed by artists who sought to capture individual character, by explorers who ventured into uncharted seas, by conquerors who carved out empires in the New World, and by merchant-capitalists who amassed fortunes.

THE RENAISSANCE OUTLOOK: HUMANISM AND SECULAR POLITICS

Humanism

The most characteristic intellectual movement of the Renaissance was *humanism,* an educational and cultural program based on the study of ancient Greek and Roman literature. The humanist attitude toward antiquity differed from the attitude of medieval scholars, who had taken pains to

Leonardo Bruni: Study of Greek Literature and a Humanist Educational Program

Leonardo Bruni (1374–1444) was a Florentine humanist who extolled both intellectual study and active involvement in public affairs, an outlook called civic humanism. In this excerpt from his History of His Own Times in Italy, *Bruni expresses the humanist's love for ancient Greek literature and language.*

Love for Greek Literature

Then first came a knowledge of Greek, which had not been in use among us for seven hundred years. Chrysoloras the Byzantine,* a man of noble birth and well versed in Greek letters, brought Greek learning to us. When his country was invaded by the Turks, he came by sea, first to Venice. The report of him soon spread, and he was cordially invited and besought and promised a public stipend, to come to Florence and open his store of riches to the youth. I was then studying Civil Law,† but . . . I burned with love of academic studies, and had spent no little pains on dialectic and rhetoric. At the coming of Chrysoloras I was torn in mind, deeming it shameful to desert the law, and yet a crime to lose such a chance of studying Greek literature; and often with youthful impulse I would say to myself: "Thou, when it is permitted thee to gaze on Homer, Plato and Demosthenes,‡ and the other [Greek] poets, philosophers, orators, of whom such glorious things are spread abroad, and speak with them and be instructed in their admirable teaching, wilt thou desert and rob thyself? Wilt thou neglect this opportunity so divinely offered? For seven hundred years, no one in Italy has possessed Greek letters; and yet we confess that all knowledge is derived from them. How great advantage to your knowledge, enhancement of your fame, increase of your pleasure, will come from an understanding of this tongue? There are doctors of civil law everywhere; and the chance of learning will not fail thee. But if this one and only doctor of Greek letters disappears, no one can be found to teach thee." Overcome at length by these reasons, I gave myself to Chrysoloras, with such zeal to learn, that what through the wakeful day I gathered, I followed after in the night, even when asleep.

Questions for Analysis

1. Why was it so important to Leonardi Bruni to learn to read Greek?
2. Who are the ancient Greek thinkers whom Bruni singles out for special praise?

---

*Chrysoloras (c. 1355–1415), a Byzantine writer and teacher, introduced the study of Greek literature to the Italians, helping open a new age of Western humanistic learning.

†*Civil Law* refers to the Roman law as codified by Emperor Justinian in the early sixth century A.D. and studied in medieval law schools.

‡Demosthenes (384–322 B.C.) was an Athenian statesman and orator whose oratorical style was much admired by Renaissance humanists.

Henry Osborn Taylor, *Thought and Expression in the Sixteenth Century* (New York: Frederick Ungar, 1930), 1:36–37.

fit classical learning into a Christian worldview. Renaissance humanists did not subordinate the classics to the requirements of Christian doctrines; rather, they valued ancient literature for its own sake—for its clear and graceful style and its insights into human nature. From the ancient classics, humanists expected to learn much that could not be provided by medieval writing: for instance, how to live well in this world and how to perform one's civic duties. For the humanists, the classics were a guide to the good life, the active life. To achieve self-cultivation, to write well, to speak well, and to live well, it was necessary to know the classics. In contrast to scholastic philosophers, who used Greek philosophy to prove the truth of Christian doctrines, Italian humanists used classical learning to nourish their new interest in a worldly life.

Whereas medieval scholars were familiar with only some ancient Latin writers, Renaissance humanists restored to circulation every Roman work that could be found. Similarly, knowledge of Greek was very rare in Latin Christendom during the Middle Ages, but Renaissance humanists increasingly cultivated the study of Greek in order to read Homer, Demosthenes, Plato, and other ancients in the original.

Although predominantly a secular movement, Italian humanism was not un-Christian. True, humanists often treated moral problems in a purely secular manner. Yet in dealing with religious and theological questions, they did not challenge Christian belief or question the validity of the Bible. They did, however, attack scholasticism for its hair-splitting arguments and preoccupation with trivial questions. They stressed instead a purer form of Christianity, based on direct study of the Bible and writings by the church fathers.

The early humanists, sometimes called the fathers of humanism, were Petrarch (1304–1374) and Boccaccio (1313–1375). Petrarch, Boccaccio, and their followers carried the recovery of the classics further by making a systematic attempt to discover the classical roots of medieval Italian rhetoric. Petrarch's own efforts to learn Greek were largely unsuccessful, but by encouraging his students to master the ancient tongue, he advanced humanist learning. Petrarch was particularly drawn to Cicero, the ancient Roman orator. Following the example of Cicero, Petrarch insisted that education should consist not only of learning and knowing things but also of learning how to communicate one's knowledge and how to use it for the public good. Therefore, the emphasis in education should be on rhetoric and moral philosophy, wisdom combined with eloquence. As Bartolommeo della Fonte (1446–1513), professor of rhetoric at Florence, said, such a program of instruction would fit a man for effective rule: that is, "to punish the wicked, to care for the good, to embellish his native land and to benefit all mankind."[1] Thus, Petrarch helped make Ciceronian values dominant among the humanists. His

followers set up schools to inculcate the new Ciceronian educational ideal.

Implicit in the humanist educational ideal was a radical transformation of the medieval (Augustinian) view of humanity. According to this view, since human beings were completely subject to divine will, not only were they incapable of attaining excellence through their own efforts and talents, but it was also wrong and sinful for them even to try. In contrast, the humanists, recalling the classical Greek concept of arête, made the achievement of excellence through individual striving the end not only of education but also of life itself. Moreover, because individuals were capable of this goal, it was their duty to pursue it as the end of life, although the pursuit was not effortless and indeed demanded extraordinary energy and skill.

People were deemed capable of excellence in every sphere and duty-bound to make the effort. This emphasis on human creative powers was one of the most characteristic and influential doctrines of the Renaissance. A classic expression of it is found in the *Oration on the Dignity of Man* (1486) by Giovanni Pico della Mirandola (1463–1494). Man, said Pico, has the freedom to shape his own life. Pico has God say to man: "We have made you a creature" such that "you may, as the free and proud shaper of your own being, fashion yourself in the form you may prefer."[2]

Pico also spelled out another implication of man's duty to realize his potential: through his own exertions, man can come to understand and control nature. One of the new and powerful Renaissance images of man was as the *magus*, the magician. The vision of the mastery of nature would continue to inspire experimentalists, such as Francis Bacon, and natural philosophers, such as Robert Boyle and Isaac Newton, until at least the early eighteenth century. A major psychological driving force of the Scientific Revolution, this vision stemmed in large part from the philosophy of Italian humanists such as Pico.

The attack on the medieval scholastics was implicit in the humanist educational ideal. From the humanist perspective, scholasticism failed not only because its terms and Latin usage were barbarous but also because it did not provide useful knowledge. This humanist emphasis on the uses of knowledge offered an additional stimulus to science and art.

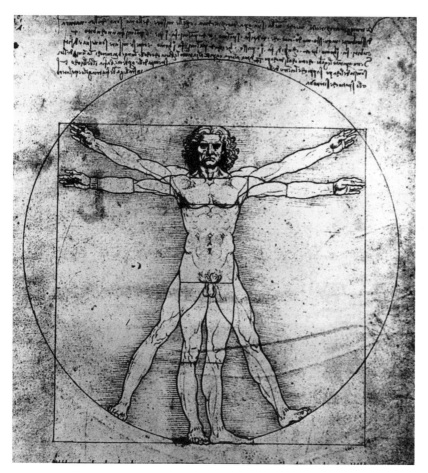

LEONARDO DA VINCI, *THE PROPORTIONS OF MAN*. Leonardo was fascinated by the human body. In his notebook, his written observations are accompanied by this marvelous drawing of the body, conceived and framed with realism and proportion. (Hulton Archive/Handout/Getty Images.)

But the new humanist and heroic image of human beings was deeply compromised and conflicted in one major area: the subject of women and gender relations. During the Renaissance, there were a few powerful female rulers, such as Elizabeth I, queen of England (1558–1603), and Catherine de' Medici, who became the regent (ruler) of France after her husband Henri II's untimely death in 1559. However, they were the exceptions. Politics and especially monarchical rule were always considered a male monopoly from which women should be excluded because they were inferior beings unsuited to holding such power.

Some aristocratic women patronized humanist scholars. Margaret Beaufort (1443–1509), mother of an English king, founded two colleges that fostered the new learning in England. Catherine of Aragon (1485–1536), the first wife of Henry VIII, king of England (1512–1547), surrounded herself with leading humanists, such as Desiderius Erasmus (1466–1536) and Juan Vives (1492–1540). The latter wrote for her a book entitled *The Instruction of a Christian Woman* (1523), which summarized humanist teaching on the subject. Vives insisted that women should be educated so that they could read serious books on religion and philosophy. But for him, like so many others, the goals of female education should be very limited. Men, he said, must be educated to act in the world and to govern. In contrast, women should be taught virtue—that is, devotion to home and family—and cheerful obedience to their husbands. In particular, women, according to Vives, should never be taught rhetoric, which was thought to be the key discipline in training men to become strong and effective leaders. Such rhetorical training would be wasted on women because their place was in the home and not in public life.

Such split thinking was repeated over and over again throughout the Renaissance. For example, Erasmus, the foremost European humanist, advocated female education, not so that educated women could act in the world but because reading was a way to banish idleness at home and was preferable to such tasks as knitting and sewing. Erasmus's friend Sir Thomas More (1478–1535) insisted on educating his daughters to a high level, not so that they could cut a figure on the public stage, but to make them better wives and daughters, that is, more virtuous and obedient. As female humanists in England and Italy, if not elsewhere, said at the time, men were jealous of educated women and afraid of losing control over them.

There were, however, a very few exceptions to this cramped and hostile view of female potential. The German physician Heinrich Cornelius Agrippa von Nettesheim (1486–1535), for instance, wrote *On the Nobility and Excellence of Women* in 1529. In this work, he held that although women are biologically different from men, they are not intellectually inferior to them. He went on to argue for the full equality of the sexes, a radical claim very far from mainstream, and even educated, opinion. Long before Agrippa, Christine de Pizan (1364–c. 1430), an extraordinary French female humanist, attacked the ancient prejudice that men are by nature not only stronger but also wiser than women. As she said in her great book, *The City of Ladies*, written in 1404, "[N]either the loftiness nor the lowliness of a person lies in the body according to sex, but in the perfection of conduct and virtues."[3] In other words, a person's worth is not about gender but about behavior. Despite this brilliant insight, which breaks through to an almost modern view of gender equality, even de Pizan could not hold

her ground but fell back on the deep-seated prejudices of her time. She said that men and women from time immemorial have played distinctly different roles in society, and so it should ever be: men are ordained to rule; women, to follow and obey. This is God's will. Thus, with the plausible exception of Agrippa, there were no modern feminists in the Renaissance, even at its most radical. The Renaissance humanists may have been overwhelmingly antifeminist, but they were also, at least in Florence and Venice, staunch republican political idealists.

In fourteenth- and fifteenth-century republican Florence, at least until the Medicis took control, Petrarchan humanism was not meant for a court elite. Humanism was a civic idea: to educate and inform citizens so that they could contribute to the common good to the greatest possible extent. In this sense, humanism was put in the service of republican values and the republican cause, and the mixture of the two is what has come to be called *civic humanism* by recent historians. This civic ideal developed furthest in the Florentine republic.

By the second half of the fifteenth century, as the Medicis gained increasing control, the civic ideal was being replaced by an ideal more fitting to the times, the ideal of princely rule. This ideal borrowed much from civic humanism, even though it was directed toward princes and courtiers and not toward citizens. The emphasis on the pursuit of virtue and honor continued. Like the ideal gentleman, the ideal prince would evolve through humanistic education, which would so prepare him for the struggle between virtue and fortune that virtue would prove victorious.

The similarities between the civic and princely ideals, however, were not as important as the differences. The aim of princely rule was not liberty but peace and security, and the best means to this end was not a republic but hereditary monarchy. This new princely ideal was reflected in a new spate of advice books, the most influential of which was *The Book of the Courtier*, written between 1513 and 1518 by Baldesar Castiglione (1478–1529). These books promoted the notion that the ideal ruler should be universally talented and skillful, equally commanding on the battlefield, at court, and in the state and virtuous throughout. These advice books, especially

Castiglione's, were to serve as indispensable handbooks for courtiers and would-be gentlemen in Renaissance Italy and throughout the rest of Europe for centuries.

A Revolution in Political Thought

One advice book transcended all the others: *The Prince,* written in 1513 by the Florentine Niccolò Machiavelli (1469–1527). It offered an indictment of the humanist ideal of princely rule and in so doing made some fundamental contributions to political theory. Indeed, Machiavelli may be called the first major modern political thinker. To Machiavelli, the humanist ideal was naïve in its insistence on the prince's virtues and eloquence to the exclusion of all other considerations. He attacked the medieval and humanist tradition of theoretical politics.

> *Since my intention is to say something that will prove of practical use to the inquirer, have thought it proper to represent things as they are in real truth, rather than as they are imagined. Many have dreamed up republics and principalities which have never in truth been known to exist; the gulf between how one should live and how one does live is so wide that a man who neglects what is actually done for what should be done learns the way to self-destruction.[4]*

NICCOLÒ MACHIAVELLI (1469–1527). Machiavelli looked back to the ancient Roman republic for his ideals and spent his life serving the city-state of Florence, but as the author of *The Prince*, his name became a byword for atheism and deceit. "Machiavellian" is still used to describe an unscrupulous politician. (Scala/Art Resource, N.Y.)

Politics, Machiavelli argued, requires the rational deployment of force, as well as, and even prior to, the exercise of virtue.

On this point, Machiavelli's advice is quite specific. He wrote *The Prince* in part as a plea. Since 1494, Italy had fallen prey to France and Spain. Their great royal armies overpowered the mercenary armies of the city-states and proceeded to lay waste to Italy in their struggle for domination of the peninsula. To prevent this, Machiavelli said, the Italians should unite behind a leader—the prince—whose first act would be to disband the mercenaries and forge a new citizen army worthy of the glorious Roman past and capable of repelling the "barbarian" invasion. "Mercenaries," Machiavelli claimed, "are useless and dangerous." They are useless because "there

is no . . . inducement to keep them on the field apart from the little they are paid, and this is not enough to make them want to die for you." And they are dangerous because their leaders, the infamous condottieri, "are anxious to advance their own greatness" at the expense of the city-state. Reliance on mercenaries was the sole cause of "the present ruin of Italy," and the cure lay in the creation of a national militia, led by a prince.[5]

This prince had to be both wily and virtuous, not just virtuous (as humanists had said): "The fact is that a man who wants to act virtuously in every way necessarily comes to grief among so many who are not virtuous." So Machiavelli scandalized Christian Europe by asserting that "if a prince wants to maintain his rule he must learn how not to be virtuous, and to make use of this or

The Renaissance

1. Filippo Brunelleschi, Church of San Lorenzo, interior, looking toward the apse, Florence, Italy.
(Erich Lessing/Art Resource, N.Y.)

The most vivid image of the Renaissance is conveyed through its architecture, sculpture, and painting. Renaissance examples of all three art forms display a style that stressed proportion, balance, and harmony. These artistic values were achieved through a new, revolutionary conceptualization of space and spatial relations. To a considerable extent, Renaissance art also reflects the values of Renaissance humanism in the use of classical models in architecture, in the rendering of the nude human figure, and in the heroic vision of human beings.

Medieval art sought to represent spiritual aspiration; the world was a veil merely hinting at the other, perfect, eternal world. Renaissance art expresses spiritual aspiration, but its setting and character differ altogether. This world is no longer a veil but the *place* where people live, act, and worship. The reference is less to the other world and more to this world, and people are treated as creatures who find their spiritual destiny as they fulfill their human one.

Renaissance artists produced revolutionary discoveries that served as the foundation of Western art up to the twentieth century. In art, as in philosophy, the Florentines played a leading role in this esthetic transformation. The first major contributor to Renaissance painting was the Florentine painter Giotto (c. 1276–1337). (See Figure 11 in the first art essay.) Giotto developed several

2. Donatello, *David*, c. 1425–1430. (Scala/Art Resource, N.Y.)

techniques of perspective, representing three-dimensional figures and objects on two-dimensional surfaces so that they appear to stand in space. Giotto's figures look remarkably alive. They are drawn and arranged in space to tell a story, and the expressions they wear and the illusion of movement they convey heighten the dramatic effect. The dramatic work of Giotto marked the end of the stiff, otherworldly style of the Middle Ages. The artists who followed Giotto diverged from his style and subject matter. Although Christianity was still an important theme, Renaissance artists also depicted subjects from Greek and Roman mythology as well as scenes from everyday life.

Painting, sculpture, architecture, and the minor arts evolved at a different pace throughout this period. It was not as if all artists declared themselves to be Renaissance figures simultaneously. Instead, styles changed with new artistic sensibilities, technological advances, and the requests of new patrons.

Rarely can one ascribe the development of an entire period of art to a single individual. Such is the case of Renaissance architecture, however. Filippo Brunelleschi (c. 1377–1446) began his career as a sculptor in Florence. He turned to architecture sometime after 1402 and traveled to Rome, where he studied the remains of imperial Roman buildings and monuments. Brunelleschi learned the theory of scientific perspective, perhaps while trying to draw on paper three-dimensional images of the monuments. He also developed a method of building double domes linked to reinforce each other. This lightened the weight of the dome, allowing the structure beneath to be built with fewer supporting elements.

One of the earliest expressions of his architectural skill can be seen in the Church of San Lorenzo in Florence (1421–1469) (Figure 1). Thanks to the benevolence of the Medici family, Brunelleschi was granted license to design an entire building himself. The Church of San Lorenzo was a new structure, not an adaptation of or an addition to an older, medieval building. Although some of its elements may have derived from earlier prototypes, the new building was distinct in its symmetry and regularity. Its floor plan shows a markedly regular repetition of equal-size squares to establish the nave, transept, and aisles. The centrally planned chapel, with its strict adherence

3. Masaccio, *The Holy Trinity*, 1425. (Scala/Art Resource, N.Y.)

to mathematical proportion, distinguishes the Church of San Lorenzo from the medieval Gothic cathedral. Brunelleschi's ability to grasp the concept of perspective in two dimensions is translated into three dimensions by the strong use of line and rhythmical arches that draw the eye to the altar.

Brunelleschi effected the same fusion of antique and Christian as his contemporaries did in other fields. Poets and writers experimented with classical and Christian styles; so too did Brunelleschi. Note, for example, the Corinthian capitals topping the San Lorenzo columns, whereas the floor plan is in the shape of a cross.

Architecture was not the only medium that combined experimentation and echoes of the past; sculpture did as well. Whereas Brunelleschi can be viewed as the father of Renaissance architecture, a host of sculptors advanced the Renaissance style in their medium. Prominent among them in the early Renaissance was Donatello (1386–1466), whose works distinguished him as a master even in his own time. The bronze *David* (c. 1425–1430) (Figure 2) is perhaps the most controversial of his best-known sculptures. The first life-size, free-standing nude sculpture since antiquity, this work is still something of an enigma.

Art historians assume that the statue was to have been exhibited outdoors, or at least in a central location, because it was meant to be viewed from all sides. The young David is wearing only a hat and high boots. Unlike the well-muscled athletes of the classical period, however, he is slender and slight, an adolescent instead of a developed adult. Donatello does pay homage to classical prototypes in the stance of his David— a *contrapposto*, or counterbalanced, pose, in which the weight on the legs is uneven (compare David's stance with Hermes' stance in Figure 1 of the first art essay).

Symbolic devices provide the key to the significance of the sculpture. David represents the city of Florence itself, and the helmet of Goliath under his feet represents the duchy of Milan, which at the time was at war with Florence. David's nudity may allude to the city's classical past, and the wreathed hat may suggest victory.

In painting, experiments in depth and linear perspective stand out as the major developments. Artists were seeking ways of making two-dimensional surfaces seem three-dimensional.

CONTVRBATIO·IESV·CHRISTI·LEGISLATORIS

4. Pietro Perugino, *The Delivery of the Keys,* 1481. (Scala/Art Resource, N.Y.)

Brunelleschi was the first to develop a system in which all parallel lines of a scene converge in one central point on the horizon; other artists adopted his scheme and carried it further.

The Holy Trinity (Figure 3), a fresco by Masaccio (1401–1428), a brilliant young artist who died at the age of twenty-seven, advanced further Brunelleschi's experiments with linear perspective. Masaccio takes a central Christian spiritual idea, the Trinity—God the Father, the Son, and the Holy Spirit—and materializes and humanizes it.

He depicts a crucified Christ on the cross with God the Father standing behind him, and the Holy Spirit descending as a dove on Christ's head. The figures of Christ, the onlooking Madonna, St. John, even the figure of God the Father, standing behind Christ on an elevated platform, are human, material figures in a three-dimensional space.

The illusion of spatial depth is created by the architectural parameters of an overarching barrel-vaulted ceiling divided into squares diminishing in size.

Masaccio here provides a point of departure for subsequent art. Henceforth, artists will increasingly portray visual space within the three-dimensional perspectival format suggested by Masaccio, and human beings as real people, solid in form and realistic in anatomy, bones, muscles, and expressions.

Pietro Perugino's *The Delivery of the Keys* (1481) (Figure 4), a fresco from the Sistine Chapel in the Vatican, illustrates the enthusiasm with which other artists achieved perspective. Note that all the parallel lines in the foreground converge at the church in the center of the background. The viewer's eye is drawn into the

5. Leonardo da Vinci, *The Last Supper*, c. 1495–1498. (© The Gallery Collection/Corbis.)

painting, and figures seem real, not flat. Compare this portrayal with the flat and linear rendering of Justinian and his retinue in the mosaic from Ravenna. There, the effect is two-dimensional, and the viewer does not expect to see beyond the layer of figures. In the Perugino, by contrast, the figures are full and exist in a three- dimensional space.

The works of Leonardo da Vinci (1452–1519)—his drawings, paintings, sculpture, innumerable inventions, and copious writings—exemplify the Renaissance spirit. He expands the idea of three-dimensional, perspectival space to include the living form of things, their mathematical proportions. He announced a new way of looking at nature and the individual. For Leonardo, visual art offered a means of arriving at nature's truths. Truth was attained when the artist brought both human reason and creative capacity to bear on the direct experience of the senses. Leonardo examined objects in all their diversity and represented them realistically. He visually delineated the natural world with unprecedented scientific

precision, and he asserted his spiritual and intellectual freedom to do so. Through his art, Leonardo helped lay the foundations for modern science.

Leonardo's *The Last Supper* (Figure 5) affords a stark contrast to that of the Magdalen Master (compare with Figure 9 in the first art essay), providing a basis for gauging the distance traversed by Western art from the Middle Ages to modernity. Leonardo's version is explosive, and the scene is depicted vibrantly. The figures, in agitated motion, arranged in three-dimensional space, huddled into four groups, exhibit a wide range of postures, attitudes, and individual reactions to Christ's pronouncement that someone among them would betray him.

Leonardo has transformed medieval and Eastern two-dimensional space into the full-volumed three-dimensional space of the modern world and the lifeless, impersonal forms of medieval and Eastern art into unique individual personalities, their feelings captured at the very instant of their reaction to Christ's announcement.

6. Michelangelo Buonarroti, *Creation of Adam*, 1510. (Sistine Chapel Ceiling: Creation of Adam, 1510 (fresco) (post restoration), Buonarroti, Michelangelo (1475–1564)/Vatican Museums and Galleries, Vatican City, Italy/The Bridgeman Art Library International.)

By the end of the fifteenth century, Renaissance art in Italy had reached its height. The High Renaissance flowered in the visual arts as well as in other areas of culture. Michelangelo, Titian, and Giorgione are among the best-known artists of this era.

The works of Michelangelo Buonarroti (1475–1564)—paintings, sculpture, literature, and architecture—epitomize the Renaissance. Looking at his paintings—for instance, *Creation of Adam* (1510) (Figure 6) on the ceiling of the Vatican's Sistine Chapel—a viewer is struck by the extent to which he learned from the art of the ancient world. Nevertheless, Michelangelo's reliance on the classical is subordinate to his Renaissance vantage point. Here, the figures float freely

through a celestial landscape and depict the biblical story of creation.

But the artists of the Renaissance looked to the classical past not only for technique; they also borrowed and adapted subject matter. Unlike the art of the Middle Ages, which concentrated on Christian themes, Renaissance paintings also illustrated the myths of ancient Greece and Rome.

The Venetian artist Titian (1488/90–1576) was well known for his use of both mythology and biblical themes. His *Bacchus and Ariadne* (1523) (Figure 7) illustrates his independence from the stylistic conventions of other High Renaissance schools. Titian offers a sensual rendering of the classical tale, in which the young Ariadne marries Bacchus (Dionysus), the god of wine, after being

7. Titian, *Bacchus and Ariadne*, 1523.

abandoned by the Greek king Theseus. Titian's use of *chiaroscuro* (alternating areas of light and dark) is pronounced. The general feeling of the work is much looser and freer than the feelings of the carefully constructed canvases produced by his contemporaries. The painting also has a roughness, as though it were unfinished—a quality that marks a departure from the meticulously realistic works of other High Renaissance artists.

As the artistic styles of the Italian Renaissance spread northward, they were adapted and superimposed on a different set of political and religious circumstances, resulting in a fusion of Renaissance method and local themes. Pieter Brueghel the Elder's (1525/30–1569) *Hunters in the Snow* (1565) (Figure 8) exemplifies this trend. The artist

uses line and motion as Titian did. But the image he presents, although it contains many elements of the old style, looks ahead to the future.

Brueghel had spent almost two years studying in Italy, where he developed a technique for dealing with the problem of landscape. In his treatment of objects in three-dimensional space, he created a recessional movement that dominates the painting. The viewer's eye is drawn into the painting at an angle from the foreground to the background through myriad intermediate, diminishing shapes—dogs, human figures, trees, houses, a flying bird—all unified by one sweeping, sloping, downward motion. Brueghel thus achieves a perspectival depth that is entirely new, relying not on the correlation of stratified forms from left to

8. Pieter Brueghel the Elder, *Hunters in the Snow*, 1565. (Erich Lessing/Art Resource, N.Y.)

right, but on the recession of foreshortened forms. In this painting, the artist has surpassed the medieval representation of space in two dimensions and has produced a boundless three-dimensional space that belongs to the modern age.

By the late fifteenth and the sixteenth centuries, the styles of the Renaissance spread from Italy to the Low Countries (the Netherlands, Belgium, and Luxembourg), Germany, France, England, and Spain. These styles were not exported wholesale; rather, elements of the Renaissance fused with local traditions to produce new styles and variants of the Italian themes. What is consistent from one country to the next, however, is the extent to which Renaissance art really was a rebirth—a departure from the style of the medieval period.

not according to his need."[6] Even more shocking, the prince must know how to dissemble, that is, to make all his actions appear virtuous, whether they are so or not. In ironic parody of conventional advice-book wisdom, Machiavelli argued that a ruler must cultivate a *reputation* for virtue rather than virtue itself. In this connection, Machiavelli arrived at a fundamental political truth: politics (and especially the relationship between the ruler and the ruled) being what it is, the road to success for the prince lies in dissimulation (the art of appearance and cover-up). As he put it, "Everyone sees what you appear to be, few experience what you really are. And those few dare not [contradict] the many who are backed by the majesty of the state."[7] Here again the Renaissance arrived at modernity.

Machiavelli broke with both the medieval and the humanist traditions of political thought. He was a secularist who tried to understand and explain the state without recourse to Christian teachings. Influenced by classical thought, especially the works of Livy, he rejected the prevailing view that the state is God's creation and the ruler should base his policies on Christian moral principles. For Machiavelli, religion was not the foundation for politics but merely a useful tool in the prince's struggle for success. The prince might even dissemble, if he thought he had to, in matters of faith, by appearing pious, whether he was or not, and by playing on and exploiting the piety of his subjects.

THE SPREAD OF
THE RENAISSANCE

The Renaissance spread to Germany, France, England, and Spain in the late fifteenth and the sixteenth centuries. In its migration northward, Renaissance culture adapted itself to conditions unknown in Italy, such as the growth of the monarchical state and the strength of **lay piety**. In England, France, and Spain, Renaissance culture tended to be court centered and hence antirepublican, as it was, for instance, under Francis I in France and Elizabeth I in England. In Germany and the Rhineland, no monarchical state existed, but a vital tradition of lay piety was present in the

Low Countries. For example, the Brethren of the Common Life was a lay movement emphasizing education and practical piety. Intensely Christian and at the same time anticlerical, the people in such lay movements found in Renaissance culture tools for sharpening their wits against the clergy—not to undermine the faith but rather to restore it to its apostolic purity.

Thus, northern humanists were profoundly devoted to ancient learning, just as the humanists in Italy had been. But nothing in northern humanism compares to the paganizing trend associated with the Italian Renaissance. The northerners were chiefly interested in the problem of the ancient church and, in particular, the question of what constituted original Christianity. They sought a model in the light of which they might reform the corrupted church of their own time.

Everywhere, two factors operated to accelerate the spread of Renaissance culture after 1450: growing prosperity and the printing press. Prosperity, brought on by peace and the decline of famine and plague, led to the founding of schools and colleges. The sons (women were excluded) of gentlemen and merchants were sent to school to receive a humanistic education imported from Italy. The purpose of such education was to prepare men for a career in the church or the civil service of the expanding state and for acceptance into higher social spheres.

Printing with movable type, which was invented in the middle of the fifteenth century, quickened the spread of Renaissance ideas. Back in the Late Middle Ages, the West had learned, through the Muslims from the Chinese, of printing, paper, and ink. However, in this block printing process, a new block had to be carved from wood for each new impression, and the block was discarded as unusable as soon as a slightly different impression was needed. About 1445, Johann Gutenberg (c. 1398–1468) and other printers in Mainz in the Rhineland invented movable metal type to replace the cumbersome blocks. It was possible to use and reuse the separate pieces of type—as long as the metal in which they were cast did not wear down—simply by arranging them in the desired order.

With the advent of the printing press, the book-publishing industry began to develop. The first printed books were religious: Bibles,

A Renaissance Man

Leonardo da Vinci (1452–1519) is a supreme example of the so-called "universal man," someone wonderfully gifted who could excel in any number of fields. Because he was born illegitimate, he was disqualified from being trained in a learned profession such as law or medicine. But recognizing his immense talent, his father saw to it that he was apprenticed to Andrea del Verrocchio (1435–1488), the esteemed Florentine painter and sculptor, who carefully developed Leonardo's skills in the visual arts. Once Leonardo had been fully trained, it is said, Verrocchio was so struck by the beauty of his pupil's work that he decided never to paint again.

Given Leonardo's restless energy and insatiable curiosity, his genius could not be channeled in only one or a few directions. He quickly gained a reputation for tremendous skill in both science and art and was highly sought after. Florence was ruled by the Medicis, and Milan was ruled by the Sforzas. Leonardo worked for both, and briefly for the Medici pope Leo X (1513–1521) in Rome as well. He spent the last three years of his life in the pay of the French king Francis I (1515–1547), living in luxury at the French court and advising his patron on a variety of building projects.

Leonardo was a quick study and took advantage of opportunities for learning wherever he found them. At the Milanese court of the Sforzas, he met Luca Pacioli (1445–1517), the foremost Renaissance mathematician, who taught him geometry and the power of numbers to explain the world. Leonardo became committed to the view that mathematics provides the basis for true understanding in every field, not only in the physical and biological sciences but in painting and music as well. Leonardo had a large library and read widely, but he also believed that there was no substitute for studying nature firsthand and making experiments in order to obtain true and certain knowledge of things.

Leonardo was deeply interested in everything, and no subject was off limits. He studied human sexuality and, in his unpublished notebooks, made scientific drawings of a human fetus in the womb, male erections, and a couple having sex. One of his main fields of

sermons, and prayer books. But other kinds soon followed because there was a ready market for books on a great variety of secular subjects. The market was enormous and continued to expand during the sixteenth century. Printed books were much cheaper than the earlier hand-copied ones, and many more people could now afford to buy them. Publishers catered to every taste in reading—learned and popular, technical and imaginative, serious and light. Books became big business, driven by both consumer demand and the profit motive. Fifteen or twenty million books had already been published by 1500, and another 150 million more a century later.

Not only were books cheaper and more numerous, but printing also made it easier to learn to read. Literacy rates were still very low, especially among women and the poor, but the clerical and genteel monopoly on reading had been broken. More and more books were also published in the **vernacular** (rather than Latin), which helped standardize written language and stimulated the development of national literatures all across Europe. Printing, moreover, provided a surer basis for scholarship and prevented the further corruption of texts through hand copying. By giving all scholars the same text to work from, it made progress in critical scholarship and science faster and more reliable.

But in early modern Europe, printing was not an unmixed blessing. Elite opinion was often divided, or at least ambivalent, on the issue. Printing was an obvious boon; the authorities, however, saw the need for censorship, for imposing controls on what was published. Today, ours investigation was human anatomy, both for how it could inform his painting and for what it could tell him about the aging process. Once he discovered a one-hundred-year-old man in a hospital in Florence and waited expectantly for his death so that he could examine his blood vessels. By comparing the corpses of the very young and the very old, he was the first to describe the disease known as arteriosclerosis, the hardening of the arteries. At this time, the church took a dim view of the carving up of human remains.

Much of Leonardo's effort was spent on practical design projects, large and small. In the prosperous and warring Italian city-states, there was always a need for industrial machinery, military fortifications, and weapons, and he received as many commissions for engineering work as he did for works of art. In 1502, he served as a military engineer to the commander of the papal army, the ruthless Cesare Borgia (d. 1507). The next year the Florentine government hired him to divert the course of the River Arno in order to cut off access to the sea by the city-state of Pisa, with which Florence was then at war. On this project, which was not successful, he collaborated with another famous Florentine, Machiavelli (see the section "A Revolution in Political Thought").

The list of Leonardo's ideas for new mechanical devices is staggering. He made some four hundred detailed drawings of machines. A short list of his proposals gives a hint of the range of his inventiveness. He came up with suggestions for a robot, a lifting fork, various cranes, machinery for making cloth, improvements on the printing press, a prototype of a car powered by springs and gears, a bicycle, and a flying machine. And then there were his ideas for weapons, including armored tanks, battering rams, scaling ladders, cannons, catapults, crossbows, and a submarine.

For all his inventive energy, Leonardo was notorious for procrastinating and sometimes never finishing his commissions for artworks and building projects, so the number of his surviving paintings is very small. This meager output has always been looked on as a great loss because his finished work sets such a high standard, including such incomparable paintings as *The Last Supper, Mona Lisa*, and *St. John the Baptist*.

is a **pluralistic** society that values new ideas and a variety of opinions, even differences of opinion, at least up to a point. Early modern Europeans were not so tolerant; in fact, they were suspicious of intellectual novelty and variety and sometimes downright hostile to **heterodox** thinking. For centuries, leaders in church and state had tried to build unity by enforcing Christian **orthodoxy** and punishing heresy. The motto of the French monarchy aptly sums up the point: "One king, one law, one faith." The Catholic church established an *Index of Prohibited Books* in the mid-sixteenth century, and books such as Machiavelli's *The Prince* were put on the list. Protestant authorities also set up machinery for regulating the book trade. Printers of "dangerous" books were punished, sometimes executed, and their book stocks confiscated. All intellectual life would be stifled by this atmosphere: the tension between the power of print and the desire to control opinion.

Erasmian Humanism

To Desiderius Erasmus (c. 1466–1536) belongs the credit for making Renaissance humanism an international movement. He was educated in the Netherlands by the Brethren of the Common Life, which was one of the most advanced religious movements of the age, combining mystical piety with rigorous humanist pedagogy. Erasmus traveled throughout Europe as a humanist educator and biblical scholar. Like other Christian humanists, he trusted the power of words and used his pen to attack scholastic theology and clerical abuses and to promote his philosophy of Christ.

Map 13.2 THE GROWTH OF PRINTING IN EUROPE The printing press was invented in the mid-fifteenth century, and its use had spread across Europe in less than a century. Even by 1500, some twenty million books had already been printed using the new technology. (Copyright © 2013 Cengage Learning.)

His weapon was satire, and his *Praise of Folly* and *Colloquies* won him a reputation for acid wit vented at the expense of conventional religion.

True religion, Erasmus argued, does not depend on dogma, ritual, or clerical power. Rather, it is revealed clearly and simply in the Bible and therefore is directly accessible to all people, from the wise and great to the poor and humble. Nor is true religion opposed to nature. Rather, people are naturally capable of both apprehending what is good as set forth in the Scriptures and living in accordance with it. Perfect harmony between human nature and true religion allows humanity to attain, if not perfection, at least the next best thing, peace and happiness in this life.

This clear but quiet voice was drowned out by the storms of the Reformation (see Chapter 14), and the weight Erasmus gave to the individual's natural capacities could not hold its own before the renewed emphasis on human sinfulness and dogmatic theology. Erasmus was caught in the middle and condemned by both sides; for him, the Reformation was both a personal and a historical tragedy. He had worked for peace and unity and was treated to a spectacle of war and fragmentation. Erasmian humanism, however, survived these horrors as an ideal, and during the next two centuries, whenever thinkers sought toleration and rational religion (Rabelais and Montaigne, for instance), they looked back to Erasmus for inspiration.

French Humanism

German and French humanists pursued Christian humanist aims. They used humanist scholarship and language to satirize and vilify medieval scholastic Christianity and to build a purer, more scriptural Christianity. These northern humanists had great faith in the power of words. The discovery of accurate biblical texts, it was hoped, would lead to a great religious awakening. Protestant reformers, including Martin Luther, relied on humanist scholarship.

French thinkers of the next generation exploited and carried the humanist legacy in more radical directions. Among them, two were outstanding: Michel de Montaigne (1533–1592) and François Rabelais (c. 1494–1553). Both thought and wrote in reaction to the religious wars resulting from the Reformation. In the face of competing religious dogmatisms—Catholic, Protestant, and sectarian—Montaigne advanced a skepticism in which he maintained that one can know little or nothing with certainty. He therefore advocated political quietism and acceptance of Christianity on faith. This skepticism also entailed tolerance. An individual was not fully responsible for his or her beliefs, given that they were the product of frail reason and force of circumstance. Thus, Montaigne argued, people should not be punished for their beliefs, and the only ones who deserved to be severely dealt with were the dogmatists in religion. These people deserved to be punished because their certainty and self-righteousness flew in the face of a fundamental epistemological fact: that

PORTRAIT OF ERASMUS (1523) BY HANS HOLBEIN THE YOUNGER. Erasmus was the leading early sixteenth-century Christian humanist. He insisted that all Christians should strive to think rationally and to live peacefully with one another, despite their differences. (© INTERFOTO/Alamy.)

reason cannot be relied on, especially in matters of religion.

Montaigne was not a systematic philosopher but devoted himself to what he could learn by Socratic self-examination, the results of which he set down in his *Essays.* In their urbane and caustic wit and their intense self-absorption, the *Essays* betray a crucial shift in humanist thought, which became more pronounced in the next century. Gone is the optimism and emphasis on civic virtue of the High Renaissance. In their place come skepticism and introspection, the attempt to base morality on the self rather than on public values. As Montaigne says, "Let us learn to be no more avid of glory than we are capable of it."[8] This shift, produced by the increasing scale and violence of religious war, represented a retreat from the idealism of Renaissance humanism.

Rabelais took a different route from Montaigne's. In response to religious dogmatism, he asserted the essential goodness of the individual and the right to be free to enjoy the world rather than being bound down, as John Calvin later would have it, by fear of a vengeful God. Rabelais's folk-epic, *Gargantua and Pantagruel,* in which he celebrates earthly and earthy life, is the greatest French work of its kind and perhaps the greatest in any literature. Rabelais said that, once freed from dogmatic religion, people could, by virtue of their native goodness, build a paradise on earth and disregard the one dreamed up by theologians. In *Gargantua and Pantagruel,* he imagined a monastery where men and women spend their lives "not in laws, statutes, or rules, but according to their own free will and pleasure." They sleep and eat when they desire and learn to "read, write, sing, play upon several musical instruments, and speak five or six . . . languages and compose in them all very quaintly." They observe one rule: "do what thou wilt."[9]

Spanish Humanism

Spanish humanism represents a special case. The church hierarchy gained such a tight grip in Spain during the late fifteenth and early sixteenth centuries that it monopolized humanist learning and exploited it for its own repressive purposes. In contrast to Germany, France, and England, there was little or no room for a dissenting humanist voice. The mastermind behind this authoritarian Spanish humanism was Cardinal Francisco Jiménez de Cisneros (1436–1517). Jiménez founded the University of Alcalá, not far from Madrid, for the instruction of the clergy. He also sponsored and published the Complutensian Polyglot Bible, with Hebrew, Latin, and Greek texts in parallel columns. Jiménez, like Christian humanists elsewhere, sought to enlighten the clergy through a return to the pure sources of religion, and he saw his Polyglot Bible as one of the chief means of realizing that goal.

A century after Jiménez, Miguel de Cervantes Saavedra (1547–1616) produced his great novel, *Don Quixote,* in which he satirized the ideals of knighthood and chivalry. Don Quixote, the victim of his own illusions, roams the countryside looking for romance and an opportunity to prove his knightly worth. To Quixote's servant Sancho Panza,

PORTRAIT OF SIR THOMAS MORE (1527) BY HANS HOLBEIN THE YOUNGER. In England, More and Erasmus were close friends and colleagues, united in their devotion to humanistic scholarship and a Christian idealism that preached rational religion and life lived in service to the larger community. (The Art Archive/Frick Collection, New York/Superstock)

Cervantes assigned the role of pointing up the inanity of his master's quest by always acting prudently and judging according to common sense. Despite his earthy realism, however, Panza must share his master's misfortunes—so much for realism in a world run by men full of illusions. Cervantes's satire is very gentle. That knightly valor was still a valid subject for satire indicates how wedded Spain was even in the early seventeenth century to the conservative values of its crusading past.

English Humanism

Christian humanism in England sharply contrasted with that in Spain. It was developed by secular men in government as much as by clerics, and its objectives were often opposed to authority and tradition. Various Italian humanists came to England during the fifteenth century as bishops, merchants, court physicians, or artists. Englishmen also studied in Italy, especially in Florence, and introduced the serious humanistic study of the classics at Oxford University toward the end of the century.

The most influential humanist of the early English Renaissance was Sir Thomas More (1478–1535), who studied at Oxford. His impact arose from both his writing and his career. Trained as a lawyer, he became a successful civil servant and member of Parliament. His most famous book is *Utopia,* the major utopian treatise to be written in the West since Plato's *Republic* and one of the most original works of the entire Renaissance.

Many humanists had attacked private wealth as the source of pride, greed, and human cruelty. But in *Utopia,* More went further. He argued that an acquisitive society is by nature both unjust and unprosperous. "For, when everyone is entitled to get as much for himself as he can, all available property . . . is bound to fall into the hands of a small minority, which means that everyone else is poor." The unscrupulous few win out over the many who remain honest and decent. For More, the conclusion was inescapable: "I am quite convinced that you will never get a fair distribution of goods . . . until you abolish private property altogether."[10] But to balance things out, he stated the economic case against communism as well. In the absence of a profit motive, "there would always tend to be shortages because nobody would work hard enough. . . . Then when things really got short, the . . . result would be a series of murders and riots."[11] But More accused those who took this view of lacking the imagination to conceive of a truly just society. In *Utopia,* he set out to make up for this deficiency by inventing an ideal society in which private ownership was abolished and poverty eliminated because everyone had to work in order to eat. Such a system even produced surpluses, which allowed people the leisure for instruction and recreation.

More succeeded Cardinal Wolsey as lord chancellor under Henry VIII. But when the king broke with the Roman Catholic church, More resigned, unable to reconcile his conscience with the king's rejection of papal supremacy. Three years later, in July 1535, More was executed for treason for refusing to swear an oath acknowledging the king's ecclesiastical supremacy.

William Shakespeare (1564–1616), widely considered the greatest playwright the world has ever produced, gave expression to conventional Renaissance values: honor, heroism, and the struggle against fate and fortune. But there is nothing conventional about Shakespeare's treatment of characters possessing these virtues. His greatest plays, the tragedies (*King Lear, Julius Caesar,* and others), explore a common theme: men, even heroic men, despite virtue, are able only with the greatest difficulty, if at all, to overcome their human weaknesses. What fascinated Shakespeare was the contradiction between the Renaissance image of nobility, which is often the self-image of Shakespeare's heroes, and man's capacity for evil and self-destruction. Thus, Ophelia says of Hamlet, her lover, in the play of the same name:

> *O, what a noble mind is here o'erthrown!*
> *The courtier's, soldier's, scholar's, eye,*
> *   tongue, sword;*
> *The expectancy and rose of the fair state,*
> *The glass of fashion and the mould of form,*
> *The observ'd of all observers, quite, quite down!*
> *[And] I, of ladies most deject and wretched,*
> *That suck'd the honey of his music vows,*
> *Now see that noble and most sovereign*
> *   reason,*
> *Like sweet bells jangled, out of tune and harsh;*
> *That unmatch'd form and feature of blown*
> *   youth*
> *Blasted with ecstasy. O, woe is me,*
> *T' have seen what I have seen, see what I see!*[12]

The plays are intensely human—so much so that humanism fades into the background. Thus, art transcends doctrine to represent life itself.

THE RENAISSANCE AND THE MODERN AGE

The Renaissance, then, marks the birth of modernity—in art, in the idea of the individual's role in history and nature, and in society, politics, war, and diplomacy. Central to this birth is a bold new view of human nature: individuals in all endeavors are free of a given destiny imposed by God from the outside—free to make their own destiny, guided only by the example of the past, the force of present circumstances, and the drives of their own inner nature. Individuals, set free from theology, are seen to be the products, and in turn the shapers, of history. Their future is not wholly determined by Providence but is partly the work of their own free will.

Within the Italian city-states, where the Renaissance was born, rich merchants were at least as important as the church hierarchy and the old nobility. The city-states were almost completely independent because of the weakness of church and empire. So the northern Italians were left free to invent new forms of government, in which merchant-oligarchs, humanists, and condottieri played a more important part than priests and nobles, who dominated politics in the rest of Europe. Along with the inventiveness, however, this newness and lack of tradition produced disorder and violence. Condottieri grabbed power from hapless citizens, and republics gave way to despotism.

But the problems created by novelty and instability demanded solutions, and the wealth of the cities called forth the talent to find them. Commercial wealth and the new politics produced a new culture: Renaissance art and humanism. Talented individuals—scholars, poets, artists, and government officials—returned to classical antiquity, which in any case lay near at hand in Italy and Greece. Ancient models in art, architecture, literature, and philosophy provided answers to their questions. This return to antiquity also entailed a rejection of the Middle Ages as dark, barbarous, and rude. The humanists clearly preferred the secular learning of ancient Greece and Rome to the clerical learning of the more recent past. The reason for this was obvious: the ancients had the same worldly concerns as the humanists; the scholastics did not.

The revival of antiquity by the humanists did not mean, however, that they identified completely with it. The revival itself was done too self-consciously for that. In the very act of looking back, the humanists differentiated themselves from the past and recognized that they were different. They were in this sense the first modern historians because they could study and appreciate the past for its own sake and, to some degree, on its own terms.

A Word of Caution

We have emphasized in this chapter that the Renaissance, especially in Italy, represented a sharp and deliberate break with medieval tradition. Thinkers crawled out from under that tradition and adopted striking new views in many fields, as, for instance, in art and science, philosophy and religion, politics and education. The result was the beginnings of a new kind of high culture, less religious and more secular, with more emphasis on individualism, artistic creativity, and political realism. The starting point for this development was to a large degree a rediscovery of the classics, that is, the writings of ancient Greek and Roman thinkers. These works were taught and translated as never before since the fall of the Roman Empire and the onset of the so-called Dark Ages a thousand years before. In other words, educated Europeans laid the foundations for a new Renaissance culture by reviving a once-powerful, dead culture and being inspired and instructed by it. Renaissance men and women undertook this project and saw it through more or less on their own initiative and without help from the outside. The Renaissance, in this view, was largely a European affair and the achievement of the northern Italian city-states in the first instance.

There is much to be said for this picture, but it is not the last word on the subject because, as historians are becoming more and more aware, southern Europe, including Italy, France and Spain, in the centuries before the Renaissance, was engaged in large-scale trade with a non-European culture, namely, the Muslim civilization stretching across the Middle East and Mediterranean. Based on Islam, this was a great civilization that had developed from the seventh century and that never experienced the long decline that Christian Europe suffered in the early Middle Ages. Instead, the Muslims conquered the Middle East and North Africa and eventually Sicily and Spain. They built up great cities like Baghdad in the east, Cairo and Alexandria in Egypt, and Córdoba in southern Spain, all linked together by a flourishing trade throughout the Mediterranean. As prosperity increased in these cities, so did education, scholarship, and research. Schools and hospitals were founded for teaching and healing and large libraries created to facilitate study and learning. In the tenth century, the great library in Muslim Córdoba already had a collection of between 400,000 and 600,000 items, thus dwarfing the holdings of any library in Christian Europe at the time. As in Europe, much of this Muslim scholarship was based on ancient Greek and Latin manuscripts that were carefully preserved, translated into Arabic, and copied. But this educational tradition never died in Muslim lands as it had in Christian Europe. So when Europeans, led by the northern Italian city-states, rediscovered ancient literature and philosophy, they did not have to rely upon themselves alone but could also draw on Muslim sources for this ancient learning, where it was still being used and taught.

The Mediterranean was a "lake" in which goods like grain, oil, and wine were traded between Europeans in the north and Muslims in the south. Venice and Bologna in Italy established themselves as two of the principal hinges in this trade. Not only were goods and money exchanged, but also information, books, and knowledge. Much further west, scholars, Italian and otherwise, rushed to Spain, and especially to Córdoba, to use its great library and to get to know the works of antiquity, Aristotle especially (see pp. 85–87 and pp. 207–208).

During the Renaissance European scholars could draw upon texts, translations and scholarship made available to them over the centuries by contact between Europeans and Muslims, both through trade and by direct intellectual exchange. This is not to detract from the European Renaissance and its achievements, from which, after all, so much of the modern world emerged, including the very idea of modernity itself. This was in large part the invention of the northern Italian city-states, but it happened with considerable support from Muslim sources. To acknowledge this complicates matters somewhat and makes for a still unfinished, and less Eurocentric, story.

❖   ❖   ❖

NOTES

1. Quoted in Quentin Skinner, *The Foundations of Modern Political Thought,* 2 vols. (Cambridge: Cambridge University Press, 1978), 1:89.

2. Giovanni Pico della Mirandola, *Oration on the Dignity of Man,* trans. A. Robert Caponigri (Chicago: Henry Regnery, 1956), 7.

3. Quoted in Margaret King, *Women of the Renaissance* (Chicago: University of Chicago Press, 1991), 221.

4. Niccolò Machiavelli, *The Prince,* trans. George Bull (Harmondsworth, England: Penguin Books, 1961), 90–91.

5. Ibid., 77–78.

6. Ibid., 91.

7. Ibid., 101.

8. Quoted in Eugen Weber, ed., *The Western Tradition,* 2 vols., 4th ed. (Lexington, Mass.: D. C. Heath, 1990), 1:395.

9. François Rabelais, *Gargantua and Pantagruel,* trans. Sir Thomas Urquhart (1883), bk. 1, chap. 57.

10. Thomas More, *Utopia,* trans. Paul Turner (Harmondsworth, England: Penguin Books, 1965), 66.

11. Ibid., 67.

12. From *Hamlet, Prince of Denmark,* in *The Complete Plays and Poems of William Shakespeare,* ed. William Allan Neilson and Charles Jarvis Hill (Boston: Houghton Mifflin, 1942), 1067.

SUGGESTED READING

Brucker, Gene A., *Renaissance Florence,* rev. ed. (1983). An excellent analysis of the city's economic and social structure, its political and religious life, and its cultural achievements.

Febvre, Lucien, and Henri-Jean Martin, *The Coming of the Book: The Impact of Printing, 1450–1800* (1997). Covers all aspects of "the print revolution."

Goody, Jack, *The Eurasian Miracle* (2010). Takes the long view and traces the origins of modernity back to the Bronze Age, offering food for thought.

Hale, John, *The Civilization of Europe in the Renaissance* (1995). An informed and entertaining survey, full of interesting illustrations.

King, Margaret L., *Women of the Renaissance* (1991). A useful survey of a burgeoning field of scholarship.

Schiffman, Zachary S., ed., *Humanism and the Renaissance* (2002). Excellent selection of brief historical interpretations of a big subject.

Writing for College History
A Short Handbook

Robert M. Frakes

Clarion University

Editor-in-Chief: Jean L. Woy Sponsoring Editor:
Sally Constable Development Editor: Leah R.
Strauss Associate Project Editor: Reba Libby
Editorial Assistant: Kendra Johnson
Production/Design Coordinator: Bethany Schlegel
Senior Manufacturing Coordinator: Marie Barnes
Senior Marketing Manager: Sandra McGuire

Cover Image: Saul Steinberg, Shadows 1972 (detail) Wood, metal,
staples, and cloth, with graphite, gouache, colored-pencils, and rubber
stamp on panel, 18 x 24 inches. ©2002 The Saul Steinberg
Foundation/Artists Rights Society (ARS), New York.

Printed in the U.S.A.

Library of Congress Control Number: 2002109450

ISBN: 0-618-30603-X

456789-CRW-10 09 08 07 06

Table of Contents

Appendices

Introduction

After more than 15 years of reading and grading student essays in a variety of teaching environments (high school, community college, regional state university, and research university), I have come to the conclusion that many students need a handbook to aid their writing for college-level history classes. The following collection of instructions has been developed on the basis of my experience together with the aid of college classes which have acted as "laboratories" for writing. It is my aim that students who follow the advice laid out in these pages will not only improve their written expression in college history classes, but also in other venues of their lives.

As you read through this handbook, you will notice it is built from the "ground up." The first chapter shows how to compose short writing assignments like the sentence, the paragraph, the journal assignment, and the letter assignment. The next chapter deals with the in-class essay. Subsequent chapters give "nuts and bolts" advice on how to write different types of papers. Along the way, I give some examples of effective and ineffective writing, modeled on (although not copied from) some of the work I have received from the approximately 5,000 students I have taught and graded since 1983. By examining these samples, and the accompanying comments, you will be able to learn important ground rules for writing various assignments. Of course, you will want to pay careful attention to any instructions or hints given by your instructor. Most instructors would agree that the ideal essay or paper today should be clear and well structured and still argue a point (and at some level a creative one). The approach presented in this handbook should be useful not just for history classes, but should also translate to college-level courses in English, Political Science, Anthropology, and Philosophy. I have aimed this handbook toward a broad audience including students at community colleges, regional state universities, small liberal arts college, and even research universities. I would like to thank Dr. David Toye (of Northeast State Technical Community College), Professor Katherine Sibley (of St. Joseph's University), Drs. Todd Pfannestiel and Janet Knepper (of the History and English Departments, respectively, of Clarion University), Anthony Maccarella (my high school teaching consultant at Parsip-pany Hills High School), and Mary Dougherty of Houghton Mifflin Company for their comments and suggestions. I also thank Susan and Catherine Frakes for once again reading several drafts and Hannah and Lilith for their patience. I encourage students to work through this handbook carefully, reflect on their own writing, and also reflect on other writing that they encounter throughout their lives.

CHAPTER 1
Short Writing Assignments

This chapter will lead the student through various kinds of short writing assignments starting with the sentence and progressing to the paragraph, the journal, and the letter. Some of these are typically given as in-class writing assignments and others may be required as homework. As you read through the sections, please pay particular attention to the examples and try to learn the ropes of what makes an effective written response.

1.1 The Sentence

All students should be familiar with the sentence as the smallest building block of writing. Typically defined as "a complete thought," the sentence should be composed of, minimally, a subject, a verb, and usually an object. Sentences that don't contain the minimum ingredients are classified as "sentence fragments," and those that are so overly-long that they contain more than one complete thought are "run-on" sentences.

Examples of Good and Bad Sentences

I use the terms "good" and "bad" throughout this handbook. While "effective" and "ineffective" might be more sensitive equivalents to "good" and "bad," it is important to remember that you are trying to write clearly and to earn a good grade in your history course.

Alexander the Great conquered Egypt around 334 B.C. (Subject: Alexander; Verb: conquered; Direct Object: Egypt. The approximate date gives additional information.)

One city state many gods around important. (This sentence is garbled because of its lack of a verb. I presume the student meant to insert the verb "had," although I'm still a little unclear on the word "important" tacked at the end. Perhaps the sentence was supposed to convey: *One city state had many gods and believed they were very important.* On the other hand, maybe the sentence should have read: *7/ is very important that one city state had many gods.*)

Theodore Roosevelt were president of the United States in 1900. (This sentence suffers from a lack of subject-verb agreement. A singular subject must have a verb form in the singular; a plural subject should use a plural verb form.)

You can see why clear sentence structure is critical. While an instructor may be generous and try to decipher the intended meaning of your words, many instructors will not and, in fact, will feel it is part of their job to teach you to write clearly. Instructors often hold to the adage: "Fuzzy writing indicates fuzzy thinking."

1.2   The Sentence as a Building Block

While instructors may require you to write a sentence in response to a question on an examination, you will more likely be required to use sentences in larger units of writing such as an identification paragraph, an essay, a book review, or a paper. In any of these units, you should effectively use various kinds of sentences such as a topic sentence (to introduce the paragraph or argument), sentences developing examples and evidence (to show your knowledge of a subject or to build an argument), transition sentences (to shift from one topic to another), and a concluding sentence (to state the significance of what you are writing).

Examples of Various Kinds of Sentences

In the following examples, determine if the sentences are playing the role of a topic sentence, a developing sentence, a transition sentence, or a concluding sentence.

There are several key reasons why the Romans were able to conquer the Mediterranean World. (This topic sentence is setting up a paragraph, essay, or paper.)

Another critical reason for the expansion of Christianity is the organization of a hierarchy in the early Church. (This topic sentence introduces a paragraph within an essay.)

While the Romans lost 50,000 troops at the Battle of Cannae in 216 B.C., they were able to go on to win the war because of their enormous manpower reserves. (This sentence develops an example as part of a greater argument.)

In his novel Babbitt, *Sinclair Lewis satirizes the middle class values of mid-twentieth century America.* (This sentence develops primary source evidence as part of a greater argument.)

In addition to taxation issues, the ideology of Enlightenment thinkers such as John Locke provided further drive for revolutionary change. (This sentence marks a transition from the treatment of one example to another.)

Although there were many reasons for Rome's expansion, the Roman concept of abstract citizenship would go on to influence many important future states, including the United States. (This sentence concludes a paragraph or essay.)

1.3   The Paragraph

A paragraph is a group of sentences (at least two), developing a central idea. Usually you start with a topic (or introductory) sentence, write several sentences developing different examples, and end with a concluding sentence. You will probably be assigned to write paragraphs either as "identification paragraphs" or as building blocks of essays (or both).

1.4   The History Identification Paragraph

A standard part of examinations in many college history courses throughout the United States is the "identification paragraph." Rather than simply requiring students to memorize events and respond to a list, the identification paragraph (sometimes called by its abbreviation "I. D.") requires the student to give not only some critical historical information, but also to interpret that information.

Although instructors are sometimes loath to explain what should be the "proper" length, try to aim for around four to five sentences. Keep in mind that the identification paragraph should be able to stand alone, with an introductory sentence, supporting sentences in a logical order, and a concluding sentence. A handy guide to remembering what should be addressed in a history I. D. paragraph are the 5 Ws:

Who?

What?

Where?

When?

and So What? (or What is the historical significance of the person, place, or event?)

Let's walk through an example. Usually the instructor will pick critical names of people, events, or developments that have been topics of the instructor's lectures. For our example, we'll write a history identification paragraph on ziggurats (a classic exam subject for an Early Western or World Civilization class).

Now, if you were constructing an I. D. paragraph on ziggurats you would want to address the 5 W's as previously mentioned.

You could accomplish this task in a minimum of about four sentences. After a quick review of your notes, you might easily come up with:

What = a temple

Where = Mesopotamia

This information could be the core of your introductory first sentence: *A ziggurat was a temple in ancient Mesopotamia.* So far, so good.

How about When? You might know that ziggurats existed in Mesopotamia for centuries. So, a safe dating would be to give a range: *A ziggurat was a temple in ancient Mesopotamia. Mesopotamians worshipped at ziggurats for centuries from c. 3000 B.C.E-1000 B.C.E.*

The <u>Who</u> aspect of this particular identification paragraph is a little more complicated. Since we cannot easily come up with an individual associated with a ziggurat, we can instead use an official, such as the priest-kings who performed sacrifices there. So, now we have a paragraph in progress that reads:

A ziggurat was a temple in ancient Mesopotamia. Mesopotamians worshipped at ziggurats for centuries from c. 3000 B.C.E-1000 B.C.E. The priest-kings of Mesopotamian cities ruled from the ziggurats and performed sacrifices there.

Thus far, we have covered <u>Who</u>, What, <u>Where</u>, and <u>When</u> and so have four of the five essential points. Since this covers 80%, our I. D. paragraph to this point might realistically be given the grade of "<u>B</u>." To complete it, we need to answer So <u>What</u>—the historical significance part. It is useful to think of this as the concluding sentence of your paragraph. A quick and simple way to set up the sentence is to write: *Ziggurats are historically significant because....*

This is where you have to do some interpretation. Ultimately, you will want to tie the specific example of ziggurats to the larger general historical view of the period (in this case, the ancient Near East). If you are taking an early Western or World Civilization course, you probably will have noticed that your textbook and instructor have stressed the religious nature of society in the ancient Near East. This would fit very well with your identification paragraph on ziggurats. So, in the end, your I. D. paragraph might read:

A ziggurat was a temple in ancient Mesopotamia. Mesopotamians worshipped at ziggurats for centuries from c. 3000 B.C.E.-1000 B.C.E. The priest-kings of Mesopotamian cities ruled from the ziggurats and performed sacrifices there. Ziggurats are historically significant because they show the central role religion had in ancient Mesopotamia and in the ancient Near East.

Time Budgeting for Identification Paragraphs

A critical point to keep in mind when you are taking in-class written examinations is how much time you have available. If you are taking a standard Monday/Wednesday/Friday class, you might have 50 minutes available for the examination. (Likewise, you might have 75 minutes if it is a Tuesday/Thursday class.) Hypothetically, you might be asked to compose three identification paragraphs and one essay in 50 minutes. If that is the case, you should plan out beforehand how much time you should devote to each section of the exam. Be sure to ask your instructor ahead of time about how the exam will be structured.

Although the amount of time for an adequate response varies from instructor to instructor, five minutes should provide enough time to develop the core of an identification paragraph. This would give you one minute to organize your thoughts and then a minute on each sentence if you were to write four sentences. If you did indeed have 50 minutes for the exam and had to write three I. D.'s and an essay, you would then spend 15 minutes on the I. D.'s and have 35 minutes left for the essay. Train yourself to immediately budget the time needed for the different parts of the exam. Practice cracking out an I. D. in five minutes.

Since that is just one scenario, ask your instructor how long you should aim to spend on each part of the test. Ideally, you would ask this question a week before the test so that you could use the information when studying. Most importantly, wear a watch and bring extra pens and pencils!

Examples of Good and Bad Identification Paragraphs

The following are some examples of identification paragraphs for lower-division introductory history courses (Western, World, and U.S.). Regardless of the course you are taking, it will be useful for you to examine these samples from a technical point of view. As you read through the examples, try to evaluate them in terms of the guidelines you have read. Do they have at least three sentences? Do they address "Who, What, Where, When, and Historical Significance"? Do they have complete sentences?

Identification Paragraph #1: <u>Ziggurat</u> *A ziggurat was a temple in ancient society. Ziggurats were very important in ancient nations.*

Comments: This I. D. paragraph defines "what" the ziggurat was, but that is about it. It needs the "where" (Mesopotamia), "when" (c. 3000 B.C.E.), "who" (the priest-kings who conducted sacrifices, issued laws, and collected taxes here), and "historical significance" (showing the central role of religion in ancient Mesopotamian society or something to that effect).

Identification Paragraph # 2: <u>Pharaoh</u> *This was a king of a town or municipality or borough in olden times. He was a priest. There was one in each town in Asia. He was in charge of sacrifices and taking care of widows and orphans.*

Comments: This paragraph is not only lacking information, it contains misinformation. While a pharaoh was a monarch and so a type of "king," he was in charge of the Kingdom of Egypt, not a city-state "in Asia." There was not a pharaoh in every "town, municipality, or borough," but one for the entire kingdom. Also, the student does not give even an approximate date, just "olden times." Again, the student needs to go through the check list of who, what, where, when, and historical significance.

Identification Paragraph #3: <u>Neolithic Revolution</u> *The Neolithic Revolution, or "New Stone Age," took place c. 10,000 B.C.E. During this development early humans shifted from hunting and gathering to agriculture as their economic basis. This happened at various places, probably simultaneously, including the Fertile Crescent, West Africa, and India. Agriculture is important because it created a surplus of food and allowed populations to rise. It also freed 10% of the population from food production and this allowed for specialization of labor. This led to the creation of towns and to government.*

Comments: This I. D. paragraph is quite good. The author deals with "who, what, where, when," and even historical significance. In comparison to the preceding two examples, an instructor would probably quickly give it an "A." The one flaw (and again this would be minor) is that the author jumps to the crea-

7

tion of government at the end of the paragraph without directly spelling out the connection to agriculture (surplus, taxes, war).

Identification Paragraph #4: <u>Articles of Confederation</u> *When the American Colonies were emerging as the winner of their revolution against Great Britain at the end of the 1770s, their leaders (such as John Hancock and Robert Morris) realized they needed to form some kind of unified government. They came up with the first Constitution of the United States of America called the "Articles of Confederation" (ratified in 1781). The articles provided for a common defense and foreign policy, but had a weak centralized executive and had trouble raising taxes to deal with debts incurred during the war of independence. This ultimately led to the writing of our current constitution in 1787 with a strong executive branch. George Washington was the first president under this second (and still existing) constitution.*

Comments: This is a solid identification paragraph. It deals with the five Ws in a clear manner. The author could give a little more clarification on the problems of the Articles of Confederation to provide a clearer analysis of how such problems led to our current constitution.

Identification Paragraph #5: <u>Charles Darwin</u> *Charles Darwin was a rich Englishman of the 19th century who is famous for his books* Origin of Species *(1859) and the* Descent of Man *(1871). After studying theology, Darwin went on a voyage around the world on the H.M.S. Beagle and was impressed by the diversity of plant and animal life which led him to develop the "Theory of Evolution " in which he argued that plants and animals evolved over a long period of time and were affected by natural selection and the survival of the fittest. In the* Descent of Man *he argued that human beings also evolved over thousands of years from earlier forms. His theories are important because they conflicted with the traditional Biblical view presented at the beginning of the Book of Genesis that states that God created the world,* *plants, animals, and humans in the course of a week (in 4004 BC according to Bishop Ussher).*

Comments: This is clearly a very strong I. D. paragraph. The student not only effectively covers the five Ws, but also develops the examples and historical significance well. The second sentence is overly long and could have been split after "diversity of plant and animal life." One possible weakness in this paragraph is that the student may have spent more than the allotted time in composing it, potentially forfeiting time on other sections of the exam. Again, make sure you have enough total time to develop your identification paragraphs and the essay (or other parts of your exam) adequately.

How to Review for Identification Paragraphs

Now you have an idea as to what you should be aiming for when you compose an identification paragraph. This knowledge alone should help you better prepare for an examination because it will allow you to sift through your notes and estimate what is likely to come up on the exam. Identification paragraph terms have to be somewhat specific, yet still able to be tied into a larger historical context. So, people, subjects, and dates such as "ziggurat, pharaoh, Constantine, Martin Luther, 1789, and Lenin" would all be potential I. D. paragraph terms for a Western Civilization or World Civilization class while "rivers, stone, and towns" would not. Likewise, "Stamp Act, Great Awakening, Dred Scott Decision, Brown vs. Board of Education, and New Deal" might be likely terms for a U.S. history survey course while "economy, religion, and America" would not. A useful exercise in preparing for an exam would be to review your lecture notes and try to come up with three potential I. D. terms for each lecture. Then look at the "master list" you have compiled and see if you are able to address the five Ws for each of your potential terms. If you cannot, it is time to review your notes and check your textbook.

1.5 The Paragraph as a Building Block of the Essay

You have now learned the basics of the historical identification paragraph. The skills you learned here should translate well into developing paragraphs as building blocks of a multi-paragraph essay. While the next chapter will treat the topic of the essay in detail, keep in mind the basics of paragraph construction. (Ideally, write more than two sentences, including a topic sentence at the beginning, sentences developing examples and evidence in the middle, and a concluding sentence at the end.)

1.6 The Journal as a Writing Assignment

Some instructors assign journal writing as part of the writing assignments for their history classes. Instructors design these journal assignments to be either reactions to readings or to lectures. Usually, students are supposed to be writing these reactions in their journals over the course of many weeks before turning them in to the instructor. The pedagogic idea behind journals is that they can offer an alternate writing environment to that of the exam and allow students to develop their writing skills in a less stressful way. Journals can also serve as a vehicle for students to develop creativity in their writing about history.

Tips for Writing Journal Entries

The following tips are compiled from the author's experiences, those of students, and advice from colleagues.
a. Ask the instructor what he or she really wants for journal entries. If you feel unsure after the explanation, meet with your instructor later during office hours and bring your first two entries to see if you are on the right track.
b. Use concrete examples, not just generalizations.
c. Don't wait until the last minute (i.e., the night before the deadline or the end of the semester) to write your journal. This creates an impossible situation for yourself in which you are desperately trying to make up for lost time. The in-

structor can read through "thin" responses where the development of thought in your analysis is unclear. d.   Don't copy your friends' or classmates' journal entries. Their writing styles are probably different and you may well be caught by your instructor.

An Example of a Journal Assignment

Analyze the Declaration of Independence *The Declaration of Independence that Thomas Jefferson and Benjamin Franklin wrote in 1776 was really important. It helped start the American Revolution and showed why North American colonists wanted to have their own country. It's got a lot of great lines in it like "All men are created equal." At the same time, though, there are some problems because some of the leaders of the American Revolution didn't really think all men were created equal because they believed in slavery. Many enslaved African Americans were not helped by the Declaration of Independence, nor were many Native Americans. It would take a long time, at least past the Civil War, before the Declaration's ideas really spread throughout the whole country.*

Comments: This is a sound enough entry in that it places the document under examination in chronological context, names the authors, cites a line, and ponders some significance. It is somewhat unpolished, but that can probably be overlooked since the student has begun to do some analysis and would be able to refine the writing if it were a more formal assignment.

1.7   The Letter as a Writing Assignment

A clever assignment given by some instructors, usually in lower-division classes, is to have students write a letter as if they are living in some different historical period (such as during the U.S. Civil War or in ancient Greece). Through such a letter, the student can show an understanding of the major issues of a historical period while being creative. The stimulation of creativity leads some students to investigate the period in greater detail.

Tips for Writing Historical Letters

The following tips are collected from the author's experiences, those of students, and advice from colleagues:

a. Ask the instructor what he or she really wants for the letter. The biggest problem with this assignment is when students exercise their creative juices but don't attend to any of the historical material.

b. Make sure to include some specific dates, political context, economic and social context, and even environmental factors.

c. Make sure that the "respondent" of your letter is clearly identified in terms of occupation, location, and connection to the "author" of the letter.

d. Don't wait until the last minute (i.e., at the end of the semester) to write your letter.

e. Try to make your letter creative and unique.

Sample Letter

Imagine that you are fighting in the trenches in France during World War I. Write a letter to someone back home. Page 11 shows an example of such a letter.

Comments: This letter assignment demonstrates that the student has an understanding of the political events of World War I France as well as some feel for life in the trenches. The context is well established, as is the author's changing viewpoint since the beginning of the war. While the reader doesn't get much insight into Molly, there is an attempt to examine the changing role of women in England during the war.

April 15, 1916
Sgt. John Hughes
The King's Own Manchester Volunteer Rifles
2nd Regiment, 3rd Co.

Miss Molly Sedgewick 14
Southeby Row Manchester,
England

Dearest Molly,

    Spring has begun again and with it, the infernal mud. We live, eat, and fight knee deep in mire. In the bloody trenches some of my mates have caught trench foot and many are lousy. Across No Man's Land sits Jerry in his lines. When the barrage begins, we dive down deep. When it lifts we man the lines and fix bayonets—we only hope there will be no more mustard gas.

    It seems like only yesterday that it was August of 1914 and we postponed our engagement so that I could sign up with my pals to join the Volunteer Rifles. Then we thought the war would be over by Christmas, and I would get my position back at the mill working the power loom. We could marry and look forward to buying a row house.

    Most in the line feel the same way. We are starting to wonder what we are fighting for. Might Jerry be feeling the same way? Some are even talking of making an action against the bloody officers.

    I know things must be hard on the home front with all the men gone and the women working in the factories. I only hope that this World War will end soon and I can come home.

Yours Fondly,

John

1.8 Conclusion: Clarity and Content

You have now encountered many varieties of shorter writing assignments. Keep in mind that clarity and content are important for all of them. Strive to write your compositions (whether I. D. paragraph, journal entry, or letter) in a way that will make them clear to the reader in terms of style and sentence structure. Make sure they have content that pertains to the assignment and the period under study.

CHAPTER 2 <u>The In-Class Essay</u>

As a standard part of most midterm and final examinations, instructors of rigorous college-level history courses usually require students to write an essay. In this written composition, the student should ideally show an overview of the material, argue a point, cite historical evidence and examples to back it up, and present the essay in a lucid, well-organized way.

This chapter will explain how to write an effective essay for an in-class examination (as opposed to a composition you work on outside of class). You will find advice on how to structure an outline for your response, how to use evidence, and how to formulate a thesis or argument. You will also encounter some examples of strong and weak essays on a variety of historical topics. When you read through these essays, try to evaluate what grade you would give them and why. Such reflection will help you build the technical skills to write your own effective in-class essays.

<u>2.1</u>   The Five-Paragraph (or more) Essay

The classic history essay is made up of at least five paragraphs, but may include more depending on the phrasing of the question. (Remember, by definition, a paragraph must have at least two sentences and will usually have more.) Your essay should have an introductory paragraph (in which you try to frame an argument and lay out the structure of your essay), body paragraphs (in which you support your argument by means of citing evidence—especially primary sources and historical examples such as events, people, and cultural institutions), and a concluding paragraph (where you hint at the long-term significance).

Essay **Structure and Outlining**

If you have at least five paragraphs in your essay, you must have at least three body paragraphs which develop core examples. A rough skeleton outline would look something like this:

I. Introduction
- Argument (traditionally called a "thesis") where you explain the main point of your essay
- Explicit structure ("By examining examples such as X, Y,and Z...")

II. Body Paragraph
- Evidence and examples

III. Body Paragraph
- Evidence and examples

IV. Body Paragraph
- Evidence and examples

V. Conclusion
- Significance

Whenever possible, try to use chronology as an organizing tool. That is, move from an earlier example to a later example. If, for instance, you are tracing the causes of a major event, or are trying to describe the most important values of a 2000-year period, choose a series of examples that supports your point and look at the examples in chronological order. Such an approach makes historical sense because earlier events often affect later events. Using chronological organization also makes you look well organized to the grader of the essay.

Students are naturally curious as to how many dates they should memorize for an exam. Using relative chronological order in an essay demonstrates an overview of the period. Working at least one date into each body paragraph shows that you have some firm historical pivots for your relative chronology.

Be sure to pick examples for your body paragraphs that actually pertain to your thesis (or argument) and to the question. You would be surprised at how many students wander off the topic (probably trying to show that they know something, at least). If an example doesn't clearly and easily pertain to the question, it is simpler and more effective not to make it one of your core examples.

Use a representative range of examples. If you are supposed to be looking at a period of 300 years, try to space out your examples in time and not have them all "clumped" together at the beginning or the end of the 300-year period.

Also, try to look at both sides of an issue. For instance, if you are looking at the causes of a war, whenever possible give examples of what is motivating both sides so your essay isn't skewed or biased. Or, if you are comparing and contrasting two cultures, try to give examples from both.

2.2   Primary Sources and Point of View

The best kind of ammunition to include in the body paragraphs of your in-class essay is primary source evidence. Primary sources are literary works (such as letters, laws, speeches, articles, and books) or material/ archaeological remains from the time period under examination. When possible, either cite the primary sources directly or at least allude to some examples (through a formula like "as can be seen in primary sources such as ..."). Primary sources are even more effective if you examine the point of view of the authors. Were they rich or poor, did they like a development or were they negatively biased against it? How might those circumstances color the way they see events?

2.3   Time Budgeting for Essays

Make sure you know beforehand how much time you will be given to write the essay and budget your time accordingly. If you are in a typical 50 minute class, you might have 30 or 35 minutes to write the essay (assuming you spend the first 15 to 20 minutes on identification paragraphs). If you are writing a classic five-paragraph essay, and if you spend five minutes planning a rough outline, you would have about five minutes per paragraph. Many, many essays that the author has graded have initial paragraphs that are huge and then two or three ending paragraphs the student desperately dashed through trying to finish before the end of the class period. Avoid that mistake by making a time plan for the exam in the first 10 seconds, budgeting your time throughout the exam, and checking your watch periodically.

Organizational Exercises

Try taking a practice run at a couple of essay questions in terms of organization. With the following questions, fill in the blank space with a major development from your history class. How many paragraphs would you write for these questions? Keep in mind that instructors use some common formats for essay questions in history classes.

1. "Trace the developments leading to ..." (a causation question)
2. "What are the most important events ..." (an overview of material question)
3. "What are the major sources for ..." (an overview of primary source material question)
4. "Analyze the following quotations. What do they tell you about changes during the period under examination?" (an analysis of primary sources and developments question)
5. "What is the better explanation, a or b ..." (a provocative interpretive question)

2-4   The Thesis

The best essays always have an argument. Indeed, a clear dividing line for instructors between a good essay and a fair to poor one is whether or not there is a clear thesis. Sometimes the essay question will help you frame your thesis, such as #5 in the preceding list which immediately demands an argument. More often, it will be up to the student to craft a thesis.

Sometimes you can make overview questions (such as #s 1-3 in the list) into argumentative essays by using a device such as "Although there are many sources for ..., only five clearly stand out." When you have a causation question (such as causes of a war or impact of a development), it will be up to you to frame the question. Again, you can demonstrate your knowledge by crafting a thesis stating that there are three major causes of the given war, for instance, or four major effects of a development. Then you can examine each of those causes or effects in a body paragraph of your essay and state in your conclusion which one might have been more influential than the others. Question #4 could be especially well suited for crafting a thesis if you can find a central theme that runs through the quotations.

A common occurrence for students is that they don't arrive at a clear thesis until they reach the end of writing their essay. In a way, this situation makes sense because the student has worked through the evidence and examples and now has reached an evaluation. If this happens to you and if you have enough time, revise your introduction and work in this clarified thesis. If you don't have enough time, it is better to write in this thesis as the last sentence of your conclusion than not to have it at all.

Examples of Good and Bad Essays

The following sample essays are typical of some written by students in lower-division survey courses. As you read through these examples, try to evaluate them in terms of the guidelines you have read for essay writing. Review the following questions as a checklist (or rubric) you aim to complete in writing your own essay:

Do the essays have an introductory paragraph that states a thesis and lays out the structure? Do they have at least five paragraphs? Do the body paragraphs develop historical examples and primary source evidence to support the central argument? Do the essays have complete sentences? Are the overall arguments convincing? (Some instructors actually use explicit rubrics in grading essays. Be sure to ask your instructor if he or she does.)

Essay #1 Question: Which was more important in the early societies we have examined thus far: technology or religion?

Religion was the most important thing in the ancient societies. In every society of ancient times, religion was very important in ancient western civilization back then. It was more important than technology.

In the early societies sometimes older societies allowed other societies they met to continue worshipping the god they worshipped before. On the other hand, sometimes that didn't always happen with ancient peoples and gods then. It's sometimes different today, but not always.

There was at one time a time period of early history in ancient societies into which where there were more than one god sometimes. Indeed, moreover there were many in some and other countries might have different gods at the same time.

However, others believed in polytheism (which is a belief in many gods, poly means many in Greek). Some had two gods, also. This was another kind of religion in some city-states. One of the ancient societies even, on the other hand, believed in monotheism, which was a belief of religion where you had one and only one god (mono means "one and only one " in Greek).

Religion had a bigger role in the ancient societies of the past world then. Now technology is more important. Who knows what the future will hold?

Comments: This essay has some severe problems. On the positive side, the student has a thesis in the introductory paragraph and is trying to have five paragraphs. The paragraphs are weak, however, because they are short and superficial and they don't cite any specific historical examples or citation of evidence. For instance, the first and second body paragraphs are very unclear as to what the student is referring (perhaps to the Persians with their tolerant religious policy and the Assyrians with their harsh one?). The last body paragraph is clearly trying to discuss monotheism. Here the student should mention the Hebrews and their scriptures, the Ten Commandments, etc. Another serious problem is the lack of any sense of chronology. The student should try to use relative chronological order going from the earliest example to later ones and also attempt to work a date into each body paragraph that ties to a specific example.

Essay #2 Question: If you could choose only five events to explain Early Western History (from c. 10,000-500 B.C.E.) to a friend, which events would you choose and why?

The five most important events of all time in Early Western History that I would explain to my friend are the Paleolithic Age, the Neolithic Age, the Stone Age, the Flint Age, the Copper Age, the Mesozoic Age, and the Steel Age. These are the most important ages in Early Western History and happened after the dinosaur ages.

The Paleolithic Age demonstrates different ways by which people hunted food. The Neolithic age, on the other hand, shows how people hunted. The Copper and Bronze ages show how people used metal for things as did the steel ages. Sometimes things changed, but other times they didn't.

These different ages are the most important events in Early Western History.

Comments: This essay has several problems. Clearly, it doesn't have enough paragraphs to develop examples. Moreover, the author actually mentions seven "ages" in the introduction instead of five "events." There is an initial problem because an age (which is a very long period of time) is not an event (which is a single historical development). Looking at the question, it would appear that the essay should have seven paragraphs (an introductory paragraph, five body paragraphs developing **five** examples, and a conclusion). The student does have an introductory paragraph, but makes a conceptual mistake in so far as the Paleolithic and Neolithic Ages are both part of the Stone Age. Additionally, I have never heard of a "Flint Age," but apparently the student didn't either in so far as it is not developed. The Mesozoic Age must have crept in from another class (perhaps in the geology department).

The second paragraph, which should be a paragraph devoted to developing the Paleolithic Age as an example, instead presents a cursory overview of the importance of some of the periods (where the author makes some sweeping overgeneralizations and mistakes). The student should instead have mentioned examples and evidence from each period in a series of successive body paragraphs before ultimately writing a concluding paragraph.

Essay #3 This is another example of a student's answer to the question in Essay #2.

While many important events occurred in early history, during the period from 10,000 BCE to 500 BCE, there were some which were even more important than others. If I had to choose only five to explain to a friend, I would probably choose the Neolithic Revolution, the discovery of bronze, the creation of the chariot, the invention of the alphabet, and the development of iron technology because of the huge effect they had in changing history.

The "Neolithic Revolution" (i.e., the shift to agriculture) was invented c. 10,000 BCE. With agriculture as a food supply (as opposed to only hunting and gathering used in the preceding Paleolithic Age) populations rose and there was enough of a surplus of food to free up 10% of the population from food production to instead be involved in crafts, trade, the military, and government. However, according to Karl Marx, with the creation of agriculture came the concept of property and wealth. So along with the creation of agriculture came the creation of conflict. To defend against internal and external conflict (or crime and war), government was created to form the abstract state which had not existed in the Paleolithic age. This government maintained justice and provided defense.

The creation of efficient bronze technology took place c. 2000 BCE somewhere on the northern frontier of Mesopotamia (although there were earlier experiments that weren't as efficient). Bronze, an alloy of copper and tin, proved superior to copper (the previous metal of choice) because it was harder and thus better for weapons. Bronze was an expensive metal because tin was a scarce resource. In order to obtain tin, extensive trade networks had to be developed that stretched all the way from the Eastern Mediterranean to Cornwall (in England).

A major important development is the invention of the alphabet (c. 1000 BCE). While earlier writing systems had been pictographic or ideograms (such as Egyptian hieroglyphics or Mesopotamian cuneiform), these writing systems had a large number of characters and only the elite could have the leisure time to learn these older scripts. It was the great merchant people of the Phoenicians who developed a 22-symbol system of writing which allowed all members of their society to learn a form of written communication and aided their great mercantile activity throughout the Mediterranean world. So, the Phoenician creation of the alphabet allowed for mass literacy. This system would be subsequently adopted by the Greeks and the Romans. The Western alphabet today stems from that of the Romans, because of the influence of the Catholic Church.

The last example from the ancient world is the invention of efficient iron technology (c.1000 BCE) somewhere in Northern Mesopotamia (although a few earlier examples made from meteoric iron have been discovered). Because this new metal was so much more plentiful than bronze, it could equip much larger armies. The Assyrians were the first people to harness the effectiveness of iron technology and equip mass armies. This development allowed the Assyrians to expand and create the first large empire stretching from Mesopotamia to Egypt.

While many important events took place in Early Western History, the most significant were the Neolithic Revolution, the creation of efficient bronze technology, the invention of the alphabet, and the creation of efficient iron technology.

Comments: This essay is clearly better than the previous examples. It has a clear structure, good examples, and some effective development. An unfortunate mistake is that the author forgot to develop example #3 (chariots). This kind of oversight does happen, so it is always a good idea to lay out your explicit structure in your introductory paragraph (which the author did), but then periodically refer back to it as you finish each body paragraph. It may be helpful to make a very rough outline on scratch paper or inside the front cover of your blue book before beginning your essay.

Aside from that, there are two more minor problems. The body paragraph on the invention of bronze technology seems underdeveloped in comparison with the others. The paragraph would have been more effective if the author alluded to a few major bronze age peoples (such as the Hittites, the New Kingdom of Egypt, and the Mycenaeans). This improvement could have been done simply by alluding to them through a formula such as "Some major societies who made use of this new bronze technology included X, Y, and Z."

Lastly, the conclusion is also a bit underdeveloped. The author basically restates the introduction. While it may be difficult in an essay question of this type to go further, you should, at least, avoid a one-sentence paragraph. Perhaps adding a final sentence such as "Without these critical developments, ancient societies would have been stuck either in the Paleolithic Age or at a very localized level" would show the long-running significance of these examples.

Essay #4 Question: What caused the U.S. Civil War?

There is no easy answer to the question of what caused the Civil War. Historians have debated (and probably will continue to debate) over economic, political, and social issues. However, three chief areas emerge after re-examination as the three biggest causes. They are 1) historical regional differences, 2) expansion, and 3) abolitionism.

The Northern and Southern colonies were always different in North America. The North (New England) was settled at first primarily by English settlers who wanted small farms or shops in cities like Boston. They believed in what scholars such as Max Weber call the "Puritan Work Ethic." Southern colonists were mostly Scotch-Irish settlers and wanted to mimic British aristocrats by having large plantations. Although there was some slavery in the North also early on, slaves worked especially well for agriculture in the South. When the Revolutionary War ended, North/South differences, especially slavery, were the biggest areas of concern in the framing of the Constitution. The Great Compromise and the 3/5th's Compromise both temporarily dealt with the difference between the North and South, but obviously didn't succeed in resolving the differences.

When the U.S. expanded during the age of "Manifest Destiny, " there was a question as to whether slavery would be allowed in new states. Both the Missouri Compromise and the Compromise of 1850 dealt with this, but neither was permanently successful. The Southerners wanted slavery in the new lands because their use of cash crops like king cotton and sot weed (or tobacco) exhausted the soil and they needed new fresh lands. The North was industrializing and needed raw materials.

The North also had a growing movement against the "peculiar institution " of slavery called abolitionism. Led by figures such as William Lloyd Garrison and Harriet Tubman, and influenced by Harriet Beecher Stowe's novel Uncle Tom's Cabin, *this movement became more and more influential in trying to not just stop slavery in the new states, but in trying to end it in the South itself.*

A series of crises (Nat Turner's Rebellion, the Dred Scott Supreme Court decision, Bleeding Kansas, John Brown's Raid) fanned the flames, and none was successfully resolved. When Lincoln was elected in 1860, South Carolina seceded, followed by the deep South. Finally, Ft. Sumter was fired upon in 1861 and the Civil War began.

Comments: The student clearly knows some things about American history leading up to the Civil War. The essay has a decent structure, cites some examples, and even provides three primary sources (the Constitution, *Uncle Tom's Cabin,* and the Supreme Court Dred Scott decision). However, the essay is not as strong as it could be. The thesis is serviceable, but weak. The first body paragraph could be developed more fully. The paragraph on expansion needs development for the Northern view.

Lastly, the shoe-horning of a series of crises in parenthesis in the concluding paragraph is not the most effective way to use and develop that evidence.

2.5 Conclusion: Studying for In-Class Essay Examinations

Knowing how to structure essay exams will help guide your ability to review for such tests. Remember to use major events and primary sources to support your essays. Try to make lists of the most critical developments, problems, and most important sources mentioned by your instructor. If a substantial amount of attention has been given to arguments between historians on the evaluation of a development, make sure you know the two sides and what the key evidence is.

Some students find it useful to construct hypothetical essay questions stressing the most critical elements of the instructor's lecture. If you make a list of four or five (and it helps to do this task with a friend from class), see if you could structure an outline with a thesis and evidence for each body paragraph for each potential question.

CHAPTER 3
<u>The Five-Page Paper</u>

A classic assignment for college history courses is the five-page paper. Unlike the in-class examination, students work on the topics of their papers at home (or in their dorm, apartment, or library) over the course of several weeks. When due, the student turns in five pages of typed (or word-processed) prose and hopes for the best. Keep in mind that a standard double-spaced $814^{x}11$ inch page with normal margins of 1 inch from the top and bottom, and 114 inch from right and left will yield about 250 words.

In Chapter 3 you will find advice on how to construct your thesis, how to structure your paper, and when and how to cite sources for a five-page paper. Like in earlier chapters, you will also find examples of effective and ineffective compositions. As you read through them, try to think about how you would grade the sample paper and why you would give it that grade. Once you start thinking about how your paper is graded, you are likely to become a better paper writer.

<u>3.1</u>   The Thesis of the Paper

Instructors will vary in how they set up their paper assignment, with some giving a list of topics from which the student chooses and others leaving the choice of topic wide open. Likewise, some instructors allow biographical papers, while others want papers based on events or on primary sources. Regardless of the choice of topic, instructors are generally more impressed by papers with a central argument in the introductory paragraph together with some kind of explicit structure (and, of course, the citation of several sources). So, even if you are writing on a person, event, or literary work, try to frame the paper as an argument. You can do this in several ways, and the topic, of course, will help determine this. A good approach is to find a central problem of interpretation.

Let's try an example. Suppose you want to write a paper on the Roman political leader Julius Caesar. Now you have to find a problem around which you can build an argument. A summary of his life would not be an argument and a tough instructor would lower your grade for it, no matter how encyclopedic it may be. Instead, you might want to offer an argument like "Why was Julius Caesar assassinated?" In the course of that paper, you will show that you know what happened in his life.

Let's look at a topic from American history. Suppose you had to write a paper on George Washington. You could choose to write a paper discussing the source of the story about George Washington and the cherry tree. This topic would force you to delve into sources about his life (and you might discover that the story comes from Parson Mason Wheems several years after Washington's death). Or, you could write a paper on the subject: "Was George Washington really the first President of the United States of America?" While this may seem like an obvious question at first, you might examine the leaders of the American states under the Articles of Confederation. You will discover that several men, including such worthies as John Hanson, held the title of president before Washington's term of office. Then you could refine the subject of your thesis to something like "First President of the United States of America: George Washington or John Hanson?" where you have sharpened your focus and, hopefully, intrigued the reader. Regardless of topic, try to find a meaty argument into which you can sink your teeth.

If you write a paper on a primary source, you will likewise want to make it into an argument. Let's say you are required to write a paper on Sophocles' tragedy *Antigone*. Instead of merely summarizing the play, you will want to hone in on a problem. Consider a topic such as why Sophocles chose to emphasize the play's moral to the audience of Athenian citizens, or discuss whether the portrayal of women in the play was supposed to represent historical reality.

As stated in the last chapter, it is fairly common to uncover your clarified thesis once you finish writing the rough draft of your paper. At this point you will definitely want to go back and revise your introductory paragraph and, quite likely, the topic sentences of several of your body paragraphs.

After laying out the thesis and structure in your introductory paragraph, you have different choices in how you might want to proceed. You could summarize the historical context or give a brief overview in a few paragraphs. Then you could determine some critical events or passages, analyze them, and offer a conclusion where you discuss the significance of your argument. You might want to skip the initial historical context section and work that material into the paragraphs in which you develop examples or passages from primary sources. **Regardless, keep in mind that you want to cite passages from primary sources to back up your argument. Without citation of sources, you will not be doing good historical writing, and your paper will surely not get a good grade.**

3.2   Sample Outlines

A key to writing a good paper is to have some kind of organization, which should be made clear to the reader in the first paragraph or two. Some writers like to organize very lengthy outlines, while others don't use them at all. However, it's important to keep in mind that you should know where you are going when you are writing.

Thus, you should have at least some kind of "basic" outline in mind. Let's try to outline some sample papers in response to different kinds of topics.

Question (a): Why was Julius Caesar assassinated?

I.   Introduction
II.   The last century of the Roman Republic (an overview)
III. Julius Caesar's career
IV.   The assassination and the assassins

V.   Analysis (e.g., What was Caesar doing that the assassins feared?)

VI.   Conclusion

Question (b): The Message of Sophocles' *Antigone*

I.   Introduction

II.   The intellectual context of Classical Greece

III. Sophocles' life and education

IV. The message of the play

V.   The audience

VI. Analysis

VII. Conclusion

Question (c): Why did Alexander Kerensky fail?

I.   Introduction

II.   The historical context of Russia in the late 19th and early 20th century

III. Kerensky's education and career

IV. Russia and World War I

V.   The February Revolution

VI. The provisional government and its policies

VII. Lenin

VIII. The October Revolution

IX. Conclusion

Again, remember to cite primary sources as often as possible to support your points. While five pages may seem like a huge amount to a beginning college student, after you write a few such papers you will come to realize that it is just enough space to make a short, well-supported argument.

3-3 Plagiarism

A critical lesson for writing any formal papers is to learn to avoid plagiarism. Indeed, recent investigations have shown that sometimes-famous historians even fall into this trap. Many students commit plagiarism without knowing what they have done.

At its simplest level, plagiarism is the use of someone else's work without attribution (from the Latin infinitive *plagiare,* to steal).

How do you avoid plagiarism? First and foremost, whenever you use the exact words of someone else (called a verbatim quotation) or a close rendering of what someone else wrote (called a paraphrase), cite the source either through a footnote, an endnote, or a parenthetical citation. The following section will show you how to approach citations.

In addition to verbatim quotations and paraphrases, you should cite information outside of the realm of "common knowledge." Students rightly ask where the border of common knowledge lies. Basically, common knowledge should include what you learned in a good high school history class. For instance, if you were writing a paper about the formation of the nation state of Bulgaria, you would not have to cite a general textbook source for stating that "Bulgaria is in southeast Europe" as a source for "World War I took place from 1914-1918." You would, however, need to cite the statement: "In late World War I, the Greek Prime Minister Venezelos launched a new front in Thessalonika that threatened Bulgaria."[1]

3.4　Citation of Sources

While the citation of sources is important to various disciplines, many have developed different standards and approaches to indicate where the author has found his or her information. So, a proper history paper will look very different from a sociology or psychology paper. Ultimately, you want to cite an author's name, the title of the work, and the relevant page numbers. To see the way historians normally accomplish this task, examine the standards set forth in *The Chicago Manual of Style?* This style manual should be your ultimate resource. If you go on to

[1]　Barbara Jelavich, *A History of the Balkans: Twentieth Century* (Cambridge: Cambridge University Press, 1983), 120-121.
[2]　*The Chicago Manual of Style,* 14th ed. (Chicago: University of Chicago Press, 1993).

become a history or social studies secondary education major, you may want to purchase your own copy of the *Chicago Manual.*

Recently, a new type of citation, called the "author-date" form, is growing in popularity. With this method, the student gives the full bibliographic information either in a first note or in a bibliography,[3] and then gives a shortened citation of the author's name (with the date of publication following in parenthesis) followed by the relevant page numbers.[4] Students who work in more "highly specialized" areas of history will find that their subfields sometimes have slight variant stylistic conventions. Since style is something that is continually evolving, it is important to know that there are standards, but these standards tend to change over time. The growth in internet use has led to the creation of a style for citing web site sources. Remember that the ultimate goal is to be clear in your written expression and to include your sources.

While this text is not intended as a substitute for a style manual, but rather a short handbook to get first year students on their way, a few tips on the citation of sources follow.

a. Footnotes and endnotes are different ways of achieving the same goal of showing your sources. With footnotes, the note appears at the bottom of the page. With endnotes, the notes are collected on a page (or pages) at the end of your paper. In the days when people wrote papers on typewriters, making footnotes was very complicated. There was a formula one used to subtract space from the bottom of a page for the text of each footnote. Endnotes were much easier. Now, with word processors and personal computers, it is no longer such a challenge to insert footnotes. Footnotes are preferable because the information is on the same page as the sentence where the citation is marked. Ask your instructor what he or

---

[3] Example: Robert M. Frakes, *Contra Potentium Iniurias: The Defensor Civitatis and Late Roman Justice* (Munich: C. H. Beck Verlag, 2001).

[4] Example: Frakes (2001), 197-203.

she prefers. If there is no preference, and if you have the "technology," go with footnotes.

b. Number your notes consecutively—that is, start with 1 (one) and go on to 2 (two), and so on. In some other disciplines you move back and forth so 1 might appear several times. Don't do this for a history paper. There should be only one footnote number 1, number 2, and so on. Examine the exam ples on the preceding page.

c. Always note direct quotations and paraphrases of primary sources (those sources from the time period under study).

d. Likewise, always note direct quotations and paraphrases from secondary or tertiary sources (from writers later than the time period under study).

e. Always try to work quotations in smoothly. That is, don't just stick the quotation in without some kind of lead in line (such as "Describing this, one historian has remarked ..." or "Even contemporaries were impressed by his abilities. One witness recounted: ...").

f. If the quotation is shorter than three lines, double space it with normal margins and use quotation marks at the begin ning and end of the quotation. If the quotation is longer than three lines, indent and single-space it, but omit the quotation marks.

g. Cite sources for informative material outside of the realm of "common knowledge." Remember that our basic definition of "common knowledge" (which is becoming harder and harder to define as the diversity of our society becomes more and more acknowledged) is the material of a rigorous high school class. That is, you should not have to footnote a high school instructor's lecture material, but rather assume that what someone in the audience of a college class knows is "common knowledge."

h. There used to be a list of Latin words and abbreviations that marked the serious student's work {ibid, idem, op. cit.₉ he. cit., passim). Most of these have fallen out of fashion in the ever-changing world of style. In this day and age it is probably best to avoid them. If the note is to a source you have cited before, cite it in a truncated way (such as "Buckler, 35."), with the appropriate page number.

3.5   The Internet as a Resource

With increasing internet availability and declining college library acquisition budgets, more and more students are using sources found on the internet as resources for research. While this topic will be dealt with more fully in the next chapter, keep in mind that not everything on the internet is true. Try to find out who the author is and what organization sponsors the web site. Also, be sure to avoid the temptation of "cutting and pasting" and not citing sources. This author has seen the number of cases of plagiarism rise dramatically with the availability of the internet. It is quite obvious to instructors when students insert a long section from another author. The change of style and voice exposes plagiarism. If the article is good, then cite it. If the source is questionable, don't use it. If the work is somewhat useful, paraphrase it and cite the source. (See the appendix on sample citations at the end of this handbook, page 52.)

3.6   Examples of Good and Bad Five-Page Papers

The following are two examples of five-page papers that might have been written for an upper-division history class. As you read through them, try to evaluate the papers in terms of the guidelines you have read. Do they have a clear structure? Is the grammar of the sentences clear? Do the papers have a solid argument? Do they include historical examples and citation of primary sources? Are they clear and convincing?

Paper #1: "The USA and the Creation of Albania"

The Triple Entente (France and Russia—nation-states at the dawn of the twentieth century), among many others was created. They were vs. the triple Alliance (Germany, Austria-Hungary, Turkey, and Italy and a number of smaller nations). The two systems postulated rationally that they could not totally control world Imperial systems. The creation of Albania took place before World War I began in 1914-1918.

The key factor was that nations in the Balkans (especially the Serbians and the Bulgarians then) were fighting for territory together with other lands of the time in Europe and elsewhere. Conflicts developed into an economic crisis. All the nation states of Europe and the Balkans argued about nationalism, historicism, and the frontiers of their nation-states. Many hot spots such as Transylvania, and the Sanjuk of Novi Pazar took place. As a result of the Ottoman wars, Austria-Hungary first administered and then seized the former military frontier. This made many people both there, like Serbians, Albanians, and Slovenians, and elsewhere unhappy (just as today).

In reprisals, the Russians had plans, since Peter and Catherine the Great, to support their desires for pan-slavism, orthodoxy, and warm-water ports by supporting the Balkan nations in alliances that they hoped at the least in Europe, would support the Habsburgs. On the other hand, the Habsburg government of Austria seized parts of the government and administration of parts of the former Ottoman Empire (a country in Europe) around the time period of 1900. The Serbians, one of the "Yugo" Slavs, desired to rebuild their greater Serbia (earlier called Servia) of the Middle Ages (1389) throughout the Balkans and asked their big Orthodox brother allies in Russia for help, while the Habsburg empire hoped to gain the support of Germans for pan-slavism at the time in Europe. However, Russia had lost a tremendous war against Japan (war), and was out of the picture. Nationalism and Imperialism reared their ugly heads because Serbia, in addition to other lands, would both have claims to lands in Europe and elsewhere in the Aegean.

Several powers made a variety of various treaties to divide and split up the Balkans for the balance of power earlier set up at the Congress of Vienna in 1815 (at the end of the French Revolution and Napoleon). In Russia, however, due to the last war against Norway (1905), the Tsars, but also the Czars, sought to try to attempt to maintain some territorial negotiations. The Russians and the Habsburg monarchy became cun-

ning and led to the Turks to follow these treaties were against their empire's lands and territories. Further treaties were made by Serbia, on the one hand, and Bulgaria (on the other)! Some ethnic groups in the European zone then felt cheated (IMRO and EMRO; see also the Ruthenians and the Galicians).

The more powerful governments in the time period (at the time period then) continued to have problems in the Balkans. The Bulgarian men and women felt because of economic and nationalistic reasons that they rationally needed a corridor to the seas. So, the Greeks wanted to take Thessaloniki. The Russian government tried to act rationally and efficiently; on the other hand, Turkey lost the war. This led to losing land and rational procedures in the Aegean. The Greeks now controlled the Aegean without Macedonia while the Italians, however, that is to say, in the "Mare Nostrum." The Greeks thus gained a "corridor to the sea" and Bulgarian men and women (especially in nationalistic sewing clubs) lost theirs. Italy gained further territory as the declining sick man of Europe lost it at that time. All this was the Turko-Italic war of 1911.

The nation-states soon watched with concern the situation in Southeastern Europe and decided to intervene but not really fight. They made everyone in Europe have a treaty, which would give the Balkan states control of the territories. The treaty was made in 1913 (and is one of the famous Treaties of London, in addition to the earlier one ending the American Revolution) and made Albania free.

The treaty changed Europe and the world. The Balkan states gained territories and lands and gave them those lands adjoining which was alot. The Turks gave Crete, part of the Aegean, to the Britains—a Balkan ally. Also, as stated earlier, Albania was made into an independent country in that time period, which was in Europe then, but would have a German king. Lastly, the so-called "great powers" would decide the face of the Aegean up to and including Mt. Blanc for all intensive purposes.

Woodrow Wilson, on the other hand, was born in the United States. He became president after William Howard Taft and Fighting Bob La Follette wanted to. He (Wilson) was a democ-

ratic who won more votes in the electoral college of representatives. Wilson's policy once he became president in 1913 was not on European affairs, but, on the contrary, was on American ones. The United States was not interested in Albania in that time period then. Indeed, they had never been, even since 1776, although Fan Noli was an Albanian bishop living in New York City who was elected by Albanian-Americans and had a vote in the Albanian parliament.

Later, World War I developed into Europe, and things changed over the course of the time period in which it was. Then Italy joined France, Great Britain and Russia in the Quadruple Alliance, against Germany, because the powers and because of the provinces of Ghent, Camucia, Trent, and Sasso Marconi and in this treaty, the pro-Slavism of Bulgaria, Russia, and Serbia was rebutted. This later treaty of London gave Italy more territory and this built nationalism at the time.

This all leads to some important conclusions. The creation of Albania was not successful in its attempt to force the two nation-states of the triple alliance to agree on land borders and frontiers in that time in the Balkans and elsewhere. This kind of nationalism led to a bloody conflict and long-lasting (that is to say, World War I). The agreement went against the Treaty to create World War I and, eventually, World War II

Comments: There are many problems with this paper. Indeed, it is difficult to say which is the biggest. Because you may not be a student of modern European history, I will not spend time on historical errors and instead will give a list of the more obvious structural problems:

1. The paper has no central thesis. It is at some level about the creation of the country of Albania in the Treaty of London of 1913 (and without the title the reader might not know even that). But what about Albania? The author doesn't actually seem to know. It might conceivably be suggested that the thesis is that the creation of Albania in 1913 did not stop World War I from breaking out, but this thought is not clear

from the text of the paper. Since the author shifts to America later in the paper, and moreover uses "USA" in the title, might he or she instead be trying to argue that the Treaty of London was pleasing to Americans? Again, this is not developed. Remember to have a central argument clearly present in your introductory paragraph.

2. The author cites no sources (primary or otherwise). A history paper must have citation of authorities and notes (footnotes or endnotes).

3. The structure and development of this paper are very weak and unorganized. Part of the problem here may be that the author does not understand what is going on historically. Early in the paper the student should have defined why Albania was made a country (i.e., What war did it end? What were the opposing sides? What were the terms of the treaty?) and then developed the rest of the paper from there. As it is, the terms of the treaty that created the country appear very late in the paper, and the point of these terms of the treaty remains unclear.

4. The sentence structure is terrible. Several sentences make no sense whatsoever. A few clunkers are: "In Russia, however, due to the last war against Norway (1905), the Tsars, but also the Czars, sought to try to attempt to maintain some territorial negotiations" or "Then Italy joined France, Great Britain and Russia in the Quadruple Alliance, against Germany, because the powers and because of the provinces of Ghent, Camucia, Trent, and Sasso Marconi and in this treaty, the pro-Slavism of Bulgaria, Russia, and Serbia was rebutted." Neither of these sentences makes sense either grammatically or historically. The author should review the earlier pages of this handbook.

Paper #2: "The Eastern Crisis and Its Reception in the USA"

The Great Eastern Crisis ending in 1878 was one of the most important developments in 19th century European History. Indeed, it brought Europe to the brink of the first wide-scale conflict since the Napoleonic Wars (which ended in 1815). Upon re-

examination of the origins and course of the Balkan Crisis together with the ensuing treaties, it becomes clear that the Great European powers were becoming increasingly interested in the Balkans—an interest that would lead to the outbreak of World War I. Closer examination will show that Americans were originally little interested in these events which would ultimately lead them some 36 years later into the "War to end all Wars" as World War I became known.

The origins of the Crisis lie in the revolt of the Orthodox Christian Bulgarians against the yoke of the oppressive Islamic Ottoman Turks, who had controlled them since the late 14th century! The Bulgarians rose in the 'April Uprising" of 1875, but were then brutally suppressed in the "Bulgarian Horrors" in which somewhere between 10,000 and 100,000 Bulgarians were executed by the Turks, to the shock of Western Europeans and Americans." The Russians, both because of Pan-Slavism and because they were co-religionists in the Orthodox Christian faith, sent aid to their little Bulgarian brothers in April of 1877? As the Bulgarians and Russians began to have success against the Turks, other Balkan peoples such as the Serbians and Greeks also attacked the Ottomans. The combined Russian and Bulgarian forces soundly defeated the Turks and in the Treaty of San Stefano redrew the map of Southeastern Europe to reward Bulgaria with a huge amount of land, access to the Sea, and also gave the Russians a presence in this new Bulgaria for two years.[4]

Many states were unhappy with the results of the Treaty of San Stefano. Obviously, the Ottoman Empire did not like losing territory. The Serbians and the Greeks felt they should have received more territory. The great powers also were concerned

[1] Mercia Macdermott, *A History of Bulgaria: 1393-1885* (London: George Allen and Unwin, 1962), 15-235.
[2] Macdermott, *A History of Bulgaria,* 275-286; Robert Lee Wolf, *The Balkans in Our Time* (New York: W. W. Norton and Co., 1967), 84.
[3] Macdermott, *A History of Bulgaria,* 292-298.
[4] Barbara Jelavich, *History of the Balkans: Eighteenth and Nineteenth Centuries* (Cambridge: Cambridge University Press, 1983), 352-359; Macdermott, *A History of Bulgaria,* 298-299; Wolf, *The Balkans,* 85.

with the large degree of new influence that Russia had gained, upsetting the Balance of Power set up by the Vienna Congress of 1815 in so far as Russia now had access to warm-water ports in the Eastern Mediterranean. Even the English were concerned that the Russian navy might now conceivably threaten the economic "life-line" of the British empire that flowed from India via the Suez canal (completed in 1869) to England[5] There was apparently popular "jingoistic" support in England for war against Russia through popular epigrams such as the famous: 'We don't want to fight, but by jingo, if we do, We've got the men, we 've got the ships, we 've got the money too! "[6]

Therefore, the great powers met in Berlin in June of 1878 to revise the Treaty of San Stefano. Representatives from the great powers as well as from the smaller Balkan states and from the Ottoman Empire were present. The great German chancellor Otto von Bismarck led the conference in the capital of the new German Empire. Mostly, the wishes of the Turks were ignored in favor of the desires of the majority of the great powers.

The Berlin Treaty greatly revised the Treaty of San Stefano and brought many changes to the boundaries of the Balkans. Bulgaria became autonomous from the Ottoman Empire. Serbia, Montenegro, and Rumania gained full independence as well as more land. Although there would be continuing problems bubbling under the surface, there would be no major political changes to the map of the Balkans after the Berlin Treaty of 1878 until the outbreak of the First Balkan War in 1912. Lastly, the power of Russia was greatly reduced in Bulgaria, thereby restoring the Balance of Power[8]

The most dramatic achievement of the Treaty of Berlin was in revising the Treaty of San Stefano's treatment of Bulgaria,

---

[5] Robert Gildea, *Barricades and Borders: Europe 1800-1914* (Oxford: Oxford University Press, 1987), 284.

[6] Recorded in R. R. Palmer and Joel Colton, *A History of the Modern World since 1815.* 8th edition (New York: McGraw-Hill, 1995), 658.

[7] Gildea, *Barricades and Borders,* 240-242; Wolf, *The Balkans,* 85.

[8] Robin Okey, *Eastern Europe; 1740-1985.* 2nd Edition (Minneapolis: University of Minnesota Press, 1982), 133-134.

especially in terms of size. What had been a "Greater" Bulgaria was cut up into smaller pieces and cut off from the eastern Mediterranean. Ultimately, the section which was the autonomous Bulgaria was about a third of the size of the Bulgaria set up by the Treatment of San Stefano.[9] Obviously, the Bulgarians and the Russians would be the most unhappy with this new treaty whereas the Serbians, Greeks, British, French, Germans, and Austrians would be happier with it.

Since this treaty, along with the revision of that of San Stefano, is so critical in both late 19th century history as well as leading up to the outbreak of World War I, it would seem plausible that there would be a large amount of reaction to it in the United States of America. Examining evidence of the "reception" of the treaty of Berlin might then lead us to understand ultimate American plans with regard to Europe in World War I. However, after reviewing a number of primary sources such as widely-read periodicals of the time like Harper's Magazine *and* The New York Times*, it becomes clear that the issues leading to the Treaty of Berlin and the treaty itself were of little importance to Americans compared to domestic affairs.*

For example, during the period from December of 1877 to May of 1879, there was no substantial article in Harper's Magazine *that had anything to do with the Eastern Crisis of 1877-78. In contrast, in the period when this conflict took place, there was an article on the Eastern Shore of New Jersey which had 17 pages.[10] Another article spent eleven pages describing "The Normal College of New York City.[11] Therefore, the periodicals discussed subjects such as schools and landscape in America instead of events in Europe.*

While coverage of the events in Harper's *was slight, one would think that the* New York Times *might have had more up-to-date coverage. However, interestingly, the coverage in ar-*

[9] **Jelavich, *History of the Balkans,* 360-361.**

[10] William H. Rideing, "Along our Jersey Shore," *Harper's Magazine* 56 (1878), 321-338.

[11] William H. Rideing, 'The Normal College of New York City," *Harper's Magazine* 56 (1878), 672-683.

guably America's greatest newspaper turns out, upon examination, to not differ much from that in Harper's. *The events from the Balkans were only mentioned a few times during these events relating the terms of the Treaty of San Stefano, the unease in various countries of the terms of San Stefano, and reporting the boundaries as set by the Treaty of Berlin.[12]*

While the New York Times *gave some coverage, other widely read periodicals apparently did not report the events at all. It is intriguing that while the Great Powers of Europe were closely monitoring power shifts in the Balkans as the Ottoman Empire ("the Sick Man of Europe ") declined further, Americans were seemingly not concerned as these events were so far away and of little interest. Americans of 1878 would have been shocked to learn that American troops would subsequently land in France in 1918 to take part in the largest war in world history up until that time ultimately as a result of Great Power interest in the Balkans.[13]*

Comments: This paper is clearly better than the first. The sentences and paragraphs are clear and the author cites both primary and secondary sources. The paper is not perfect, however. The thesis could be tightened a bit in the introductory paragraph to focus on why America is being brought into the paper. One way to do this would be to set up how many Americans served (or died) in World War I and then analyze backward from that to the Balkan crisis as an underlying cause. The author is anticipating this approach at the end of the concluding paragraph. As we have seen, in rough drafts the thesis often appears at the end of the paper because the author has finally figured out what the point of the paper should be. In this situation the student should revise the paper by moving the thesis to the beginning and reorganizing.

Also, the treatment of American periodicals could be handled more efficiently. The author clearly looked at some articles but casually cites many of them loosely together (especially

[12] *The New York Times* (1877-1879).
[13] Palmer and Colton, *A History of the Modern World,* 716.

from *The New York Times)*. As a whole, the kind of primary source evidence that this paper uses can be classified as "negative" evidence. This is defined as a lack of coverage of a development in a primary source that may suggest something specific. Such an approach is certainly a kind of evidence, but "positive" evidence is much stronger ammunition to use. Whenever possible, use positive evidence that actually says something specific, rather than build an argument "from silence." The author should cast his or her net more widely and look into sources such as the *Congressional Record and* more politically oriented journals.

3.7 Conclusion: Revising the Draft

You have now worked through the process of organizing and building a paper. The ideal way to approach writing a paper is to contemplate the sources, frame a thesis, compose a structure and outline, and then begin the writing process. After writing a draft, the key to good written expression is to revise your early drafts. In this process, you can first accomplish such obvious tasks as cleaning up typographical and grammatical errors. Then you can think about polishing the structure of your paper. Do you have the thesis in the first or second paragraph, or did you finally discover your thesis in the last two pages? Does your organization of examples flow logically, or should you reorder them?

CHAPTER 4

<u>The Research Paper</u>

A hallmark of advanced historical study at the undergraduate level, and indeed of a liberal arts education, is the research paper. Here the student encounters a wide body of information, reads widely until discovering a problem, defines a topic, and writes an extended argument over many pages that is supported by primary and secondary sources. The process of writing such a paper demands that the student delve deeply into library holdings and take accurate notes for subsequent formulation of the argument and for use as source citations.

The research paper draws upon all the skills taught in this handbook including structure, use of evidence, and clarity of argument. A student's involvement in such an exercise is not only the culmination of undergraduate education, but it also provides useful skills in the workplace where one may well have to research a problem and write a report, regardless of profession. This section will guide you through the process of choosing and defining a topic, conducting research, using sources, and organizing and writing the paper. It will end with an examination of sample introductions and conclusions of research papers.

<u>4.1</u>   Types of Papers

The types of assignments mentioned earlier in this handbook all lead toward the research paper. The identification paragraph requires that students show what they know in a limited and structured way. The essay requires that students show what they know, but through an argumentative form where possible. The five-page paper requires that students make an argument, but its length limits how long and detailed this argument can be.

Traditionally, students were taught that there were three kinds of writing: narrative, descriptive, and expository. A narrative composition involves the telling of a story. The "trace the developments leading to ..." type of essay question would fall under the rubric of narrative. A descriptive composition, as the name implies, describes something such as a place or an object. While various kinds of fiction and nonfiction use description, many students[5] essays and papers fall into a blend of narrative and descriptive. In an expository composition, the writer makes an argument. As we have seen earlier, the best kind of five-page paper is one that is framed as an argument, or an expository composition. This approach is even more critical for research papers. So, the ideal research paper will be an expository piece, which will include narrative and descriptive elements.

How long should a research paper be? This is a difficult question. Many instructors will answer "as long as it takes to make an effective argument that is well-supported by sources." This answer, of course, does not help a student new to history research papers. This author usually tells students to aim for 10 to 15 pages, but not to worry if it grows beyond that limit. Realize, however, that some instructors expect at least 25 pages (following the philosophy that students learn to write by writing a lot!). The best answer to the question of length is to ask your instructor what he or she expects. If the instructor does not give a clear answer, ask what length most "A" papers seem to have. Regardless of the potential length, the good research paper will have a focused thesis, will be supported by evidence and examples, and will have a clear organization.

4.2 Defining the Topic

One of the most challenging initial parts of writing a research paper is defining the topic. A good topic allows the author the opportunity to make an extended argument based on primary sources, and, at some level, to also treat interpretations in secondary sources. Obviously, establishing a good topic is difficult to do immediately, so it is best to work toward this goal in stages. First, you need to find an **area** of interest. An area could be a time period (i.e., Medieval Europe), an event (i.e., World War

II), or a process (i.e., Western relations with Imperial China). Then, you need to start reading broadly, in textbooks at first, and then in more specialized works, to find an aspect of that area that is especially interesting and also has the feel of a "problem" that you can engage. When reading widely, check the bibliography at the ends of chapters and books to track down further resources.

While conducting further research in some of these resources, keep your mind open for any problems of interpretation. You will discover that scholars have differences of interpretation over sources and events. Such a difference of opinion or debate will provide a good way to approach the material. When you find a potential topic, discuss it with your instructor. So, while we started with broad areas like Medieval Europe, World War II, or Western relations with Imperial China, after wide reading and discussion with an instructor, we might end up with topics such as "The Evolution of the Drawbridge in Castles in Medieval Wales," or "The Depiction of World War II in African-American Newspapers from 1941-1945," or "The British Government's View of the Opium Trade in China (1839-1840)." Not only are these topics more focused and detailed than the broad areas, but they also suggest the kind of primary source data with which the students might work (i.e., physical remains of castles, African-American newspapers, or British government documents). Think of the process of identifying a research paper topic as being similar in design to a funnel: it is very broad at the top, but as you read more widely, the topic focuses more and more.

Good and Bad Topics

The process of identifying the topic is the critical first step in writing the research paper. If you don't have a focused topic, and you don't have primary sources on which to base your research, your paper is doomed. Examine the following titles of papers and evaluate whether or not they are good research topics. (Keep in mind that the role of the title is both to grab the reader's interest and to state the topic clearly at the very beginning of the paper.)

"The Story of the Destruction of the Kulaks"

"Witches in Early Modern Europe"

"What has Athens to do with Missouri?: The Greek Civil War and the Truman Doctrine"

"Critias of Athens: Oligarchic Reactionary or Democratic Radical?"

"Out of the Loop?: The USA and the Creation of Albania"

"Early Colonial Guatemala"

"The Development of the Steamship and the USA's Annexation of Hawaii"

You probably noticed that some of these seem to be very broad topics verging on an "area" while others clearly suggest a focused topic. Thus, "The Story of the Destruction of the Kulaks," "Witches in Early Modern Europe," and "Early Colonial Guatemala" all appear to be narrative or descriptive papers. The more focused papers ("What has Athens to do with Missouri?: The Greek Civil War and the Truman Doctrine," "Critias of Athens: Oligarchic Reactionary or Democratic Radical?," "Out of the Loop?: The USA and the Creation of Albania," and "The Development of the Steamship and the USA's Annexation of Hawaii") all suggest a process of research and focused thought that leads to good, provocative research topics.

4.3   Using Primary and Secondary Sources

We have seen earlier in this handbook that primary sources (sources actually from the time period under study) are the most powerful kind of evidence to use in historical writing. This rule holds for research papers also. Primary sources for a research paper might include literary sources (such as histories, diaries, magazines, newspapers, novels, and poems), documentary sources (laws, treaties, numerical data like census figures), or material remains (such as archaeological evidence).

You will also want to examine secondary sources in the research paper. Secondary sources are works written after an event by historians or biographers who are trying to interpret the event based upon primary sources. For the purposes of your research paper, secondary sources would include books, articles, and book reviews by scholars. Such works will help you define your topic further because you will find disagreements of interpretation in them, and you might find some arguments more interesting than others. Published book reviews in scholarly journals (such as the *American Historical Review, The Historian,* or others that your instructor may recommend) may give you some useful ideas about how to revise arguments laid out in books and monographs. Check *Book Review Digest* for references to major book reviews.

Research in the Library

While reading in textbooks and following up bibliographic references are good beginnings to your research, you will find that you must use the resources of your college library effectively to accumulate the critical mass of primary and secondary source material necessary to write an effective paper. There are several reference guides available (probably in the reference room of your library) to aid in historical research which will help you find secondary sources. In turn, the secondary sources, if they are sound, should cite primary sources in their notes. For topics in American history, examine the indices of *America: History and Life* (Santa Barbara: ABC-Clio) which currently has over 450,000 entries. For topics in world history since 1450, search through *Historical Abstracts* (Santa Barbara: ABC-Clio) which has over 600,000 entries.

Most academic libraries also have search engines available to students (often via the library's home page on the internet). Through such databases as "EBSCO" and others, students can gain further access to a wide body of secondary literature. In beginning your library research, consult one of the reference librarians at your institution about your working topic and be sure to ask what printed and computer-based reference works are available.

Not to be ignored is the old-fashioned approach of "walking the stacks." Before elaborate databases existed, and even before many printed reference sources were available, college students found that an effective way of doing historical research was to look up key words relating to their topic in the library catalog and then to search the shelf of the library where those call numbers appeared. In addition to the book discovered in the catalog, look at books to the right and the left of it on surrounding shelves and browse through the tables of contents, indices, end-notes/footnotes, and bibliographies for information related to your topic. Some of the best insights can occur from examining related works.

Note Cards

When conducting research with library materials, it is imperative to note key arguments and quotations that might be helpful in writing your paper. While you will not know for certain whether every single quotation will be important, by the time you are leafing through works in the library aisles, you probably have some idea as to whether something may be remotely useful. Put a slip of paper in the book to mark the page and write down the passage and related thoughts you have as soon as possible.

Students long ago discovered that noting such passages on 3 x 5 inch cards was a good tactic. While you could use sheets of paper or a laptop computer for notes, the advantage to note cards is that you have a separate card for each important citation. Be sure to note the bibliographic reference for each passage, so you can cite it adequately in the writing of your paper. When you reach the stage of actually formulating the structure of your argument, you can play out variant approaches by lining up the note cards in different arrangements. This author remembers resorting to the floor of my dorm room as a display surface to layout different alternatives for my paper's structure because my desk top wasn't big enough. Once you have a good working structure, write your outline with references to the respective note cards.

Types of Citations

Because of the large number of primary and secondary sources you will examine, your research paper will naturally have many notes citing sources (and your instructor will expect it to). If it does not, your topic, research approach, and/or source material available may be problematic. You may want to rethink your paper, and discuss options with your instructor.

For citing sources, follow the rules suggested in the five-page paper section in Chapter 3 as well as the Appendix on Citations at the end of this handbook. Keep in mind that a research paper may have other kinds of notes in addition to the classic note that cites a primary or secondary source. These include descriptive and provocative notes. The descriptive, or textual, note is for information which you may have discovered through the course of your research that is interesting and somewhat useful, but tangential to your argument.[1] If you had the information in the text of your paper it might distract the reader, but in a note you can still use it effectively. In a similar fashion, the provocative note is useful for ideas that have occurred to you in examining primary or secondary sources that, while not directly germane to your argument, are insights that you would like to share. Occasionally, some very creative ideas emerge out of such notes.

4.4   The Internet as a Resource

As you no doubt know, the internet is becoming more and more important as a resource for all kinds of research. This is especially the case for history students at colleges with smaller libraries. Through intelligent and effective use of the internet,

---

Example: It is interesting that writing guides and handbooks from the 1950s gave concrete evidence and examples, while works from the 1970s and 1980s moved away from such practical advice.

students can access both primary and secondary sources not easily available through local collections.

As you might also know, in addition to some very useful sources, there is a great deal of "garbage" on the internet that ranges from totally useless material, to that which is downright wrong, unsubstantiated, biased, and/or hate-filled. Naturally, you want to use the good sources, and not the bad, in writing your paper. For a student beginning the research process, differentiating the former from the latter is not always easy. One hint is to lean toward "edu" and "org" addresses over "com," "net," and other domains. "Edu" signifies an accredited institution of higher learning in the United States. Often you can find web sites created by professors who are specialists in their fields. However, "edu" sites also may include college student work which varies significantly in its quality and accuracy. Be careful to find out who the author or compiler of the site is. "Org" signifies a nonprofit organization. Many of these sites are scholarly and well-documented. However, some "org" addresses are non-scholarly (and some of the organizations might even be classified as hate groups, so be sure to learn who has authored or compiled the web site). It proves useful to move from the web page that may have initially appeared as a search engine result (i.e., Yahoo!, Altavista, Google, etc.) to the home page for that respective web site. On the home page you can find more information about the person or organization sponsoring the source. If the sponsor is an association of professional historians at various well-known universities, the site is probably more valid than a site created by someone claiming to have been kidnapped by aliens.

As stated earlier, be careful about lifting information directly from an internet source to your paper. While this might seem quick and easy, the author is not trying to make the same argument you are, and the change in style and voice will suggest plagiarism to your instructor.

Some Useful Internet Sites

Here is a list of scholarly web sites for different subgroups of professional historians which may provide useful links for your research. If any of these sites appears to be a potential area for your research, navigate around the site and look for further links and resources. Keep in mind that internet addresses change, and new scholarly web sites are created frequently. If these particular examples don't work, you may have to plug the name of the association into a search engine.

Association of Ancient Historians
(**www.trentu.ca/ahc/aah/welcome.shtml**)

Encyclopedia of Roman Emperors
(**www.roman-emperors.org**)

American Society for Eighteenth-Century Studies
(**www.asecs.press.jhu.edu**)

American Society for Environmental History
(**www2.h-net.msu.edu/~environ/membership.html**)

American Society of Church History
(**www.churchhistory.org**)

Committee on Lesbian and Gay History
(**www.usc.edu/isd/archives/clgh**)

Conference on Latin American History
(**www.h-net.msu.edu/~clah/**)

Renaissance Society of America
(www.r-s-a.org)

Society for Historians of the Early American Republic
(**www2.h-net.msu.edu/~shear/**)

Society for Historians of the Gilded Age and Progressive Era
(**www.h-net.msu.edu/~shgape**)

World War Two Studies Association
(**www2.h-net.msu.edu/~war/wwtsa/**) Society for Historians of American Foreign Relations
(**www.shaff.history.ohio-state.edu/**)

4.5   Structure and Organization

While the structure of the essay, and even of the five-page paper, is simple enough to lay out without knowing the particulars of the topic and of the sources, giving a general statement on the structure and organization of a research paper is more difficult. Every research paper is fundamentally different because of the nature of the process of defining the topic, working with the sources, and laying out an argument. There are, however, some basic elements of structure that must still be stressed for a research paper:

a. Write an introduction. This first paragraph or two should introduce the reader to the topic and to your thesis. It may be that your introduction will take more than one or, in special circumstances, more than two paragraphs.

b. Give some background (or context) to your topic. You will want to do this in a couple of paragraphs. Be careful not to let it overwhelm your reader early in the paper and muddy your topic. By using topic and concluding sentences well in these paragraphs, you will be able to keep the reader on track.

c. Develop your interpretation of primary and secondary sources well. Your reader will especially be looking for this interpretation in your paper. Here is where effective organi zation of your note cards will pay dividends. After several pages of such examination, you will want to build your analysis in greater detail.

d. Lastly, have a solid concluding paragraph (or two or three) where you detail the significance of your research and pre sent your conclusion.

4.6   Rules for Layout or Appearance

While we began to discuss the physical appearance of a history paper in the last chapter, since the research paper is longer and is seen as a more formal piece of composition, the lay out will be even more important. Make sure to comply with your instructor's rules or suggestions. Ultimately, your paper will have three to four parts:

1. *Title Page.* Try to think of a title that grabs the reader's attention and demonstrates that your work is an analysis of a problem, rather than a summary or a narrative. The title of your paper should be centered, about one-fourth of the way down from the top. Type your name below the title and center it as well. About one-third of the way up from the bottom, type the course number and title, the instructor's name, and the date on separate lines.

2. *Text of the Paper.* The text should be double-spaced and should run anywhere from 10 to 25 pages. (Again, check with your instructor even before you begin doing research so that you have an idea of the scale of your presentation.) Use a 12-point font such as New York or Times. Most people still prefer the old-fashioned look of the uneven right margin or "ragged right." Speaking of margins, try to follow the traditional approach of having 1.25 inch margins for the left and right margins and 1 inch margins for the top and bottom (or "headers" and "footers"). Be sure to have a page number in the upper-right corner (after the title page). Try to avoid "widow" and "orphan" lines (single lines of text, such as the first or last lines of a paragraph) at the top or bottom of a page.

   If your instructor doesn't have a specific preference, decide whether to have footnotes (at the bottom of each page) or endnotes (at the end of all your pages of text). If you are working with a good word-processing program, and making footnotes is just as simple as making endnotes, go for the footnotes. This way, the text or citation is handy for the reader and he or she won't have to keep flipping back and forth. If you are using footnotes, skip the next section and go straight to the bibliography.

3. *Endnotes.* If you have decided to use endnotes, (this section will follow the body of your paper) type a centered subtitle

("Notes") at the top of the page and then number your notes consecutively. 4. *Bibliography.* Your last section should be the bibliography. Center this term as your subtitle. List all the primary and secondary sources you consulted in the writing of your paper. Some instructors prefer that you compile a "Select Bibliography" where a full citation is given for any work that has been cited in the notes more than once. Ask your instructor which approach he or she would prefer. For bibliography style, check Appendix 3 on page 54 of this handbook.

4.7 Conclusion: Revising the Research Paper

While the last chapter gave some preliminary remarks on revising a five-page paper, this section will treat the topic of revising a research paper in more depth. Often, students work on research papers in history courses classified as "seminars." The history seminar was the creation of the German scholar Leopold von Ranke in the early nineteenth century at the University of Berlin. In his concept of a seminar, students would work on research projects using primary sources under the direction of a professor, report on the progress of their work, and write up their results. History seminars in American universities follow this model fairly closely.

An important part of the seminar experience is to have the instructor and the other students "critique" a given student's work in progress (either an oral report, or even more importantly, a written draft). At the outset, students should keep in mind that the purpose of this exercise is to improve the student's methodology and to improve the paper (and thus to improve the grade the student will receive). Remember, there is a difference between "critiquing" (pointing out problems that can be improved and how to improve them) and "criticizing." If you are in this situation, try to be helpful to your fellow students. Give them the kind of good advice that you yourself would appreciate receiving (and try to give it in a manner that you would appreciate). Remember also, the time will come when you will be the one receiving a critique.

Sometimes, to start off a critiquing session, an instructor will ask you to give a five-to-fifteen-minute presentation about your own (or someone else's) paper. If you are going to make such a presentation, plan out what you are going to say, practice it, and time it. Give the broad context for the area of history, state the thesis of the paper, and present the organization the paper follows, the kind of sources the paper uses, and the significance of the results.

A Check List for Revisions

___ Does your title catch the reader's interest and pertain to your paper?

___ Is your thesis in the first one or two paragraphs of your paper?

___ Does your introduction match the paper you have written?

___ Did you follow through on your thesis?

___ Can you refine your thesis (after rereading your paper)?

___ Do you adequately cite your sources in notes?

___ Do you cite primary and secondary sources?

___ Do you have balanced examples?

___ Do the first sentences of each paragraph suggest what each paragraph will be about?

___ Have you cleaned up typographical errors?

___ Have you cleaned up grammatical errors?

___ Have you had a friend proofread the paper to catch additional errors?

___ Have you given yourself time to revise?

___ How can you make your paper better?

4.8 Examples of Introductions and Conclusions of Research Papers

The following examples show the introductions and conclusions to three research papers for an upper-division class on the history of the Roman Empire. The only direction for research was to "find a problem in a primary source for the Roman Empire." As you read through the introductions, ask yourself how clearly developed the thesis is and how well organized the paper seems. I have also included the concluding paragraphs for comparison and contrast with the introductions. Comments for improvement will follow each sample. Try to gauge which example is the best in terms of clarity of thesis.

1. "Ammianus Marcellinus: The Last Roman Historian"

Introduction *In studying a historian of a period so remote in time and culture from ours such as the fourth century A.D. Ammianus Marcellinus, one must try to appreciate the way that he might have viewed the world in order to read his history fairly. By this, one tries to read history as the author, Ammianus, wanted it to be read. This process yields, at the very least, three products. First, one gains insight into the life and thought of an ancient author and what his political and social worlds were. Second, one sees a detailed narrative of a decisive time in western history. This account is the most complete source on the period from the death of Constantine to the death of Valens in 378. This historical period saw the establishment of Christianity as the firm religion of the Roman world as well as the inroads of Gothic invaders into the Roman state that was destined to collapse from their effect. Third, one gains self-knowledge. For in critically analyzing and attempting to re-create the world of a historian writing over a millennium and a half ago, one changes inwardly. One's own historical conceptions, mind set, and world view cannot help but be changed. This is not to say that one would adopt the world view of a certain fourth-century man. Rather, by critically examining his work, by trying to abandon early twenty-first century values and preconceptions to see him clearly, those same values and preconceptions will be altered. This process cannot help but be ever continuing. Thus, the view of history and historical men, as well as the conceptions of one's own history will be continually growing and continually evolving as one studies history.*

Conclusion *Ammianus saw that the traditional Roman values of Fortune and Virtue had become alienated from each other in the fourth-century Roman world. His message was a warning to the cultivated aristocracy of that state. The twin threats of internal decadence and external invasions of Germans and Persians were going to overcome the Roman state if something was not done. Ammianus presents the image of the Emperor Julian as a prototype of correct conduct, of a possible return to greatness and strength. By accepting responsibility for the Roman state, by cultivating traditional Roman virtues, the aristocracy could save the Roman world from the impending disaster (in Ammianus' eyes). Virtue and Fortune could be realigned and the Roman state could return to its rightful position in the world. To this end, Ammianus Marcellinus, an ethnic Greek of the Roman state, fought in its army for over ten years, and wrote this moral history, this last Roman history, as a further defense of his world.*

Comments: A close reading of these two paragraphs shows that the author does not reach his or her thesis until the conclusion. In the rather long and sweeping introduction, the author attempts to be philosophical about the purpose of studying history (and at some level it is an endearing attempt). However, the conclusion doesn't match the introduction. In the conclusion we come upon what has clearly evolved as a thesis in the paper—the purpose of Ammianus' history. The author should purge the second half of the introductory paragraph and instead anticipate what the focus of the paper will be.

2. "Eunapius of Sardis: Historian and Historical Controversy"

Introduction *Eunapius of Sardis is a frequently disputed source for the later Roman Empire. Scholars from the Byzantine lexicographer Photius onward have presented different theories regarding Eunapius and the nature of his work. Eunapius, a fourth-century pagan historian, wrote two (or perhaps three) works. The only one extant is his* Lives of the Philosophers and

Sophists. *The other one or two were of a political/ historical nature. This political history (hereafter the* Universal History) *is preserved only in fragments in Byzantine compilations and in other authors' works. When one tries to read Eunapius, one finds himself inevitably drawn into the fascinating world of secondary scholarship that analyzes Eunapius'* Quellenforschung *(German for "Source Research").*

Conclusion *In the midst of all this heady research, one is apt to lose sight of the simplest facts of a problem. Eunapius, as far as we know, lived in Sardis from 369 until his death in c. 414. Ammianus, on the other hand, probably lived and wrote in the city of Rome in the western part of the empire around 400. We have seen that many scholars have argued Eunapius read Ammianus' history (written c. 388-395) and based his history (which was written anywhere from 378-393) upon that earlier work. However, this theory is not necessarily true. The publication process of the late Roman world was not as instantaneous as our own. Moreover, the work of Oribasius, who we have seen was a doctor who accompanied Julian and wrote an account (now lost) of his war against Persia, may not have influenced either Eunapius or Ammianus. Ammianus also accompanied Julian's expedition and probably based his account upon his own experiences. Since there are so many lines of demarcation between these works, and because the chronology is so unclear, it is safest to assume that Eunapius and Ammianus wrote independently of each other (and probably of Oribasius) in describing a tumultuous period of Roman history.*

Comments: The introduction of this second paper is more succinct and to some degree more clear than the first, but the author is also cagier. He or she hints that a thesis will be emerging in the course of the paper ("the reader finds himself... drawn into... secondary scholarship") without actually explaining what the thesis will be. Again, only in the conclusion do we discover that the key problem is the interrelationship of the work of Eunapius with that of Ammianus, and here the author ultimately argues that they wrote independently of each other. So far, this paper is a good draft, but it could be revised by moving the thesis to the introduction and re-examining the subsequent organization of the paper.

3. "A Study of Documentary Papyri from the Reign of Elagabalus"

Introduction *Since the late nineteenth century, the discovery of Egyptian papyri has contributed greatly to our knowledge of ancient history. Whereas before that point we had only literary sources and some inscriptions for knowledge of ancient Roman administration, now we have many official documents that shed light on how a Roman province was governed and upon social life in the ancient world. One particular use of documentary papyri is to use it to compare and contrast with traditional literary sources to evaluate the reigns of Roman emperors. Few Roman emperors match up to the image of Elagabalus (who reigned from 218-222) for sheer depravity in traditional literary sources like that of Herodian, Dio Cassius, and the anonymous* Historia Augusta. *However, re-examination of the documents surviving on papyrus in the province of Egypt, if not exactly contradicting the traditional sources, demonstrates that for the average Roman in the provinces life went on relatively unchanged no matter who was emperor.*

Conclusion *Was Elagabalus an insane "catamite" or a religious political theorist? The papyri cannot tell us. However, documents surviving from the sands of Egypt can tell us that the emperor's behavior did not rock the empire, only the senators whose position he ignored. Augustus' provincial apparatus ran on with even inexperienced favorites of the ruler as political appointees, just as some agencies do in some modern countries. Thus, the papyri serve to illustrate problems and gaps in the literary sources of antiquity and to shed even more light on how the common man lived in the provinces of the Roman Empire.*

Comments: Here the student has clearly worked through an earlier draft and revised his or her paper. We see a clear, focused thesis at the end of a succinct first introductory paragraph. We can imagine that, in the rest of the paper, the student laid out the standard traditional descriptions of the emperor's reign, followed by a description of the contents of surviving documents on papyri. The conclusion draws the reader into the wider significance of such an argument.

APPENDIX 1
Common Mistakes

The following is a list of mistakes in writing that this author has often noticed over the course of 15 years of grading student assignments. Try to read them over before beginning the process of writing your essay or papers. If you are writing a formal research paper, it might serve you well to reread them before proofreading your paper during the revision process.

Lack of clarity.

Lack of structure.

Lack of evidence.

Absence of notes and citations.

Lack of time budgeting. This too often means the first part of an essay is swimming in so much detail that all the major points are lost, and the second part of the essay is pathetically thin.

One-sentence paragraphs.

Overly-long paragraphs with too many disparate topics included.

Paragraphs with no topic sentences.

Indenting at the tops of pages when in the middle of a sentence or paragraph.

Incomplete sentences without subject, verb, or object.

Run-on sentences.

Subject-verb agreement (he is, they were; not he were, they is).

Consistency in tenses. ("The treaty was a temporary agreement that did not solve the problem." rather than "The treaty is a temporary agreement that did not solve the problem.")

Sweeping generalizations (including inaccurate statements that have nothing to do with either lectures or the textbook) with no support from evidence or examples.

Use of the first person in formal writing such as identification paragraphs or essays (i.e., avoid sentences starting with "I feel ..." or "I think ..." or "It seems to me ...").

The apostrophe s ('s). Use it for possession, not to make nouns plural! That is, "Alexander the Great's conquests" not "The Roman's had many conquests."

The stylistic jury is still out on whether to use a simple apostrophe or an apostrophe s when denoting possession of nouns that end in -s. So either Julius' or Julius's is acceptable.

"Their" vs. "There."

"Its" vs. "It's."

"Where" vs. "were."

"Alot" vs. "A lot."

"Would've" = "would have," not "would of."

Spelling. If you are using a word processing computer, use the spell check and grammar check programs.

APPENDIX 2
<u>Sample</u> <u>Citations</u>

Here are examples of the most common types of notes you might use in writing five-page or research papers. Read them over to get a feel for how to write citations of sources. Find the appropriate example when you are writing your papers. If you cannot find the type of note you need here, you should consult the *Chicago Manual of Style.*

<u>Primary Sources</u>

1. Citation of Primary Source—Book:
George Orwell, *1984* (New York: Harcourt, Brace, 1949).

2. Citation of Primary Source—Article:
William H. Rideing, "The Normal College of New York City," *Harper's Magazine* 56 (1878), 672-683.

3. Citation of Primary Source within Edited Collection: *Priscus of Panium, An Embassy to the Huns,* ed. and trans. James H. Robinson, *Readings in European History* (Boston: Ginn and Company, 1904), vol. 1, 30-33, following C. W. Hollister, Joe W. Leedom, Marc A. Meyer, and David S. Spear, eds., *Medieval Europe: A Short Sourcebook,* 2d ed. (New York: McGraw Hill, 1992), 20-21.

4. Citation of Primary Source from Internet Site: Sir Francis Bacon, *The New Atlantis* (**http://www.perseus.org**)**;** accessed July 8, 2002.

<u>Secondary Sources</u>

1. Citation of Secondary Source—Book:
Crane Brinton, *The Anatomy of Revolution* (New York: Prentice Hall, 1952).

Robert M. Frakes, *Contra Potentium Iniurias: The Defensor Civitatis and Late Roman Justice* (Munich: C. H. Beck Verlag,2001).

2. Citation of Secondary Source—Article:
Frank J. Frost, "Akakallis, a Divinity of Western Crete," *Ancient Worldll* (1996), 53-58.

3. Citation of Secondary Source from Edited Collection: David L. Toye, "Plutarch on Poetry, Prose, and Politeia," in *The Dance of Hippocleides: A Festschrift for Frank J. Frost,* ed. Robert M. Frakes and David L. Toye (Golden, CO: Ares Publishers, 2002), 173-181.

4. Citation of Secondary Source from Internet Site: Michael DiMaio, Jr., "Maxentius (306-312 A.D.)," *De Im-peratoribus Romanis* (**http://www.roman-emperors.org/maxentiu.htm**), 1-3;
accessed July 8, 2002.

APPENDIX 3
Sample Bibliography

Here are the major types of entries you will use in writing the bibliography for your five-page or research papers. Read them over to get a feel for how to write such entries. Find the appropriate example when you are writing your papers.

Primary Sources

1. Primary Source—Book:
Orwell, George. *1984.* New York: Harcourt, Brace, 1949.

2. Primary Source—Article:
Rideing, William H. "The Normal College of New York City," *Harper's Magazine* 56 (1878), 672-683.

3. Primary Source from Internet Site:
    Bacon, Sir Francis. *The New Atlantis*
    (**http://www.perseus.org**); accessed July 8, 2002.

Secondary Sources

1. Secondary Source—Book:
Brinton, Crane. *The Anatomy of Revolution.* New York: Prentice Hall, 1952.
Frakes, Robert M. *Contra Potentium Iniurias: The Defensor Civitatis and Late Roman Justice.* Munich: C. H. Beck Verlag, 2001.

2. Secondary Source—Article:
Frost, Frank J. "Akakallis, A Divinity of Western Crete," *Ancient World 21* (1996), 53-58.

3.   Secondary Source from Edited Collection:
Toye, David L. "Plutarch on Poetry, Prose, and Politeia," in *The Dance ofHippocleides: A Festschrift for Frank J. Frost,* ed. Robert M. Frakes and David L. Toye, 173-181. Golden, CO: Ares Publishers, 2002.

4.   Secondary Source from Internet Site:
DiMaio, Michael J., Jr. "Maxentius," *De Imperatoribus Romanis* **(http://www.roman-emperors.org/maxentiu.htm),** 1-3; accessed July 8, 2002.

APPENDIX 4

Classic History Essay Questions

The following list is made up of typical history essay questions drawn from survey courses in Western Civilization, World Civilization, and U.S. History. It is based on the author's own experience and contributions from colleagues at a variety of institutions (regional state universities, private liberal arts colleges, and community colleges).

While the list is no guarantee of what will show up on the student's examination, it will provide an idea of the scale of importance of what might appear and provide different approaches one can take in organizing responses. Look through the list of questions for the type of course you are taking, and contemplate how you might approach an essay question that covers material you have learned. Also, think about how you might structure your response in terms of the number of paragraphs and what kinds of examples and evidence you would use to support your argument.

Western /World Civilization:

1. Which was more important in the early civilizations (c. 3000-800 B.C.E.) we have examined so far—technology or religion?

2. To what extent have modern scholars changed the traditional view of early history?

3. If you had to choose only five major pieces of evidence to best explain the history of Early Western Civilization from 8000-500 B.C.E., what would you choose and why?

4. Why did the Romans, and not the Greeks, successfully conquer the Mediterranean World?

5. Choose five authors of primary sources that best explain Early Western Civilization from c. 800 B.C.E.-100 A.D./C.E.

6. Choose five individuals (they can be historical people or literary characters from primary sources) who best explain important developments in Early Western Civilization from c. 800B.C.E.-100A.D./C.E.

7. In 64 A.D./C.E., Peter and Paul were martyred in the city of Rome by the emperor Nero. However by 1100 A.D., bishops of Rome were dictating foreign and domestic policy to kings. How did this change come about?

8. In 390 A.D., the Mediterranean World was still rule by a unified Roman Empire. By 750, the political map of the Mediterranean looked very different. Explain the differences.

9. If you had to select only five primary sources to explain the most important developments in the history of Western Civilization from c. 100-1200 A.D./C.E., what would they be and why?

10. What was more important, the Renaissance or the Reformation? Give examples and evidence and be sure to examine both.

11. In the first half of the nineteenth century, the Balkan nations were secondary to European great power interest. In 1914, however, they were the cause of the "Great War." Explain this transformation.

12. Compare and contrast the Vienna Congress and the Paris Peace Conference of 1919.

13. Choose five authors who best exemplify changing ideas from the mid-nineteenth century to the mid-twentieth century. Justify your choices.

14. What killed more people in the 20th century: ideology or the machine gun?

U.S. **History:**

1. What motivated people more to settle in the American colonies, the desire for economic opportunity or the desire for religious freedom? Support your answer with examples.

2. Discuss the ways in which historical development (i.e., wars, revolutions, political struggles, and economic hardship) in Europe and Africa shaped die course of history in the original 13 colonies from their foundation to 1763.

3. If you were to arrive in the American colonies in the late 1600s, what groups of people would you expect to find there? Which groups settled where, and with what goals?

4. What were the origins of the American Revolution?

5. What were the strengths and weaknesses of the Constitution when it was written? Be sure to think about what events came before and afterwards in American history.

6. Trace the developments leading to the outbreak of the Civil War.

7. Why did the North win the Civil War?

8. What were the three most important developments in American history from the end of the Civil War to America's entry into World War I?

9. Why did the U.S.A. enter World War I?

10. What was the effect of the Great Depression on the United States?

11. What was the effect of World War II on the United States?

12. What was the effect of the Cold War on the United States?

13. Describe the five most important developments in U.S. history since the end of the Civil War.

14. If you could choose only five people from American history (from the colonial period to the present) to best explain the nation's history to you, which five would you choose and why?

Index

Note: Page numbers followed by *ph* refer to photographs. Page numbers followed by *m* refer to maps.